Tutorials in
Visual Cognition

MACQUARIE MONOGRAPHS IN COGNITIVE SCIENCE

The *Macquarie Monographs in Cognitive Science* series publishes original monographs dealing with any aspect of cognitive science. Each volume in the series covers a circumscribed topic and provides readers with a summary of the current state of the art in that field. A primary aim of volumes is also to advance research and knowledge in the field through discussion of new theoretical and experimental advances.

PUBLISHED TITLES

Routes to Reading Success and Failure: Toward an Integrative Cognitive Psychology of Atypical Reading, Nancy Ewald Jackson and Max Coltheart.

Cognitive Neuropsychological Approaches to Spoken Word Production, Lyndsey Nickels (Ed.).

Rehabilitation of Spoken Word Production in Aphasia, Lyndsey Nickels (Ed.).

Masked Priming: The State of the Art, Sachiko Kinoshita and Stephen J. Lupker (Eds.).

Individual Differences in Theory of Mind: Implications for Typical and Atypical Development, Betty Repacholi and Virginia Slaughter (Eds.).

From Mating to Mentality: Evaluating Evolutionary Psychology, Kim Sterelny and Julie Fitness (Eds.).

Speech Production: Models, Phonetic Processes, and Techniques, Jonathan Harrington and Marija Tabain (Eds.).

Cognitive Neuropsychology Twenty Years on, Max Coltheart and Alfonso Caramazza (Eds.).

Delusion and Self-Deception: Affective and Motivational Influences on Belief-Formation, Timothy Bayne and Jorge Fernández (Eds.).

Tutorials in Visual Cognition, Veronika Coltheart (Ed.).

Tutorials in Visual Cognition

edited by
Veronika Coltheart

Psychology Press
Taylor & Francis Group

New York   London

Psychology Press
Taylor & Francis Group
270 Madison Avenue
New York, NY 10016

Psychology Press
Taylor & Francis Group
27 Church Road
Hove, East Sussex BN3 2FA

© 2010 by Taylor and Francis Group, LLC
Psychology Press is an imprint of Taylor & Francis Group, an Informa business

Printed in the United States of America on acid-free paper
10 9 8 7 6 5 4 3 2 1

International Standard Book Number: 978-1-84872-853-0 (Hardback)

Library of Congress Cataloging-in-Publication Data

Tutorials in visual cognition / editor, Veronika Coltheart.
        p. cm. -- (Macquarie monographs in cognitive science)
    Based on presentations at a meeting held at the Macquarie Center for
Cognitive Science in Sydney, Australia.
    Includes bibliographical references and index.
    ISBN 978-1-84872-853-0 (hardcover : alk. paper)
    1. Visual perception--Congresses. 2. Cognition--Congresses. I. Coltheart,
Veronika.

BF241.T868 2010
152.14--dc22
                                                                        2009043480

Visit the Taylor & Francis Web site at
http://www.taylorandfrancis.com

and the Psychology Press Web site at
http://www.psypress.com

Contents

Contributors   vii

1   Introduction   1

   Veronika Coltheart

2   Iterative Reentrant Processing: A Conceptual Framework for
Perception and Cognition (The Binding Problem? No Worries, Mate)   9

   Vincent Di Lollo

3   Dissecting Spatial Visual Attention   43

   William Prinzmetal and Ayelet N. Landau

4   Top-Down and Bottom-Up Control of Visual Selection:
Controversies and Debate   67

   Jan Theeuwes and Artem Belopolsky

5   Getting Into Guided Search   93

   *Jeremy M. Wolfe, Todd S. Horowitz, Evan M. Palmer,
Kristin O. Michod, and Michael J. Van Wert*

6   Eyeblinks and Cognition   121

   David E. Irwin and Laura E. Thomas

7   Visual Spatial Attention and Visual Short-Term Memory:
Electromagnetic Explorations of the Mind   143

   *Pierre Jolicœur, Roberto Dell'Acqua, Benoit Brisson,
Nicolas Robitaille, Kevin Sauvé, Émilie Leblanc, David Prime,
Stéphan Grimault, René Marois, Paola Sessa, Christophe Grova,
Jean-Marc Lina, and Anne-Sophie Dubarry*

8   A Review of Repetition Blindness Phenomena and Theories   187

   Veronika Coltheart

9   Spatial Attention and the Detection of Weak Visual Signals   211
        Philip L. Smith

10   Face and Object Recognition: How Do They Differ?   261
        Elinor McKone

11   Is Face Processing Automatic?   305
        Romina Palermo and Gillian Rhodes

12   Visuospatial Representation of Number Magnitude   337
        Carlo Umiltà, Konstantinos Priftis, and Marco Zorzi

13   Visual Memories   349
        Max Coltheart and Veronika Coltheart

Author Index   367
Subject Index   375

Contributors

Artem Belopolsky
Vrije University
Amsterdam, the Netherlands

Benoit Brisson
University of Montreal
Montreal, Quebec, Canada

Max Coltheart
Macquarie Centre for Cognitive
    Science
Macquarie University
New South Wales, Australia

Veronika Coltheart
Macquarie Centre for Cognitive
    Science
Macquarie University
New South Wales, Australia

Roberto Dell'Acqua
University of Padua
Padua, Italy

Vincent Di Lollo
Department of Psychology
Simon Fraser University
Burnaby, British Columbia, Canada

Anne-Sophie Dubarry
University of Montreal
Montreal, Quebec, Canada

Stéphan Grimault
University of Montreal
Montreal, Quebec, Canada

Christophe Grova
University of Montreal
Montreal, Quebec, Canada

Todd S. Horowitz
Visual Attention Lab, Brigham and
    Women's Hospital
Cambridge, Massachusetts
Department of Ophthalmology,
    Harvard Medical School
Boston, Massachusetts, USA

David E. Irwin
Department of Psychology
University of Illinois
Champaign, Illinois, USA

Pierre Jolicœur
University of Montreal
Montreal, Quebec, Canada

Ayelet N. Landau
Department of Psychology
University of California
Berkeley, California, USA

Émilie Leblanc
University of Montreal
Montreal, Quebec, Canada

Jean-Marc Lina
University of Montreal
Montreal, Quebec, Canada

René Marois
Vanderbilt University
Nashville, Tennessee, USA

Elinor McKone
School of Psychology
Australian National University
Canberra, Australia

Kristin O. Michod
Department of Psychology
University of Delaware
Newark, Delaware, USA

Romina Palermo
Macquarie Centre for Cognitive
    Science
Macquarie University
New South Wales, Australia

Evan M. Palmer
Visual Attention Lab, Brigham and
    Women's Hospital
Cambridge, Massachusetts
Department of Ophthalmology,
    Harvard Medical School
Boston, Massachusetts, USA

Konstantinos Priftis
Department of General Psychology
University of Padua
Padua, Italy

David Prime
University of Montreal
Montreal, Quebec, Canada

William Prinzmetal
Department of Psychology
University of California
Berkeley, California, USA

Gillian Rhodes
School of Psychology
University of Western Australia
Perth, Australia

Nicolas Robitaille
University of Montreal
Montreal, Quebec, Canada

Kevin Sauvé
University of Montreal
Montreal, Quebec, Canada

Paola Sessa
University of Padua
Padua, Italy

Philip L. Smith
University of Melbourne
Melbourne, Australia

Jan Theeuwes
Department of Cognitive Psychology
Vrije University
Amsterdam, the Netherlands

Laura E. Thomas
Department of Psychology
University of Illinois
Champaign, Illinois, USA

Carlo Umiltà
Department of General Psychology
University of Padua
Padua, Italy

Michael J. Van Wert
Visual Attention Lab
Brigham and Women's Hospital
Cambridge, Massachusetts, USA

Jeremy M. Wolfe
Visual Attention Lab, Brigham and
    Women's Hospital
Cambridge, Massachusetts
Department of Ophthalmology,
    Harvard Medical School
Boston, Massachusetts, USA

Marco Zorzi
Department of General Psychology
University of Padua
Padua, Italy

1

Introduction

VERONIKA COLTHEART

INTRODUCTION

*T*utorials in Visual Cognition is the outcome of a meeting held at the Macquarie Centre for Cognitive Science in Sydney, Australia, to discuss current topics in a variety of areas of visual cognition. The chapters of the book are based on the contributions presented at this meeting and intended to provide a tutorial review of each topic and the methods used to study it. The readership includes postgraduate and postdoctoral researchers who want to become acquainted with research in various areas of visual cognition.

THE REENTRANT PROCESSING ACCOUNT OF PERCEPTION AND COGNITION

A highlight of this volume is the account of iterative reentrant processing proposed by Vincent Di Lollo in Chapter 2. Di Lollo presents a model that accounts for the mechanisms of information processing by all the sensory modalities (though he focuses on vision) and by higher level cognitive processes. He points out that visual perception has been attributed to the results of feed-forward mechanisms but that more recent neurophysiological investigations have demonstrated the existence of feedback mechanisms as well; it is the feedback mechanisms that constitute reentrant processing.

The ideas of feedback and feed-forward activation and cascaded processing have been a feature of various cognitive theories (e.g., of word recognition), but only now are such ideas being formulated in terms of explicit brain mechanisms. Di Lollo presents a lively review of ideas throughout the ages about how the brain works; these ideas were heavily influenced by the technology of the day—aqueducts, telephone switchboards, and computer hardware. All of these function solely in feed-forward mode.

Di Lollo points out that the integration of separate sorts of visual information, color, form, orientation, etc. (the "binding problem") presents a major theoretical obstacle to the understanding of visual perception and cognition. He goes on to argue that the feed-forward and feedback reentrant processing concepts remove the binding problem. The chapter considers the possible mechanisms and evidence for them in detail. The reentrant processing model is applied to the explanation of object recognition, inhibition of return, motion perception, visual search, object substitution masking, and other phenomena.

SPATIAL VISUAL ATTENTION

A number of the chapters in this volume are concerned with various aspects of visual attention—specifically, spatial attention. In Chapter 3, interest has focused on voluntary and involuntary attention, a distinction made by Wundt (1902) as cited by Bill Prinzmetal and Ayelet Landau, who argue that these forms of attention have different mechanisms. They use the spatial cueing paradigm devised by Posner (1980) in which observers have to detect or identify a target in one of two locations. The target is preceded by a valid cue (one that predicts the target location), an invalid cue, or no cue at all. Typically, the majority of the cues are valid so that the cue will encourage subjects to shift attention to the cued location. Voluntary attention can be deployed only when the cue–target SOA (stimulus onset asynchrony) is at least 200 ms.

Prinzmetal and Landau report that when task conditions were manipulated so that either response accuracy or reaction time was used as the response measure, different conclusions were indicated concerning voluntary and involuntary attention. They report experiments using functional magnetic resonance imaging (fMRI) measures indicating different patterns of brain activity for voluntary attention to a predictive cue compared to those for involuntary attention.

CONTROL OF VISUAL SELECTION

Effective response to the complex visual environment we inhabit requires effective attentional selection, which may be controlled by the observer (top-down processing) or may be elicited by properties of visual stimuli in the field of view (bottom-up processing). The extent to which these two processes determine visual selection is the concern of Chapter 4 by Jan Theeuwes and Artem Belopolsky. They investigated this question using a feature singleton visual search task. The target possesses a unique basic feature (e.g., it may be the sole red item in the display, or the red item may be an irrelevant distractor—the "irrelevant singleton" paradigm). Their chapter reviews the extensive evidence concerning the long-standing debate in this field and concludes that the size of the attentional window determines the likelihood of visual capture by a salient singleton.

VISUAL SEARCH

The paradigms used by Prinzmetal and Landau and by Theeuwes and Belopolsky involved small arrays of visual stimuli; however, the visual field frequently contains a large array of items. The observer frequently has to search the array to determine whether a required item is present. The processes involved in visual search have been the subject of intensive study since Treisman's research and theorizing ignited interest in this field in the 1980s. An impressive and substantial body of research and theorizing has been assembled by Jeremy Wolfe and his colleagues.

In Chapter 5, Wolfe, Horowitz, Palmer, Michod, and Van Wert present the 4.0 version of their guided search model, focusing on the nature of the visual-search guidance process, specifically on its temporal features. Early investigations reported evidence of parallel search for targets possessing a simple unique basic visual feature such as color, size, or orientation; targets defined by a conjunction of features could be found only after a slow serial search process. However, as Wolfe has noted in an earlier review (1998), search is frequently neither clearly parallel nor clearly serial, and it might more properly be termed more, or less, efficient. Processes of guidance are hypothesized to play a role in search, and object recognition is represented as a diffusion process in the current 4.0 model.

In many studies of visual search, a target definition is given at the outset of the task. In contrast, Wolfe et al. asked subjects to search for the unique item in an array without telling them about the possible target attributes. They introduced some clever manipulations to control guidance and contrasted unguided conditions with those in which different types of cue were provided at varying intervals before the array appeared. Guidance can be viewed as the "reentrant process" postulated by Di Lollo in his earlier papers (e.g., Di Lollo, Enns, & Rensink, 2000) and further developed and extended in his theoretical review chapter in this volume. Wolfe et al. present evidence to suggest that it takes time (a few hundred milliseconds) for search guidance to be established.

DISRUPTING VISION: EYE BLINKS AND COGNITION

In Chapter 6, David Irwin and Laura Thomas took as an index of cognitive processes the mundane occurrence of frequent eye blinks whose disruption to vision typically goes unnoticed. People usually blink 12–15 times per minute in normal daily conditions, with vision obscured for 100–150 ms each time. Vision is also suppressed briefly just before and after each blink.

Irwin and Thomas point out that people blink less often during difficult visual tasks and generally less often during cognitively taxing tasks. Their research investigated the question of whether blinking affects thinking—specifically, whether it impairs cognition. They report that blinking disrupted information maintained in iconic memory. Some evidence indicates that blinks suppress activity in primary visual cortex (V1) as well as in posterior parietal cortex. The latter is thought to be involved in spatial working memory and spatial attention, and Irwin and Thomas report some of their findings on effects of blinks on allocation of attention in space.

VISUAL SPATIAL ATTENTION AND
VISUAL SHORT-TERM MEMORY

Chapter 7 by Pierre Jolicœur (with colleagues Dell'Acqua, Brisson, Robitaille, Sauvé, Leblanc, Prime, Grimault, Marois, Sessa, Grova, Lina, and Dubarry) is concerned with the interaction between early and late attentional mechanisms in selection and retention of visual information. They report research using visual cognition tasks with electrophysiological, magnetoencephalographic (MEG), and fMRI measures to study visuospatial attention and visual short-term memory. The N2pc has been shown to be a correlate of visuospatial attention to lateralized visual stimuli and the SPCN (sustained posterior contralateral negativity) has been associated with the use of visual short-term memory.

These authors studied visual attention in a temporal visual search task using rapid serial visual presentation (RSVP). In the typical task, two targets are inserted at various distances apart in a long sequence of 10 or more distractors; each item is shown for about 100 ms. The first target (T1) is usually easily identified, but the second target (T2) is frequently missed if it occurs within an interval of about 500 ms after T1. This difficulty in T2 detection or identification is known as the *attentional blink;* it is a transitory deficit because the T2 report recovers as the interval between T1 and T2 increases beyond 500 ms.

Jolicœur et al. used a peripherally presented colored T2 at the left or right of the central stream (as well as an irrelevant distractor on the opposite side). This procedure allowed them to measure the N2pc used to track the deployment of visual spatial attention. In a series of experiments, they found N2pc attenuation during the attentional blink interval (when T2 was missed). In a single target condition (report T2 only), the SPCN thought to reflect visual short-term memory (STM) activation was large. Noting subjects' difficulty in ignoring a T1 that was the same color as T2 in the single target condition, they explored the mechanisms of contingent capture using event-related potential (ERP) N2pc measures. In addition to the likelihood that a red target would not be reported when a peripheral distractor was red, there was an N2pc that did not occur when the peripheral distractor was another color.

REPETITION BLINDNESS

It is difficult not only to detect and identify two targets in an RSVP sequence of items shown at a rate of about 10 per second, but also to detect and report a second (repeated) occurrence of an item shown in similar temporal conditions. This phenomenon was termed repetition blindness by Kanwisher (1987) and is reviewed in Chapter 8 by Veronika Coltheart. Repetition blindness (RB) is large when the first item and its repetition are close in a sequence and diminishes with increased lag (or SOA). However, the time course of RB is usually shorter than that of the attentional blink.

Repetition blindness is also found when distractor/mask similarity to the to-be-reported items is low; the attentional blink is likely to be diminished or absent under these conditions (Chun, 1997). The paradigms in which RB occurs can include short or long sequences of to-be-reported items. When long sequences are presented, the items are typically words that form a grammatical sentence if all words are reported. Several accounts of RB have been proposed with varying attributions of the role of memory in causing the repetition deficit, and these are evaluated in the chapter.

DETECTION OF WEAK VISUAL SIGNALS

In Chapter 9, Philip Smith considers the ways in which observers detect weak visual signals and the possible role of attention in the processes involved. The approach taken is both empirical and theoretical, with mathematical modeling of mask-dependent cueing effects. His concern is with covert attention in the absence of eye movements and hence with the use of stimuli shown too briefly to permit eye movements. The detection task merely requires a presence/absence judgment about Gabor patches (simple sinusoidal grating displays). These are presented in arrays of distractors in a search task with numbers of distractors manipulated or with a spatial cue varying in validity. This is a form of the spatial cueing paradigm used in Prinzmetal's research and described in his chapter.

Smith points out that the determination of whether detection is limited by capacity has been far from straightforward with weak stimuli in noisy conditions. The empirical work he reports was based on a psychophysical method of multiple testing of a small number of observers. Smith's modeling of the data led to the conclusion that increasing display size (the number of distractors) increased the level of noise present. Detection in spatial cueing tasks, specifically in the poststimulus probe tasks (probe presented after stimulus offset), indicates visual short-term memory capacity limits, whereas visual search performance showed no such limits. Smith concludes by describing a dynamic model of visual encoding, attention, masking, and visual short-term memory and their role in perceptual decision making.

FACE PERCEPTION AND RECOGNITION

The topic of face perception and recognition has attracted a great deal of interest in recent years. In Chapter 10, Elinor McKone tackles the much debated question of whether the perceptual and recognition processes required to identify human faces are simply those used to identify any other types of objects or patterns. She argues that holistic/configural processing is an integral part of face recognition and that this form of processing is not required for recognition of other types of objects, even though many other stages of processing may be common to all classes of objects (including faces). Her chapter also reviews and discusses paradigms used to study holistic processing.

The remarkably high level of performance demonstrated in recognition of individual faces has been attributed to the expertise with faces that humans acquire through experience from an early age. It has further been assumed that this expertise is responsible for observed differences between recognition of faces and recognition of other classes of objects. McKone reviews the literature on this topic and concludes that, although children at least as young as 4 years show configural face processing, the expertise studies have failed to demonstrate convincing levels of configural processing for other objects of expertise (e.g., specific breeds of dogs when these are displayed as stimuli to dog-breeding experts). This leads her to conclude that some form of specialized face-specific processing mechanisms has evolved. These mechanisms might possibly be innate to humans; alternatively, they might arise from the close experience newborn infants have with human faces from the earliest moments of life.

Given the extraordinary skill humans have in recognizing and identifying hundreds of individual faces personally encountered or encountered from media sources, we can ask whether face processing is automatic. This is the question tackled by Romina Palermo and Gillian Rhodes in Chapter 11. As they point out, one can perform a number of tasks with faces: detection, categorization, identification of individuals, and detection and identification of facial expressions.

Palermo and Rhodes consider the neural mechanisms involved in these various face-processing tasks. The evidence indicates that face detection occurs very rapidly and that recognition of individuals takes only a little extra time. Expression discrimination is also rapid. However, the evidence concerning specific emotion processing differences is not so clear-cut. The chapter also considers the various interacting brain areas and pathways involved in face perception and recognition.

VISUOSPATIAL REPRESENTATION
OF NUMBER MAGNITUDE

It has been argued that a covert form of visuospatial analogue code underlies our semantic representation of numbers—a view dating back to Galton (1880). This is an internal "number line" on which numbers are distributed in order of magnitude from left to right for people who read from left to right. The direction is reversed for those whose script requires that words be read from right to left. Evidence for the mental number line is reviewed in Chapter 12 by Carlo Umiltà, Konstantinos Priftis, and Marco Zorzi, who discuss the work of Dehaene and his colleagues in particular. For example, it is easier to respond to the larger of two dissimilar numbers than it is to respond to the larger of two similarly sized numbers (termed the distance effect).

The association of small numbers with left-side responses and large ones with responses on the right (the SNARC—spatial number associations of response codes—effect) provides further evidence of the spatial representation of numbers. Umiltà and colleagues review evidence concerning representations of other ordered sets of items, such as letters of the alphabet or days of the week. They also consider possible effects on spatial attention prompted by number perception, and they present their own neuropsychological studies with unilateral neglect patients. The data from "neglect" patients indicate a dissociation between explicit and implicit access to the number line.

VISUAL MEMORIES

In Chapter 13, the final chapter, Max and Veronika Coltheart consider distinctions among the forms of visual memories that are assumed to play a role in visual cognition. These forms of visual memory include visible persistence and informational persistence (often conflated and referred to as "iconic memory"). Both these forms of memory are of very brief duration and can be distinguished from a more lasting but low-capacity visual short-term memory and also from a slow, effortfully operated but higher capacity visual imagery generation system.

However, when the original, partial-report iconic memory experiments were theoretically analyzed, it was proposed that, for information to outlast the brief displays, items had to be encoded in durable storage—a system that can represent phonological codes and therefore the names of the to-be-reported items indicated by the cue. Clearly, this durable storage cannot be a form of visual memory, but rather can be equated to the phonological short-term store whose input codes arise through visual-to-phonological recoding processes.

The roles of visuospatial attention and visual STM in the attentional blink have been studied by using electrophysiological indices, as noted earlier. Chapter 13 considers the possible ways that these indices might reveal more about the nature of the relationship of early visual informational persistence, visual STM, and durable storage.

REFERENCES

Chun, M. M. (1997). Types and tokens in visual processing: A double dissociation between the attentional blink and repetition blindness. *Journal of Experimental Psychology: Human Perception and Performance, 23,* 738–755.

Di Lollo, V., Enns, J. T., & Rensink, R. A. (2000). Competition for consciousness among visual events: The psychophysics of reentrant visual pathways. *Journal of Experimental Psychology: General, 129*(3), 481–507.

Galton, F. (1880). Visualized numerals. *Nature, 21,* 352–356.

Kanwisher, N. G. (1987). Repetition blindness: Type recognition without token individuation. *Cognition, 27,* 117–143.

Posner, M. I. (1980). Orienting of attention. *Quarterly Journal of Experimental Psychology, 32,* 3–25.

Wolfe, J. M. (1998). Visual search. In H. Pashler (Ed.), *Attention* (pp. 13–74). Hove, East Sussex, England: Psychology Press Ltd.

Wundt, W. (1902). *Outlines of psychology.* Leipzig: W. Engelman.

2

Iterative Reentrant Processing
A Conceptual Framework for Perception and Cognition (The Binding Problem? No Worries, Mate)

VINCENT DI LOLLO

INTRODUCTION

*I*n the past few decades, we have learned a good deal about the brain. We have a fair idea of its structure, and we are discovering what regions become active when specific tasks are performed. On the other hand, this research has produced an aggregate of facts that are interconnected only loosely, if at all. As Francis Crick noted some time ago, what is conspicuously lacking is a broad framework of ideas capable of encompassing all these findings. Described in this chapter is a first approximation to such a framework. The framework builds on ideas of earlier researchers and is intended as a general model of how information is processed in the brain. As such, it applies to all sense modalities and cognitive processes. The bulk of the examples, however, have been drawn from the field of vision.

Visual perceptions have been said to emerge from a sequence of processing stages. That sequence has been regarded as being mainly feed-forward; processing advances from simple to increasingly complex attributes along brain pathways that converge to a common area in which conscious perceptions occur. This view is disconfirmed by advances in neuroanatomy and neurophysiology, which implicate reentrant two-way signaling as the predominant form of communication between brain regions.

In agreement with the neuroanatomical evidence, I hold to a scheme in which perceptions emerge from iterative exchanges between brain regions linked by reentrant pathways. In this scheme, the brain is seen as a repository of memories in the form of neural networks (cell assemblies and phase sequences) established through Hebbian learning. Those networks are used in cortical reentrant loops to set up moment-to-moment action plans for perceiving objects and for predicting behavior sequences.

Long-standing problems, including the establishment of perceptual categories (invariant representations) and the "binding" problem, are resolved naturally within a conceptual framework based on reentrant processing. This viewpoint is buttressed by converging evidence from behavioral manifestations such as visual masking, by neural activity recorded from single brain cells or populations of cells, by electrophysiological evidence from event-related potentials (ERPs), and by brain-imaging evidence from magnetoencephalography (MEG) and functional magnetic resonance imaging (fMRI).

FEED-FORWARD MODELS AND THEIR DEFICIENCIES

Some Historical Highlights

How does the brain work? How does it go about identifying objects? How does it plan for action? Nobody really knows, but there have been guesses. Early hominids knew enough about the vital importance of the brain—or at least the head—to aim their clubs at it. Of some 40 baboon skulls found at australopithecine sites in South Africa, 64% reveal fractures of the skull, mainly in the parietal area (Le Gros Clark, 1967). Some time later, the ancient Egyptians finessed the issue by denying that the brain had anything to do with cognition or thought; its principal function, they proposed, was to lubricate the nose. They got away with this hypothesis, perhaps because it had not been submitted to peer reviewing.

Throughout more recent times, the brain was said to function in the manner of the currently prevailing technological marvels. In keeping with the wonders of civil engineering that were the aqueducts, the Romans used a hydrodynamic metaphor that is still with us in the nomenclature of the structure that links the third and fourth ventricles in the brain. This metaphor was used until the 16th century. Then the hydrodynamic theory of ventricular localization of function was debunked by Vesalius, a professor of anatomy at the University of Padua, which also housed Galileo in what was then the hub of the scientific Renaissance.

Within the lifetime of at least some of the readers of this chapter (certainly within mine), the brain has been likened to another technological marvel: the telephone switchboard. Messages were said to enter the system through the sense organs and to be routed to the relevant brain regions through the appropriate pathways. One of those pathways was the thalamus, which was said to act as a multipurpose relay switching station.

Connectionist models and computer analogies then followed, spurred by the landmark paper of McCulloch and Pitts (1943), who pointed out that neurons could function as logical gates such as AND, NOT, and OR. McCulloch and Pitts showed how groups of such gates linked together in neural networks could duplicate the logical functions performed by the circuits in digital computers. To be sure, McCulloch and Pitts never asserted that the brain actually works like a computer: They merely regarded it as a possibility. But this subtle distinction was missed by many who built on these ideas and forged ahead with the field of artificial intelligence.

One critical element of the telephone-switchboard and the brain-as-a-computer models that has persisted to the present day is the notion that the sequence of information-processing events in the brain is mainly feed-forward. One of the earliest schemes based on feed-forward processing is Selfridge's (1959) "pandemonium" model, in which notional demons, each specializing in a different visual or cognitive function, marshal the stream of incoming stimuli to a high-level cognitive demon who eventually makes a decision as to what will reach the observer's conscious awareness.

Pandemonium was broadly accepted in the 1960s and 1970s as the default model of brain functioning. Its acceptance was bolstered by the widely publicized progression in the receptive field properties of cortical visual neurons, aptly characterized as simple, complex, and hypercomplex (Hubel & Wiesel, 1962, 1977). The feed-forward structure of this model lent itself readily to computer analogies and provided the frame of reference for introductory textbooks of psychology (e.g., Frisby, 1980; Lindsay & Norman, 1977).

Among the feed-forward models, perhaps the most influential was that of David Marr (1982). In its day, Marr's model was widely regarded as a milestone in the field. The model comprises several successive levels of neural computation. At the lowest level is the primal sketch, in which the local elements of the decomposed image begin to form two-dimensional (2D) luminance borders. Next comes the 2½D sketch in which the elements from the two-dimensional sketch accrue additional attributes such as position and orientation in depth. Processing culminates in a three-dimensional representation that corresponds to conscious awareness of the object or scene.

Marr's feed-forward analysis involving the progressive accumulation of perceptual elements up to a global three-dimensional representation was highly influential in the fields of both perceptual psychology and artificial intelligence, especially in the 1970s and 1980s. By the 1990s, however, researchers began to realize that the model could not provide a conceptual framework capable of directing the field of artificial intelligence toward the ambitious goals that had been set for it. An important consideration was that the model's feed-forward architecture was not consistent with the picture of massively reentrant brain connectivity that was emerging from discoveries in neuroanatomy and neurophysiology. In a nutshell, the feed-forward conceptualization of cortical connectivity could not provide a realistic underpinning for a functional model of the visual system.

Deficiencies of the Feed-Forward Scheme

On the face of it, the feed-forward theoretical framework is parsimonious and intuitively appealing. These desirable qualities have made it the framework of choice for theories up to the present day (e.g., Bundesen, 1990). In spite of its intuitive appeal, however, the feed-forward scheme is beset by at least two major problems: the so-called *binding problem* and the mounting evidence from neuroanatomical and brain-imaging studies that reveal massive reentrant pathways linking separate regions throughout the brain (e.g., Felleman & Van Essen, 1991; Posner & Raichle, 1994).

The Binding Problem   First formulated as a theoretical problem by von der Malsburg (1981), the binding problem applies to all sensory modalities but has been investigated principally in vision. A large portion of an entire issue of the journal *Neuron* was once dedicated to that topic (1999, vol. 24, issue 1). At the root of the problem is the well-founded view that the visual system consists of a set of modules, each optimally tuned to a different stimulus attribute such as orientation and color.

Suppose that we display a vertical red bar and a horizontal green bar for 10 ms in different spatial locations. The onset of the display will trigger activity in the red and in the green color modules, as well as in the vertical and the horizontal orientation modules. What needs to be explained is how activities in the vertical and red modules become linked (bound) together so as to yield the perception of a red vertical bar instead of, say, a green vertical bar.

In other words, why is it that—except for rare binding errors such as illusory conjunctions—we invariably perceive such displays veridically? It is important to note that, by the time the activation reaches the primary visual cortex, the brief display is no longer on the screen. What the visual system has available to reconstruct the image consists mostly of the activity in disconnected units in primary visual cortex, at least initially.

The problem becomes almost intractable if, instead of simple geometrical shapes, we present a naturalistic scene, such as a bowl of fruit, that triggers activity in many largely independent modules. What guides the visual system to assign the appropriate colors and shapes to the banana, the apple, and the bunch of grapes? Put in more general terms, the binding problem arises when one feature of an object, such as its shape, is to be associated with another feature, such as its color, to yield a coherent and veridical representation of that object. A generally agreed-upon solution to the binding problem is yet to be formulated within a conceptual framework based exclusively on feed-forward principles. In this chapter, I argue that feature binding ceases to be a problem when viewed from the perspective of reentrant processing.

Contrary Neuroanatomical and Neurophysiological Evidence   It has been known for some time that communication between brain regions is seldom one way. If a source area sends signals to a target area, then the target area sends signals back to the source area through reentrant pathways (Felleman & Van Essen, 1991; Zeki, 1993). In the brain's architecture, reentrant connections are the proverbial 600-lb gorilla. For example, in the network that links the cortex and the thalamus, descending fibers outnumber ascending fibers by a factor of at least 10.

An excellent example of cortical interconnectivity has been reported by Shipp and Zeki (1989), who traced the units that project from V1 to V5 and the corresponding reentrant connections from V5 to V1. A notable aspect of this two-way link is that the reentrant fibers do not merely complete a feedback loop from low-level neuron to high-level neuron and back, but are distributed widely on their return, including many terminals in the spaces between the source neurons. This arrangement constitutes a powerful means by which a target area can not only influence the outputs of currently active units in the source area but can also selectively sensitize or inhibit other neighboring units to modulate future incoming signals. Two-way pathways are not limited to cortical regions; they include subcortical structures such as the perigeniculate nucleus, which is known to receive direct excitatory input from the prefrontal cortex (Skinner & Yingling, 1977; Steriade, Domich, & Oakson, 1986).

Exchanges of information between brain regions can take place at remarkably fast rates. Using transcranial magnetic stimulation (TMS) to interfere with signals between Areas V1 and V5, Pascual-Leone and Walsh (2001) reported cycle-time estimates of around 10 ms. Similar estimates have been reported by Sillito, Jones, Gerstein, and West (1994), who recorded the reciprocal signaling between units in dorsal lateral geniculate nucleus (LGN) and cortical Area 17 in the cat: One complete cycle from LGN to cortex and back to LGN takes between 5 and 10 ms.

CORTICAL CONNECTIVITY FOR REENTRANT PROCESSING

Two aspects of cortical connectivity are critical for reentrant-processing models. First is the notion that all major visual centers have reentrant connections with Area V1, which is where stimulation first enters the cortex. Thus, neurons in the primary visual area can be activated not only by ascending signals from the optic pathways but also by reentrant signals arriving from higher brain regions (Bullier, McCourt, & Henry, 1988; Mignard & Malpeli, 1991).

Second, it is a general rule that the size of the receptive fields is smallest in V1 and increases progressively at higher centers. Because its receptive field is small, any given unit in an orientation column in V1 has no way of "knowing" whether the external stimulus is an isolated line segment or part of a more complex configuration. By the same token, a high-level unit might "know" the total configuration, but not its exact spatial location. Figure 2.1 is a schematic illustration of the hierarchical organization of the visual system and its two-way connectivity.

How is the functional connectivity of the system established and what functions does it serve? We begin by considering Hawkins's (2004) view that the brain can be regarded as a vast repository of memories housed in a hierarchical structure similar to that illustrated in Figure 2.1. This memory system contains a model of the world. As such, it serves to identify objects and to predict the temporal course of environmental regularities (e.g., the trajectory of a ball flying through the air) and learned behavior sequences (e.g., the sequence of actions involved in opening one's front door). For this reason, this system is called the "memory-prediction system."

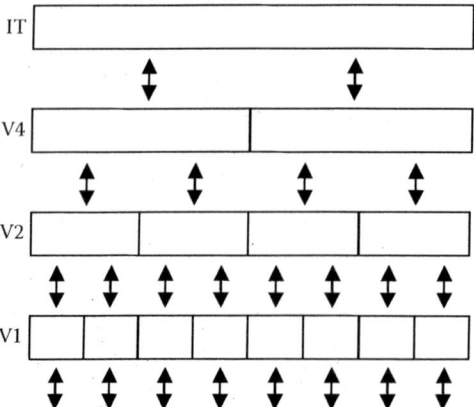

Figure 2.1   Schematic diagram of the cortical areas involved in the initial stages of visual perception.

How the System's Functional Connectivity Is Established

In discussing the origin and development of the memory-prediction system, Hawkins (2004) makes use of the concept of *autoassociative memories*. In the world of computers, autoassociative memories consist of networks that represent objects or learned sequences in the environment. What makes autoassociative memories especially useful is that they can be activated not only by the entire object but also by parts of the object or action sequence that they represent. Thus, the sound of a familiar voice can bring to mind an image of the speaker. From this it is clear that autoassociative memories are multidimensional representations that comprise cross-modal links.

The biological equivalent of an autoassociative memory is the concept of Hebb's (1949) *cell assembly*. This concept holds that the connection between two neurons can be strengthened through neurobiotaxis—namely, the growth of new knobs at the synaptic junctions. If the pre- and postsynaptic neurons are active at the same time, new knobs are produced that increase the strength of the synapse. As the dictum goes in neuroscience circles, "what fires together wires together."

A cell assembly is formed when more than two neurons are involved in a firing sequence. Consider three neurons connected in such a way that the firing of neuron A activates neuron B, which then activates neuron C, which finally activates neuron A again. Suppose that the firing of neuron A is triggered by the sight of a given object in the environment. Repeated presentations of that object or of other objects that share critical features with it will cause repeated firing of neuron A and its attendant network (neurons B and C). This will result in a strengthening of the connections linking the neurons in that network. This, in turn, will lead to an increment in the probability that the entire network will be activated again in the future.

In practice, cell assemblies comprise many thousands of neurons. An important attribute of a cell assembly is that, like an autoassociative memory, it can be activated by parts of the object that it represents. A second important attribute is that when activated by a briefly presented stimulus, the cell assembly continues to be active for a while. Hebb referred to this as a *reverberating circuit* and likened it to the ringing of a bell after a single strike with a hammer.

Hierarchical Organization of Autoassociative Memories

Figure 2.2 is a schematic illustration of how a system of autoassociative memories might work. For simplicity, the hierarchical structure in Figure 2.2 has only three levels. The low level corresponds broadly to cortical Area V1. The middle level corresponds to extrastriate cortex and the high level to higher brain regions, such as inferotemporal cortex.

The two hatched boxes in Figure 2.2(a) represent two cell assemblies that have been established through repeated concurrent activation of its component neurons. We can think of these low-level units as consisting of neurons in primary visual cortex. At that level, the images are decomposed into primitive features such as orientation and color. Repeated concurrent activation of the neurons within each hatched box will result in a strengthening of the connections among those neurons, thus giving rise to a cell assembly. Each of the two low-level cell assemblies feeds into a unit at the next (middle) level singled out by the segmented oval shape.

An important characteristic of the stimulus representation in the middle-level unit is that it has lost some of the spatial resolution relative to low-level representations, but it has gained in generality in that it can be activated by a larger population of inputs (e.g., by branches as well as leaves in Figure 2.2a). In this sense, the middle-level representation possesses a degree of invariance that is higher than that of the representations at the lower level.

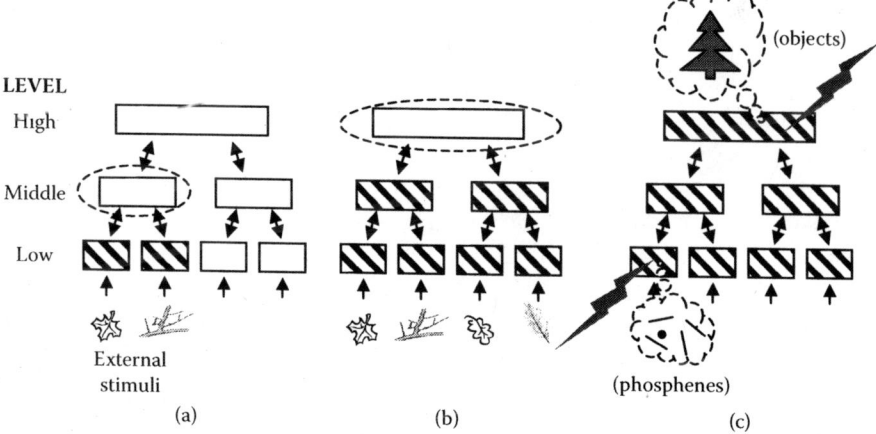

Figure 2.2   Schematic illustration of how a system of autoassociative memories might work. For simplicity, the hierarchical structure has only three levels. The low level corresponds broadly to cortical Area V1. The middle level corresponds to extrastriate cortex and the high level to higher brain regions such as inferotemporal cortex.

Figure 2.2(b) shows the state of the system after more low-level units have been activated repeatedly by other stimuli. As indicated by the segmented oval shape, repeated concurrent activation of the two middle-level units will lead to the establishment of a cell assembly that has an even greater degree of invariance relative to that in Figure 2.2(a). Figure 2.2(c) shows a fully established autoassociative memory system.

Evidence consistent with the hierarchical coding structure illustrated in Figure 2.2 comes from studies involving direct electrical stimulation of units at different cortical levels. The type of perceptions triggered by direct stimulation of low-level units has been studied by Brindley and Rushton (1974), who implanted electrodes in the primary visual cortex of a peripherally blind patient. Upon stimulation, the patient reported seeing spots and bars of achromatic or colored lights, as illustrated in the lower part of Figure 2.2(c). Brindley and Rushton referred to these experiences as phosphenes.

A corresponding investigation involving high-level units has been reported by Penfield and Perot (1963). Upon direct stimulation of units in inferotemporal cortex, patients reported seeing and hearing meaningful objects and sounds, as illustrated in the upper part of Figure 2.2(c).

Several attributes of the kind of memory system illustrated in Figure 2.2 must be emphasized. First, each level beyond primary cortex contains representations that are, to some degree, spatially invariant. The degree of invariance increases as we ascend from low to higher levels. Second, because it receives input from units at lower levels, any given high-level unit can be activated by only part of the object or action sequence that it represents. Thus, the sight of only a portion of a partly occluded object will bring to mind the entire object. Third, high-level representations are not templates that faithfully mirror objects in the real world. Rather, they are abstractions based on the commonalities that characterize the objects that participated in the establishment of that particular high-level representation.

In this sense, important invariant relationships in the world are encoded in the high-level units, independent of details. They form the mechanism underlying J. J. Gibson's (1977) concept of "affordances" and they correspond to what Konorski (1967) called "gnostic units." In contrast, what is encoded in the cell assemblies at the lowest level are primitive features such as line orientation and color.

But the abstract, detail-free nature of the high-level representations creates a problem. If our perceptions are mediated by those abstract high-level representations, why do we perceive the objects in the world in rich details and fine spatial registration rather than as notional abstractions? This is where reentrant processing plays a crucial role.

REENTRANT PROCESSING MODELS

Many studies have provided existence proof of reentrant (top-down) effects. The general strategy in such studies has been to demonstrate that some attribute of a stimulus is detected more accurately or rapidly when it is presented in a context that is familiar and meaningful (Reicher, 1969; Weisstein & Harris, 1974). Some of these effects have even been simulated using parallel distributed networks in which reciprocal activation of units at different levels has been a central feature (McClelland & Rumelhart, 1981).

However, the main emphasis in these studies has been on the existence and importance of top-down influences. Much less emphasis has been placed on the temporal course of the reentrant signaling and on the question of whether the descending signals merely perform a classical handshake with the low-level units or whether the activity in the lower levels is actually modified by descending signals.

We now turn to theoretical models that have sought to answer the question of what functions are served by the brain's ubiquitous and massive reentrant pathways. It goes without saying that any comprehensive theory must include at least an educated guess as to the role played by reentrant signaling in perception and cognition. This is not to say that feed-forward processes are irrelevant. Rather, I argue that the role of feed-forward processes, while necessary, is relatively minor.

Behavioral implications of the reentrant pattern of brain connectivity were realized early by Hebb (1949), whose conception of the visual system was remarkably modern. In addition to feed-forward projections, Hebb's conceptualization included reentrant projections between striate and extrastriate cortex (e.g., Figure 8 in Hebb, 1949). Hebb saw in this architecture a way to make concrete the then-subjective ideas of attention and imagery.

One of the most comprehensive models of brain functioning based on reentrant processing is that proposed by Mumford (1991, 1992). The brain organization envisaged in Mumford's model is similar to that illustrated in Figure 2.1. Not shown in this figure is a connection between cortical Area V1 and the thalamus, to which Mumford assigns an important role in determining which of several alternative stimulus representations will actually be seen.

According to Mumford (1991, 1992), the feed-forward sweep of neural activity triggered by an external stimulus is first handled by the lower cortical areas (Areas V1, V2, and V4 in Figure 2.1), which deal with stimulus-bound details. The feed-forward sweep then reaches the higher cortical areas (inferotemporal [IT] in Figure 2.1) in which abstract representations of information about the world are stored. Depending on complexity, the incoming signals can activate many such abstract representations, thus generating multiple, often conflicting perceptual hypotheses regarding the identity of the external stimulus.

The perceptual hypotheses (autoassociative memories) activated at the higher level are then sent back to the lower levels, having first been translated from the abstract code of the higher area to the more concrete codes suitable for comparison with the still active (reverberating circuits) representations triggered by the feed-forward sweep at the lower level. Comparisons between the ascending and the reentrant patterns are carried out in parallel and involve all alternative hypotheses simultaneously. The comparison is said to take place in the thalamus, where a kind of voting takes place as to the best fit between ascending and reentrant representations; the outcome is sent back to the higher area. Several iterations of this kind take place, resulting in a dynamic modification of the prevailing perceptual hypothesis by means of a relaxation algorithm. This iterative-looping sequence culminates in the confirmation of the perceptual hypothesis that best fits the input data. Conscious awareness of the initial stimulus then follows.

Variations on this theme have been proposed by a number of theorists. Notable among them are the adaptive-resonance theory of Carpenter and Grossberg (1987); the ALOPEX optimization algorithm of Harth, Unnikrishnan, and Pandya (1987); the reentrant model of Tononi, Sporns, and Edelman (1992), designed to deal with the integration of activity in separate cortical regions; Vidyasagar's (1999) neuronal model of the attentional spotlight; and the object-substitution model of Di Lollo, Enns, and Rensink (2000). A comprehensive outline of the neurophysiology of reentrant connections has been presented by Bullier (2001) as the basis for an integrated model of visual processing. A model in which perception of moderately complex stimuli arises from comparisons between the sensory input and conceptual information in long-term memory has been proposed by Potter (1999). Many of these ideas, as well as new ideas, have been incorporated in Hawkins's (2004) recent memory-prediction model.

In the next section, I present a reentrant model distilled from the contributions of all these theorists. While not losing sight of individual contributions, the emphasis is on encompassing these ideas within a coherent account of perception and cognition based on iterative reentrant processing.

A General Model of Visual Perception and Cognition

Considered collectively, extant models point to two main functions mediated by the reentrant projections in the brain. One is the identification of objects in the environment, and the other is the prediction of the next step in a learned sequence.

Object Identification   Assuming that a system of autoassociative memories has been established (mainly during the first couple of years of human life), the process of object identification might take place as illustrated in Figure 2.3.

Suppose that we display an object—a banana in this case—on a screen and ask an observer to identify it. Although differing in details, extant models agree on the main reentrant processes that are presumed to take place in the course of identifying that object. In Figure 2.3(a), stimulus presentation triggers a feed-forward sweep that carries the signals through the system. Upon reaching the highest levels (e.g., prefrontal cortex, inferotemporal cortex), the ascending signals activate a large number of autoassociative memories (represented inside the bubble in Figure 2.3a). Exactly which memories are activated will depend on the number of features that any given autoassociative memory has in common with the stimulus object. Following the practice of Di Lollo et al. (2000), I use the term *perceptual hypothesis* to refer to any given autoassociative memory activated in the feed-forward sweep.

Once activated, perceptual hypotheses must be regarded as being in need of confirmation for at least two reasons. First, the multiplicity of perceptual hypotheses triggered by the ascending signals creates an ambiguity for perception that can be resolved by comparing each perceptual hypothesis with the ongoing pattern of activity at the lower level. Reentrant pathways enable such a comparison. Second, because the receptive fields at the higher levels are large, sensitivity to location is reduced. Spatial information can be regained, however,

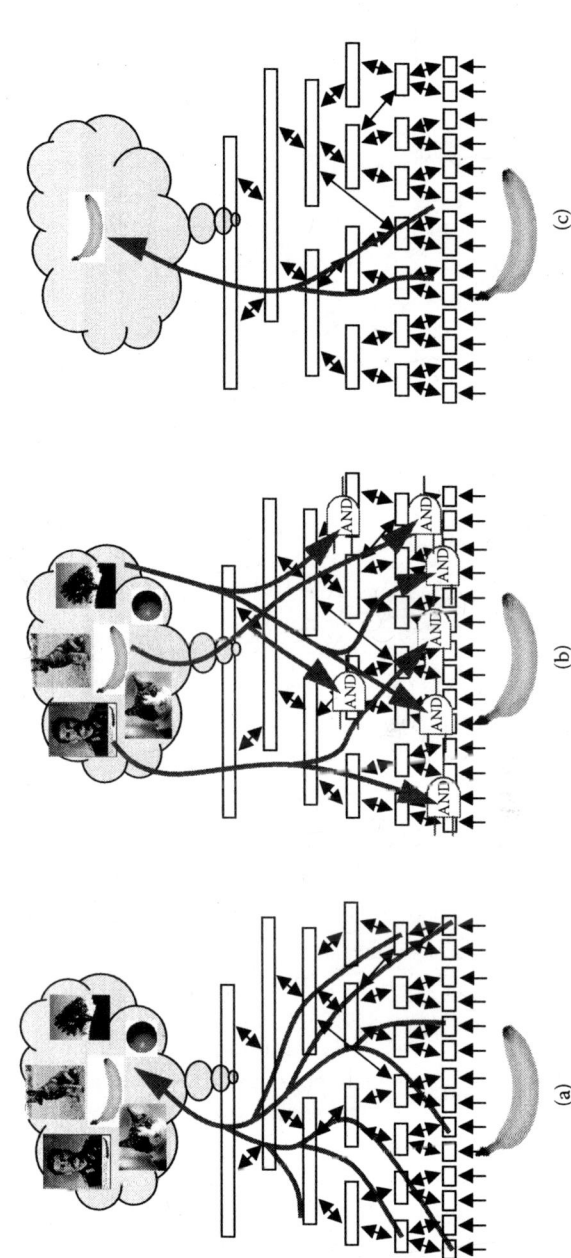

Figure 2.3   (See color insert following page 150.) Schematic illustration of how the process of object identification might take place within a hierarchical cortical architecture based on iterative reentrant signaling between brain regions connected by two-way pathways.

by sending the high-level codes back to the lower areas in which small receptive fields maintain high-precision spatial maps. This is illustrated in Figure 2.3(b).

It is assumed that all perceptual hypotheses, suitably coded to match the low-level signals, are compared with the ongoing activity at the lower level, perhaps through a process of correlation (e.g., Eggermont, 1990), symbolized by the AND gates in Figure 2.3(b). The comparisons take place in parallel, with each perceptual hypothesis attempting to match itself to the pattern of activity at the lower level. Through iterative exchanges between the two levels, the hypotheses that yield low correlations are discarded, and the hypothesis that yields the highest correlation is confirmed and eventually leads to conscious awareness (Figure 2.3c).

Whether the comparisons take place at the level of primary visual cortex, as illustrated in Figure 2.3(b), or in the thalamus, as suggested by Mumford (1991, 1992), remains to be determined. In view of the extensive feedback projections between the thalamus and the primary visual cortex, thalamic involvement is highly likely. But it is also possible that the correlation may be carried out, partly or wholly, in Area V1. The circuitry and logical gating required for correlating two signals is readily available within each columnar structure in Area V1. As summarized by Hawkins (2004), cells in Layer 4 (where signals arrive from lower levels) project to Layers 2 and 3, as do cells from Layer 1 (where reentrant signals arrive from higher levels). Thus, both ascending and reentrant signals meet in Layers 2 and 3, where they can be correlated by forming the inputs to a third neuron that performs a logical AND operation.

The next thing to note is that many neurons in Layers 2 and 3 project to the input layer (Layer 4) of the next higher region. Conceivably, these projections could carry the outcome of the correlations—performed in Layers 2 and 3—between reentrant perceptual hypotheses and the ongoing activity triggered by the incoming stimulus. At any rate, the option must not be ignored that the comparison might involve cooperative and iterative activity in both the thalamus and Area V1.

A word of caution is in order. The diagrams in Figure 2.3 do not do total justice to the hierarchical organization that they are meant to illustrate. For example, the stimulus input provided by the banana is shown as impinging on the same low-level units in each of the figure's three panels. This might convey the impression that if the stimulus occupied different spatial locations in the three panels, perceptual processing of the banana would be disrupted.

This is not what Figure 2.3 is meant to convey. Rather, in the system illustrated here, perception of a given object depends on the activation of high-level invariant representations that become active when the object appears and continue to be active while the object remains on view anywhere in the visual field. In this respect, the high-level representations correspond to the high-level units investigated by Moran and Desimone (1985) in inferotemporal cortex of the monkey.

The main idea to bear in mind is that in successive stages of the processing cycle, from retina to inferotemporal cortex, the functional characteristics of the units at each level change dramatically. In primary visual cortex, the outputs of the units are transient, rapidly changing, and spatially specific. In contrast, in inferotemporal cortex, the unit outputs are sustained, spatially nonspecific, and detail free.

Predicting the Next Step in a Sequence   Stored in high-level autoassociative memories are not only invariant representations of objects but also action
sequences and expectations based on physical laws and environmental regularities. These expectations govern many, if not most, aspects of everyday functioning.
Hawkins (2004, pp. 87–89) has provided a splendid example of the ubiquity and
importance of this type of autoassociative memory:

> When you come home each day, you usually take a few seconds to go through
> your front door or whichever door you use. You reach out, turn the knob, walk
> in, and shut it behind you. It's a firmly established habit, something you do
> all the time and pay little attention to. Suppose while you are out, I sneak
> over to your home and change something about your door. It could be almost
> anything. I could move the knob over by an inch, change a round knob into a
> thumb latch…change [the door's] color.…When you come home that day and
> attempt to open the door, you will quickly detect that something is wrong. It
> might take you a few seconds' reflection to realize exactly what is wrong, but
> you will notice the change very quickly.…There is only one way to interpret
> your reactions to the altered door: your brain makes low-level sensory predic-
> tions about what it expects to see, hear, and feel at every given moment, and it
> does so in parallel. All regions of your neocortex are simultaneously trying to
> predict what their next experience will be.…"Prediction" means that the neu-
> rons involved in sensing your door become active in advance of them actually
> receiving sensory input. When the sensory input does arrive, it is compared
> with what was expected.

Figure 2.4 is a sketch of the type of network that might mediate such expectations and attendant predictions. Endogenous activation of an autoassociative memory (driving a car, in the case of Figure 2.4) sets up a pattern of activation throughout
the system in readiness for the corresponding sensory input. When the correct sensory input arrives, it is treated as a confirmation of an expectation, and the chain of
events in the action sequence continues automatically from there. If the expectation
is disconfirmed, as in the case of the altered door, the automatic sequence is disrupted and control is transferred to mechanisms that involve focal attention.

Expectations based on physical laws and environmental regularities can
account naturally for a variety of findings in the perceptual and attentional literature. A case in point is the well-known phenomenon of *inhibition of return* (IOR;
Posner & Cohen, 1984) in which responses to a target presented at a previously
cued location are slower and less accurate than responses to a target presented at
an uncued location.

The typical display consists of two placeholders, one on either side of a fixation
point. The display sequence begins with a cue flashed briefly at the location of one
of the placeholders. After a brief interval, the cue is flashed again at fixation. This
is known as the *reorienting event* because attention is assumed to be focused first
at the cued location and then to be redeployed to the fixation location. A target
stimulus is then presented at either the cued or the uncued location. Observers are
instructed to respond (e.g., by pressing a button) as quickly as possible upon target

Figure 2.4   (See color insert following page 150.) Sketch of a hypothetical reentrant network capable of mediating expectations and predictions.

onset. As noted, IOR is evidenced by slower and less accurate responses to targets presented at the previously cued location.

Initially, Posner and Cohen (1984) attributed IOR to the buildup of inhibition at the cued location. They also considered two alternative, but not necessarily incompatible, accounts. One was based on the hypothesis that the observer might develop an expectation that a stimulus (the target) would not be presented again at the same location as an immediately preceding stimulus (the cue). The other option was based on the hypothesis that attention has momentum: "the movement of attention away from the cued stimulus in order to return to the center…may [lead the observer to] have more difficulty in reversing it back to the cued position than in allowing attention to continue to the uncued side" (Posner & Cohen, 1984, p. 537). Both these options were dismissed by Posner and Cohen in favor of the inhibition hypothesis.

The results of recent studies, however, strongly suggest that the noninhibitory alternatives were dismissed prematurely. A number of researchers have reported that observer expectation plays a role in IOR, whether it is based on attentional momentum or on other learned regularities, such as reading habits (e.g., Jefferies, Wright, & Di Lollo, 2005; Spalek & Di Lollo, 2007; Spalek & Hammad, 2004, 2005). In these studies, observer expectations were inferred indirectly from reaction times. This pattern of results has been confirmed with *direct* estimates of observer expectation (Spalek, 2007). Collectively, these studies provide convincing evidence that IOR is influenced by learned expectations based on physical laws and environmental regularities that, according to the present theoretical conviction, are encoded in high-level invariant representations called cell assemblies or autoassociative memories.

Many more examples along these lines can be gathered from everyday living. I learned to drive in Australia, where cars keep to the left-hand side of the road and the steering wheel is by the right-hand door. After I moved to Canada, where driving is on the right side of the road and steering wheels on the left in cars, it took me weeks, if not months, to walk to the correct door when approaching my car with the intention of driving it. Conversely, when approaching a friend's car as a passenger, I went to the driver's side, prompting embarrassing denials on my part of any intention to take control of my friend's car. As far as possible, I kept this embarrassing evidence of slow learning strictly to myself until a colleague joined me for a sabbatical period from Japan where, as in Australia, steering wheels are on the right. To my profound relief and solace, he kept on approaching his Canadian car from the wrong side for the longest time. This, I later found out, is quite a common experience.

An important thing to note in this example is that the tendency to approach the wrong door could not have been mediated by specific features of my Canadian car that differed markedly in shape and color from the car I drove in Australia. Clearly, the autoassociative memory that governed my behavior was triggered by my intentions and was not feature bound in a purely stimulus–response fashion. What guided my behavior was an invariant representation of an action sequence that was abstract and detail free. To make predictions involving action sequences, the brain must set up invariant representations that can be applied (successfully, in most cases) under changing circumstances.

Routine daily tasks, such as the motions we go through when showering or getting dressed, are governed by autoassociative memories, most of which are established early in life. Once triggered, these sequences are implemented smoothly and effortlessly, with a minimum of focal attention. They are instances of what Shiffrin and Schneider (1977) called "automaticity." When I or my Japanese colleague thought of driving a car, an action plan in the form of an autoassociative memory (pun not intended) unfolded automatically, leading us to the wrong door.

Autoassociative memories are parsimonious devices because they free us from the requirement to attend to every detail of tasks that we perform routinely in everyday living. They require little or no attentional resources and, as such, they allow us to deploy attention to other, more pressing tasks. But attentional resources are suddenly called upon if the input from the environment does not match the expected pattern set up at the system's low level (see Figure 2.4). Returning to our example, the sight of the passenger seat disconfirmed my system's expectation for a steering wheel and caused it to switch from effortless "autopilot" mode to the laborious type of processing, illustrated in Figure 2.3, that Di Lollo, Smilek, Kawahara, and Ghorashi (2005) called "template matching."

INSTANTIATIONS OF REENTRANT PROCESSING

By its very nature, the concept of "expectation" tends to have somewhat subjective overtones and to be rather difficult to pin down experimentally. For these reasons, the highly specific mechanism proposed in the preceding section might seem unduly speculative. In fact, examples of how expectations can be implemented are readily available in the neurophysiological literature. Discussed in the present section is an example of how expectations based on directional-motion perception can be implemented neurophysiologically through reentrant processing (Sillito, 1992; Sillito et al., 1994).

Also discussed in this section are three other instantiations of reentrant processing. Two are physiological: multiplexing the function of a given neuron at different stages of the processing cycle (Lamme, 1995; Lamme & Roelfsema, 2000; Zipser, Lamme, & Schiller, 1996) and improving the signal-to-noise ratio in noisy and ill-defined perceptual representations (Hupé et al., 1998). The third is psychophysical: a new form of visual masking called object-substitution masking (Di Lollo et al., 2000).

Expectation in Perception of Directional Motion

An example of how expectations based on physical laws and environmental regularities may be implemented in a biological system has been reported by Sillito et al. (1994). The experiment involved monitoring the activity along the two-way pathways between the LGN and Area 17 in the cat in response to moving stimuli. Area 17 is where the projections from LGN first enter the cortex, and it corresponds broadly to Area V1 in primates. The stimuli were bar-gratings drifting coherently on a screen in a predetermined direction.

The finding of major interest to the present discussion was that the firing threshold of LGN neurons located just ahead in the motion path—but not yet activated by the moving grating—was significantly lowered. Because of the lowered threshold, these neurons fired more readily and more strongly when eventually stimulated by the moving grating. The sequence of events is illustrated in Figure 2.5.

In Figure 2.5(a), a bar-grating is displayed in front of the cat's eye. Signals from the eye are sent to the LGN and thence to the primary visual cortex. Illustrated at the level of the LGN are three neurons: the leftmost has been painted black to indicate that it had been activated by the onset of the grating on the screen. Activation is then relayed to the corresponding neuron in Area 17. The structure illustrated in Area 17 is a Reichardt directional motion sensor (Reichardt, 1961). Reichardt sensors have two inputs and one output. When the two inputs are triggered sequentially at the optimal temporal interval, a directional motion signal is issued at the sensor's output. At the processing stage illustrated in Figure 2.5(a), the grating is not yet seen as being in motion because only one input to the motion sensor has been activated.

In Figure 2.5(b) the grating has moved to the right, thus activating the next LGN unit and, in turn, providing the second input to the motion sensor. With both

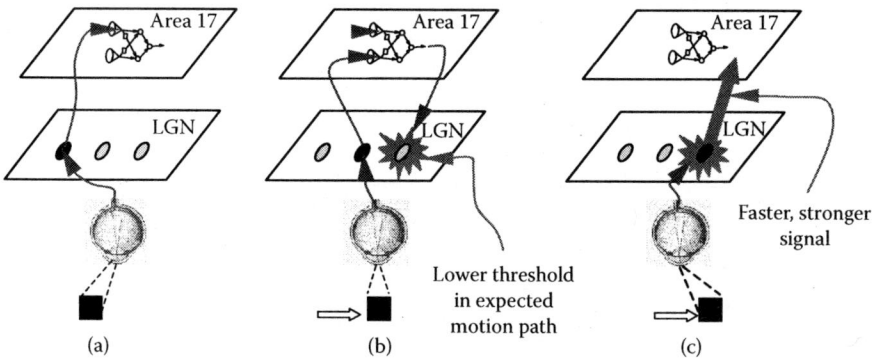

Figure 2.5 (See color insert following page 150.) Schematic representation of the sequence of processing events leading to greater sensitivity to stimuli in the expected direction of motion. (After Sillito, A. M. et al., 1994, *Nature, 369*, 479–482.)

inputs activated at the optimal temporal interval, the motion sensor generates an output in the form of a directional motion signal back to LGN. As illustrated in Figure 2.5(b), an important end product of that motion signal is to lower the firing threshold of the LGN unit that lies next to the source unit in the expected path of motion. To understand how this is done, we need to be reminded of two important aspects of cortical wiring related to motion perception.

First, the primary visual cortex contains a very large number of motion sensors that are set in many different orientations and are optimally tuned to different spatial and temporal frequencies. For example, had the grating in Figure 2.5(a) been oriented differently or moved in a different direction, another suitably tuned motion sensor would have been activated in Area 17.

The second consideration pertains to the wiring between primary visual cortex and LGN. Each motion unit in Area 17 projects to both higher and lower brain regions. The ascending projections go to Area V5, which is beyond the present concerns. The descending projections are connected to the corresponding LGN cells in such a way as to facilitate the firing of cells located next to the initial source cell in the direction to which the cortical motion sensor is optimally tuned. This circuitry provides an anticipatory coordinating influence by lowering the firing threshold of the LGN cells that are about to be activated by the moving grating. Thus, upon receiving input from the moving grating, the LGN neurons that lie directly ahead in the expected path of motion fire more readily and more strongly, as illustrated in Figure 2.5(c).

The main point to be gathered from this discussion is that, even in the absence of physical stimulation, reentrant signals to LGN can prepare the system for a stimulus that is about to occur at a location in the expected path of motion. This is a specific instance of the class of expectancies discussed in the foregoing and illustrated in Figure 2.4.

It must be noted, at least in passing, that not all reentrant projections from primary visual cortex to LGN are excitatory: Some are inhibitory. When directed at LGN units that have fired recently, the inhibitory feedback serves to reduce motion smear. This has been shown by Sillito (1992), who studied suppression of motion smear in the cat's LGN. He concluded that suppression of motion smear can be ascribed to the action of inhibitory reentrant signals from primary visual cortex to LGN following the establishment of an expected motion trajectory. These findings can be tied directly to expectation in human observers by reference to a study by Hogben and Di Lollo (1985), who found that motion smear is suppressed to a far greater extent when the motion path is predictable than when it is not predictable.

Finally, it is of interest to note that the suppression of motion smear is impaired when the reentrant pathways are damaged. This has been reported by Tassinari, Marzi, Lee, Di Lollo, and Campara (1999), who found that suppression of motion smear was significantly impaired in patients with compression of the anterior visual pathways.

Multiplexing Neuronal Function

Among the arguments put forth in support of feed-forward models, parsimony is often cited as the most obvious advantage. Why invoke complicated reentrant schemes when most findings in the perceptual and cognitive literature can be explained by some combination of feed-forward factors? Intuitively, feed-forward accounts do seem more parsimonious than reentrant schemes. On closer inspection, however, reentrant processing reveals a degree of parsimony that goes beyond what can be achieved with feed-forward circuitry alone.

A splendid example of the parsimony inherent in reentrant processing has been provided by Lamme and coworkers (e.g., Lamme, 1995; Lamme & Roelfsema, 2000; Zipser et al., 1996). In a series of clever experiments, they have shown that reentrant signals can redefine the function of the same neurons to perform several very different tasks in successive phases of the processing cycle. This multiplexing makes for a leaner and more efficient system than one with enough neurons to do the same job in a feed-forward fashion.

Lamme and colleagues (Lamme, 1995; Lamme, Zipser, & Spekreijse, 1997, 1998; Zipser et al., 1996) recorded responses from V1 neurons in awake monkeys fitted with chronic microelectrode implants. The monkeys viewed textured stimuli similar to those illustrated in Figure 2.6(2). Some of the stimuli contained a figure superimposed on the background, as in Figure 2.6(1). In the present example, responses were recorded from a V1 neuron that was optimally sensitive to lines oriented at 45°—"c" in Figure 2.6(1). The white disks in Figures 2.6(1) and 2.6(2) represent different locations at which the classical receptive field of the neuron was centered in different stages of the experiment. The responses of the neuron are illustrated in Figures 2.6(3), 2.6(4), and 2.6(5).

Two sets of experimental outcomes are especially pertinent here. The first revealed functional multiplexing: The same neuron responded to vastly different stimulus attributes at different stages of the processing sequence. The second showed that this multiplexing was governed by reentrant signals.

Functional Multiplexing   The first set of results was obtained by placing the neuron's receptive field in different locations of the stimulus pattern: on the background, on the figure boundary, or at the center of the figure. Figure 2.6(3)

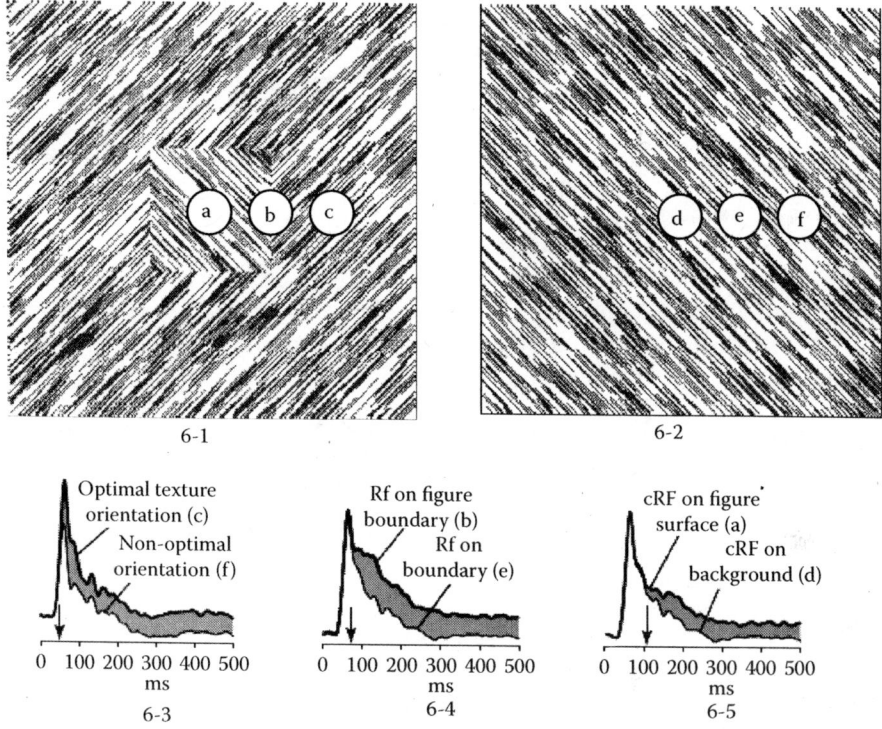

Figure 2.6 Functional multiplexing of neurons in area V1 at different stages of figure–ground processing. (After Lamme, V. A. F. & Roelfsema, P. R., 2000, *Trends in Neuroscience*, 23, 571–579; see text for details.)

illustrates the temporal course of the neuron's activity when its receptive field was placed on the background. As might be expected, the neuron responded more vigorously when the stimulus orientation in its receptive field was optimal—"c" in Figure 2.6(1)—than when it was not—"f" in Figure 2.6(2). The thing to be noted in Figure 2.6(3) is that the response functions for optimal and suboptimal stimuli began to separate as early as 40 ms after stimulus onset. To wit, the neuron "knew" very quickly whether the stimulus in its receptive field was oriented optimally.

Figure 2.6(4) shows the neuron's activity when its receptive field was centered on the figure's boundary—"b" in Figure 2.6(1)—relative to when it was centered on the corresponding location of a figureless field—"e" in Figure 2.6(2). The neuron responded more strongly when its receptive field was on the figure's boundary. The important thing to notice in Figure 2.6(4) is that the two response functions did not begin to diverge until some 80 ms had elapsed since stimulus onset.

Finally, Figure 2.6(5) shows the neuron's activity when its receptive field was centered on the figure—"a" in Figure 2.6(1)—relative to when it was centered on the corresponding location of a figureless field—"d" in Figure 2.6(2). The neuron responded more strongly when its receptive field was centered on the figure than when it was centered on the corresponding location of a figureless field, even though the orientation of the line stimuli within its receptive field was identical in the two situations. Again, an important thing to notice in Figure 2.6(5) is that the two response functions did not begin to diverge until about 120 ms had elapsed since stimulus onset.

In summary, the results revealed three distinct stages in the neuron's response. In the first stage (up to about 80 ms from stimulus onset) the neuron responded only to local features presented within its receptive field. In the second stage (80–120 ms), the same neuron began to respond to figure boundaries. In the third stage (beyond about 120 ms), the neuron responded to the surface of the figure. Unquestionably, the neuron performed very different functions at successive stages of the processing cycle. It was selective for orientation in Stage 1, for contour in Stage 2, and for figure–ground relationships in Stage 3. In the feed-forward heydays of the 1960s and 1970s, one might have said that the neuron could function indifferently as an orientation detector, as a subjective-contour detector, and as a figure–ground detector.

We must not lose sight of the fact that these findings were based exclusively on neurons in Area V1. Until recently, that area was believed to function automatically in a rigidly fixed manner. Its main function was believed to be the coding of low-level stimulus features such as orientation and color. Furthermore, it was believed to be totally impervious to high-level influences such as attention. These notions have now been dispelled, not only by the types of results outlined earlier, but also by other neurophysiological studies (e.g., Motter, 1993) and brain-imaging studies (e.g., Bahrami, Lavie, & Rees, 2007; Kastner, Pinsk, De Weerd, Desimone, & Ungerleider, 1999; Kastner & Ungerleider, 2000). The question that now needs to be asked is: How is this impressive feat of multiplexing achieved? Predictably, the answer lies in reentrant signaling.

Reentrant Signaling

Evidence that the multiplexing of function in Area V1 is governed by reentrant signals from higher brain regions has been reported by Lamme et al. (1997, 1998). The same monkeys tested in the experiment described previously were retested after having undergone extensive lesions to extrastriate cortex ipsilateral to the recording site.

After surgery, the V1 activity corresponding to Stages 1 and 2 continued to be very much in evidence, but the activity corresponding to Stage 3 was missing. Behaviorally, the monkeys were no longer capable of distinguishing figure from ground. A very similar outcome was obtained when the monkeys were tested before ablation surgery but under anesthesia. When the monkeys were anesthetized, neurons in V1 continued to respond to local features (Stage 1) and remained sharply tuned to stimulus orientation, but Stages 2 and 3 were missing.

These findings confirm that, within a processing cycle, signals from higher centers reenter the primary visual cortex and are instrumental in redefining the functions performed by neurons at that level. More important, when the reentrant flow is disrupted, local nonfigural attributes of the stimulus can still be processed, but global attributes relating to the overall configuration are lost. This pattern of results is entirely consistent with the functional connectivity illustrated in Figure 2.4.

Boosting the Signal-to-Noise Ratio

An important function performed by reentrant connections in the visual brain is to improve the visibility of stimuli that are noisy or poorly defined. This has been shown by Hupé and colleagues (1998), who studied the role of reentrant connections from Area V5—a brain region involved in motion integration—and visual Areas V1, V2, and V3 in the macaque monkey. Activity was recorded from single units and multiple units in each of the three lower areas. The stimulus was an optimally oriented bar that moved on a visually noisy background populated by many small square patches. The luminance of the background noise patches was varied systematically but was always lower than that of the moving bar.

The main experimental manipulation was aimed at inactivating Area V5 so as to disable the reentrant signals to the lower areas. In practice, V5 was inactivated reversibly by cooling an area of superior temporal sulcus that included V5. The principal objective of the cooling manipulation was to find out whether the inactivation of Area V5 altered the response characteristics of the neurons in the lower areas. The results showed that during the period of V5 cooling, the frequency of neuronal firing at the lower areas in response to the moving bar was drastically reduced. The reduction was in evidence in all three lower areas, but was most pronounced in Area V2, where response strength was reduced by as much as 91%. Notably, the reduction was greatest when the luminance ratio between the moving bar and the noisy background (i.e., the signal-to-noise ratio) was lowest.

On the basis of these results, Hupé et al. (1998) concluded that reentrant signals from Area V5 have a facilitatory effect on the responses of neurons at the lower areas. In the words of the authors,

> [F]eedback connections act more as a gain enhancer, or gater, of activity already present, rather than as an activator of otherwise silent neurons, a role presumably reserved to feedforward connections....[The finding that the effects of V5 cooling] were at their strongest for low-salience stimuli...implies that feedback projections serve to improve the visibility of features that activate the receptive field centre in the stimulus and may thus contribute to figure–ground segregation, breaking of camouflage, and psychophysically demonstrated pop-out effects. (p. 786)

This hypothesized gating function for reentrant signals is entirely consistent with the network illustrated in Figure 2.4.

Behavioral phenomena congruent with the neurophysiological findings of Hupé et al. (1998) are readily available, and are consistent with the sequence of reentrant processing events illustrated in Figure 2.3. A simple example comes from the visual-search literature. In visual-search experiments, observers are required to find a target item hidden among distractor items. In attentionally demanding tasks, it is usually the case that the time to find the target (reaction time, RT) increases with the number of distractors. Efficiency of visual search, therefore, is indexed by the slope of the function relating RT to the number of distractors. The shallower the slope is, the more efficient is the search.

Tasks that yield efficient shallow slopes (e.g., finding a red apple among green apples) are said to be carried out preattentively—namely, with little or no drain on attentional resources. In these tasks, the target is said to "pop out" from the display. Preattentive processing was thought to be performed by built-in analyzers that respond automatically to specific stimulus attributes such as color, orientation, and spatial frequency.

The preattentive hypothesis, however, has been seriously questioned by the finding that the same target can yield either an efficient shallow slope or an inefficient steep slope, depending not on whether it is characterized by a primitive visual feature (color, orientation), but on whether its salience is high relative to the distractors (Duncan & Humphreys, 1989; Theeuwes & Belopolsky, Chapter 4). Although they disconfirm the preattentive hypothesis, the findings of Duncan and Humphreys are entirely consistent with Hupé and colleagues' (1998) conclusion that perception of low-salience stimuli depends critically on reentrant signaling between higher and lower regions in the visual system. With reference to Figure 2.3 and its attendant discussion, we would expect that the number of iterative loops required to find a target in a search display would increase as the salience of the target relative to the distractors is decreased.

Object Substitution Masking

On a stormy winter evening in the early 1990s, serendipity alighted in my laboratory at the University of Alberta. Waiting for the snow ploughs to clear the roads so that I could get home, I idled away the hours fiddling with various display sequences on my point-plotting oscilloscopes. My intent was to explore the spatiotemporal parameters that govern temporal integration in vision. What I saw in one of those stimulus sequences, however, was so strange and unexpected that I rewrote the C-code in several different ways to ensure that I was seeing a real perceptual effect, not a programming artifact. It turned out that I had discovered a new form of masking that has come to be known as *object substitution masking* (OSM). What is more, I could think of no plausible way of accounting for it within an exclusively feed-forward framework. This is when I began to think of reentrant processing and to read the pertinent literature.

First studied and modeled by Di Lollo et al. (2000; see also Di Lollo, Bischof, & Dixon, 1993; Enns & Di Lollo, 1997), OSM is obtained with a display sequence consisting of two successive images, as is illustrated in Figure 2.7. The first image is displayed very briefly (e.g., 10 ms) and contains between 1 and 16 rings, each with a small gap at one of the cardinal orientations. The target ring is singled out by four dots at the corners of an imaginary square surrounding the ring. The second image, which contains only the four dots, is displayed for a duration that is varied systematically between zero (no second image) and several hundred milliseconds. In other words, the display sequence begins with a brief combined display of rings and dots and continues with the dots alone. The subject's task is to indicate the orientation of the gap in the target ring.

This experiment yields two main results. First, when the display consists of only a brief single image (i.e., when the duration of the second image in Figure 2.7 is equal to zero), the subjects have no difficulty in naming the orientation of the gap in the target ring. But when the second image (the four dots alone) remains on

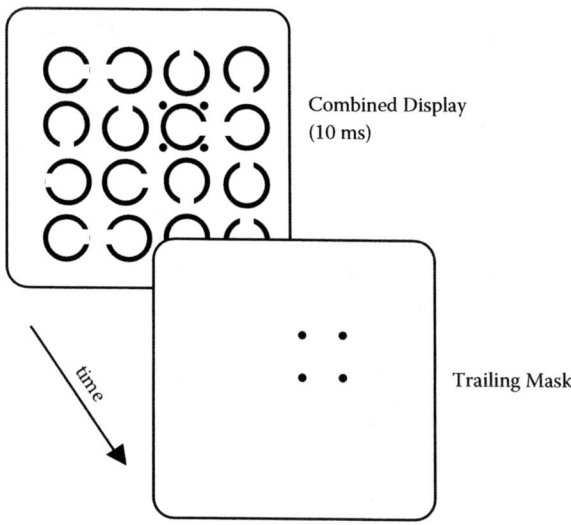

Figure 2.7 Display sequence in common-onset masking. Observers indicate the orientation of the gap in the ring singled out by four dots. Accuracy is severely impaired when a brief presentation of the search display continues with an extended presentation of the four dots alone. (After Di Lollo, V. et al., 2000, *Journal of Experimental Psychology: General*, *129*, 481–507.)

the screen beyond the disappearance of the rings, subjects make a large number of errors. Phenomenologically, the area inside the four dots appears to be blank, even though the remaining rings seem quite visible.

The second result of interest is that the magnitude of OSM is directly related to the number of items in the leading image. No OSM occurs when the leading image contains only a single item (i.e., the target and the four dots), but the magnitude of OSM increases as the number of items is increased. This shows that OSM is critically dependent on the target *not* being at the focus of attention. This pattern of results is illustrated in Figure 2.8. Demonstrations of OSM are available on the Web at http://www.sfu.ca/~enzo/ (follow the current-projects/object-substitution links).

To appreciate the importance of OSM as a window on the mind and brain, we need to take a brief excursion to masking land. Visual masking is typically classified in two types, based on the spatial relationships that exist between the contours of the target and the contours of the mask. Masking that involves spatial superimposition of contours is commonly referred to as *pattern masking*. Masking that involves closely adjacent but nonoverlapping contours is called *metacontrast* (Breitmeyer, 1984; Breitmeyer & Höğmen, 2006). Because it does not involve superimposition of contours, OSM cannot be classified as an instance of pattern masking. However, it cannot be classified as an instance of metacontrast because the OSM paradigm differs from the classical metacontrast paradigm in both the timing and the spatial extent of the masking stimuli.

The timing difference relates to stimulus-onset asynchrony (SOA) between the target and the mask. Metacontrast masking is critically dependent on the

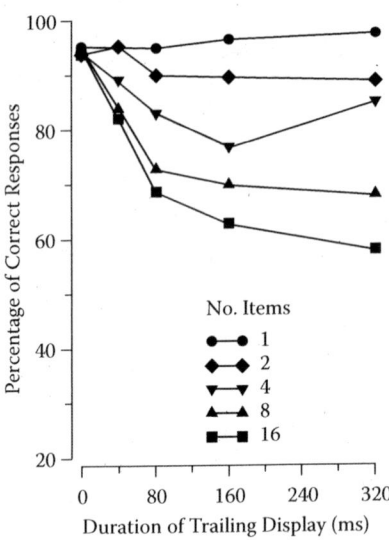

Figure 2.8   Percentage of correct responses in identifying the orientation of the gap in the display illustrated in Figure 2.7 as a function of the period for which the four-dot pattern remains on the screen alone, after a brief presentation of the search display. (After Di Lollo, V. et al., 2000, *Journal of Experimental Psychology: General, 129,* 481–507.)

presence of an optimal SOA. No masking occurs when the SOA is equal to zero. Object-substitution masking, on the other hand, occurs in full force at an SOA of zero. This is why it has also been called "common-onset masking." The main spatial difference relates to the amount of contours in the masking stimulus. For metacontrast masking to occur, the mask must have substantial contours that must be located in close proximity to the contours of the target. A mask consisting of four small dots is demonstrably inadequate for metacontrast masking. The same four-dot pattern, on the other hand, makes for a powerful mask in OSM, even when the dots are separated from the contours of the mask by a substantial margin.

Feed-forward models based on inhibitory contour interactions cannot account for the findings illustrated in Figure 2.8 or for other related findings involving OSM (e.g., Dehaene et al., 2001; Jang & Chun, 2001; Lleras & Moore, 2003). Likely reasons for this failure have been discussed extensively by Di Lollo et al. (2000). One of the main reasons is that, in conventional models, masking is said to be triggered by the *onset* of the trailing mask, whereas no such trailing onset is part of the OSM paradigm. The seemingly paradoxical aspect of OSM is that the target display (rings and dots in Figure 2.7) is masked by parts of itself (the dots alone). No new stimuli are presented in the display sequence, as in conventional metacontrast-masking paradigms.

In contrast to the difficulties encountered by feed-forward schemes, OSM is explained naturally within the reentrant framework advocated in the present work. In brief, OSM is said to take place when a mismatch arises between the reentrant signal and the ongoing activity at the lower level. The sequence of events is illustrated in Figure 2.9.

Figure 2.9(a) illustrates the feed-forward sweep leading to the establishment of a low-level representation of the initial display in primary visual cortex. Figure 2.9(b) illustrates the two-way exchanges between high- and low-level cortical regions. At this stage, the exchanges are aimed at locating the four dots within the low-level representation. Finding the four dots is essential because they mark the location of the target ring. For example, no OSM occurs if the location of the four dots is revealed (e.g., by spatial cueing) before the onset of the display sequence. This is because the number of iterations required to locate the four dots is drastically reduced, permitting the perceptual hypotheses to be checked directly against the low-level image inside the four dots.

This is not the case when the contents of the screen are replaced by the trailing image before the four dots have been located, as illustrated in Figure 2.9(c). In this case, when the four dots are eventually located, a mismatch arises between the perceptual hypothesis (four dots plus target ring) and the ongoing activity at the lower level (four dots alone). Because of this mismatch, the correlation between the perceptual hypothesis and the activity in primary visual cortex is low (see Figure 2.9b). The low correlation causes a new perceptual hypothesis to be

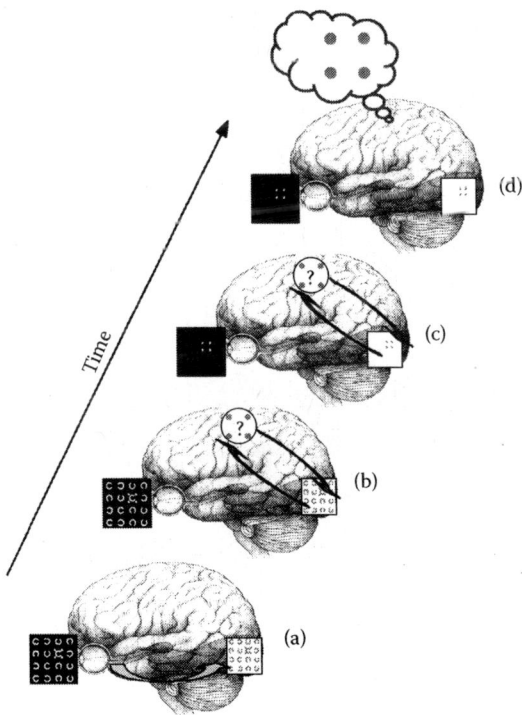

Figure 2.9   (See color insert following page 150.) Schematic representation of the sequence of reentrant-processing events involved in object-substitution masking. See text for explanation.

formed that is consistent with the currently predominant low-level activity and the "mask alone" percept replaces the "target plus mask" percept, as illustrated in Figure 2.9(d).

Not shown in Figure 2.9 is an account of the dependence of OSM on the number of nontarget items in the display. Within the reentrant-processing framework, this is explained on the assumption that the number of iterations required to locate the four dots within the search display increases with the number of nontarget items. If only a few iterations are required, the process of target identification might be completed before the image on the screen has changed. If more iterations are needed, however, a new perceptual hypothesis is formed that is consistent with the currently predominant low-level activity and the "mask alone" percept replaces the "target plus mask" percept.

This description of the sequence of events in OSM is necessarily sketchy. A more detailed description, as well as a computer simulation of the phenomenon, can be found in the paper by Di Lollo et al. (2000). What is important for the present purposes is that this new type of masking, which defies explanation in terms of feed-forward processing, is explained easily and coherently within a conceptual framework based on reentrant processing.

WHAT REENTRANT SCHEMES DO THAT FEED-FORWARD SCHEMES DO NOT DO

We have noted how reentrant processing is more efficient than feed-forward processing, how it can clean up noisy signals and implement expectations, and how it stems naturally from the way in which the brain is wired. Here, we go on to consider how reentrant processing resolves the binding problem (actually, it shows it not to be a real problem at all) and how a system such as that illustrated in Figures 2.1–2.4 offers a solution to an ancient problem in the philosophy of mind. This problem is variously known as the "problem of universal," "problem of categorization," or "problem of invariant representations."

Feature Binding: Not a Problem

What mechanisms ensure that we see the features of objects in the correct combination—for example, a red roof as red and a white house as white, and not the reverse? I noted earlier in this chapter that the binding problem arises when attempts are made to answer this question in strictly feed-forward terms.

Since von der Malsburg (1981) first formulated it, the binding problem has undergone some serious metamorphoses. The term "binding" now seems to denote not one but many disparate processes. Treisman (1996) identified no fewer than seven binding problems:

property binding (assigning the correct features to objects);
part binding (linking separate parts of an object to one another, and segregating them from the background);

range binding (assigning a specific value to a given feature (e.g., "green" for color, 25° for orientation);

hierarchical binding (linking specific features to surface-defining properties);

conditional binding (in which interpretation of one property depends on another—for example, visual illusions);

temporal binding (in which two objects displayed in rapid sequence are perceived as a single object); and

location binding (in which objects are linked to their current locations).

To this we might add a recent suggestion that the term "binding" might refer to the establishment of an association *between* objects. Colzato, Raffone, and Hommel (2006, p. 705) have defined the binding problem as involving "difficulties in relating the codes of a given entity or processing unit (e.g., visual object) to each other."

On an indulgent day, we might regard all these phenomena as belonging to the same class of events because they all subsume some form of association between distinct entities. But that would hardly help in finding a solution to the binding problem if it is the case that these phenomena are based on different underlying mechanisms. To paraphrase Coltheart (1980, p. 207), if the assignment of correct features to objects depends on visual process X and the integration of successive displays depends on visual process Y, then we can call process X "binding" and process Y something else, or call process Y "binding" and process X something else. What we cannot do without creating the utmost chaos is to use the term "binding" to refer to both X and Y if it is indeed the case that X and Y are different things.

At the outset of this chapter, I stated that the hierarchical reentrant system advocated in these pages offers a natural solution to the binding problem. To avoid chaos, I would like to make it clear that, in making that statement, what I had in mind was the problem of assigning the correct features (color, orientation, etc.) to objects. This is not to say that the remaining problems in Treisman's list are not interesting or worth pursuing or that solutions to those problems cannot be found within a reentrant scheme. But what is offered here is a solution only to the classical binding problem—namely, the *feature binding* problem.

This said, the denouement comes almost as a letdown. Within the conceptual framework of reentrant processing, the binding question simply does not arise. It is an ill-posed question. In the reentrant scheme, there is no need for features to coalesce or be bound into objects. Rather, objects are perceived realistically (i.e., as having the correct features) through the process of correlation illustrated in Figure 2.3.

Once activated by the feed-forward sweep, the high-level perceptual hypotheses (autoassociative memories) descend through the hierarchical structure where they attempt to match themselves to the patterns of activity at the lower levels through a process of correlation. Matches that yield low correlations are discarded, while the hypothesis that yields the highest correlation is confirmed and eventually leads to conscious awareness. The important consideration is that, in the present view, no separate binding process actively assigns features to objects, except perhaps in the trivial sense that objects are ultimately perceived as possessing the correct features. Within the reentrant processing account advocated here, binding is inherent in the workings of the system.

To be sure, the present approach to the binding problem is not entirely novel. Individual neurons ("grandmother cells") or dedicated cell assemblies have been proposed as forming high-level templates activated by specific combinations of input features (e.g., Barlow, 1972). In some sense, these high-level units resemble the autoassociative memories postulated in the reentrant account. These schemes were beset, however, by the combinatorial proliferation of features, objects, perspectives, sizes, etc., each requiring separate templates. What was missing from the schemes and what avoids the problem of proliferating templates is the notion of dynamic iterative reentrant processing advocated in the present work.

Invariant Representations

Among the ancient problems in the philosophy of mind is the epistemological question of how we come to know the world and all its contents. The central issue relates to the ontogeny of invariant (universal) representations: How do we know that the object we are looking at is a tree even though we have never seen this particular tree before? Two viewpoints have dominated this issue through the ages: the analytical and the holistic. These viewpoints are ostensibly in opposition to one another, but arguments have been brought forward to the effect that they are not necessarily incompatible (e.g., Prinzmetal, 1995).

First articulated in Athens's αγορά, the distinction between the two viewpoints has persisted to the present day. The holistic (also known as "nativist") view was championed by Plato (c. 427–347 b.c.). In his *Theory of Forms*, Plato postulated a transcendental universe in which perfect exemplars (forms) of all objects in the world exist in timeless invariance. Imperfect copies of these forms are immanent in the soul (which also comes from that transcendent universe) and mediate the flawed perception of objects in the world. The critical notion for our purposes is that, being immanent in the soul, invariant representations are necessarily innate. Different versions of this line of thinking are recognizable in such modern nativist theories as Gestalt psychology (e.g., Psotka, 1978).

The analytical viewpoint was championed by Aristotle (384–322 b.c.), one of Plato's graduate students. In his peripatetic school, he taught that object perception begins with experience of the features of objects in the world. Through repeated exposure to different exemplars, knowledge of a class of objects is established and object identification follows. This bottom-up process of establishing invariant representations is discernable in the theories of the British empiricists (e.g., Berkeley, Hume), who believed that the mind begins as a tabula rasa on which life experiences leave their marks. In modern times, Hebb's approach was clearly analytical: The cortex begins as a blank matrix of cells that coalesce into cell assemblies and phase sequences as a result of repeated exposure to objects and action sequences.

As was the case with the binding problem, a solution to the problem of invariant representations is trivially simple within the framework of reentrant processing. The solution was first articulated by Hawkins (2004) in his memory-prediction model of cortical functioning. Consider the system illustrated in Figure 2.2. The hatched boxes at the low level in Figure 2.2(a) are separate from one another and represent units in different locations at a low level in visual cortex. However, both units feed into the same unit at the middle level. Thus, activation of either of the two low-level units leads to activation of the middle-level unit and, not incidentally, to activation of the other low-level unit through reentrant signaling. The important consideration is that the middle-level unit in Figure 2.2(a) contains an invariant representation of the information coded in greater detail but lesser generality in the two low-level units.

In this sense, we can say that invariant representations are coded not only at the highest level (e.g., inferotemporal cortex) but at every level of the system. According to Hawkins (2004, pp. 124–125):

> [T]he subregions of V4, V2, and V1 create invariant representations based on what flows into them. They may only see a tiny part of the world, and the vocabulary of sensory objects they deal with is more basic, but they are performing the same job as IT. Also, association regions above IT form invariant representations of patterns from multiple senses. Thus all regions of cortex form invariant representations of the world underneath them in the hierarchy.

In other words, invariant representations are inherent in the structure and function of the hierarchical system. It is worth emphasizing that coded within the system are not only representations of objects but also representations of learned action sequences and environmental regularities on which expectations are based. In this context, Gestalt laws become examples of invariant representations (autoassociative memories) arising from repeated experiences with environmental regularities and physical laws. It was Aristotle all the way.

CONCLUSIONS

Throughout this chapter, I have juxtaposed feed-forward and reentrant viewpoints and the reentrant viewpoint has clearly come out ahead. In the interest of disclosure and accountability, I declare that I am something in the way of a "born-again" theorist. In my first incarnation as a vision scientist, I was interested in such phenomena as temporal integration and directional motion perception in low-level vision. In that pursuit, I used the tools of linear systems analysis to couch theoretical accounts entirely in feed-forward terms. My mantra in those days was that I wanted to see how far linear systems could go in accounting for visual perceptions.

This was not very far, it turned out—not even as far as primary visual cortex, as we have seen. In at least partial exculpation and to reduce my period of confinement in that place where wayward theorists are detained before gaining admission to visual Nirvana, I point out that my early work was done before the currently available cortical wiring diagrams became widely accessible. In my second incarnation, having seen the light, I adopted the conceptual framework of reentrant processing advocated in these pages, and I have never looked back (although, to be true to my theoretical convictions, that is precisely what I should have done).

Recent discoveries in neurobiology fit naturally within this conceptual framework. A case in point is the discovery of "mirror neurons." In 1996, Gallese, Fadiga, Fogassi, and Rizzolatti reported a happenstance finding in their laboratory. When a monkey fitted with chronic electrode implants in premotor cortex witnessed someone reaching for a raisin, the pattern of activity at the electrode site was the same as that evoked when the monkey itself performed the reaching action. Gallese et al. concluded that the function of these mirror neurons was to match observation of a motor action with its execution.

Since Gallese and colleagues' initial report in 1996, mirror neurons have been found in many regions of the cortex. What is more, they have been shown to be activated not only when witnessing a motor action, but also in response to a verbal description of or the intention to perform a motor action. It goes without saying that mirror neurons are not, strictly speaking, single neurons: They are neural networks involved in identifying objects and in monitoring and predicting action sequences. These are precisely the functions of the autoassociative memories discussed in the present work and postulated in Hawkins's (2004) memory-prediction model.

Principles of iterative reentrant processing offer more than a realistic conceptual framework for perception, cognition, and action. As has been pointedly noted by Hawkins (2004), the logic of reentrant processing could profitably replace or at least augment the feed-forward logic so prominent in the field of artificial intelligence. In this connection, Hawkins's comments regarding the concept of *back propagation* are worth pursuing in some detail.

In the field of artificial intelligence, neural networks based on back-propagation principles are established through a form of Hebbian learning involving feedback from higher to lower levels of the network when errors occur. Back propagation, however, cannot be regarded as an instance of the class of reentrant processing events discussed in the present chapter. This is because the feedback occurs only during the learning phase. Once the network has been established, processing is exclusively feed-forward, and it does not involve the kind of iterative signaling between connected regions advocated in the reentrant models outlined previously.

Hawkins (2004) points out how current artificial intelligence models encounter almost insurmountable difficulties in solving perceptual problems—such as face recognition—that biological systems can solve easily and rapidly. The problem, Hawkins believes, lies in the predominantly feed-forward architecture of these models. If ways could be found to endow them with the kind of reentrant processing that seems so prevalent in biological systems, the capabilities of artificial intelligence systems would be vastly increased.

ACKNOWLEDGMENTS

This work was sponsored by a Discovery Grant from the Natural Sciences and Engineering Research Council of Canada. I thank my colleague, Thomas M. Spalek, for thoughtful and constructive comments on earlier versions of this chapter and for enjoyable and stimulating discussions on related topics. Correspondence concerning this work should be addressed to Vincent Di Lollo, Department of Psychology, Simon Fraser University, Burnaby, B.C., Canada. Electronic mail may be sent to enzo@sfu.ca.

REFERENCES

Bahrami, B., Lavie, N., & Rees, G. (2007). Attentional load modulates responses of human primary visual cortex to invisible stimuli. *Current Biology, 17*, 509–513.

Barlow, H. B. (1972). Single units and cognition: A neuronal doctrine for perceptual psychology. *Perception, 1*, 371–394.

Breitmeyer, B. G. (1984). *Visual masking: An integrative approach.* New York: Oxford University Press.

Breitmeyer, B. G., & Högmen, H. (2006). *Visual masking: Time slices through conscious and unconscious vision.* New York: Oxford University Press.

Brindley, G. S., & Rushton, D. N. (1974). Implanted simulators of the visual cortex as visual prosthetic devices. *Transactions of the American Academy of Ophthalmology & Otolaringology, 78*, 74–745.

Bullier, J. (2001). Integrated model of visual processing. *Brain Research Reviews, 36*, 96–107.

Bullier, J., McCourt, M. E., & Henry, G. H. (1988). Physiological studies on the feedback connection to the striate cortex from cortical areas 18 and 19 of the cat. *Experimental Brain Research, 70*, 90–98.

Bundesen, C. (1990). A theory of visual attention. *Psychological Review, 97*, 523–547.

Carpenter, G., & Grossberg, S. (1987). A massively parallel architecture for a self-organizing neural pattern recognition machine. *Computer Vision, Graphics, and Image Processing, 37*, 54–115.

Coltheart, M. (1980). Iconic memory and visible persistence. *Perception & Psychophysics, 27*, 183–228.

Colzato, L. S., Raffone, A., & Hommel, B. (2006). What do we learn from binding features? Evidence for multilevel feature integration. *Journal of Experimental Psychology: Human Perception and Performance, 32*, 705–716.

Dehaene, S., Naccache, L., Cohen, L., Le Bihan, D., Mangin, J.-F., Poline, J.-B., et al. (2001). Cerebral mechanisms of word masking and unconscious repetition priming. *Nature Neuroscience, 4*, 752–758.

Di Lollo, V., Bischof, W. F., & Dixon, P. (1993). Stimulus-onset asynchrony is not necessary for motion perception or metacontrast masking. *Psychological Science, 4*, 260–263.

Di Lollo, V., Enns, J. T., & Rensink, R. A. (2000). Competition for consciousness among visual events: The psychophysics of reentrant visual processes. *Journal of Experimental Psychology: General, 129*, 481–507.

Di Lollo, V., Smilek, D., Kawahara, J., & Ghorashi, S. M. S. (2005). System reconfiguration, not resource depletion, determines the efficiency of visual search. *Perception & Psychophysics, 67*, 1080–1087.

Duncan, J., & Humphreys, G. (1989). Visual search and stimulus similarity. *Psychological Review, 96*, 433–458.

Eggermont, J. J. (1990). *The correlative brain.* Berlin: Springer–Verlag.

Enns, J. T., & Di Lollo, V. (1997). Object substitution: A new form of masking in unattended visual locations. *Psychological Science, 8*, 135–139.

Felleman, D. J., & Van Essen, D. C. (1991). Distributed hierarchical processing in primate visual cortex. *Cerebral Cortex, 1*, 1–47.

Frisby, J. (1980). *Seeing. Illusion, brain and mind.* Oxford: Oxford University Press.

Gallese, V., Fadiga, L., Fogassi, L., & Rizzolatti, G. (1996). Action recognition in premotor cortex. *Brain, 119*, 593–609.

Gibson, J. J. (1977). The theory of affordances. In R. E. Shaw & J. Bransford (Eds.), *Perceiving, acting, and knowing*. Hillsdale, NJ: Lawrence Erlbaum Associates.

Harth, E., Unnikrishnan, K. P., & Pandya, A. S. (1987). The inversion of sensory processing by feedback pathways: A model of visual cognitive functions. *Science, 237*, 184–187.

Hawkins, J. (2004). *On intelligence*. New York: Holt.

Hebb, D. O. (1949). *The organization of behavior*. New York: John Wiley & Sons.

Hogben, J. H., & Di Lollo, V. (1985). Practice reduces suppression in metacontrast and in apparent motion. *Perception & Psychophysics, 35*, 441–445.

Hubel, D. H., & Wiesel, T. N. (1962). Receptive fields, binocular interaction and functional architecture in the cat's visual cortex. *Journal of Physiology, London, 160*, 106–154.

Hubel, D. H., & Wiesel, T. N. (1977). Functional architecture of macaque visual cortex. *Proceedings of the Royal Society, London (B), 198*, 1–59.

Hupé, J. M., James, A. C., Payne, B. R., Lomber, S. G., Girard, P., & Bullier, J. (1998). Cortical feedback improves discrimination between figure and ground by V1, V2 and V3 neurons. *Nature, 394*, 784–787.

Jang, Y., & Chun, M. M. (2001). The spatial gradient of visual masking by object substitution. *Vision Research, 41*, 3121–3131.

Jeffries, L. N., Wright, R. D., & Di Lollo, V. (2005). Inhibition of return to an occluded object depends on expectation. *Journal of Experimental Psychology: Human Perception and Performance, 31*, 1224–1233.

Kastner, S., Pinsk, M. A., De Weerd, P., Desimone, R., & Ungerleider, L. G. (1999). Increased activity in human visual cortex during directed attention in the absence of visual stimulation. *Neuron, 22*, 751–761.

Kastner S., & Ungerleider, L. G. (2000). Mechanisms of visual attention in the human cortex. *Annual Review of Neuroscience, 23*, 315–341.

Konorski, J. (1967). *Integrative activity of the brain. An interdisciplinary approach*. Chicago: University of Chicago Press.

Lamme, V. A. F. (1995). The neurophysiology of figure–ground segregation in primary visual cortex. *Journal of Neuroscience, 15*, 1605–1615.

Lamme, V. A. F., & Roelfsema, P. R. (2000). The distinct modes of vision offered by feedforward and recurrent processing. *Trends in Neuroscience, 23*, 571–579.

Lamme, V. A. F., Zipser, K., & Spekreijse, H. (1997). Figure–ground signals in V1 depend on extrastriate feedback. *Investigative Ophthalmology & Visual Science, 38*, S969 (abstract).

Lamme, V. A. F., Zipser, K., & Spekreijse, H. (1998). Figure–ground activity in primary visual cortex is suppressed by anesthesia. *Proceedings of the National Academy of Sciences USA, 95*, 3263–3268.

Le Gros Clark, W. (1967). *Man–apes or ape–men?* New York: Holt, Rinehart, & Winston.

Lindsay, P. H., & Norman, A. D. (1977). *Human information processing: An introduction to psychology*. New York: Academic Press.

Lleras, A., & Moore, C. M. (2003). When the target becomes the mask: Using apparent motion to isolate the object-level component of object substitution masking. *Journal of Experimental Psychology: Human Perception and Performance, 29*, 106–120.

Marr, D. (1982). *Vision*. San Francisco: W. H. Freeman.

McClelland, J. L., & Rumelhart, D. E. (1981). An interactive activation model of context effects in letter perception: Part 1. An account of basic findings. *Psychological Review, 88*, 375–407.

McCulloch, W. S., & Pitts, W. (1943). A logical calculus of the ideas immanent in nervous activity. *Bulletin of Mathematical Biology, 5*, 115–133.

Mignard, M., & Malpeli, J. G. (1991). Paths of information flow through visual cortex. *Science, 251,* 1249–1251.

Moran, J., & Desimone, R. (1985). Selective attention gates visual processing in extrastriate cortex. *Science, 229,* 782–784.

Motter, B. C. (1993). Focal attention produces spatially selective processing in visual cortical areas V1, V2, and V4 in the presence of competing stimuli. *Journal of Neurophysiology, 70,* 909–919.

Mumford, D. (1991). On the computational architecture of the neocortex I. The role of the thalamo-cortical loop. *Biological Cybernetics, 65,* 135–145.

Mumford, D. (1992). On the computational architecture of the neocortex II. The role of cortico-cortical loops. *Biological Cybernetics, 66,* 241–251.

Pascual-Leone, A., & Walsh, V. (2001). Fast back projections from the motion to the primary visual area necessary for visual awareness. *Science, 292* (April), 510–512.

Penfield, W. G., & Perot, P. (1963). The brain's record of auditory and visual experience: A final summary and discussion. *Brain, 86,* 595–696.

Posner, M. I., & Cohen, Y. A. (1984). Components of visual orienting. In H. Bouma & D. G. Bouwhuis (Eds.), *Attention and performance X* (pp. 531–556). Hillsdale, NJ: Lawrence Erlbaum Associates.

Posner, M. I., & Raichle, M. E. (1994). *Images of mind.* New York: Scientific American Library.

Potter, M. C. (1999). Understanding sentences and scenes: The role of conceptual short-term memory. In V. Coltheart (Ed.), *Fleeting memories: Cognition of brief visual stimuli* (pp. 13–46). Cambridge, MA: MIT Press.

Prinzmetal, W. (1995). Visual feature integration in a world of objects. *Current Directions in Psychological Science, 4,* 90–94.

Psotka, J. (1978). Perceptual processes that may create stick figures and balance. *Journal of Experimental Psychology: Human Perception and Performance, 4,* 101–111.

Reichardt, W. (1961). Autocorrelation, a principle for the evaluation of sensory information. In W. A. Rosenblith (Ed.), *Sensory communication* (pp. 303–317). Cambridge, MA: MIT Press.

Reicher, G. M. (1969). Perceptual recognition as a function of meaningfulness of stimulus material. *Journal of Experimental Psychology, 81,* 275–280.

Selfridge, O. (1959). Pandemonium: A paradigm for learning. In *Symposium on the mechanization of thought processes.* London: HM Stationery Office.

Shiffrin, R. M., & Schneider, W. (1977). Controlled and automatic human information processing II. Perceptual learning, automatic attending, and a general theory. *Psychological Review, 84,* 127–190.

Shipp, S., & Zeki, S. (1989). The organization of connections between areas V5 and V1 in the macaque monkey visual cortex. *European Journal of Neuroscience, 1,* 309–332.

Sillito, A. M. (1992). GABA mediated inhibitory processes in the function of the geniculo-striate system. *Progress in Brain Research, 90,* 349–384.

Sillito, A. M., Jones, H. E., Gerstein, G. L., & West, D. C. (1994). Feature-linked synchronization of thalamic relay cell firing induced by feedback from the visual cortex. *Nature, 369,* 479–482.

Skinner, J. E., & Yingling, C. D. (1977). Central gating mechanisms that regulate event-related potentials and behavior. In J. E. Desmedt (Ed.), *Progress in clinical neurophysiology* (Vol. 1, pp. 30–69). Basel: Karger.

Spalek, T. M. (2007). A direct assessment of the role of expectation in IOR. *Psychological Science, 18,* 783–787.

Spalek, T. M., & Di Lollo, V. (2007). The time required for perceptual (nonmotoric) processing in IOR. *Psychonomic Bulletin & Review, 14,* 327–331.

Spalek, T. M., & Hammad, S. (2004). Supporting the attentional momentum view of inhibition of return: Is attention biased to go right? *Perception & Psychophysics, 66,* 219–233.

Spalek, T. M., & Hammad, S. (2005). The left-to-right bias in inhibition of return is due to the direction of reading. *Psychological Science, 16,* 15–18.

Steriade, M., Domich, L., & Oakson, G. (1986). Reticularis thalami neurons revisited: Activity changes during shifts in states of vigilance. *Journal of Neuroscience, 6,* 68–81.

Tassinari, G., Marzi, C. A., Lee, B. B., Di Lollo, V., & Campara, D. (1999). A possible selective impairment of magnocellular function in compression of the anterior visual pathways. *Experimental Brain Research, 127,* 391–401.

Tononi, G., Sporns, O., & Edelman, G. M. (1992). Reentry and the problem of integrating multiple cortical areas: Simulation of dynamic integration in the visual system. *Cerebral Cortex, 2,* 310–335.

Treisman, A. (1996). The binding problem. *Current Opinion in Neurobiology, 6,* 171–178.

Vidyasagar, T. R. (1999). A neuronal model of attentional spotlight: Parietal guiding the temporal. *Brain Research Reviews, 30,* 66–76.

von der Malsburg, C. (1981). The correlation theory of brain function. MPI Biophysical Chemistry, internal report 81–82. Reprinted in E. Domany, J. L. van Hemmen, and K. Schulten (Eds.), *Models of neural networks II* (1994), Berlin: Springer–Verlag.

Weisstein, N., & Harris, C. S. (1974). Visual detection of line segments: An object-superiority effect. *Science, 186,* 752–755.

Zeki, S. (1993). *A vision of the brain.* Oxford, England: Blackwell.

Zipser, K., Lamme, V. A. F., & Schiller, P. H. (1996). Contextual modulation primary visual cortex. *Journal of Neuroscience, 16,* 7376–7389.

3

Dissecting Spatial Visual Attention

WILLIAM PRINZMETAL and AYELET N. LANDAU

INTRODUCTION AND BACKGROUND

*T*he study of attention had a prominent place at the birth of psychology as a scientific discipline. Wundt devoted the first chapter of his *Einfuhrung in die Psychologie (Introduction to Psychology)* to attention. He commented, for example,

> If we practise letting our attention wander over the different parts of the field of vision while keeping the same fixation-point, it will soon become clear to us that the fixation point of attention and the fixation-point of the field of vision are by no means identical. (1912/1973, p. 20)

It has been recognized that at least two forms of spatial attention can be found in vision. For example, Wundt (1902) observed that attention could be involuntary or voluntary. A variety of distinctions have been made that more or less correspond to Wundt's distinction, including goal-directed attention versus stimulus-driven capture and endogenous attention versus exogenous attention. The terms used to label these forms of attention are not important. The critical question is whether these two forms of attention involve the same or different mechanisms, and, if they involve different mechanisms, what are those mechanisms?

Modern investigators have largely been unclear whether voluntary and involuntary forms of attention are mediated by different mechanisms or whether they are simply different means of controlling a single mechanism. Rather, most contemporary investigations have focused on the properties of different methods of summoning attention. The assumption is often made that involuntary attention has the same effect on perceptual processes as voluntary attention (Rauschenberger, 2003) and that they affect the same neural mechanisms (Gazzaniga, Ivry, & Mangun, 1998).

The research reported here challenges this assumption. Three separate behavioral paradigms demonstrate that voluntary and involuntary forms of attention have different consequences. Furthermore, neural imaging (Esterman et al., 2007) and electroencephalograph (EEG) studies (Landau, Esterman, Robertson, Bentin, & Prinzmetal, 2007) demonstrate that they involve different neural mechanisms. Voluntary attention enhances the perceptual representation so that the observer has a more veridical perceptual representation of stimuli in an attended location than in an unattended location (e.g., Lu & Dosher, 1998; Prinzmetal, 2005). Involuntary attention, on the other hand, does not enhance the perceptual representation, but rather works by nonperceptual mechanisms that only affect response time.

Although we are interested in the distinction between voluntary and involuntary attention in a variety of paradigms, an excellent way of separating voluntary and involuntary spatial attention in vision is the spatial cueing paradigm developed by Posner and his colleagues (Posner, 1980). In this paradigm, subjects engage in a simple target detection or target identification task. Before the target appears, a location is "cued"—for example, with a box changing color or brightening. A version of this paradigm is illustrated in Figure 3.1.

In this version, the task was to indicate which of two target faces was presented by pressing a button. The cue consisted of one of the boxes getting thicker and turning red (dashed line in the figure). There were two kinds of trials. In valid trials, the cue indicated the target location. In invalid trials, it indicated a nontarget location. Eye movements were monitored. Subjects were trained not to move their eyes, and trials on which eye movements were made were eliminated from the analysis. The general idea was that subjects would "attend" to the cued location and that target detection or identification would be better on valid trials than on invalid trials.

Posner and his colleagues (e.g., Posner, Snyder, & Davidson, 1980) had subjects engage in various detection and identification tasks designed to examine voluntary attention. The onset of the cue preceded the onset of the target by 1 s, and the cue was always informative of the target location. For example, 75% of the trials may have been valid and 25% invalid. Subjects were faster on valid trials than on invalid trials in both detection and identification tasks. The notion was that the cue

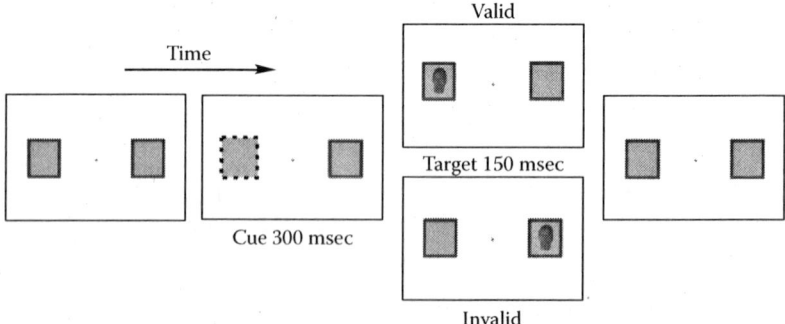

Figure 3.1   A example of the spatial-cueing task. One of two target faces was briefly presented. The task was to indicate which face was presented. The target was preceded by a cue, which consisted of one of the frames turning red (shown as a dashed black frame).

enabled subjects to shift their attention voluntarily to the cued location. When the target appeared in the cued location (valid trials), subjects were already attending to the relevant location. On invalid trials, subjects had to switch their attention, causing longer reaction times (RTs).

Jonides (1976, 1981) demonstrated how this task could be used to investigate both voluntary and involuntary attention. With the experiment described in Figure 3.1, to study voluntary attention, the cue was made informative or predictive about the target location as in the Posner et al. studies. In this situation, it is strategically advantageous for the subject to attend voluntarily to the cued location. To study involuntary attention, the cue was made noninformative or nonpredictive as to the target location. Thus, with two possible target locations, 50% of the trials would be valid and 50% would be invalid. Jonides found that both predictive and nonpredictive cues affected performance in RT experiments: Subjects were faster on valid trials than on invalid trials. Thus, simple RT experiments do not discriminate voluntary and involuntary attention.

Posner and his colleagues used a central cue that was predictive of the target location, whereas Jonides often used a peripheral cue. For many years, investigators believed that the main difference between these experiments was whether the cue was in central vision and symbolic of the target location or in peripheral vision and directly indicated the target location (e.g., Briand & Klein, 1987). However, since that time, numerous investigators have found the peripheral nature of the cue is not necessarily critical for involuntary attention, and some central cues can behave identically to cues in the periphery (Driver et al., 1999; Friesen & Kingstone, 1998; Lambert & Duddy, 2002; Langton, Watt, & Bruce, 2000; Ristic, Friesen, & Kingstone, 2002; Ristic & Kingstone, 2006; Tipples, 2002).

In order to engage voluntary attention, at least two requirements must be met. First, the cue must be predictive of the target location. Second, the time between the onset of the cue and the onset of the target must be sufficiently long (~200 ms; e.g., see Posner, Cohen, & Rafal, 1982; Sereno & Holzman, 1996; Warner, Juola, & Koshino, 1990).

In all of the studies reported in this chapter, we compared predictive and nonpredictive cues; all other stimulus parameters were identical. That is, we used the same task, stimuli, timing, and cues so that the differences we found could only be attributed to the predictability of the cues. Interestingly, different results can be obtained between predictive and nonpredictive cues even if the subjects are not aware of the proportion of valid trials (e.g., Bartolomeo, Decaix, & Siéroff, 2007; Decaix, Seíroff, & Bartolomeo, 2002).[1] In addition, voluntary attention can be summoned by merely instructing the participants to attend to the cues even if these cues are uninformative (Jonides, 1981). Thus, both probability and instructional manipulations can engage the voluntary attention mechanisms.

The second criterion for engaging voluntary attention is that the stimulus-onset asynchrony (SOA) must be sufficiently long, over about 200 ms. (Luck, Hillyard, Mouloua, & Hawkins, 1996). Involuntary attention has its effect almost immediately, and then its effect dissipates with time (e.g., Wright & Richard, 2000). The difference in time course of voluntary and involuntary attention is seen most clearly in the anticueing paradigm (Posner et al., 1982; Sereno & Holzman, 1996; Warner et al., 1990). In this paradigm, a location is cued, as in the standard spatial cueing paradigm. However, the probability that the target will be in the cued location is low, and the probability that it will be in the opposite (uncued) location is high.

To illustrate this, in an unpublished study (Prinzmetal & Wang, 2005), we had four possible target locations around the fixation point (above, below, left, and right). Subjects identified a target (the letters F or T) and there were two SOAs (40 and 600 ms). On 20% of the trials, the target was in the cued location, but on 80% of the trials it was in the location opposite the cue. Subjects averaged about 92% correct, and the dependent variable was RT on correct trials (Figure 3.2). On the short SOA condition, subjects were faster when the target was in the cued (low probability) location. This effect represents involuntary attention. At the longer SOA, subjects were faster when the target appeared in the opposite location (also see, for example, Decaix et al., 2002; Posner et al., 1982; Sereno & Holzman, 1996; Warner et al., 1990). The interaction shown in Figure 3.2 is significant ($F(1,15)$ = 3.15, $p < .05$).

Hence, voluntary and involuntary forms of attention clearly differ in their temporal properties. Involuntary attention is transient in nature and has its largest effect at short SOAs, and voluntary attention has its largest effect at longer SOAs (also see Berger, Henik, & Rafal, 2005). The issue is whether they differ only in their time courses or whether they are also different in their effects on behavior and their neural mechanisms. We argue that they have different effects and are mediated by different mechanisms. Voluntary attention enhances the perceptual representation so that more information is available about an attended object. Involuntary attention does not affect perception. Later, we will outline two possible mechanisms that could mediate involuntary attention: (1) a postperceptual serial mechanism and (2) a response-decision priming mechanism.

In the following sections, we illustrate three behavioral differences between voluntary and involuntary attention. We also demonstrate differences between voluntary and involuntary attention in cortical response seen in functional magnetic

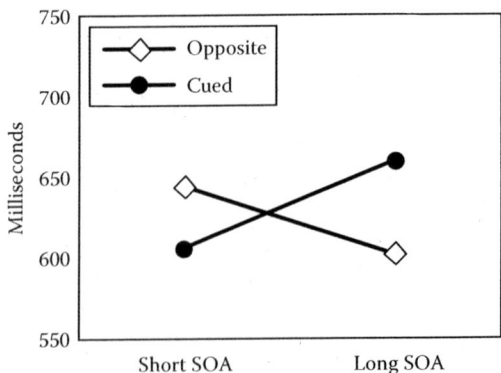

Figure 3.2   Results from an anticueing experiment. There were four possible target locations. A cue in one location indicated that the target would appear in the opposite location with a probability of .8 and in the cued location with a probability of .2.

resonance imaging (fMRI) and in EEG gamma band response. In all of the experiments, we either manipulate SOA or use an SOA that is suitable for both voluntary and involuntary attention. All of the experiments use a peripheral cue and hence evoke involuntary attention. In most cases, the important independent variable is whether the cue is informative of the target location or not. To study involuntary attention, the cue is made nonpredictive of the target location. To study voluntary attention, we make the cue predictive of the target location, thus adding a voluntary component.

ACCURACY AND REACTION TIME

The inspiration for these experiments was a series of studies on the effect of attention on stimulus qualia (e.g., Prinzmetal, Amiri, Allen, & Edwards, 1998; Prinzmetal & Wilson, 1997). For example, one set of experiments examined the effect of attention on phenomenal brightness and contrast (Prinzmetal, Nwachuku, Bodanski, Blumenfeld, & Shimizu, 1997). In these experiments, attention was manipulated in various ways and the dependent variable was related to the accuracy of perception. In several cases, we failed to obtain an effect of attention using the spatial-cueing task unless location uncertainty was present (discussed later). However, all of these early experiments were designed around accuracy as the dependent variable. In these cases, we may have found RT effects if we had emphasized speed in the experiments.

To determine whether a dissociation between RT and accuracy could exist, we carried out a series of experiments in which we first conducted the usual RT experiment in which subjects were over 90% correct and RT was the variable of interest (Prinzmetal, McCool, & Park, 2005). In every experiment, subjects were faster on valid trials than on invalid trials, regardless of whether the cue was predictive of the target location (voluntary attention) or not (involuntary attention). In each of these experiments, the voluntary and involuntary attention conditions were run with different groups of subjects.

Having ascertained that we obtained the usual RT effects of Posner and colleagues, and Jonides, we ran accuracy versions of the same experiments. In the accuracy experiments, we made the discrimination difficult by changing some aspect of the stimulus. For example, in the face discrimination task shown in Figure 3.1, we morphed the faces to be more similar to each other. Subjects were instructed to take their time and be as accurate as possible. Immediate feedback was given when subjects erred.

Typical results for the face stimuli are show in Figure 3.3. The left panel shows the results of an RT experiment in which the face discrimination was easy, subjects were quite accurate (>90% correct), and speed was emphasized. (The RT data are from Landau et al., 2007.) The right panel shows the results of a separate experiment in which the faces were morphed to yield a difficult discrimination and accuracy was emphasized. In each RT experiment, subjects were significantly faster on valid trials than on invalid trials. In every accuracy experiment, subjects were more accurate on valid than on invalid trials, but only when the cue was predictive

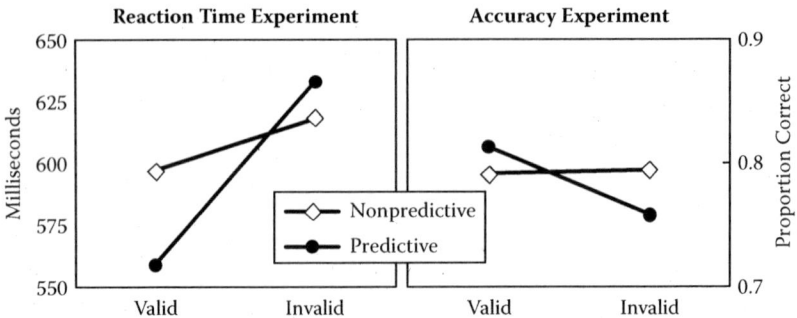

Figure 3.3   Results from typical RT and accuracy experiments. Subjects had to discriminate faces. In the RT experiment, accuracy was over 90% correct. In the accuracy experiment, the faces were morphed to make the discrimination difficult and subjects were urged to take their time and be as accurate as possible.

of the target location (i.e., voluntary attention). When the cue was not predictive, no difference in accuracy was found between valid and invalid trials.

Prinzmetal, McCool, and Park (2005) obtained this pattern of results not only with faces as stimuli, but also with letter discrimination (e.g., the target was the letter F or T) and line orientation discrimination (horizontal or vertical). This pattern of results was obtained with and without poststimulus masks (cf. Smith, 2000), on a white background or black background, and with SOAs from 0 ms (simultaneous onset of cue and target) to 300 ms. Different cues were used, including visual onsets, auditory cues from speakers located to the left and right of the subject (see Spence, 2001), and gaze direction cues (Prinzmetal, Leonhardt, & Garrett, 2008).

In 19 experiments reported by Prinzmetal, McCool, et al., and other experiments in our lab (e.g., Prinzmetal, Leonhardt, & Garrett, 2008), we found the same pattern across the different stimulus types and procedures. In experiments designed around RT, subjects were faster on valid trials than on invalid trials, regardless of whether the cue was predictive or not. However, in experiments designed around accuracy, subjects were more accurate on valid than on invalid trials only with voluntary attention (e.g., predictive cues).

A few previous investigators had found that subjects were more accurate on valid than on invalid trials with nonpredictive spatial cues (e.g., Awh & Oh 2005; Carrasco, Ling, & Read, 2004; Dufour, 1999; Handy et al., 1996; Klein & Dick, 2002). We were able to replicate each of these studies and demonstrate that the results were due to a factor confounded with involuntary attention. For example, Dufour (1999) did not monitor eye movements. We replicated his results, but when we monitored eye movements, the effect disappeared (Prinzmetal, Park, & Garrett, 2005). Other results could be accounted for by other confounds (see Prinzmetal, Park, & Garrett).

Many of the results in the spatial cueing paradigm can be accounted for by location uncertainty (Luck & Thomas, 1999; Shiu & Pashler, 1994). Location uncertainty arises when several possible stimulus locations are present and subjects are uncertain as to which contains the target. The quality of the perceptual representation might be the same in both cued and uncued locations; however, if subjects have a tendency to base their responses on information in the cued location, they will be more accurate on valid trials (where target information is in the cued location) than in invalid trials (where target information is in the uncued location).[2]

We have demonstrated that the results of Carrasco et al. (2004) could be accounted for by location uncertainty (Prinzmetal, Long, & Leonhardt, 2008; also see P. Smith, Chapter 9). The effect of location uncertainty can be very subtle. Consider a recent experiment by Awh and Oh (2005): Each trial began with a fixation point (see Figure 3.4A), followed by a nonpredictive spatial cue (Figure 3.4B), a stimulus that contained a digit (Figure 3.4C), and a mask (Figure 3.4D). The stimulus consisted of a cluster of nine alphanumeric characters; the center character was a digit.

The task was to indicate which digit had been presented; the cluster of characters could appear in four possible locations. In previously unpublished data, Prinzmetal and Le (2005) replicated Awh and Oh: Subjects were more accurate with valid than invalid trials ($t(13) = 4.36$, $p < .05$; see diamonds in Figure 3.5). Awh and Oh argued that because it was clear to subjects which of the four quadrants contained the target, there was no location uncertainty.

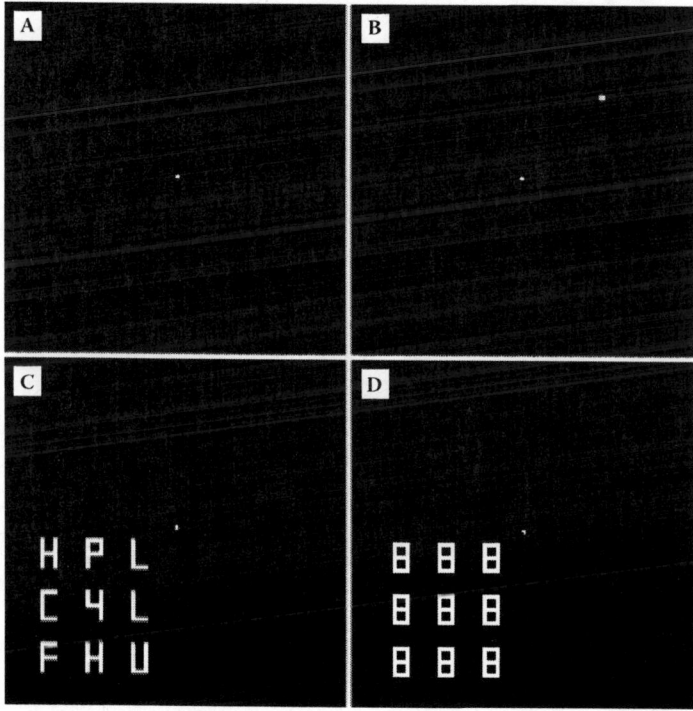

Figure 3.4 The stimuli used in the replication of Awh & Oh (paper presented at the Cognitive Science Association for Interdisciplinary Learning, Hood River, OR, 2005). The trial begins with a fixation point (A), followed by a cue (B), a stimulus (C), and a mask (D).

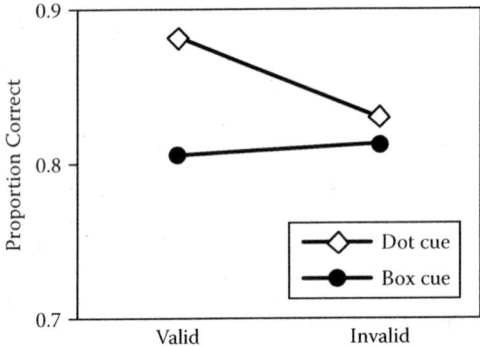

Figure 3.5   The results of the replication of Awh & Oh (paper presented at the Cognitive Science Association for Interdisciplinary Learning, Hood River, OR, 2005). The dot cue indicated a specific location in the cluster of items reducing spatial uncertainty. The box cue surrounded all of the items.

However, given that, with a brief exposure, the perceived location of an object may be different from the actual location (Prinzmetal, 2005), perhaps the dots helped subjects know which item within the cluster was the digit. We tested this by replacing the dot cue with a box that surrounded the entire cluster of characters. The effect of the cue vanished. The difference between valid and invalid trials did not approach significance (t(13) = 0.20; see solid circles in Figure 3.5).

In summary, in every RT study that we have conducted, subjects were faster on valid trials than on invalid trials, regardless of whether the cue was predictive or not. In every study designed around accuracy with voluntary attention that we have conducted, subjects are more accurate on valid than on invalid trials. However, across a large number of studies with only involuntary attention, we have not observed even one study where involuntary attention improved accuracy.

REACTION TIME AND PERCEPTUAL DIFFICULTY

The results in the previous section demonstrate a dissociation between voluntary and involuntary attention across different dependent variables. We have conducted another series of experiments within RT where we varied the perceptual difficulty of the task (Prinzmetal, Zvinyatskovskiy, Gutierrez, & Dilem, 2008). The preferential allocation of processing resources should have its greatest effect with a perceptually difficult task rather than with a perceptually easy task. A perceptually easy task—one that can be accomplished without much "attention"—should show a relatively small effect of an attentional manipulation. Thus, in an experiment with predictive spatial cues, the effects of the cue (difference between invalid and valid RTs) should be larger with a perceptually demanding task than with an easy task (e.g., Briand & Klein, 1987; Soetens, Deroost, & Notebaert, 2003; cf. Johnston, McCann, & Remington 1995).

We made the opposite prediction for involuntary attention: The effect of attention should be less with a perceptually difficult task. The effect of involuntary attention is transient; it decreases with time (e.g., Berger et al., 2005; Nakayama & Mackeben, 1989). Hence, making the task perceptually difficult would increase the time before response selection, and the transient benefit of the cue would have had time to dissipate. Thus, we predicted that increasing perceptual difficulty would increase the effect of a predictive spatial cue (voluntary attention) but decrease the effect of a nonpredictive spatial cue (involuntary attention).

We have found this interaction in a number of studies (Prinzmetal, Zvinyatskovskiy, et al., 2008). One of the experiments is illustrated in Figure 3.6. There were four possible target positions. One of the positions was cued with a box 280 ms before the target appeared. Subjects indicated whether the display contained an F or T. For the easy task, the target was surrounded by the letter O (e.g., OFO—left panel). This task was easy because the targets can be discriminated by a single feature (the "–" in the F). Hence, this task was called the feature condition.

For the difficult task, the target was surrounded by the letter H (e.g., HFH— right panel). The targets cannot be discriminated by a simple feature, and subjects must correctly conjoin the features, a process that has been shown to require attention (e.g., Prinzmetal et al., 1986; Treisman & Schmidt, 1982). We called this the conjunction condition. For half the subjects, the cue was predictive of the target location (voluntary attention) and for half it was random with respect to the target location (involuntary attention). Each group contained 12 subjects.

Interaction in the predictive group was significant in that the effect of attention was larger in the conjunction condition than in the feature condition (Figure 3.7a). This result replicates Briand and Klein (1987) and Soetens et al. (2003). Significant interaction was also present in the nonpredictive group, but the results were in the opposite direction: The feature task had a significantly larger attention effect than

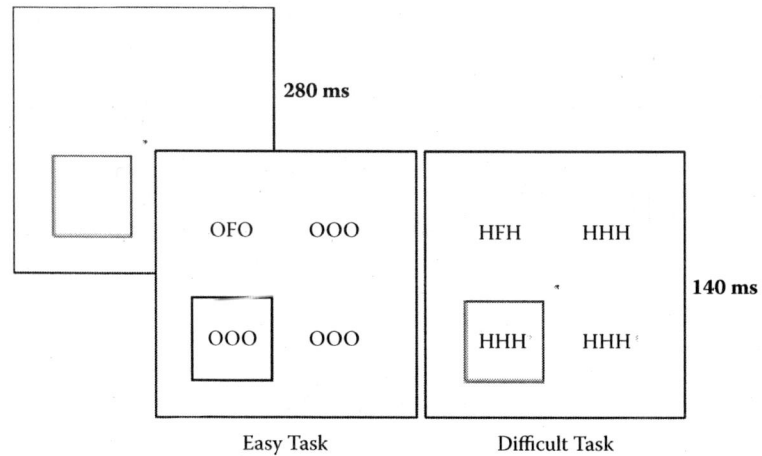

Easy Task   Difficult Task

Figure 3.6   The stimuli used by Prinzmetal, Zvinyatskovsky, et al. (2008).

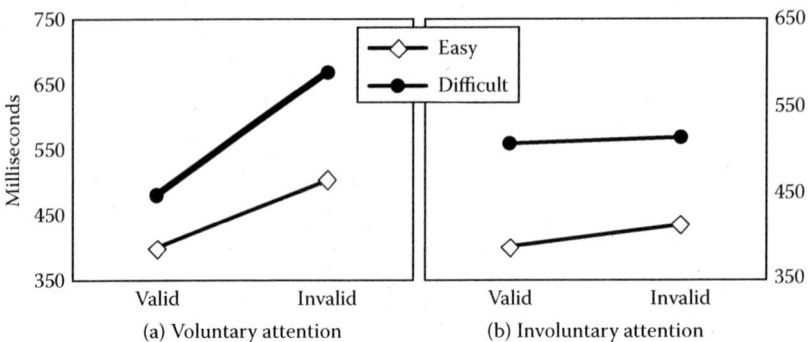

Figure 3.7 The results of Prinzmetal et al. (2007).

the conjunction task (Figure 3.7b). The three-way interaction of group, cue valid-ity, and difficulty was significant. We replicated this finding twice with small pro-cedural variations. Interpreting interactions in RT is difficult, but a strong aspect of these data is that no simple monotonic transformation can lead to the pattern in Figure 3.7 (Loftus, 1978).

The results for the nonpredictive group were in contrast to those of Briand (1998), who reported that both predictive and nonpredictive peripheral cues led to the same results (i.e., the pattern in Figure 3.7a). We were able to demonstrate that Briand's results were due to the uncontrolled eye movements.

In summary, one would expect that a perceptually difficult task would demand more "attention" than an easy task. Hence, the effect of a spatial cue (measured in RT) should be greater for a difficult task than for an easy task. We found this effect only with predictive cues. With involuntary attention, we obtained the opposite effect: a larger cueing effect with the easy rather than the difficult task. Recently, Kerzel, Zarian and Souto (2009) have replicated these results with a different manipulation of perceptual difficulty.

CHARACTERIZING INVOLUNTARY ATTENTION

Voluntary attention is easy to characterize: It enhances the perceptual representa-tion so that we have a more veridical view of objects to which we are attending than of objects to which we are not attending. Voluntary attention leads to higher accuracy. The effect of voluntary attention is greater with a perceptually demand-ing task than it is with an easy task. The goal of this section is to characterize invol-untary attention. Few theories of involuntary attention do not involve perceptual processes. Here, we briefly describe two theories and report a preliminary test that compares these theories.

The first theory is part of the class of accumulator models (e.g., Grice, 1972; Smith & Vickers, 1988). In particular, we use aspects of the "leaky accumulator model" of Usher and McClelland (2001; see P. Smith, Chapter 9, for a similar use of accumulator models). The model we describe is to account for performance in a direct cueing experiment, with two targets and two possible stimulus locations.

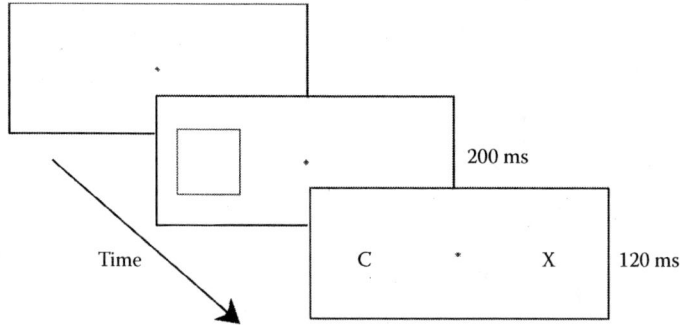

Figure 3.8   A sample stimulus from the multiple-targets experiment. A single-target cued (valid) trial is shown.

The model assumes four accumulators: two accumulators sum evidence for targets 1 and 2 in the left display position and two accumulators sum evidence for targets 1 and 2 in the right display (see Figure 3.8). Unlike previous models, we assume that evidence for the alternative targets accumulates separately for each display position. This assumption is consistent with the claim that independent decisions are made for targets at each location. Considerable evidence supports this claim (Shaw, 1982). When evidence in any one of the accumulators reaches a threshold, the subject responds.

When a location is cued (left location in this example), both target accumulators in the cued location are incremented (diagonal stripes in Figure 3.8). This activation "leaks" away with time, so the effect of the cue is transient. When a target appears, evidence for that target/location accumulates on top of the cue related activity. If the target appears in the cued location shortly after the cue, activation will reach threshold rapidly (valid trials, solid arrow, left panel). However, on an invalid trial, it will take longer for activation to reach threshold (dashed arrow, right panel). In the model, activation related to the cue (striped bars) is not information that enables one to discriminate the targets. Information represented by the arrows does discriminate targets. That is, the rate of accumulation of information indicated by the arrows is identical for *involuntary* attention. In contrast, voluntary attention does affect the rate of information accrual. In speeded experiments, the response is determined by which accumulator reaches a threshold first.

The second model is a serial checking model. This model assumes items in all display locations are encoded into a buffer to the same degree. The buffer could be visual working memory. A serial processor checks the items one at a time. The tendency is to begin the process at the cued location. If the target is in the cued location, subjects will respond faster than if it is in another location. The spatial cueing effect occurs because, on invalid trials, the target is not in the cued location and subjects must move to another location.

To compare these theories of involuntary attention, we conducted a standard spatial cueing task with two possible target locations and nonpredictive cues (Prinzmetal & Choi, 2005). The sequence of events is shown in Figure 3.8. There were two kinds of trials. Half of the trials had a target and a nontarget. These are called "one-target trials." The targets were randomly chosen from the letters A, B, C, and D. The non-targets were chosen from the letters W, X, Y, and Z. Subjects responded vocally, and reaction times were measured with a voice-operated relay. After the subject responded, the experimenter entered the response into the computer. On the trials with one target and one nontarget, both the accumulator and the serial processing models predict that subjects should be faster on valid than on invalid trials.

The other half of trials had a target in each location. The targets were randomly selected, as before, but with the constraint that they could not contain the same letter in both positions. On these two-target trials, subjects were told that they could respond to either target. They were to blurt out the first target that they saw (see Prinzmetal & Taylor, 2006). For example, if the targets were B and D, a response of "B" or "D" would be correct, and a response of "A" or "C" would be incorrect.

One- and two-target trials were randomly mixed within each block. On the two-target trials, the accumulator model predicts that subjects should be faster when they respond with the cued location than the uncued location because responses to anything that appears in the cued location will be primed. The serial model predicts no difference in RT in responses to the cued versus uncued locations because, whether subjects begin their search at a cued or uncued location, it will have a target and the search will terminate.

The results are shown in Figure 3.9. For both the one-target trials and two-target trials, subjects were faster when they responded with a target in the cued location compared to the uncued location. This difference was reliable for both the one-target ($t(5) = 3.83$, $p < .05$) and two-target ($t(5) = 2.74$, $p < .05$) trials. This result is consistent with the accumulator model because responses will be primed to anything that occurs in the cued location. However, the difference between cued and uncued trials is inconsistent with the serial processing model because, with a

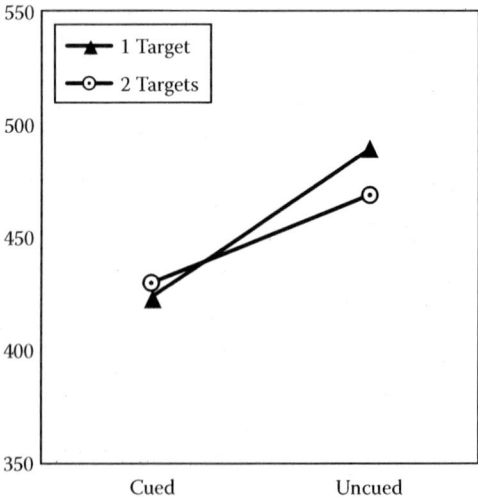

Figure 3.9   Results from the multiple-targets experiment.

target in each location, wherever the search begins, there will be a target. On the two-target trials, subjects were more likely to respond to the cued target than to the uncued target (80.7% vs. 19.3%), but when they responded to the uncued location, they were slower than when they responded to the cued location.

The accumulator model has a number of nice features. It is a possible account for "contingent capture" (e.g., Folk, Remington, & Johnston, 1992), which is the finding that effectiveness of the cue is related to the extent that target and cue share stimulus features. We assume that the cue activates target accumulators in the cued position—presumably because the cue shares features with the target. For example, if the target is defined by color (the red letter), then a cue of the same color will be more effective than a cue of a different color (e.g., Ansorge & Heumann, 2003).

Although the results of the present experiment favored the accumulator model over the serial search model for involuntary attention, in some circumstances the serial search model might be a better descriptor of performance. This experiment had only two target locations, so locating the target was relatively easy. It may be that when locating the target is easy, the accumulator model is a better predictor of performance. However, when locating the target is difficult, the serial search model might be a better predictor of performance. In summary, involuntary attention might affect RT in at least two ways that do not involve enhancing the perceptual representation. Preliminary evidence favors the accumulator model, at least in situations where locating the target is easy.

Behavioral data demonstrate that voluntary attention enhances the perceptual representation such that subjects are more accurate in identifying targets to which they are attending; involuntary attention does not have this effect. In an RT task, the more perceptually demanding the task is, the greater is the attention effect. Involuntary attention by itself can show the opposite pattern of responses. Finally, involuntary attention seems to prime responses to any stimulus (similar to the target) that appears in the cued location. Hence, its effect could be described as of priming motor responses to stimuli in a particular location. This is similar to lowering a decision threshold for stimuli in the cued location. Given these differences in behavior, we expected differences in neural mechanisms; these differences are explored in the next two sections.

FUNCTIONAL MAGNETIC RESONANCE IMAGING

The previous experiments using faces (Prinzmetal, McCool, & Park, 2005, Experiments 9, 10, 11; Figure 3.1) in the spatial cueing task were ideally suited for fMRI. Faces are known selectively to activate a region in the fusiform gyrus, referred to as the face fusiform area (FFA) (e.g., Ishai, Ungerleider, Martin, Schouten, & Haxby, 1999; Kanwisher, 2000). When presented with faces, this region manifests a higher response compared to when other categories of objects are presented. In addition, the FFA response has been shown to be modulated by task relevance (e.g., Beck, Rees, Frith, & Lavie, 2001; Wojciulik, Kanwisher, & Driver, 1998). By the use of faces as stimuli, we were able to make specific predictions that were easily tested in a constrained region of interest (ROI) analysis. Therefore, FFA response enabled a measure of the consequences of voluntary and involuntary attention while focusing on a functionally localized ventral region and hence overcame limitations present in previous imaging attempts of spatial attention.

Since the landmark PET (positron emission tomography) study of Corbetta, Miezin, Shulman, and Petersen (1993), dozens of functional imaging studies of the spatial cueing task have been conducted. A curious finding is that no spatial cueing study using the paradigm where the cues precede the target by a few hundred milliseconds has found evidence of spatially specific activation.[3] For example, Corbetta et al. (2005) commented that "a rather puzzling observation, one that has been replicated several times, is that preparatory signals…show weak evidence for spatial specificity during tasks that force subjects…to switch attention between locations" (p. 2052). In other words, heretofore, cortical activation in spatial cueing tasks has not shown spatial specificity. We hoped that by looking at a specific stimulus-sensitive ROI, we would find evidence of greater activation in the FFA contralateral to the target (face) location.

Until very recently, there was no clear evidence, using fMRI, showing distinctly different neural systems for voluntary (endogenous) and involuntary (exogenous) attention. Three studies compared noninformative peripheral cues to informative central cues and found no difference or very little difference in brain activation (Kim et al., 1999; Peelen, Heslenfeld, & Theeuwes, 2004; Rosen et al., 1999). Two more recent studies (Kincade, Abrams, Astafiev, Shulman, & Corbetta, 2005; Mayer, Seidenberg, Dorflinger, & Rao, 2004) found differences, but the studies are problematic. First, both studies confounded voluntary and involuntary attention with other factors—for example, by comparing a central symbolic cue with a long SOA with a peripheral cue and short SOA. Using direct spatial cueing, we compared voluntary and involuntary attention cues using the same cues and temporal parameters. We only varied the proportion of valid to invalid trials.

We have completed an fMRI study using a task that is identical to that shown in Figure 3.1 (Esterman et al., 2007). We used the RT version so that subjects were between 95 and 100% correct. Ten subjects participated in a practice session in a simulated scanner and then were scanned the next day. Both the practice session and scanning session consisted of three blocks of 64 trials with a predictive cue and three blocks with a nonpredictive cue; the order was counterbalanced across subjects. In the scanning session, the predictive and nonpredictive blocks of trials were separated by an additional task aimed at localizing each participant's FFA.

The only difference between the voluntary and involuntary attention sessions was the proportion of valid and invalid trials. In the voluntary attention session, in 75% of the trials the face appeared in the cued location. In the involuntary attention version, the face appeared in the cued location in 50% of the trials. The subjects were aware of the validity manipulation. We used an event-related design, where each event begins with the onset of the cue. During the task, 18 axial slices with full brain coverage were obtained every 2 s.

We found numerous areas where voluntary and involuntary attention differed. Here, we will limit the discussion to the FFA because this structure has

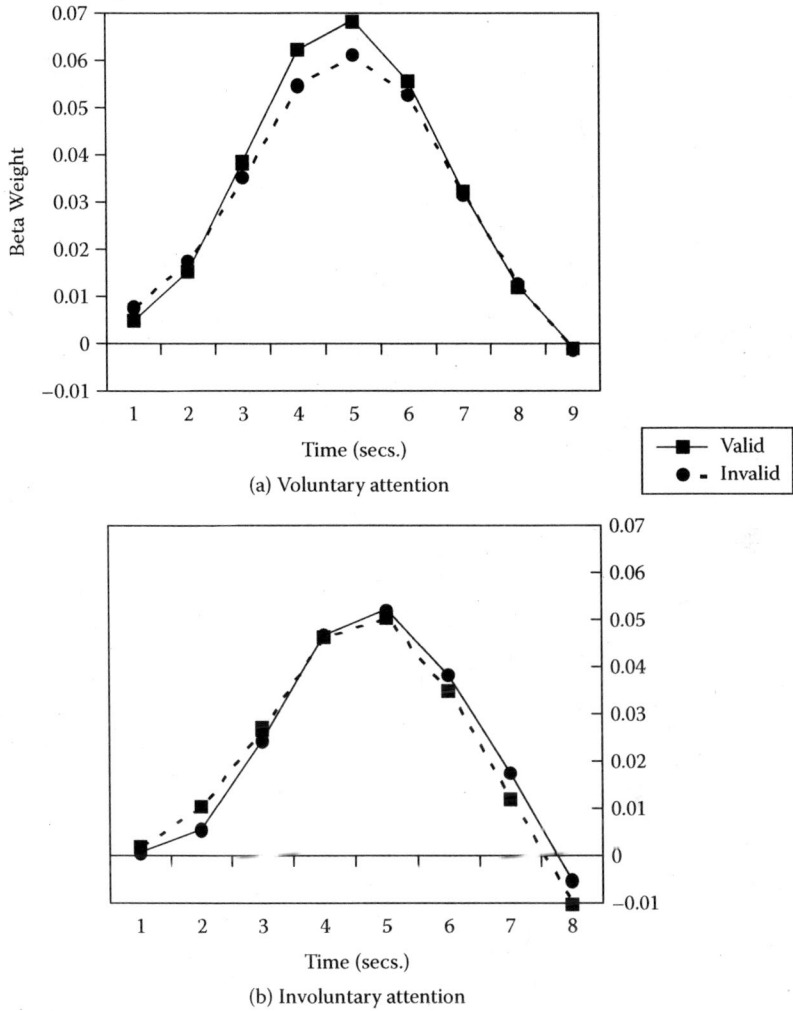

Figure 3.10   Activation in the FFA contralateral to the target face.

been related to the perceptual processing of faces. Significantly greater activation in the FFA was contralateral to the target than ipsilateral to the target. Hence, for a cueing effect, we examined processing in the FFA contralateral to the target face. The BOLD response is plotted in Figure 3.10 as a function of the type of cue. The predictive session showed significantly more activation in valid trials than invalid trials. However, BOLD response did not differ between valid and invalid trials in the nonpredictive session. Both sessions yielded the typical RT effect. By examining a stimulus-specific perceptual area, we found cue-specific enhancement in brain activity. Thus, in the voluntary condition, the cue modulated the FFA, but in the involuntary condition it did not.

ELECTROENCEPHALOGRAPHY

The advantage of fMRI is that it has terrific spatial resolution. The analysis in Figure 3.10 is based on 15 voxels in each left and each right FFA. The disadvantage is that temporal resolution is poor. We do not know whether the activation shown in Figure 3.10 is due to the cue, the target, or some combination of the two. To obtain a good picture of temporal changes with voluntary and involuntary attention, we used the same face stimuli that we used in the fMRI study and similar temporal parameters (Landau et al., 2007).[4] Each of 16 subjects participated in two sets of approximately 600 trials: In one set the cue was predictive and in one set the cue was not. We also included approximately 15% of the trials with only the cue, and no face (cue-only trials). On these trials, subjects were to press a "face-absent" button. We included the cue-only trials to obtain a measure of the electrophysiological activity uniquely evoked by the cue (independent of the target).

We conducted two different types of analyses. In the ERP (event-related potential) analysis, we averaged multiple trials in each condition and compared these averaged responses. This analysis did not reveal any interesting differences between voluntary and involuntary attention conditions.

Event-related potentials only include information about phase-locked electrical activity under about 15 Hz. Higher frequencies that are not time and phase locked are averaged out and do not influence the ERP. Previous research has found signatures of voluntary attention in higher frequencies, called gamma-band response (Gruber, Müller, Keil, & Elbert, 1999). Therefore, we convolved the epoched EEG data with a Gaussian-windowed sinusoidal wavelet of two-cycle duration. At each frequency band, the mean spectral energy of the prestimulus baseline was subtracted from the pre- and poststimulus time frequency energy. The absolute power measure was converted to decibels (dB; 10 ° log [microvolts squared]). This procedure describes power values as relative to the corresponding baseline level of each frequency band. The resulting time-frequency maps were averaged across trials for each subject to form the event-related spectral perturbation (ERSP; Makeig, 1993).

The spectral analysis from the contralateral posterior cluster of channels is illustrated in Figures 3.11–3.13. In these figures, time is represented on the abscissa. The stimuli appear at 0 ms in the figure. Frequency is plotted on the ordinate. Color denotes a measure of power intensity (in decibels).

The spectral data plotted in Figures 3.11–3.13 (see color insert) illustrate a strong correspondence between shifts of voluntary attention and spectral power in the gamma range. On the cue-only trials, beginning about 130 ms after the appearance of the cue, significantly greater activity occurs in the 30- to 70-Hz range when the cue is predictive than when the cue is not predictive (Figure 3.11). This activity reaches its peak about 200 ms after the cue appears.

The results from the valid trials are shown in Figure 3.12. For both the predictive and nonpredictive attention conditions, there is activity in the 30- to 70-Hz range related to the target, about 130 ms after the onset of the target and peaking about 200 ms after the target appears. This activity is significantly *less* in the predictive session. This is reasonable because, if subjects have done cue-related

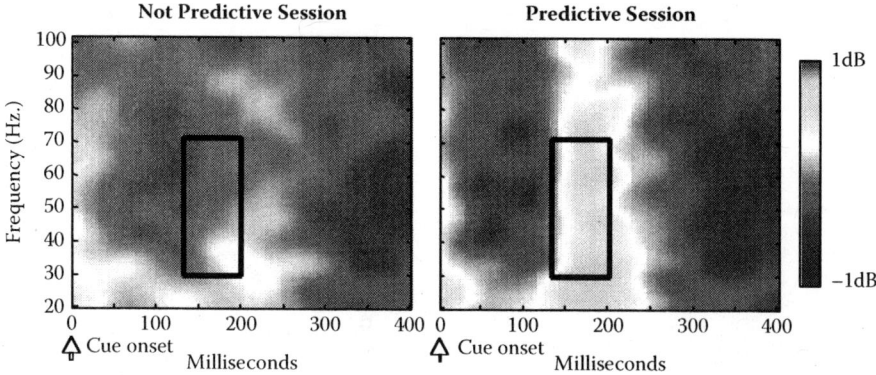

Figure 3.11 (See color insert following page 150.) Time-frequency plot for cue-only trials.

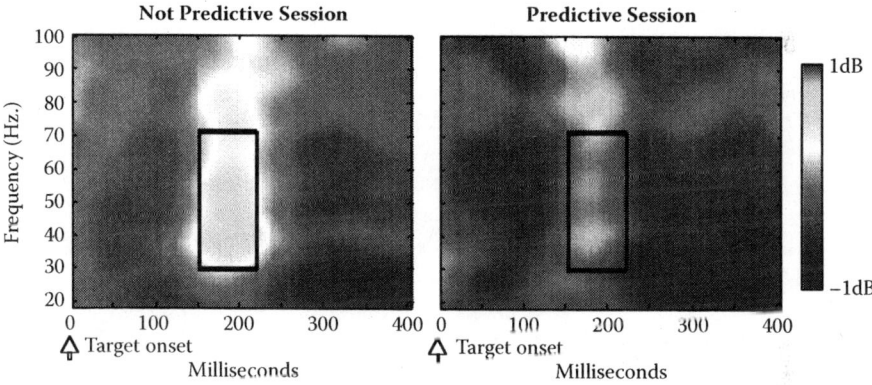

Figure 3.12 (See color insert following page 150.) Time-frequency plot for valid trials.

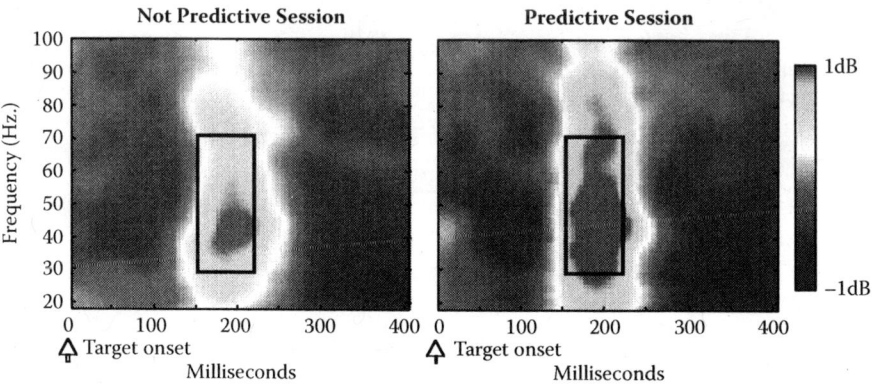

Figure 3.13 (See color insert following page 150.) Time-frequency plot for invalid trials.

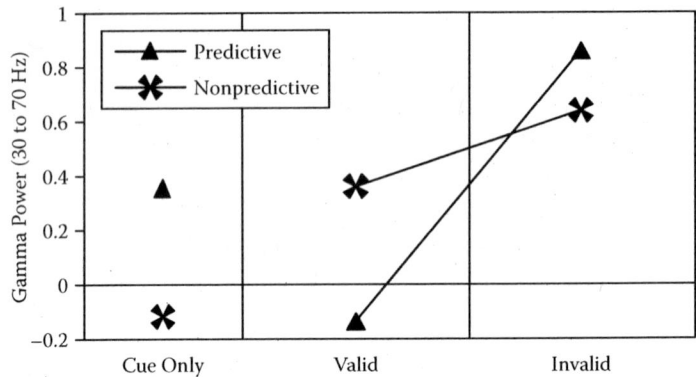

Figure 3.14 The power averaged over all electrode sites, subject from 30 to 70 Hz, and a temporal window 70 ms wide centered around cue-related activity for cue-only trials and target-related activity for valid and invalid trials.

preparatory processing in the predictive session (i.e., shifting attention), there is less target processing to do (or it is easier because attention has been deployed to that location). In the nonpredictive session, there was little preprocessing related to the cue, so a larger shift of attention was required.

Finally, the activity in invalid trials is shown in Figure 3.14. Here the relative magnitude of the target-related activity reverses: Greater activation is seen in the predictive cue session. This pattern is expected because, in the predictive session, subjects have oriented attention to the cued location—*but that is the wrong location*. They have to reorient attention to the target location, and this is expressed in increased gamma band response.

One interpretation of the gamma band response is that it reflects shifts of voluntary attention. In the predictive session, subjects shift their attention when the cue appears, and this is seen in the gamma activity. Almost no cue-related activity occurs in the nonpredictive session. When the target appears in the nonpredictive session, subjects have to shift their attention to the target. With the predictive session, subjects have already done this, so there is less gamma activity than in the nonpredictive session. On invalid trials, in the predictive session subjects have to reorient their attention, leading to a large burst of activity.

Gamma band activity has been linked in the literature to different cognitive capacities (e.g., Tallon-Baudry & Bertrand, 1999). Here we report three significant differences between voluntary and involuntary attentional conditions in the gamma band response. A summary of these findings is illustrated in Figure 3.14 depicting the average of 30–70 Hz in the 70-ms window around the cue and target peak activity (averaged over contralateral posterior electrode sites and subjects). Three important findings can be listed:

On cue-only trials, significantly greater cue-related activity takes place in the predictive than in the nonpredictive session.

When the target appears, significantly greater target-related activity occurs in valid trials for the nonpredictive session than for the predictive session. This pattern reverses on invalid trials.

Thus, voluntary attention to a predictive cue results in a different pattern of brain activity than involuntary attention, which in turn affects responses to targets.

CONCLUSIONS

We have followed a "divide and conquer" strategy in understanding visual attention. We hypothesized that voluntary and involuntary attention involved different mechanisms. This distinction is not based on any logical consideration, but rather on empirical dissociations between the two kinds of attention. We manipulated attention in the spatial cueing paradigm, using a peripheral cue. When the cue was nonpredictive of the target location, any effects were involuntary because there was no reason to allocate processing resources to the cued location. To study voluntary attention, we added a voluntary component to the task by making the cue predictive of the target location.

We found several differences between voluntary and involuntary attention manipulated in this way. Both affect RT, but only voluntary attention affects accuracy as long as subjects are not under speed pressure, there is no location uncertainty, and there are no confounds, such as eye movements (Prinzmetal, McCool, & Park, 2005). In a pure RT experiment, we found that manipulations of perceptual difficulty can have the opposite effect for voluntary and involuntary attention (Prinzmetal, Zvinyatskovskiy, et al., 2008). With a predictive spatial cue, increasing difficulty increased the cueing effect; however, with a nonpredictive cue, increasing difficulty decreased the cueing effect. In an fMRI study with faces as stimuli, we found voluntary attention enhanced activity in the FFA (a face-specific processing area) but involuntary attention did not. In gamma band EEG response, predictive and nonpredictive cue sessions showed three clear differences.

Given the existence of separable mechanisms for voluntary and involuntary attention, what are these mechanisms? Several different mechanisms have been proposed for voluntary attention; many of them are equivalent to the "more samples" hypothesis proposed by Luce (1977). This hypothesis could be implemented in neural hardware in many different ways (see Prinzmetal, 2005). The consequence of the more samples model is that voluntary attention should increase the accuracy of perception for attended objects.

Involuntary attention has been a bit of a puzzle. How can a mechanism affect RT, yet not accuracy? We proposed two models: the accumulator model and the serial search model. The results of the multiple-targets experiment favored the accumulator model. In effect, the cue primes responses to any stimulus appearing in the cued location that is similar to the target.

Having dissected visual attention in the spatial-cueing task, one might wonder whether further divisions would be useful. Involuntary attention can be accounted for by the accumulator model. However, in some situations the serial search model might be a better descriptor of the results. Thus, involuntary attention can potentially be divided further.

Does more than one mechanism of voluntary attention exist? In fact, many regions of the brain contain cells that behave in a manner that could account for attention effects (Colby, 1991). One question that we have is whether the mechanisms involved when subjects are aware or unaware of the cue-target contingencies differ. It may be that there are few differences behaviorally between aware and unaware conditions (e.g., Bartolomeo et al., 2007; Decaix et al., 2002), but there may be neural differences (e.g., see Hazeltine, Grafton, & Ivry, 1997). We now have powerful imaging and EEG methods to study voluntary attention that will be useful for exploring different kinds of attention.

Our ultimate goal is to understand the mechanisms of attention. In order to do this, we need to know whether there is one phenomenon or many. If distinctly different phenomena exist, a single theory of "attention" (singular) ultimately will not be successful. Hence, in order to understand attention, we need an empirically based taxonomy of attention. Dividing voluntary and involuntary attention is a first step in this process.

NOTES

1. One might argue that "voluntary" is not an appropriate term when the effects can be obtained without awareness of the probabilities of valid and invalid trials. The reason we use the terms "voluntary" and "involuntary" attention is that they were first used by Wundt (1902) well before terms such as endogenous and exogenous (Posner, 1978). In this chapter, we use the terms with a precise operational definition based on whether the cue provides information about the target location or not.
2. Note that location uncertainty could also account for accuracy effects with voluntary attention, as in Prinzmetal, McCool & Park (2005). However, they designed their stimuli so that there was no uncertainty as to which location contained the target.
3. Note that this is in contrast to numerous studies that use sustained attention to a particular location (e.g., Hopfinger, Buonocore, & Mangun, 2000).
4. The only difference was that the SOA was 250 ms for the EEG study and 300 ms for the fMRI study.

REFERENCES

Ansorge, U., & Heumann, M. (2003). Top-down contingencies in peripheral cuing: The roles of color and location. *Journal of Experimental Psychology: Human Perception and Performance*, 29(5), 937–948.

Awh, E., & Oh, S. H. (2005). *Automatic attention and accuracy: An alliterative account.* Paper presented at the Cognitive Science Association for Interdisciplinary Learning, Hood River, OR.

Bartolomeo, P., Decaix, C., & Siéroff, E. (2007). The phenomenology of endogenous orienting. *Consciousness and Cognition, 16*(1), 144–161.

Beck, D. M., Rees, G., Frith, C. D., & Lavie, N. (2001). Neural correlates of change detection and change blindness. *Nature Neuroscience, 4,* 645–650.

Berger, A., Henik, A., & Rafal, R. (2005). Competition between endogenous and exogenous orienting of visual attention. *Journal of Experimental Psychology: General, 134*(2), 207–221.

Briand, K. A. (1998). Feature integration and spatial attention: More evidence of a dissociation between endogenous and exogenous orienting. *Journal of Experimental Psychology: Human Perception & Performance, 24*(4), 1243–1256.

Briand, K. A., & Klein, R. M. (1987). Is Posner's "beam" the same as Treisman's "glue"? On the relation between visual orienting and feature integration theory. *Journal of Experimental Psychology: Human Perception and Performance, 13,* 228–241.

Carrasco, M., Ling, S., & Read, S. (2004). Attention alters appearance. *Nature Neuroscience, 7*(3), 308–313.

Colby, C. L. (1991). The neuroanatomy and neurophysiology of attention. *Journal of Child Neurology, 6,* S90–S118.

Corbetta, M., Miezin, F., Shulman, G., & Petersen, S. (1993). A PET study of visuospatial attention. *Journal of Neuroscience, 13,* 1202–1226.

Corbetta, M., Tansy, A. P., Stanley, C. M., Astafiev, S. V., Snyder, A. Z., & Shulman, G. L. (2005). A functional MRI study of preparatory signals for spatial location and objects. *Neuropsychologia, 43,* 2041–2056.

Decaix, C., Seíroff, E., & Bartolomeo, P. (2002). How voluntary is "voluntary" orienting in attention? *Cortex, 38*(5), 841–845.

Driver, J., Davis, G., Ricciardelli, P., Kidd, P., Maxwell, E., & Baron-Cohen, S. (1999). Gaze perception triggers reflexive visuospatial orienting. *Visual Cognition, 6,* 509–540.

Dufour, A. (1999). Importance of attentional mechanisms in audiovisual links. *Experimental Brain Research, 126,* 215–222.

Esterman, M., Prinzmetal, W., DeGutis, J., Landau, A., Hazeltine, E., Verstynen, T., & Robertson, L. (2008). Voluntary and involuntary attention affect face discrimination differently. *Neuropsychologia, 46,* 1032–1040.

Folk, C. L., Remington, R. W., & Johnston, J. C. (1992). Involuntary covert orienting is contingent on attentional control settings. *Journal of Experimental Psychology: Human Perception & Performance, 18,* 1030–1044.

Friesen, C. K., & Kingstone, A. (1998). The eyes have it! Reflexive orienting is triggered by nonpredictive gaze. *Psychonomic Bulletin & Review, 5*(3), 490–495.

Gazzaniga, M. S., Ivry, R. B., & Mangun, G. R. (1998). *Cognitive neuroscience: The biology of the mind.* New York: W. W. Norton.

Grice, G. R. (1972). Application of a variable criterion model to auditory reaction time as a function of the type of catch trial. *Perception & Psychophysics, 12*(1-B), 103–107.

Gruber, T., Müller, M. M., Keil, A., & Elbert, T. (1999). Selective visual-spatial attention alters induced gamma band responses in the human EEG. *Clinical Neurophysiology, 110*(12), 2074–2085.

Handy, T. C., Kingstone, A., & Mangun, G. R. (1996). Spatial distribution of visual attention: Perceptual sensitivity and response latency. *Perception & Psychophysics, 58,* 613–627.

Hazeltine, E., Grafton, S. T., & Ivry, R. (1997). Attention and stimulus characteristics determine the locus of motor-sequence encoding a PET study. *Brain: A Journal of Neurology, 120*(1), 123–140.

Hopfinger, J. B., Buonocore, M. H., & Mangun, G. R. (2000). The neural mechanisms of top-down attention control. *Nature Neuroscience, 3*(3), 284–291.

Ishai, A., Ungerleider, L. G., Martin, A., Schouten, J. L., & Haxby, J. V. (1999). Distributed representation of objects in the human ventral visual pathway. *Proceedings of the National Academy of Science USA, 96*(16), 9379–9384.

Johnston, J., McCann, R. S., & Remington, R. W. (1995). Chronometric evidence for two types of attention. *Psychological Science, 6*, 365–369.

Jonides, J. (1976). *Voluntary versus reflexive control of the mind's eye's movement.* Paper presented at the meeting of the Psychonomic Society, St. Louis, MO.

Jonides, J. (1981). Voluntary versus automatic control over the mind's eye's movement. In J. B. Long & A. D. Baddeley (Eds.), *Attention and performance IX* (pp. 187–204). Hillsdale, N.J: Lawrence Erlbaum Associates.

Kanwisher, N. (2000). Domain specificity in face perception. *Nature Neuroscience, 3*(8), 759–763.

Kim, Y. H., Gitelman, D. R., Nobre, A. C., Parrish, T. B., LaBar, K. S., & Mesulam, M.-M. (1999). The large-scale neural network for spatial attention displays mutifunctional overlap but differential asymmetry. *NeuroImage, 9*, 269–277.

Kincade, J. M., Abrams, R. A., Astafiev, S. V., Shulman, G. L., & Corbetta, M. (2005). An event-related functional magnetic resonance imaging study of voluntary and stimulus-driven orienting of attention. *Journal of Neuroscience, 25*(18), 4593–4604.

Klein, R. M., & Dick, B. (2002). Temporal dynamics of reflexive attention shifts: A dual-stream serial visual presentation. *Psychological Science, 13*, 176–179.

Lambert, A., & Duddy, M. (2002). Visual orienting with central and peripheral precues: Deconfounding the contributions of cure eccentricity, cue discrimination and spatial correspondence. *Visual Cognition, 9*, 303–336.

Landau, A. N., Esterman, M., Robertson, L. C., Bentin, S., & Prinzmetal, W. (2007). Different effects of voluntary and involuntary attention on EEG activity in the gamma band. *Journal of Neuroscience, 27*(44), 11986–11990.

Langton, S. R. H., Watt, R. J., & Bruce, V. (2000). Do the eyes have it? Cues to the direction of social attention. *Trends in Cognitive Sciences, 4*(2), 50–59.

Loftus, G. R. (1978). On interpretation of interactions. *Memory & Cognition, 6*, 312–319.

Lu, Z. L., & Dosher, B. (1998). External noise distinguishes attention mechanisms. *Vision Research, 38*, 1183–1198.

Luce, R. D. (1977). Thurstone's discriminal processes fifty years later. *Psychometrika, 42*, 461–489.

Luck, S., Hillyard, S., Mouloua, M., & Hawkins, H. (1996). Mechanisms of visual-spatial attention: Resource allocation or uncertainty reduction? *Journal of Experimental Psychology: Human Perception and Performance, 27*, 725–737.

Luck, S. J., & Thomas, S. J. (1999). What variety of attention is automatically captured by peripheral cues? *Perception & Psychophysics, 61*(7), 1424–1435.

Makeig, S. (1993). Auditory event-related dynamics of the EEG spectrum and effects of exposure to tones. *Electroencephalography and Clinical Neurophysiology, 86*(4), 283–293.

Mayer, A. R., Seidenberg, M., Dorflinger, J. M., & Rao, S. M. (2004). An event-related fMRI study of exogenous orienting: Supporting evidence for the cortical basis of inhibition of return? *Journal of Cognitive Neuroscience, 16*(7), 1262–1271.

Nakayama, K., & Mackeben, M. (1989). Sustained and transient components of focal visual attention. *Vision Research, 29*, 1631–1647.

Peelen, M. V., Heslenfeld, D. J., & Theeuwes, J. (2004). Endogenous and exogenous attention shifts are mediated by the same large-scale neural network. *NeuroImage, 22*, 822–830.

Posner, M. I. (1980). Orienting of attention. *Quarterly Journal of Experimental Psychology, 32*, 3–25.

Posner, M. I., Cohen, Y., & Rafal, R. D. (1982). Neural systems control of spatial orienting. *Philosophical Transactions of the Royal Society London, 298,* 187–198.

Posner, M. I., Snyder, C. R. R., & Davidson, B. J. (1980). Attention and the detection of signals. *Journal of Experimental Psychology: General, 109,* 160–174.

Prinzmetal, W. (2005). Location perception: The X-files parable. *Perception & Psychophysics, 67,* 48–71.

Prinzmetal, W., Amiri, H., Allen, K., & Edwards, T. (1998). The phenomenology of attention part 1: Color, location, orientation, and "clarity." *Journal of Experimental Psychology: Human Perception and Performance, 24,* 261–282.

Prinzmetal, W., & Choi, J. (2005). *Cueing with multiple targets.* Unpublished study.

Prinzmetal, W., & Le, D. (2005). *Awh–Oh revisited: A case of location uncertainty.* Unpublished study.

Prinzmetal, W., Leonhardt, J., & Garrett, R. (2008). Does gaze direction affect accuracy? *Visual Cognition, 16,* 567–584.

Prinzmetal, W., Long, V., & Leonhardt, J. (2008). Attention and contrast. *Perception & Psychophysics, 70,* 1139–1150.

Prinzmetal, W., McCool, C., & Park, S. (2005). Attention: Reaction time and accuracy reveal different mechanisms. *Journal of Experimental Psychology: General, 134*(1), 73–92.

Prinzmetal, W., Nwachuku, I., Bodanski, L., Blumenfeld, L., & Shimizu, N. (1997). The phenomenology of attention part 2: Brightness and contrast. *Consciousness and Cognition, 6,* 372–412.

Prinzmetal, W., Park, S., & Garrett, R. (2005). Involuntary attention and identification accuracy. *Perception & Psychophysics, 67*(8), 1344–1353.

Prinzmetal, W., Presti, D. E., & Posner, M. I. (1986). Does attention affect visual feature integration? *Journal of Experimental Psychology: Human Perception and Performance, 12,* 361–369.

Prinzmetal, W., & Taylor, N. (2006). Color singleton pop-out does not always poop-out: An alternative to visual search. *Psychonomic Bulletin and Review, 13,* 576–580.

Prinzmetal, W., & Wang, V. (2005). *The difference between automatic and voluntary attention.* Unpublished study.

Prinzmetal, W., & Wilson, A. (1997). The effect of attention on phenomenal length. *Perception, 26,* 193–205.

Prinzmetal, W., Zvinyatskovsky, A., Gutierrez, P., & Dilem, L. (2008). Voluntary and involuntary attention have different consequences: The effect of perceptual difficulty. *Quarterly Journal of Experimental Psychology, 62,* 352–369.

Rauschenberger, R. (2003). Attentional capture by auto- and allo-cues. *Psychonomic Bulletin & Review, 10*(4), 814–842.

Remington, R. W., & Folk, C. L. (2001). A dissociation between attention and selection. *Psychological Science, 12*(6), 511–515.

Ristic, J., Friesen, C. K., & Kingstone, A. (2002). Are eyes special? It depends on how you look at it. *Psychonomic Bulletin & Review, 9*(3), 507–513.

Ristic, J., & Kingstone, A. (2006). Attention to arrows: Pointing to a new direction. *Quarterly Journal of Experimental Psychology, 59,* 1921–1930.

Rosen, A. C., Rao, S. M., Caffarra, P. A. S., Bobholz, J. A., Woodley, S. J., et al. (1999). Neural basis of endogenous and exogenous spatial orienting. A functional MRI study. *Journal of Cognitive Neuroscience, 11*(2), 135–152.

Sereno, A. B., & Holzman, P. S. (1996). Spatial selective attention in schizophrenic, affective disorder and normal subjects. *Schizophrenia Research, 20*(1–2), 33–50.

Shaw, M. L. (1982). Attending to multiple sources of information: I. The integration of information in decision making. *Cognitive Psychology, 14,* 353–409.

Shiu, L., & Pashler, H. (1994). Negligible effect of spatial precuing on identification of single digits. *Journal of Experimental Psychology: Human Perception and Performance, 20*, 1037–1054.

Smith, P. L. (2000). Attention and luminance detection: Effects of cues, masks, and pedestals. *Journal of Experimental Psychology: Human Perception & Performance, 26*, 1401–1420.

Smith, P. L., & Vickers, D. (1988). The accumulator model of two-choice discrimination. *Journal of Mathematical Psychology, 32*(2), 135–168.

Soetens, E., Deroost, N., & Notebaert, W. (2003). *Is Treisman's "glue" related to Posner's "beam"?* Paper presented at the Psychonomics Society meeting, Vancouver, BC.

Spence, C. (2001). Cross-modal attentional capture: A controversy resolved. In C. L. Folk & B. S. Gibson (Eds.), *Attraction, distraction and action: Multiple perspectives on attentional capture* (pp. 231–262). (*Advances in Psychology: 133*). Elsevier Science B.V.: Amsterdam.

Tallon-Baudry, C., & Bertrand, O. (1999). Oscillatory gamma activity in humans and its role in object recognition. *Trends in Cognitive Neuroscience, 3*(4), 151–162.

Tipples, J. (2002). Eye gaze is not unique: Automatic orienting in response to uninformative arrows. *Psychonomic Bulletin & Review, 9*, 314–318.

Treisman, A., & Schmidt, H. (1982). Illusory conjunctions in the perception of objects. *Cognitive Psychology, 14*, 107–141.

Usher, M., & McClelland, J. L. (2001). The time course of perceptual choice: The leaky, competing accumulator model. *Psychological Review, 108*(3), 550–592.

Warner, C. B., Juola, J., & Koshino, H. (1990). Voluntary allocation versus automatic capture of visual attention. *Perception & Psychophysics, 48*, 243–251.

Wojciulik, E., Kanwisher, N., & Driver, J. (1998). Covert visual attention modulates face-specific activity in the human fusiform gyrus: fMRI study. *Journal of Neurophysiology, 79*, 1574–1578.

Wright, R. D., & Richard, C. M. (2000). Location cue validity affects inhibition of return of visual processing. *Vision Research, 40*(17), 119–126.

Wundt, W. (1902). *Outlines of psychology*. Leipzig: W. Engelman.

Wundt, W. (1912/1973). *An introduction to psychology*. London: George Allen & Company.

4

Top-Down and Bottom-Up Control of Visual Selection
Controversies and Debate

JAN THEEUWES and ARTEM BELOPOLSKY

VISUAL SELECTION

*T*he amount of information available to the visual system is much greater than the amount we can fully process. Therefore, it is important that we select relevant information from the environment and ignore information that is irrelevant, particularly when this information may disrupt our actions. Selection implies that some objects or events are excluded from processing. This process of prioritizing information can be accomplished covertly or overtly (Posner, 1980).

When selection occurs covertly, only attention (and not the eyes) is directed to a location in space. For example, without moving one's eyes one is able to detect an approaching car from a side street by directing attention to the left side of the visual field. When selection occurs overtly, not only attention but also the eyes are moved to the selected location. Although it is possible to direct spatial attention to a location without moving the eyes, in order to make a saccade it is necessary that attention be first directed to the location to which the eyes will ultimately go (e.g., Deubel & Schneider, 1996; Godijn & Theeuwes, 2003).

Theories of attention are concerned with how people select information to provide the basis for responding and with how information irrelevant to that response is treated. A very basic question that has spurred a heated debate over the last 15 years is whether we have full control over the process of visual selection. Selection processes may be controlled by the observer in a top-down way or may be controlled by the properties of the stimulus field in a bottom-up way (e.g., reviews by Burnham, 2007; Corbetta & Shulman, 2002; Rauschenberger, 2003; Ruz & Lupiañez, 2002, Theeuwes & Godijn, 2001).

One aspect that is crucial for this debate is the time course of bottom-up and top-down processes. For example, it has recently been suggested that in early vision, selection is primarily driven by bottom-up factors and that only later in time can top-down processes play a role (Theeuwes, Atchley, & Kramer, 2000; Theeuwes & Van der Burg, 2007; Van Zoest, Donk, & Theeuwes, 2004).

From a neurophysiological point of view, it can be assumed that bottom-up signals, mediated primarily by magnocellular visual inputs, are combined with top-down signals at several cortical (e.g., frontal, parietal) and subcortical (e.g., basal ganglia, superior colliculus, thalamus) stages. Bottom-up and top-down control of attention represent the interplay of exogenous (feed-forward) and endogenous (feedback) neuronal activities within the cortex. Early visual areas such as lateral geniculate nucleus (LGN) and V1 have relatively small receptive fields and respond primarily to simple features. Upstream, inferotemporal (IT) and posterior parietal cortex (PPC) have much larger receptive fields and can respond to more complex and abstract features.

Imagine a situation in which the visual system is confronted with two different objects in different locations in the visual field (see Figure 4.1). Within the system, these two objects are in competition, and the question is which object wins this competition and stimulates neurons throughout the visual system, forming an ensemble of neurons that represent this one single object. In line with the biased competition model of Desimone and Duncan (1995), it is conceivable that attention biases these competitive interactions such that attended stimuli receive priority over unattended stimuli.

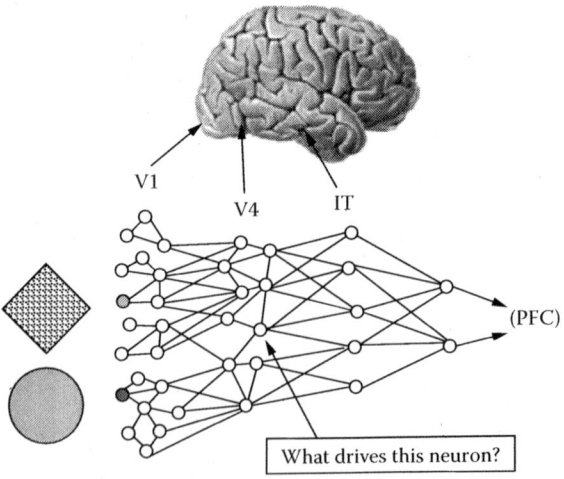

Figure 4.1 A schematic drawing of the visual system. In this example, two different objects in different locations are in competition. The question is which object will win the competition and drive the neuron. Bottom-up and top-down activity can resolve this competition. (Adapted from Serences, J. T., & Yantis, S., 2006, *Trends in Cognitive Sciences*, *10*, 38–45.)

Attentional effects on resolving this competition are the result of bottom-up and top-down factors. The bottom-up signal depends on the properties of the stimulus field. Objects that are highly salient and stand out from the background may immediately receive attentional priority. Indeed, it is likely that before top-down influences can have an effect, the visual system is biased toward salient stimuli that resolve the competition simply on the basis of the bottom-up input (e.g., see Reynolds & Desimone, 2003; Theeuwes, 1992, 1994a; Van Zoest et al., 2004). This type of selection is basically exogenous and automatic and is often referred to as stimulus-driven attentional control.

Another way to bias the competition within the visual system is through top-down feedback signals that depend on the goals, intentions, and expectations of the observer. Directing voluntary attention to a location in space increases the sensory gain for features at that location (e.g., Theeuwes & Van der Burg, 2007) and appears to alter the apparent stimulus contrast (e.g., Carrasco, Ling, & Read, 2004). These results imply that directing attention to a location results in greater neuronal sensitivity (i.e., a decreased threshold). This type of selection is endogenous and is often referred to as goal-driven control. As noted before, over the last 15 years a heated debate has been conducted on the extent to which visual selection is controlled by stimulus-driven and goal-driven factors (e.g., see Burnham, 2007; Corbetta & Shulman, 2002; Rauschenberger, 2003; Ruz & Lupiañez, 2002; Theeuwes & Godijn, 2001).

On the one hand, a group of researchers claim that visual selection is basically under top-down control (e.g., Egeth & Yantis, 1997; Folk & Remington, 1998; Folk, Remington, & Johnston, 1992; Müller, Reimann, & Krummenacher, 2003; Wolfe, 1994; Wolfe, Butcher, Lee, & Hyle, 2003). On the other hand, others have claimed that the initial selection is basically bottom up and only later does top-down control have its effect (e.g., Theeuwes, 1991a, 1992, 1994a, 1994b, 1996, 2004; Theeuwes et al., 2000, Van Zoest et al., 2004). Before we discuss the empirical findings that spurred this debate, it is important to define what should be considered to be visual selection and the processes that are often associated with visual selection but are in fact processes that are postselection—that is, processes that occur later, after the initial selection of one object over another.

For several decades, there has been agreement that visual selection involves two functionally independent stages of processing (e.g., Broadbent, 1958; Neisser, 1967; Treisman & Gelade, 1980). An early visual stage, sometimes referred to as preattentive, operates in parallel across the visual field; a later stage, often referred to as attentive, can deal with only one item (or a few items) at a time. Even though it appears that the dichotomy between these two stages is not as strict as originally assumed, in almost all past and present theories of visual attention, this basic architecture is more or less still present (e.g., Itti & Koch, 2001; Li, 2002; Treue, 2003; Wolfe, 1994).

Given the two-stage framework, it is generally assumed that visual selection depends principally on the outcome of the early stage of visual processing. Processing occurring during the initial wave of stimulation through the brain determines which element is selected and passed on to the second stage of processing. In line with the two-stage approach, passing on an item to the second stage of processing implies that this item has been selected for further processing (e.g., Broadbent, 1958; Treisman & Gelade, 1980).

According to this notion, each time one of the objects present in the visual field (and available at the preattentive stage of processing) is passed on the final stage of processing, this object will affect decision making and responding (see Figure 4.2). This passing on from the initial stage of preattentive processing to attentive processing is what is considered to be selection. As noted earlier, this distinction between early parallel and later serial processing is present explicitly or implicitly in most classic and recent theories of visual selection (e.g., Broadbent, 1958; Itti & Koch, 2001; Li, 2002; Neisser, 1967; Treisman & Gelade, 1980; Treue, 2003; Wolfe, 1994).

However, theories that are based on the classic conception of "late-selection" (Deutsch & Deutsch, 1963) do not make a distinction between early and later processing and assume that everything is processed in parallel up to a high level (e.g., Bundesen, 1990). Theoretically, these theories cannot make a distinction between early visual selection processes and processes that are involved in decision making and response selection.

Given the preceding framework, the question that needs to be considered is whether the output of the preattentive stage, which basically represents bottom-up activity, can be modulated in a top-down way (see Figure 4.2). We will discuss evidence that stems from paradigms in which a salient target is in competition with a salient distractor. The question is whether it is possible to suppress the bottom-up activity of a distractor so that the target is selected. In other words, on the basis of top-down knowledge, is it possible to change the bottom-up selection priority?

If one wants to answer the very basic question of whether the initial selection of stimuli is affected in a top-down way, one has to use a visual search task known as a feature singleton search task. In this type of task, the target is unique in a basic

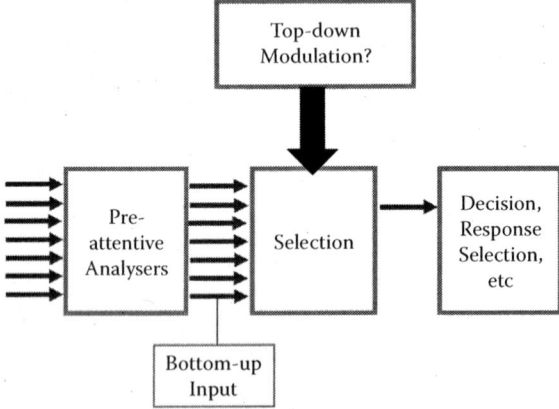

Figure 4.2 A schematic drawing of the classic two-stage model of visual selection. When an object is passed on from the preattentive to the attentive stage of processing, the object is thought to be selected. The question is whether selection can be influenced in a top-down way.

feature dimension (e.g., a red element surrounded by green elements) and therefore "pops-out" from the display. Using a feature singleton task makes it possible to investigate top-down modulation on early (feed-forward) vision, thereby excluding later top-down modulations arising from massive recurrent processing from extrastriate areas to primary visual areas. Indeed, pop-out detection tasks have been claimed to subserve the first stage of visual processing, and single unit studies have implicated primary visual cortex in mediating bottom-up pop-out saliency computations (e.g., Nothdurft, Gallant, & Van Essen, 1999).

OVERVIEW OF PARADIGMS

Studies investigating initial attentional control typically use displays in which the target is defined as a feature singleton. When confronted with this display (such as one in which one element is red and the others are green), one is able immediately to detect this element without any effort. Typically, search time to determine whether such a feature singleton is present or not is independent of the number of elements in the display. Finding these flat search functions is important because it implies that we are dealing with parallel preattentive searches (see Figure 4.2). Only when a parallel, preattentive search is involved can we determine whether the initial selection is controlled in a top-down or bottom-up way. If search is slow and effortful (e.g., in conjunction search), there is ample time to have massive feedback from higher to lower areas, making it impossible to investigate top-down modulation on early (feed-forward) vision.

The finding that a feature singleton can immediately be detected has led to the suggestion that feature singletons receive attentional priority independently of the intentions of the observer. In other words, when a person is searching for a prespecified target (such as a red circle between green circles), selection occurs in a purely bottom-up way. When objects or events receive priority independent of the observer's goals and beliefs, one refers to attentional capture (e.g., Theeuwes, 1992, 1994a); one refers to oculomotor capture when such an event triggers an exogenous saccade to the location of the object or event (Theeuwes, Kramer, Hahn, & Irwin, 1998).

Even though it seems reasonable to assume that a unique feature singleton (such as a red element in a display of green elements) captures attention in a purely exogenous way, such a claim is not necessarily correct. Indeed, when the feature singleton is also the element that observers are instructed to look for, one cannot determine whether this immediate selection of the feature singleton is the result of bottom-up or top-down control. As pointed out by Yantis and Egeth (1999), one can only speak of selection in a purely stimulus-driven fashion when the stimulus feature in question is completely task irrelevant so that there is no incentive for the observer to attend to it deliberately. Yantis and Egeth assert that "if an object with such an attribute captures attention under these conditions, then and only then can that attribute be said to capture attention in a purely stimulus-driven fashion" (p. 663).

Irrelevant Singleton Paradigm

To investigate perceptual selection in early vision, Theeuwes (1991a, 1992, 1994a) developed a paradigm that has become known as the "irrelevant singleton" paradigm (e.g., Yantis & Egeth, 1999). In terms of the earlier outlined model, the paradigm allows one to determine whether top-down information can resolve competition between two salient objects: One is task relevant (i.e., the target) and the other is task irrelevant (i.e., the distractor). The logic underlying this paradigm is simple: Participants perform a visual search task in which two salient singletons are simultaneously present. One singleton is the target; the other singleton is a distractor. Participants are told that the irrelevant singleton is never the target, implying that there is no reason to attend to this item from a top-down point of view. This condition is then compared to a condition in which such an irrelevant singleton is not present.

For example, Theeuwes (1992) presented participants with displays consisting of green circles or diamonds appearing on the circumference of an imaginary circle. Line segments of different orientations appeared in the circles and diamonds. Participants had to determine the orientation of the line segment appearing in the target shape. The target shape that participants searched for was a shape singleton because it was the only diamond present in the display (see Figure 4.3, left panel). In the distractor condition, an irrelevant color singleton was also present in the display (Figure 4.3, right panel). Time to find the diamond (the shape singleton) increased when one of the circles had a different color (Figure 4.3, bottom panel). Even though participants had a clear top-down set to search for the shape singleton (i.e., the single green diamond), the presence of an irrelevant singleton (i.e., the single red circle) caused interference.

In subsequent experiments, Theeuwes (1991a, 1992, 1994a) showed that an irrelevant singleton only causes interference when it is more salient than the target. When the color singleton was made less salient than the shape singleton (by reducing the color difference between the target and the nontarget elements), the shape singleton interfered with search for the color singleton, but the color singleton no longer interfered with the search for the shape singleton. These findings are important because they indicate that the bottom-up salience signal of the stimuli in the visual field determines the selection priority. Even though observers knew that the red singleton was never the target, they could not apply enough top-down control to prevent the selection of the irrelevant singleton.

In one study (Theeuwes, 1992; Experiment 2), participants were trained for up to 1,800 trials to determine whether enough training would allow top-down control and reduce the interference caused by the irrelevant distractor. The results showed that even though the extensive training reduced overall search times, the interference effect caused by the irrelevant distractor remained present. Thus, Theeuwes concluded that extensive training cannot induce a top-down set that can overcome the interference caused by a salient distractor.

The increase in search time in conditions in which an irrelevant singleton was present was explained in terms of attentional capture (Theeuwes, 1991a, 1992, 1994a, 1994b, 2004). Because the irrelevant singleton was selected exogenously and thus captured spatial attention, it required more time before a response could

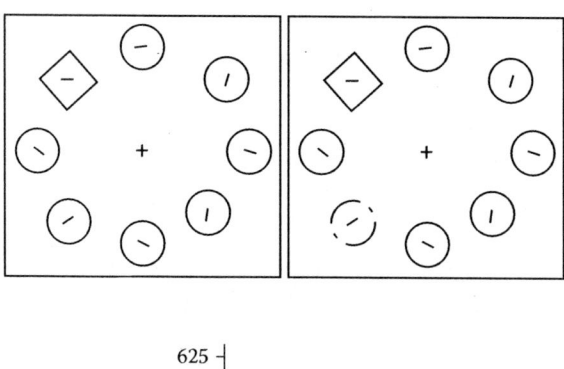

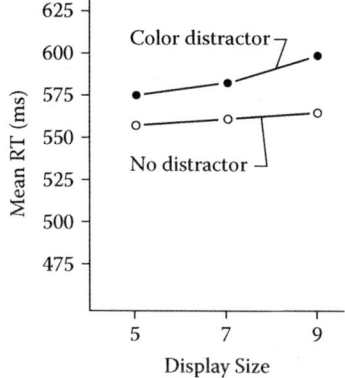

Figure 4.3 Stimuli and data from Theeuwes (1992). Top: A vertical and horizontal bar appeared within a diamond (the other bars were oblique). On the left, all elements are green (solid lines); on the right, one of the elements is red (dashed line). Participants were to report the orientation of the bar in the diamond. Bottom: The presence of the irrelevant color singleton slowed search for a unique shape (the diamond). (Adapted from Theeuwes, J , 1992, *Perception & Psychophysics*, 51, 599–606; Experiment 1.)

be emitted. Given the observation that selectivity completely depended on the relative salience of the singleton target and the distractor singleton, it was suggested that early visual preattentive processing is only driven by bottom-up factors.

Considering Figure 4.1, this implies that early on, during the first sweep of information through the brain, the competition between the two salient objects is resolved by bottom-up salience signals. These signals drive the neurons at higher levels that create a perceptual coherence field, an ensemble of neurons that jointly represent the single selected object (Serences & Yantis, 2006). Top-down control over feature selection (i.e., knowing that the target is a diamond and not a red circle) and extensive training cannot influence these early bottom-up salience signals.

Theeuwes (1992, 1994a, 2004) argued that, irrespective of the attentional set of the observer, spatial attention is automatically and involuntarily captured by the location containing the most salient singleton. The shift of spatial attention to the location of the singleton causes the singleton to be selected for further processing. If this singleton is the target, a response is made. If it is not the target, attention is directed to the next most salient singleton. The initial shift of attention to the most salient singleton is thought to be the result of relatively inflexible, "hardwired" mechanisms, which are triggered by the presence of a feature difference signal. It is assumed that, at each location in the visual field, a local feature contrast is calculated that represents how different that object is from its surroundings within a particular primitive feature dimension (e.g., color, shape, contrast, etc.).

The notion suggested by Theeuwes is similar to that of Koch and Ullman (1985), who introduced the idea of a salience map that accomplishes preattentive selection. This two-dimensional map encodes the salience of objects in their visual environment. Neurons in this map compete among each other, giving rise to a single winning location (cf. winner take all) that contains the most salient element. If this location is inhibited, the next salient location will receive spatial attention (see also Itti & Koch, 2000; Nothdurft, 2000; Sagi & Julesz, 1985).

Since 1991, when Theeuwes introduced the irrelevant singleton paradigm, various other labs have replicated the basic finding that the presence of a salient singleton can interfere with search for a target singleton (see, for example, Bacon & Egeth, 1994, Exp. 1; Joseph & Optican, 1996; Kawahara & Toshima, 1996; Kim & Cave, 1999; Kumada, 1999; Lamy, Leber, & Egeth, 2004; Mounts, 2000; Todd & Kramer, 1994), indicating that the singleton capture effect is highly reliable.

The Contingent Capture Paradigm

In the previous section, we discussed the view that, in early vision, selection is completely data driven. At the other end of the spectrum is the view that selection is completely under top-down control. According to this alternative view, which is known as the contingent capture hypothesis (e.g., Folk et al., 1992), selection depends critically on the explicit or implicit perceptual goals held by the observer at any given time. For example, it is assumed that when people perform a task, such as searching for a traffic sign while approaching a busy intersection, they activate a template (e.g., "red" and "triangle") that guides their search processes.

In a series of experiments, Folk et al. (1992) showed that visual selection depends critically on the top-down attentional set of the observer. These researchers used a spatial cueing paradigm in which a cue display was followed in rapid succession by a target display that had four elements. In the target display, which could consist of a color or an onset display, one element was a singleton, and observers were required to identify the unique element. In the color display, the target was red while the other three elements were white. In the onset display, only one element was presented, so the target was characterized as being the only element with an abrupt onset.

Immediately preceding the target display at 150-ms stimulus-onset asynchrony (SOA), a cue display was presented. This display consisted of color cues (in which one location was surrounded by red dots and the other three locations were surrounded by white dots) or onset cues (in which one location was surrounded by an abrupt onset of white dots and the remaining locations remained empty). All conditions were factorially combined (see Figure 4.4).

The critical finding of Folk and colleagues' (1992) studies was that the cue captured attention only when the search display was preceded by a to-be-ignored featural singleton (the "cue") that matched the singleton for which observers were

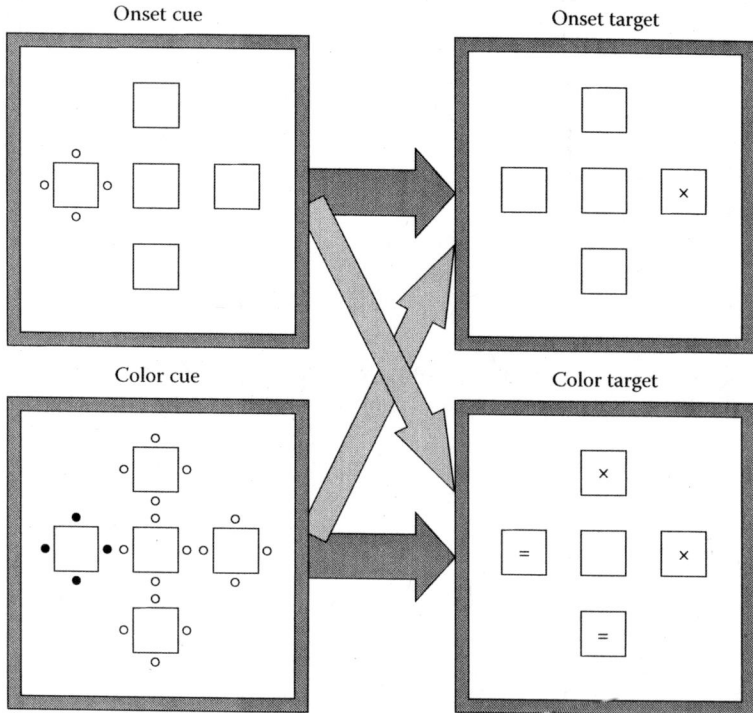

Figure 4.4 The contingent capture paradigm of Folk, C. L. et al. (1992, *Journal of Experimental Psychology: Human Perception and Performance, 18,* 1030–1044). Participants had to respond to a target singleton (either an "X" or an "="). The target was defined as a singleton that had a unique color (color target) or was the only element presented as an onset (onset target). Each target display was preceded by either an onset or a color cue display.

searching. Thus, when subjects were searching for a red target singleton, their attention automatically shifted to the location of the irrelevant red cue that preceded the search display, and the irrelevant onset had no effect on performance. The result clearly indicated that the top-down attentional set determines the selection priority: When set for a particular feature singleton, one will select each element that matches this top-down set; feature singletons that do not match top-down attentional sets will not be selected and will simply be ignored. Obviously, according to this view, the attentional readiness adopted by the observer determines selection.

Search Experiments of Yantis and Colleagues

In the late 1980s, Yantis and Jonides (1984; Jonides & Yantis, 1988; see also Yantis & Egeth, 1999) conducted several studies investigating whether feature singletons receive attentional priority. Yantis and colleagues adopted a visual search task in which the search target was a nonsingleton letter. This type of search is not efficient because search times increase with the number of elements present in the display. Each search display always contained one salient element, and the question addressed was whether search would automatically start at the salient element. With N as the number of elements in the display, the salient element was the target on 1/N of the trials, indicating that the chance that the salient element was the target was the same as that for any other letter. Because the salient element was the target at chance level, there was no incentive deliberately to start searching at the salient singleton (see Figure 4.5).

Jonides and Yantis (1988) showed that subjects did not start searching at the salient element in the display. When the unique element happened to be the target (e.g., an element with a unique color or unique luminance), the search slopes were basically the same as for the condition in which a nonunique element was the target (see panels B and C in Figure 4.5; compare the "unique" and "common" search slopes). It was concluded that salient static singletons are treated in the same way

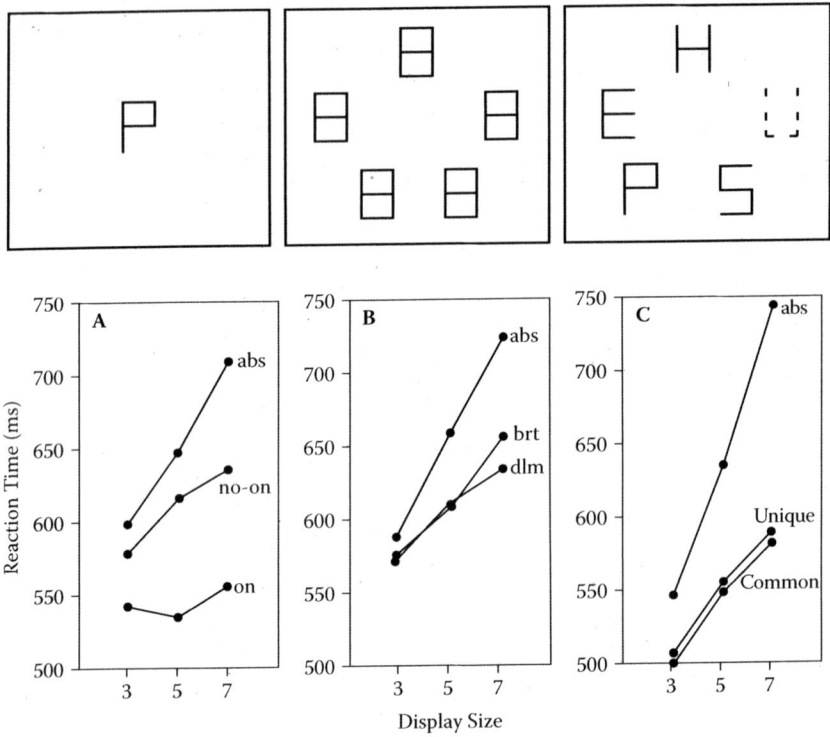

Figure 4.5 Paradigm and data from Jonides, J. and Yantis, S. (1988, *Perception & Psychophysics, 43*, 346–354). In the first display, a target letter was displayed for 1,000 ms (in this case, the letter P), followed by a premask display for 1,000 ms. In the search display, one letter had a unique color (dotted lines). At chance level, this letter could be the target. The results show that participants do not start searching at the unique feature (panel B: unique brightness; panel C: unique color). Note that when the unique feature is an abrupt onset (panel A), participants do start searching at the unique feature (i.e., the abrupt onset).

as other nonsalient elements in the visual field. Uniqueness in color or luminance is not sufficient to capture attention when it is irrelevant to the top-down goal. Jonides and Yantis showed that only elements appearing with an abrupt onset have a special status in capturing attention irrespectively of the top-down settings (see panel A in the figure).

Overall, Jonides and Yantis (1988; see also Yantis & Egeth, 1999) claimed that a feature singleton (such as an element with a unique color or brightness) is not automatically selected. Only when the element is presented with abrupt onset does it receive attentional priority. Yantis and Egeth claimed that selection is very much under top-down control except for elements that are presented with abrupt onset, constituting a new object.

Singleton Detection and Singleton Search Experiments

The studies conducted by Bacon and Egeth (1994) became important in resolving several controversies in the literature. On one hand, Theeuwes (1992) claimed there was no top-down control in early vision; at the same time, Folk et al. (1992) claimed that selection was completely under top-down control. The Bacon and Egeth study was an attempt to resolve this apparent contradiction.

Bacon and Egeth (1994) first replicated Theeuwes's (1992) experiment in which a color singleton interfered with search for a shape singleton. In the following experiment, they added additional shapes (i.e., squares and triangles) to the display so that the shape singleton was no longer unique. In this condition, the color singleton did not interfere anymore. Bacon and Egeth suggested that under these conditions, observers could not simply use uniqueness to find the target. They argued that when additional shapes are present, participants can no longer rely on a difference signal detection (referred to as "singleton detection" mode) and had to switch strategies and rely on the so-called "feature search" mode. In a feature search mode, observers are able to direct their attention exclusively to the relevant feature, so irrelevant singletons no longer interfere. These results suggest that once the feature search mode is set, it is used throughout a whole block of trials.

Bacon and Egeth concluded that "goal-directed selection of a specific known featural singleton identity may override stimulus-driven capture by salient singletons" (1994, p. 493). These results suggest that when observers "choose" a feature search mode, attentional capture by irrelevant singletons can be eliminated. The notion that choosing a search strategy allows attentional control suggests that selection is very much under top-down control.

In summary, over the past 15 years, a heated discussion has taken place on the extent to which visual selection is under top-down control. On one hand is Theeuwes's view that no top-down control is present in early vision and that the initial sweep of information is basically bottom up. On the other hand are views that assume full top-down control (Folk et al., 1992) or that assume top-down control under specific conditions (such as Jonides & Yantis, 1988, and Bacon & Egeth, 1994). Even though it may appear that this is an old discussion, there is still no clear answer to the question. Over the years, many attempts have been made to reconcile these differences. Most studies appeared to have argued that findings from Theeuwes's irrelevant singleton paradigm showing bottom-up selection were flawed. In the next section, we will discuss those claims and provide arguments why we believe that initial claims that selection is basically bottom up in early vision still stand.

BOTTOM-UP SELECTION: DEBATE AND DISCUSSION

Filtering Costs

As noted, Theeuwes (1991a, 1992, 1994a) observed an increase in reaction time for those conditions in which the irrelevant singleton was present (see Figure 4.3). The increase in reaction time (RT) was explained in terms of attention capture: Attention moved exogenously to the location of the salient singleton before it could move to the location of the (less salient) singleton target. Folk and Remington (1998) offered an alternative explanation for the increase in RT in conditions in which a distractor was present. They argued that "filtering costs" (Kahneman, Treisman, & Burkell, 1983) lead to an increase in search time caused by the irrelevant singleton. The idea of filtering costs is that the presence of an irrelevant singleton may slow the deployment of attention to the target item by requiring an effortful and time-consuming filtering operation.

According to this line of reasoning, attention is employed in a top-down way and goes directly to the singleton target; simply because another irrelevant singleton is present, directing attention to the target may take more time than when no such irrelevant singleton is present. Note that this view does not entail a shift of spatial attention to the location of the irrelevant singleton. In other words, according to this view, the irrelevant singleton is not selected. The filtering cost argument can explain how the results of Theeuwes (1991a, 1992, 1994a) are compatible with a view in which there is full top-down control over the visual selection processes.

The explanation of Theeuwes's findings in terms of filtering costs seems to be reasonable. In these early studies, Theeuwes (1991a, 1992, 1994a) never showed that spatial attention shifted to the location of the irrelevant singleton. In other words, Theeuwes had no direct evidence that the irrelevant singleton was indeed selected. In recent years, various studies have provided evidence that spatial attention first shifts to the highly salient singleton before it goes to the target.

In 1996, Theeuwes conducted a study that provides strong evidence that attention shifts to the irrelevant singleton. In his study, participants performed typical "irrelevant singleton" searches (as in Theeuwes, 1992). Instead of having slightly tilted line segments at all display elements (see Figure 4.1), the letters R and L were placed inside all display elements (see Figure 4.6). Participants responded to the letter placed inside the diamond. The letter placed inside the color distractor could be congruent or incongruent with the response to the letter inside the color singleton. In other words, in half of the trials, the character at the distractor location was associated with the same response as that required by the target; in the other half, it was associated with the opposite response.

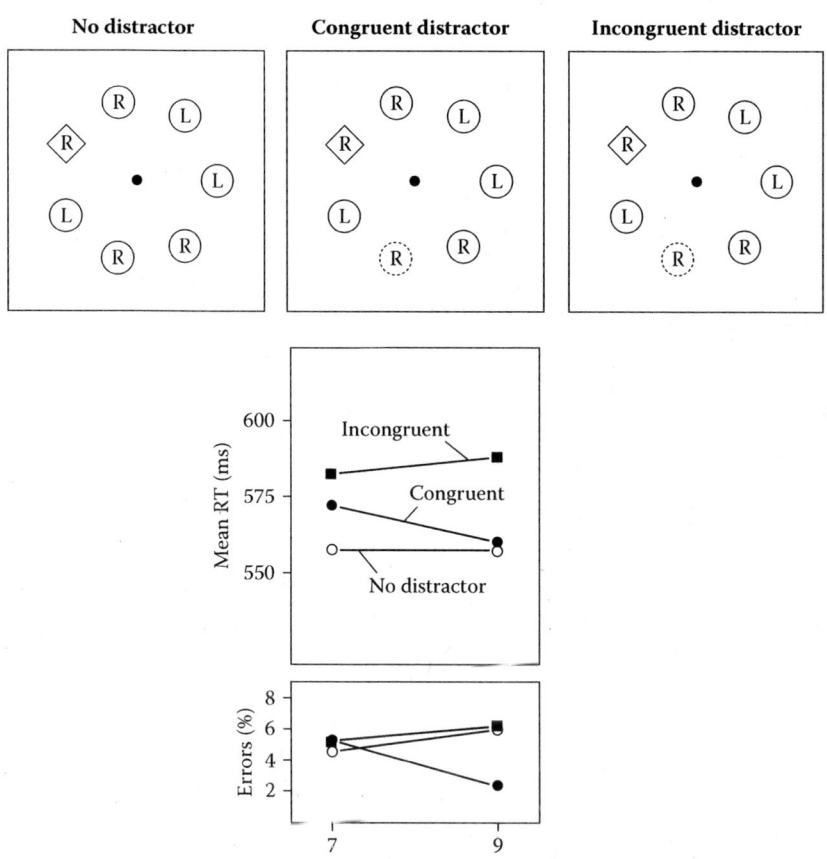

Figure 4.6   Stimuli and data from Theeuwes (1996). Top: Sample stimulus display (display size 7). In the no-distractor condition (top left), the green diamond shape appears among green circles. In the congruent condition (top middle), the letter inside the green diamond target shape (in this case, the letter R) is identical to the letter inside the red circle distractor. In the incongruent condition (top right), the letter inside the green diamond target shape is different from the letter inside the red circle distractor. Solid lines indicate green and dotted lines indicate red. Bottom: Data from Theeuwes (1996, Experiment 1). The incongruent condition is significantly slower than the congruent condition, suggesting that the letter at the location of the to-be-ignored singleton was processed. This finding indicates that spatial attention was captured by the irrelevant colored singleton, enabling the processing of the letter inside the irrelevant singleton. (From Theeuwes, J., 1996, In A. F. Kramer, M. G. H. Coles, & G. D. Logan (Eds.), *Converging operations in the study of visual attention,* pp. 297–314; Experiment 1. Washington, DC: American Psychological Association.)

Theeuwes (1996) argued that the identity of the character at the location of the irrelevant singleton could only have an effect on responding if at some point spatial attention had been employed at the location of the distractor. Figure 4.6 presents an example of the stimulus material and the data.

In line with Folk and Remington's (1998) filtering notion, if attention is deployed directly and exclusively to the target location, then there should be no congruency effect of a character presented at the irrelevant singleton location. In other words, if attention never goes to the location of the irrelevant singleton, it is impossible that the identity of a character can have any effect on responding. However, as is clear from Figure 4.6, Theeuwes (1996) did find clear congruency effect of about 20 ms, which provided strong evidence that, before a response was given, spatial attention was at the location of the irrelevant singleton. This finding completely supports the notion that spatial attention first moved to the irrelevant singleton. In other words, initially the salient but irrelevant singleton was selected before the relevant target singleton was selected.

A more recent study by Hickey, McDonald, and Theeuwes (2006) provided converging evidence for the claim that the irrelevant distractor singleton was initially selected. In this study, displays similar to those of Theeuwes (1991a, 1992) were used. Instead of just examining RT effects, in this study Hickey et al. measured the N2pc, a component of the event-related potential (ERP). The N2pc is defined as a larger negative voltage at electrodes contralateral to the selected stimulus than at electrodes ipsilateral to that stimulus. The N2pc is thought to reflect the attentional selection of an item in a search array via the suppression of surrounding items (Luck, Girelli, McDermott, & Ford, 1997). This study showed that the irrelevant distractor singleton caused an N2pc. More importantly, Experiment 2 showed that both the distractor and the target elicited an N2pc component when the two stimuli were presented on opposite sides of the search array. Critically, the distractor-elicited N2pc preceded the target-elicited N2pc on these trials. These results show that first the salient irrelevant distractor was selected before the target was selected. This pattern of results supports Theeuwes's claims that selection is basically stimulus driven.

Early Selection: Top Down or Bottom Up?

Some claims hold that the early selection of the irrelevant singleton is not truly exogenous. One claim is that participants endogenously choose to select the irrelevant singleton as part of some kind of strategy (e.g., the strategy to use a singleton-detection mode). Others have claimed that it may be easier to let attention be captured by whatever salient stimulus is present in the visual field (e.g., Rauschenberger, 2003).

In a series of recent experiments, Theeuwes and colleagues (Theeuwes & Godijn, 2002; Theeuwes & Chen, 2005) provided evidence that the initial shift of spatial selection is indeed truly exogenous. These studies used the phenomenon of "inhibition of return" (IOR; Posner & Cohen, 1984) to resolve the dispute concerning whether the initial shift of attention is indeed exogenous. When attention is exogenously drawn to a location of an abrupt onset (see Posner & Cohen, 1984), one typically obtains a biphasic pattern in which initial facilitation is followed by inhibition. Note that such a biphasic pattern can only be obtained when attention is exogenously captured.

According to Klein (2000), IOR is the hallmark of exogenous orienting. Typically, IOR does not follow a shift of attention that is under top-down control (Posner & Cohen, 1984; Pratt, Kingstone, & Khoe, 1997). In other words, finding initial facilitation followed by IOR can only be the result of a shift of exogenous attention. As recently shown by Pratt, Sekuler, and McAuliffe (2001), if participants use a top-down attentional control setting such as a singleton-detection mode, one will not find IOR effects. Finding IOR in the present study adds to the notion that attentional capture by static singletons is not due to some top-down strategy used by the participant but rather genuinely exogenous in origin.

Theeuwes and Godijn (2004) presented a stimulus display consisting of eight outline circles equally spaced around the fixation point on an imaginary circle. In the center of each of the eight outline circles was a small gray dot. All outline circles were gray, except for one red circle, which constituted the uniquely colored irrelevant singleton. This colored singleton was completely irrelevant for the task. Participants viewed the display for 1,300 ms and then had to detect whether or not one of the small dots was turned off. The results showed that participants were slower to detect the offset of the small gray dot when it was located in the irrelevant distractor singleton than when the gray dot was extinguished in another nonsingleton circle. The observation of an IOR effect to the location of the salient red distractor outline circle strongly suggests that attention was captured to that location (see Folk & Remington, 2006, for a replication of this effect).

In another study, Theeuwes and Chen (2005) provided evidence that at the location of the irrelevant distractor singleton, one obtains the classic biphasic pattern (facilitation followed by IOR) signifying exogenous orienting. In this study, Theeuwes and Chen systematically manipulated the singleton target and distractor locations. Similarly to the spatial cueing task of Folk et al. (1992), the irrelevant distractor singleton could appear at a location at which the target would appear somewhat later. Instead of using RT as a dependent measure, Theeuwes and Chen (2005) determined the sensitivity (d-prime) in detecting the target singleton.

The most important finding from this study was that at the location of the distractor singleton, increased sensitivity was followed by reduced sensitivity relative to a condition in which no distractor was present. The increased sensitivity implies that spatial attention was directed at the location of the distractor singleton; the reduced sensitivity suggests inhibition at the location of the distractor. As noted, this pattern of results showing initial facilitation followed by inhibition can only be obtained when attention is exogenously shifted to a location in space.

Feature Search and Singleton Detection Mode

Up until now, we have established that initial selection involves a shift of spatial attention ("Filtering Costs" section) and we have shown that it is likely to be the result of an exogenous shift of attention (preceding section). The question that remains unanswered is why Bacon and Egeth (1992) found top-down selectivity (which they referred to as "feature search" mode) in the irrelevant singleton paradigm. Even though no evidence has ever indicated that these search modes exist, the interpretation of Bacon and Egeth in terms of search strategies ("singleton detection" vs. "feature search" mode) is the generally accepted way to explain differences in viewpoints on top-down selectivity. Recent literature reviews (see Egeth & Yantis, 1997; Rauschenberger, 2005; Ruz, & Lupiañez, 2002; Yantis, 1996, 2000) all embrace the concept of search strategies (see also Leber & Egeth, 2006).

As described previously, Bacon and Egeth (1994) took the original displays of Theeuwes (1992) and added additional shapes (i.e., squares and triangles) to the display so that the shape singleton was no longer unique. In this condition, the color singleton did not interfere anymore. Bacon and Egeth argued that, under these conditions, observers could not simply use "uniqueness" to find the target. They argued that because of the additional shapes, participants could no longer rely on a difference signal detection (the "singleton detection" mode) and thus switch their strategy to the so-called "feature search" mode.

Even though such a strategy is possible, one aspect of Bacon and Egeth's (1994) data was troublesome: When the additional shape singleton was added, search was no longer efficient. Instead of being conducted in parallel across the display (as in Theeuwes, 1991a, 1992), search became partly serial. In Bacon and Egeth, slopes were relatively flat (up to 11.5 ms/item); however, they always differed significantly from zero, suggesting that search may have been partly serial. This suggests that when additional shapes are present (such as squares and triangles), the stimulus field becomes less homogenous (i.e., more noisy); this may have rendered the irrelevant color singleton less salient.

Indeed, theories like those of Duncan and Humphreys (1989) recognize that search performance depends to a large extent on how similar distractors are to each other and how dissimilar they are from the target. Therefore, in Bacon and Egeth's (1994) displays, the irrelevant color singleton may not have captured attention because the color singleton was simply not salient enough to capture attention rather than because of some search strategy chosen by the observer. As Theeuwes (1992) demonstrated, color singletons may fail to capture attention when they become less salient.

Theeuwes (2004) tested this idea. He used exactly the same displays as Bacon and Egeth (1994) with three differently shaped singletons, forcing observers to engage in a feature search mode. At the same time, he increased the salience of target and distractor singleton by adding more nontarget elements (see Figure 4.7, top). The key point of his findings (Figure 4.7, bottom) was that even though participants were forced to use a feature search mode, the color singleton caused a large interference effect. At the same time, Theeuwes showed that by adding the additional nontarget circles, the search became parallel, producing virtually no search slope. In an additional experiment, Theeuwes replicated Bacon and Egeth data using fewer nontarget elements—producing a small search slope (of about 12 ms/item) and virtually no interference of the color singleton.

Theeuwes (2004) concluded that the assumed search modes of Bacon and Egeth may not be a viable concept. Indeed, in various studies, the claims have been made that whenever interference is present, observers must have engaged in a singleton detection mode, and whenever interference is not present, observers

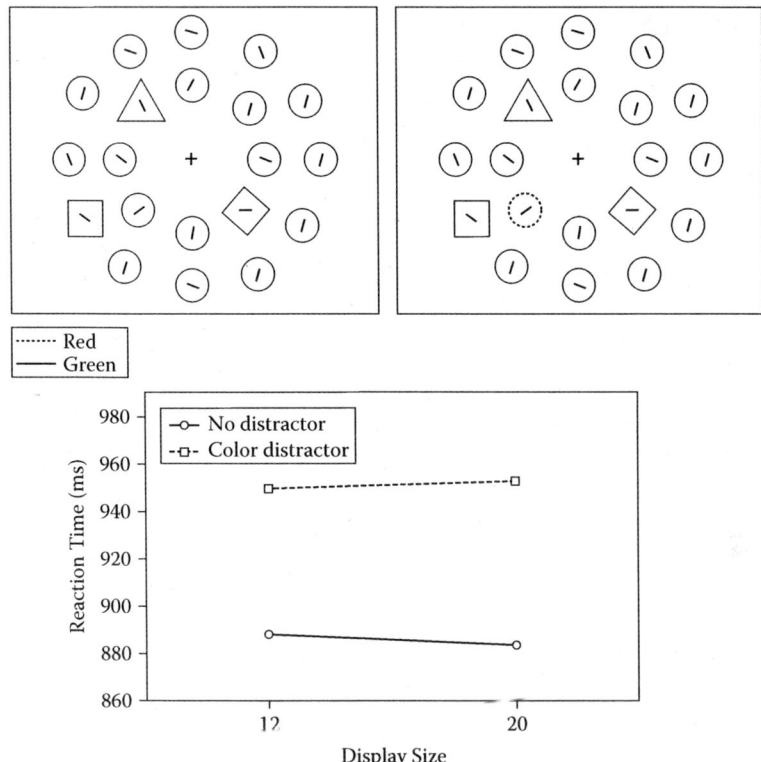

Figure 4.7   Stimuli and data from Theeuwes, J. (2004, *Psychonomic Bulletin & Review*, *11*, 65–70). Top: Sample stimulus display (display size 20). The top left presents the condition without a distractor; top right presents the condition with a color distractor singleton. Observers searched for a shape singleton (a diamond between circles) while other unique-shape singletons (a square and a triangle) were also present. The presence of the additional unique shape singletons (square and triangle) should induce a feature search mode, which should eliminate attentional capture by the irrelevant color singleton. The data clearly show that this is not the case: The color distractor causes a large interference effect.

must have been in a feature search mode. This type of reasoning is also used to explain interference effects in Theeuwes (1992), even though in those experiments observers had ample opportunity to engage in the feature search mode because they searched for more than 1,800 trials for the very same target singleton (i.e., a green diamond). It will be clear that this reasoning is circular and does not add anything above and beyond the data: If interference is present, then it is assumed that a singleton detection mode is used; if interference is not present, then it is assumed a feature search mode is used.

Without claiming the existence of nonobservable search modes, one can simply argue that when displays are more heterogeneous, target and distractor singletons become less salient, resulting in search performance that is serial or partly serial (clump-wise search). When search is serial or partly serial, the distracting effects of the irrelevant singleton are attenuated or may even be absent. However, this does not mean that visual selection becomes goal driven. The extent to which distracting effects are reduced is completely dependent on the bottom-up salience of the display elements.

The Time Course of Selection

An important question that needs to be answered is why there appears to be full top-down control over selection in Folk and colleagues' spatial cueing paradigm (see Figure 4.4), and why there is no top-down control in Theeuwes's irrelevant singleton paradigm (see Figure 4.3). The answer may lie in the procedural differences between the paradigms. Folk et al. used a spatial cueing paradigm in which participants had to ignore a "cue" that appeared 150 ms prior to the presentation of the target display (see Folk et al., 1992). Participants responded to a character shape ("X" vs. "="), which had a unique color or a unique abrupt onset. When the search display was preceded by a to-be-ignored featural singleton (the "cue") that matched the singleton for which the subject was searching, the cue captured attention, as evidenced by a prolonged reaction time to identify the target (i.e., when the cue and target appeared in different spatial locations).

On the other hand, if the to-be-ignored featural singleton "cue" did not match the singleton for which the subject was searching, its appearance apparently did not have an effect on responding (i.e., the cue did not capture attention). The critical finding in these studies was that a cue that did not match the top-down search goal (i.e., the defining property of the target) did not affect RT (i.e., a zero effect), but a cue that matched the search goal had an effect on RT.

Rather than the spatial cueing paradigm, Theeuwes (1992) used the previously described irrelevant singleton search task in which the target and distractor singletons were simultaneously present. He showed that, independent of any top-down goal, an irrelevant singleton that was more salient than the singleton target interfered with search. The increase in RT (always 15–25 ms) was taken as evidence that attention was captured by the salient distractor singleton. Given that the distraction effects in basically all of the experiments of Theeuwes were relatively small, it is entirely feasible that attention shifts to the irrelevant singleton for a relatively brief time before it moves on the singleton target. As Theeuwes et al. (2000) have argued, it is quite feasible that, in Folk and colleagues' spatial cueing paradigm also, the irrelevant cue did capture attention. Because of a delay of 150 ms between the presentation of the cue and the search display, participants may have been able to overcome the attentional capture by the time the search display was presented (see also Theeuwes, 1994a, 1994b).

Disengagement of attention from the cue may have been relatively fast when the cue and target did not share the same defining properties (e.g., the cue is red and the target is an onset), and disengagement from the cue may have been relatively slow in the case where the cue and target shared the same defining properties (e.g., both were red). Such a mechanism could explain why there are RT costs when the cue and target have the same defining characteristics and no costs when cue and target are different. In this view, the contingent capture hypothesis can explain why it may be easier to disengage attention from a particular location when an element presented at that location is not in line with the top-down control settings. However, this does not imply that attention is not captured by the irrelevant cue singleton; it simply indicates that after a certain time participants are able to exert top-down control over the erroneous capture of attention by the irrelevant singleton.

To test this notion Theeuwes et al. (2000) used a task that was very similar to the irrelevant singleton task. Again, observers had to search for a shape singleton (a single gray diamond among eight gray circles). Prior to the presentation of the target display at different SOAs (50, 100, 150, 200, 250, and 300 ms), a color singleton was presented. The results showed that the presence of an irrelevant salient distractor had an effect only when the singleton target and distractor were presented in close succession (at SOAs of 50 and 100 ms). Theeuwes et al. argued that in conditions in which target and distractor were presented in close temporal proximity, there was not enough time to exert top-down control that could have overcome attentional capture by the salient distractor. However, when the distractor singleton was presented a considerable time (SOAs of 150–300 ms) before the presentation of the singleton target, it was possible to exert sufficient top-down control so that, by the time the singleton target was presented, there was no sign of attentional capture by the distractor anymore.

The results of Theeuwes et al. (2000) showing no sign of attentional capture when the interval between the target and distractor singleton is more than 100 ms provide some new insights regarding the findings obtained with the spatial cuing paradigm of Folk and colleagues (1992; Folk & Remington, 1998). As noted before, in the spatial cueing paradigm, participants have to ignore a cue that appears 150 ms before the search display.

The critical finding is that a cue that does not match the top-down search goal (e.g., in Theeuwes's experiments where the search goal is a shape singleton and the cue is a color singleton) does not affect RT; however, a cue that does match the search goal slows search. The finding of an effect on RT in Folk and colleagues' experiments when the cue and target share the same defining property (e.g., the cue is red and the target is red) is not surprising: It is likely that disengagement and redirection of attention from the distractor location will take much longer when the distractor and target have the same defining property.

The current interpretation fits very well with data reported by Kim and Cave (1999) employing the irrelevant singleton search task (as in Theeuwes, 1992) in combination with a probe detection task. Kim and Cave presented probes 60 or 150 ms after the presentation of the search display at the location of the target and the location of the distractor. It was hypothesized that if the early preattentive processing is solely driven by bottom-up salience, as suggested by Theeuwes (1991a, 1992), then the location of the salient distractor singleton should be attended to first. Therefore, the probe RT at the distractor location should be faster than at any of the other locations in the short SOA condition, regardless of whether the unique feature is relevant or not. On the other hand, if top-down control is possible somewhat later in time, as the current experiments suggest, then it is expected that in the late SOA condition, attention will no longer be at the distractor location but instead at the location of the singleton target.

For those conditions in which target and distractor were locally unique (and therefore salient enough), Kim and Cave (1999) did indeed find these results. At the 60-ms SOA, the probe RT at the location of the distractor singleton was about 20 ms faster than at the singleton target location. At the 150-ms SOA, however, this pattern was reversed: The probe RT at the target location was about 15 ms faster than at the distractor location. The bottom line is that Kim and Cave also showed that, after 150 ms, attention was no longer at the location of the distractor, but instead at the location of the target.

Recently, Kim and Cave (1999) replicated these findings using a focused-attention task in which participants responded to a central letter that was flanked on one side by a letter having the same color as the target letter and on the other side by a uniquely colored letter. Again, it was shown that at 60 ms, attention was first captured by the uniquely colored distractor, while soon thereafter (at 150 ms), the flanker that shared the target color received more attentional activation. Given the findings of Kim and Cave (1999, 2001) and those of Theeuwes et al. (2000), it is likely that it takes between 100 and 150 ms to disengage attention from the location of the distractor and redirect it to the location of the singleton target, at least when the distractor and singleton target have different defining properties.

Attentional Window

A final question that needs to be resolved is why the most salient element (e.g., a color singleton) in Theeuwes's additional singleton paradigm is always selected first and why, in the Jonides and Yantis's paradigm (see Figure 4.5), the salient color singleton is basically ignored. Recently, Theeuwes (2004) suggested that the size of the "attentional window" of observers could be one of the factors explaining why salient color singletons fail to capture attention in some experiments (as in Bacon & Egeth, 1994; Jonides & Yantis, 1988). In studies that do not find capture by a color singleton, visual search often occurs in a serial or partly serial fashion such that the search elements are examined individually or in small clusters.

According to this hypothesis, when observers expect a difficult search task, the size of the attentional window is reduced such that the window does not encompass the whole display. This increases the chance that the unique element is not included in the salience computations and does not capture attention. However, when the target is a unique object, as in the task used by Theeuwes (1992, 1994a), the optimal strategy is to attend to the whole display at once to find the target. As a consequence, the uniquely colored item falls inside the attentional window, is processed preattentively, and captures attention. This idea is supported by a well-known finding that when a target location is known in advance, even abrupt onset does not capture attention (Theeuwes, 1991b; Yantis & Jonides, 1990).

In a recent study, Belopolsky, Zwaan, Theeuwes, and Kramer (2007) tested this idea. They used a design similar to that of Jonides & Yantis (1988), but in addition manipulated the size of the attentional window of observers. To ensure that observers spread their attention across the whole display, the observers had to make a judgment regarding the spatial layout of all the elements before they could start searching. Specifically, observers had to decide whether the elements formed an upward-pointing triangle. In order to make this judgment about the layout of the display, observers had to spread their attention. In another condition, Belopolsky et al. ensured that observers focused their attention before they could start searching: Only when the fixation point was a circle were they allowed to search.

The results showed that when attention was initially focused in the center (focused attention condition), the salient color singleton was basically ignored, confirming the findings of Jonides and Yantis (1988). However, when attention was initially diffused over the global stimulus arrangement (diffuse attention condition), in many trials the irrelevant color singleton was selected first.

The findings of Belopolsky et al. (2007) suggest that the size of attentional window is an important factor in determining whether an irrelevant color singleton will capture attention. When attention is spread, visual search may be conducted across all items in the visual field in parallel (as in the irrelevant singleton task of Theeuwes, 1991a, 1992), incurring the expense that a salient irrelevant singleton would also be automatically selected. However, when, in anticipation of a difficult search, the attentional window is set to a small size, visual search will become serial (as in Jonides & Yantis, 1988) or partly serial (as in Bacon & Egeth, 1994). In these conditions, a salient singleton outside the attentional window will not capture attention.

CONCLUSIONS

We discussed the very basic issue of whether top-down knowledge can modulate the selection priority within the first sweep of information through the brain. We show that the initial selection during this first sweep of information is basically bottom up and depends on the saliency of the stimuli in the visual field. We argue that the only way to demonstrate top-down control is by varying the extent to which observers must spread attention across the visual field. If attention is focused on a limited, special area, then salient elements outside the attentional window do not affect performance. If attention is spread across the visual field, salient elements, irrespective of whether they are task relevant or not, compel selection and seize attention.

REFERENCES

Bacon, W. F., & Egeth, H. E. (1994). Overriding stimulus-driven attention capture. *Perception & Psychophysics, 55*, 485–496.

Belopolsky, A. V., Zwaan, L., Theeuwes, J., & Kramer, A. F. (2007). The size of attentional window modulates attentional capture by color singletons. *Psychonomic Bulletin and Review, 14*, 934–938.

Broadbent, D. E. (1958). *Perception and communication.* New York: Pergamon Press.

Bundesen, C. (1990). A theory of visual attention. *Psychological Review, 97,* 523–547.

Burnham, B. R. (2007). Displaywide visual features associated with a search display's appearance can mediate attentional capture. *Psychonomic Bulletin and Review, 14,* 392–422.

Carrasco, M., Ling, S., & Read, S. (2004). Attention alters appearance. *Nature Neuroscience, 7,* 308–313.

Corbetta, M., & Shulman, G. L.(2002). Control of goal-directed and stimulus-driven attention in the brain. *Nature Review Neuroscience 3,* 201–215.

Desimone, R., and Duncan, J. ((1995). Neural mechanisms of selective visual attention. *Annual Review of Neuroscience 18,* 193–222.

Deubel, H., & Schneider, W. X. (1996). Saccade target selection and object recognition: Evidence for a common attentional mechanism. *Vision Research, 6,* 1827–1837.

Deutsch, J. A., & Deutsch, D. (1963). Attention: Some theoretical considerations. *Psychological Review, 70,* 51–61.

Duncan, J., & Humphreys, G. W. (1989). Visual search and stimulus similarity. *Psychological Review, 96,* 433–458.

Egeth, H. E., & Yantis, S. (1997). Visual attention: Control, representation and time course. *Annual Review of Psychology, 48,* 269–297.

Folk, C. L., & Remington, R. W. (1998). Selectivity in distraction by irrelevant featural singletons: Evidence for two forms of attentional capture. *Journal of Experimental Psychology: Human Perception and Performance, 24,* 847–858.

Folk, C. L., & Remington, R. (2006). Top-down modulation of preattentive processing: Testing the recovery account of contingent capture. *Visual Cognition, 14,* 445–465.

Folk, C. L., Remington, R. W., & Johnston, J. C. (1992). Involuntary covert orienting is contingent on attentional control settings. *Journal of Experimental Psychology: Human Perception and Performance, 18,* 1030–1044.

Godijn, R., & Theeuwes, J. (2003). Parallel allocation of attention prior to the execution of saccade sequences. *Journal of Experimental Psychology: Human Perception and Performance, 29,* 882–896.

Hickey, C., McDonald, J. J., & Theeuwes, J. (2006), Electrophysiological evidence of attentional capture. *Journal of Cognitive Neuroscience, 18,* 604–613.

Itti, L., & Koch, C. (2000). Saliency based search mechanism for overt and covert shifts of visual attention. *Vision Research, 40,* 1489–1506.

Itti, L., & Koch. C. (2001) Computational modeling of visual attention, *Nature Reviews Neuroscience, 2,* 194–203.

Jonides, J., & Yantis, S. (1988). Uniqueness of abrupt visual onset in capturing attention. *Perception & Psychophysics, 43,* 346–354.

Joseph, J. S., & Optican, L. M. (1996). Involuntary attentional shifts due to orientation differences. *Perception & Psychophysics, 12,* 201–204.

Kahneman, D., Treisman, A., & Burkell, J. (1983). The costs of visual filtering. *Journal of Experimental Psychology: Human Perception and Performance, 9,* 510–522.

Kawahara, J., & Toshima, T. (1996). Stimulus-driven control of attention: Evidence from visual search for moving target among static nontargets. *Japanese Journal of Psychonomic Science, 15,* 77–87.

Koch, C., & Ullman, S. (1985). Shifts in selective visual attention: Towards the underlying neural circuitry. *Human Neurobiology, 4,* 219–227.

Kim, M. S., & Cave, K. R. (1999). Top-down and bottom-up attentional control: On the nature of interference from a salient distractor. *Perception & Psychophysics, 61,* 1009–1023.

Klein, R. M. (2000). Inhibition of return. *Trends in Cognitive Science, 4,* 138–147.

Kumada, T. (1999). Limitations in attending to a feature value for overriding stimulus-driven interference. *Perception & Psychophysics, 61*, 61–79.

Lamy, D., Leber, A., & Egeth, H. E. (2004). Effects of stimulus-driven salience within feature search mode. *Journal of Experimental Psychology: Human Perception and Performance, 30*(6), 1019–1031.

Leber, A. B., & Egeth, H. E. (2006). It's under control: Top-down search strategies can override attentional capture. *Psychonomic Bulletin & Review, 13*(1), 132–138.

Li, Z. (2002). A saliency map in primary visual cortex. *Trends in Cognitive Sciences, 6*, 9–16.

Luck, S. J., Girelli, M., McDermott, M. T., & Ford, M. A. (1997). Bridging the gap between monkey neurophysiology and human perception: An ambiguity resolution theory of visual selective attention. *Cognitive Psychology, 33*, 64–87.

Mounts, J. R. W. (2000). Attentional capture by abrupt onsets and feature singletons produces inhibitory surrounds. *Perception & Psychophysics, 62*, 1485–1493.

Müller, H. J., Reimann, B., & Krummenacher, J. (2003). Visual search for singleton feature targets across dimensions: Stimulus- and expectancy-driven effects in dimensional weighting. *Journal of Experimental Psychology: Human Perception and Performance, 29*(5), 1021–1035.

Neisser, U. (1967). *Cognitive psychology.* Englewood Cliffs, NJ: Prentice Hall.

Nothdurft, H. C. (2000). Salience from feature contrast: Variations with texture density. *Vision Research, 40*, 3181–3200.

Nothdurft, H. C., Gallant, J. L., & Van Essen, D. C. (1999). Response modulation by texture surround in primate area V1: Correlates of "pop-out" under anesthesia. *Visual Neuroscience, 16*, 15–34.

Posner, M. I. (1980). Orienting of attention. *Quarterly Journal of Experimental Psychology, 32*, 3–25.

Posner, M. I., & Cohen, Y. (1984). Components of visual orienting. In H. Bouma & D. Bouwhuis (Eds.), *Attention & performance X* (pp.531–556). Hillsdale, NJ: Lawrence Erlbaum Associates.

Pratt, J., Kingstone, A., & Khoe, W. (1997). Inhibition of return in allocation and identity based choice decision tasks. *Perception and Psychophysics, 59*, 964–971.

Pratt, J., Sekuler, A., & McAuliffe, J. (2001). The role of attentional set on attentional cueing and inhibition of return. *Visual Cognition, 8*, 33–46.

Rauschenberger, R. (2003). Attentional capture by auto- and allo-cues. *Psychonomic Bulletin & Review, 10*, 814–842.

Reynolds, J. H., and Desimone, R. (2003). Interacting roles of attention and visual salience in V4. *Neuron, 37*(5), 853–863.

Ruz, M., & Lupiañez, J. (2002). A review of attentional capture: On its automaticity and sensitivity to endogenous control. *Psicologica, 23*, 283–309.

Sagi, D., & Julesz, B. (1985). Detection versus discrimination of visual orientation. *Perception, 14*, 619–628.

Serences, J. T., & Yantis, S. (2006). Selective visual attention and perceptual coherence. *Trends in Cognitive Sciences, 10*, 38–45.

Theeuwes, J. (1991a). Cross-dimensional perceptual selectivity. *Perception & Psychophysics, 50*, 184–193.

Theeuwes, J. (1991b). Exogenous and endogenous control of attention: The effect of visual onsets and offsets. *Perception & Psychophysics, 49*, 83–90.

Theeuwes, J. (1992). Perceptual selectivity for color and form. *Perception & Psychophysics, 51*, 599–606.

Theeuwes, J. (1994a). Stimulus-driven capture and attentional set: Selective search for color and visual abrupt onsets. *Journal of Experimental Psychology: Human Perception and Performance, 20*, 799–806.

Theeuwes, J. (1994b). Endogenous and exogenous control of visual selection. *Perception, 23*, 429–440.

Theeuwes, J. (1996). Perceptual selectivity for color and form: On the nature of the interference effect. In A. F. Kramer, M. G. H. Coles, & G. D. Logan (Eds.), *Converging operations in the study of visual attention* (pp. 297–314). Washington, DC: American Psychological Association.

Theeuwes, J. (2004). Top-down search strategies cannot override attentional capture. *Psychonomic Bulletin & Review, 11*, 65–70.

Theeuwes, J., Atchley, P., & Kramer, A. F. (2000). On the time course of top-down and bottom-up control of visual attention. In S. Monsell & J. Driver (Eds.), *Attention & performance* (Vol. 18). Cambridge, MA: MIT Press.

Theeuwes, J., & Chen, C. Y. D (2005). Attentional capture and inhibition (of return): The effect on perceptual sensitivity. *Perception & Psychophysics, 67*(8), 1305–1312.

Theeuwes, J., & Godijn, R. (2001). Attention and oculomotor capture. In C. Folk and B. Gibson (Eds.), *Attraction, distraction, and action: Multiple perspectives on attentional capture* (pp. 121–150). New York: Elsevier Science B.V.

Theeuwes, J., & Godijn, R. (2002). Irrelevant singletons capture attention: Evidence from inhibition of return. *Perception & Psychophysics, 64*, 764–770.

Theeuwes, J., Kramer, A. F., Hahn, S., & Irwin, D. E. (1998). Our eyes do not always go where we want them to go: Capture of the eyes by new objects. *Psychological Science, 9*, 379–385.

Theeuwes, J., & Van der Burg, E. (2007). The role of spatial and nonspatial information in visual selection. *Journal of Experimental Psychology: Human Perception and Performance, 33*(6), 1335–1351.

Todd, S., & Kramer, A. F. (1994). Attentional misguidance in visual search. *Perception & Psychophysics, 56*, 198–210.

Treisman, A., and Gelade, G. (1980). A feature integration theory of attention. *Cognitive Psychology, 12*, 97–136.

Treue, S. (2003). Climbing the cortical ladder from sensation to perception. *Trends in Cognitive Science, 7*, 469–471.

Van Zoest, W., Donk, M., & Theeuwes, J. (2004). The role of stimulus-driven and goal-driven control in visual selection. *Journal of Experimental Psychology: Human Perception and Performance, 30*, 746–759.

Wolfe, J. M. (1994). Guided search 2.0: A revised model of visual search. *Psychonomic Bulletin and Review, 1*, 202–238.

Wolfe, J. M., Butcher, S. J., Lee, C., & Hyle, M. (2003). Changing your mind: On the contribution of top-down and bottom-up guidance in visual search for feature singletons. *Journal of Experimental Psychology: Human Perception and Performance, 29*, 483–502.

Yantis, S. (1996). Attentional capture in vision. In A. F. Kramer, M. G. H. Coles, & G. D. Logan (Eds.). *Converging operations in the study of visual attention* (pp. 45–76). Washington, DC: American Psychological Association.

Yantis, S. (2000). Goal directed and stimulus driven determinants of attentional control. In S. Monsell & J. Driver (Eds.), *Attention & performance* (Vol. 18). Cambridge, MA: MIT Press.

Yantis, S., & Egeth, H. E. (1999). On the distinction between visual salience and stimulus-driven attentional capture. *Journal of Experimental Psychology: Human Perception and Performance 25*, 661–676.

Yantis, S., & Jonides, J. (1984). Abrupt visual onsets and selective attention: Evidence from selective search. *Journal of Experimental Psychology: Human Perception and Performance, 10*, 601–621.

Yantis, S., & Jonides, J. (1990). Abrupt visual onsets and selective attention: Voluntary versus automatic allocation. *Journal of Experimental Psychology: Human Perception and Performance, 16*, 121–134.

5

Getting Into Guided Search

JEREMY M. WOLFE, TODD S. HOROWITZ,
EVAN M. PALMER, KRISTIN O. MICHOD, and
MICHAEL J. VAN WERT

INTRODUCTION

*T*he world delivers more input than the visual system can handle. In response, the visual system has developed a variety of ways to limit the amount of information that it processes. For example, our foveated retina transmits the most detailed information from only a very small part of the visual field. Because we cannot see the entire world at once, we must move our eyes in order to get that level of detail from a different portion of the visual field. That retinal image still contains more information than the system can process. Visual selective attention is a set of mechanisms to restrict processing further to a subset of the input (e.g., a single location or object) at one time. As a consequence, if we want to know if a specific object is present, we will often need to search for it, even if it is easily visible. Thus, in Figure 5.1, the medium size, light gray diamond is perfectly visible but not immediately discovered until we search for and direct our attention to it.

A vast body of empirical information on visual search has accumulated over the past quarter century (for reviews, see Kinchla, 1992; Pashler, 1998; Sanders & Donk, 1996; Wolfe, 1998a and b) and numerous models have been developed to account for portions of the data (e.g., Cave, 1999; Deco, Pollatos, & Zihl, 2002; Grossberg, Mingolla, & Ross, 1994; Hamker, 2006; Herd & O'Reilly, 2005; Hubner, 2001; Parkhurst, Law, & Nicbur, 2002; Thornton & Gilden, 2007). "Guided Search" is our model of human visual search that has been in development for almost 20 years (Wolfe, 1994, 2007; Wolfe, Cave, & Franzel, 1989; Wolfe & Gancarz, 1996). It is currently in its fourth incarnation, guided search 4.0 (GS4).

Guided Search 4.0 accounts for reaction time (RT) and error data in a range of visual search tasks as well as or better than other models. Still, one might think

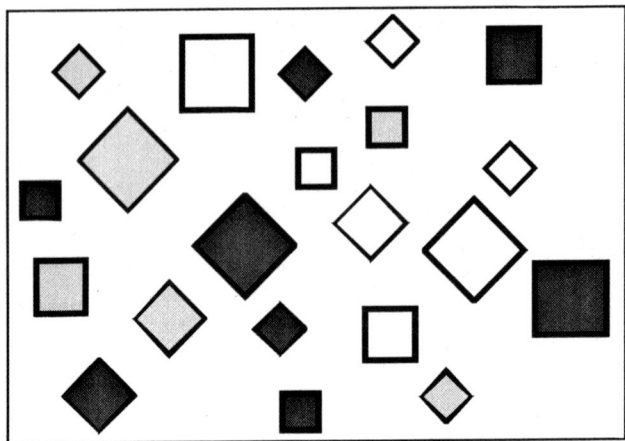

Figure 5.1   A simple visual search stimulus.

that, after 20 years, it is time for a model to explain the data or quietly retire. Of course, as with any active field of science, the "problem" lies in the data. Some aspects of the data have always proved difficult to model (e.g., target absent trials, Chun & Wolfe, 1996; Cousineau & Shiffrin, 2004; Hong, 2005; Zenger & Fahle, 1997). In other cases, new data provide fresh challenges for a model.

This chapter will describe several lines of research that modify our understanding of the dynamics of guidance in GS4. The results are not specific to our model, but rather provide constraints for any model of search.

The "guided" part of GS4 can be illustrated in Figure 5.1. When we searched for that medium size, light gray diamond, we might have intuitively felt that we did not search at random. We were more likely to attend to items of the correct color, shape, or size. These basic visual attributes "guide" the deployment of selective attention (Wolfe & Horowitz, 2004). This chapter is concerned with the temporal dynamics of this guidance. The data reviewed here make the following points about the time course of guidance:

- It takes several hundred milliseconds for guidance to become effective after the guiding information is available.
- Curiously, it seems to take a similar amount of time for guidance to become effective each time a new stimulus is presented, even if the guidance is the same as on the previous trial. That is, if we search another version of Figure 5.1 for another medium, gray diamond; the guidance settings from the first search would not be immediately available to the second search.
- More generally, the earliest moments of an extended visual search are different from later moments. The processes of attentional selection evolve over the course of a search.
- Different aspects of search evolve at different rates. Here we describe the example of guidance to scene-based properties like surface type (e.g., is there a target on top of a block?). This sort of guidance appears to take

much longer to develop on each trial than guidance to simpler properties like color or orientation.

A QUICK OUTLINE OF GUIDED SEARCH 4.0

Guided Search 4.0 is an effort to explain why some targets take longer to find in a visual search than others. A red dot among green dots will be found quickly and the number of green dots will not have much impact on the RT. A search for a specific letter among a variety of different letters will take longer and, even if the letters are big enough to make eye movements unnecessary, each additional distractor letter will add something like 20–30 ms to the average RT. Real-world search tasks exaggerate these effects. A fire engine, racing through the parking lot, will be found rapidly and independently of the number of cars; however, the proverbial needle in a haystack will take much more time, even if the needle is visible, and that time will scale with the size of the haystack.

In her highly influential feature integration theory (FIT), Treisman (1988; Treisman & Gelade, 1980) argued that the efficient searches for red dots, fire engines, and so forth were those searches where the target was defined by a single, salient, basic feature like red color or leftward motion. Such searches could proceed in parallel across the whole search display. If target identification required the *binding* together of features, as in the letter search, then attention would need to be directed to each item in turn in a serial manner. The model proposed an initial, "preattentive," parallel feature processing stage and a subsequent, "attentive" serial binding stage (cf. Broadbent, 1958; Hoffman, 1979; Neisser, 1967).

Guided search borrowed this two-stage architecture and added the core principle that information from the first stage could guide attentional deployments in the second stage. The core example is a conjunction search for a target defined by the conjunction of two features—for example, a small blue square among big blue and small yellow squares. Because identification of a small blue item requires the binding of color and size, it requires attention. Nevertheless, search for such stimuli is quite efficient (Egeth, Virzi, & Garbart, 1984; McLeod, Driver, & Crisp, 1988; Nakayama & Silverman, 1986; Wolfe, 1998b; Wolfe et al., 1989). Guided search proposes that the first-stage color processing would guide attention toward blue items while, at the same time, first-stage size processing would guide attention toward small items.

More precisely, attention is deployed to the most active location in an "activation map." Activation is based on a weighted average of bottom-up salience and top-down guidance. A limited set of basic feature dimensions contribute to the activation map (reviewed in Wolfe & Horowitz, 2004). Bottom-up, stimulus-driven salience is based on local differences in a dimension. Thus, a vertical line surrounded by horizontals is salient. The same line surround by lines tilted 10° off vertical is not salient (Julesz, 1984; Moraglia, 1989; Nothdurft, 1993).

Numerous sophisticated models of the computation of bottom-up salience have been developed (Hamker, 2004; Itti & Koch, 2000; Krummenacher, Muller, & Heller, 2001; Z. Li, 2002; Parkhurst et al., 2002; Zhaoping & Koene, 2007). They are broadly similar, though they differ importantly in, for example, their proposed neural substrates and the degree of modularity of processing of different dimensions (size, orientation, etc.). Top-down, user-driven guidance is more complex. We believe it to be based on categorical representations of features (e.g., "steep" and "shallow," rather than 12° and 75°; Wolfe, Friedman-Hill, Stewart, & O'Connell, 1992). Guided search proposes that a target object would be described in a very limited vocabulary of these categorical attributes. Other models have different, usually richer descriptions of the top-down information (Hamker, 2006; Hochstein & Ahissar, 2002; Navalpakkam, Rebesco, & Itti, 2004; Torralba, Oliva, Castelhano, & Henderson, 2006). This topic awaits more data.

Also open for debate is exactly how the system sets weights to use some signals and ignore others (e.g., from irrelevant singletons; Bacon & Egeth, 1994; Lamy & Egeth, 2003; Lamy & Tsal, 1999; Rauschenberger, 2003; Theeuwes, 1991; Yantis, 1993). Some of this weight setting seems to be essentially a priming effect in which the last stimulus configures the search for the next (e.g., DiLollo, Kawahara, Zuvic, & Visser, 2001; Hillstrom, 2000; Kristjansson, Wang, & Nakayama, 2002; Olivers & Humphreys, 2003); however, as discussed later, that cannot be the whole story (Muller, Reimann, & Krummenacher, 2003; Wolfe, Butcher, Lee, & Hyle, 2003).

Returning to the example of a search for a small blue item, dimensional weights would be adjusted so that size and color information made more of a contribution to the activation map than other dimensions like motion and orientation. Feature weights would be adjusted to favor blue and small over yellow and big. It does not seem to be possible to set the weight on bottom-up saliency to zero. In this case, yellow items near blue and big near small all produce salience signals that act as noise in this particular task. Combined with noise within the visual system, this will degrade the activation map so that the small blue target is not necessarily the most active item. Search will be biased toward the target, but not perfectly—resulting in search that is moderately efficient, falling between the easiest feature searches and the hardest inefficient searches where no feature guidance is possible (illustrated, in black and white, in Figure 5.2).

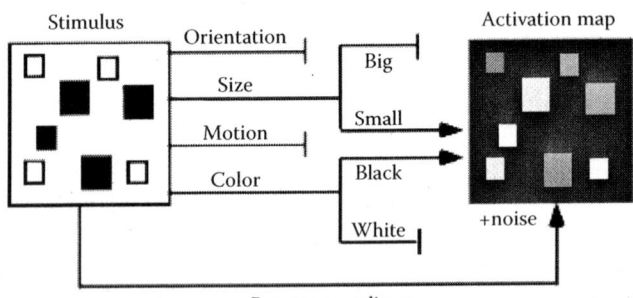

Figure 5.2   In a search for small, black items, the activation map guiding attention would be based on inputs from size and color. Weights for other dimensions (e.g., motion and orientation) would be reduced. Within the dimension, weights for black and small would be increased while other features (e.g., white and big) would be decreased. Noise and a mandatory contribution from bottom-up salience complete the inputs to the activation map.

In earlier versions of GS, it was proposed that attention was directed to the most active locus in the activation map. If that did not prove to be the target, attention would move to the next most active, and so on, until the target was found or all (or almost all) items had been rejected. This simple serial search model is inadequate for several reasons. First, as will be discussed in the second part of this chapter, subsequent research has shown that observers do not keep track of rejected distractors in a way that would permit this sort of sampling without replacement (Horowitz & Wolfe, 1998, 2001, 2003, 2005). Second, depending on the assumptions about memory in search, simple items are being processed at a rate of one object every 20–40 ms in standard search tasks. However, the lower bound of estimates for the time required to identify a single item is on the order of 100 ms (Thorpe, Fize, & Marlot, 1996).

Accordingly, GS4 models object recognition as an asynchronous diffusion process (Ratcliff, 1978, 2006). Specifically, as shown in Figure 5.3, when an item is selected, information begins accumulating. If that information reaches a target threshold, a target-present response is generated. If that information reaches a distractor threshold, the item is rejected as a possible target. Identification of one object need not end before the process begins for the next item. Attention can be

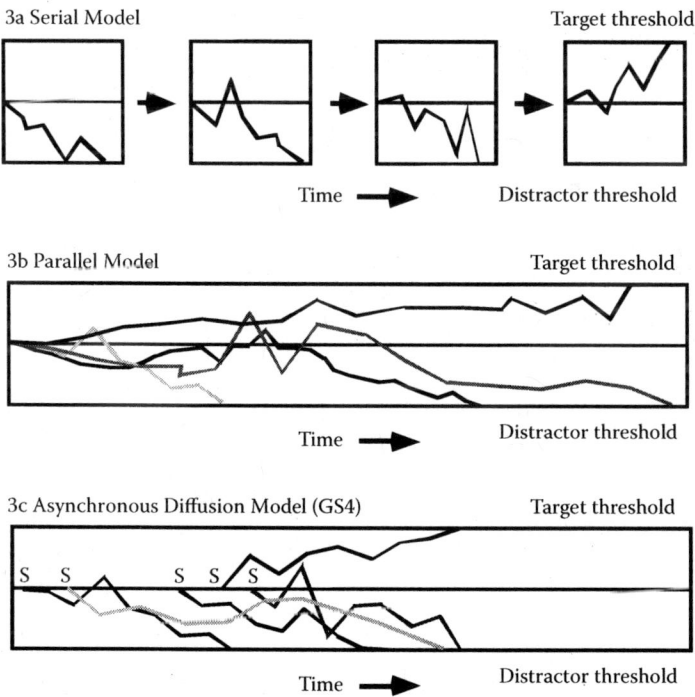

Figure 5.3   Using a diffusion process to model the categorization of an item as target or distractor, this figure illustrates serial and parallel accounts of visual search as well as the hybrid GS4 account. Each "S" in (c) marks the selection of a new item. In (a) and (b), all selections occur at the left-hand axis.

deployed to the next item while the prior item is still in the process of being identified. At that point, two items would be in the identification process at the same
time. The maximum number of items that can be in the identification stage at the
same time is a parameter of the model. A number on the order of four seems to
work well in current simulations (and, perhaps coincidentally, fits nicely with capacity estimates for visual working memory; Cowan, 2001; Luck & Vogel, 1997).

The asynchronous diffusion aspects of GS4 blur the distinction between serial
and parallel models of visual search. If the diffuser can handle only one item at a
time, we have a strict serial model (Figure 5.3a). If all items can begin diffusing at
the same time, we have a parallel model (Figure 5.3b). If the rate of diffusion varies inversely with the number of items that are diffusing, we have a limited-capacity parallel model. Guided search 4.0 is a limited-capacity serial/parallel hybrid
model (Figure 5.3c). It places a limit on the number of items that can be diffusing
toward recognition at any moment. Therefore, once the set size is above that limit,
there must be some serial aspect to the process of search. However, multiple items
can be in the process of recognition at the same time, giving the model a parallel
aspect as well. More details can be found in Wolfe (2007).

One final introductory note about the architecture of GS4: In the spirit of
feature integration theory, GS4 holds that object identification requires selective attention of the object in order to permit binding. If we cannot recognize an
object before we attend to it, what do we *see* at that object's location before attention is directed there? This topic has been the subject of a great deal of debate.
Positions range from the claim that if we do not attend to something, we do not
see it (Mack & Rock, 1998; Mack, Tang, Tuna, & Kahn, 1992; Noe, Pessoa, &
Thompson, 2000; O'Regan & Noe, 2001) to claims that objects (Thorpe et al.,
1996; VanRullen & Thorpe, 2001) or whole scenes (F. Li, VanRullen, Koch, &
Perona, 2002) can be recognized without attention or, at least, without much
attention. It is always a methodological challenge to claim that a task is being
done "without attention." This mirrors the classic debate (reviewed in Pashler,
1998) between early selection (Broadbent, 1958) and late selection (Deutsch &
Deutsch, 1963; reviewed in Pashler, 1998a and b) models.

Rather like its response to the serial/parallel debate, GS4 wants to have it both
ways on the early/late selection debate. The debate centers on the position of a
bottleneck on a pathway from eye to conscious perception. Suppose, however, that
there are two pathways through the visual system, a common enough idea (Goodale,
1996; Held, 1970; Ungerleider & Mishkin, 1982). Guided search 4.0 proposes that
one pathway gives rise to object recognition. The bottleneck of selective attention
lies in this pathway, making it the embodiment of an early selection model.

The second pathway is nonselective and not bottlenecked, but it is severely
limited in its capabilities. It is capable of quickly registering image statistics (Ariely,
2001; Chong & Treisman, 2003) and global scene properties that might give rise
to an understanding of the layout of a scene or even its semantic category (e.g.,
"beach scene"; Oliva & Torralba, 2001; Torralba et al., 2006). From the vantage
point of conscious visual perception, it would be this nonselective pathway that
fills the visual field with some sort of perceptual "stuff." Note that the nonselective
pathway is not a magic end run around the limitations of selective attention. Each

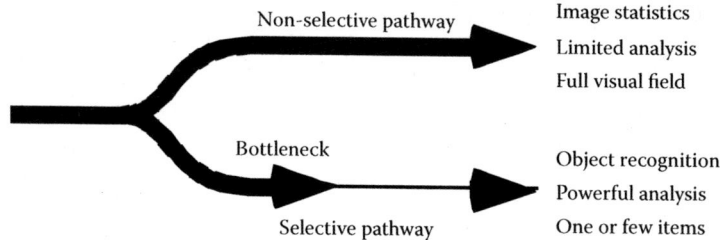

Figure 5.4 The large-scale architecture of GS4 differentiates between a selective pathway that does object recognition on a very limited subset of the stimulus at any one time and a nonselective pathway that does a very limited analysis of the entire scene in parallel.

pathway is severely limited: the selective pathway in its capacity and the nonselective pathway in its abilities (Figure 5.4).

HOW LONG DOES IT TAKE TO CHANGE ONE'S MIND?

Consider that basic conjunction search for a small, blue target, described in the previous section. This search will be reasonably efficient because observers can use the information about the color and size of the target to guide the deployment of attention. What is the time course of this guidance? Returning yet again to Figure 5.1, we can look at the array without a task, in an unguided way. If we are then asked to look for a small, dark square, we can reconfigure our visual system to guide our attention to those targets. We are interested in the temporal dynamics of that act of getting into guided search. Here we describe four sets of experiments that reveal the dynamics of the start of guidance. The first set asks how long it takes to change a person's mind, switching from one search goal to another.

Consider a search task in which the observer did not know the identity of the target because it could change on each trial. We asked observers to search for the unique item in an array composed of rectangles that could be red or green, big or small, vertical or horizontal (Wolfe, Horowitz, Kenner, Hyle, & Vasan, 2004). On each trial, one pair of attributes defined the unique target (e.g., BIG GREEN—CAPS denote target attributes), but the participant was not informed of the target attributes before the search display was presented. The two types of distractors on that trial each shared one target attribute—in this case, *BIG red* and *small GREEN* distractors. On this trial, the orientation would be irrelevant and uniform.

In the absence of information about target identity, one might do this task in a number of ways. One might look for an oddball in a set defined by color or size. One might figure out that multiple *BIG red* and *small GREEN* distractors mandate either a BIG GREEN or a small red target. Whatever our observers were doing, it took about 1,250 ms on average to find the target in this "uninformed" condition. Unsurprisingly, if the target did not change over trials, observers learned what to look for and they could do the task more quickly. Thus, when the observers searched for BIG GREEN or some other fixed target on every trial in a "blocked" condition, mean RT was about 600 ms.

In the critical conditions, observers were cued about target identity at some time prior to the appearance of the search array. In these conditions, a cue was presented at fixation, some time prior to the onset. The cue could be a copy of the actual target or the words describing the target.

Figure 5.5 shows the basic result. When the cue was physically identical to the target, 200 ms was adequate advance warning to make the cued RT indistinguishable from the blocked RT. It is not surprising that it took longer for the word cues to become fully effective. After all, the words needed to be read. More interesting was the fact that word cues were never as good as picture cues. Even after hundreds of trials, writing "BIG GREEN" produced guidance that was less effective than showing the observer the big green item.

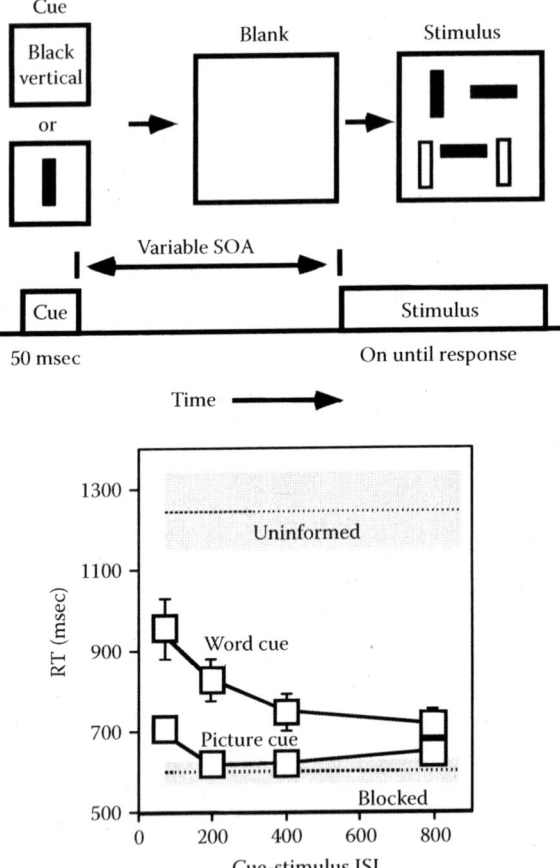

Figure 5.5   The design and sample results from the "advance warning" experiments. Dashed lines represent the blocked and uninformed baseline conditions. Gray regions are 95% confidence limits. (Data figure redrawn from Wolfe et al., 2004, *Vision Research*, *44*(12), 1411–1426.)

That penalty went away when target type repeated by chance. Thus, even if word cues were used, if the cue and the target were BIG GREEN for two trials in a row, then the RT for the second trial was as fast, on average, as the picture-cued trials. This is consistent with the idea that seeing the target on one trial primes the observer to find it on the next (priming of pop-out; Hillstrom, 2000; Kristjansson, 2006; Lamy, Bar-Anan, Egeth, & Carmel, 2006; Maljkovic & Martini, 2005; Maljkovic & Nakayama, 1994). It suggests that the picture cue acted not only as top-down information but also as a prime.

These data indicate that it takes a minimum of about 200 ms to change the setting of the top-down guiding weights so that attention can be guided to items of the correct color, size, or orientation. In these 200 ms, the weights get to the same state as that on trials in the blocked condition, where the weights can remain more or less fixed over many trials. One might think that this represents the time to get guidance going. However, that is not quite right, as the next set of experiments will show.

EVEN CONSISTENTLY MAPPED GUIDANCE TAKES TIME TO GET STARTED

The preceding experiment measures the time to start guidance only if we assume that guidance is fully in place at the start of a trial under blocked conditions, when the target identity is consistent and known. This would imply a model in which guidance was something like a filter, eliminating (or, at least, attenuating) items with the wrong attributes.

Figure 5.6 illustrates this point with stimuli from a new set of experiments. The observer was faced with a set of Cs in four possible orientations. All but one opened up or down. The target, present on each trial, opened to the left or right, and observers were asked to report its orientation. Each C was placed on a colored disk. Suppose that observers knew that the target was always on a gray disk. If the top-down guidance to gray acted like a filter, then search for the target should be like search through the set of four gray items. If no guidance were available, this would be a search through the 16 Cs on the left side of the figure.

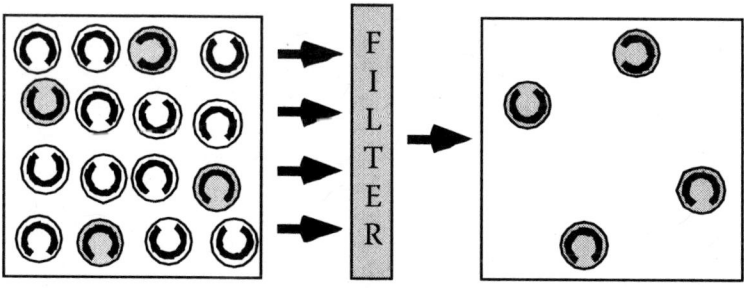

Figure 5.6   Guidance as a filter.

To examine the temporal dynamics of guidance, the appearance of the colored disks was offset in time from the appearance of the Cs, as illustrated at the top of Figure 5.7.

Consider a simple, two-state model. At any moment, observers are either searching through all 16 items in an unguided manner, or they are restricting their search to the four items of the target color. For simplicity, assume that there is a sharp transition between those two states. Suppose that the Cs appear 400 ms before the color cue (stimulus-onset asynchrony [SOA] = −400 in Figure 5.7). When the Cs appear, observers must search through 16 items because no guiding information is available. After 400 ms, the color information appears. Once it becomes effective, this is a search through four items. The RT, therefore, is a mixture distribution of some purely unguided searches, when the observer finds the target before the color ever appears, and some that benefit from eventual guidance.

As the SOA becomes increasingly negative, the chance is greater that the search will finish before the color becomes available. At the longest negative SOAs, RTs should approximate the 16-item baseline—the time required to find a target when no color guidance is offered. The four-item baseline is the RT for an unguided search through a set of just four items. Figure 5.7 shows the predictions of such a model for the case where guidance starts as soon as the guiding information is presented (solid line) and a second case where guidance starts some time after the onset of the guiding information (dashed line). In this case, that delay is arbitrarily set to about 300 ms. Note that the declining function hits the four-item baseline RT at the SOA corresponding with the delay in the onset of guidance. This is marked by the arrows at 0 ms for the solid line and 300 ms for the dashed line.

The data in Figure 5.8 show the average of the median RTs for 15 observers. Each observer was tested for 30 trials at each of 13 SOAs. Each observer also completed 27

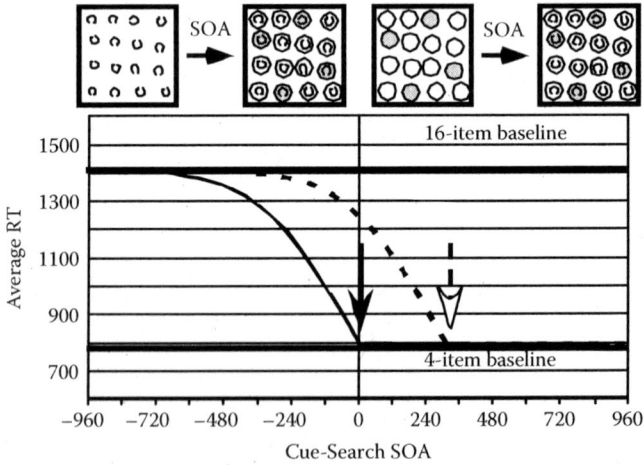

Figure 5.7   Hypothetical outcomes for the time-to-guide experiments. Solid line assumes that color guidance is available as soon as the color is available. Dashed line assumes that guidance begins about 300 ms after the color becomes available.

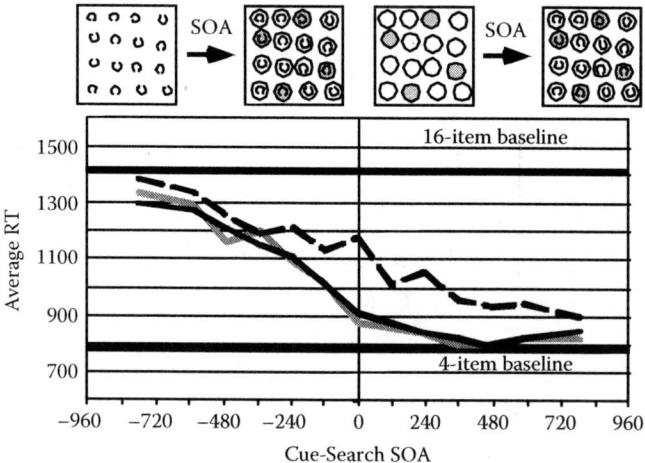

Figure 5.8 Results for one set of time-to-guide experiments. Black line shows data from blocked trials. Gray line shows data for mixed trials with consistent mapping of target and distractor colors. The dashed line shows data for mixed trials with inconsistent mapping.

trials of unguided search with set sizes of 4 and 16 items to establish the baselines, plotted as horizontal lines at their median value. A full account of these experiments is presented in Palmer, Van Wert, Horowitz, and Wolfe (in preparation).

The data plotted with a dashed line are most analogous to the data from the previous "advance warning" experiments. On these trials, observers did not know from trial to trial which color set would contain the target. Moreover, a target color on one trial could be a distractor color on another (inconsistent mapping; Schneider & Shiffrin, 1977; Shiffrin & Schneider, 1977). Clearly, guidance is not fully effective in this condition until hundreds of milliseconds after the onset of the color. Why is guidance so delayed? In this experiment, observers had to figure out the target color for themselves. They were told that there would be 12 items of one color and 4 of another and that the target was always in the smaller set. When a target color on one trial could become a distractor color on the next, substantial penalties, akin to task-switching costs, are seen (e.g., Mayr & Kliegl, 2003; Wylie & Allport, 2000).

The data plotted in gray show the results when observers do not know the color of the target on this trial but do know that the set of target colors and the set of distractor colors are distinct from each other (consistent mapping). This speeds the onset of fully effective guidance; however, critically, at an SOA of 0 ms, performance is significantly worse than the four-item baseline and has not reached asymptote. This is the sign that guidance is not fully effective at the onset of the guiding colors.

The most important data for the present argument are those plotted in black. They show the results for the blocked condition where observers knew that the four-item subset containing the target would always be the same color. The 12 distractors also preserved the same color for the entire block. It is obvious that this blocked condition produced the same results as the consistent mapping condition. Even when observers knew that the target was always, for example, in the pink subset, they were not able to begin fully effective guidance at the moment of color onset. These data cannot pinpoint the precise time when guidance is fully available, but clearly it takes at least 200 ms. We can firmly reject the hypothesis that guidance is fully available from stimulus onset even under conditions when an observer can maintain the same "guiding principles" for an entire block of hundreds of trials.

The data shown in Figure 5.8 came from a study using relatively desaturated colors; the actual search stimuli (i.e., the Cs) were black, but placed on colored placeholders that carried the guiding information. However, we have replicated this result several times, including experiments using saturated hues and experiments where the Cs themselves carry the guiding color. In all cases, the basic result is the same: at SOA = 0, guidance is not fully active. We can reject the model of Figure 5.6. Guidance is not a simple filter that, once established, can sit athwart the visual pathway, ready and waiting for the next stimulus. Instead, guidance must be reestablished on every trial, and that takes several hundred milliseconds.

WHERE, IN THEORY, IS THE GUIDING REPRESENTATION?

In Treisman's original formulation, a preattentive stage could process a limited set of basic features in parallel. It was followed by an attentive stage that accomplished the binding of features into object representations in a serial manner, one object at a time (Treisman & Gelade, 1980). Guided search (Wolfe et al., 1989) borrowed this essentially linear architecture and added the notion that the preattentive stage could guide the deployment of attention in the attentive stage.

Subsequent work has revealed problems with this architecture. Attention seems to be guided by a specific abstraction of the traditional "preattentive features." For example, guidance by orientation seems to be based on a categorical representation of orientation. Guidance is more effective if the target is categorically unique: the only steep, shallow, left- or right-tilted item (Hodsoll & Humphreys, 2005; Wolfe et al., 1992). Moreover, in guidance by orientation, a 90° representation provides the greatest orientation contrast. Guidance seems to be quite insensitive to the 180° difference between upright and inverted, even for clearly polar objects (Wolfe, Klempen, & Shulman, 1999). These findings pose a problem because, if preattentive information is a coarse categorization of the input, how do later stages recover information? After all, the end user of all this visual processing can determine which end is up and can tell the difference between 20 and 30° "steep" orientations.

The point is perhaps made more clearly in the case of preattentive processing of intersection type (Bergen & Julesz, 1983; Gurnsey & Browse, 1989; Julesz & Krose, 1988; Wolfe & DiMase, 2003). The distinction between a "T" junction and a "+" intersection can be used by early visual processes—for example, to make initial inferences about occlusion of one object by another (e.g., Rensink & Enns, 1995; Yantis, 1995). Later processes also have access to this distinction. After all, we can easily distinguish between an uppercase "T" and a lowercase "t" on the basis of the intersection type. Nevertheless, visual search for + junctions among

T junctions or vice versa is very inefficient (Wolfe & DiMase, 2003). In a linear scheme, it is awkward to explain how intersection information can be available before and after guidance but is not available to guide.

In the latest versions of guided search (GS4), we have argued for a "guiding representation" that is not in the main pathway from visual input to object recognition (Wolfe, 2007; Wolfe & Horowitz, 2004). Instead, we propose that guidance sits (figuratively) to one side of the pathway, controlling the bottleneck between early visual processes and later object recognition processes. The guiding representation is abstracted from the visual input but cannot be directly perceived, and it is not one of the building blocks of later, perceptual representations. In this view, it is a separate control device. The findings concerning the timing of guidance fit into this framework, as shown in Figure 5.9.

Imagine that the observer is looking for a black vertical line. The cartoon in Figure 5.9(a) shows an essentially unguided, initial, feed-forward sweep of activity after stimulus onset. At the same time, information about the stimulus is being fed

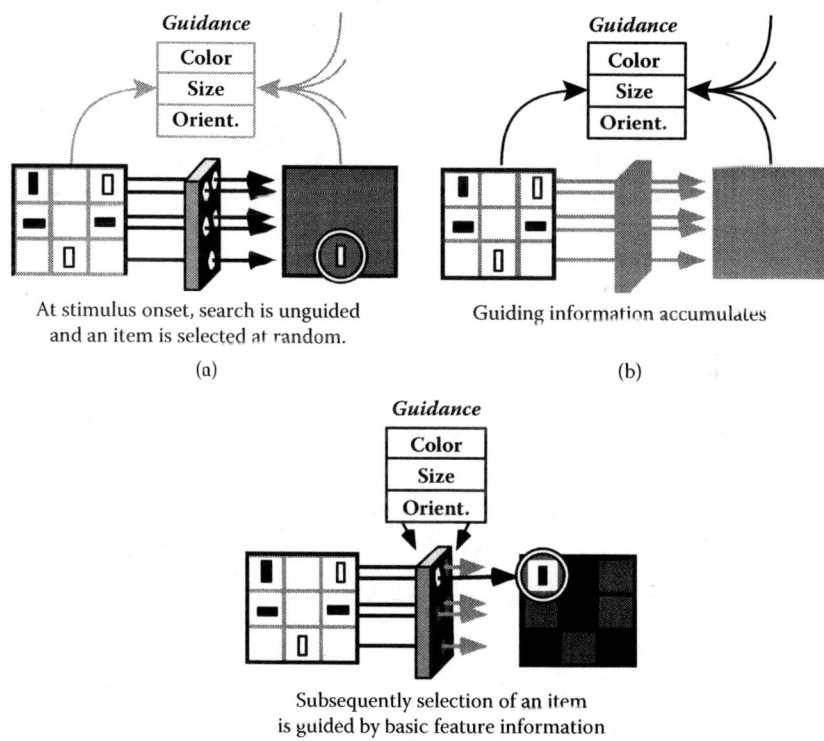

At stimulus onset, search is unguided and an item is selected at random.

(a)

Guiding information accumulates

(b)

Subsequently selection of an item is guided by basic feature information

(c)

Figure 5.9   Guided Search 4.0 proposes that guidance is based on a representation that lies off the main pathway from early vision to object recognition. In this view, the deployments of attention (marked by the circle) in a search would initially be unguided (a). Guiding information would accumulate over time (b), and subsequent deployments would be guided (c).

to the guiding representation (Figure 5.9b). This might be feed-forward information from early visual stages or feedback information from some later stage. Guided search is currently agnostic on this point—hence the various input arrows with unspecified origins. As shown in Figure 5.9(c), after some period of time, the guiding representation has enough information to determine where "black" and "vertical" items might be. At that point, guidance can be used to constrain selection and it becomes more likely that attention will be directed to a black vertical target. This view is broadly consistent with the notion of guidance as "reentrant process" (Di Lollo, Enns, & Rensink, 2000; Di Lollo et al., 2001; Lamme & Roelfsema, 2000) and models like the reverse hierarchy theory (Ahissar & Hochstein, 1997; Hochstein & Ahissar, 2002).

ARE THE FIRST MOMENTS OF STANDARD GUIDED SEARCHES "UNGUIDED"?

The account illustrated in Figure 5.9 makes the prediction that visual search is initially unguided, with available guidance developing as search progresses. The experiments presented thus far point in that direction, but some converging evidence would be helpful. The results of the blocked condition of the time-to-guide experiments show that, at SOA = 0, guidance to four items is not exactly the same as search through four items, presented without other distractors. However, that task differs from a standard search task in its dissociation of the guiding color information from the rest of the stimulus. In this section, we describe evidence for a delayed onset of full guidance in standard visual search.

The logic of these experiments is very simple. In standard visual search experiments, set size is varied to allow estimation of the slope of the RT × set size function. Because that function is assumed to be linear, three or four set sizes are typically considered adequate. However, if guidance takes time to develop, searches through small set sizes should be relatively unguided and should produce relatively steep slopes compared to larger set sizes. In other words, the RT × set size function should be curved instead of linear, with large set sizes having shorter RTs than would be predicted by linear extrapolation from small set size RTs.

This should be especially true for guided search tasks like conjunction search and less evident for unguided search tasks such as a spatial configuration search for a T among Ls or a two among fives. In the following experiments, we tested observers on both conjunction search and spatial configuration search; we used eight set sizes spanning a large range and sampled densely at the smallest set sizes.

In the first experiment, set sizes were mixed within blocks. The conjunction search consisted of search for a red vertical bar among green vertical and red horizontal bars, and the spatial configuration search consisted of search for a T among Ls ("TvL"), where both Ts and Ls could appear in any of four 90° rotations. The upper left panel in Figure 5.10 shows the mean RTs for correct target-present trials for the conjunction and TvL tasks. The accompanying regression lines were computed only on set sizes one to four. This figure makes three points:

- The initial slopes are very similar: Over the first four items, conjunction search is just as inefficient as spatial configuration search.
- Reaction times for the larger set sizes were systematically faster than would be predicted by linear extrapolation from the smaller set sizes.
- This compressive nonlinearity is greater for the conjunction data than for the TvL data.

These three points are reinforced in the lower left panel of Figure 5.10, which plots the target-present slopes for the two search tasks for small and large set size ranges. Note that we are using this approach only to illustrate that the functions are compressive. We are not making any claim that the functions are bilinear, because any set of four set sizes would be roughly linear.

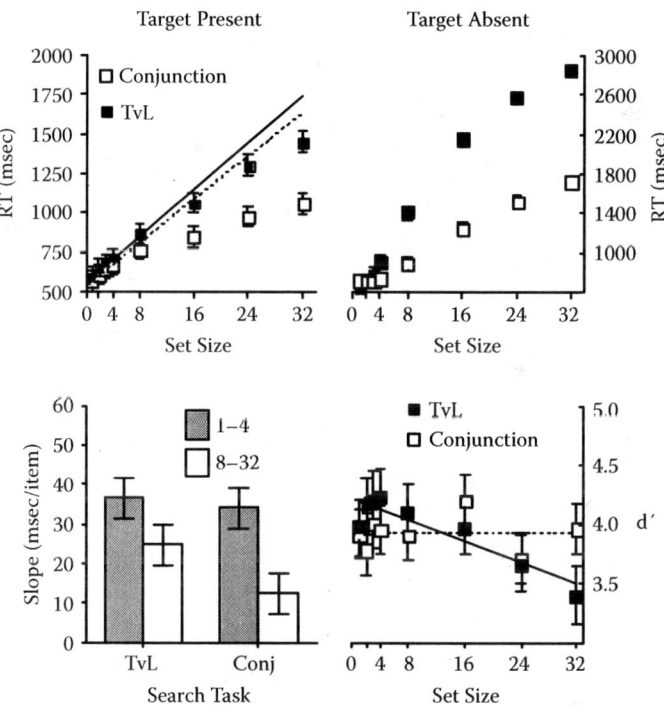

Figure 5.10 Compressively nonlinear RT × set size functions in visual search. Upper left panel plots the target-present RT × set size functions for the TvL (solid symbols) and the conjunction (open symbols) search tasks. Regression lines are based on set sizes 1–4 for TvL (solid line) and conjunction (dashed line). Upper right panel plots the target-absent RT × set size functions. Lower left panel shows target-present slopes for set sizes of 1–4 (shaded bars) and 8–32 (open bars) as a function of task. Lower right panel shows d' as a function of set size for TvL (solid symbols) and conjunction (open symbols) tasks. Error bars in all figures except the d' figure are within-subjects 95% confidence intervals based on the interaction shown. In the d' figure, confidence intervals are based on the simple effect of set size for that task.

These data are consistent with the hypothesis that guidance takes some time to become effective. For the fast searches through small set sizes, the "guided" conjunction search is no more efficient than the presumably unguided TvL task. The tasks diverge at larger set sizes—after, we would argue, color and orientation have had a chance to guide the selection of items effectively.

Can we explain these results as a product of speed–accuracy trade-offs? Remember that RTs for the two search tasks were comparable at the small set sizes, diverging only at the larger set sizes. Thus, a speed–accuracy trade-off account must predict that errors at large set sizes should be substantially greater for the conjunction task than for the TvL task. If we convert those errors into d' measures, a speed–accuracy trade-off would be reflected in a decline in d' as set size increases.

The lower right panel of Figure 5.10 shows that the TvL task shows more of a decline than the conjunction task. In fact, d' did not vary with set size for the conjunction task, so the compressive nonlinearity in those data cannot be explained by a speed–accuracy trade-off. The smaller nonlinearity in the TvL data, however, can be at least partially accounted for by a speed–accuracy trade-off. This analysis suggests that the difference between TvL and conjunction search is actually underestimated in these data: If we could have held TvL accuracy constant across set sizes, we would have seen even less compression.

A plausible account of the data from this experiment would make three points:

- When examined with sufficient resolution, RT × set size functions from standard search tasks are not necessarily linear. This point, by itself, is worthy of note because it has been assumed that the functions are basically linear and most models produce linear functions.
- At least part of the nonlinearity in the TvL data is likely due to a speed–accuracy trade-off. Modeling this sort of nonlinearity would require correctly specifying the "quitting rule" for visual search. When do observers give up on unsuccessful searches? This has been a hard problem in the modeling of search.
- The nonlinearity in the conjunction search data does not appear to be readily explained as a speed–accuracy trade-off because d' remains constant across set sizes. Search efficiency for conjunction and TvL tasks is initially very similar but diverges at larger set sizes. This is consistent with the idea that the initial stages of the search are relatively unguided but become guided as time goes on.

The slope at low set sizes would be consistent with a rate of processing of 35–70 ms per item (depending on modeling assumptions). If we propose that search becomes increasingly guided after four or five items have been examined, this would produce an estimate of about 200–300 ms for the onset of guidance, comparable to the estimates from the previous experiments in this chapter.

A REPLICATION AND SOME COMPLICATIONS

Thus far, the data presented here fit with the cartoon in Figure 5.9. The initial phase of a search appears to be unguided, with guidance gradually developing to full strength over the course of several hundred milliseconds. In this section, we wish to consider two matters that complicate this account. First, in a second experiment (described next), we again sampled set sizes densely in conjunction and spatial configuration searches. We successfully replicated the decelerating function for conjunction search. However, compared to the TvL task of the previous experiment, we obtained more marked nonlinearity in the nominally "unguided" spatial configuration search. This cannot be attributed to a simple speed–accuracy trade-off. The second complication is that the estimates of the time required to get guidance going seems long. In some physiological studies, reentrant processes have latencies on the order of 200 ms, but others have shorter latencies (Lamme & Roelfsema, 2000). Why does it seem to take so long to start simple guidance by a feature like a color?

The second experiment was motivated by our concern that the shape of the RT × set size functions might be strongly influenced by the mixture of set sizes. The average set size was 11.25. Perhaps observers quit searching through the longer set size displays because they had set a quitting threshold based on the smaller set sizes. Accordingly, in the second experiment, the set size variable was blocked. We maintained the same conjunction search task for comparison purposes but employed a different spatial configuration task: search for a digital two among digital fives ("2v5").

Figure 5.11 shows the data in the same format as in Figure 5.10. The conjunction search data replicated the previous experiment in every aspect. RTs at large set sizes were substantially faster than predicted by linear extrapolation from the small set sizes (open symbols in the upper left panel of Figure 5.11). The slopes for search through one to four items were again around 35–40 ms/item, but the slopes for the larger set sizes were substantially shallower (lower left panel of Figure 5.11). This cannot be explained by a speed–accuracy trade-off because d' was constant across set sizes (open symbols in the lower right panel of Figure 5.11). This close replication suggests that search strategies were not affected by whether the set sizes were mixed or blocked.

However, the data for the 2v5 task were different from what we observed for the TvL task in the first experiment. The 2v5 task was substantially less efficient than the conjunction task for small set sizes and its RT × set size function was markedly compressive (filled symbols in the upper left-hand panel of Figure 5.11), more so than TvL search (lower left-hand panel of Figure 5.10). This is not the result we would predict for unguided spatial configuration search. Some of the nonlinearity in the 2v5 task can be explained due to speed–accuracy trade-offs, because d' again declined as a function of set size. However, while d' drops off with set size at roughly the same rate in the two experiments, the compressive nonlinearity is much greater for the 2v5 task. Some additional explanation is required.

The current architecture of GS4 contains a possible source for a nonlinearity not associated with guidance. Recall from Figure 5.3 that GS4 models search as an asynchronous diffusion process. Information about each item, as it is selected,

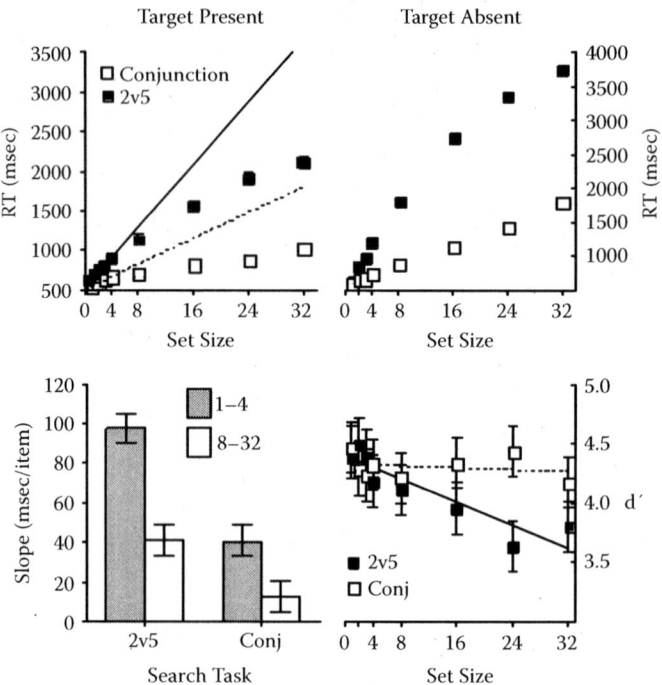

Figure 5.11 Compressively nonlinear RT × set size functions in visual search (blocked set size version). Upper left panel plots the target-present RT × set size functions for the 2v5 (solid symbols) and the conjunction (open symbols) search tasks. Regression lines are based on set sizes 1–4 for 2v5 (solid line) and conjunction (dashed line). Upper right panel plots the target-absent RT × set size functions. Lower left panel shows target-present slopes for set sizes of 1–4 (shaded bars) and 8–32 (open bars) as a function of task. Lower right panel shows d' as a function of set size for 2v5 (solid symbols) and conjunction (open symbols) tasks. Error bars in all figures except the d' figure are within-subjects 95% confidence intervals based on the interaction shown. In the d' figure, confidence intervals are based on the simple effect of set size for that task.

diffuses toward a target or distractor boundary. If the item is rejected as a distractor, it is removed from the diffuser and a new item is selected. The parameters of this process are discussed elsewhere (Wolfe, 2007). One important parameter for present purposes is the capacity of the diffuser. How many items can be diffusing at the same time? Again, a reasonable estimate might be about four (Cowan, 2001; Luck & Vogel, 1997). For present purposes, the exact number is not important; what is important is that this architecture predicts differences between the beginning of a search and its later stages.

Suppose that capacity is four. What happens at the first moment of selection? One possibility is that four items are selected at the same time. Subsequent items are selected only as each of the initially selected items is dropped from the diffuser. Thus, there is a transition from parallel selection of multiple items to a steady-state selection at a rate related to the slope in unguided search tasks (on the order of one every 50 ms). If the set size is small, most or all of the items in the display might be selected in this initial phase. If four items are selected as efficiently as one, why does the RT increase quite steeply with small set sizes? One possibility is that more resources can be devoted to processing each item if the diffuser is not loaded to capacity. Thus, one might imagine that information in the diffuser would accumulate four times as fast when one item was in the diffuser than when four items were in the diffuser.

Suppose that only one item can be selected at a time—a strict serial bottleneck, even if up to four could be in the diffuser at one time. In that case, the beginning of each search would be characterized by a steady increase in the number of items, up to the capacity of the diffuser. If the rate of accumulation of information about an item is proportional to the number of items in the diffuser, then the rate of accumulation for the first selected item would slow as other items were selected into the diffuser.

The point of this delineation of possibilities is to show that many variants of the GS4 architecture are characterized by an early period of search that is different from steady-state search and that will evolve into the steady state if the search is reasonably prolonged. For those searches that have very small set sizes, the entire search will have characteristics of the early period of search.

Simulations of these various GS4 configurations tend to produce decelerating, nonlinear RT × set size functions. If capacity is about four, and if the throughput rate is about 50 ms per item, the transition from the early stage of search to the steady state will take about 200 ms, which is broadly consistent with the data. At the present time, the data do not constrain the model to the point where it is possible to specify a capacity firmly or to determine if the initial act of selection involves one or several items. All of these options propose some sort of transition over the course of an extended period of search.

If curvilinear functions fall out of the GS4 architecture, is there any need to propose that guidance takes time to develop? The time-to-guide experiments (Figures 5.7 and 5.8) suggest that the answer is yes. If guidance were in place at the beginning of a trial, like the filter of Figure 5.6, then the initial loading of the diffuser would only include items of the correct color in those experiments. If that were the case, then the RT for SOA = 0 should be the same as the RT for a set size of four. In either case, the diffuser should be loaded with a set of four items that must include the target. Apparently this is not the case. Fully effective guidance develops after stimulus onset.

GUIDANCE BY SURFACE TYPE

As a final example of the evolution of search process during a single search, consider the problem of looking for people in a real scene. In some sense, this must be a guided search. We look for people in places where people might be—on horizontal surfaces that will support them, for example, rather than in less plausible places like midair or on the wall (Torralba et al., 2006). This sort of guidance is not the feature guidance of a standard conjunction search (Wolfe et al., 1989), and it is not the location guidance of spatial cueing experiments (Posner & Cohen, 1984).

Some of our recent data suggest that it is a form of guidance with its own very slow time course. Perhaps this guidance is slow because it involves feedback from the "nonselective" pathway illustrated in Figure 5.4.

Figure 5.12 is a grayscale illustration of the stimuli we used. Actual stimuli were vividly colored. Observers looked for a T among the Ls. A single T was present on half the trials. The other half of the trials contained only Ls. Five conditions were tested:

In the *unguided* condition, observers searched for a T among Ls.

In the *blocked color* condition, observers searched for a T of a specific color (red, blue, or yellow) among Ls of various colors.

In the *mixed color* condition, the guiding color was changed on each trial. A word cue was given 1,000 ms in advance of each trial to specify the color.

In the *blocked surface* condition, observers searched for a T on a specific type of cube surface (top, left, or right) for 300 trials in a row.

In the *mixed surface* condition, the guiding surface was changed on each trial. A word cue was given in advance of each trial to specify the surface.

In all of the guided searches, the guiding property defined a subset of one third of the items. That is, if the target was a red T, one third of the Ls were also red. If the target was a T on top of a cube, one third of the Ls were on top of cubes.

The results for target-present trials are shown in Figure 5.13. Color guidance replicated standard guided search results. One third of the items were of the guiding color. Consequently, slopes dropped by a factor of three relative to the unguided condition. Results for guidance by surface showed much less evidence

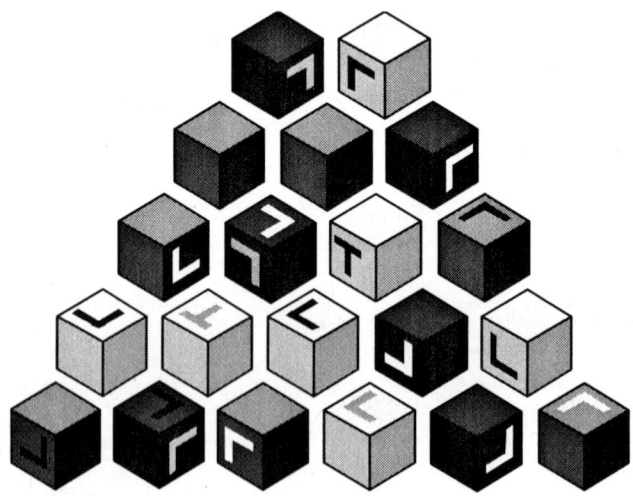

Figure 5.12   Stimuli for search by surface type. Observers could be asked to look for a "T" ("look for a T of any color on any surface"), a colored T ("look for the black T"), or a T on a particular surface ("look for the T on the top of a cube").

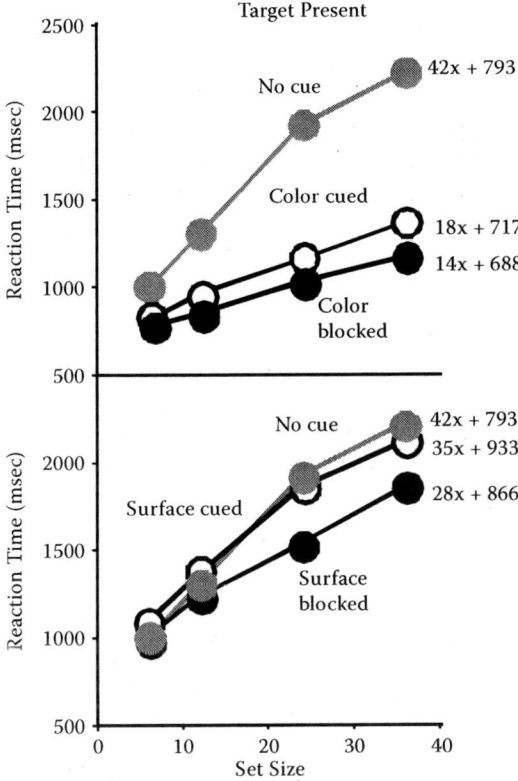

Figure 5.13 Mean target-present RT data for searches guided by color and surface information. Unguided baseline data are shown in gray.

for guidance. Indeed, when the surface was changed on each trial (surface cued), there was no significant guidance for target-present trials.

Why did this experiment "fail"? It is intuitively clear that guidance of this sort *must* exist. If we are told that our child's missing sock is *somewhere* on the floor, we will be able to guide attention to the floor and away from the walls, ceilings, and shelves of his room. One possibility is that guidance to surface properties is a different form of guidance, one that takes a long time to develop. Figure 5.13 shows a hint of this in the surface-blocked conditions. Here, the RTs are the same as the unguided RTs for smaller set sizes. They deviate for the larger set sizes.

This hypothesis is supported more clearly by the target-absent data shown in Figure 5.14. When surface was the guiding property, RTs for the blocked and cued versions of the task were very similar to the unguided baseline for set sizes of 6 and 12. They deviate at set sizes of 24 and 36. This cannot be attributed to a simple speed–accuracy trade-off.

Work on guidance by scene properties is in its infancy. For the present, we offer as a working hypothesis the idea that guidance by surface is similar to guidance by classical features like color. However, it involves reentrant processes operating on

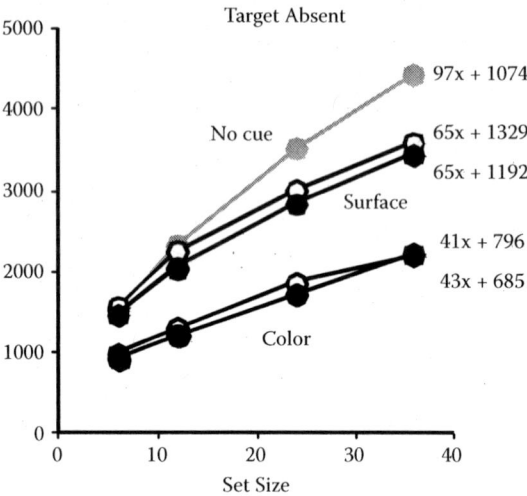

Figure 5.14   Target-absent data for search using the stimuli illustrated in Figure 5.12. Filled symbols indicate blocked conditions. Open symbols indicated that the guiding feature or surface was specified by cue on each trial.

a much slower time scale. It would be unsurprising to find that the nervous system might use the same trick in two different ways. Examples abound. If we stay within the realm of visual attention, we find that illusory conjunctions occur for basic features. An observer might report seeing red vertical in a display containing red horizontal and green vertical stimuli (Treisman & Schmidt, 1982); at a slower time scale, illusory words can be seen when letters are incorrectly combined (Treisman & Souther, 1986).

CONCLUSIONS

Twenty-five years ago, models of visual search had a linear feel to them: a series of boxes, connected by arrows that flowed from input to perception. Models of vision and visual physiology tended to have similar architectures. The output of retinal receptive fields was used to build simple cells that built complex cells and so on until cells that responded to faces and yellow Volkswagens were reached (Barlow, 1985; Weisstein, 1973).

   It is clear that this was an oversimplification. For example, we now know that more fibers feed back from cortex to LGN than feed forward (Cudeiro & Sillito, 2006). Current theories recognize that understanding the feed-forward sweep of information from eye to brain probably only accounts for the first 100 ms or so of visual experience (Serre, Oliva, & Poggio, 2007). After that, reentrant feedback mechanisms will tend to alter and complicate any feed-forward story. Steady-state visual perception—the visual experience of an observer looking for an extended period of time at a scene—is different from the initial experience of the first moments of input.

In this chapter, we have seen evidence for this temporal evolution of the processes of vision in the context of the guidance of visual search. Even if we know what we are looking for, and even if we have been looking for the same thing on trial after trial, visual search at the moment of stimulus onset is not as effectively guided as it will be a couple of hundred milliseconds later. On the initial, feedforward sweep, guidance does not appear to be engaged fully. Only with time are those aids to selection used to their full effect.

REFERENCES

Ahissar, M., & Hochstein, S. (1997). Task difficulty and visual hierarchy: Counterstreams in sensory processing and perceptual learning. *Nature, 387,* 401–406.

Ariely, D. (2001). Seeing sets: Representation by statistical properties. *Psychological Science, 12*(2), 157–162.

Bacon, W. F., & Egeth, H. E. (1994). Overriding stimulus-driven attentional capture. *Perception and Psychophysics, 55*(5), 485–496.

Barlow, H. B. (1985). The twelfth Bartlett memorial lecture: The role of single neurons in the psychology of perception. *Quarterly Journal of Experimental Psychology, 37A,* 121–145.

Bergen, J. R., & Julesz, B. (1983). Rapid discrimination of visual patterns. *IEEE Transactions on Systems, Man, and Cybernetics, SMC-13,* 857–863.

Broadbent, D. E. (1958). *Perception and communication.* London: Pergamon Press.

Cave, K. (1999). The FEATUREGATE model of visual selection. *Psychological Research, 62*(2–3), 182–194.

Chong, S. C., & Treisman, A. (2003). Representation of statistical properties. *Vision Research, 43*(4), 393–404.

Chun, M. M., & Wolfe, J. M. (1996). Just say no: How are visual searches terminated when there is no target present? *Cognitive Psychology, 30,* 39–78.

Cousineau, D., & Shiffrin, R. M. (2004). Termination of a visual search with large display size effects. *Spatial Vision, 17*(4–5), 327–352.

Cowan, N. (2001). The magical number 4 in short-term memory: A reconsideration of mental storage capacity. *Behavioral and Brain Sciences, 24*(1), 87–114; discussion: 114–185.

Cudeiro, J., & Sillito, A. M. (2006). Looking back: Corticothalamic feedback and early visual processing. *Trends in Neuroscience, 29*(6), 298–306.

Deco, G., Pollatos, O., & Zihl, J. (2002). The time course of selective visual attention: Theory and experiments. *Vision Reseach, 42*(27), 2925–2945.

Deutsch, J A., & Deutsch, D. (1963). Attention: Some theoretical considerations. *Psychological Review, 70,* 80–90.

Di Lollo, V., Enns, J. T., & Rensink, R. A. (2000). Competition for consciousness among visual events: The psychophysics of reentrant visual pathways. *Journal of Experimental Psychology: General, 129*(3), 481–507.

Di Lollo, V., Kawahara, J.-I., Zuvic, S. M., & Visser, T. A. W. (2001). The preattentive emperor has no clothes: A dynamic redressing. *Journal of Experimental Psychology General, 130*(3), 479–492.

Egeth, H. E., Virzi, R. A., & Garbart, H. (1984). Searching for conjunctively defined targets. *Journal of Experimental Psychology: Human Perception and Performance, 10,* 32–39.

Goodale, M. A. (1996). One visual experience, many visual systems. In T. Inui & McClelland (Eds.), *Attention and performance XVI* (Vol. 16, pp. 369–393). Cambridge, MA: MIT Press.

Grossberg, S., Mingolla, E., & Ross, W. D. (1994). A neural theory of attentive visual search: Interactions of boundary, surface, spatial and object representations. *Psychological Review, 101*(3), 470–489.

Gurnsey, R., & Browse, R. A. (1989). Asymmetries in visual texture discrimination. *Spatial Vision, 4*(1), 31–44.

Hamker, F. H. (2004). A dynamic model of how feature cues guide spatial attention. *Vision Research, 44*(5), 501–521.

Hamker, F. (2006). Modeling feature-based attention as an active top-down inference process *Biosystems, 86*(1–3), 91–99.

Held, R. (1970). Two modes of processing spatially distributed visual stimuli. In F. O. Schmitt (Ed.), *The neurosciences: Second study program* (pp. 317–324). New York: Rockefeller University.

Herd, S., & O'Reilly, R. (2005). Serial search from a parallel model. *Vision Research, 45*(24), 2987–2992.

Hillstrom, A. P. (2000). Repetition effects in visual search. *Perception and Psychophysics, 62*(4), 800–817.

Hochstein, S., & Ahissar, M. (2002). View from the top: Hierarchies and reverse hierarchies in the visual system. *Neuron, 36*, 791–804.

Hodsoll, J. P., & Humphreys, G. W. (2005). The effect of target foreknowledge on visual search for categorically separable orientation targets. *Vision Research, 45*(18), 2346–2351.

Hoffman, J. E. (1979). A two-stage model of visual search. *Perception and Psychophysics, 25*, 319–327.

Hong, S.-K. (2005). Human stopping strategies in multiple-target search. *International Journal of Industrial Ergonomics, 35*, 1–12.

Horowitz, T. S., & Wolfe, J. M. (1998). Visual search has no memory. *Nature, 394*(Aug 6), 575–577.

Horowitz, T. S., & Wolfe, J. M. (2001). Search for multiple targets: Remember the targets, forget the search. *Perception and Psychophysics, 63*(2), 272–285.

Horowitz, T. S., & Wolfe, J. M. (2003). Memory for rejected distractors in visual search? *Visual Cognition, 10*(3), 257–298.

Horowitz, T. S., & Wolfe, J. M. (2005). Visual search: The role of memory for rejected distractors. In L. Itti, G. Rees, & J. Tsotsos (Eds.), *Neurobiology of attention* (pp. 264–268). San Diego, CA: Academic Press/Elsevier.

Hubner, R. (2001). A formal version of the guided search (GS2) model. *Perception & Psychophysics, 63*(6), 945–951.

Itti, L., & Koch, C. (2000). A saliency-based search mechanism for overt and covert shifts of visual attention. *Vision Research, 40*(10–12), 1489–1506.

Julesz, B. (1984). A brief outline of the texton theory of human vision. *Trends in Neuroscience, 7*(Feb), 41–45.

Julesz, B., & Krose, B. (1988). Features and spatial filters. *Nature, 333*, 302–303.

Kinchla, R. A. (1992). Attention. *Annual Review of Psychology, 43*, 711–742.

Kristjansson, A. (2006). Simultaneous priming along multiple feature dimensions in a visual search task. *Vision Research, 46*(16), 2554–2570.

Kristjansson, A., Wang, D., & Nakayama, K. (2002). The role of priming in conjunctive visual search. *Cognition, 85*(1), 37–52.

Krummenacher, J., Muller, H. J., & Heller, D. (2001). Visual search for dimensionally redundant pop-out targets: Evidence for parallel-coactive processing of dimensions. *Perception and Psychophysics, 63*(5), 901–917.

Lamme, V. A., & Roelfsema, P. R. (2000). The distinct modes of vision offered by feedforward and recurrent processing. *Trends in Neuroscience, 23*(11), 571–579.

Lamy, D., Bar-Anan, Y., Egeth, H. E., & Carmel, T. (2006). Effects of top-down guidance and singleton priming on visual search. *Psychonomic Bulletin & Review, 13*(2), 287–293.

Lamy, D., & Egeth, H. E. (2003). Attentional capture in singleton-detection and feature-search modes. *Journal of Experimental Psychology: Human Perception and Performance, 29*(5), 1003–1020.

Lamy, D., & Tsal, Y. (1999). A salient distractor does not disrupt conjunction search. *Psychonomic Bulletin & Review, 6*(1), 93–98.

Li, F., VanRullen, R., Koch, C., & Perona, P. (2002). Rapid natural scene categorization in the near absence of attention. *Proceedings of the National Academy of Sciences USA, 99*(14), 9596–9601.

Li, Z. (2002). A salience map in primary visual cortex. *Trends in Cognitive Science, 6*(1), 9–16.

Luck, S. J., & Vogel, E. K. (1997). The capacity of visual working memory for features and conjunctions. *Nature, 390*(20 Nov), 279–281.

Mack, A., & Rock, I. (1998). Inattentional blindness: Perception without attention. In R. D. Wright (Ed.), *Visual attention* (Vol. 8, pp. 55–76). New York: Oxford University Press.

Mack, A., Tang, B., Tuna, R., & Kahn, S. (1992). Perceptual organization and attention. *Cognitive Psychology, 24*, 475–501.

Maljkovic, V., & Martini, P. (2005). Implicit short-term memory and event frequency effects in visual search. *Vision Research, 45*(21), 2831–2846.

Maljkovic, V., & Nakayama, K. (1994). Priming of popout: I. Role of features. *Memory & Cognition, 22*(6), 657–672.

Mayr, U., & Kliegl, R. (2003). Differential effects of cue changes and task changes on task-set selection costs. *Journal of Experimental Psychology: Learning, Memory and Cognition, 29*(3), 362–372.

McLeod, P., Driver, J., & Crisp, J. (1988). Visual search for conjunctions of movement and form is parallel. *Nature, 332*, 154–155.

Moraglia, G. (1989). Display organization and the detection of horizontal lines segments. *Perception and Psychophysics, 45*, 265–272.

Muller, H. J., Reimann, B., & Krummenacher, J. (2003). Visual search for singleton feature targets across dimensions: Stimulus- and expectancy-driven effects in dimensional weighting. *Journal of Experimental Psychology: Human Perception and Performance, 29*(5), 1021–1035.

Nakayama, K., & Silverman, G. H. (1986). Serial and parallel processing of visual feature conjunctions. *Nature, 320*, 264–265.

Navalpakkam, V., Rebesco, J., & Itti, L. (2004). Modeling the influence of knowledge of the target and distractors on visual search. *Journal of Vision, VSS04* (abs E123).

Neisser, U. (1967). *Cognitive psychology.* New York: Appleton, Century, Crofts.

Noe, A., Pessoa, L., & Thompson, E. (2000). Beyond the grand illusion: What change blindness really teaches us about vision. *Visual Cognition, 7*(1), 93–106.

Nothdurft, H.-C. (1993). Saliency effects across dimensions in visual search. *Vision Research, 33*(5/6), 839–844.

Oliva, A., & Torralba, A. (2001). Modeling the shape of the scene: A holistic representation of the spatial envelope. *International Journal of Computer Vision, 42*(3), 145–175.

Olivers, C. N. L., & Humphreys, G. W. (2003). Attentional guidance by salient features depends on intertrial contingencies. *Journal of Experimental Psychology: Human Perception and Performance, 29*(3), 650–657.

O'Regan, J. K., & Noe, A. (2001). A sensorimotor account of vision and visual consciousness. *Behavioral and Brain Sciences, 24*, 957.

Parkhurst, D., Law, K., & Niebur, E. (2002). Modeling the role of salience in the allocation of overt visual attention. *Vision Research, 42*(1), 107–123.

Pashler, H. (1998a). *The psychology of attention.* Cambridge, MA: MIT Press.

Pashler, H. E. (1998b). *Attention.* Hove, East Sussex, England: Psychology Press Ltd.

Posner, M. I., & Cohen, Y. (1984). Components of attention. In H. Bouma & D. G. Bouwhuis (Eds.), *Attention and performance X* (pp. 55–66). Hillside, NJ: Lawrence Erlbaum Associates.

Ratcliff, R. (1978). A theory of memory retrieval. *Psychological Review, 85*(2), 59–108.

Ratcliff, R. (2006). Modeling response signal and response time data. *Cognitive Psychology, 53*(3), 195–237.

Rauschenberger, R. (2003). Attentional capture by auto- and allo-cues. *Psychonomic Bulletin & Review, 10*(4), 814–842.

Rensink, R. A., & Enns, J. T. (1995). Preemption effects in visual search: Evidence for low-level grouping. *Psychological Review, 102*(1), 101–130.

Sanders, A. F., & Donk, M. (1996). Visual search. In O. Neumann & A. F. Sanders (Eds.), *Handbook of perception and action, vol. 3: Attention* (pp. 43–77). London: Academic Press.

Schneider, W., & Shiffrin, R. M. (1977). Controlled and automatic human information processing: I. Detection, search, and attention. *Psychological Review, 84*, 1–66.

Serre, T., Oliva, A., & Poggio, T. (2007). A feedforward architecture accounts for rapid categorization. *Proceedings of the National Academy of Sciences USA, 104*(15), 6424–6429.

Shiffrin, M. R., & Schneider, W. (1977). Controlled and automatic human information processing: II. Perceptual learning, automatic attending, and a general theory. *Psychological Review, 84*, 127–190.

Theeuwes, J. (1991). Exogenous and endogenous control of attention: The effect of visual onsets and offsets. *Perception and Psychophysics, 49*(1), 83–90.

Thornton, T. L., & Gilden, D. L. (2007). Parallel and serial processes in visual search. *Psychological Review, 114*(1), 71–103.

Thorpe, S., Fize, D., & Marlot, C. (1996). Speed of processing in the human visual system. *Nature, 381*, 520–552.

Torralba, A., Oliva, A., Castelhano, M. S., & Henderson, J. M. (2006). Contextual guidance of eye movements and attention in real-world scenes: The role of global features on object search. *Psychological Review, 113*(4), 766–786.

Treisman, A. (1988). Features and objects: The 14th Bartlett memorial lecture. *Quarterly Journal of Experimental Psychology, 40A*, 201–237.

Treisman, A., & Gelade, G. (1980). A feature-integration theory of attention. *Cognitive Psychology, 12*, 97–136.

Treisman, A., & Souther, J. (1986). Illusory words: The roles of attention and of top-down constraints in conjoining letters to form words. *Journal of Experimental Psychology: Human Perception and Performance, 12*, 3–17.

Treisman, A. M., & Schmidt, H. (1982). Illusory conjunctions in the perception of objects. *Cognitive Psychology, 14*, 107–141.

Ungerleider, L. G., & Mishkin, M. (1982). Two cortical visual systems. In D. J. Ingle, M. A. Goodale, & R. J. W. Mansfield (Eds.), *Analysis of visual behavior* (pp. 549–586). Cambridge, MA: MIT Press.

VanRullen, R., & Thorpe, S. J. (2001). Is it a bird? Is it a plane? Ultrarapid visual categorization of natural and artifactual objects. *Perception, 30*(6), 655–668.

Weisstein, N. (1973). Beyond the yellow Volkswagen detector and the grandmother cell: A general strategy for the exploration of operations in human pattern recognition. In R. L. Solso (Ed.), *Contemporary issues in cognitive psychology: The Loyola symposium* (pp. 17–51). Washington, DC: Winston/Wiley.

Wolfe, J. M. (1994). Guided search 2.0: A revised model of visual search. *Psychonomic Bulletin and Review, 1*(2), 202–238.

Wolfe, J. M. (1998a). Visual search. In H. Pashler (Ed.), *Attention* (pp. 13–74). Hove, East Sussex, England: Psychology Press Ltd.

Wolfe, J. M. (1998b). What do 1,000,000 trials tell us about visual search? *Psychological Science, 9*(1), 33–39.

Wolfe, J. M. (2007). Guided search 4.0: Current progress with a model of visual search. In W. Gray (Ed.), *Integrated models of cognitive systems* (pp. 99–119). New York: Oxford University Press.

Wolfe, J. M., Butcher, S. J., Lee, C., & Hyle, M. (2003). Changing your mind: On the contributions of top-down and bottom-up guidance in visual search for feature singletons. *Journal of Experimental Psychology: Human Perception and Performance, 29*(2), 483–502.

Wolfe, J. M., Cave, K. R., & Franzel, S. L. (1989). Guided search: An alternative to the feature integration model for visual search. *Journal of Experimental Psychology: Human Perception and Performance, 15*, 419–433.

Wolfe, J. M., & DiMase, J. S. (2003). Do intersections serve as basic features in visual search? *Perception, 32*(6), 645–656.

Wolfe, J. M., Friedman-Hill, S. R., Stewart, M. I., & O'Connell, K. M. (1992). The role of categorization in visual search for orientation. *Journal of Experimental Psychology: Human Perception and Performance, 18*(1), 34–49.

Wolfe, J. M., & Gancarz, G. (1996). Guided search 3.0: A model of visual search catches up with Jay Enoch 40 years later. In V. Lakshminarayanan (Ed.), *Basic and clinical applications of vision science* (pp. 189–192). Dordrecht, the Netherlands: Kluwer Academic.

Wolfe, J. M., & Horowitz, T. S. (2004). What attributes guide the deployment of visual attention and how do they do it? *Nature Reviews Neuroscience, 5*(6), 495–501.

Wolfe, J., Horowitz, T., Kenner, N. M., Hyle, M., & Vasan, N. (2004). How fast can you change your mind? The speed of top-down guidance in visual search. *Vision Research, 44*(12), 1411–1426.

Wolfe, J. M., Klempen, N. L., & Shulman, E. P. (1999). Which end is up? Two representations of orientation in visual search. *Vision Research, 39*(12), 2075–2086.

Wylie, G., & Allport, A. (2000). Task switching and the measurement of "switch costs." *Psychological Research, 63*(3–4), 212–233.

Yantis, S. (1993). Stimulus-driven attentional capture. *Current Directions in Psychological Science, 2*(5), 156–161.

Yantis, S. (1995). Perceived continuity of occluded visual objects. *Psychological Science, 6*(3), 182–186.

Zenger, B., & Fahle, M. (1997). Missed targets are more frequent than false alarms: A model for error rates in visual search. *Journal of Experimental Psychology: Human Perception and Performance, 23*(6), 1783–1791.

Zhaoping, L., & Koene, A. R. (2007). Feature-specific interactions in salience from combined feature contrasts: Evidence for a bottom–up saliency map in V1. *Journal of Vision, 7*(7), article 6, 1–14.

6

Eyeblinks and Cognition

DAVID E. IRWIN and LAURA E. THOMAS

INTRODUCTION

*E*yeblinks are easily observable behavioral phenomena that people engage in every few seconds. They serve to cleanse and irrigate the eyes, spreading moisture as the lids close and reopen. People tend to blink much more often than the two to four times per minute necessary for this purpose alone, however (Doane, 1980; Evinger, 1995; Ponder & Kennedy, 1927). Rather, people blink for a variety of reasons.

Some blinks are *reflexive,* generated as a protective response to environmental events such as a loud noise, a puff of air, an electrical shock to the skin, a foreign object in the eye, or virtually any sudden intense stimulus. Other blinks are *voluntary,* made as a purposeful response to external stimuli or simply of one's own will. Still other blinks occur in the absence of any readily identifiable evoking stimulus. These spontaneous blinks, sometimes called *endogenous* eyeblinks, comprise the majority of our blinking behavior (Stern, Walrath, & Goldstein, 1984).

The kinematic characteristics of these different kinds of eyeblinks vary; reflexive and voluntary blinks have shorter and less variable durations than endogenous eyeblinks (VanderWerf, Brassinga, Reits, Aramideh, & Ongerboer de Visser, 2003). All eyeblinks are produced by antagonistic interactions between two skeletal eyelid muscles: the levator palpebrae superioris (LPS) and the orbicularis oculi (OO) muscles (Evinger, Manning, & Sibony, 1991). Immediately before a blink, LPS motoneurons briefly stop firing while OO motoneurons fire briefly, causing a rapid lowering of the upper eyelid; OO motoneurons stop firing and LPS motoneurons resume firing to return the upper eyelid to its original position (Bour, Aramideh, & Ongerboer de Visser, 2000). The eyes themselves rotate down and toward the nose during an eyeblink (Collewijn, Van der Steen, & Steinman, 1985; Riggs, Kelly, Manning, & Moore, 1987); the extent of eye rotation depends on the initial eye position (Bour et al.).

Although the physical characteristics of different kinds of eyeblinks are some-what different, in all cases vision is almost completely blocked by the closed eyelids for approximately 100–150 ms (Riggs, Volkmann, & Moore, 1981). Interestingly, we rarely notice these blank periods, even though dimming the lights in a room for the same duration is very noticeable (Volkmann, Riggs, & Moore, 1980). This implies that perception of the blank is suppressed during the blink, and experimental evidence (reviewed later) supports this introspection. In the present chapter, we review evidence that suggests that cognition, as well as vision, is affected by eyeblinks.

BLINKING AND VISUAL PERCEPTION

Eyeblinks occur 12–15 times each minute under normal circumstances, with the eyelid covering the pupil for approximately 100–150 ms (Riggs et al., 1981). Despite their frequency, magnitude, and duration, the perceptual effect of these visual interruptions is usually quite small, going almost unnoticed. Volkmann et al. (1980) hypothesized that a central inhibitory signal must accompany each blink to suppress vision and thereby minimize its perceptual consequences. To test this hypothesis, they placed a fiber-optic bundle against the roof of the mouth to present light through the back of the eyeball to the retina, bypassing the normal route through the pupil. All other sources of light were eliminated by opaque goggles, so the only visual stimulation arrived through the back of the eye.

Volkmann et al. found that visual sensitivity for brief decrements in this visual stimulus was reduced by about 0.5 log units during a blink and, to a lesser extent, 100 ms before and up to 200 ms after a blink as well, even though the light source itself was never physically impeded (see Figure 6.1). These results show that vision is indeed suppressed around the time of a blink and that this suppression is at least partly the result of a central (rather than optical) inhibitory mechanism. Subsequent experiments showed that visual suppression occurs for reflexive blinks as well as for voluntary blinks (Manning, Riggs, & Komenda, 1983) and that the

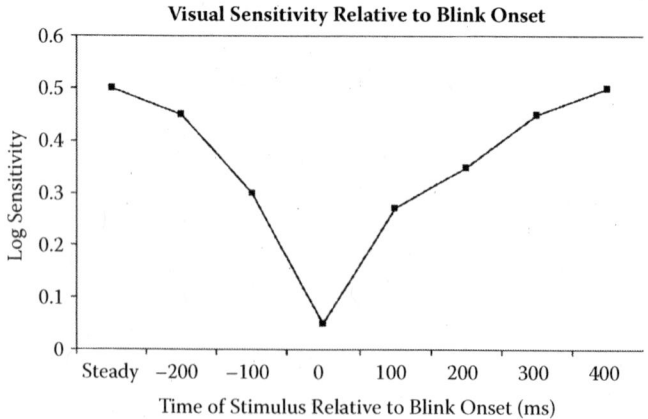

Figure 6.1 Visual sensitivity relative to blink onset in Volkmann et al. (1980, *Science, 207*, 900–902).

magnitude of visual suppression increases as blink amplitude increases (Stevenson, Volkmann, Kelly, & Riggs, 1986).

In order to measure the subjective magnitude of the visual interruption accompanying eyeblinks, Riggs et al. (1981) had people compare the phenomenal experience of a momentary luminance decrement (i.e., a simulated blink) in an otherwise constantly illuminated Ganzfeld (viewed with the eyes open) with the phenomenal effect of an actual eyeblink. The luminance decrement (i.e., simulated blink) had a 20-ms ramp onset, a 45-ms minimum, and a 60-ms return to the level of steady illumination.

Averaged across participants and background illumination levels in the Ganzfeld, a luminance decrement of 46% was judged subjectively equal to an eyeblink, even though during an actual eyeblink the physical luminance decrement is nearly 100%. In other words, luminance decrements that participants perceived to be subjectively equivalent to eyeblinks had a smaller magnitude and a shorter duration than the physical values generated by an eyeblink (which, of course, provides additional evidence that visual input is suppressed during eyeblinks).

Because visual input is suppressed during eyeblinks, it is perhaps not surprising that people reduce their rate of blinking during visually demanding tasks, presumably in order to minimize the probability of missing important information (Baumstimler & Parrot, 1971; Drew, 1951; Kennard & Glaser, 1964; Stern & Skelly, 1984). People also blink less often when engaged in a task that is cognitively demanding irrespective of its visual demands (Stern et al., 1984). These findings suggest that thinking affects blinking; we review this in more detail next.

THINKING AFFECTS BLINKING

It is intuitively obvious that blinking during a visually demanding task would be detrimental to task performance because vision is occluded during a blink. As noted before, blinks occur 12–15 times each minute under ordinary circumstances, with the eyelid covering the pupil for approximately 100–150 ms. Thus, vision is obscured for approximately 20–30 minutes during the course of a 16-hour waking day. As described previously, in addition to the occlusion caused by the eyelids, vision is also suppressed prior to blink onset and after blink completion (Manning et al., 1983; Riggs et al., 1981; Volkmann et al., 1980; Wibbenmeyer, Stern, & Chen, 1983).

This additional visual suppression associated with blinks occurs during voluntary, reflexive, and endogenous blinks (Volkmann, 1986). Presumably, vision is suppressed during blinks in order to minimize the disruptive effects produced by the physical occlusion of the visual world during the blink. As noted earlier, although an external interruption of visual input (such as turning out the lights in a room) of durations even shorter than an eyeblink is quite noticeable, the visual disruption that occurs during a blink typically goes unnoticed (Volkmann et al., 1980).

Although people typically do not consciously notice the interruption in visual input that blinks cause, early investigations of spontaneous blink rate suggested that the human information processing system does take these disruptions into account when people are engaged in visually demanding tasks. For example, Ponder and Kennedy (1927) found that people blink less frequently when performing tasks involving visual activity such as reading than during nonvisual activities such as conversation.

The experimenters also found that blink rate increased when people were induced to become excited or angry, and that people blinked more during courtroom cross-examination than when giving their initial testimony. The experimenters concluded that blinking was associated with "mental tension," whereby blinks serve as a relief mechanism for nervous energy; however, subsequent research showed that this claim did not adequately explain the occurrence of most blinks. Nevertheless, the researchers did provide the first evidence that blinks are centrally controlled and linked to cognitive states.

Drew (1951) pursued a more direct examination of the relationship between spontaneous blink rates and the visual demands of a task. The experiment tested the hypotheses that individuals with higher blink rates will be less efficient in performing visual tasks and more likely to have accidents (Lawson, 1948) and that intra-individual variations in blink rate should reflect the difficulty of a visual task. Drew asked participants to perform a tracking task in which they traced a straight or oscillating line while their blinks were monitored. As the difficulty of the tracking task and the complexity of the required motor response increased, participants blinked less frequently than they did under resting conditions or under conditions in which they were tracing lines that were less curved. In fact, participants tended to inhibit blinking completely during periods of maximum task difficulty, spacing their blinks so that they occurred just before or just after these periods.

However, contrary to the hypothesis that individuals with the highest resting blink rates should be the least efficient in tracking task performance, Drew found no relationship between participants' relative blink rates and their relative accuracy on the tracking task. Those who blinked frequently under resting conditions blinked less frequently as task difficulty increased, and those who blinked infrequently at rest blinked even less frequently when the tracing task became more challenging. Regardless of their baseline behavior, participants reduced their blink rates when performing a visually demanding task, presumably to decrease the likelihood of missing important information.

In a similar study on blinks during visual tracking, Poulton and Gregory (1952) were able to expand upon the conclusions of Drew (1951). They too found that blink rate decreased as tracking task difficulty increased and that participants tended to concentrate their blinks during easy portions of the task and to avoid blinking during the most difficult portions. Additionally, when participants in their experiment did happen to blink as they attempted to trace difficult courses, these blinks had a detrimental effect on performance.

Perhaps even more interestingly, Poulton and Gregory (1952) also found that when participants were asked to make voluntary blinks during the tracking task, these blinks were more detrimental to task performance than were blackouts of the stimulus that occurred at the same rate. This suggested that blinks' interference with performance went beyond simple visual interference. Further support for the conclusion that blinks' detrimental effect on tracking performance can be attributed to sources in addition to visual interference is provided by the fact that participants showed increased errors in performance even 1 s after a blink occurred; visual interference effects should not persist so long after the eyes reopen.

Additional evidence that blink inhibition is not solely tied to preventing visual interference is provided by experiments demonstrating that, as difficulty in non-visual tasks such as auditory tracking, mental arithmetic, and digit span recall increases, the spontaneous blink rates of participants performing these tasks decreases (Gregory, 1952; Holland & Tarlow, 1975). When these results are considered with those of Drew (1951) and Poulton and Gregory (1952), they suggest that blink rate can serve as an indicator of the attentional demands of a cognitive task. The more attention a task requires, the less often people blink.

These early studies of blink rate during continuous tasks provided evidence that the attentional demands of a task are reflected in blinks' occurrence. Later experiments that included a more detailed investigation of blink timing and blink characteristics during discrete trial paradigms showed more specifically how blinks are tied to the cognitive demands of a task. In one such experiment, Baumstimler and Parrot (1971) asked participants to perform a choice reaction time (RT) task in which they responded by pressing one of five keys mapped to the presentation of specific digits. On a small portion of trials, the digits were paired with a peripheral stimulus that acted as a cue to inhibit making a response on that trial.

Supporting earlier conclusions that blink rate is tied to task demands, the experimenters found that spontaneous blinking was inhibited during stimulus presentations. They also found that the majority of blinks tended to be deferred until after participants made their key press response. On the small percentage of trials in which the peripheral cue indicated that participants should inhibit their response, the experimenters found that blinking was inhibited to an even greater extent. Based upon these findings, they concluded that blink inhibition was tied to inhibition of making a motor response; when responses are inhibited, blinks are also inhibited, but when participants make a response, it releases this inhibition so that blinks then occur.

Baumstimler and Parrot's (1971) interpretation of their results contradicts the notion that blinks are a useful indicator of underlying cognitive processes, suggesting instead that spontaneous blinks are tied to motor rather than cognitive processes. However, these results are also consistent with the hypothesis that blinks were inhibited while participants processed and made decisions about whether or how to respond to stimuli and then programmed those responses. This hypothesis is consistent with the idea that blinks do reflect cognitive processes.

According to this hypothesis, participants inhibited blinks until after making a response because they were busy identifying the stimulus, mapping it to the correct key, and then programming this response. Participants did not blink during the trials in which they withheld responses because they were busy processing the more complicated and rare peripheral stimulus and then making the decision to inhibit the key press response.

The results of several other studies support the hypothesis that the timing of blinks reflects underlying cognitive processes and that blink inhibition is not strictly tied to response inhibition, as Baumstimler and Parrot (1971) suggested. In one such study, Fukuda and Matsunaga (1983) found that blinks were deferred until some time after stimulus onset in a discrete trial paradigm, regardless of whether or not a motor response was required for that trial. In their tasks, participants made discriminations about visual and auditory stimuli.

Although participants blinked less frequently overall when presented with visual stimuli, blinks tended to be inhibited until after stimulus presentation in both visual and auditory conditions. The authors interpreted these results as suggesting that blinks were inhibited during their task when participants' attention level increased in anticipation of a stimulus; that is, the cognitive response to stimuli, rather than motor responses, influenced when blinks would occur in a trial.

Two other studies designed to examine the relationship of blinking, the cognitive demands of a task, and response programming demonstrated that the timing and characteristics of blinks are sensitive to processing demands (Bauer, Strock, Goldstein, Stern, & Walrath, 1985; Goldstein, Walrath, Stern, & Strock, 1985). In both of these studies, the experimenters examined blink latency with respect to a trial's imperative stimulus in duration discrimination tasks. Goldstein et al. presented participants with visual and auditory signals either 200 or 400 ms in duration. Participants were required to make a motor response only to the shorter duration stimuli.

The experimenters found that blinks occurring on trials with the briefer stimulus (that required a response) had longer latencies with respect to the visual or auditory stimulus than blinks occurring on trials with the longer duration stimulus (that did not require a response). Opposing Baumstimler and Parrot's (1971) theory that blink inhibition is tied to response inhibition, Goldstein et al. (1985) found no differences in the blink rate between response and nonresponse trials. These results led the researchers to propose that response programming inhibits blinking and, more specifically, that the latency of a blink is determined by the duration of processing events within trials, such that blinks tend to occur when there are breaks in the flow of decision processes (e.g., after participants identify a stimulus and select and program a response).

Additional evidence supporting the claim that a centrally initiated mechanism defers blinks until after participants have made decisions about stimuli and programmed their responses came from a follow-up study by Bauer et al. (1985). Stimulus duration and the requirement to respond were confounded in the Goldstein et al. (1985) study, making it difficult for them to draw conclusions about the effects of these factors and which, if either, held more sway on blink latency. However, Bauer et al. unconfounded these variables in their study. Their participants performed in separate conditions where 200-ms auditory tones required a response but 400-ms tones did not and vice versa.

These researchers found that both stimulus duration and the response requirement influenced blink latency; blinks occurring after 400-ms stimuli had longer latencies than those occurring after 200-ms stimuli. Blinks occurring after stimuli that required a response had longer latencies than those occurring after nontarget stimuli. When a stimulus was long, it took more time for participants to process it, and this delayed blink onset. Similarly, when a stimulus required a response, it took more time for participants to program this response, delaying blink onset in this condition as well.

Additional evidence in favor of the notion that blinks reflect the processing demands of particular stimuli comes from a study by Fukuda (2001). In this study, participants viewed a set of cards and chose one that they defined as the relevant stimulus. Following this choice, participants viewed each card in the initial set one at a time and were required to make identical responses to each card, saying that each one was not the card they had chosen, regardless of whether or not it was the relevant stimulus.

Fukuda (2001) found that participants had lower blink rates during the intervals in which they viewed and responded to relevant cards and that blinks occurring after presentation of a relevant card had longer latencies than blinks associated with other cards from the set. These results show that, once again, when a stimulus demands more processing resources—in this case, the stimulus participants had to lie—participants defer blinks associated with this stimulus.

Fogarty and Stern (1989) performed another study demonstrating that endogenous blinks are triggered by aspects of information processing in a cognitive task. In their experiment, participants viewed a centrally presented letter and then had to detect or identify and then compare to the central letter, a peripheral letter stimulus presented 15 or 50° to the left or right of fixation. Participants had to make eye movements to the peripheral stimuli in order to *identify* them correctly, but no eye movements were required in order to *detect* the peripheral stimuli. This design allowed Fogarty and Stern to examine three questions:

- By including both detect and identify conditions, they were able to investigate how the information processing demands of a task influence blink timing. An examination of blink latency showed that blinks occurring following peripheral stimulus presentation in the identify condition occurred later than in the detect condition. This result suggests that the timing of blinks was a function of the amount of information a participant needed to abstract from a stimulus. In the case of detection, once participants confirmed that a stimulus was present, they could quickly make a response to it; in the identify condition, they had not only to detect and identify the stimulus, but also to compare it to a stored representation of the central stimulus, determine if it was a match, and then program the appropriate response.
- The experimenters were able to look at the influence of large versus smaller amplitude saccades on blink occurrence. They hypothesized that because visual information intake is suppressed during saccades (e.g., E. Matin, 1974; Riggs, Merton, & Morton, 1974; Volkmann, 1986; Zuber & Stark, 1966), just as it is during blinks, an efficient strategy for minimizing the loss of visual information would be for participants to perform blinks in tandem with their saccades. Pairing blinks with long saccades would be particularly efficient because 50° saccades allow the most time for a blink to occur strategically without causing any additional disruption of information intake. They found that blinks did indeed tend to co-occur with saccades and that blinks were more often paired with long than with short saccades. This offered support to the notion that participants minimize

visual disruption during an information-processing task by performing blinks together with long duration saccades.

- The experimenters were able to investigate differences between blinks that occurred close in time with saccades directed toward critical stimuli as well as blinks paired with return saccades to fixation. They found that blinks were more likely to be paired with return saccades than with saccades made to a peripheral stimulus. Participants presumably did not frequently pair blinks with saccades to peripheral stimuli because they did not want to miss pertinent information. Therefore, as in many other experiments examining the timing of blinks during stimulus presentations in discrete trial paradigms, they found that blinks were inhibited until participants gained and processed the information they needed from a stimulus.

Blinks tend to co-occur strategically with specific types of saccades during laboratory information processing tasks, and they are also often paired with particular eye movements associated with reading. As was previously noted, in their early investigation of blinking, Ponder and Kennedy (1927) found that the spontaneous blink rate during normal reading was lower than during activities such as engaging in conversation, a finding later replicated by Hall (1945). Although part of the inhibition of blinking during reading may be explained by noncognitive factors such as the fact that gaze is typically directed downward during reading and reading often takes place in silent environments (Doughty, 2001), Hall's study suggested that the distribution of blinks during reading is under perceptual and cognitive control.

Hall (1945) found that when participants read passages aloud, blinks were not randomly distributed. Instead, he observed that people tended to blink during events such as page turns, column shifts, and punctuation marks—events in the reading process where the disruption of information intake would be minimized. However, participants in Hall's study read very short passages of text, limiting the amount of data upon which he based his conclusions. In addition, the fact that participants in his study were reading aloud may have been a potential confound; many experiments find that blinks are linked to speech production (Stern et al., 1984).

Orchard and Stern (1991) pursued an updated examination of blinks during reading in which participants silently read handheld pages of text. They found that significantly fewer blinks were paired with fixation pauses and that more blinks occurred in conjunction with saccades than would be expected on the basis of chance. Breaking the data down further, Orchard and Stern found that the largest proportion of blinks was associated with line change saccades and the second largest proportion occurred in conjunction with regressive saccades. These results provide additional support for the hypotheses put forward by Fogarty and Stern (1989) and extend their findings to the more naturalistic activity of reading; blinks tended to occur in conjunction with saccades, thereby minimizing the time during which visual information intake was disrupted.

The fact that blinks co-occurred most frequently with long saccades during line changes or saccades to previously viewed information during regressive eye movements also supports the hypothesis that blinks occur when information intake and processing are least likely to be disrupted. Orchard and Stern suggested that blinks take place after a person has abstracted information or made a decision. They serve almost as a mental punctuation mark, signaling the end of one stage of information processing and the start of another (such as at the end of a paragraph), and they occur most often when they will not disrupt information processing.

Although the placement and timing of blinks during reading led researchers to hypothesize that blinks tend to take place when people conclude one cognitive process and start another, a series of experiments using a modified Sternberg (1966) memory scanning task provided evidence that blinks signal the conclusion of one specific process: stimulus encoding (Bauer, Goldstein, & Stern, 1987; Goldstein, Bauer, & Stern, 1992). In these studies, participants first viewed a cue that indicated the number of items that would subsequently appear in a memory set. Some time after this cue was presented, a memory set of letters would appear and offset, followed some time later by presentation of a test letter. Participants were instructed to respond whether the test letter was a member of the memory set.

Both Bauer et al. (1987) and Goldstein et al. (1992) found that memory set size influenced blinks. When the memory set contained five or six items, thereby challenging participants' short-term memory capacity, the experimenters found increased blink latencies and lower blink rates than under conditions in which participants viewed memory sets with fewer items. Interestingly, following the initial depression of blink rate during memory set presentation, there was a subsequent increase in blink rate. The experimenters interpreted this increase as an indicator of the conclusion of the encoding process. Participants not only inhibited blinking as memory sets were presented in order to avoid missing visual information, but also refrained from blinking for up to a second after the memory set appeared. They blinked only after they had presumably encoded the set.

Interim Summary: Thinking Affects Blinking

An examination of the various studies investigating how thinking affects blinking leads to several conclusions. Blinks are generally inhibited during visually demanding tasks, occurring at such times as to maximize stimulus perception. Beyond merely reflecting perceptual concerns, blinks also tend to be inhibited during attentionally demanding tasks as task-relevant stimuli are processed, regardless of modality.

Blink occurrence is regulated as a function of the information content and task demands associated with particular stimuli. Blinks may also signal a time of transition from one stage of information processing to another. When blinks do occur, they are often paired with saccades, when vision is already obscured because of saccadic suppression. In sum, considerable evidence indicates that both visual and cognitive demands influence blinking.

BLINKING AFFECTS THINKING

Although many studies have investigated whether thinking affects blinking, very little research has investigated the converse question—that is, whether blinking affects thinking. This question has been the focus of much research in our laboratory recently. The motivation for our research has been twofold:

- Because vision is suppressed by central, neural mechanisms during a blink (Volkmann et al., 1980), it seemed possible that blinking might suppress central cognitive processes as well, particularly visually related cognitive processes.
- Considerable evidence now indicates that saccadic eye movements interfere with cognition (e.g., Brockmole, Carlson, & Irwin, 2002; Irwin, 2003; Irwin & Brockmole, 2000, 2004; Irwin & Carlson-Radvansky, 1996; Irwin & Thomas, 2007).

Because saccades and blinks rely on some of the same neural mechanisms (Ridder & Tomlinson, 1995, 1997; Uchikawa & Sato, 1995; Volkmann, 1986), we hypothesized that eyeblinks, as well as saccades, might interfere with cognition.

Our first investigation of this hypothesis examined the effect of eyeblinks on iconic memory (Thomas & Irwin, 2006). Iconic memory is a short-lived memory for the contents of a visual display and has frequently been investigated using a partial-report procedure (e.g., Sperling, 1963). In this procedure, an array of letters is presented visually for a brief time; then, some time after stimulus offset, an auditory cue is presented to indicate that some part of the array should be reported. Because iconic memory decays rapidly, accuracy of report declines quickly as the interval between array offset and response cue increases.

The duration of iconic memory is sensitive to visual factors such as the luminance of the visual fields preceding and following the stimulus array, and generally only partial-report cues that signal report based on some physical property of the array (such as location or color) have proven to be effective. These facts led early investigators to believe that iconic memory consisted of a raw, unprocessed, literal copy of the stimulus (e.g., Neisser, 1967).

However, later research demonstrated that the partial-report paradigm actually measures both precategorical and postcategorical (i.e., cognitive) sources of information (Coltheart, 1980; Di Lollo, 1978; Loftus & Irwin, 1998). For example, most errors in partial-report tasks are mislocation errors, rather than item intrusion errors (e.g., Dick, 1969; Irwin & Yeomans, 1986; Townsend, 1973), suggesting that the stimulus items have been identified but that memory for their locations has faded.

It has also been shown that familiarity with the letter array reduces the number of intrusion, but not mislocation, errors (Mewhort, Campbell, Marchetti, & Campbell, 1981). Thus, it appears that the partial-report procedure measures not only a visual memory for the display, but also some postcategorical (i.e., cognitively processed) information as well.

Because the partial-report procedure appears to tap into representations at the interface between perception and cognition, it seemed an ideal starting point for investigating whether blinks interfere with cognitive processing. Thus, Thomas and Irwin (2006) investigated performance in a partial-report task under blink and no-blink conditions. The basic procedure is shown in Figure 6.2.

In each trial, a 3 × 3 letter array was presented for 106 ms, followed 50, 150, or 750 ms later by the presentation of a cue tone. The pitch of the tone cued participants to recall the top, middle, or bottom row of the array. In some blocks of trials,

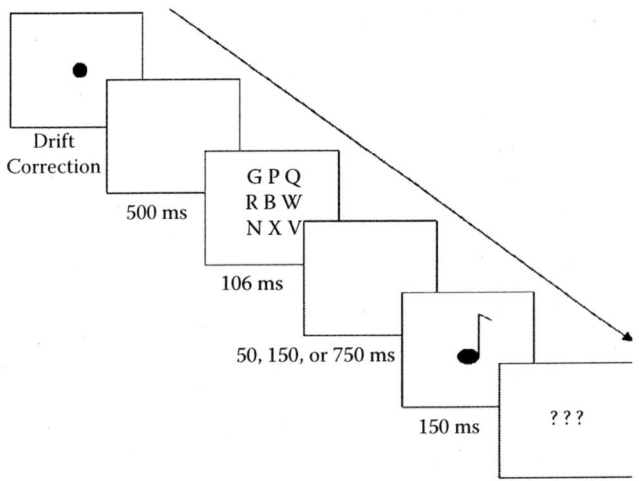

Figure 6.2   Sequence of events (from left to right and top to bottom) for a no-blink partial report trial in Thomas & Irwin (2006, *Perception & Psychophysics, 68,* 475–488).

participants were instructed to blink as soon as the letter array was presented; in other blocks, they were told to keep their eyes open and steady. Blink latency exceeded the duration of the stimulus array by over 100 ms, so the blink did not prevent participants from seeing the array.

Nonetheless, partial-report accuracy was lower when participants blinked than when they did not, but only at the shortest cue delay of 50 ms (see Figure 6.3). This finding indicates that blinking disrupted the maintenance of stimulus information

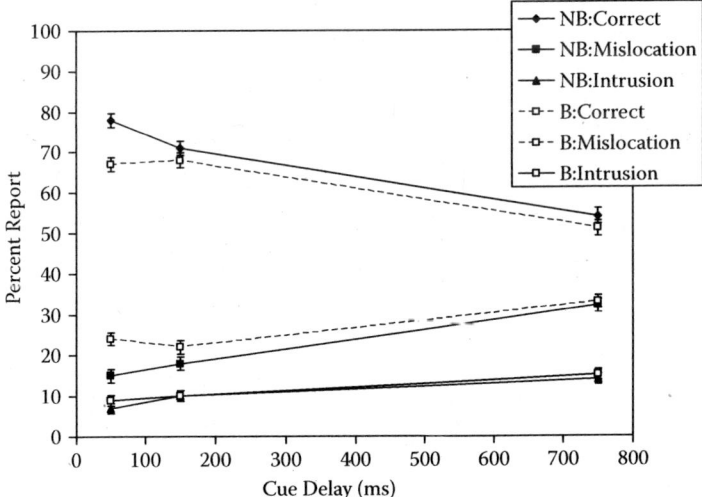

Figure 6.3   Mean percentages of correct responses, mislocation errors, and intrusion errors as a function of cue delay for blink (B) and no-blink (NB) trials in Thomas & Irwin (2006, *Perception & Psychophysics, 68,* 475–488).

in iconic memory (which has a very short duration) but not in short-term memory (which has a longer duration). Importantly, the decrease in accuracy at the 50-ms delay under blink conditions was accompanied by an increase in the number of mislocation errors. In other words, blinking disrupted the binding between letter identity and letter position information in iconic memory.

In order to strengthen the conclusion that blinks interfere with cognitive processing, Thomas and Irwin (2006) conducted several control experiments to rule out possible alternative explanations for their results. In one control experiment, they had participants press a button (instead of blink) as soon as the letter array was presented. These button presses (or "finger blinks") had no disruptive effect on partial-report performance, even though their latency and duration were similar to those of eyeblinks. This ruled out the possibility that the deleterious effects of blinking on partial-report performance were due to the requirement to make an irrelevant motor response in reaction to the onset of the stimulus display.

In another control experiment, participants were instructed to close their eyes when the letter array appeared and keep them closed until the response cue was presented. This too had no effect on partial-report performance, indicating again that blinks are special in their ability to interfere with the maintenance of information in iconic memory. A final control experiment demonstrated that the effect of blinking was not due to visual masking; this experiment showed that "simulated blinks" in which the display went from light to dark to light again after stimulus offset (while the eyes were open) did not produce a pattern of results like those found when eyeblinks occurred after stimulus offset.

Thomas and Irwin (2006) speculated that eyeblinks might disrupt iconic memory because the parts of the visual pathway activated by blink programming and blink execution are the same parts required for maintaining an iconic representation of the stimulus display. This hypothesis is consistent with physiological evidence regarding the locus of iconic memory and of the neural activity associated with blinks.

For example, one locus of iconic memory is primary visual cortex (V1), where it has been shown that neurons continue to fire even after a visual stimulus has been terminated (e.g., Duysens, Orban, Cremieux, & Maes, 1985; Engel, 1970; Supèr, Spekreijse, & Lamme, 2001). Blinks suppress the activity of neurons in V1 (Gawne & Martin, 2000), however, and a consequence of this suppression may be interference with iconic memory representations that also rely on V1. Thus, the suppression of iconic memory by blinks that was observed by Thomas and Irwin (2006) may be the result of neural interference in primary visual cortex.

Thomas and Irwin (2006) hypothesized that blinks might affect higher levels of the visual/cognitive processing stream as well, however. In addition to V1, blinks have been shown to influence activation in posterior parietal cortex (Bodis-Wollner, Bucher, & Seelos, 1999; Bristow, Haynes, Sylvester, Frith, & Rees, 2005; Hari, Salmelin, Tissari, Kajola, & Virsu, 1994). This area is thought to be an essential part of the spatial working memory system (e.g., Awh et al., 1999; D'Esposito et al., 1998; Jonides et al., 1993), and it is also instrumental in the allocation of visual spatial attention (e.g., Colby & Goldberg, 1999; Corbetta, Kincade, Ollinger, McAvoy, & Shulman, 2000).

Because Thomas and Irwin (2006) found that blinks appear to interfere selectively with the binding of position information with identity information (i.e., most errors in partial report were mislocation errors rather than item intrusion errors), it seems possible that the deleterious effects of blinks occur at this level rather than at the level of V1. This might happen because blinking interferes with memory for spatial position or because blinking interferes with the allocation of visual attention required to bind position and identity information together into a stable representation (Treisman & Gelade, 1980).

Recent investigations in our laboratory have examined both of these possibilities. Higgins, Irwin, Wang, and Thomas (in preparation) explored whether blinking interferes with memory for spatial position. The procedure was as follows. On every trial, a single dot was presented on a display for 100 ms and then extinguished; then, either 50 or 750 ms later, the dot was re-presented above, below, left, or right of its initial position. The participants' task was to indicate the direction of displacement.

Performance was compared across two experimental conditions. In one, participants were instructed to blink as soon as they saw the first dot; in the other, they kept their eyes open. Blink latency was sufficiently long to ensure that both dots were seen before the blink started. Higgins et al. found that accuracy was lower in the blink condition than in the no-blink condition. This was true even when the dot displacement took place before the eyes started to blink (i.e., in trials where an interstimulus interval (ISI) of only 50 ms separated the two presentations of the target dot).

This indicates that merely the intention to blink (i.e., blink motor programming) is sufficient to interfere with the representation of spatial position in memory. It is interesting that similar findings appear in the saccadic eye movement literature, where numerous studies have shown that memory for spatial position is distorted before, during, and after a saccade (see L. Matin, 1986, for a review). We are exploring these relationships further in our laboratory.

In a second line of research, we are investigating whether blinks exert their effect on performance by influencing the allocation of visual attention. In the case of saccadic eye movements, it is well known that visual attention precedes the eyes to the saccade target location. This is demonstrated by the fact that the detection and the identification of stimulus items presented at the saccade target location are facilitated relative to items presented at other spatial locations (e.g., Deubel & Schneider, 1996; Henderson, 1993; Hoffman & Subramaniam, 1995; Irwin & Gordon, 1998; Klein, 1980; Kowler, Anderson, Dosher, & Blaser, 1995; Rayner, McConkie, & Ehrlich, 1978; Shepherd, Findlay, & Hockey, 1986).

This is true even if the stimulus is presented and removed before the saccade actually begins and even if participants are instructed to attend to a location other than the saccade target (e.g., Deubel & Schneider, 1996; Hoffman & Subramaniam, 1995; Irwin & Gordon, 1998; Kowler et al., 1995). This indicates that saccade programming causes visual attention to be allocated to the saccade target location in an obligatory fashion.

Given the similarities between the neural characteristics of saccades and eyeblinks, we wondered whether blinking might also cause visual attention to be allocated systematically in some fashion. Recall that during a blink, the eyes rotate down and toward the nose (Collewijn et al., 1985; Riggs et al., 1987). If attention precedes the movements of the eyes during a blink, as it does during a saccade, then we would expect to find facilitative effects on processing of material in the lower visual field preceding an eyeblink.

Support for this hypothesis was found when we looked more closely at the data from Thomas and Irwin (2006). In the partial-report task, attention must be directed to the cued row quickly and accurately so that information can be read from iconic memory before it decays. If blinking drives attention in a downward fashion, then we would expect to find differences in partial-report performance based on which row of the array is cued. When we re-analyzed the data from Thomas and Irwin (2006) to investigate this possibility, we found that blinking interfered with partial-report accuracy only when the top or middle row of the array had been cued for report (see Figure 6.4). Blinking had no effect on accuracy when the bottom row was cued, as though attention had been driven downward by the blink, ensuring that information in the bottom row was maintained and easily retrieved from iconic memory.

Encouraged by this post hoc analysis, we decided to investigate this hypothesis more systematically. To do this, we conducted another partial-report experiment similar to that of Thomas and Irwin (2006), but using a more spatially distributed letter array (see Figure 6.5). The letter array in this experiment consisted of four triplets of letters—one above central fixation, one to the left, one to the right, and

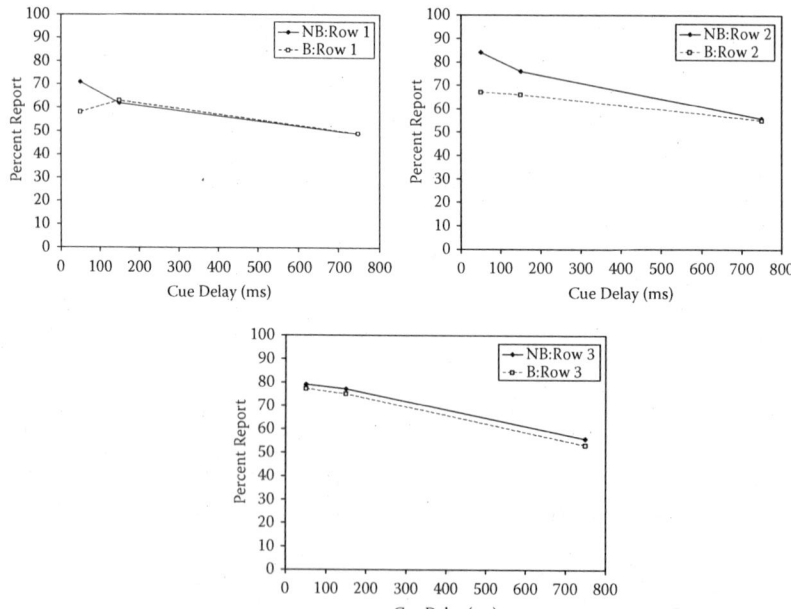

Figure 6.4   Mean percentages of correct responses as a function of cue delay and row for blink (B) and no-blink (NB) trials in Thomas & Irwin (2006, *Perception & Psychophysics*, 68, 475–488).

NGW

DFK   >   CPB

XRM

Figure 6.5   Example stimulus for the spatially distributed letter array partial report experiment.

one below. On each experimental trial, a letter array was presented for 106 ms, followed 0, 50, or 750 ms later by a partial-report cue.

The partial-report cue in this experiment (also shown in Figure 6.5) was an arrow pointing up, down, left, or right that signaled which letter triplet should be reported. Each triplet position was cued equally often, with the cued position sequenced randomly across trials. As in Thomas and Irwin (2006), participants completed blocks of trials in which they were told to blink as soon as the letter array was presented as well as blocks of trials in which they kept their eyes open and steadily fixated in the center of the letter array.

The results of this study are shown in Figure 6.6. When the top row of the array was cued, partial-report accuracy was higher at all cue delays on no-blink trials than on blink trials. The decrease in correct reports on blink trials was due to an increase in mislocation errors. There was no difference in accuracy between blink and no-blink trials when the left or right triplets in the letter array were cued. Interestingly, when the bottom row of the array was cued, accuracy was actually higher on blink trials than on no-blink trials, and mislocation errors were lower.

These results provide good support for the hypothesis that attention moves downward before a blink. For accurate performance in a partial-report task, attention is required in order to bind letter identities with letter positions. If attention moves downward before a blink, then binding of items at the bottom of the letter array will be facilitated and binding of items at the top of the letter array will be inhibited. In sum, these results indicate that blinking affects the allocation of visual attention during task performance.

In a follow-up study, we investigated whether this blink-induced allocation of attention is obligatory, as is true for saccadic eye movements. In this experiment, we cued one position in the array much more often than the other positions, balancing which position was cued with higher frequency across participants. Participants were informed of the position bias. Despite this, they were unable to allocate attention flexibly to the high-probability position on blink trials; instead, accuracy on blink trials was low when the top position was cued and high when the bottom position was cued, just as in the unbiased position experiment. This result indicates that the downward movement of attention that precedes eyeblinks is obligatory in nature.

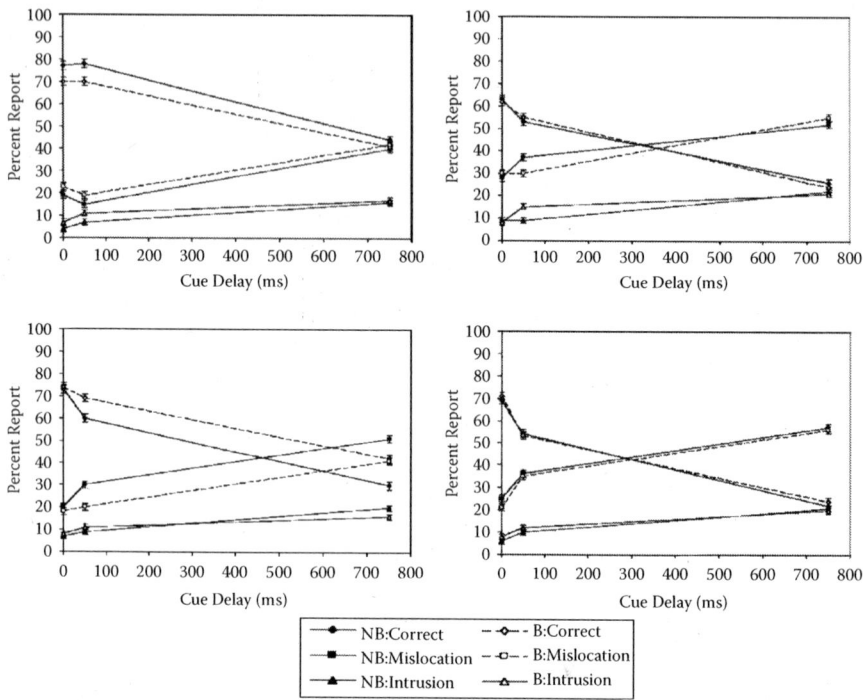

Figure 6.6 Mean percentages of correct responses, mislocation errors, and intrusion errors as a function of location and cue delay for blink (B) and no-blink (NB) trials in the spatially distributed letter array partial report experiment. Clockwise from top left, the results are shown for the top, left, right, and bottom array locations.

Additional evidence that memory and attention are disrupted by eyeblinks is demonstrated by the finding that people are poor at detecting changes in a visual display that take place during a blink. This can be observed casually if one happens to blink when the computer display is updated during a screen refresh, but it has also been shown experimentally by O'Regan, Deubel, Clark, and Rensink (2000). These investigators employed a change-detection procedure in which a picture displayed on a computer screen changed in some fashion (e.g., an object appeared or disappeared, changed color, or changed position) during an eyeblink.

Participants were instructed to look for changes, but were not told that the changes occurred during eyeblinks. O'Regan et al. (2000) found that changes were frequently undetected, even when the change occurred at the exact location that the participant was fixating before and after the blink. They called this "looking without seeing" and suggested that the failure to detect changes that occur during a blink might be due to failures of either memory or attention.

The studies summarized here all used accuracy as a dependent measure to investigate how blinks affect performance. We have also conducted a number of RT experiments to investigate cognitive blink suppression. Unfortunately, the results of these experiments are somewhat ambiguous. The general experimental procedure is as follows. On each trial, participants are presented with a stimulus and instructed to make some judgment about the stimulus as quickly and as accurately as they can. On some trials, they are also instructed to blink as soon as the stimulus appears. Accuracy and RT are measured for both blink and no-blink trials.

We have used this procedure to examine the effects of blinks on several different cognitive tasks (e.g., mental rotation, lexical decision) and the results are the same in every experiment: RT is about 100 ms longer on blink trials than on no-blink trials. This is consistent with the hypothesis that blinks interfere with cognitive processing. However, the problem is that we have not been able to rule out the possibility that blink interference occurs simply because participants must perform some irrelevant motor response (the blink) in addition to their primary task on blink trials.

We ruled out this possibility in our experiments that used accuracy as a dependent measure by showing that blinks were unique in their ability to disrupt performance; for example, Thomas and Irwin (2006) showed that button presses and eye closures did not disrupt partial-report performance even though eyeblinks did. In the RT domain, however, we have found that button presses and eye closures cause at least as much interference as eyeblinks do. In sum, it is possible that blinks slow cognitive processing (as measured by RT), but it is also possible that this is just a general dual-task cost and not something that is unique to blinks per se.

Interim Summary: Blinking Affects Thinking

Although many studies have shown that cognitive factors influence blinking, only recently have investigators begun to examine whether blinking might affect cognition as well. Recent findings from our laboratory have suggested that blinks interfere with visual memory and that they influence the allocation of visual attention as well. Memory for spatial position suffers when a blink occurs, and the binding of identity information with position information is hindered as well. Both of these effects may be due to a blink-induced involuntary reallocation of visual attention similar to what is observed for saccadic eye movements.

There may be several neural loci for these effects. Blinks have been shown to influence activity in V1, in posterior parietal cortex, and, more recently, in V3 and prefrontal areas as well (Bristow et al., 2005). This latter finding is of interest because these higher cortical areas have been associated with conscious awareness of environmental change (Beck, Rees, Frith, & Lavie, 2001), which may help explain the change detection results of O'Regan et al. (2000) and may also account for why we generally do not notice the blackout that accompanies each eyeblink.

CONCLUSION

A wealth of research from the past 80 years shows that thinking affects blinking. Blinks are a useful indicator of cognitive processing, showing sensitivity to demands in a variety of cognitive tasks in both continuous and discrete trial paradigms.

Recent research from our laboratory indicates that blinking affects thinking as well, although additional research is needed to discover in which circumstances this occurs and why it occurs. As a final observation, it is interesting to note that many experimental studies discard blinks as uninteresting artifacts; this is particularly true in the domain of reading. The studies we have summarized in this chapter suggest that investigation of the relationship between thinking and blinking and blinking and thinking may prove very fruitful in our attempts to understand human cognition.

ACKNOWLEDGMENT

The research reported in this chapter was supported by NSF grant BCS 01-32272.

REFERENCES

Awh, E., Jonides, J., Smith, E., Buxton, R., Frank, L., Love, T., et al. (1999). Rehearsal in spatial working memory: Evidence from neuroimaging. *Psychological Science, 10,* 433–437.

Bauer, L. O., Goldstein, R., & Stern, J. A. (1987). Effects of information-processing demands on physiological response patterns. *Human Factors, 29,* 213–234.

Bauer, L. O., Strock, B. D., Goldstein, R., Stern, J. A., & Walrath, L. C. (1985). Auditory discrimination and the eyeblink. *Psychophysiology, 22,* 636–641.

Baumstimler, Y., & Parrot, J. (1971). Stimulus generalization and spontaneous blinking in man involved in a voluntary activity. *Journal of Experimental Psychology, 1,* 95–102.

Beck, D. M., Rees, G., Frith, C. D., & Lavie, N. (2001). Neural correlates of change detection and change blindness. *Nature Neuroscience, 4,* 645–650.

Bodis-Wollner, I., Bucher, S. F., & Seelos, K. C. (1999). Cortical activation patterns during voluntary blinks and voluntary saccades. *Neurology, 53,* 1800–1805.

Bour, L. J., Aramideh, M., & Ongerboer de Visser, B. (2000). Neurophysiological aspects of eye and eyelid movements during blinking in humans. *Journal of Neurophysiology, 83,* 166–176.

Bristow, D., Haynes, J-D., Sylvester, R., Frith, C. D., & Rees, G. (2005). Blinking suppresses the neural response to unchanging retinal stimulation. *Current Biology, 15,* 1296–1300.

Brockmole, J. R., Carlson, L. A., & Irwin, D. E. (2002). Inhibition of attended processing during saccadic eye movements. *Perception and Psychophysics, 64,* 867–881.

Colby, C., & Goldberg, M. (1999). Space and attention in parietal cortex. *Annual Review of Neuroscience, 22,* 319–349.

Collewijn, H., Van der Steen, J., & Steinman, R. M. (1985). Human eye movements associated with blinks and prolonged eyelid closure. *Journal of Neurophysiology, 54,* 11–27.

Coltheart, M. (1980). Iconic memory and visible persistence. *Perception & Psychophysics, 27,* 183–228.

Corbetta, M., Kincade, J. M., Ollinger, J. M., McAvoy, M. P., & Shulman, G. L. (2000). Voluntary orienting is dissociated from target detection in human posterior parietal cortex. *Nature Neuroscience, 3,* 292–297.

D'Esposito, M., Aguirre, G., Zarahn, E., Ballard, D., Shin, R., & Lease, J. (1998). Functional MRI studies of spatial and nonspatial working memory. *Cognitive Brain Research, 7,* 1–13.

Deubel, H., & Schneider, W. X. (1996). Saccade target selection and object recognition: Evidence for a common attentional mechanism. *Vision Research, 36,* 1993–1997.

Dick, A. O. (1969). Relations between the sensory register and short-term storage in tachistoscopic recognition. *Journal of Experimental Psychology, 82,* 279–284.

Di Lollo, V. (1978). On the spatiotemporal interactions of brief visual displays. In R. H. Day & G. V. Stanley (Eds.), *Studies in perception* (pp. 39–55). Perth: University of Western Australia Press.

Doane, M. G. (1980). Interactions of eyelids and tears in corneal wetting and the dynamics of the normal human eyeblink. *American Journal of Ophthalmology, 89,* 507–516.

Doughty, M. J. (2001). Consideration of three types of spontaneous eyeblink activity in normal humans: During reading and video display terminal use, in primary gaze, and while in conversation. *Optometry and Vision Science, 78,* 712–725.

Drew, G. C. (1951). Variations in reflex blink-rate during visual-motor tasks. *Quarterly Journal of Experimental Psychology, 3,* 73–88.

Duysens, J., Orban, G. A., Cremieux, J., & Maes, H. (1985). Visual cortical correlates of visible persistence. *Vision Research, 25,* 171–178.

Engel, G. R. (1970). An investigation of visual responses to brief stereoscopic stimuli. *Quarterly Journal of Experimental Psychology, 22,* 148–160.

Evinger, C. (1995). A brain stem reflex in the blink of an eye. *News in Physiological Sciences, 10,* 147–153.

Evinger, C., Manning, K. A., & Sibony, P. A. (1991). Eyelid movements. Mechanisms and normal data. *Investigative Ophthalmology and Visual Science, 32,* 387–400.

Fogarty, C., & Stern, J. A. (1989). Eye movements and blinks: Their relationship to higher cognitive processes. *International Journal of Psychophysiology, 8,* 35–42.

Fukuda, K. (2001). Eye blinks: New indices for the detection of deception. *International Journal of Psychophysiology, 40,* 239–245.

Fukuda, K., & Matsunaga, K. (1983). Changes in blink rate during signal discrimination tasks. *Japanese Psychological Research, 25,* 140–146.

Gawne, T. J., & Martin, J. M. (2000). Activity of primate V1 cortical neurons during blinks. *Journal of Neurophysiology, 84,* 2691–2694.

Goldstein, R., Bauer, L. O., & Stern, J. A. (1992). Effect of task difficulty and interstimulus interval on blink parameters. *International Journal of Psychophysiology, 13,* 111–117.

Goldstein, R., Walrath, L. C., Stern, J. A., & Strock, B. D. (1985). Blink activity in a discrimination task as a function of stimulus modality and schedule of presentation. *Psychophysiology, 22,* 629–635.

Gregory, R. L. (1952). Variations in blink-rate during nonvisual tasks. *Quarterly Journal of Experimental Psychology, 4,* 165–169.

Hall, A. A. (1945). The origin and purposes of blinking. *British Journal of Ophthalmology, 29,* 445–467.

Hari, R., Salmelin, R., Tissari, S. O., Kajola, M., & Virsu, V. (1994). Visual stability during eyeblinks. *Nature, 367,* 121–122.

Henderson, J. M. (1993). Visual attention and saccadic eye movements. In G. d'Ydewalle & J. Van Rensbergen (Eds.), *Perception and cognition: Advances in eye-movement research* (pp. 37–50). Amsterdam: North–Holland.

Hoffman, J. E., & Subramaniam, B. (1995). The role of visual attention in saccadic eye movements. *Perception and Psychophysics, 57,* 787–795.

Holland, M. K., & Tarlow, G. (1975). Blinking and thinking. *Perceptual and Motor Skills, 41,* 403–406.

Irwin, D. E. (2003). Eye movements and visual cognitive suppression. In D. E. Irwin & B. H. Ross (Eds.), *Cognitive vision, Vol. 42, Psychology of learning & motivation* (pp. 265–293). San Diego: Academic Press, Elsevier.

Irwin, D. E., & Brockmole, J. R. (2000). Mental rotation is suppressed during saccadic eye movements. *Psychonomic Bulletin and Review, 7,* 654–661.

Irwin, D. E., & Brockmole J. R. (2004). Suppressing *where* but not *what*: The effect of saccades on dorsal- and ventral-stream visual processing. *Psychological Science, 15,* 467–473.

Irwin, D. E., & Carlson-Radvansky, L. A. (1996). Suppression of cognitive activity during saccadic eye movements. *Psychological Science, 7,* 83–88.

Irwin, D. E., & Gordon, R. D. (1998). Eye movements, attention, and transsaccadic memory. *Visual Cognition, 5,* 127–155.

Irwin, D. E., & Thomas, L. E. (2007). The effect of saccades on number processing. *Perception & Psychophysics, 69,* 450–458.

Irwin, D. E., & Yeomans, J. M. (1986). Sensory registration and informational persistence. *Journal of Experimental Psychology: Human Perception and Performance, 12,* 343–360.

Jonides, J., Smith, E., Koeppe, R., Awh, E., Minoshima, S., & Mintun, M. (1993). Spatial working memory in humans as revealed by PET. *Nature, 363,* 623–625.

Kennard, D. W., & Glaser, G. H. (1964). An analysis of eyelid movements. *Journal of Nervous and Mental Disease, 139,* 31–48.

Klein, R. (1980). Does oculomotor readiness mediate cognitive control of visual attention? In R. S. Nickerson (Ed.), *Attention and performance VIII* (pp. 259–276). Hillsdale, NJ: Lawrence Erlbaum Associates.

Kowler, E., Anderson, E., Dosher, B., & Blaser, E. (1995). The role of attention in the programming of saccades. *Vision Research, 35,* 1897–1916.

Lawson, R. W. (1948). Blinking: Its role in physical measurement. *Nature, 161,* 154.

Loftus, G. R., & Irwin, D. E. (1998). On the relations among different measures of visible and informational persistence. *Cognitive Psychology, 35,* 135–199.

Manning, K. A., Riggs, L. A., & Komenda, J. K. (1983). Reflex eyeblinks and visual suppression. *Perception & Psychophysics, 34,* 250–256.

Matin, E. (1974). Saccadic suppression: A review and an analysis. *Psychological Bulletin, 81,* 899–917.

Matin, L. (1986). Visual localization and eye movements. In K. R. Boff, L. Kaufman, & J. P. Thomas (Eds.), *Handbook of perception and human performance* (Vol. 1, pp. 20.1–20.45). New York: John Wiley & Sons.

Mewhort, D. J. K., Campbell, A. J., Marchetti, F. M., & Campbell, J. I. D. (1981). Identification, localization, and "iconic" memory: An evaluation of the bar-probe task. *Memory & Cognition, 9,* 50–67.

Neisser, U. (1967). *Cognitive psychology.* New York: Appleton–Century–Crofts.

Orchard, L. N., & Stern, J. A. (1991). Blinks as an index of cognitive activity during reading. *Integrative Physiological and Behavioral Science, 26,* 108–116.

O'Regan, J. K., Deubel, H., Clark, J. J., & Rensink, R. A. (2000). Picture changes during blinks: Looking without seeing and seeing without looking. *Visual Cognition, 7,* 191–211.

Ponder, E., & Kennedy, W. P. (1927). On the act of blinking. *Quarterly Journal of Physiology, 18,* 89–110.

Poulton, E. C., & Gregory, R. L. (1952). Blinking during visual tracking. *Quarterly Journal of Experimental Psychology, 4,* 57–65.

Rayner, K., McConkie, G., & Ehrlich, S. (1978). Eye movements and integrating information across fixations. *Journal of Experimental Psychology: Human Perception and Performance, 4,* 529–544.

Ridder, W. H., & Tomlinson, A. (1995). Spectral characteristics of blink suppression in normal observers. *Vision Research, 35,* 2569–2578.

Ridder, W. H., & Tomlinson, A. (1997). A comparison of saccadic and blink suppression in normal observers. *Vision Research, 37,* 3171–3179.

Riggs, L. A., Kelly, J. P., Manning, K. A., & Moore, R. K. (1987). Blink-related eye movements. *Investigative Ophthalmology and Visual Science, 28,* 334–342.

Riggs, L. A., Merton, P. A., & Morton, H. B. (1974). Suppression of visual phosphenes during saccadic eye movements. *Vision Research, 14,* 997–1010.

Riggs, L. A., Volkmann, F. C., & Moore, R. K. (1981). Suppression of the blackout due to blinks. *Vision Research, 21,* 1075–1079.

Shepherd, M., Findlay, J., & Hockey, R. (1986). The relationship between eye movements and spatial attention. *Quarterly Journal of Experimental Psychology, 38A,* 475–491.

Sperling, G. (1963). A model for visual memory tasks. *Human Factors, 5,* 19–31.

Stern, J. A., & Skelly, J. J. (1984). The eye blink and workload consideration. *Proceedings of the Human Factors Society, 28,* 942–944.

Stern, J. A., Walrath, L. C., & Goldstein, R. (1984). The endogenous eyeblink. *Psychophysiology, 21,* 22–33.

Sternberg, S. (1966). High speed scanning in human memory. *Science, 153,* 652–654.

Stevenson, S. B., Volkmann, F. C., Kelly, J. P., & Riggs, L. A. (1986). Dependence of visual suppression on the amplitudes of saccades and blinks. *Vision Research, 26,* 1815–1824.

Supèr, H., Spekreijse, H., & Lamme, V. (2001). A neural correlate of working memory in the monkey primary visual cortex. *Science, 293,* 120–124.

Thomas, L. E., & Irwin, D. E. (2006). Voluntary eyeblinks disrupt iconic memory. *Perception & Psychophysics, 68,* 475–488.

Townsend, V. M. (1973). Loss of spatial and identity information following a tachistoscopic exposure. *Journal of Experimental Psychology, 98,* 113–118.

Treisman, A., & Gelade, G. (1980). A feature-integration theory of attention. *Cognitive Psychology, 12,* 97–136.

Uchikawa, K., & Sato, M. (1995). Saccadic suppression of achromatic and chromatic responses measured by increment-threshold spectral sensitivity. *Journal of the Optical Society of America A, 12,* 661–666.

VanderWerf, F., Brassinga, P., Reits, D., Aramideh, M., & Ongerboer de Visser, B. (2003). Eyelid movements: Behavioral studies of blinking in humans under different stimulus conditions. *Journal of Neurophysiology, 89,* 2784–2796.

Volkmann, F. C. (1986). Human visual suppression. *Vision Research, 26,* 1401–1416.

Volkmann, F. C., Riggs, L. A., & Moore, R. K. (1980). Eyeblinks and visual suppression. *Science, 207,* 900–902.

Wibbenmeyer, R., Stern, J. A., & Chen, S. C. (1983). Elevation of visual threshold associated with eyeblink onset. *International Journal of Neuroscience, 18,* 279–286.

Zuber, B. L., & Stark, L. (1966). Saccadic suppression: Elevation of visual threshold associated with saccadic eye movements. *Experimental Neurology, 16,* 65–79.

7

Visual Spatial Attention and Visual Short-Term Memory
Electromagnetic Explorations of Mind

PIERRE JOLICŒUR, ROBERTO DELL'ACQUA,
BENOIT BRISSON, NICOLAS ROBITAILLE, KEVIN SAUVÉ,
ÉMILIE LEBLANC, DAVID PRIME, STÉPHAN GRIMAULT,
RENÉ MAROIS, PAOLA SESSA, CHRISTOPHE GROVA,
JEAN-MARC LINA, and ANNE-SOPHIE DUBARRY

INTRODUCTION

Visual short-term memory has a very limited storage capacity of about three objects. Some stages of categorization and decision making appear also to have very sharp capacity limitations, sometimes as low as one representation. Early visual processing, on the other hand, is massively parallel and can deliver many more stimuli for further processing than can be stored or acted upon. In this chapter, we review recent work from our laboratories that explores how early and late attentional mechanisms interact to select and store information of interest to the observer. The studies are based on the analysis of electrophysiological and magnetoencephalographic recordings using paradigms that allowed us to track the moment-to-moment deployment of visual spatial attention and the participation of visual short-term memory in ongoing cognitive processing.

These studies showed that visual spatial attention modulates early cortical responses to attended stimuli, whether attention was deployed voluntarily or involuntarily; that the deployment of spatial attention is impaired by concurrent processing in the attentional blink and psychological refractory period paradigms; and that transfer to visual short-term memory is impaired and/or delayed by concurrent central processing. Finally, converging evidence from functional magnetic resonance imaging (fMRI), event-related potentials, event-related magnetic fields, and time-frequency analysis of magnetoencephalography data showed that activity of neurons in parietal cortex plays an important role in the representation of objects in visual short-term memory.

For thousands of years, thoughtful men and women have wondered how human beings perceive the world through vision, hearing, and other senses, and how they feel, remember, and think. Recent advances in physics, engineering, and psychology are enabling cognitive neuroscientists to provide answers with heretofore unparalleled accuracy and detail to these fundamental questions concerning the human psyche. In this chapter, we summarize recent work that combines basic methods of cognitive psychology with recent advances in electrophysiology, magnetoencephalography, and functional magnetic resonance imaging. This work illustrates how the convergence of these methods is enabling us to understand basic mechanisms of human visuospatial attention and visual short-term memory at the functional and neural levels.

Despite the wondrous complexity of the human brain, we are often severely limited in how we perceive and process information about the world. Although we would often like to think every possible thought at the same time, ample empirical evidence confirms the common-sense conclusion based on everyday experience that we can only entertain a small number of ideas at any given time. The number of ideas that we can entertain at the same time, in some cases, appears to be as few as one.

On the other hand, it is clear that the world often affords us the opportunity to process a great many different stimuli, each of which is capable of triggering a cascade of perceptions, object recognitions, associated memories, and reflections. Somewhere between the image on the retina and conscious awareness, there are massive restrictions in the transmission of information and restrictions in terms of representational and storage capacity that limit what we can perceive and remember from a visual scene.

Psychophysical studies have shown that the storage capacity of visual short-term memory is about three objects, on average (Vogel, Woodman, & Luck, 2001; see also Cowan, 2001). Given the severe processing rate and storage capacity limitations in later stages of processing, attentional selection of a subset of the possible inputs for further processing is often desirable (Sperling, 1960). In this chapter, we summarize recent work that enables us to track the encoding and maintenance of information in visual short-term memory.

Visual spatial attention consists of a set of mechanisms that selects one or more locations in the visual display for further processing. The selected information can then be subjected to more detailed processing, possibly leading to an overt response, and/or to storage in one or more types of memory. Single-cell electrophysiology has shown that the firing rate of cells in early visual cortex (i.e., as early as V1) increases when the cell participates in the processing of an attended stimulus (Roelfsema & Spekreijse, 2001). Interestingly, recent work using human electrophysiology has revealed a component of the event-related potential, called the N2pc, that appears to be a correlate of the deployment of visuospatial attention to lateralized visual stimuli (Luck & Hillyard, 1994).

Another event-related potential component, which we call the sustained posterior contralateral negativity (SPCN), tracks the involvement of visual short-term memory in stimulus processing (Jolicœur, Sessa, Dell'Acqua, & Robitaille, 2006a). The chapter is divided into two major parts. In the first part, we describe the N2pc and recent work showing how we can use this component to determine when and how subjects can or cannot deploy visuospatial attention to a visual target. In the second part, we review recent work focusing on the SPCN as an index of visual short-term memory.

THE ATTENTIONAL BLINK AND VISUAL SPATIAL ATTENTION

Impaired Deployment of Visual Spatial Attention During the Attentional Blink

Recent work in our laboratories focused on the ability to deploy visual spatial attention to a second visual target (in the periphery) while processing of another, previously presented target was still ongoing, during the period of the attentional blink. Initially, our motivation was to demonstrate the independence of the attentional blink and visual spatial attention. The independence assumption was based on previous work that had shown that the attentional blink appeared to be confined to relatively late stages of processing, such as the short-term consolidation of information in memory (Jolicœur, 1998; Jolicœur & Dell'Acqua, 1998, Sessa, Luria, Verleger, & Dell'Acqua, 2007; Vogel, Luck, & Shapiro, 1998). We quickly discovered that our initial assumption of independence between the attentional blink and the ability to deploy visuospatial attention was incorrect, as we summarize next.

The attentional blink paradigm usually presents two targets, T_1 and T_2, briefly; each is followed by a mask, often in the context of other distractor stimuli presented using rapid serial visual presentation. Jolicœur et al. (2006a) modified the attentional blink procedure, as illustrated in Figure 7.1; this enabled them to use human electrophysiology to track the deployment of spatial attention and encoding in visual short-term memory associated with the processing of the second target.

In the initial portion of each trial, we presented a sequence of distractor letters at fixation at a rate of 10 items per second. One of the letters in the sequence was replaced by a digit, and this was the first target, or T_1. The degree of central processing involvement was manipulated by instructing subjects to encode and remember this digit (report-T_1) or to ignore it (ignore-T_1). The second target, T_2, was presented following T_1 after one additional item in the central stream (lag 2, at a stimulus-onset asynchrony [SOA] of 200 ms, illustrated in Figure 7.1) or after seven additional items (lag 8, SOA of 800 ms). T_2 was also a digit; it was presented to the left or right of fixation and was either red (for half of the subjects) or green (for the others).

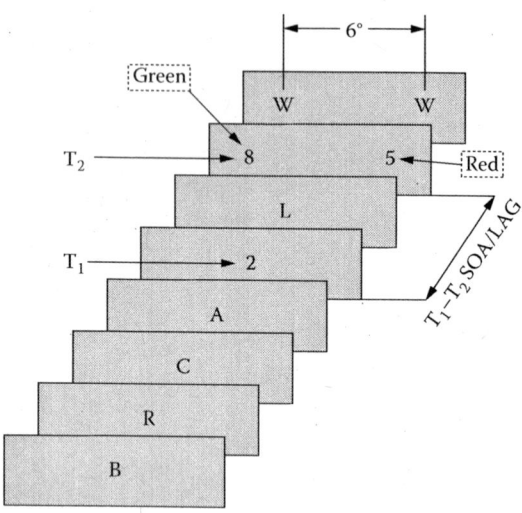

Figure 7.1   Modified attentional blink paradigm used in the experiment of Jolicœur et al. (2006a, *Psychological Research, 70,* 414–424). T_1 was a white digit presented at the center, followed by one distractor. T_2 was red (half of the subjects) or green, presented 3° to the left or right of fixation and followed by a pattern mask. T_1 was followed by one letter at fixation in the lag-2 condition (shown here) and by seven letters in the lag-8 condition (not shown).

Another digit was presented concurrently with T_2 on the other side of fixation and in the other color (e.g., in green if the target was red). The two digits in the T_2 time frame were followed by a bilateral mask (the letter W) to ensure that we would observe an attentional blink (Giesbrecht & Di Lollo, 1998; Jolicœur, 1999b). The task for T_2 was to encode and later report the identity of T_2, without moving the eyes. Recordings of the horizontal oculogram allowed us to verify that no subject moved his or her eyes more than 0.2° in the direction of the target, on average.

The logic of the design was as follows. In the report-T_1 condition, encoding T_1 should occupy central mechanisms and this should produce the conditions required to observe an attentional blink (e.g., Jolicœur, 1999a; Vogel et al., 1998). When T_2 is presented at lag 2, only a short time after T_1, some aspect of the processing of T_2 suffers because a central mechanism or capacity is occupied by the ongoing processing of T_1 (Jolicœur, 1999a). When T_2 is presented at lag 8 and thus a relatively long time after T_1, the encoding of T_1 should be completed and any interference on T_2 would likely be attributable to the load of maintaining a memory representation of T_1 until the end of the trial (Jolicœur & Dell'Acqua, 1998).

Trial blocks in which T_1 could be ignored provided a control condition with identical physical stimulation to that in the report-T_1 condition, but without the processing costs associated with the encoding and retention of a representation of T_1 (Jolicœur, 1999a; Raymond, Shapiro, & Arnell, 1992).

But how would we know whether subjects succeeded or failed to deploy visuospatial attention to T_2? The behavioral results alone would be ambiguous. Failing to report the correct identity of T_2 could occur because of a failure to deploy attention to T_2 or to a failure at later stages of processing (e.g., memory encoding) despite successful deployment of spatial attention.

This is where we capitalized on the potential of human electrophysiology to track processing at intermediate stages of processing between stimulus and response. The selection of a visual target for further processing is often associated with an electrophysiological response, called the N2pc, that has been studied extensively by several researchers—most particularly by Luck and his colleagues (e.g., Dell'Acqua, Pesciarelli, Jolicœur, Eimer, & Peressotti, 2007; Eimer, 1996; Girelli & Luck, 1997; Jolicœur et al., 2006a; Luck, Girelli, McDermott, & Ford, 1997; Luck & Hillyard, 1994; Woodman & Luck, 2003). The N2pc event-related potential (ERP) is a lateralized response characterized by a greater negativity over the hemisphere contralateral to the visual field of a target relative to the response over the hemisphere ipsilateral to the target.

The N2pc difference waveform is computed by subtracting the ipsilateral from the contralateral responses of corresponding electrode pairs positioned symmetrically about the midline (e.g., T5, T6; O1, O2; Jasper, 1958) for lateralized visual targets. It is usually found from about 180–280 ms after target onset and is maximal at posterior electrode sites—often between O1 and T5, and O2 and T6, in the 10-20 system (Jasper, 1958) or PO7/PO8 as this position is named in the 10-10 system (American Electroencephalographic Society, 1994) (e.g., see Brisson & Jolicœur, 2007a, 2007b; Luck & Hillyard, 1994; Robitaille & Jolicœur, 2006a). Note that we used a minimum of 200 trials per condition (for each subject) in experiments in which the N2pc component was measured to ensure an adequate signal-to-noise ratio in the event-related electrophysiological results. This is many times more trials per condition than are typically used in behavioral studies and required modifications of the typical experimental designs (e.g., including fewer SOA conditions).

In short, when attention is deployed on a target in the left visual field, we should observe a greater negativity at right-sided posterior electrodes relative to the voltage recorded at corresponding left-sided electrodes. Conversely, when attention is deployed to the right, we should observe a negativity on the left relative to the voltage on the right. Woodman and Luck (2003) used the N2pc to track the deployment of visuospatial attention in the context of a visual search task. In the present work, we used a simple search task in which one target (T_2) was presented in isolation in one visual field and one distractor was presented in the other visual field.

This combination of different paradigms allowed us to study the relationship between the mechanisms that mediate visuospatial attention and those that mediate central attentional operations. By "central attention" we mean post-perceptual operations that encompass response selection, memory retrieval, and short-term consolidation and have been shown to impose large-capacity demands when performed concurrently with other operations (e.g., Jolicœur & Dell'Acqua, 1998).

Other research had shown that increases in central attentional load can lead to an increase in the degree to which distracting stimuli interfere with processing of a target (de Fockert, Rees, Frith, & Lavie, 2001; Jiang & Chun, 2001). These authors argued that spatial selection is impaired when central attention is engaged on a concurrent task. This conclusion regarding spatial attention is somewhat indirect, however, because intruding information from distractors could result from a loss of control at other, later stages of processing (e.g., response selection).

The experiment of Jolicœur et al. (2006a) provided a more direct test of the dependence or independence of the control of spatial attention on central attentional mechanisms because the N2pc can only arise as a result of a differential processing of T_2 relative to the distractor in the T_2 visual display. The presence of this distractor is important for a number of reasons.

The first is to equate the low-level sensory responses to the T_2 display across the left and right hemispheres. Had we presented T_2 by itself, large interhemispheric differences would have been observed at posterior electrode sites because of the structure of the visual system, and these interhemispheric differences would not be informative regarding the locus of visuospatial attention. Stimuli presented in the left visual field project initially only to the right hemisphere, whereas stimuli in the right visual field project initially only to the left hemisphere in primary visual cortex (e.g., Coren, Ward, & Enns, 1994; Zeki, 1993). Event-related potentials to a single stimulus in the left or right visual field would thus have produced large interhemispheric differences (e.g., Bayard, Gosselin, Robert, & Lassonde, 2004; Luck & Hillyard, 1994), making it more difficult to distinguish attentional effects from purely low-level sensory effects. The presence of an equivalent equiluminant form in each hemifield produces a balanced electrophysiological response of early visual cortex across the two hemispheres (counterbalancing eliminates any small residual differences). Differences in ERPs across the hemispheres for such displays can only arise as a function of differential processing due to attentional selection of one of the two stimuli (see Luck & Hillyard, 1994, and Woodman & Luck, 2003, for further discussion).

The second reason to use a digit as a lateral distractor was to increase the probability that subjects would deploy visuospatial attention to T_2 by making the use of a late-selection strategy less useful. In order to give the correct response, subjects had to select the correct digit—namely, the one in the target color. If the display contained only one digit (e.g., paired with a letter), then subjects might have been able to perform the task without deploying visuospatial attention to the target location. They might have been able to use differences in semantic activation to perform the task (see Duncan, 1980, 1983). Although prior work showed that an N2pc could be observed even when a single alphanumeric character was used with a distractor that was not a letter (e.g., Eimer, 1996), the presence of two digits in the display was meant to encourage subjects to use color to guide visuospatial attention to one of them. Doing so would then engage differential processing at the location of T_2, which should lead to a greater contralateral negativity at posterior electrode sites, thus producing an N2pc ERP.

Figure 7.2 shows the mean accuracy of report for T_2 for 16 observers who performed a total of about 800 trials: 400 in a block in which they had to report the identities of T_1 and T_2 and 400 in a block in which they reported only the identity of T_2. Within each block, trials with a lag of 2 between T_1 and T_2 (SOA of 200 ms) and trials with a lag of 8 (SOA of 800 ms) were intermixed at random. The

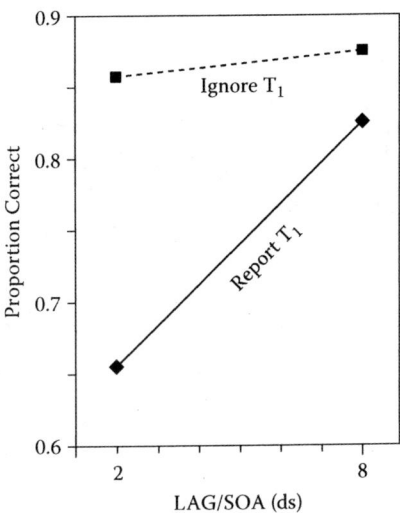

Figure 7.2   Proportion correct report of T_2, for each lag, in the ignore-T_1 and the report-T_1 conditions in the experiment of Jolicœur et al. (2006a, *Psychological Research, 70,* 414–424).

results replicated the typical attentional blink pattern: Accuracy was generally high and unaffected by lag when T_1 could be ignored; in contrast, accuracy decreased sharply as lag was reduced when T_1 had to be encoded and remembered for later report.

Figure 7.3 shows the most important electrophysiological results. The waveforms were computed by averaging electroencephalographic activity at each electrode and in each condition (attend/ignore T_1 by lag) across trials, time locked to the onset of T_2 (*time* = 0 in the figure). The displayed N2pc difference waveforms were computed by subtracting the waveform recorded at a particular electrode ipsilateral relative to the side of the target from the waveform recorded at the corresponding electrode on the contralateral side.

It is clear that our original supposition that the attentional blink would not influence the deployment of visuospatial attention was soundly refuted by the results. Had this hypothesis been correct, the amplitude of the N2pc would have been the same in all conditions. Clearly, this was not the case. The N2pc was largest when T_1 could be ignored (and when there was no attentional blink deficit) and smallest when T_1 had to be reported. Furthermore, when T_1 had to be reported and the T_1–T_2 lag was short (maximum attentional blink), the N2pc was completely abolished.

A control experiment showed that the location of T_2 was well perceived despite the attentional blink, ruling out a failure of color perception as an explanation for the results (Jolicœur et al., 2006a).

The results suggest that increasing the processing load associated with T_1 systematically reduced the differential allocation of attention to T_2.

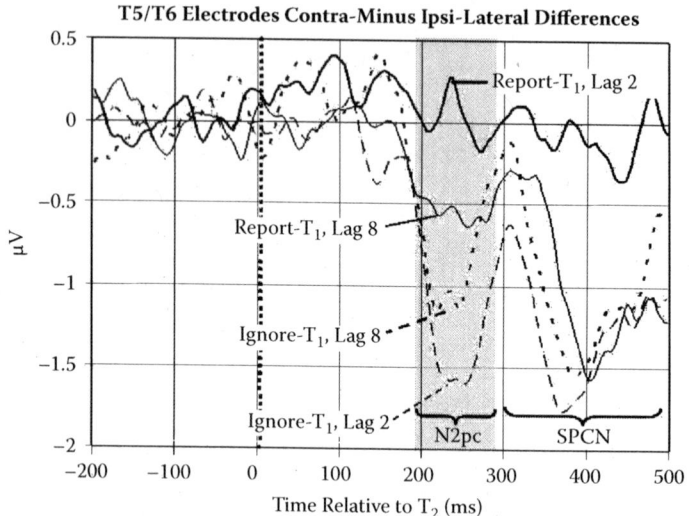

Figure 7.3   Contralateral minus ipsilateral difference waves used to isolate the N2pc and the SPCN at electrode sites T5/T6, for the four conditions in the experiment of Jolicœur et al. (2006a, *Psychological Research*, 70, 414–424). The shaded region shows the time window used to quantify the N2pc.

Spatial Capture in the Attentional Blink Paradigm

We wondered whether the sharply suppressed N2pc in the report-T_1, lag-2 condition could have resulted from a failure to disengage from the central position on the screen, at the location of T_1, rather than from interference taking place at later, central stages of processing. We performed several experiments to address this issue.

Consider first the experiment of Jolicœur, Sessa, Dell'Acqua, and Robitaille (2006b). This experiment had the same structure as the one just described, except that the color of T_1 matched the color of T_2. In the experiment just reviewed, T_1 was white and only T_2 and the T_2 distractor were colored. Perhaps the reason spatial attention could not be deployed efficiently to T_2 in that experiment was that a different selection filter had to be used for T_1 and T_2, and changing from selection on the basis of category (digit vs. letter, for T_1) to selection on the basis of color (red vs. green, for T_2) could not be done in parallel with mechanisms that redeploy visuospatial attention.

We reasoned that coloring T_1 and T_2 in the same way would allow subjects to adopt a single selection filter to pull out T_1 and T_2 from distractors. Once a selection filter was in place, it might be possible for attention to shift to T_2 despite simultaneous processing of T_1 (despite the attentional blink) because the same top-down selection filter could be used for T_1 and T_2.

The results, shown in Figure 7.4, were clear-cut: There was a large and statistically significant reduction in the amplitude of the N2pc as lag was reduced when T_1 had to be reported. Thus, despite the fact that T_1 and T_2 could be selected on the

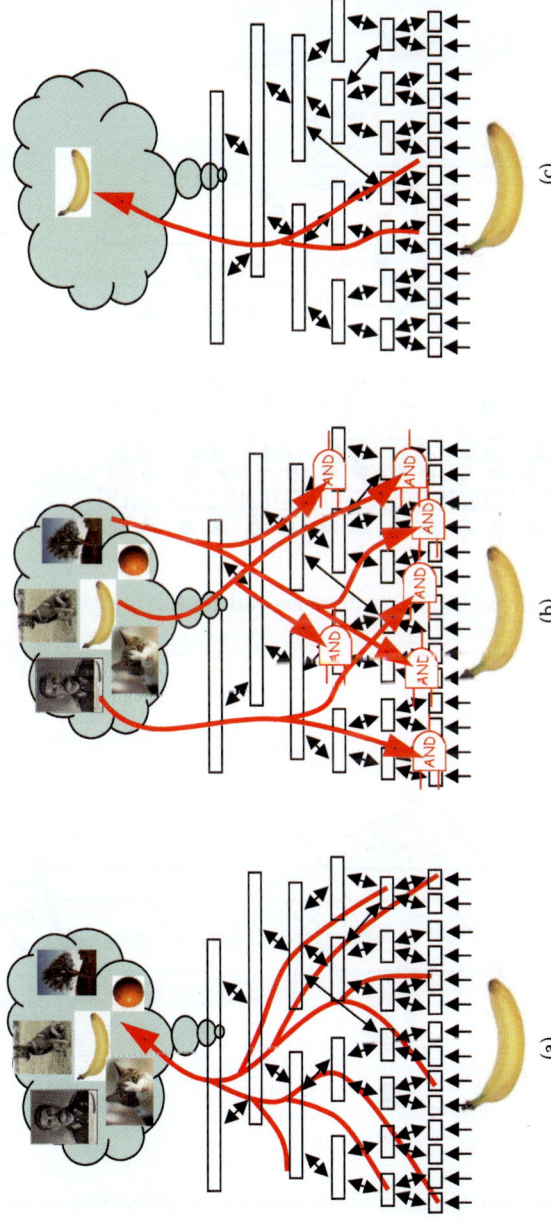

Figure 2.3 Schematic illustration of how the process of object identification might take place within a hierarchical cortical architecture based on iterative reentrant signaling between brain regions connected by two-way pathways.

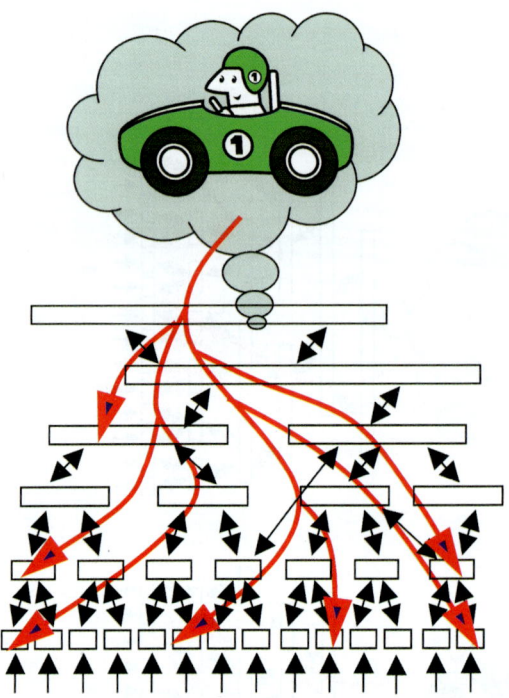

Figure 2.4 Sketch of a hypothetical reentrant network capable of mediating expectations and predictions.

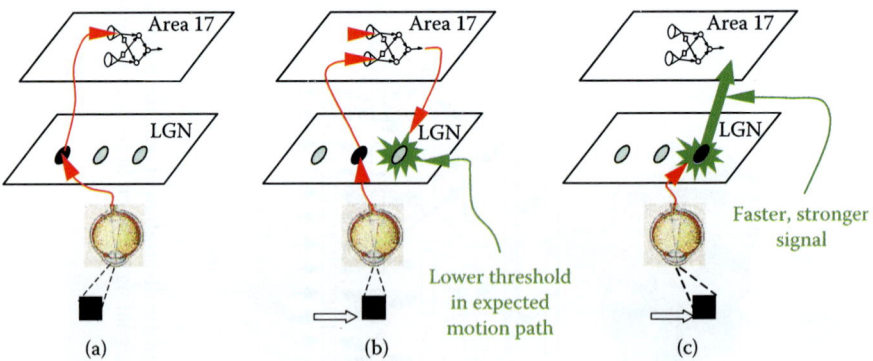

Figure 2.5 Schematic representation of the sequence of processing events leading to greater sensitivity to stimuli in the expected direction of motion. (After Sillito, A. M. et al., 1994, *Nature*, 369, 479–482.)

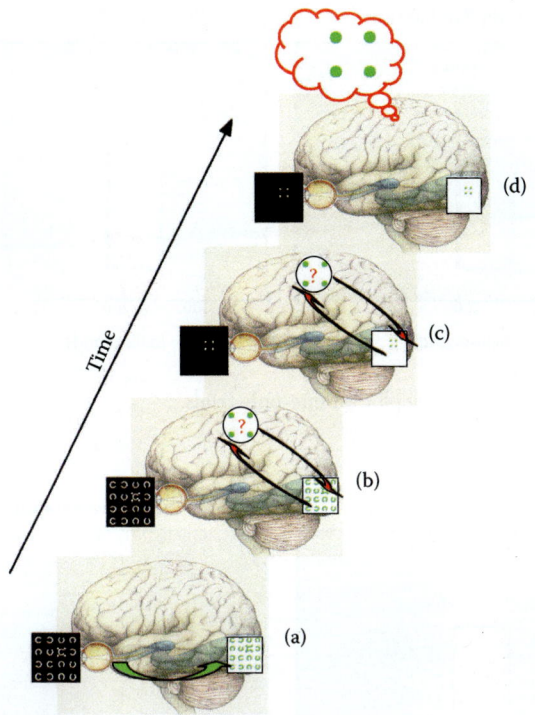

Figure 2.9 Schematic representation of the sequence of reentrant-processing events involved in object-substitution masking. See text for explanation.

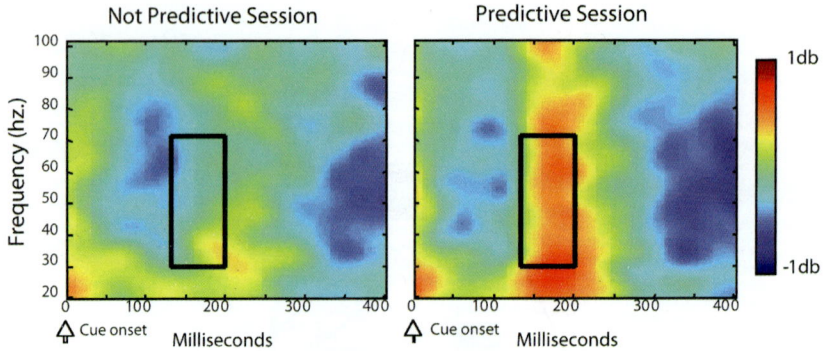

Figure 3.11　Time-frequency plot for cue-only trials.

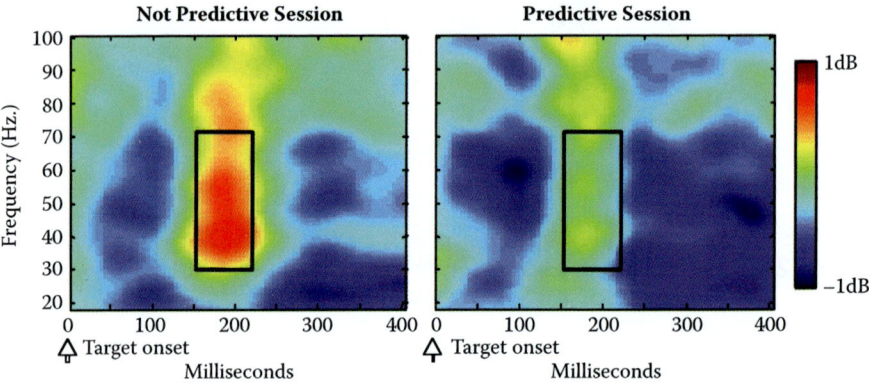

Figure 3.12　Time-frequency plot for valid trials.

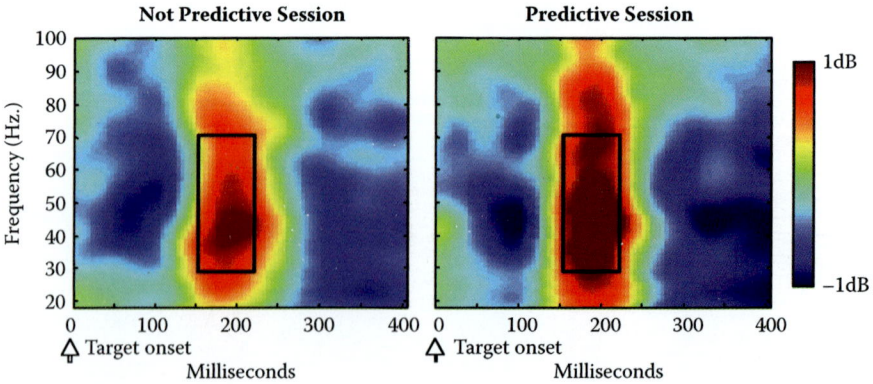

Figure 3.13　Time-frequency plot for invalid trials.

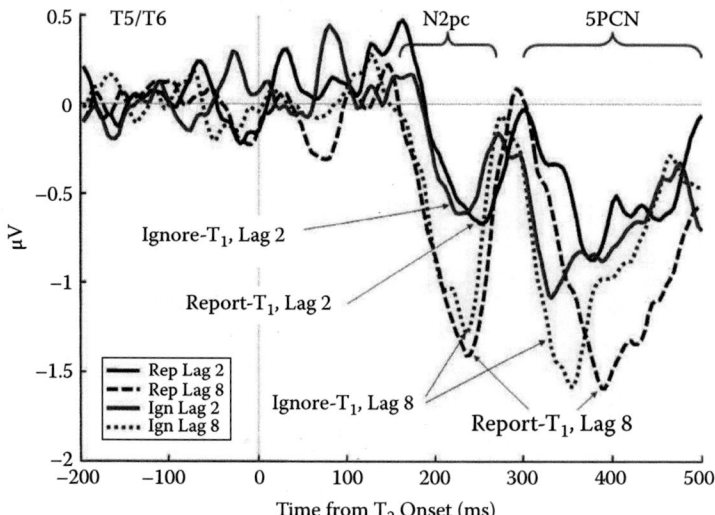

Figure 7.4 Electrophysiological results from the experiment of Jolicœur et al. (2006b, *European Journal of Cognitive Psychology, 18,* 560–578). Contralateral minus ipsilateral difference waves for the T5/T6 electrode pair, for each condition (ignore-T_1 vs. report-T_1, at lags 2 vs. 8). The N2pc component is visible in the 160- to 270-ms time window. Note the sustained posterior contralateral negativity observed from 300 to 500 ms.

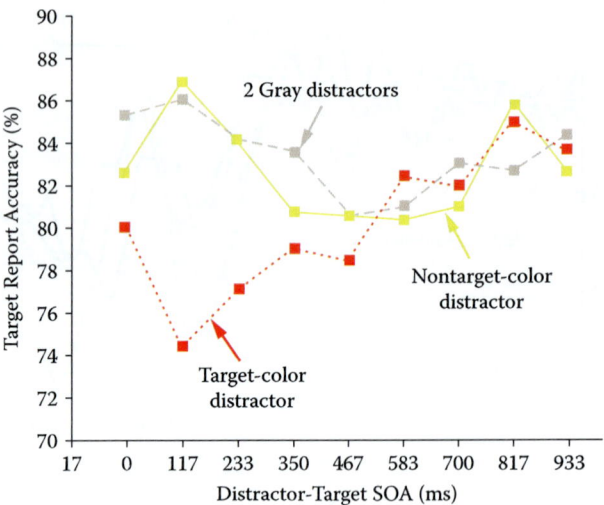

Figure 7.10   Results of Leblanc & Jolicœur (2005, *Canadian Journal of Experimental Psychology*, 59, 124–131). Percent correct report of the identity of a colored digit, presented at fixation in a rapid serial visual presentation stream of digits in other colors, as a function of the color of the two lateralized distractors and of the distractors-target SOA. Both distractors could be gray, one could be gray and the other the target color, or one could be gray and the other a nontarget color.

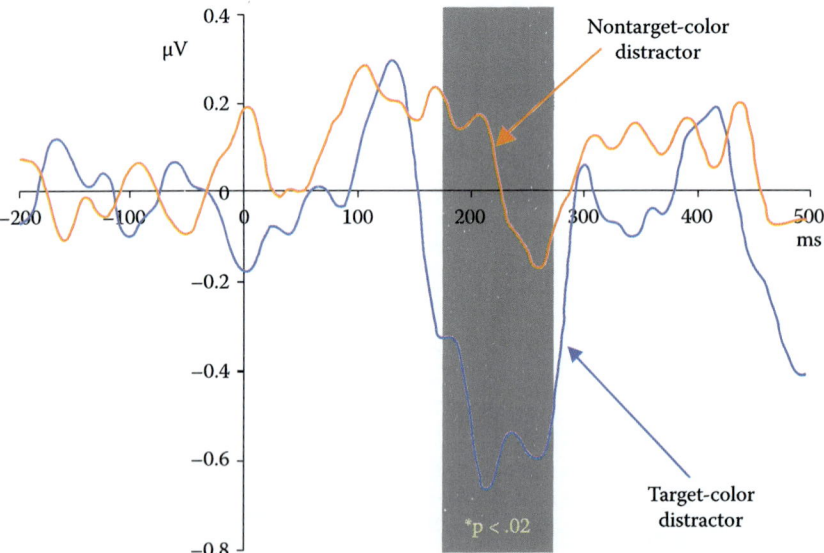

Figure 7.11   Results of Leblanc et al. (2008, *Journal of Cognitive Neuroscience*, 20, 657–671), Experiment 1. Electrophysiological, event-related difference waves, contralateral minus ipsilateral, relative to the side of presentation of the colored distractor, time locked with the onset of the distractor frame, as a function of the color of the lateralized distractors.

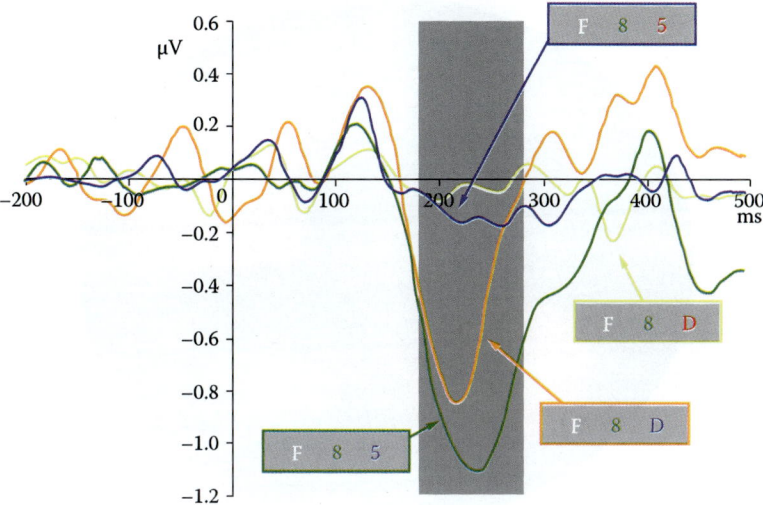

Figure 7.12 Results of Leblanc et al. (2008, *Journal of Cognitive Neuroscience, 20*, 657–671), Experiment 2. Electrophysiological, event-related difference waves, contralateral minus ipsilateral, relative to the side of presentation of the colored distractor, time locked with the onset of the distractor frame. The labels show the possible content of a distractor frame (just prior to the target digit) for a subject searching for a blue digit in the central rapid serial visual presentation stream. A blue digit distractor is thus a target-color distractor in the target category (blue waveform); a blue letter is a target-color distractor in the nontarget category (yellow waveform). Notice the N2pc for these conditions and the larger and longer N2pc for the target-color, target-category, distractor (blue waveform). Peripheral distractors in other colors would be in nontarget colors for this subject (green and orange waveforms), for which N2pc amplitude was not statistically different from zero.

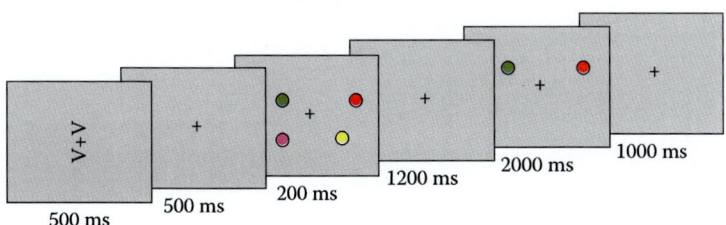

Figure 7.15 Sequence of events in the experiment of Robitaille et al. (2009, *Neurophysiology, 46*, 1080–1089. The stimuli were disks in different color).

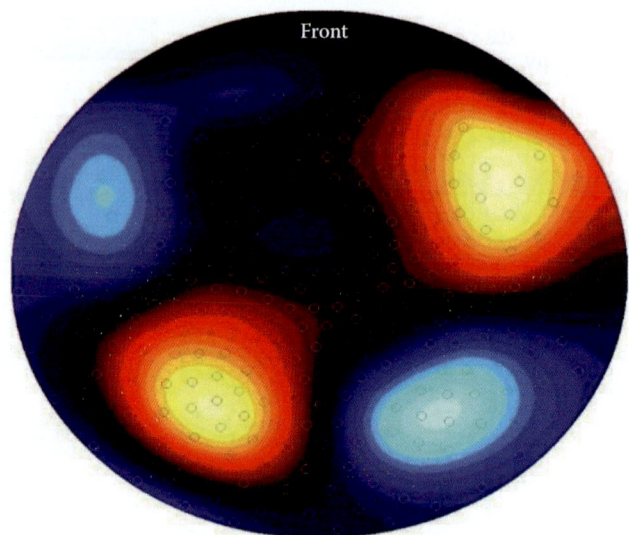

Front

Time: 0.733333s

Figure 7.16 Grand average event-related magnetic field distribution obtained by subtracting the average magnetic field distribution observed when subjects held two objects in visual short-term memory from the distribution observed when they held four objects in visual short-term memory (experiment of Robitaille et al., 2009, *Psychophysiology, 46*, 1080–1089). The averages were taken over a wide time window during the retention interval (500–1,000 ms). Blue indicates an outward field and red an inward one.

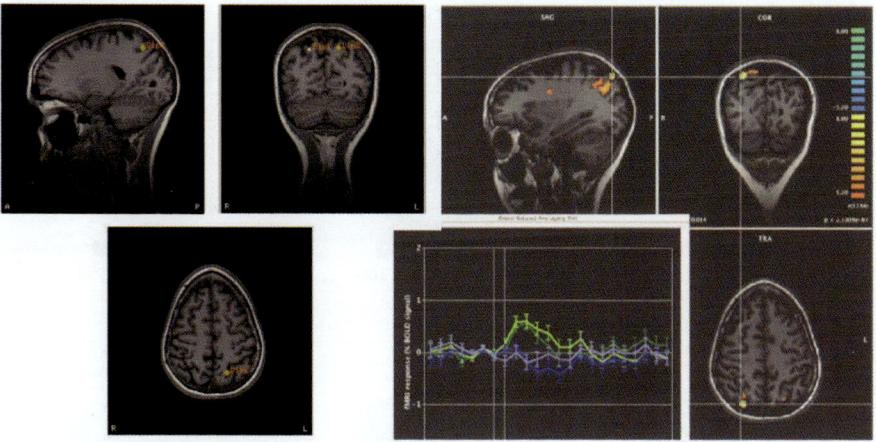

Figure 7.17 Results from a single observer in an unpublished study by Robitaille et al. (2009, manuscript in preparation, Department of Psychology, University of Montreal) using the paradigm illustrated in Figure 7.15. The left side shows a dipole fit analysis for magnetoencephalography results using a pair of symmetric dipoles fit to the memory load effect illustrated in Figure 7.16. The right side shows that, as in the study of Todd & Marois (2004), increasing the load in visual short-term memory produces a BOLD response activation peak at the border between occipital and parietal cortex when the same subject was tested using fMRI using a close variant of the paradigm (adapted for fMRI testing). Note that one of the dipole pairs in the magnetoencephalography results was localized in the same region as the fMRI activation peak, suggesting that the two methods converge nicely in suggesting that a region in the occipitoparietal border plays a special role in the retention of information in visual short-term memory.

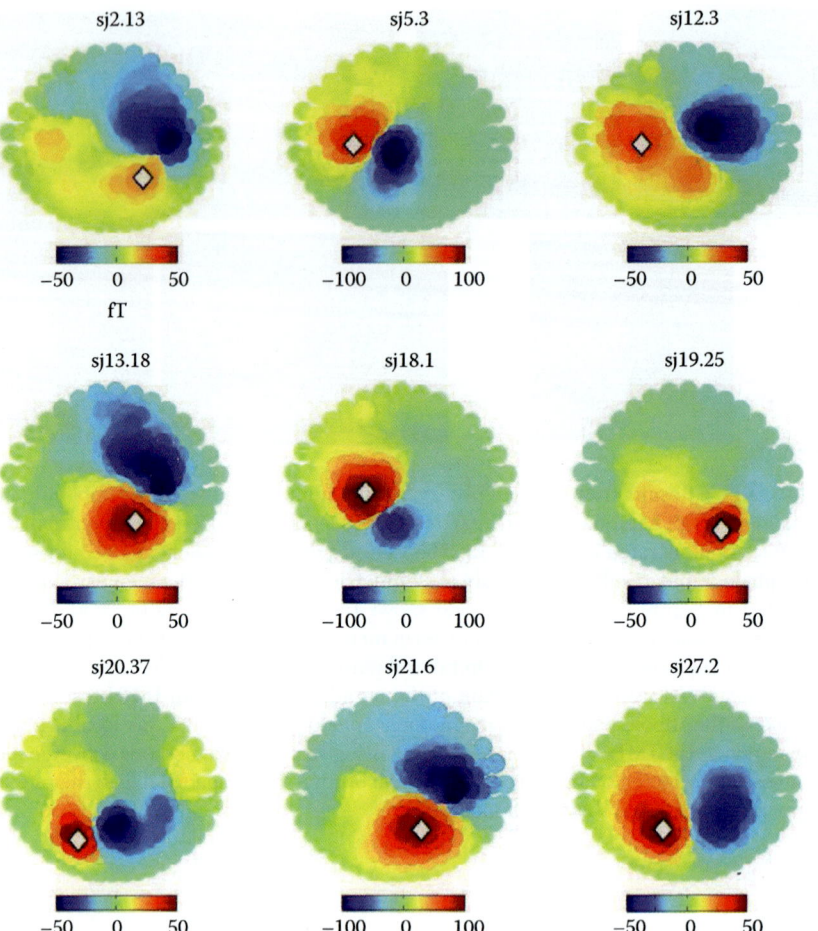

Figure 7.18 Magnetic field across 275 sensors for the parietal component exhibiting a large memory load difference extracted from the independent components analysis in each of nine subjects. Red indicates an outward magnetic field and blue an inward one. Most subjects exhibit a dipolar field over parietal cortex indicating an upward-oriented current located midway between the maximum outgoing sensor (diamond) and maximum ingoing sensor (darkest blue). This dipolar pattern occurred in the left hemisphere in some subjects (sj5, sj18) and the right hemisphere (sj13, sj21) in others. Some subjects (sj2, sj12) exhibited an apparent mixture of parietal sources in two hemispheres. In other subjects (sj20, sj27), the parietal source maximally sensitive to load was located more posteriorly. Most of these subjects had several other dipolar components in other areas that also exhibited load differences. Top sensors cover anterior cortex. The diamond denotes the maximal positive sensor (whose time course is shown in the next figure).

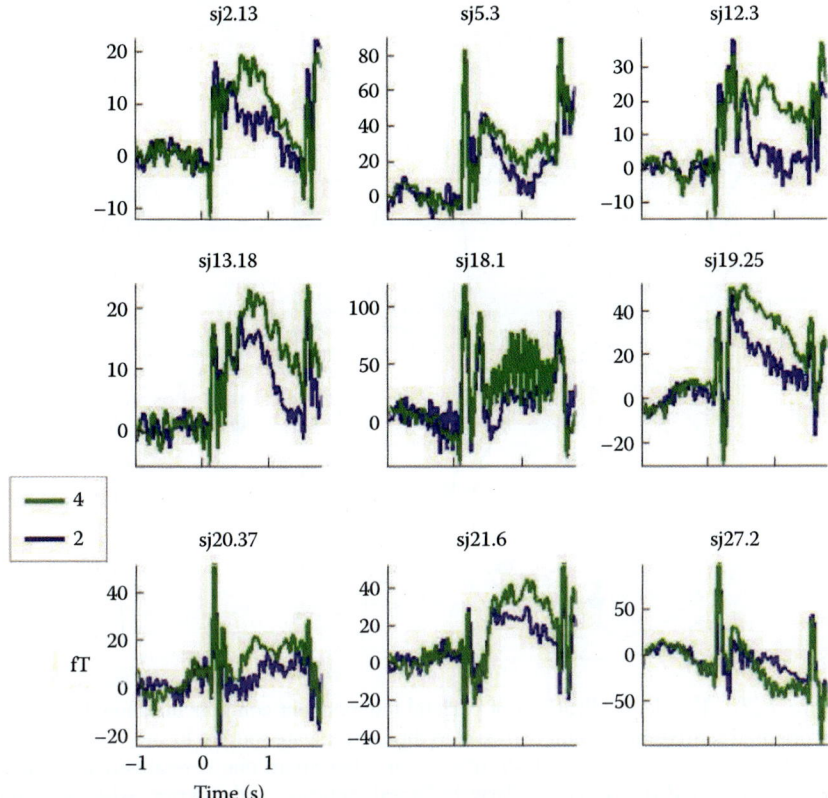

Figure 7.19 Waveforms of independent components exhibit large amplitude responses during retention of four objects versus two objects. All subjects but one show activation in both memory load conditions; however, retention of four objects results in higher amplitude activation of this source, specifically during the retention period, where the differences in mean amplitude (500–1,400 ms) were significant (in a within-subjects *t*-test over trials) for all these subjects; $p < .001$ for all subjects except Subject 27. Note also the sharp wave preceding and following the memory retention period, which may indicate the arrival of visual information into this parietal source. The first sharp wave (at about 100–200 ms) does not show large memory-load differences, but the latter one does (at about 1,800 ms). These activation patterns suggest that the parietal source maintains visual information during the retention interval.

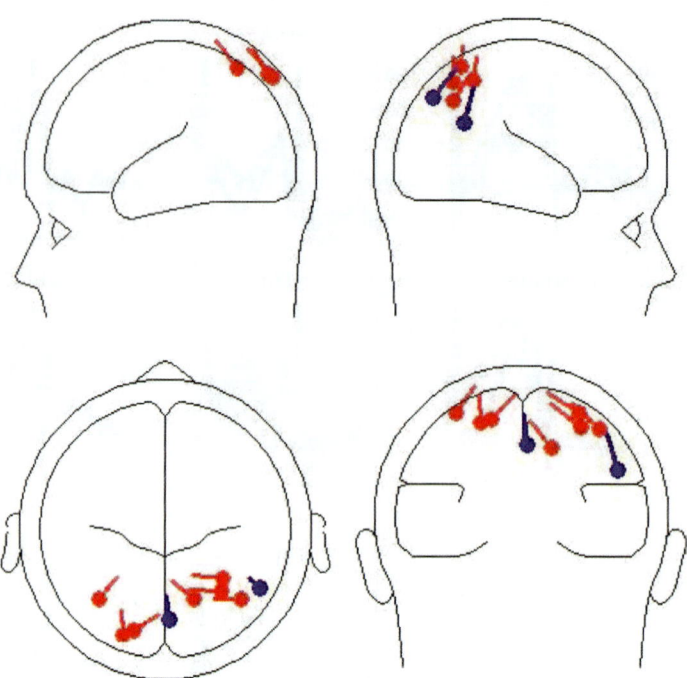

Figure 7.20 Dipole localizations of parietal independent components show many similarly oriented sources in parietal cortex. Red dipoles indicate sources located clearly within parietal cortex. Blue dipoles indicate sources in other areas: one is relatively medial and posterior (sj27) and the other is relatively lateral, anterior, and inferior (sj19). The most anterior left hemisphere dipole location is similar to those on the right, with an opposite (mirror) orientation. The mean goodness of fit of the red dipoles was 90.1%. The mean Talairach coordinates for the red dipoles is X: 27.1, Y: −46.04, Z: 50.0, after all the X axis (left–right) values are made positive for averaging.

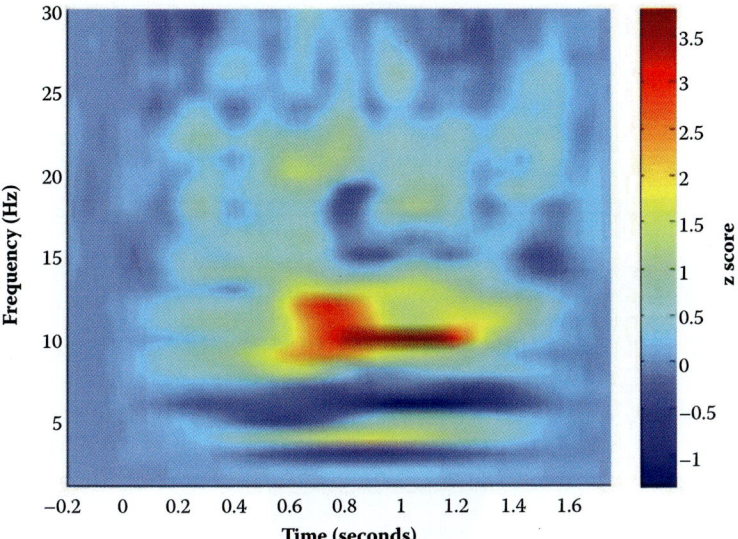

Figure 7.21 Results of time-frequency analysis (z-score relative to prestimulus baseline averaged over 11 subjects) for the contralateral sensor with the largest power in the alpha band, during the retention interval. This map shows the difference in z-score for the load-4 condition and the load-2 condition. Frequency is plotted on the ordinate and time (in seconds) on the abscissa. The color in the graph indicates the value of the z-score at that frequency and time. Note the large yellow-red band at about 10 Hz, from 500 to 1,400 ms, that indicates that α-band power increased significantly during the retention interval as memory load increased. See Grimault et al., 2009, *Human Brain Mapping, 30*, 3378–3392 for further details.

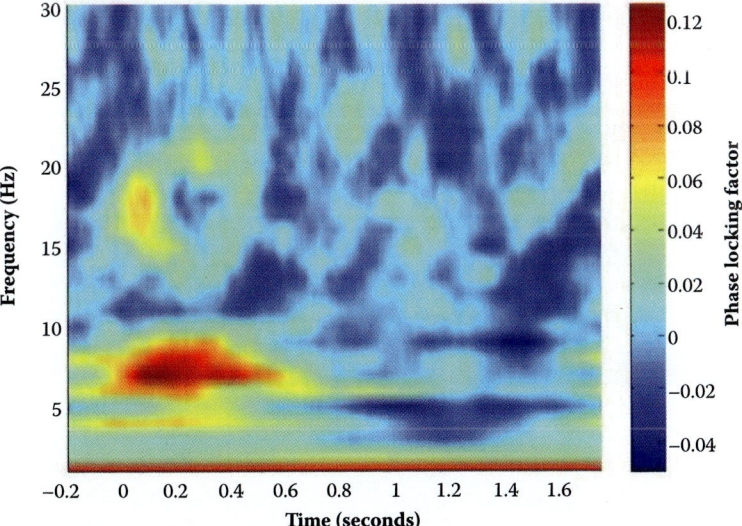

Figure 7.22 Differences in trial-by-trial phase locking across the load-4 encode right condition and the load-2 encode right condition. Time (in seconds) is on the abscissa and frequency on the ordinate. The color in the figure codes the degree to which an occurs at the same relative phase from one trial to the next. In this difference map, we examined how trial-by-trial phase locking varied across memory loads. There was greater phase locking in load-4 trials than load-2 trials, but only immediately after the onset of the memory array, probably indicating a greater event-related response in load-4 trials.

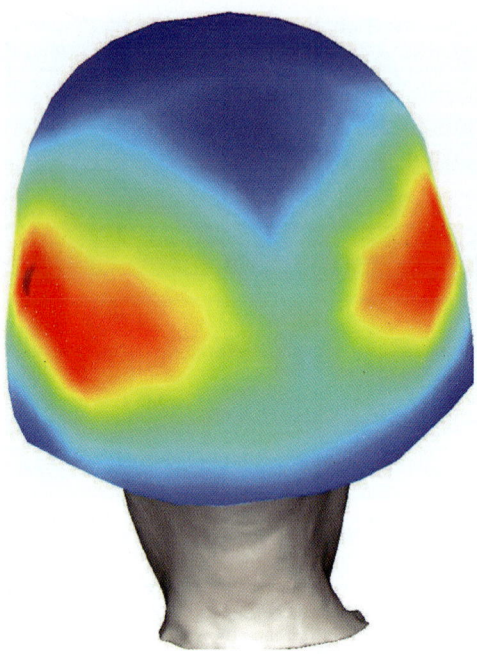

Figure 7.23 Sensor distribution of the power in the α-band during the retention interval (500–1,200 ms) based on time-frequency analysis for one observer in the load-4, right, condition.

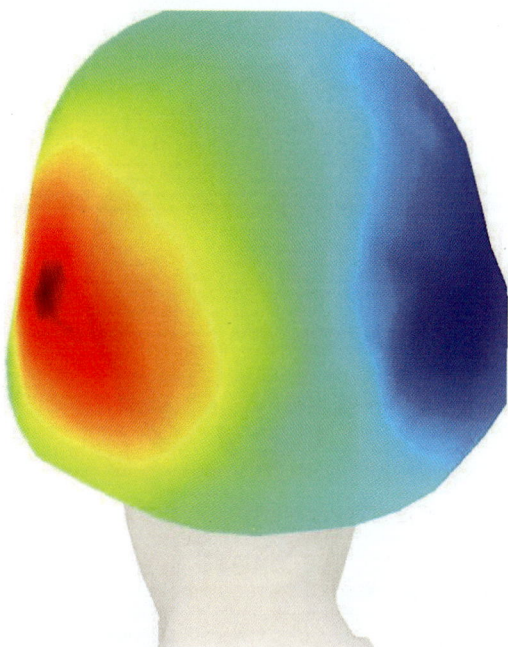

Figure 7.24 Sensor map of aligned α-band signal amplitude, using a sensor over the left hemisphere as the reference sensor. This map shows a strong peak over the left hemisphere, indicating phase-locked activity, and a peak over the right hemisphere, also indicating phase-locked activity (relative to the reference sensor), but also indicating a significant phase shift (indicated by the change in sign of the induced activity).

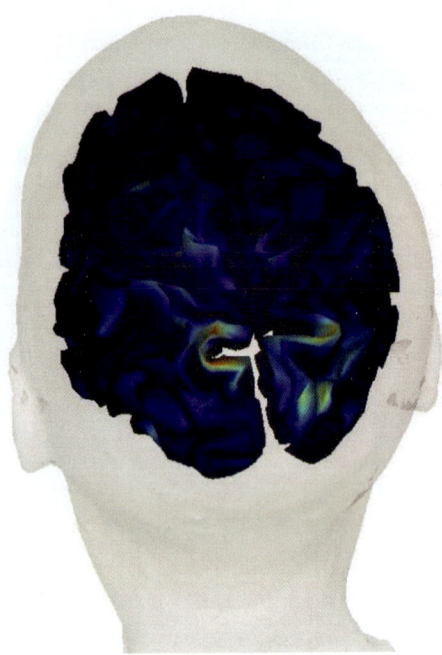

Figure 7.25 Source localization of induced activity in the α-band using the method of maximum entropy on the mean (Grova et al. 2006), using the method developed by Grimault et al. (2009, *Human Brain Mapping*, *30*, 3378–3392). The reconstructed surface at the border between gray and white matter was used to constrain the inverse problem. Note the peaks on the occipitoparietal girus, at the border between parietal and occipital cortex.

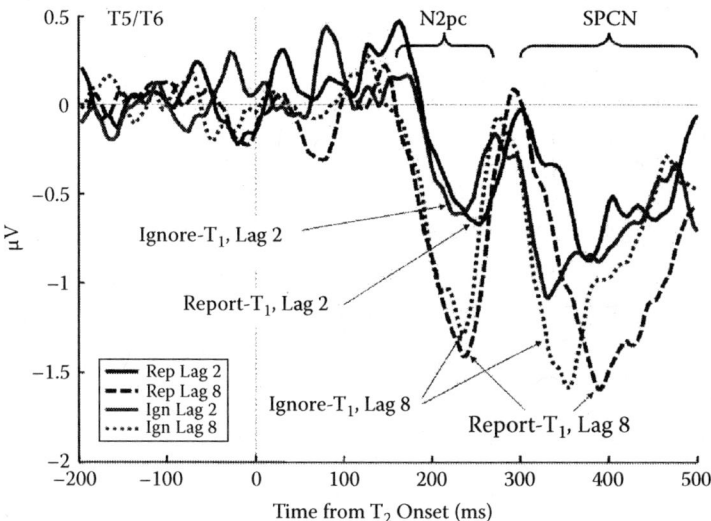

Figure 7.4   (See color insert following page 150.) Electrophysiological results from the experiment of Jolicœur et al. (2006b, *European Journal of Cognitive Psychology, 18,* 560–578). Contralateral minus ipsilateral difference waves for the T5/T6 electrode pair, for each condition (ignore-T_1 vs. report-T_1, at lags 2 vs. 8). The N2pc component is visible in the 160–270-ms time window. Note the sustained posterior contralateral negativity observed from 300–500 ms.

basis of color—indeed, the same color—the attentional blink sharply attenuated the N2pc, suggesting that spatial attention could not be allocated to T_2 as efficiently during the attentional blink a few hundred milliseconds later.

Although subjects could use color to select T_1, they could also use the category difference between T_1 (digit) and central stream distractors (letters). Perhaps this experiment produced results similar to those of the previous one because, again, different selection criteria were used for T_1 and T_2. However, the results from the control condition, in which T_1 could be ignored (in principle), suggest that this alternative account of results is unlikely. As can be seen in Figure 7.4, we observed a reduction in N2pc amplitude as lag was reduced in the ignore-T_1 condition that was equivalent to the reduction observed in the report-T_1 condition.

Why should this occur, if T_1 was ignored? We suppose that, in fact, adopting a selection filter for a particular color to select T_2 made it difficult to ignore T_1 when T_1 was also in the same color. Indeed, accuracy of report for T_2 was about the same in the ignore-T_1 condition as in the report-T_1 condition and exhibited a large lag effect. This suggests that T_1 could not be easily ignored, as shown in Figure 7.5. The fact that color had such a powerful effect on the pattern of results in the ignore-T_1 condition (comparing across the first two experiments, Figures 7.2 and 7.5) suggests to us that it was unlikely that subjects attempted to select T_1 based on another, more complex attribute.

The results of the Jolicœur et al. (2006b) study, in which the attenuation of N2pc was no larger in the encode-T_1 condition than in the ignore-T_1 condition, raised the possibility that the modulations of N2pc occurred mainly at the level of

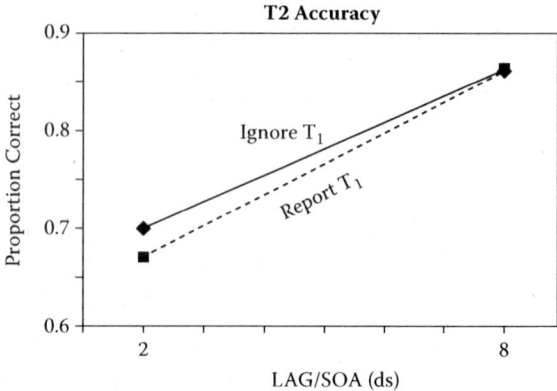

Figure 7.5 Proportion correct report of T_2 (contingent on correct report of T_1 in the report-T_1 condition) for each condition (ignore-T_1 vs. report-T_1) and each lag (2 vs. 8) in the experiment of Jolicœur et al. (2006b, *European Journal of Cognitive Psychology, 18,* 560–578).

visuospatial attention, per se, rather than via mediations at later stages of processing. In the case of the experiment in which T_1 and T_2 had the same color, perhaps the effect was mainly due to contingent capture (Folk, Leber, & Egeth, 2002; Folk, Remington, & Johnston, 1992).

According to the contingent capture hypothesis, a distractor can involuntarily draw visuospatial attention to the location it occupies by virtue of a top-down attentional set to find a target with the same features. Here, attention would have been captured at the location of T_1 and remained there for a sufficiently long time (presumably in the order of 100 ms or more) to make it difficult to redeploy attention to T_2, to the left or right of fixation, in time to engage on T_2 before T_2 was overwritten by the T_2 mask.

In the first experiment, perhaps the issue was one of a need to disengage from monitoring the central stream when T_1 had to be attended and that monitoring activity at a particular location made it difficult to reorient attention when T_2 was presented. With a long T_1–T_2 lag, subjects would have time to disengage from the central stream in preparation for the onset of T_2.

Spatial Attention Freezes During the Attentional Blink

We addressed these issues in two additional experiments involving visual stimulation for T_1 and T_2. In the first of these, Dell'Acqua, Sessa, Jolicœur, and Robitaille (2006) presented two concurrent rapid serial visual presentation streams, one to either side of fixation, as illustrated in Figure 7.6. The distractors were letters. T_1 was composed of a pair of digits on 50% of the trials. In the other trials, T_1 was a pair of equal ("=") signs.

When T_1 was composed of digits, the digits were the same on 50% of the trials and different in the other trials. T_1 was then followed by a pair of letters that served

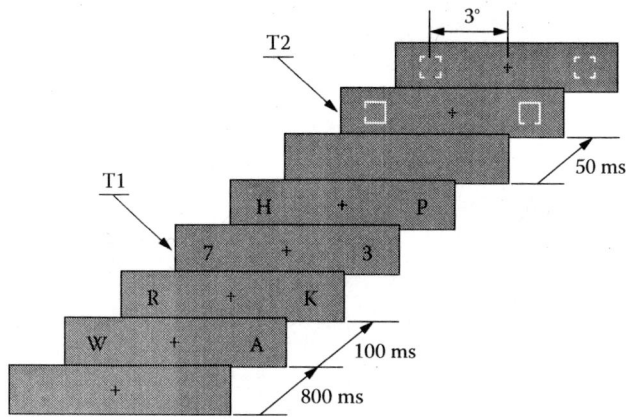

Figure 7.6 Stimulus events in each trial of the experiment of Dell'Acqua et al. (2006, *Psychophysiology*, *43*, 394–400). The squares of the T_2 frame were red and green in the actual experiment (shading is used here for illustrative purposes).

as masks for the T_1 characters. After a blank interval of 50 ms, a frame including two squares, one green and one red (green and red were equated for luminance), was displayed. Each of these squares had a small gap in one randomly chosen side. T_2 was the red square for half of the subjects, and the green one for the others. The T_2 frame was followed by a pair of light gray squares with a gap on each side that served as masks (Figure 7.6).

The subjects were assigned at random to one of two groups of equal size (*N* = 15 each). Subjects in the dual-task group monitored the two concurrent rapid serial visual presentation streams of alphanumeric characters for both T_1 and T_2. When T_1 was a pair of digits, subjects had to decide whether they were the same or different. They reported their decision at the end of the trial without speed pressure by button press. When T_1 was a pair of "=" signs, they pressed the spacebar. In addition, they had to determine whether the T_2 target square had a gap in the top, bottom, left, or right side. They used keys on the numeric keypad to report the position of the gap using a spatially compatible mapping that was learned quickly and enabled subjects to respond without looking at their fingers (and hence without moving their eyes from the fixation point) during the EEG recording session.

Subjects in the single-task group were instructed to ignore all stimuli except the T_2 square and to report the position of the gap in the target square. The same stimuli were presented to these observers as in the dual-task group, but no task was associated with T_1.

Each participant performed one block of 24 practice trials and eight blocks of 48 experimental trials. Our intention was to require subjects to monitor both rapid serial visual presentation streams throughout the initial presentation up to and including the processing of T_1, which required encoding and comparing two digits (one from each stream) in half of the trials (in the dual-task condition). Thus, at the time of presentation of T_2, attention should have been spread over the two streams, in contrast to the initial attentional state in the experiments of Jolicœur et al. (2006a, 2006b) reviewed earlier. In these earlier experiments, T_1 was presented at the center of the screen and presumably attention was focused at this location when T_1 had to be encoded or when T_1 captured attention. In the present experiment, however, it was much more likely that attention would be distributed over both peripheral locations in order to be prepared to encode the two digits in the T_1 frame (when those were presented). In the single-task condition, we suppose that attention was initially spread over the two streams in order to be able to determine as quickly as possible where to focus attention upon detection of the T_2 frame (the two colored squares).

If the attenuation of N2pc observed in the experiments of Jolicœur et al. (2006a, 2006b) was due to difficulty in disengaging from focused attention at fixation, the results of Dell'Acqua et al. (2006) should be different because attention was presumably distributed over the locations that would ultimately contain T_2.

Interestingly, the behavioral results for accuracy of report of T_2 exhibited a typical attentional blink pattern. Accuracy of report of T_2 (gap location in the target square) is plotted in Figure 7.7 for the single-task group (filled squares) and the dual-task group (unfilled circles), and for each T_1 condition (digits vs. "=" signs). As anticipated, the nature of the T_1 stimulus did not influence accuracy for T_2 in the single-task group, given that T_1 could be ignored. In contrast, for the dual-task group, the task associated with T_1 caused an attentional blink. The attentional blink was larger when T_1 required encoding and comparing the symbols in the T_1 frame (to determine whether the two digits were the same or different), compared with when the symbols in T_1 simply signaled that nothing more had to be done with T_1 (i.e., when "=" signs were presented in the T_1 frame).

The electrophysiological results are shown in Figure 7.8 (note that negative is plotted up in this figure). These are event-related potentials, time locked to the onset of T_2. The results were quite clear: An N2pc was found in the results of

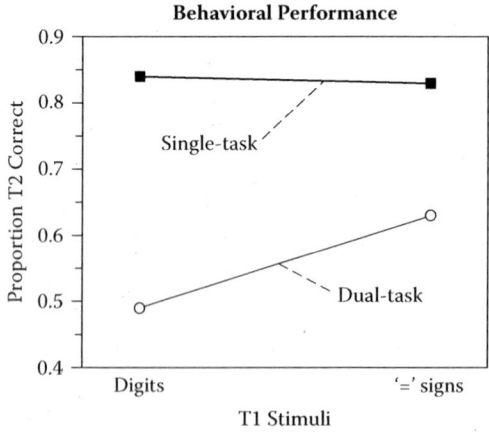

Figure 7.7 Mean percent correct report of the location of the gap in T_2 in the experiment of Dell'Acqua et al. (2006, *Psychophysiology, 43,* 394–400).

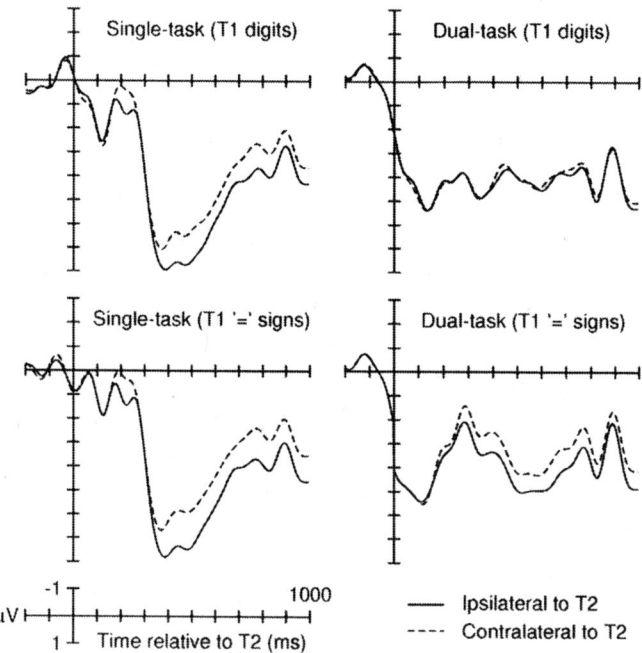

Figure 7.8 Electrophysiological results in the experiment of Dell'Acqua et al. (2006, *Psychophysiology, 43,* 394–400). The contralateral response is plotted using a dashed line and the ipsilateral response is plotted using a solid line. Note that positive is plotted down.

the single-task group, and this N2pc was unaffected by whether T_1 consisted of digits or "=" signs. The N2pc was attenuated, overall, in the dual-task group and completely suppressed when T_1 consisted of digits (required encoding and comparison). The suppression of N2pc in the T_1-digits, dual-task condition suggests that encoding and operating on the T_1 digits prevented the differential allocation of visual spatial attention to the location of the T_2 target square.

This, in turn, suggests that a substantial dual-task effect on N2pc can be observed even under conditions that were meant to encourage an initial state of divided attention. Subjects appear to have been unable to shift from an initial state in which attention was allocated equally to the two peripheral locations to a state in which attention would have been differentially allocated to the side of T_2. Note also the very large impact of the attentional manipulations on the amplitude of the SPCN, which was largest in the single-task conditions; clearly present in the low-load, dual-task condition; and completely suppressed in the high-load, dual-task (T_1-digits) condition. On the assumption that the SPCN reflects activation in visual short-term memory, the results suggest that this transfer of information into visual short-term memory was impaired by the attentional blink.

Impaired Deployment of Spatial Attention During the Attentional Blink in the Absence of Task Switching or Visual Capture

In a fourth study on N2pc and the attentional blink, Robitaille, Jolicœur, Dell'Acqua, and Sessa (2007) manipulated the relative frequency of the category into which T_1 and T_2 had to be categorized. T_1 and T_2 were squares with a gap, and the task for both targets was to decide whether the gap was in one particular side or not (e.g., top vs. not-top). Targets with a gap at the top, bottom, left, or right were equally likely throughout the test session. Consequently, a target was categorized into one of two categories that had a probability of either .25 (e.g., top) or .75 (e.g., not-top: bottom, left, or right).

Previous work had shown that the attentional blink is larger and longer when T_1 is categorized into a low-frequency category than when T_1 is categorized into a high-frequency category (Crebolder, Jolicœur, & McIlwaine, 2002). This frequency effect was useful because it enabled us to manipulate the magnitude of the attentional blink effect while holding the SOA between T_1 and T_2 constant. Furthermore, we were able to create a frequency effect while presenting virtually the same stimulus (simply by moving the location of the gap in a colored square). This equated for the relevant low-level physical characteristics of the stimulus from a bottom-up electrophysiological point of view.

In this experiment we also ensured that the tasks associated with each target were the same, thus eliminating possible contributions of task switching to the attentional blink effects reported in the preceding experiments (Potter, Chun, Banks, & Muckenhoupt, 1998; Visser, Bischof, & Di Lollo, 1999). The targets were red and the distractors green (equiluminant to red) for half of the subjects; this assignment was reversed for the other half. Each target frame contained two stimuli, one red and one green (a target and a distractor), and both squares had a gap. The gap was never in the same location in the two squares. For the T_1 frame, the squares were presented on the vertical midline, one above and one below fixation. This ensured that no differentially lateralized event-related potentials were associated with processing T_1. For the T_2 frame, the target and distractors were presented so that one was in the left and one in the right visual fields. A single, constant T_1–T_2 SOA of 350 ms was used.

The behavioral results showed that the relative frequency of categorization of the targets had the desired effects: a larger attentional blink when T_1 belonged to the less frequent category. The most important electrophysiological results are shown in Figure 7.9. Processing T_2 elicited an N2pc, and the N2pc was smaller when the attentional blink was larger (namely, when T_1 was in the less frequent category). This smaller N2pc suggests that visuospatial attention could not be redeployed to T_2 as efficiently when processing T_1 produced a larger attentional blink. This result is important because the physical stimuli leading to the differential attentional blink effects on T_2 were essentially identical. Each T_1 target square was presented equally often (each with a probability of .25), but they were ultimately categorized into either a low-frequency or high-frequency category. The categorization effect in this range of relative frequencies has been shown to take place at a central stage of processing in the context of the psychological refractory period

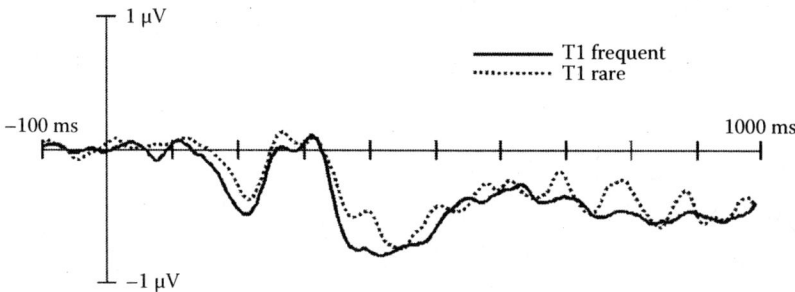

Figure 7.9   Electrophysiological results in the experiment of Robitaille et al. (2007, *Brain Research, 1185*, 158–169). Event-related difference waves, contralateral minus ipsilateral, relative to the side of presentation of T_2, time locked to T_2 onset, for frequent and infrequent T_1 targets.

paradigm (i.e., additive effects of the frequency manipulation in $Task_2$ with SOA; Crebolder et al., 2002). Consequently, the present attenuation of the N2pc had to be due to a longer period of central processing when T_1 was categorized into the less frequent category. Importantly, T_1 and T_2 required the same processing, ensuring that the attentional blink we observed had no contributions from task switching.

The attentional blink experiments all converge to show that visuospatial attention cannot be deployed as efficiently during the attentional blink. This conclusion may seem at odds with the view that the attentional blink results from a postperceptual processing bottleneck relatively late in the information processing stream. Indeed, our initial expectation was that the attentional blink would not impede visuospatial attention. Nonetheless, the consistency of the finding and the sometimes impressive magnitude of the effect (complete suppression of the N2pc) show that our expectations were incorrect and point to the importance of performing experiments to test even widely and strongly held expectations.

ELECTROPHYSIOLOGICAL TESTS OF VISUOSPATIAL CAPTURE IN THE CONTINGENT CAPTURE PARADIGM

The results of the control condition in the second attentional blink experiment, in which T_1 and T_2 had the same color, suggested that subjects found it difficult to ignore T_1, even when instructed to do so and when the task required processing only T_2. In that experiment, visual capture by T_1 brought and maintained attention at fixation and thus prevented a redeployment of spatial attention to T_2 in the near periphery. We decided to devise some experiments to investigate the notion of contingent spatial capture more directly and more carefully by using the N2pc as a measure of the locus of visuospatial attention. Attention can be guided in either a voluntary or involuntary fashion. Voluntary shifts of attention are usually driven by the goals of the individual, whereas involuntary shifts occur in response to the characteristics of the stimuli; the most salient stimuli attract attention exogenously.

There is general agreement that salient visual stimuli can capture attention; however, the degree to which the observer's goals and search strategies can affect attentional capture is controversial. According to the contingent attentional capture hypothesis (Folk, Remington, & Johnston, 1992), a distractor can elicit an involuntary shift of attention to the location it occupies if it matches the top-down attentional control settings required to perform the task. Hence, if the task is to respond to a red target, the presentation of a concurrent red distractor will impair performance, but the presentation of a blue or yellow distractor will not (Folk, Leber, & Egeth, 2002; Folk & Remington, 1998; Lamy, Leber, & Egeth, 2004; Leblanc & Jolicœur, 2005; Serences et al., 2005). Such contingent capture effects have been observed for color, shape, movement, and sudden onset (Bacon & Egeth, 1994; Folk, Remington, & Wright, 1994).

By contrast, Theeuwes (1991, 1992, 1994, 1996) suggests that attentional capture depends solely on the sensory salience of stimuli and that the item generating the strongest bottom-up signal within the visual display will attract attention regardless of the observer's goals. Consistent with this view, Kim and Cave (1999) observed different time courses for capture by salient stimuli and attentional shifts following top-down attentional control settings—the former happening earlier than the latter. However, these results can be explained by the adoption of a single-ton search mode.

When participants are forced to adopt a feature search mode in paradigms similar to the ones used by Theeuwes (1991, 1992, 1994, 1996) and Kim and Cave (1999), no attentional effects arise from the presence of salient distractors that do not match the target feature (Bacon & Egeth, 1994; Lamy, Tsal, & Egeth, 2003). Moreover, a distractor that matches the top-down attentional control settings does not have to be a singleton or create a pop-out effect within the visual search array to capture attention (Lamy et al., 2004; Leblanc & Jolicœur, 2005).

The contingent capture hypothesis states that the effect of salient distractors on behavioral performance results from a shift of visual spatial attention to the location of the distractor. However, a number of nonspatial explanations of the interference observed in capture studies have been proposed, such as filtering of the distractors (Folk & Remington, 1998; delayed allocation of attention to the target (Remington, Folk, & McLean, 2001), processing of the salient distractor (Ghorashi, Zuvic, Visser, & Di Lollo, 2003), or late selection of the target (Folk & Remington, 1998).

Several behavioral studies have addressed these possibilities and yielded results consistent with the spatial attention interpretation. For example, Folk and colleagues (Folk & Remington, 1998; Folk et al., 1992) have found an interaction between the distractor and the target location. Responses were facilitated when the distractor preceded the target in the same location and impaired when the target followed the distractor in a different location.

Similarly, compatibility effects of the identity of the distractor on target processing have been observed, as expected if attention was focused on the distractor (Ansorge & Heumann, 2004; Remington et al., 2001; Theeuwes, 1996; Theeuwes & Burger, 1998). Finally, the time course of the contingent capture effect seems to be consistent with rapid shifts of attention to and from the location of the distractor

(Leblanc & Jolicœur, 2005; Remington et al., 2001). However, overt responses depend on a wide range of processes and it is difficult to identify the stages of processing at which differences in behavioral performance arise.

The event-related potential technique and, in particular, the N2pc component provide a way to infer the locus of visuospatial attention over time as processing unfolds, even in the absence of a response to the particular stimulus that may attract attention. In the case of attentional capture, the N2pc allowed us to monitor whether spatial attention was indeed drawn, involuntarily, to the location of a distractor that matched the target feature, and whether attention was drawn to the location of equally salient distractors that did not match the target feature.

We performed several experiments, reported by Leblanc, Prime, and Jolicœur (2008). We summarize only one here to illustrate how the N2pc allowed us to answer an important psychological question concerning the underlying nature of contingent capture—namely, whether contingent capture involved capture at a low level of visuospatial attention or whether the phenomenon is due to later stages of processing (e.g., late selection).

Participants performed a task similar to the one used by Leblanc and Jolicœur (2005), adapted from the study by Folk et al. (2002). In this paradigm, participants were looking for a target-colored digit embedded in a rapid serial visual presentation (RSVP) stream of heterogeneously colored digits. Capture was induced by presenting two irrelevant, peripheral pound ("#") signs along with the digit preceding the target digit in the RSVP stream. One of the peripheral distractors was always gray. The color of the other distractor was the same as, or different from, the target. Leblanc and Jolicœur and Folk et al. found attentional capture—a drop in report accuracy of the identity of the target digit—when a target-colored distractor, rather than a nontarget-colored distractor, preceded the presentation of the target. The results of Leblanc and Jolicœur are shown in Figure 7.10.

If the contingent capture effect is due to a shift of visuospatial attention to the location of the target-colored distractor, we should observe an N2pc in response to the presentation of a target-colored distractor, but not of a nontarget-colored distractor. However, if the interference is due to nonspatial mechanisms, no N2pc should arise in either condition. Leblanc et al. (2008; Experiment 1) recorded EEG while subjects performed the Leblanc and Jolicœur (2005) task, simplified to include a single distractor-target SOA. The most important electrophysiological results are displayed in Figure 7.11.

A clear N2pc was found when the colored distractor was in the target color but not when the colored distractor was in a nontarget color. These results provide strong electrophysiological evidence for capture at the visuospatial level in the contingent capture phenomenon, supporting the model proposed by Folk et al. (2002). As suggested by Folk et al., the N2pc found when a distractor matched the target-defining color shows that spatial attention was engaged at this location.

The absence of an N2pc wave when the distractor was in another color is equally important. Given the structure of the experimental design (counterbalancing of target colors across subjects and equiluminance of the colors), the absence of N2pc for nontarget colored distractors rules out bottom-up salience of the colored

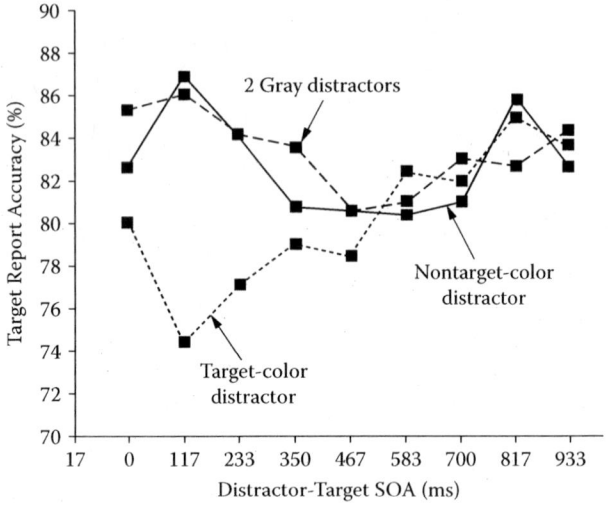

Figure 7.10   (See color insert following page 150.) Results of Leblanc & Jolicœur (2005, *Canadian Journal of Experimental Psychology*, 59, 124–131). Percent correct report of the identity of a colored digit, presented at fixation in a rapid serial visual presentation stream of digits in other colors, as a function of the color of the two lateralized distractors and of the distractors-target SOA. Both distractors could be gray, one could be gray and the other the target color, or one could be gray and the other a nontarget color.

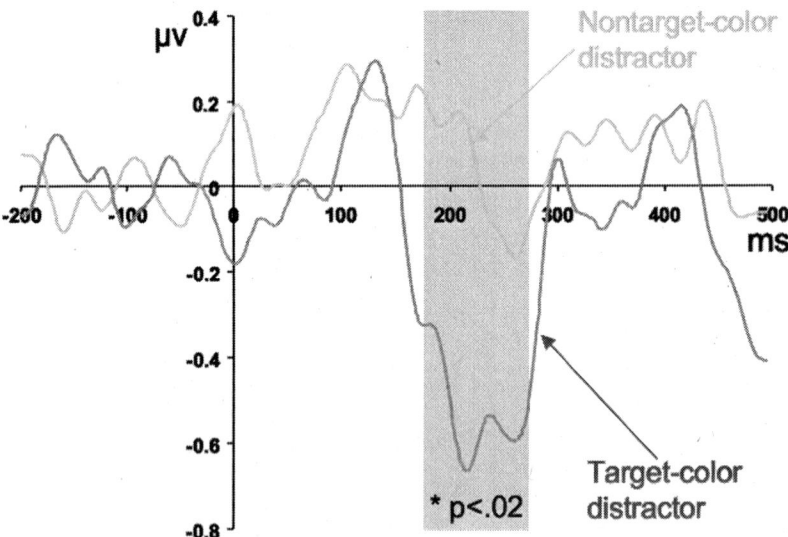

Figure 7.11   (See color insert following page 150.) Results of Leblanc et al. (2008, *Journal of Cognitive Neuroscience*, 20, 657–671), Experiment 1. Electrophysiological, event-related difference waves, contralateral minus ipsilateral, relative to the side of presentation of the colored distractor, time locked with the onset of the distractor frame, as a function of the color of the lateralized distractors.

distractor as a cause of capture in this experiment (and several others reported by Leblanc et al., 2008).

The results of Leblanc et al. (2008) provided the first electrophysiological evidence specifically implicating a shift of visuospatial attention in the contingent capture phenomenon. Other sources of interference (e.g., via late selection) could also contribute to the contingent capture effect. Indeed, Leblanc et al. (Experiment 2) provided support for an interaction between early and late selection in the contingent capture paradigm. In one condition, targets were a digit in a particular color among other digits (in different colors) at fixation. One of the distractors could be in the target color or in a distractor color. Furthermore, this distractor could be a digit (same category as the target) or a letter (different category). The other distractor was a gray letter (nontarget category). The preceding were the conditions used for half of the subjects. For the other half, the stimuli at fixation were letters; the distractors were a gray digit (on one side of fixation) and either a letter (target category) or digit (nontarget category) in the target color or in a distractor color.

The results are summarized in Figure 7.12. There was no N2pc for nontarget color distractors, despite the physical (bottom-up) equivalence of nontarget colors with the target color (despite the fact that, across observers, they were exactly the

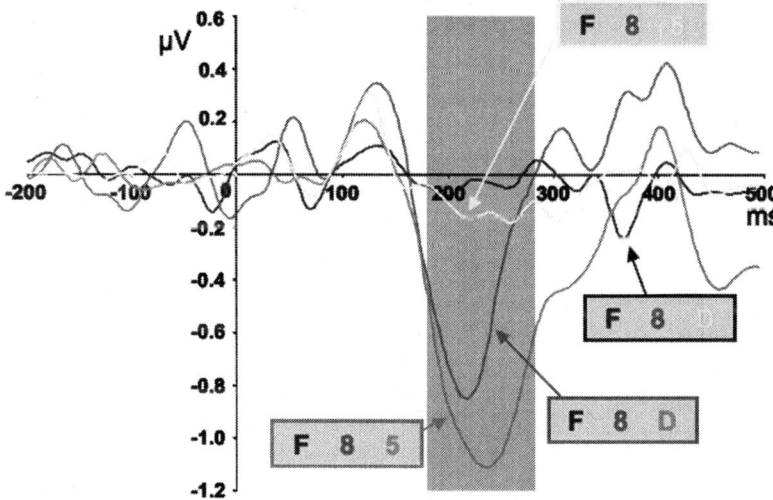

Figure 7.12 (See color insert following page 150.) Results of Leblanc et al. (2008, *Journal of Cognitive Neuroscience, 20,* 657–671), Experiment 2. Electrophysiological, event-related difference waves, contralateral minus ipsilateral, relative to the side of presentation of the colored distractor, time locked with the onset of the distractor frame. The labels show the possible content of a distractor frame (just prior to the target digit) for a subject searching for a blue digit in the central rapid serial visual presentation stream. A blue digit distractor is thus a target-color distractor in the target category (blue waveform); a blue letter is a target-color distractor in the nontarget category (yellow waveform). Notice the N2pc for these conditions and the larger and longer N2pc for the target-color, target-category, distractor (blue waveform). Peripheral distractors in other colors would be in nontarget colors for this subject (green and orange waveforms), for which N2pc amplitude was not statistically different from zero.

same colors). As before, there was a significant N2pc for target-color distractors, showing that visuospatial attention had been captured by target-colored distractors by virtue of a match with the top-down set adopted by subjects for selection of the target at fixation.

Moreover, the duration of the N2pc was longer when the target-colored symbol was in the same category as the target than when it was not in the same category. The results were consistent with the notion that visuospatial attention was captured by distractors presented in the target-defining color and that spatial attention mechanisms took longer to disengage from this location when the category of the distractor character matched the target category than when the distractor was in a different category. See Leblanc et al. (2008) for further details.

VISUAL SPATIAL ATTENTION DURING THE PSYCHOLOGICAL REFRACTORY PERIOD

At the beginning of the chapter, we reviewed work that examined the ability to deploy visuospatial attention during the attentional blink period. Concurrently with this work, we also examined whether the deployment of visuospatial attention would be impaired by possibly another type of dual-task interference—namely, the interference observed during the so-called psychological refractory period.

The psychological refractory period paradigm is the name for a class of experiments in which subjects perform two speeded responses to two stimuli (one response for each stimulus). The stimuli are usually shown sequentially and the SOA between them is varied. The typical result is that response times (RT_2) for the second target, T_2, increase as SOA is reduced, with a slope approaching -1 at very short SOAs. Response times to T_1 (1) remain relatively flat across SOAs. This pattern of results is generally consistent with an all-or-none bottleneck model with serial response selection (see Pashler, 1994, for a review).

Nonetheless, RT_2 often also lengthens with decreasing SOA (although almost always much less than for RT_2), which is not easily accounted for by the all-or-none bottleneck model, but can be accommodated if some degree of capacity sharing can take place at central stages of processing (Navon & Miller, 2002; Tombu & Jolicœur, 2003). Recent empirical and theoretical advances in understanding dual-task interference can be found in two special journal issues on the topic, one edited by Band and Jolicœur (2006) and the other by Koch and Jolicœur (2006).

Brisson and Jolicœur (2007a) had several reasons for examining the influence of central attention, as engaged in the psychological refractory period paradigm, and visuospatial attention. As in the attentional blink domain, there were reasons to expect that visuospatial attention would be independent from central attention. Earlier work, particularly that of Pashler (1991), suggested that the interference observed in the psychological refractory period paradigm occurred at later stages of processing relative to spatial attention (see also Johnston, McCann, & Remington, 1995). Jolicœur and colleagues (Crebolder et al., 2002; Jolicœur, 1998, 1999a, 1999b, 1999c; Jolicœur & Dell'Acqua, 1998, 1999) argued and provided evidence for a functional similarity between interference in the attentional blink and the psychological refractory period paradigm (see also Dell'Acqua, Jolicœur, Pesciarelli, Job, & Palomba, 2003, for electrophysiological evidence).

On the other hand, differences also exist across the paradigms in terms of masking and methods of presentation leading to differences in patterns of results. These differences suggest that the detailed causes of observable performance in the two paradigms are often quite different. Consequently, results from the attentional blink paradigm are not necessarily predictive of results in the psychological refractory period paradigm.

Another reason to examine the N2pc in the psychological refractory period paradigm was to provide clear-cut evidence for central interference on the deployment of visuospatial attention in the absence of possible effects of visual capture by T_1. We eliminated the possibility of visual capture by T_1 by presenting an auditory stimulus (a pure tone) for T_1, rather than a visual stimulus, as had been the case in the attentional blink experiments.

Brisson and Jolicœur (2007b) used an auditory stimulus (pure tone) for T_1, and simple visual forms (squares with a gap in one side) for T_2, as illustrated in Figure 7.13. A speeded, four-alternative discrimination was associated with each stimulus. For the tone T_1, there were four frequencies and the task was to indicate which one had been presented. For the target square (red for half of the subjects and green for the other half), the task was to indicate the location of the gap (top, bottom, left, or right). Both responses were made by button press, using four fingers of different hands for the different tasks.

As expected, response times in Task$_2$, RT_2 increased sharply as SOA was reduced, showing that the paradigm produced a large psychological refractory period effect. The main question was whether subjects would be able to deploy visuospatial attention to T_2 as efficiently during the period of dual-task interference as they could in the absence of interference. The behavior of the N2pc component across the three SOAs can answer this question, and the results were very clear, as shown in Figure 7.14. The amplitude of the N2pc decreased systematically as SOA was reduced, showing that interference during the psychological refractory period impairs the ability to deploy visuospatial attention to a lateralized visual target.

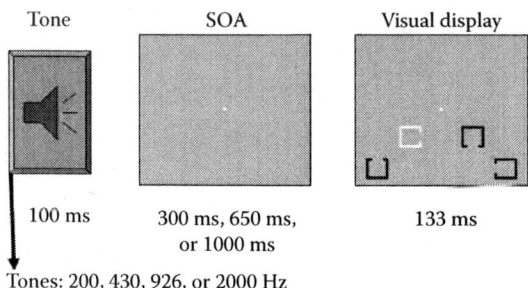

Figure 7.13   Sequence of events in the experiment of Brisson & Jolicœur (2007b, *Psychophysiology*, *44*, 323–333). The squares in the display were either red or green (represented with different shades of gray in this figure) and had the same luminance to equate bottom-up sensory responses.

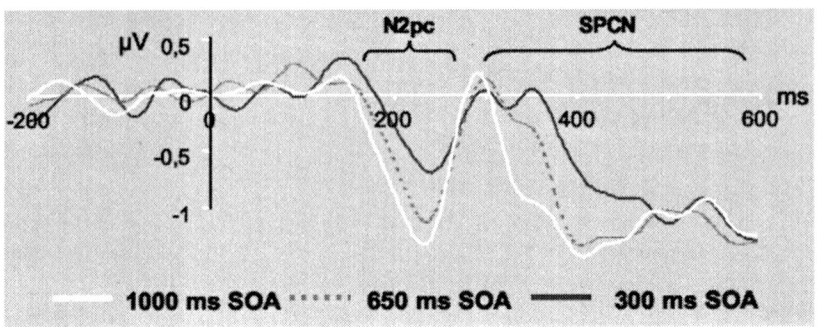

Figure 7.14   Electrophysiological results in the experiment of Brisson & Jolicœur (2007b, *Psychophysiology*, *44*, 323–333). The waveforms show the difference between contralateral and ipsilateral waveforms, pooled (bottom panel) across three posterior electrode sites (top three panels) near the peak of the N2pc wave. In the N2pc time window (180–260 ms), the amplitude of the contralateral negativity was maximal for long-SOA trials (1,000-ms SOA) and it decreased sharply as SOA was reduced. Note the later SPCN, which eventually reached the same amplitude in all SOA conditions, but with an onset that was delayed as SOA was reduced.

Brisson and Jolicœur (2007a) showed a similar pattern of results in an experiment in which the difficulty of Task$_1$ was manipulated while holding the T$_1$–T$_2$ SOA constant, showing that uncertainty about the time of presentation of T$_2$, or overlap of the event-related components from the two stimuli, cannot explain the reduction in the amplitude of N2pc. The fact that T$_1$ was an auditory stimulus eliminates the possibility of visual capture by T$_1$ (as was possible in some, but not all, of the attentional blink experiments).

In general, the attentional blink and psychological refractory period experiments present a rather consistent pattern of results in which the N2pc to a highly salient colored peripheral target is systematically attenuated as dual-task interference increases. We can think of the N2pc as an electrophysiological consequence of the deployment of visual spatial attention to a particular visual target. Our results show that this consequence of attention is suppressed under high concurrent central attentional load; however, they do not yet allow us to pinpoint how or where the interference occurs.

Several control experiments have ruled out a failure of color perception per se during the attentional blink or the psychological refractory period as a principal cause. For the moment, we hypothesize that dual-task interference in the attentional blink and psychological refractory period paradigms originates primarily at relatively late stages of processing, such as short-term consolidation or response selection, and that these mechanisms interfere with the mechanisms that control the deployment of visuospatial attention.

ELECTROPHYSIOLOGICAL AND NEUROMAGNETIC INDICES OF VISUAL SHORT-TERM MEMORY

Dual-Task Paradigms and Sustained Posterior Contralateral Negativity (SPCN)

The experiments described in the preceding sections focused on visual spatial attention in dual-task and capture paradigms. As we performed them and focused on the N2pc event-related potential component, we discovered what appeared to be a second posterior contralateral negativity, often with a much longer time course than the N2pc. We will refer to this component as the sustained posterior contralateral negativity (SPCN).

Similar posterior contralateral negative waves have been found in tasks requiring the encoding and retention of simple visual stimuli in reports by Klaver, Talsma, Wijers, Heinze, and Mulder (1999) and Vogel and Machizawa (2004). Klaver et al. called their component the CNSW (for contralateral negative slow wave). Vogel and Machizawa called their component the CDA (for contralateral delay activity). It seems very likely that all of these contralateral negativities are closely related. Thus, we will refer to all of them using the label SPCN because of their common sustained duration, posterior and contralateral scalp distribution, and sign (more negative at electrodes contralateral relative to the encoded information).

Vogel and Machizawa (2004) showed that the amplitude of the SPCN grows as the number of visual stimuli to be remembered increases, but only up to the capacity of storage in visual short-term memory (on a subject-by-subject basis). These very interesting results suggest that we can track the amount of information maintained in visual short-term memory and the time course of passage through visual short term memory by measuring the amplitude and latency of the SPCN.

Consider again the electrophysiological results of Jolicœur et al. (2006a) shown in Figure 7.3. Recall that these results show the contralateral minus ipsilateral difference waves relative to the side of presentation of a lateralized T_2 in the context of an attentional blink experiment (paradigm illustrated in Figure 7.1). In the preceding discussions, we focused on factor effects (T_1–T_2 SOA, and Task$_1$ attend vs. ignore) on the N2pc (shaded region in Figure 7.3). As can be seen in Figure 7.3, however, after the N2pc time window, the *contra–ipsi* difference waves for three of the four conditions all exhibit negative deflections that converge to a common amplitude of about –1.5 µV.

Interestingly, these are the conditions for which report accuracy of T_2 was generally high (and about equal). In contrast, accuracy in the report-T_1 condition, at lag 2, was very low, and the SPCN was essentially 0 for this condition. These results suggest to us that the SPCN was tracking the passage of T_2 into visual short-term memory. Interestingly, the onset of the SPCN appeared to be slightly earlier when T_1 could be ignored (a result that converges nicely with one we will present later in the context of the SPCN results of Brisson & Jolicœur, 2007b).

Next, consider again the results of Jolicœur et al. (2006b) shown in Figure 7.4. Again, the results suggest the presence of two separable components: First, an

N2pc, followed by an SPCN. As in Figure 7.3, the pattern of amplitudes of the SPCN correlated well with the pattern of report accuracy of T_2. In this case, T_2 could be reported well at lag 8 in both $Task_1$ attention conditions and poorly at lag 2 in both $Task_1$ conditions. Although the SPCN was not completely abolished in the conditions with reduced T_2 report accuracy, it was significantly reduced in these conditions relative to the amplitude in conditions with high report accuracy. Furthermore, as in Figure 7.3, the SPCN onset appears systematically delayed when subjects had to report T_1 compared with when they could ignore T_1.

A similar pattern of results is also apparent for the results of Dell'Acqua et al. (2006) shown in Figure 7.8. A clear SPCN was found when subjects could report T_2 with high accuracy, and the SPCN was attenuated (eliminated in this case) when report accuracy for T_2 was low.

The SPCN for the results of Robitaille, Jolicœur, Dell'Acqua, and Sessa (2007) (Figure 7.9) also showed a trend in this direction, although much less so given that the SPCN amplitude for the two 1 conditions converged to a common level, despite different levels of report accuracy for T_2. Nonetheless, the initial amplitude of the SPCN (at around 380 ms) was higher when T_1 was frequent than when T_2 was rare (i.e., in the expected direction). It is possible that something about T_2 was encoded in visual short-term memory on most trials in this experiment (i.e., the fact that T_2 was a square on a given side of fixation), but that the location of the gap could not be extracted with equal accuracy for frequent versus rare T_1 stimuli from this representation.

The results from the contingent capture experiments of Leblanc et al. (2008), shown in Figures 7.11 and 7.12, are particularly interesting in the present context. In contrast with the previously considered paradigms in which subjects were actively trying to encode form information from a lateralized target, this was not the case in the capture experiments. Information at the capture location could only hinder performance in the primary task (report the identity of a letter or digit shown at fixation), so we expect that subjects never tried to encode information at the distractor locations. It is thus most interesting that there was no obvious SPCN immediately following the N2pc waves in either of the two capture experiments summarized in Figures 7.11 and 7.12, suggesting that subjects were largely successful in not encoding distractor information into visual short-term memory.

In the psychological refractory period experiments, subjects were trying to encode a lateralized T_2 and generally achieved very good accuracy in all conditions (in part because T_2 was not masked, in contrast with the typical procedure in attentional blink experiments). As can be seen in Figure 7.14, there was a clear SPCN and its amplitude converged to a common voltage in all conditions, consistent with the creation of a stable and functionally equivalent trace in visual short-term memory in all conditions.

Most interestingly, however, the onset latency of the SPCN was systematically delayed as T_1–T_2 SOA was reduced. Although subjects were able to encode T_2 into visual short-term memory with equal probability at all SOAs, the delayed onset latency of the SPCN, suggests strongly that it took more time to transfer a representation of T_2 into visual short-term memory when central attention was engaged on the tone (T_1). The results of Brisson and Jolicœur (2007a, 2007b) thus provided the first demonstration for delayed transfer of visual information into visual short-term memory as a result of central interference in the psychological refractory period paradigm.

Magnetoencephalographic Study of the Magnetic Equivalent of the Sustained Posterior Contralateral Negativity

In the final portion of this chapter, we summarize research seeking convergence between electrophysiology, magnetoencephalography, and functional magnetic resonance imaging. This work involves three collaborative projects, by Robitaille, Grimault, and Jolicœur (2009), Grimault et al. (2009), and Robitaille, Jolicœur, and Marois (2009).

Most of what we present here is based on magnetoencephalography data recorded while subjects performed a visual short-term memory task known to elicit the SPCN electrophysiological component. The aim of the work is to understand the functional and neural basis of visual short-term memory in the human brain. The paradigm used the sequence of events depicted in Figure 7.15. A pair of greater than (">") or smaller than ("<") symbols was presented at the beginning of each trial. Subjects were instructed to encode information on the right of fixation following a ">" symbol and to the left following a "<" symbol. Following a blank screen (except for a fixation cross present throughout the trial), a set of colored disks was presented for 200 ms. We call this display the memory array. The memory array contained either two colored disks on each side of fixation (total of four) or four colored disks on each side (total of eight) in colors and locations that changed randomly from trial to trial.

There was then a 1,200-ms blank retention interval. This interval was chosen to be long enough to avoid an influence of visible persistence on the memory results (Coltheart, 1980) but short enough to discourage verbal encoding (Vogel et al., 2001). Visual memory was tested by presenting a pair of disks, one on each side of fixation and each at the location of one of the disks in the memory array for that trial. The task was to decide whether the color of the test disk was the same as or different from the color of the disk in the memory array at that location.

As expected, we found an expected SPCN in data from a simultaneous recording of the electroencephalogram at PO7 and PO8, posterior electrode sites where the N2pc and SPCN are typically maximal (Brisson & Jolicœur, 2007a, 2007b;

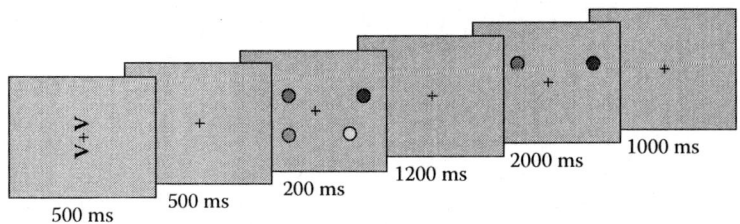

Figure 7.15   (See color insert following page 150.) Sequence of events in the experiment of Robitaille et al. (2009, *Neurophysiology*, 46, 1080–1089. The stimuli were disks in different color).

Klaver et al., 1999; Luck & Hillyard, 1994; McCollough, Machizawa, & Vogel, 2007; Robitaille & Jolicœur, 2006a, 2006b). We do not show these results; instead, we focus on the magnetoencephalography results.

Figure 7.16 shows the grand average event-related magnetic field distribution obtained by subtracting the grand average magnetic field distribution observed when subjects held two objects in visual short-term memory from the distribution observed when they held four objects in visual short-term memory. These means were computed over a time window well into the retention interval (500–1000 ms), ensuring that they reflected memory retention, rather than initial ERPs associated with stimulus onset. The map shows the magnetic field pattern as seen from above, looking down on the sensor array; the front of the head is at the top of the figure.

The pattern of the event-related magnetic field associated with the memory-load effect was beautifully bipolar and suggested approximately symmetric dipoles in parietal cortex. Recall from an introductory physics course on electromagnetism that moving charges are accompanied by a magnetic field orthogonal to the direction of current. If the current is in the direction indicated by the thumb of the right hand, the direction of the magnetic field is indicated by the direction of the curl of the fingers (the "right-hand rule").

In our lab, we also remember this relationship between the direction of the current and the lines of force of the magnetic field by imagining the direction of movement of a corkscrew as it penetrates the cork (direction of current) and the

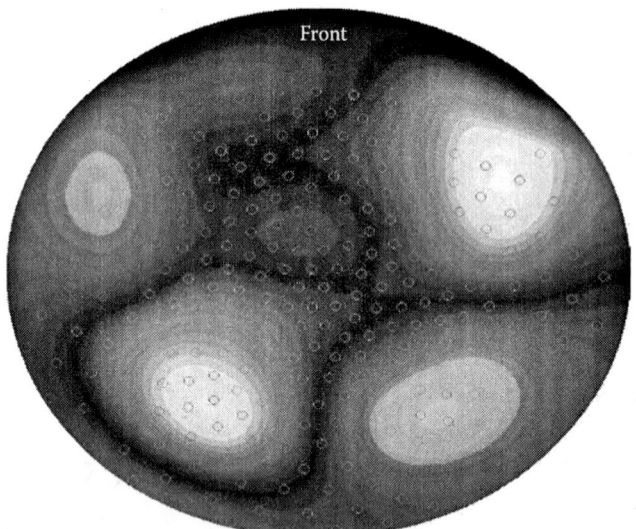

Time: 0.733333s

Figure 7.16   (See color insert following page 150.) Grand average event-related magnetic field distribution obtained by subtracting the average magnetic field distribution observed when subjects held two objects in visual short-term memory from the distribution observed when they held four objects in visual short-term memory (experiment of Robitaille et al., 2009, *Psychophysiology, 46,* 1080–1089). The averages were taken over a wide time window during the retention interval (500–1,000 ms). Blue indicates an outward field and red an inward one.

direction in which the corkscrew rotates (lines of force). In the figure, red to yellow to white indicates magnetic lines of force of increasing intensity going into the head; blue to turquoise to white indicates magnetic lines of force of increasing intensity going out of the head. An underlying current dipole is generally indicated by a pair of blue-red patches in the field map—one red patch going with one blue patch.

To interpret the distribution pattern in Figure 7.16, the reader can turn his or her right hand so that the thumb points up and to the left slightly; the palm is down and the fingers should be curling down. Now, line up the fingers with the red-yellow blob on the right side of the map; the thumb should point to the left, halfway between the red and blue blobs (on the right side). Imagine that the thumb is under the figure and that the hand has freakishly long fingers that curl out of the figure at the blue blob and back into the figure at the red blob (on the right). This offers some intuition for how to interpret this kind of magnetic field distribution map.

Now, rotate the right hand so that the palm is up, fingers curling up out of the head where the blue blob was found on the left side of the field map in Figure 7.16. The reader should see that now this hand configuration can be aligned with the blue-white and red-yellow pair of blobs on the left of the figure, indicating an underlying dipole in the left hemisphere pointing up and to the right—that is, a dipole that is symmetric with the one found in the right hemisphere. Note, therefore, that the reversed red-blue patterns on the left and right sides of the map are consistent with a pair of symmetrically located and oriented dipoles, one in each hemisphere. (One of the authors of this chapter confesses to some excitement when his graduate student first computed this grand average event-related field pattern. It was evident, at a glance, that magnetoencephalography would be an excellent tool with which to study and understand the neural basis of visual short-term memory!)

Figure 7.17, left, shows a dipole-fit solution in a model for results from a single subject in the magnetoencephalography experiment, who also participated in a functional magnetic resonance imaging study involving the same task (Robitaille, Jolicœur, & Marois, 2007). We were thus able to superimpose the dipole fits on the subject's anatomical brain scan (from the magnetic resonance imaging scan). A dipole fit model that included a single pair of symmetrically positioned dipoles, one in each hemisphere, could explain about 75% of the variance in the magnetic field map, whereas two pairs of symmetric dipoles explained about 96% of the variance.

One of these pairs of dipoles was located in parietal cortex, near the border with occipital cortex, as shown in Figure 7.17. On the right side of the figure, we show the functional magnetic resonance imaging activation for the memory load effect for this subject (see Todd & Marois, 2004, for details of the functional magnetic resonance imaging recording and analysis procedures used to isolate the activation shown in Figure 7.17). Interestingly, increasing visual short-term memory load was associated with activation of the parietal cortex near the border with the occipital cortex.

Our interpretation of the dipolar field pattern on each side of the grand average field map is supported by infomax independent components analysis of the magnetoencephalography data. Independent components analysis refers to a family

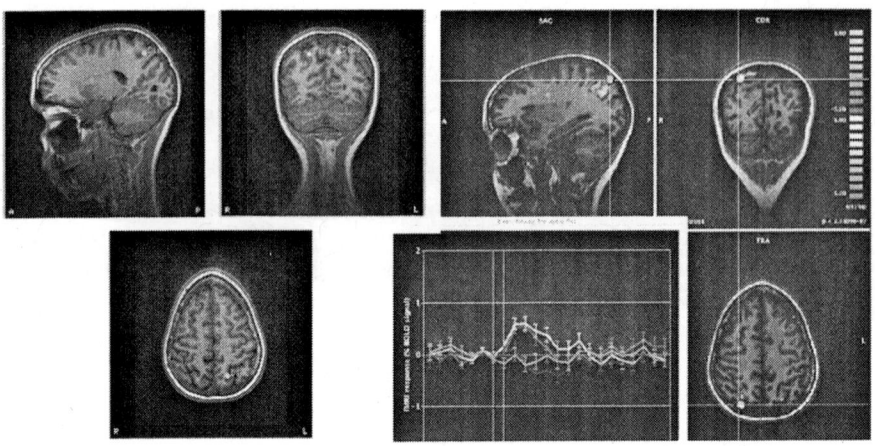

Figure 7.17   (See color insert following page 150.) Results from a single observer in an unpublished study by Robitaille et al. (2009, manuscript in preparation, Department of Psychology, University of Montreal) using the paradigm illustrated in Figure 7.15. The left side shows a dipole fit analysis for magnetoencephalography results using a pair of symmetric dipoles fit to the memory load effect illustrated in Figure 7.16. The right side shows that, as in the study of Todd & Marois (2004), increasing the load in visual short-term memory produces a BOLD response activation peak at the border between occipital and parietal cortex when the same subject was tested using fMRI using a close variant of the paradigm (adapted for fMRI testing). Note that one of the dipole pairs in the magnetoencephalography results was localized in the same region as the fMRI activation peak, suggesting that the two methods converge nicely in suggesting that a region in the occipitoparietal border plays a special role in the retention of information in visual short-term memory.

of "source separation" algorithms that decompose multisensor data into a linear combination of independent sources, called components. Typically, independent components analysis algorithms separate components that are completely independent of each other: Activity in one source only randomly predicts activity in any other (Cichocki & Amari, 2002).

We used infomax independent components analysis, which maximizes the independence (information) of each component without enforcing complete independence—a more physiologically realistic assumption (Makeig, Jung, Bell, Ghahremani, & Sejnowski, 1997). Each component comprises a distribution across sensors (a spatial map) and a single waveform showing how the amplitude of that source changes over time. The independent components analysis decomposition is perfect; the original data can be perfectly reconstructed by recombining activity of all the components. Infomax independent components analysis assumes that the actual sources generating the data are spatially stable (the brain does not move relative to the magnetoencephalograph sensors) and combine linearly (magnetic fields do).

However, the method makes no a priori assumptions concerning experimental conditions or brain structures and is thus a form of "blind source separation" (Makeig, Bell, Jung, & Sejnowski, 1996). In physiological terms, if the amplitude of a neural source changes over time independently of other sources at other locations, independent components analysis should isolate each source's particular magnetic pattern across the 275 magnetoencephalograph sensors.

We performed infomax independent components analysis on the data from subjects in the magnetoencephalography experiment using the paradigm outlined in Figure 7.15. Each subject's data were analyzed separately. Even if a common neural generator subsumed a psychological function (such as visual short-term memory) across subjects, it cannot be assumed that this source would be in exactly the same orientation and position in each subject relative to the sensor array (because of anatomical differences from one brain to the next and differences in the position of the head relative to the sensors). Nonetheless, we found components in several individuals that were very similar in their spatial field distribution.

Figure 7.18 shows selected components from the independent components analysis results for nine subjects. Some of these components are remarkably similar across subjects. For example, compare the components shown for Subjects 2, 13, and 21, which have similar spatial structures; also compare those for Subjects 5, 18, and (to a lesser extent) 20. We also show a number of other components from other subjects that have well-defined and simple spatial structure. Some components appear to reflect a source in the left hemisphere, whereas others are for a source in the right hemisphere, converging with the evidence from functional magnetic resonance imaging and ERPs suggesting that visual short-term memory engages neural activity in both hemispheres.

Each component isolated by independent components analysis has an associated activation time course. We performed a separate event-related average of these time courses for trials in which two items were in memory and for trials with four items in memory. Figure 7.19 shows these event-related averages for the activation patterns associated with the components shown in Figure 7.18.

All of these components show differential activity levels during the retention interval for trials with different memory loads. This is not entirely surprising because this was one of our criteria for selecting these particular components. The vast majority of components have activation profiles that do not show this effect. Nonetheless, it is most interesting that the independent components analysis allowed us to extract components that appear to reflect neural activity specifically related to the maintenance of information in visual short-term memory.

Dipole fits were computed for the independent components analysis spatial maps shown in Figure 7.18. The results are shown in Figure 7.20. As would be expected from the similarity of some of these component spatial maps, their associated equivalent current dipoles tended to cluster. Interestingly, many of the dipoles were in the posterior parietal region in the same general region found by Todd and Marois in a functional magnetic resonance imaging experiment designed to discover the neural locus of retention in visual short-term memory (see also Figure 7.17).

We also included two components with activity profiles suggesting a participation in visual short-term memory (a clear load effect in the component activation time courses), which did not localize in the same regions. These dipoles are shown in blue in Figure 7.20. One of them was clearly more medial than the others (in

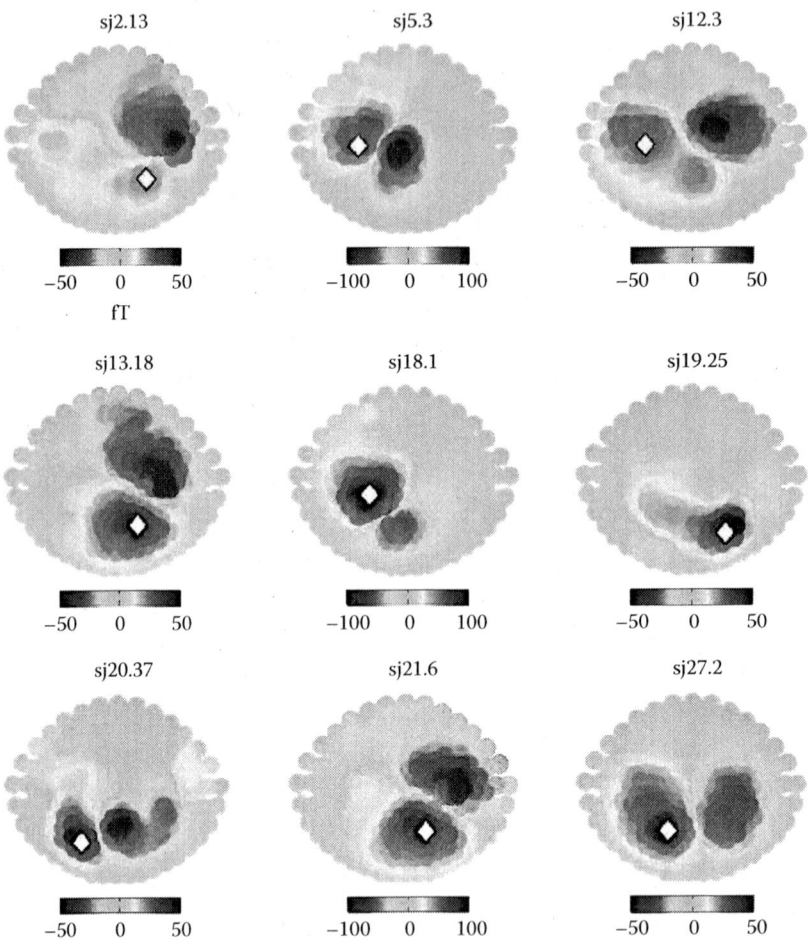

Figure 7.18   (See color insert following page 150.) Magnetic field across 275 sensors for the parietal component exhibiting a large memory load difference extracted from the independent components analysis in each of nine subjects. Red indicates an outward magnetic field and blue an inward one. Most subjects exhibit a dipolar field over parietal cortex indicating an upward-oriented current located midway between the maximum outgoing sensor (diamond) and maximum ingoing sensor (darkest blue). This dipolar pattern occurred in the left hemisphere in some subjects (sj5, sj18) and the right hemisphere (sj13, sj21) in others. Some subjects (sj2, sj12) exhibited an apparent mixture of parietal sources in two hemispheres. In other subjects (sj20, sj27), the parietal source maximally sensitive to load was located more posteriorly. Most of these subjects had several other dipolar components in other areas that also exhibited load differences. Top sensors cover anterior cortex. The diamond denotes the maximal positive sensor (whose time course is shown in the next figure).

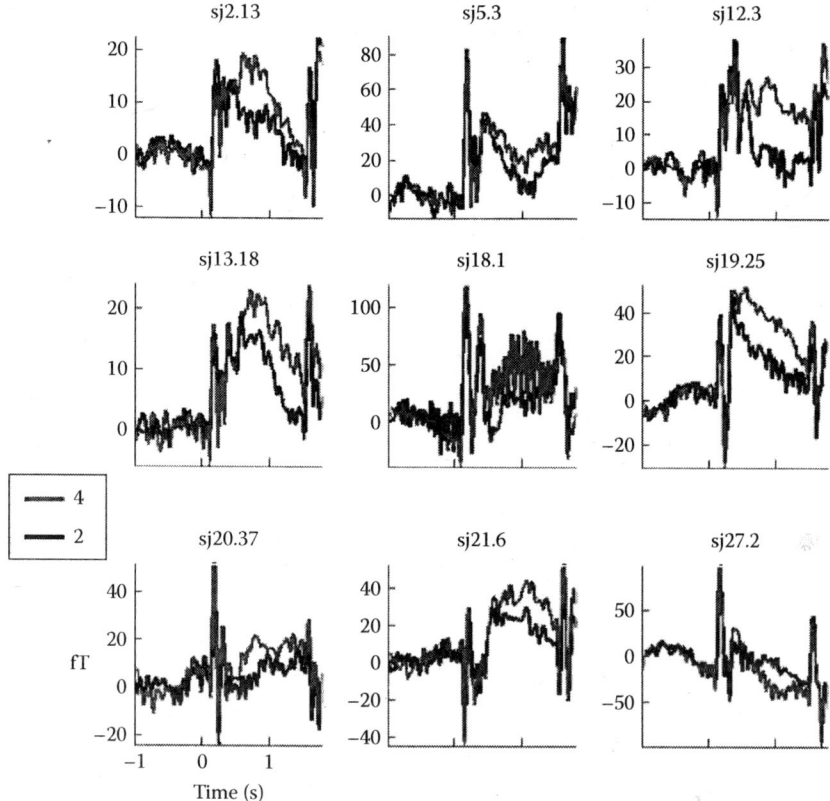

Figure 7.19 (See color insert following page 150.) Waveforms of independent components exhibit large amplitude responses during retention of four objects versus two objects. All subjects but one show activation in both memory load conditions; however, retention of four objects results in higher amplitude activation of this source, specifically during the retention period, where the differences in mean amplitude (500–1,400 ms) were significant (in a within-subjects t-test over trials) for all these subjects; $p < .001$ for all subjects except Subject 27. Note also the sharp wave preceding and following the memory retention period, which may indicate the arrival of visual information into this parietal source. The first sharp wave (at about 100–200 ms) does not show large memory-load differences, but the latter one does (at about 1,800 ms). These activation patterns suggest that the parietal source maintains visual information during the retention interval.

red), and the other was clearly lower and more lateral. The independent components analysis results suggest that the posterior parietal region contributes to the observed event-related magnetoencephalography results shown in Figure 7.16, but that other regions also participate in a broader network involved in retention in visual short-term memory.

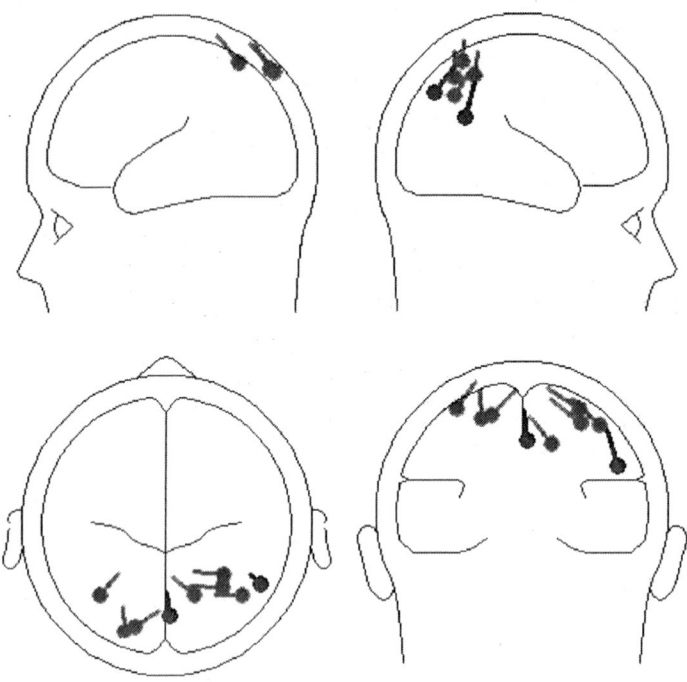

Figure 7.20   (See color insert following page 150.) Dipole localizations of parietal independent components show many similarly oriented sources in parietal cortex. Red dipoles
indicate sources located clearly within parietal cortex. Blue dipoles indicate sources in other
areas: one is relatively medial and posterior (sj27) and the other is relatively lateral, anterior,
and inferior (sj19). The most anterior left hemisphere dipole location is similar to those on
the right, with an opposite (mirror) orientation. The mean goodness of fit of the red dipoles
was 90.1%. The mean Talairach coordinates for the red dipoles is X: 27.1, Y: −46.04, Z: 50.0,
after all the X axis (left–right) values are made positive for averaging.

Source Localization of the Neural Generators of Induced
Activity During Visual Short-Term Memory Retention

In this final section, we summarize analyses of induced activity discovered in time-
frequency analyses of magnetoencephalography recordings made while subjects
performed the visual memory task illustrated in Figure 7.15. We subjected trial-
by-trial data in each of 271 channels of data to wavelet analysis, and we plotted
power, at different frequencies, over time. The time-frequency maps were computed for 11 subjects for which the data were sufficiently well behaved. We found
that power at about 10–12 Hz (in the so-called α-band) tended to increase just
before the onset of the to-be-encoded memory array and then to decrease sharply,
followed by a large increase in power during the retention interval (roughly from
600 to 1,400 ms).

We quantified these patterns by computing the average power in 1-Hz intervals at each moment during a 500-ms prememory array interval, and we used the
mean and standard deviation of the baseline power to compute a z-score for the

power observed in a window of −500 to +1,400 ms relative to the onset of the memory array. For each subject and each memory load condition (encode left load 2, encode right load 2; encode left load 4, encode right load 4), we found the magnetoencephalography sensor over the hemisphere contralateral to the encoded colored disks that had the maximum mean power in the α-band, in a window of 600–1,400 ms. We then averaged the z-score maps across subjects and also computed difference maps by subtracting the z-score map for load-2 trials from the map for load-4 trials for each encoding side (encode left vs. encode right). The resulting z-score time-frequency map for encode-right trials (sensors over left hemisphere) is shown in Figure 7.21. The results for encode-left trials were essentially the same.

It is evident in Figure 7.21 that the α-band power during the retention interval is significantly larger for load-4 trials than for load-2 trials, thus demonstrating that our visual short-term memory load manipulation caused significant changes in induced brain oscillatory activity during the retention interval. Interestingly, these changes in neural oscillations are not visible in the event-related averages because of variations in the phase of the oscillations relative to the onset of the memory array (Tallon-Baudry, Bertrand, Peronnet, & Pernier, 1998).

The trial-by-trial phase vectors were averaged for each condition (left-2, right-2, left-4, right-4), averaged over trials and subjects, and then subtracted (right-4 minus right-2; left-4 minus left-2). In Figure 7.22, we show the load-4 right minus load-2 right difference in degree of phase locking. Soon after the onset of the memory array, the increase in phase-locked activity was greater for load-4 trials than for load-2 trials, probably reflecting a larger ERP when more disks were in the visual display. No obvious differences were observed in trial-by-trial phase locking during the retention interval, where we found the greatest change in α-band power related to memory retention. This pattern of results was the same for the presubtraction phase maps for each load condition.

The results shown in Figures 7.21 and 7.22 highlight the importance of looking at induced activity (caused by the stimulus, but not phase locked with the stimulus) in addition to looking at event-related averages (evoked, or phase-locked, activity). Tallon-Baudry et al. (1998) reported significant increases in γ-band (20–80 Hz) power during retention in visual short-term memory. Our experiment was not ideally designed to observe γ-band activity because our sampling rate was only 240 Hz (imposing a low-pass filter at acquisition at 60 Hz, which may have attenuated induced γ). Although there are hints of changes in power related to memory load— at about 20 Hz and perhaps at 35 Hz (Figure 7.21), it is clear that these effects are much smaller than the changes in power in the 10- to 12-Hz region.

In a more recent experiment, we sampled magnetic activity at 600 Hz to ensure that γ-band activity would not be attenuated by filtering. Again, the most prominent effects on induced power were in the α-band. It is possible that induced γ may be stronger for memory for visual shape (Tallon-Baudry et al., 1998; Tallon-Baudry, Kreiter, & Bertrand, 1999) than for memory for color (present work). We will address this interesting possibility in future research.

For the moment, it is clear from our results that visual short-term memory for colored disks caused induced activity mainly in the α-band. In order to determine

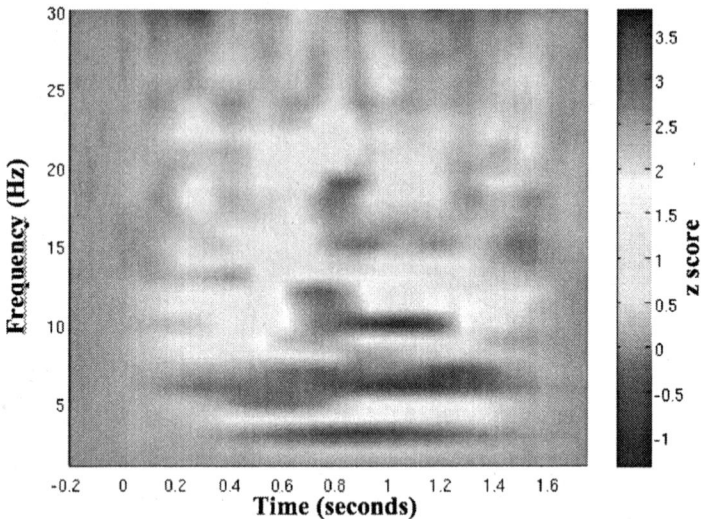

Figure 7.21 (See color insert following page 150.) Results of time-frequency analysis (z-score relative to prestimulus baseline averaged over 11 subjects) for the contralateral sensor with the largest power in the alpha band, during the retention interval. This map shows the difference in z-score for the load-4 condition and the load-2 condition. Frequency is plotted on the ordinate and time (in seconds) on the abscissa. The color in the graph indicates the value of the z-score at that frequency and time. Note the large yellow-red band at about 10 Hz, from 500 to 1,400 ms, that indicates that α-band power increased significantly during the retention interval as memory load increased. See Grimault et al., 2009, *Human Brain Mapping*, *30*, 3378–3392 for further details.

the neural sources of this memory-related activity, we computed the average power in a window from 500 to 1,200 ms after memory array onset in the α-band for each sensor. We created a sensor map of the resulting values (shown in Figure 7.23) for one observer for whom we had a structural magnetic resonance image of the brain and for one condition (load-4 right). Most interestingly, the distribution of α-band power had two clear peaks at posterior sensors over occipitoparietal cortex. Similar distributions were found in maps for the other conditions (with varying amplitudes) for each of the five subjects in our analyses (the five for whom we had a structural magnetic resonance image).

The very similar bilateral posterior distribution of memory-related α-band power across conditions and subjects encouraged us to develop a method to find the neural sources of this activity. Existing source localization techniques could not be used, however, because the mathematics of the forward solution (computing the expected sensor activity given a known source) used to compute solutions to the inverse problem (inferring sources given an observed pattern of activity at the sensors) have been worked out for linear models and power is a nonlinear value.

Grimault et al. (2009) devised a way around this problem. For each trial, the time of peak activity in the α-band in the retention interval (500–1,200 ms) was

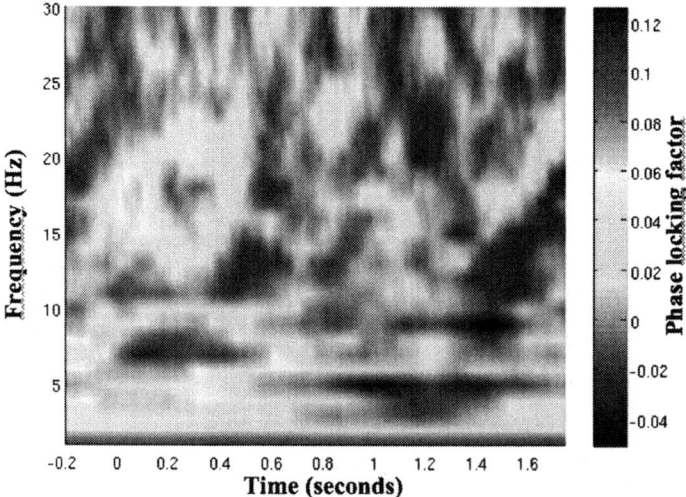

Figure 7.22   (See color insert following page 150.) Differences in trial-by-trial phase locking across the load-4 encode right condition and the load-2 encode right condition. Time (in seconds) is on the abscissa and frequency on the ordinate. The color in the figure codes the degree to which an oscillation occurs at the same relative phase from one trial to the next. In this difference map, we examined how trial-by-trial phase locking varied across memory loads. There was greater phase locking in load-4 trials than load-2 trials, but only immediately after the onset of the memory array, probably indicating a greater event-related response in load-4 trials.

found for a given sensor (called the reference sensor, chosen to be in the zone of maximum power in the map of power distribution, Figure 7.23). This time defined an event of interest that was later used to compute a new event-related average of the original magnetoencephalography signals.

In other words, we shifted the signals, trial by trial, so as to align the moment of peak activity in the frequency of interest across all trials. We shifted the signals from all other sensors using the event time stamps from the reference sensor, and we averaged the signals using this new event-related alignment. This event-related average, like any other event-related average, is in the original metric of the data and could thus be localized with existing source localization methods.

Because the method aligns the data from all sensors based on events defined for the reference sensor, averages for other sensors reflect the degree to which α-power is phase locked with α at the reference sensor. The method revealed strong phase synchrony among sensors close to the reference sensor (which is not very surprising), as well as for sensors near the α peak over the opposite hemisphere. These results suggest that cortical regions in the two hemispheres responding to load in visual short-term memory likely participate in a bilateral neural network. We are actively pursuing these very interesting preliminary findings.

Figure 7.24 shows the sensor map of the intensity of the aligned α-band signals for the encode-4, right, condition. The map shows a nice peak at posterior sensors that are out of phase for left versus right sensors.

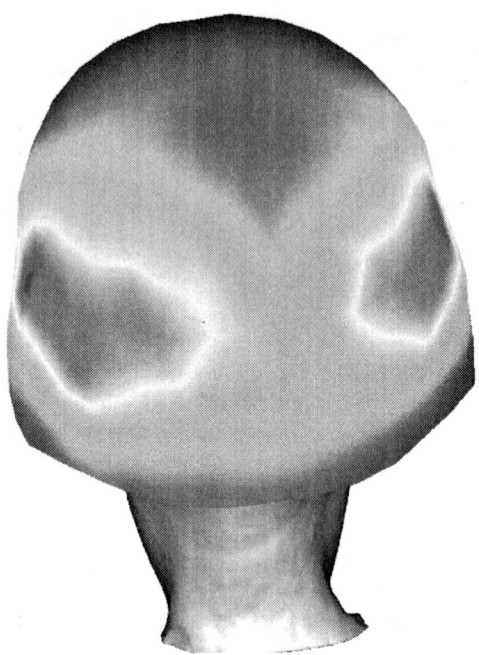

Figure 7.23   (See color insert following page 150.) Sensor distribution of the power in the α-band during the retention interval (500–1,200 ms) based on time-frequency analysis for one observer in the load-4, right, condition.

Figure 7.25 shows the results of distributed source localization of induced peak α activity during the retention interval, using the method of maximum entropy of the mean (Grova et al. 2006), for the activations computed using the method of Grimault et al. (2009) described earlier (Figure 7.23). This distributed source localization method constrains the inverse solution using a reconstruction of the cortical surface of each observer, extracted from their anatomical magnetic resonance imaging scan. A strong peak in the occipitoparietal gyrus was found, providing very good convergence with other indications that this region appears to play an important role in the maintenance of information in visual short-term memory.

SUMMARY AND CONCLUSIONS

By making use of recent advances in electrophysiology, magnetoencephalography, and functional magnetic resonance imaging, we gained a better understanding of the functional and neural basis of visuospatial attention and visual short-term memory. Our research team combined recordings of the electroencephalogram and the ERP technique with several dual-task paradigms. We focused on a component of the ERP called the N2pc and used it to track the efficiency and time course of the deployment of visuospatial attention.

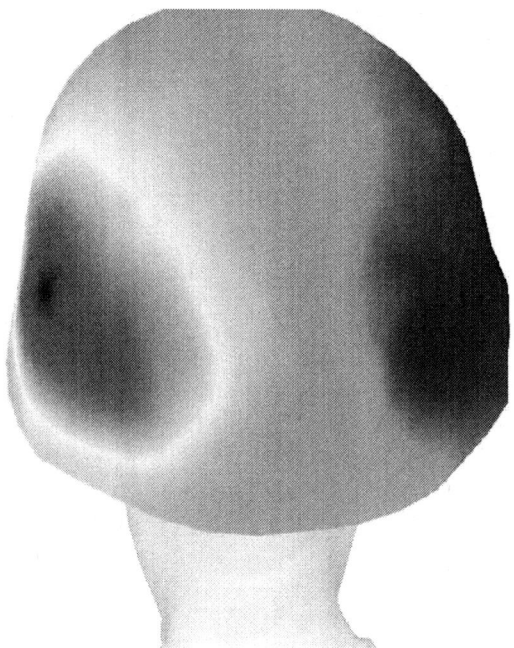

Figure 7.24   (See color insert following page 150.) Sensor map of aligned α-band signal amplitude, using a sensor over the left hemisphere as the reference sensor. This map shows a strong peak over the left hemisphere, indicating phase-locked activity, and a peak over the right hemisphere, also indicating phase-locked activity (relative to the reference sensor), but also indicating a significant phase shift (indicated by the change in sign of the induced activity).

We discovered that the deployment of visuospatial attention is less efficient and sometimes appears to be severely impaired during concurrent central processing. This was true for the attentional blink paradigm, using unimodal visual stimuli, and for the psychological refractory period paradigm, using cross-modal auditory–visual stimuli. The N2pc ERP component, a moment-to-moment index of the deployment of visuospatial attention, was attenuated or abolished under concurrent central processing load.

Overall, the results suggest that the control of visuospatial attention depends on mechanisms that overlap with central bottleneck mechanisms implicated in the attentional blink and psychological refractory period paradigms. Interestingly, these results were not originally anticipated, given the belief that spatial attention is a relatively early mechanism, whereas dual-task bottlenecks involve relatively late central processing mechanisms (such as response selection or short-term consolidation in working memory systems).

Electrophysiology in the context of contingent capture experiments enabled us to show that contingent capture is accompanied by a significant N2pc wave. This result provides strong evidence for capture at the level of visuospatial attention (as opposed to later stages of processing). Interestingly, in these studies, the later SPCN wave was not evident. In contrast, in tasks in which subjects

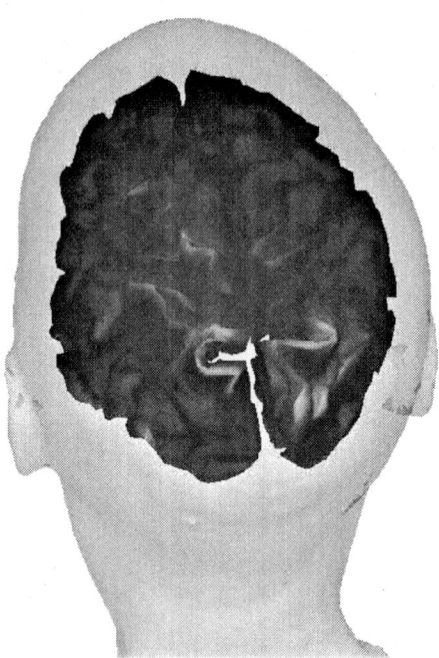

Figure 7.25 (See color insert following page 150.) Source localization of induced activity in the α-band using the method of maximum entropy on the mean (Grova et al. 2006), using the method developed by Grimault et al. (2009, *Human Brain Mapping, 30,* 3378–3392). The reconstructed surface at the border between gray and white matter was used to constrain the inverse problem. Note the peaks on the occipitoparietal girus, at the border between parietal and occipital cortex.

actively tried to process peripheral targets, we typically observed both an N2pc and an SPCN.

Although the N2pc appears to track the locus of visuospatial attention, the SPCN appears to track encoding and retention in visual short-term memory. The fact that there are no SPCNs in the capture experiments and significant SPCNs when peripheral stimuli are targets suggests that subjects have good control over what enters and what does not enter visual short-term memory. Indeed, one of the paradigms used to study visual short-term memory (illustrated in Figure 7.15) critically hinges on the ability to select information on one side of fixation at the expense of information on the other side. In most experiments, the amplitude of the SPCN provided a very good correlate of report accuracy for the targets, giving rise to the SPCN. This reinforced our interpretation that the SPCN reflects passage through visual short-term memory and that encoding in visual short-term memory may be necessary for conscious report.

In the final portion of the chapter, we summarized recent magnetoencephalography results that focused on understanding the neural basis of visual short-term memory. This is work in progress and we may have raised more questions than we provided answers. Nevertheless, we are strongly encouraged by our preliminary results, based on analyses of evoked and induced activity and on the exciting prospects for convergence across different neuroimaging techniques. Although it is likely that multiple areas in the brain contribute to visual short-term memory, it appears that a particularly important node in this network is located in parietal cortex, at the border with occipital cortex.

REFERENCES

American Electroencephalographic Society. (1994). Guidelines for standard electrode position nomenclature. *Journal of Clinical Neurophysiology, 11*, 111–113.

Ansorge, U., & Heumann, M. (2004). Peripheral cuing by abrupt-onset cues: The influence of color in S–R corresponding conditions. *Acta Psychologica, 116*, 115–143.

Bacon, W. F., & Egeth, H. E. (1994). Overriding stimulus-driven attentional capture. *Perception & Psychophysics, 55*, 485–496.

Band, G., & Jolicœur, P. (guest eds.). (2006). Special issue on shared and unique processing limitations in dual-task performance. *European Journal of Cognitive Psychology, 18*(5).

Bayard, S., Gosselin, N., Robert, M., & Lassonde, M. (2004). Inter- and intrahemispheric processing of visual event-related potentials in the absence of the corpus callosum. *Journal of Cognitive Neuroscience, 16*, 1–14.

Brisson, B., & Jolicœur, B. (2007a). Electrophysiological evidence of central interference on the control of visual-spatial attention. *Psychonomic Bulletin & Review, 14*, 126–132.

Brisson, B., & Jolicœur, B. (2007b). A psychological refractory period in access to visual short-term memory and the deployment of visual-spatial attention: Multitasking processing deficits revealed by event-related potentials. *Psychophysiology, 44*, 323–333.

Cichocki, A., & Amari, S. (2002). *Adaptive blind signal and image processing: Learning algorithms and applications.* New York: John Wiley & Sons.

Coltheart, M. (1980). Iconic memory and visible persistence. *Perception & Psychophysics, 27*, 183–228.

Coren, S., Ward, L. M., & Enns, J. T. (1994). *Sensation & perception*, 4th Ed. Orlando, FL: Hartcourt Brace Jovanovich.

Cowan, N. (2001). The magical number four in short-term memory: A reconsideration of mental storage capacity. *Behavioral and Brain Sciences, 24*, 87–114.

Crebolder, J. M., Jolicœur, P., & McIlwaine, J. D. (2002). Loci of signal probability effects and of the attentional blink bottleneck. *Journal of Experimental Psychology: Human Perception and Performance, 28*, 695–716.

de Fockert, J. W., Rees, G., Frith, C. D., & Lavie, N. (2001). The role of working memory in visual selective attention. *Science, 291*, 1803–1806.

Dell'Acqua, R., Jolicœur, P., Pesciarelli, F., Job, R., & Palomba, D. (2003). Electrophysiological evidence of visual encoding deficits in a cross-modal attentional blink paradigm. *Psychophysiology, 40*, 629–639.

Dell'Acqua, R., Jolicœur, P., Vespignani, F., & Toffanin, P. (2005). Central processing overlap modulates P3 latency. *Experimental Brain Research, 165*, 54–68.

Dell'Acqua, R., Pesciarelli, F., Jolicœur, P., Eimer, M., & Peressotti, F. (2007). The interdependence of spatial attention and lexical access as revealed by early asymmetries in occipitoparietal ERP activity. *Psychophysiology, 44*, 436–443.

Dell'Acqua, R., Sessa, P., Jolicœur, P., & Robitaille, N. (2006). Spatial attention freezes during the attentional blink. *Psychophysiology, 43*, 394–400.

Duncan, J. (1980). The locus of interference in the perception of simultaneous stimuli. *Psychological Review, 87,* 272–300.

Duncan, J. (1983). Perceptual selection based on alphanumeric class: Evidence from partial reports. *Perception & Psychophysics, 33,* 533–547.

Eimer, M., (1996). The N2pc component as an indicator of attentional selectivity. *Electroencephalography and Clinical Neurophysiology, 99,* 225–234.

Folk, C. L., Leber, A. B., & Egeth, H. E. (2002). Made you blink! Contingent attentional capture produces a spatial blink. *Perception & Psychophysics, 64,* 741–753.

Folk, C. L., & Remington, R. W. (1998). Selectivity in distraction by irrelevant featural singletons: Evidence for two forms of attentional capture. *Journal of Experimental Psychology: Human Perception and Performance, 24,* 847–858.

Folk, C. L., Remington, R. W., & Johnston, J. C. (1992). Involuntary covert orienting is contingent on attentional control settings. *Journal of Experimental Psychology: Human Perception and Performance, 18,* 1030–1044.

Folk, C. L., Remington, R. W., & Wright, J. H. (1994). The structure of attentional control: Contingent attentional capture by apparent motion, abrupt onset, and color. *Journal of Experimental Psychology: Human Perception and Performance, 20,* 317–329.

Ghorashi, S. M. S., Zuvic, S. M., Visser, T. A. W., & Di Lollo, V. (2003). Focal distraction: Spatial shifts of attentional focus are not required for contingent capture. *Journal of Experimental Psychology: Human Perception and Performance, 29,* 78–91.

Giesbrecht, B. L., & Di Lollo, V. (1998). Beyond the attentional blink: Visual masking by object substitution. *Journal of Experimental Psychology: Human Perception and Performance, 24,* 1454–1466.

Girelli, M., & Luck, S. J. (1997). Are the same attentional mechanisms used to detect visual search targets defined by color, orientation, and motion? *Journal of Cognitive Neuroscience, 9,* 238–253.

Grimault, S., Robitaille, N., Lina, J.-M., Grova, C., Dubarry, A.-S., & Jolicœur, P. (2009). Oscillatory activity in parietal and dorsolateral prefrontal cortex during retention in visual short-term memory: Additive effects of spatial attention and memory load. *Human Brain Mapping, 30,* 3378–3392.

Grova, C., Daunizeau, J., Lina, J. M., Benar, C. G., Benali, H., & Gotman, J. (2006). Evaluation of EEG localization methods using realistic simulations of interictal spikes. *Neuroimage, 29,* 734–753.

Hickey, C., McDonald, J., & Theeuwes, J. (2006). Electrophysiological evidence of the capture of visual attention. *Journal of Cognitive Neuroscience, 18,* 604–613.

Jasper, H. H. (1958). The ten-twenty electrode system of the International Federation. *Electroencephalography & Clinical Neurophysiology, 10,* 371–375.

Jiang, J., & Chun, M. M. (2001). The influence of temporal selection on spatial selection and distractor interference: An attentional blink study. *Journal of Experimental Psychology: Human Perception and Performance, 27,* 664–679.

Johnston, J. C., McCann, R. S., & Remington, R. W. (1995). Chronometric evidence for two types of attention. *Psychological Science, 6,* 365–369.

Jolicœur, P. (1998). Modulation of the attentional blink by on-line response selection: Evidence from speeded and unspeeded task₁ decisions. *Memory & Cognition, 26,* 1014–1032.

Jolicœur, P. (1999a). Concurrent response selection demands modulate the attentional blink. *Journal of Experimental Psychology: Human Perception and Performance, 25,* 1097–1113.

Jolicœur, P. (1999b). Dual-task interference and visual encoding. *Journal of Experimental Psychology: Human Perception and Performance, 25,* 596–616.

Jolicœur, P. (1999c). Restricted attentional capacity between sensory modalities. *Psychonomic Bulletin & Review, 6,* 87–92.

Jolicœur, P., & Dell'Acqua, R. (1998). The demonstration of short-term consolidation. *Cognitive Psychology, 36,* 138–202.

Jolicœur, P., & Dell'Acqua, R. (1999). Attentional and structural constraints on visual encoding. *Psychologische Forschung, 62,* 154–164.

Jolicœur, P., Sessa, P., Dell'Acqua, R., & Robitaille, N. (2006a). On the control of visual spatial attention: Evidence from human electrophysiology. *Psychological Research, 70,* 414–424.

Jolicœur, P., Sessa, P., Dell'Acqua, R., & Robitaille, N. (2006b). Attentional control and capture in the attentional blink paradigm: Evidence from human electrophysiology. *European Journal of Cognitive Psychology, 18,* 560–578.

Kim, M.-S., & Cave, K. R. (1999). Top-down and bottom-up attentional control: On the nature of interference from a salient distractor. *Perception & Psychophysics, 61,* 1009–1023.

Klaver, P., Talsma, D., Wijers, A. A., Heinze, H-J., & Mulder, G. (1999). An event-related brain potential correlate of visual short-term memory. *NeuroReport, 10,* 2001–2005.

Koch, I., & Jolicœur, P. (guest eds.). (2006). Special issue on process-based and code-based interference in dual tasks. *Psychological Research, 70.*

Lamy, D., Leber, A. B., & Egeth, H. E. (2004). Effects of task relevance and stimulus-driven salience in feature-search mode. *Journal of Experimental Psychology: Human Perception and Performance, 30,* 1019–1031.

Lamy, D., Tsal, Y., & Egeth, H. E. (2003). Does a salient distractor capture attention early in processing? *Psychonomic Bulletin & Review, 10,* 621–629.

Leblanc, É., & Jolicœur, P. (2005). The time course of the contingent spatial blink. *Canadian Journal of Experimental Psychology, 59,* 124–131.

Leblanc, É., Prime, D., & Jolicœur, P. (2008). Tracking the location of visuospatial attention in a contingent capture paradigm. *Journal of Cognitive Neuroscience, 20,* 657–671.

Luck, S. J., Girelli, M. T., McDermott, M. A., & Ford, M. A. (1997). Bridging the gap between monkey neurophysiology and human perception: An ambiguity resolution theory of visual selective attention. *Cognitive Psychology, 33,* 64–87.

Luck, S. J., & Hillyard, S. A. (1994). Spatial filtering during visual search: Evidence from human electrophysiology. *Journal of Experimental Psychology: Human Perception and Performance, 20,* 1000–1014.

Makeig, S., Bell, A. J., Jung, T. P., & Sejnowski, T. J. (1996). Independent component analysis of electroencephalographic data. In D. Touretzky, M. Mozer, & M. Hasselmo (Eds.), *Advances in neural information processing systems* (pp. 145–151). Cambridge, MA: MIT Press.

Makeig, S., Jung, T. P., Bell, A. J., Ghahremani, D., & Sejnowski, T. J. (1997). Blind separation of auditory event-related brain responses into independent components. *Proceedings of the National Academy of Science, USA, 94,* 10979–10984.

McCollough, A. W., Machizawa, M. G., & Vogel, E. K. (2007). Electrophysiological measures of maintaining representations in visual working memory. *Cortex, 43,* 77–94.

Navon, D., & Miller, J. (2002). Queuing of sharing? A critical evaluation of the single-bottleneck notion. *Cognitive Psychology, 44,* 193–251.

Pashler, H. (1991). Shifting visual attention and selecting motor responses: Distinct attentional mechanisms. *Journal of Experimental Psychology: Human Perception and Performance, 17,* 1023–1040.

Pashler, H. (1994). Dual-task interference in simple tasks: Data and theory. *Psychological Bulletin, 116,* 220–244.

Potter, M. C., Chun, M. M., Banks, B. S., & Muckenhoupt, M. (1998). Two attentional deficits in serial target search: The visual attentional blink and an amodal task-switch deficit. *Journal of Experimental Psychology: Learning, Memory, and Cognition, 24,* 979–992.

Raymond, J. E., Shapiro, K. L., & Arnell, K. M. (1992). Temporary suppression of visual processing in an RSVP task: An attentional blink? *Journal of Experimental Psychology: Human Perception and Performance, 18*, 849–860.

Remington, R. W., Folk, C. L., & McLean, J. P. (2001). Contingent attentional capture or delayed allocation of attention? *Perception & Psychophysics, 63*, 298–307.

Robitaille, N., & Jolicœur, P. (2006a). Fundamental properties of the N2pc as an index of spatial attention: Effects of masking. *Canadian Journal of Experimental Psychology, 60*, 79–89.

Robitaille, N., & Jolicœur, P. (2006b). Effect of cue-target interval on the N2pc. *NeuroReport, 17*, 1655–1658.

Robitaille, N., Jolicœur, P., Dell'Acqua, R., & Sessa, P. (2007). Short-term consolidation of visual patterns interferes with visuo-spatial attention: Converging evidence from human electrophysiology. *Brain Research, 1185*, 158–169.

Robitaille, N., Jolicœur, P., & Marois, R. (2007). *Comparative neuroimagery of visual short-term memory: Evidence from functional magnetic resonance imaging, magnetoencephalography, and human electrophysiology.* Manuscript in preparation, Department of Psychology, University of Montreal.

Robitaille, N., Grimault, S., & Jolicœur, P. (2009). Bilateral parietal and contralateral responses during the maintenance of unilaterally-encoded objects in visual short-term memory: Evidence from magnetoencephalography. *Psychophysiology, 46*, 1080–1089.

Robitaille, N., Marois, R., Todd, J., Grimault, S., Cheyne, D., & Jolicœur, P. (2009). Distinguishing between lateralized and nonlateralized brain activity associated with visual short-term memory: fMRI, MEG, and EEG evidence from the same observers. Manuscript in preparation, Departement of Psychology, University of Montreal.

Roelfsema, P. R., & Spekreijse, H. (2001). The representation of erroneously perceived stimuli in the primary visual cortex. *Neuron, 31*, 853–863.

Serences, J. T., Shomstein, S., Leber, A. B., Golay, X., Egeth, H. E., & Yantis, S. (2005). Coordination of voluntary and stimulus-driven attentional control in human cortex. *Psychological Science, 16*, 114–122.

Sessa, P., Luria, R., Verleger, R., & Dell'Acqua, R. (2007). P3 latency shifts in the attentional blink: Further evidence for second target processing postponement. *Brain Research, 1137*, 131–139.

Sperling, G. (1960). The information available in brief visual presentations. *Psychological Monographs: General and Applied, 74*, 1–29.

Tallon-Baudry, C., Bertrand, O., Peronnet, F., & Pernier, J. (1998). Induced γ-band activity during the delay of a visual short-term memory task in humans. *Journal of Neuroscience, 18*, 4244–4254.

Tallon-Baudry, C., Kreiter, A., & Bertrand, O. (1999). Sustained and transient oscillatory response in the gamma and beta bands in a visual short-term memory task in humans. *Visual Neuroscience, 16*, 449–459.

Theeuwes, J. (1991). Exogenous and endogenous control of attention: The effect of visual onsets and offsets. *Perception & Psychophysics, 49*, 83–90.

Theeuwes, J. (1992). Perceptual selectivity for color and form. *Perception & Psychophysics, 51*, 599–606.

Theeuwes, J. (1994). Stimulus-driven capture and attentional set: Selective search for color and visual abrupt onsets. *Journal of Experimental Psychology: Human Perception and Performance, 20*, 799–806.

Theeuwes, J. (1996). Perceptual selectivity for color and form: On the nature of the interference effect. In A. F. Kramer, M. G. H. Coles, & G. D. Logan (Eds.), *Converging operations in the study of visual selective attention* (pp. 297–314). Washington, DC: American Psychological Association.

Theeuwes, J., & Burger, R. (1998). Attentional control during visual search: The effect of irrelevant singletons. *Journal of Experimental Psychology: Human Perception and Performance, 24,* 1342–1353.

Tombu, M., & Jolicœur, P. (2003). A central capacity sharing model of dual-task performance. *Journal of Experimental Psychology: Human Perception and Performance, 29,* 3–18.

Visser, T. A. W., Bischof, W. F., & Di Lollo, V. (1999). Attentional switching in spatial and nonspatial domains: Evidence from the attentional blink. *Psychological Bulletin, 125,* 458–469.

Vogel, E. K., Luck, S. J., & Shapiro, K. L. (1998). Electrophysiological evidence for a postperceptual locus of suppression during the attentional blink. *Journal of Experimental Psychology: Human Perception and Performance, 24,* 1656–1674.

Vogel, E. K., & Machizawa, M. G. (2004). Neural activity predicts individual differences in visual working memory capacity. *Nature, 428,* 748–751.

Vogel, E. K., Woodman, G. F., & Luck, S. J. (2001). Storage of features, conjunctions, and objects in visual working memory. *Journal of Experimental Psychology: Human Perception and Performance, 27,* 92–114.

Woodman, G. F., & Luck, S. J. (2003). Serial deployment of attention during visual search. *Journal of Experimental Psychology: Human Perception and Performance, 29,* 121–138.

Zeki, S. M. (1993). *A vision of the brain.* Oxford, England: Blackwell Scientific Publications.

8

A Review of Repetition Blindness Phenomena and Theories

VERONIKA COLTHEART

INTRODUCTION

*I*n a review of rapid serial visual presentation (RSVP) phenomena, Potter (1984) remarked on the surprising inadvertent discovery in her laboratory by Helene Intraub that a pictured object shown twice within a sequence of pictures was frequently seen only once. This was an unexpected observation because, in most circumstances, when an item such as a word is shown twice, the identification of the second occurrence is facilitated; responding to the repeated word is faster and more likely to be correct than response to that word when preceded by an unrelated word or neutral item.

The enhanced responding to the second item, known as facilitatory repetition priming, was observed in word recognition tasks by Scarborough, Cortese, and Scarborough (1977) and has been replicated in many studies. In most studies both occurrences of the repeated word can be identified because the exposure durations exceed half a second. However, facilitated recognition of the second word also occurs with brief exposures and even when the first occurrence, termed the prime, is briefly presented for 50–60 ms, forward masked by hash marks, and backward masked by the immediately following target word (Forster & Davis, 1984).

The difficulty in seeing a repeated picture in an RSVP sequence noted by Intraub was investigated in a series of experiments using words by Kanwisher (1986), Potter's PhD student, who observed the deficit in several tasks and termed it "repetition blindness." Many subsequent experiments by Kanwisher and by others followed using a variety of paradigms and stimulus types, and a number of competing explanations were offered to explain repetition blindness phenomena. This chapter presents a review of the findings observed with different paradigms and stimulus types and of explanations proposed.

PARADIGMS IN WHICH REPETITION BLINDNESS OCCURS

Reporting the Repeated Item

In the first experiment, Kanwisher (1987) used a task similar to the one in which Intraub had observed repetition blindness. Subjects saw different sequences of seven words preceded and followed by masks composed of computer symbol strings (#######, %%%%%). These sequences were shown at one of several fixed exposure durations per word, and a word occurred twice in every list. Letter case alternated between adjacent words, and the repeated word appeared in a different case on its two occurrences.

The subject's task was to report which word was repeated in each list, and Kanwisher varied both the serial positions of the repeated words and the RSVP rate, the fixed exposure duration of each word, in a range from 117 to 250 ms per word. The repeated word was not detected or was inaccurately reported with exposure durations below 180 ms per word and when the repetition was in close temporal contiguity with the first occurrence. As exposure duration increased and as the lag between first and second occurrence increased, repeated words were more and more likely to be reported correctly.

Sequence Recall: Report All Items in the Sequence

In subsequent experiments, subjects were asked to report all words in the sequence and were explicitly instructed to report repeated words twice. This task cannot be performed with high accuracy for unrelated list items of more than a few words when these are shown at rates of 8–10 per second (Potter, 1984). Consequently, the lists Kanwisher (1987) presented consisted of words that formed a sentence, because sentences can be recalled with high accuracy even when shown serially at high rates (Potter, 1984).

In fact, when sentences included a repeated word, the nonrepeated words were recalled with accuracy of 80–90%. The first instance of the repeat (C1) was similarly well reported, and it was the second instance (C2) that was usually omitted in recall (e.g., "when she spilled the ink there was ink all over" vs. "when she spilled the liquid, there was ink all over"). The omissions occurred despite the fact that omitting the repeated word rendered the sentence (and recall) semantically and syntactically anomalous.

MEASURES OF REPETITION BLINDNESS

Critical Item Report

When the task involves reporting the repeated item, accuracy in report of the repeated word is the measure and accuracy is compared for sequences shown at different rates or as a function of lag—the number of words intervening between the first and second occurrence of the repeated word. With sentences requiring full report, Kanwisher (1987) and subsequent researchers included a control condition in which the first occurrence of the repeated word is replaced by another word that is appropriate in the sentence. They contrast recall of these critical words (C1 and C2) in the control and repeat conditions.

As noted before, recall of the second word (C2), the repetition, is reduced relative to report of that word when preceded by a dissimilar word in the C1 location. "Catch" trials are presented in which the second critical word is excluded and subjects are informed that some sentences might have missing words or not make sense. They are requested not to "fix them up" but rather to report only words seen.

Joint Report of Both Critical Items

Because the nonrepeated words are well recalled for RSVP sentences, it is relatively straightforward to determine which of a repeated C1 or C2 has been reported. This is not so when sequences consist of unrelated words or other items such as individual letters or digits. Recall of unrelated items is considerably lower, as noted earlier, and it is frequently unclear whether report of one of a repeated item represents C1 or C2. The solution to this problem adopted initially by Bavelier and Potter (1992) was to use the percentage of trials on which both C1 and C2 were reported in the repeat and control conditions as a measure of repetition blindness. This measure indicated that repetition blindness occurred when performance in the repeat and control conditions was compared.

In dual target search of RSVP sequences, another paradigm, a conditional measure, is typically used—namely, the incidence of C2 (termed T2) report when C1 (termed T1) has been successfully reported. Because the targets are different items, there is no ambiguity over whether the first has been reported. However, with repeated items, this determination is unclear, so the conditional measure is inappropriate.

Repetition Blindness Index (RBI)

Park and Kanwisher (1994) introduced another measure, the repetition blindness index (RBI). The RBI is calculated as a proportion equal to the number of trials on which both C1 and C2 are reported in the repeat condition divided by the number of trials on which C1 and C2 are reported in repeat and control conditions. This index has values ranging from 0 to 1, where values significantly below .5 indicate repetition blindness and values above .5 indicate repetition benefit or advantage: namely, that joint report in the repeat condition exceeds joint report in the control condition. This index was intended to deal with the problems posed by baseline variation in control trial performance when comparing the magnitude of repetition blindness across conditions.

However, the RBI can give a misleading picture of performance and can spuriously produce an appearance of low variability in highly variable performance. Take as an example a task with 50 repeat and 50 control trials. Subject 1 obtains joint C1.C2 scores of 20 on repeat trials and 40 on control trials; Subject 2 scores 1 on repeat trials and 2 in the control condition. These look very different and, although Subject 1 clearly shows evidence of repetition blindness, one would hesitate to conclude that the low-scoring Subject 2 reliably does so.

If these scores are analyzed (along with others in the sample tested), the standard deviations in both conditions may be rather high. If, on the other hand, each subject's scores are entered into the RBI formula, this yields exactly the same value of .33 and the variability of these two derived scores becomes zero. Because performance levels in RSVP tasks can vary greatly between individuals and between experimental conditions, individual item or joint C1.C2 report seems preferable to use of the RBI.

ADDITIONAL PARADIGMS FOR STUDYING REPETITION EFFECTS

Subspan List Report

When the sequences constitute well-formed sentences, verbatim report can be remarkably accurate, as noted earlier. However, semantic and syntactic properties of the sentences vary between items and may influence repetition effects in unknown ways. Thus, the use of sentences introduces additional linguistic variables to the task. Some possible influences of such variables were discussed by Whittlesea and Wei (1997). The effects of these unwanted variables can be eliminated through the use of short lists of simpler stimuli, such as unrelated letter or digit sequences; these were used in the research reported next.

An early attempt at investigating repetition effects with simple stimuli and reduced memory load was conducted by Bavelier and Potter (1992). They devised a task in which at most only three items had to be reported, although these items were sandwiched among other to-be-ignored items (all items were presented at a fixed exposure duration of 100 ms/item). For example, subjects were presented with three letters sandwiched between punctuation and other symbol distractors (e.g., %, &, #. $, +, °, etc.); letters were the only items to be reported. An example is shown in Figure 8.1.

The six stimuli on all trials included two or three letters plus three or four symbols. In the repeat condition, the first and third letters were the same and were separated by another letter or a letter and a symbol; in the control condition, the three letters were all different. Two-letter trials included an extra symbol and served to provide genuine two-item trials and to establish the extent to which spurious reports of repetitions might occur. Letter case (upper or lower case) and lag (one or two items between C1 and C2) were manipulated. Reducing memory load of the task produced control C1.C2 recall ranging between 64.5% and 71.5% along with repetition blindness. Joint C1.C2 recall was significantly worse on repeat than on control trials: repetition deficit varied between 12.5% and 34.5%. Although the magnitude of repetition blindness was unaffected by a difference in letter case between C1 and C2, it was greater when C2 was lower case than when C2 was upper case (regardless of the case of C1).

Of course, the finding of repetition blindness across case change was consistent with results from Kanwisher's (1987) initial experiment using repetition detection because the repeated words differed in case. These findings of repetition blindness across different letter case indicate that the deficit cannot be due to early sensory or perceptual inhibitory processes operating at the letter feature level.

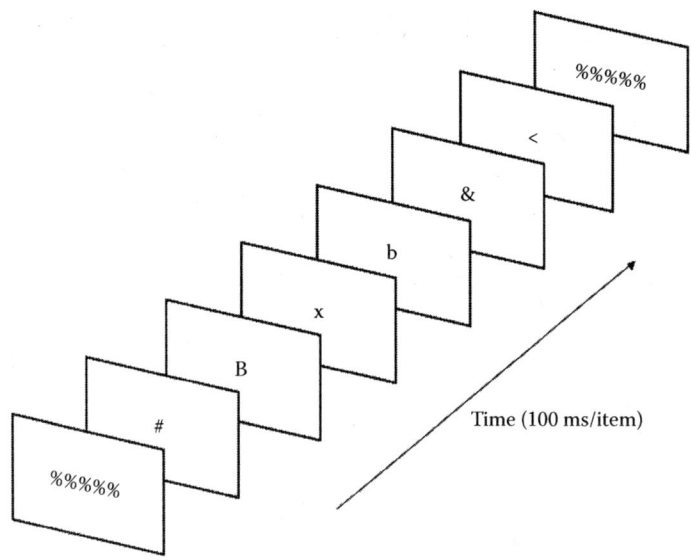

Figure 8.1   Example sequence from Bavelier & Potter (1992, *Journal of Experimental Psychology: Human Perception and Performance, 18,* 134–147).

Online Detection Accuracy and Response Time

A few investigators have used two alternative forced-choice speeded or unspeeded repetition detection or online item detection ("Is there an 'A' or a 'B' present?"), the latter with letter sequences (e.g., Dux & Marois, 2007; Johnston, Hochhaus, & Ruthruff, 2002). Reporting the number of items in short sequences of two or three items sandwiched between visual masks is another task (Coltheart & Langdon, 2003). These tasks also provide evidence of repetition blindness. Thus, subjects more frequently fail to detect the second target letter "A" when the first target letter was also "A" than when it was "B" (Johnston et al.), and they are more likely to decide erroneously that a three-word sequence contained only two words when the first and third words are the same than when they are different (Coltheart & Langdon).

Spatially Distributed Sequences

Luo and Caramazza (1995) assessed repetition effects with a task having minimal memory demands: two letters that were the same or different. They avoided the problem of fusion of two successive identical letters by displaying the letters serially in different spatial locations, each exposed for 50 ms. In Experiment 1, the location of letters varied randomly in a circular array with eight possible locations; these locations were simultaneously filled with backward masking "$" symbols after each 50-ms letter. Although with stimulus-onset asynchrony (SOA) of 50 and 100 ms the magnitude of repetition blindness was comparable to that observed with three-letter sequences by Bavelier and Potter (1992), at 150 ms the effect was significantly reduced, especially with increased spatial separation between the letters.

In Experiment 2, the same two predictable locations were used on every trial, but the location (left or right) of C1 varied randomly (with C2 presented in the other location) and both C1 and C2 were followed by a "%" symbol as backward mask. Although only the 50-ms C2 had to be identified, repetition blindness occurred when C1 durations varied between 50 and 100 ms, with no effects for C1 of 25 ms. Thus, these two-item studies have shown that repetition blindness occurs with minimal memory load and can be found even when only the second item (C2) had to be reported. The findings are inconsistent with memory retrieval and reconstruction accounts of the mechanisms responsible for repetition blindness.

Simultaneous Spatial Arrays

Does repetition blindness occur for concurrent, spatially separated, identical items in a simultaneously presented array? Kanwisher (1991) observed repetition blindness for simultaneous spatially distributed letters and color patches. Luo & Caramazza (1996) compared the effects of repetition in RSVP sequences and simultaneous arrays of letters. In both conditions, five letters appeared inside a circle in one of eight possible positions; the remaining positions were occupied by "$" signs. In the RSVP condition, the sequence began at a randomly selected position with at least one "$" sign and items appeared clockwise in adjacent positions for 100 ms each. In the simultaneous displays, the five upper positions were filled with letters and the three lower ones with "$" signs. The exposure duration for these displays was individually set and averaged at 300 ms.

Both types of display were followed by a backward mask of eight "$" signs. Repeats were separated by one letter (e.g., R D K D H). Subjects were required to report letters in serial order for the RSVP condition and from left to right for the simultaneous displays. Repetition blindness occurred for the second repeat (C2) and, to a lesser extent, for the first (C1).

In further experiments with simultaneous arrays, the spatial separation between the repeats was increased and repetition blindness did not decrease with spatial separation. Furthermore, there was an increase in repetition blindness from zero lag (adjacent repeats) to lag 1 (one letter between the repeats). Luo and Caramazza (1996) argued that with both RSVP and simultaneous arrays, items were coded serially so that the effects could be attributed to coding onset asynchrony determined by the number of items between C1 and C2.

Effects of repetition on identification of temporally and spatially distributed pairs of letters were investigated by Neill, Neely, Hutchison, Kahan, and VerWys (2002), who adapted the paradigms used by Luo and Caramazza (1995, 1996). Neill et al. presented just two successive backward masked letters, A or B, each exposed for 50 ms, yielding an SOA of 50 ms. The sequence of events is shown in Figure 8.2. This procedure allowed them to present two letters without producing visual fusion in the repeat condition. It also enabled them to investigate reports of individual stimuli using temporal (first letter, second letter) or spatial (left letter, right letter) cues. Subjects reported the cued letter and then the other letter, given a spatial or temporal cue for first or second presented letter. Substantial repetition blindness was observed for the first letter as well as for the second, and repetition blindness for the first was especially marked with the spatial cue.

ATTENTIONAL BLINK AND REPETITION BLINDNESS

Another information processing deficit found with RSVP sequences occurs when people have to search for two targets inserted in a sequence of 10 or more distractors (see Chapter 7 by Jolicœur and colleagues). The first target is usually accurately identified, but the second target is frequently missed when it occurs 200–300 ms after the first. As the between-target SOA increases, accuracy in second target detection progressively improves with no impairment at SOA of 600–800 ms. This deficit was termed an "attentional blink" by Raymond, Shapiro, and Arnell (1992). A number of studies showed that target–distractor similarity and backward masking of T1 and T2 were essential determinants of the occurrence of the attentional blink (Chun & Potter, 1995; Seiffert & Di Lollo, 1997; Shapiro et al., 1994). Given the similarity in exposure durations and time course between the attentional blink and repetition blindness, we can ask whether these are essentially manifestations of the same underlying process.

A series of experiments by Chun (1997) demonstrated that different variables affect the occurrence of these two phenomena. For example, the attentional blink does not occur if the distractors are not very similar to the targets—when targets are letters and distractors are punctuation and other symbols (#, ?, %, &). On the

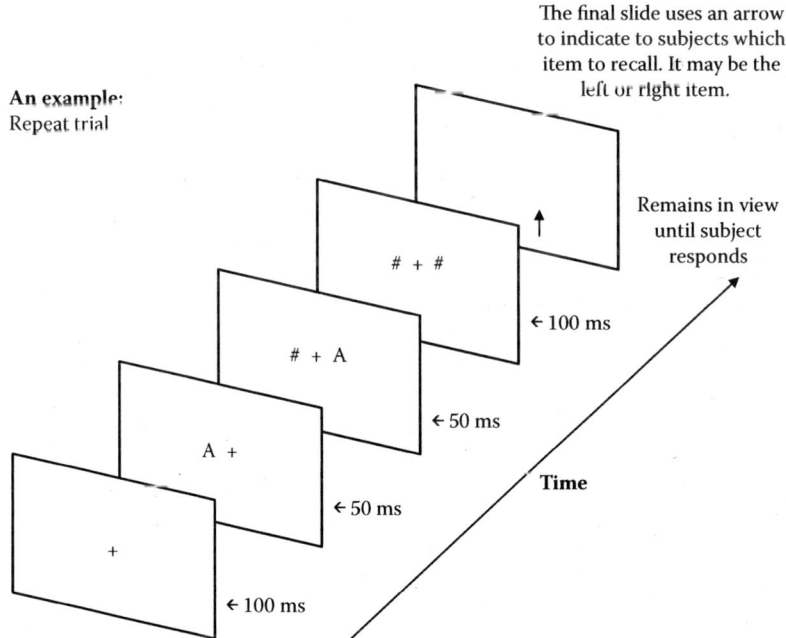

Figure 8.2 Example sequence from Neill et al. (2002, *Journal of Experimental Psychology: Human Perception and Performance, 28*, 137–149).

other hand, repetition blindness does occur with these sorts of distractors. Yet, repetition blindness was eliminated when targets were letters differing in color from distractors—a condition in which the attentional blink was clearly manifest. In addition, repetition blindness in the dual target search task had a shorter time course between T1 and T2 (200–300 ms) than did the attentional blink (600+ ms). Increasing the central processing demands of the task by requiring a speeded response to T1 increases the magnitude of the attentional blink but not that of repetition blindness (Dux & Marois, 2007). These results suggest that repetition blindness has an earlier processing locus than does the attentional blink.

EXPLANATIONS OF REPETITION BLINDNESS

The Token Individuation Account

Various possible explanations of repetition blindness were discussed by Kanwisher (1987). Influenced by the notion of object files proposed by Kahneman and Treisman (1984) to account for perception of objects in visual arrays, she suggested that rapidly presented words, letters, or numbers are initially processed through activation of their type nodes in long-term memory. However, this processing is insufficient for conscious recognition that a particular item has been seen. For that to be possible, the new occurrence of the item must be recorded as an episode. This requires the establishment of token nodes representing spatiotemporal and other forms of contextual information. The token node is linked to the activated type node, a process termed token individuation. By this means, the occurrence of the stimulus becomes a reportable episode.

Kanwisher (1987) proposed that repetition blindness occurred through a failure of the token individuation process. When a type node has just been assigned to a token, that process cannot recur for the same type for a brief period, although token individuation can occur for other activated types. The nature of "type" units was unspecified, but Kanwisher conducted further experiments that were aimed at establishing empirically the underlying basis of types. These experiments will be discussed later, after discussion of alternative explanations of repetition blindness.

Memory Retrieval Limitations

The study of repetition blindness for stimuli shown in RSVP sequences is complicated by the memory demands imposed when lists of unrelated items are shown at high rates, typically 8–10 per second. The undoubted existence of these memory demands led some investigators to argue that repetition blindness is due to memory retrieval limitations or to other retrieval phenomena. Thus, Fagot and Pashler (1995) pointed out that research on short-term memory (STM) serial recall had demonstrated the existence of a bias against reporting a previously recalled item—a finding named the Ranschburg effect after the investigator who initially noted it (Ranschburg, 1902, cited by Crowder, 1968; Jahnke, 1969). Subjects might be biased against reporting an item already recalled (censorship bias) or are more likely to guess another list item that has not yet been recalled (guessing bias).

Fagot and Pashler (1995) found no difference between repeat and control conditions when subjects recalled the lists backwards. However, recall levels were low and there was ambiguity about which of C1 or C2 had been recalled on repeat trials. As noted by Neill et al. (2002), the between-subjects manipulation of recall mode may have promoted different encoding strategies in the backward and forward recall conditions.

Another technique for reducing retrieval load was adopted by Armstrong and Mewhort (1995). They presented five- or seven-letter lists and tested cued report of the item following the cue. When the cued item was C2, no difference was observed between the repeat and control conditions, although full report showed repetition blindness. However, as Johnston et al. (2002) pointed out, cued recall levels were low in both conditions and repetition effects might have been obscured by floor effects. Consequently, the partial-report experiments do not provide unequivocal support for the retrieval hypothesis as the basis of repetition blindness. Moreover, although difficulties in recalling repeated items do occur in STM tasks, a systematic investigation by Henson (1998) demonstrated that the temporal and lag effects in STM tasks differ markedly from the parameters governing repetition deficits in RSVP tasks.

Construction–Attribution Account

Whittlesea, Dorken, and Podrouzek (1995) initially argued that reconstructive processes impede recall of repetitions because context is insufficiently encoded at RSVP rates of presentation. They further claimed that memory migrations of C2 to the C1 location may occur.

In a more recent development of these ideas, Whittlesea and Masson (2005) asserted that theoretical explanations involve metaphors and that their metaphors are those of construction and attribution. Their claim is that representations in memory are of "processing experiences…not stimulus structures or abstract meanings" and that performance is controlled by distributed representations in memory. "Construction and attribution can be based on stimulus interpretations controlled by intuitive theories of cause and effect. Perception is always an act of interpretation and attribution" (p. 54).

These are very general assertions and do not lead to clearly testable predictions; as Masson (2004) acknowledged, "It is difficult to generate precise predictions from [the construction account]" (p. 1287). Furthermore, few current theorists adopt the view that their own theoretical proposals merely involve the development of metaphorical descriptions. The underlying assumption of the Masson–Whittlesea theoretical approach appears to be an instrumental view of scientific explanation theories seen as "convenient fictions" or analogies, whereas most cognitive theorists adopt the realist assumption. This is the view that a theory should represent a true state of affairs concerning the storage and processing mechanisms underlying cognitive functions. For example, the theoretical account of word recognition and reading, the dual route cascaded processing model of M. Coltheart, Rastle, Perry, Langdon, and Ziegler (2001), attempts to explain the processes of reading aloud in real time as performed by skilled adult readers. Of course, the many electrophysiological and imaging studies conducted in recent years also represent the realist approach to theoretical explanation. Similarly, in Chapter 2 Di Lollo presents an account of visual perception and attention that explains phenomena such as visual feature binding with reference to known neural mechanisms.

Modified Token Individuation Theory

The finding by Neill et al. (2002) of substantial repetition blindness for the first of the repeated items is problematical for the original token individuation account because it assumes that repetition blindness occurs after successful tokenization of the first occurrence, with failure of token individuation for the second occurrence. Downing and Kanwisher (1995) considered the possibility that, with temporally close events, tokenization of the second occurrence might be completed first because processes overlap in time. However, this would be an uncommon event: although repetition blindness for the first of the repeats could sometimes occur, the overall repetition deficit across trials would be weaker than the deficit for the second item.

Neill et al. (2002) considered possible explanations from existing theories of repetition blindness and argued that, because repetition blindness was unaffected by report order (i.e., report first presented letter vs. report second presented letter), their results were inconsistent with memory accounts based on output interference or guessing censorship bias. Furthermore, the fact that repetition blindness could be comparable in magnitude for first and second items was inconsistent with the type refractoriness hypothesis proposed by Luo and Caramazza (1995, 1996). As noted before, the large repetition blindness effect for the first item was also inconsistent with Kanwisher's (1987) token individuation account because the failure of tokenization should involve the second item more frequently than the first.

Neill et al. (2002) argued that a modification of the token individuation hypothesis could account for their data as well as other previous results. This account assumes that a first stage of type activation is necessary and that this process occurs for both of the critical items whether they are repeated or not. It also assumes that token individuation is a necessary second stage, but Neill et al. asserted that this stage consists of two subprocesses: instantiation and contextualization. Instantiation involves registration that an item of a particular type has occurred and this process fails when the same type has recently been instantiated.

However, for successful report of an item, contextualization is also required. This process locates the instantiated item in a specific temporal and spatial context. Contextualization may be inaccurately applied when only one of the repeats has been instantiated; the result is that the first rather than the second occurrence is "lost" because the first instantiated item is contextualized as the second occurrence.

Neill et al. (2002) speculated that task demands imposed by the cued report, spatial or temporal, can influence the contextualization process. Temporal cues emphasize the first occurrence ("When did I first see 'A'?"), whereas spatial cues might emphasize the most recent location ("Where did I last see 'A'?"). When the occurrence of temporal and spatial report cues was unpredictable, the magnitude of repetition blindness was comparable for C1 and for C2 if these were temporally cued. The magnitude of repetition blindness was 26% for C1 and C2 when C1 was the first item reported—the usual condition in repetition blindness experiments in which items are reported in serial order.

TYPES OR UNITS UNDERLYING REPETITION BLINDNESS

Repetition blindness occurs with repeated written words (Kanwisher, 1987), as well as with repeated single letters or Arabic numerals (Bavelier & Potter, 1992). Both the original token individuation and the modified accounts assume that items undergo some form of initial processing, activation of "type nodes" (Kanwisher, 1987), or a brief form of identification: Stage 1 processing (Chun & Potter, 1995). However, the nature of these processes was not specified in any detail, although it might be assumed that the normal processes of letter, number, or word recognition would be involved. Which of the outputs of the various subprocesses of initial recognition fails to be registered in reportable short-term memory for the repeated items remains an open question.

Kanwisher and Potter (1990) pointed out that the loss of whole words in repetition blindness does not imply that the units that fail to be registered are necessarily lexical. The units underlying the deficit could involve repetitions of abstract letter identities, of letter clusters, of lexical entries, or of lexical–semantic representations. Therefore, Kanwisher and Potter conducted experiments to determine the nature of the units responsible for the repetition deficit.

Lexical and Morphological Units

Kanwisher and Potter (1990) considered whether susceptibility to repetition blindness was affected by a word's form class. There was, however, no difference in repetition blindness for open and closed class words (such as "the," "of," "then"). Polysemous homographs (river bank, money bank) whose meanings were conveyed by their sentence context generated as much repetition blindness as did repeated words having a single meaning. Repetition blindness also occurred for words sharing a morpheme with a compound (e.g., hot and hot dog [or hotdog], with the second "hot" omitted in sentence recall).

Bavelier, Prasada, and Segui (1994) investigated report of morphologically related words such as WRITE and WRITER and observed reduced joint recall of these pairs relative to the report of unrelated word pairs. Interestingly, the deficit was no worse than that observed for orthographically similar but morphologically unrelated words such as WAND and WANDER. Thus, orthographic overlap between a pair of words is sufficient to cause reduced report for that pair. This form of deficit was referred to as "orthographic repetition blindness."

Chialant and Caramazza (1997) argued that repetition blindness has a lexical basis and that the critical words must share an orthographic lexical entry. Thus, the report deficit for a repeated word should be distinguished from effects occurring for homographs that have separate lexical entries or for orthographically similar word pairs such as "barn" and "yarn." They compared recall of identical word pairs, homographs, and orthographically similar word pairs presented at various lags in sentences. The report deficit relative to the control conditions differed as a function of lag for identical and for similar word pairs. They therefore concluded that repetition blindness involved activation and inhibition at the lexical level for repeated words, but that different, intralexical inhibitory mechanisms caused reduced recall for homographs and orthographically similar words. Mackay and Miller (1994) similarly argued that lexical nodes were responsible for repetition blindness.

Orthographic Units and Similarity Effects

Kanwisher and Potter (1990) investigated recall of pairs of words that were merely similar rather than identical and found a recall deficit (relative to dissimilar pairs of words); however, the deficit was lower than it was for a repeated pair. Similar results were observed by Bavelier et al. (1994), who presented pairs of words that differed by one letter but were phonologically dissimilar (e.g., REACH and REACT). These orthographically similar pairs of words differed only by one letter, had shared letters in the same positions, and were termed orthographic neighbors by M. Coltheart, Davelaar, Jonasson, and Besner (1977).

The size of a word's orthographic neighborhood (N, a count of the number of neighbors) is a determinant of ease of written word recognition (M. Coltheart et al., 1977; Forster & Shen, 1996): A large neighborhood facilitates lexical decision "yes" RTs to (low-frequency) words and slows rejection RTs to nonwords. Orthographic neighborhood effects are attributed to early stages of the word recognition process (e.g., to activation patterns in the orthographic input lexicon in the dual route cascaded model) (M. Coltheart, Curtis, Atkins, & Haller, 1993; M. Coltheart et al., 2001).

Given that the recall deficit for orthographically similar pairs of words is less pronounced than for repeated words, one can then ask about the type and degree of orthographic similarity that reduce recall. Kanwisher and Potter (1990) found no evidence for reduced recall for words overlapping in a single letter (e.g., "t" in "fault" and "heart") or for anagram pairs (e.g., early/layer). Thus, Bavelier et al. (1994) proposed that the units responsible for reduced recall were ordered letter clusters. Subsequently, Chialant and Caramazza (1997) manipulated lag—the number of words between the critical pair—in sentences that included orthographically similar word pairs. They obtained different lag functions for recall of similar and repeated word pairs and concluded that the mechanisms underlying the repetition and similarity effects differed.

Subsequently, using a different set of sentences, Harris and Morris (2004) were unable to replicate the crossover interaction between type of critical pair (repeated or similar) and lag. They concluded that a common mechanism, a form of letter deletion, is responsible for both types of deficit. However, many differences in stimulus materials and procedure might account for the discrepant results. An important difference between these lag studies and most others is that exposure duration was individually set and determined on a small number of practice trials and that "lag" durations differed for different individuals and between the experiments.

Another important difference was that practice trials used to determine individual exposure durations included repetitions in the Chialant–Caramazza study but not in the Harris–Morris experiments, where the exposure duration was determined without inclusion of repeated and similar words. Given that repetition blindness can readily be observed with a common fixed exposure duration of 100–130 ms/item, it seems undesirable to introduce the additional variable of differing stimulus durations for different subjects.

Because of these atypical features of the Chialant–Caramazza and Harris–Morris experiments, it is difficult to conclude whether repetition and similarity deficits for word report have a common or different underlying mechanism. Furthermore, in experiments using repeated words in sentences, the report of words other than the repeated one is typically high (Bavelier & Potter, 1992; Kanwisher & Potter, 1990). This occurs even when considerable orthographic overlap is present between the noncritical words. For example, in the sentence, *We were anxious for autumn well before autumn arrived,* orthographic overlap occurs between *we/ were, anxious/autumn, were/well,* and *for/before* and initial letter overlap between *autumn/arrived.* However, there is no difficulty in reporting words other than the repeated word, *autumn* (Kanwisher & Potter).

Phonological Units

Kanwisher and Potter (1990) considered the possibility that phonological similarity might be the basis of repetition blindness. They presented homophone pairs (e.g., threw/ through) in sentences and observed reduced report for the second of these relative to control words in one experiment (4A) but no difference in a second experiment (4B) when the orthographic similarity between the homophones was low (e.g., eye/I, size/ sighs). They concluded that repetition blindness was not phonologically mediated.

However, subsequently, Bavelier and Potter (1992) found that items with the same name, such as "8" and "eight," and homophones such as "one" and "won" were less likely to be recalled than were orthographically matched control pairs. They termed this deficit "phonological repetition blindness" and found it with homophones presented in RSVP sentences and in lists. The report deficit for homophone pairs (won/one) was smaller than for identical pairs (one/one and won/won), but it was significant when compared to the control condition of orthographically matched word pairs (age/get). These experiments demonstrated that shared lexical-level phonological representations can induce a form of repetition blindness.

Semantic Units

Semantic or conceptual similarity of word pairs (e.g., students/pupils) did not reduce report (Kanwisher & Potter, 1990), and, indeed, these types of word pairs are frequently used as the control items for repeated words in sentences (e.g., sofa/couch). Similarly, with three-word lists, Kanwisher, Yin, and Wojciulik (1999) found that synonyms or semantically related word pairs did not exhibit "semantic blindness," but instead were significantly more accurately reported than were unrelated word pairs. Thus, for written words, the pair of words has to be identical or must have a high degree of orthographic or phonological similarity for report to be impaired, and semantic overlap cannot be the basis of repetition blindness.

Conceptual/Language Level Units

Studies of bilingual subjects' RSVP word list recall have shown repetition blindness for repeated words in both of the languages (Spanish and English) spoken by the subjects (Altarriba & Soltano, 1996). However, Altarriba and Soltano found that, with mixed language lists of three words translation equivalents, words in two languages sharing a meaning (e.g., horse/caballos) were significantly *better* recalled than were word pairs unrelated in meaning, although a recall deficit was reported by MacKay and Miller (1994) for mixed language sentences.

DOES REPETITION BLINDNESS OCCUR FOR NONWORDS?

Nonwords With Unfamiliar Phonology

Coltheart and Langdon (2003) investigated this question using four-letter mono-syllabic pronounceable nonwords as items in short lists of three items preceded and followed by symbol string masks. The method of Bavelier and Potter (1992) was used in an attempt to minimize memory load for such unfamiliar stimuli. The nonwords varied in orthographic similarity to real words (assessed by orthographic neighborhood size, N) and were presented for slightly longer durations than usual (128 vs. 100–117 ms per item). Performance was compared to that with three-word lists having similar length (four letters) and neighborhood sizes (high or low N) shown for the same exposure durations. We investigated whether a word or a nonword with many orthographic neighbors was more susceptible to repetition blindness than one sharing orthographic segments with few words.

We failed to observe repetition blindness for nonwords; instead, there was a repetition benefit or advantage. Pairs of repeated nonwords were recalled significantly more frequently than were pairs of unrelated (control) nonwords. At the same time, there was substantial repetition blindness for repeated words. Nonwords with many word neighbors were better recalled than nonwords with few neighbors. In contrast, for word sequences, low N enhanced recall. The repetition advantage for nonwords occurred even after the subjects were familiarized with the nonwords. Nonword report improved after this practice, but the repetition advantage remained.

Nonwords With Lexical Phonology

We also studied the effects of repetition of nonwords possessing a lexical phonological representation (namely, pseudohomophones) that sounded identical to English words. The orthographic similarity of the pseudohomophones to their real-word mate was another manipulation (e.g., "sckool" differs by only one letter from school, whereas "skule" differs by many letters). There was a repetition advantage for both of these sorts of pseudohomophone pairs rather than repetition blindness. Thus, lexical phonology was insufficient to reinstate repetition blindness. However, even a reduced memory task of only three items resulted in low performance levels on control trials, leading to a concern that repetition blindness might not be observed at such low levels of performance. Consequently, an alternative task was devised in which subjects merely had to decide whether a sequence contained two or three letter strings after viewing the same two or three pseudohomophone and word sequences described previously.

Reporting the Number of Items

Here the subjects were merely asked to decide whether a sequence contained two or three letter strings. For sequences of three words, subjects were *less* likely to judge that three words had been presented when the first and third words were the same than when they differed. When the items were pseudohomophones, repetition enhanced correct decisions: subjects were more accurate at judging that three items had been presented than they were when the three pseudohomophones were different.

Thus, repetition blindness occurred in a task that required no item report and the items were words, whereas when the items were nonwords, repetition enhanced accurate frequency judgments. The decision RTs confirmed these results: repetition slowed decisions to word sequences but speeded decisions to pseudohomophone sequences. Similarity to their base word did not affect performance. Thus, even with minimal memory demands, repetition blindness occurred for words and repetition advantage occurred for nonwords.

Repetition Benefits With Nonwords

The results of all six experiments reported in Coltheart and Langdon (2003) suggest that the orthographic type units that induce a repetition deficit over a brief interval are lexical rather than sublexical units. The findings of repetition advantage along with repetition blindness in the same task are inconsistent with the censorship bias or guessing bias accounts of repetition blindness by Fagot and Pashler (1995) Thus, the nature of the items determined the pattern of recall or decision accuracy rather than some general extra-task response strategy.

It was noted earlier that when recall levels are low, it might be difficult to obtain repetition blindness and that repetition advantage might simply be due to extreme task difficulty. This is unlikely for several reasons:

- Repetition advantage for nonwords was also found when subjects had merely to decide whether two or three letter sequences had been shown.
- Practice with the nonwords improved recall levels but did not remove repetition advantage.
- It is possible to observe repetition blindness with low levels of recall—for example, when the stimuli are pictures of familiar faces (Coltheart, Bornhofen, Mondy, & Stephenson, 2004).
- It is also possible to observe repetition advantage in RSVP dual target letter search when levels of performance are high (Chun, 1997; Dux & Coltheart, 2008).

Consequently, performance levels per se do not determine whether repetition deficits or benefits are observed.

Identity of orthographic or phonological form is sufficient to induce repetition blindness provided that the items are words, numbers, or single letters. This may indicate that repetition blindness arises only for items that have familiar preexisting representations in long-term memory. These representations can be rapidly identified and sequentially registered in short-term memory; however, as Potter (1999) argued, two of the same (or very similar) activated items are likely to be collapsed into a single memory code if they occur in close temporal contiguity.

Because items that are nonwords have no preexisting representations in the word recognition system, initial identification will take longer and registration in short-term memory (token individuation) is likely to be slower and might be incomplete before the next item arrives. However, if the first nonword is successfully encoded, the initial identification of the repeated item, as a consequence of priming, will be faster. Also, its registration in memory may begin earlier than will recognition and memory encoding of an unrelated new nonword for which the recognition processes will take longer. Consequently, repetition will benefit report of these novel items relative to report of two different items.

Repetition Blindness for Nonwords?

The conclusion that repetition blindness does not occur with repeated nonwords has not gone unchallenged. Harris and her colleagues (Harris, 2001; Harris & Morris, 2002, 2004), who frequently used an atypical two-word task and procedure, argued that repetition blindness is due to overlap of letter clusters with common letters "deleted" in the second word. Although their claim was initially confined to accounts of orthographic repetition blindness, they subsequently argued that letter deletion explains repetition blindness in the usual sense when the same word is shown twice. Using a two-item task in which the critical pair was separated by a symbol string mask, Harris and Morris reported findings of repetition blindness for nonwords and orthographic repetition blindness for similar nonwords.

The paradigms devised by Harris and Morris (2004) differ in a number of ways from those of Coltheart and Langdon (2003) and most other investigators (e.g., Bavelier & Potter, 1992; Kanwisher, 1987), as noted earlier. Most investigators embed the critical pair within a list of other items or, at the very least, insert a to-be-reported dissimilar word between the critical words. This ensures that the processing episodes for the repeat pair are clearly separated by another to-be-recognized and reported word. In the two-word task, a mask of briefer duration than that of either C1 or C2 intervened between a word and its second occurrence. These conditions might occasionally induce letter-feature-level fusion for repeated words despite the fact that the words differ in case.

Cross-case fusion effects were observed by Davis and Forster (1994) in a masked priming paradigm with primes and targets differing in case. The interposition of a brief symbol string might not be effective in preventing fusion effects. Consequently, the deficit with repeated or similar items in the two-item task might have mechanisms differing from those found with sequences of words shown for exposure durations of 100–130 ms per word. Although we suggest that the repetition deficit in the two-word task may have an earlier processing basis than that underlying repetition blindness, we do not mean to suggest that the effects are due to low-level visual fusion.

Instead, we refer to the process of merging a pair of successively presented brief stimuli proposed by Davis and Forster (1994). These authors demonstrated that superimposed upper- and lowercase versions of the same word can produce a recognizable version of a single uppercase word. For example, tile-TILE produces a single, slightly noisy looking TILE even when a brief energy mask intervened or when the word pair was misaligned by one character (tile=/=TILE). Furthermore, these fusion effects occurred for repeated nonword pairs as well as word pairs. Consequently, lexicality and repetition may have different effects in briefly displayed two-item tasks and for lists shown for fixed item durations in the range of 100–130 ms.

However, it is not necessary to present items at individually selected exposure durations because reliable repetition effects can be obtained with a common fixed duration in the range 100–130 ms per item; this has been the standard procedure in most of the previous research. Use of varied exposure durations between subjects makes the possibility of successful replication of effects less likely. Consequently, we used the fixed rate exposure conditions to investigate orthographic similarity effects with words and nonwords in RSVP sequences. Orthographic similarity deficits have been reliably obtained with words in list and sentence tasks in a number of studies cited earlier, and we explored the effects of similarity and lexicality in three experiments using the three-item list paradigm. We observed a similarity deficit in report (relative to dissimilar controls) for both words and nonwords, suggesting that different mechanisms underlie repetition and similarity effects (Coltheart, Stephenson & Langdon, 2006).

REPETITION EFFECTS WITH OTHER CATEGORIES OF VISUAL STIMULI

Repetition of Colors

Repetition blindness was first informally observed with repeated pictures of objects, as noted in the introduction to this chapter. The initial systematic investigations used linguistic stimuli: words, letters, and digits. However, Kanwisher (1987) assumed that repetition blindness was a visual phenomenon that would be observed with other types of visual stimuli. She demonstrated repetition blindness for repeated colors when the task was to report the colors of a fixed set of ASCII symbols that were difficult to label (Kanwisher, 1991). Furthermore, repetition blindness occurred for repeated colors (as well as for letter identities) when pairs of colored letters were simultaneously presented in different spatial locations and immediately followed by a pair of multicolored pattern masks (Kanwisher, Driver, & Machado, 1995).

In these experiments with simultaneous item pairs, when subjects missed a repeated item they frequently reported an incorrect letter and were less likely to report absence of any letter. Thus, with spatial arrays, the difficulty appeared to involve binding a specific letter identity with the spatial location—termed type-token binding failure—rather than a complete lack of awareness of the presence of a letter in the second location. With sequentially presented stimuli, awareness that some item had been present was less likely.

Repetition of Objects

Bavelier (1994) reported several experiments in which line drawings of common objects were presented in RSVP sentences in place of nouns and in short, three-item lists of pictures and their names. Repetition blindness occurred for repeated pictured objects as well as for their names. In this study, only a small pool of eight pictured items per task was used. Kanwisher et al. (1999) investigated recall of repeated pictures of objects in a larger scale study using more items. They presented both line-drawn and photographed objects (in different experiments), manipulating size and orientation differences between critical repeated and unrelated control items in sequences of three items sandwiched between masks. Their interest was in establishing the level of abstractness of the representation derived in the early stages of object recognition.

Repetition blindness occurred for repeated objects and was not reduced by changes in size or viewing angle for objects rotated in a two-dimensional picture plane or in depth (e.g., side view or top view of a shoe). Further evidence for the viewpoint independence of repetition blindness comes from studies by Harris and Dux, who presented line-drawn objects rotated in the picture plane through various angles to 180 degrees. Repetition blindness occurred through all rotations, with the exception of a 180° difference between the orientation of the repeated pair (upright vs. upside down).

Visual, Phonological, and Semantic Similarity Effects

Report was impaired for unrelated similarly drawn objects that were visually similar at a depiction level (e.g., guitar/pear, carrot/closed umbrella). However, Kanwisher et al. (1999) acknowledge that in these cases the items might have been visually confused and the effects could have arisen at an early perceptual level. There was no evidence of repetition blindness for visually dissimilar and semantically unrelated pictured objects that shared a name (e.g., [drinking] glasses/glasses [spectacles]). The finding of repetition blindness for depth rotated objects indicates that viewpoint-invariant representations are extracted rapidly for sequences of objects shown for a tenth of a second and these codes are not phonological.

Kanwisher et al. (1999) observed a reduced but significant report deficit for semantically related objects, a "semantic blindness" effect for pictures of helicopter/plane and horse/cow. However, it is possible that the "semantic blindness" observed by Kanwisher et al. was due to visual similarity at the object level and not to semantic relatedness. Thus, the codes registered during object sequences that are vulnerable to repetition blindness are visual and are largely viewpoint independent.

Repetition of Novel Objects

Do objects have to have preexisting representations for repetition blindness to occur? The answer appears to be no. Arnell and Jolicœur (1997) observed repetition blindness for drawn novel patterns adopted from Kroll and Potter's nonobjects (devised for an object decision task). Similarly, Coltheart, Mondy, and Coltheart (2005) found repetition blindness for colored, novel, three-dimensional objects even when, on the second presentation, the object was rotated in depth by 10° or 20°. Consequently, repetition blindness is a phenomenon of some generality across visual stimuli, although it does not involve low-level features; it occurs across letter case changes and across disparate views of familiar and unfamiliar objects.

Repetition Effects with Faces

An obvious next question is whether repetition blindness occurs with the rather special class of stimuli humans have to distinguish in daily life, namely, human faces. People are able to recognize and identify many individual human faces. This ability is remarkable because it requires a level of detailed visual memory for unique stimuli not demanded by other categories of visual items.

Moreover, known faces can be identified when viewed from different angles (provided faces are not inverted; Yin, 1969). Faces are also recognizable when transformed by cosmetics and hairstyle changes and after age-related changes. Face recognition has been regarded as a form of expert pattern or object recognition, but experts do not usually have to discriminate many unique exemplars. For example, the expert ornithologist learns to identify many species of birds but does not have to identify unique individuals.

In most research using familiar faces, the stimuli are faces of celebrities and people known through the media, rather than faces of individuals known personally by the subjects. It is well known that name retrieval is slow and effortful, but familiarity or semantic decisions ("Is it an actor or politician?") show these decisions can be made quickly and accurately in under a second (e.g., Ellis et al., 1996).

Stone and Valentine (2004) reported the intriguing finding that covert recognition of disliked famous persons (e.g., Stalin) can occur even after masked presentations of no longer than 17-ms duration because they can induce an avoidance response. Consequently, the face recognition system can respond to very brief stimuli and its response may be faster than that of the word recognition system, which shows little or no evidence of facilitation by masked primes below 30-ms duration.

Research on face recognition thus reveals both rapid access to stored representations of faces and slow access to proper names. Naming RTs are slower than object name retrieval (which is slower than reading object names aloud). These aspects of face recognition and identification might indicate that faces are encoded in episodic memory differently from the ways in which objects and written words are registered. For example, are perception of and memory for briefly presented faces vulnerable to the repetition deficit observed with other classes of repeated visual stimuli?

Coltheart, Bornhofen, Mondy and Stephenson (2004) investigated whether repetition blindness occurs with face stimuli and, if so, whether it occurs across changes in viewing angle of the same face. Repetition blindness was observed in four experiments when the stimuli were familiar faces of actors, politicians, and other celebrities. It was undiminished in magnitude when the viewing angle of the face changed between first and second occurrence, indicating that the activated types registered in memory tokens are at least at the level of view-independent descriptions. In this regard, repetition blindness for known faces resembles repetition blindness for objects (Kanwisher et al., 1999).

Another similarity between repetition blindness for the two classes of visual stimuli was the finding of a report deficit when the faces (and hair) differed across the two occurrences and were clearly photographs taken on different occasions. The results indicate the existence of within-domain repetition blindness for a class of visual stimuli for which name retrieval is unusually slow and difficult. Indeed, it is unlikely that the task of name recall of two or three faces, each shown for a tenth of a second, would have been possible without the prior familiarization of the photographs and their names.

Reporting the names of three faces shown at RSVP rates can be assumed to involve the face recognition system and phonological output subsystems shared by word and face (and object) recognition systems. The results of our experiments indicate that the information encoded in the early memory representations is independent of viewpoint and may include face recognition units as well as name-level phonological codes. When stimuli sharing these codes occur in close temporal contiguity, the memory representations are likely to be collapsed into one. Given the high level of recency in report of the third face on control trials, repetition blindness is possibly largely due to loss of C1. When all three faces were different, the third face was twice as likely to be recalled as the first.

CONCLUSIONS

Repetition blindness is a difficulty in perceiving and reporting repeated items in RSVP sequences shown at a rate of 7–10 items per second. One of the repeats is detected and reported with high accuracy and it is usually, but not always, the second repetition that is missed. The temporal and lag characteristics distinguish repetition blindness from other difficulties with repeated items such as the Ranschburg effect in STM tasks. Additionally, a number of other tasks demonstrate impairment in processing repetitions. These include repetition detection, list and sentence recall, report of two or three items from subspan lists, online speeded item detection, and item counting tasks.

Repetition blindness has been observed with a range of visual stimuli, letters, digits, words, drawn and photographed familiar and novel objects, and photographed familiar faces. It is not due to visual similarity at a simple visual feature level because repetition blindness occurs undiminished across letter case for both single letters and for words and is largely unaffected by size and viewpoint changes for pictures of objects and faces. Although there have been controversies over the locus of repetition blindness, there is a growing consensus that the effects arise at early stages during the registration of information in reportable immediate memory.

REFERENCES

Altarriba, J., & Soltano, E. G. (1996). Repetition blindness and bilingual memory: Token individuation for translation equivalents. *Memory and Cognition, 24,* 700–711.

Armstrong, I. T., & Mewhort, D. J. K. (1995). Repetition deficit in rapid serial visual presentation displays: Encoding failure or retrieval failure? *Journal of Experimental Psychology: Human Perception and Performance, 21,* 1044–1052.

Arnell, K. M., & Jolicœur, P. (1997). Repetition blindness for pseudo-object pictures. *Journal of Experimental Psychology: Human Perception and Performance, 23,* 999–1013.

Bavelier, D. (1994). Repetition blindness between visually different items: The case of pictures and words. *Cognition, 51,* 199–236.

Bavelier, D., & Potter, M. C. (1992). Visual and phonological codes in repetition blindness. *Journal of Experimental Psychology: Human Perception and Performance, 18,* 134–147.

Bavelier, D., Prasada, S., & Segui, J. (1994). Repetition blindness between words: Nature of the orthographic and phonological representations involved. *Journal of Experimental Psychology: Learning, Memory, and Cognition, 20,* 1437–1455.

Chialant, D., & Caramazza, A. (1997). Identity and similarity factors in repetition blindness: Implications for lexical processing. *Cognition, 63,* 79–119.

Chun, M. M. (1997). Types and tokens in visual processing: A double dissociation between the attentional blink and repetition blindness. *Journal of Experimental Psychology: Human Perception and Performance, 23,* 738–755.

Chun, M. M., & Potter, M. C. (1995). A two-stage model for multiple target detection in rapid serial visual presentation. *Journal of Experimental Psychology: Human Perception and Performance, 21,* 109–127.

Coltheart, M., Curtis, B., & Atkins, P., & Haller, M. (1993). Models of reading aloud: Dual-route and parallel-distributed-processing approaches. *Psychological Review, 100,* 589–608.

Coltheart, M., Davelaar, E., Jonasson, J. T., & Besner, D. (1977). Access to the internal lexicon. In S. Dornie (Ed.) *Attention and performance. IV* (pp. 535–555). Hillsdale, N.J.: Lawrence Erlbaum Associates.

Coltheart, M., Rastle, K., Perry, C., Langdon, R., & Ziegler, J. (2001). DRC: A dual route cascaded model of visual word recognition and reading aloud. *Psychological Review, 108,* 204–256.

Coltheart, V., Bornhofen, C., Mondy, S., & Stephenson, L. (2004). Repetition blindness for famous faces. *Perception, 33*(Suppl. 1), 14.

Coltheart, V., & Langdon, R. (2003). Repetition blindness for words yet repetition advantage for nonwords. *Journal of Experimental Psychology: Learning, Memory, and Cognition, 29,* 171–185.

Coltheart, V., Mondy, S., & Coltheart, M. (2005). Repetition blindness for novel objects. *Visual Cognition, 12*(3), 519–540.

Coltheart, V., Stephenson, L., & Langdon, R. (2006). Repetition blindness and effects of lexicality, similarity and task. *Australian Journal of Psychology, 58*(Suppl. 1), 69.

Crowder, R. G. (1968). Intraserial repetition effects in immediate memory. *Journal of Verbal Learning & Verbal Behavior. 7,* 446–451.

Davis, C., & Forster, K. I. (1994). Masked orthographic priming: The effect of prime-target legibility. *Quarterly Journal of Experimental Psychology A: Human Experimental Psychology, 47A*(3), 673–697.

Downing, P., & Kanwisher, K. (1995). Types and tokens unscathed: A reply to Whittlesea, Dorken, and Podrouzek (1995) and Whittlesea and Podrouzek (1995). *Journal of Experimental Psychology: Learning, Memory, and Cognition, 21*, 1698–1702.

Dux, P. E. & Coltheart, V. (2008). Repetition blindness and repetition priming: Effects of featural differences between targets and distractors on RSVP dual-target search. *Memory & Cognition, 36*, 776–790.

Dux, P. E. & Marois, R. (2007). Repetition blindness is immune to the central bottleneck. *Psychonomic Bulletin & Review, 14*, 729–734.

Ellis, A. W., Flude, B. M., Young, A., & Burton, A. M. (1996). Two loci of repetition priming in the recognition of familiar faces. *Journal of Experimental Psychology: Learning, Memory, and Cognition, 22*, 295–308.

Fagot, C., & Pashler, H. (1995). Repetition blindness: Perception or memory failure? *Journal of Experimental Psychology: Human Perception and Performance, 21*, 275–292.

Forster, K. I. (1970). Visual perception of rapidly presented word sequences of varying complexity. *Perception & Psychophysics, 8*, 215–221.

Forster, K. I. & Shen, D. (1996). No enemies in the neighborhood: Absence of inhibitory neighborhood effects in lexical decision and semantic categorization. *Journal of Experimental Psychology: Learning, Memory, & Cognition, 22*, 696–713.

Harris, C. L. (2001). Are individual or consecutive letters the unit affected by repetition blindness? *Journal of Experimental Psychology: Learning, Memory & Cognition, 27*, 761–774.

Harris, C. L., & Morris, A. L. (2004). Repetition blindness occurs in nonwords. *Journal of Experimental Psychology: Human Perception and Performance, 30*, 305–318.

Henson, R. N. A. (1998). Item repetition in short-term memory: Ranschburg repeated. *Journal of Experimental Psychology: Learning, Memory, and Cognition, 24*, 1162–1181.

Jahnke, J. C. (1969). The Ranschburg effect. *Psychological Review, 76*, 592–605.

Johnston, J. C., Hochhaus, L., & Ruthruff, E. (2002). Repetition blindness has a perceptual locus: Evidence from online processing of targets in RSVP streams. *Journal of Experimental Psychology: Human Perception and Performance, 28*, 477–489.

Kahneman, D., & Treisman, A. (1984). Changing views of attention and automaticity. In R. Parasuraman & D. R. Davies (Eds.), *Varieties of attention.* New York: Academic Press,

Kanwisher, N. G. (1986). *Repetition blindness: Type recognition without token individuation.* Unpublished doctoral dissertation, Massachusetts Institute of Technology, Cambidge.

Kanwisher, N. G. (1987). Repetition blindness: Type recognition without token individuation. *Cognition, 27*, 117–143.

Kanwisher, N. (1991). Repetition blindness and illusory conjunctions: Errors in binding visual types with visual tokens. *Journal of Experimental Psychology: Human Perception and Performance, 17*, 404–421.

Kanwisher, N., Driver, J., & Machado, L. (1995). Spatial repetition blindness is modulated by selective attention to color or shape. *Cognitive Psychology, 29*, 303–337.

Kanwisher, N. G., & Potter, M. C. (1990). Repetition blindness: Levels of processing. *Journal of Experimental Psychology: Human Perception and Performance, 16*, 30–47.

Kanwisher, N., Yin, C., & Wojciulik, E. (1999). Repetition blindness for pictures: Evidence for the rapid computation of abstract visual descriptions. In V. Coltheart (Ed.), *Fleeting memories: Cognition of brief visual stimuli* (pp. 119–150). Cambridge, MA: MIT Press.

Luo, C. R., & Caramazza, A. (1995). Repetition blindness under minimum memory load: Effects of spatial and temporal proximity and the encoding effectiveness of the first item. *Perception & Psychophysics, 57,* 1053–1064.

Luo, C. R., & Caramazza, A. (1996). Temporal and spatial repetition blindness: Effects of presentation mode and repetition lag on the perception of repeated items. *Journal of Experimental Psychology: Human Perception and Performance, 22,* 95–113.

McKay, D. G., & Miller, M. D. (1994). Semantic blindness: Repeated concepts are difficult to encode and recall under time pressure. *Psychological Science, 5,* 52–55.

Masson, M. E. J. (2004). When words collide: Facilitation and interference in the report of repeated words from rapidly presented lists. *Journal of Experimental Psychology: Learning, Memory, and Cognition, 30,* 1279–1289.

Neill, W. T., Neely, J. H., Hutchison, K. A., Kahan, T. A., & VerWys, C. A. (2002). Repetition blindness, forward and backward. *Journal of Experimental Psychology: Human Perception and Performance, 28,* 137–149.

Park, J., & Kanwisher, N. G. (1994). Determinants of repetition blindness. *Journal of Experimental Psychology: Human Perception and Performance, 20,* 500–519.

Potter, M. C. (1984). Rapid serial visual presentation (RSVP): A method for studying language processing. In D. E. Kieras & M. A. Just (Eds.), *New methods in reading comprehension research* (pp. 91–118). Hillsdale, NJ: Lawrence Erlbaum Associates.

Potter, M. C. (1999). Understanding sentences and scenes: The role of conceptual short-term memory. In V. Coltheart (Ed.), *Fleeting memories: Cognition of brief visual stimuli* (pp. 13–46). Cambridge, MA: MIT Press.

Raymond, J. E., Shapiro, K. L., & Arnell, K. M. (1992). Temporary suppression of visual processing in an RSVP task: An attentional blink? *Journal of Experimental Psychology: Human Perception and Performance, 18,* 849–860.

Scarborough, D. L., Cortese, C., & Scarborough, H. S. (1977). Frequency and repetition effects in lexical memory. *Journal of Experimental Psychology: Human Perception and Performance, 3,* 1–17.

Seiffert, A. E., & Di Lollo, V. (1997). Low-level masking in the attentional blink. *Journal of experimental psychology. Human perception and performance, 23,* 1061–1073.

Shapiro, K. L., Raymond, J E., & Arnell, K. M. (1994). Attention to visual pattern information produces the attentional blink in RSVP. *Journal of Experimental Psychology: Human Perception and Performance, 20,* 357–371.

Stone, A., & Valentine, T. (2004). Better the devil you know? Non-conscious processing of identity and affect of famous persons. *Psychonomic Bulletin & Review, 11,* 469–474.

Whittlesea, B. W. A., Dorken, M. D., & Podrouzek, K. W. (1995). Repeated events in rapid lists: Part 1. Encoding and representation. *Journal of Experimental Psychology: Learning, Memory, and Cognition, 21,* 1670–1688.

Whittlesea, B. W. A., & Masson, M. E. J. (2005). Repetition blindness in rapid lists: Activation and inhibition versus construction and attribution. *Journal of Experimental Psychology: Learning, Memory, and Cognition, 31,* 54–67.

Whittlesea, B. W. A., & Wai, K. H. (1997). Reverse "repetition blindness" and release from "repetition blindness": Constructive variations on the "repetition blindness" effect. *Psychological Research, 60,* 173–182.

Yin, R. K. (1969). Looking at upside down faces. *Journal of Experimental Psychology, 81,* 141–145.

9

Spatial Attention and the Detection of Weak Visual Signals

PHILIP L. SMITH

INTRODUCTION

*M*odern attention research had its beginnings in the 1950s, with the dichotic listening studies of Cherry in 1953 and, subsequently, with Broadbent's filter theory, described in his monograph *Perception and Communication* in 1958. Research in attention burgeoned during the following decades and its focus switched increasingly from audition to vision. These decades were marked by successive waves of fashionable research topics, each driven by the discovery of new phenomena and accompanied by a proliferation of new theories to explain them. Throughout these changes in fashion, however, two core ideas—the legacy of the first decade of attention research—continued to provide researchers with fruitful ways to think about attention.

The first of these was the idea that "attention" is a set of mechanisms that control a limited-capacity processing mechanism. Capacity has been conceived in a variety of ways by different researchers, but the common underlying notion is that the brain is unable to identify and respond to all of the stimuli in the ambient environment at any given moment. Its processing resources must therefore be concentrated on the subset of stimuli deemed most relevant to current goals. The mechanisms that determine how these resources are allocated are what we collectively refer to as "attention." Limited capacity and selectivity thus become two sides of the same coin: Because capacity is limited, processing is necessarily selective.

The second is the idea that mental processes do not all benefit from or require attention to the same extent. In the jargon of attention theory, mental processes do not all draw on the brain's limited-capacity attentional resources equally. This led to the idea, which had its origins in Cherry's groundbreaking papers (Cherry, 1953; Cherry & Taylor, 1954), that mental processes can be divided into two classes: a class of processes that require access to a limited-capacity system and another class of processes that do not. The latter processes were termed *preattentive* processes by Neisser (1967); the former he termed processes of *focal attention*. This led to the realization that a fruitful way to study attention was to study capacity limitations to understand which mental processes can be performed preattentively and which can only be performed with focal attention. This approach has continued to provide researchers with new insights for more than 50 years.

The subject of this chapter, visual signal detection, lies at the heart of the contemporary debate about preattention, selectivity, and capacity limitations. It does so because of a view, which had its origins in the first decade of attention research, that detection is a preattentive task. According to this view, simply detecting whether a visual stimulus is or is not present in the visual field does not benefit from or require attention (Egeth, 1977). This idea has been expressed in a variety of ways, but perhaps the most influential contemporary statement of it has been Anne Treisman's feature integration theory (Treisman & Gelade, 1980). Treisman's theory holds that detection of simple features is performed preattentively and that focal attention is required only to glue features together into identifiable compounds. The purpose of this chapter is to assess whether this is true for stimuli near threshold and, if so, to characterize the particular sense in which it is true and the particular circumstances under which it is true.

Of course, we need to qualify this immediately by making clear that what we mean by "attention" is what researchers term *covert* attention—that is, attention independent of eye movements. In normal visual functioning, shifts of attention are almost always accompanied by saccadic eye movements that bring the object of attention into central vision. This allows perception to benefit from the finer spatial resolution afforded by the higher density of cone receptors in the fovea. Naturally, many perceptual tasks can be performed more accurately when the stimulus is in foveal vision, for reasons quite unrelated to attention. It is therefore imperative to be certain that comparisons of performance with attended and unattended stimuli are not confounded with differences in acuity between foveal and peripheral vision. Most of the tasks we will be discussing in this chapter will be tasks in which acuity factors of this kind can be discounted because the displays were too brief to allow stimuli to be refixated.

We should also acknowledge at the outset that the question of how to define "detection" in a satisfactory way is not a completely straightforward matter. The reader is referred to Kawahara, Di Lollo, and Enns (2001) for a useful discussion of this issue. What we would like is a definition that distinguishes detection unambiguously from other, more complex perceptual judgments, such as discrimination, or recognition of form. Typically, by "detection," we mean performance on what in signal detection theory is known as a yes/no task (Green & Swets, 1966; Macmillan & Creelman, 1991).

In a yes/no task, observers are required to judge whether a stimulus, defined by a simple visual feature or attribute, is present in or absent from the visual field. It does not require that observers be able to localize the stimulus or, indeed, to report anything about it, other than its presence. Later, we will relax our definition and allow certain kinds of easy discrimination tasks also to count as detection.

According to this more inclusive definition, detection tasks are tasks in which performance is limited by the absolute intensity or contrast of the stimulus. Discrimination tasks are tasks in which performance is limited by the similarity of the stimulus alternatives.

Even as it stands, however, our definition of detection begs the question of what counts as a "simple visual feature or attribute." This is actually quite a deep question that has significant implications for theories of visual attention (e.g., Treisman, Cavanagh, Fischer, Ramachandran, & von der Heydt, 1990). We will make no attempt in this chapter to answer this question in any definitive way. Most of the experiments we consider here used sinusoidal grating patches (so-called Gabor patches) as stimuli. Because the luminance profiles of Gabor patches match the receptive fields of oriented simple cells in primary visual cortex, at least approximately (Webster & DeValois, 1985), such stimuli can reasonably be deemed to be "simple" from the standpoint of the visual system. We therefore define "simple" in terms of the known physiology of the visual cortex and sidestep the issue of whether it can be defined psychophysically in any principled way.

The tasks we consider in this chapter are of two kinds. One is a detection analogue of the visual search task, in which a low-contrast target is presented in an array of distractor stimuli. In such tasks, processing load is manipulated by varying the number of stimuli in the display. It is typically assumed that capacity limitations will be revealed under these circumstances via a degradation or decrement in performance as the load increases. The other kind of task uses the Posner (1980) spatial cuing paradigm. In this task, cues are used to attract or summon attention to a particular location in the visual field. The cue is followed after a brief interval by a stimulus, either at the attended location or elsewhere in the visual field. It is assumed that capacity limitations will be revealed as a decrement in performance for unattended stimuli relative to performance for attended stimuli. These two kinds of tasks provide complementary pictures of the role of capacity limitations in detection.

ATTENTION, CAPACITY LIMITATIONS, AND NOISE

The question of whether detection is, in some sense or other, a capacity-limited process appears on the face of it to be a simple one to which a reader might feel entitled to expect a straightforward answer. However, a review of the literature on attention and detection, which extends back about 25 years, will quickly dash any expectations of this kind. What one finds instead is continuing controversy, disagreement over methods, and an inconsistent body of experimental findings, with roughly equal numbers of studies supporting the capacity-limited view as rebutting it (Smith, 2000). One group of studies, (Bonnel & Hafter, 1998; Brawn & Snowden, 2000; Davis, Kramer, & Graham, 1983; Foley & Schwarz, 1998; Graham, Kramer, & Haber, 1985; Lee, Koch, & Braun, 1997; Müller & Findlay, 1987; Palmer, 1994; Palmer, Ames, & Lindsey, 1993; Shaw, 1984) which investigated the effects of attention on detection using a variety of methods, found no evidence that detection is a capacity-limited process.

A number of these studies (Bonnel & Hafter, 1998; Brawn & Snowden, 2000; Lee et al., 1997; Müller & Findley, 1987; Palmer, 1994; Palmer et al., 1993; Shaw, 1984) also compared detection with more complex judgments, such as discrimination or recognition. Their results supported the classical attention–preattention dichotomy: there was little evidence of capacity limitations in detection, but large and systematic effects for more complex judgments. In contrast to these findings, a second group of studies (Bashinski & Bacharach, 1980; Cameron, Tai, & Carrasco, 2002; Carrasco, Penpeci-Talgar, & Eckstein, 2000; Downing, 1988; Hawkins et al., 1990; Luck et al., 1994; Müller & Humphreys, 1991; Smith, 1998) found evidence supporting the idea that detection is capacity limited. To the reader unfamiliar with the area, this will probably seem a strange state of affairs. Why should the answer to such an apparently simple question prove so elusive?

The answer is that, when one is dealing with near-threshold stimuli, the problem of distinguishing the effects of stimulus noise from those of capacity limitations becomes acute. To characterize performance on detection tasks, we need to begin with the assumption, articulated in Thurstone's law of comparative judgment (1927) and formalized in signal detection theory, that the representation of stimuli in the central nervous system is inherently noisy. The noise may arise because of trial-to-trial variation in the quality of the stimulus information encoded by the sensory receptors or because of moment-by-moment fluctuations in the level of neural noise within the nervous system; it may even be added into the stimulus display by the experimenter, with the objective of making the task more difficult. Regardless of where the noise originates, however, what makes the task of distinguishing signal from noise difficult perceptually is that the strength of the signal is small relative to the level of noise in the system.

The theoretical and mathematical framework of signal detection theory provides a way to characterize a human observer's perceptual sensitivity to a stimulus in these situations. It does so in a way that is independent of the observer's response bias—that is, of his or her propensity to label the perceptual experience produced by a stimulus as "signal" rather than "noise." Sensitivity is defined in signal detection theory as the perceptual distance between the means of the noise and the signal distributions, scaled in noise standard deviation units (Green & Swets, 1966). Response bias is defined by the placement of the observer's decision criterion along an underlying axis of sensory effect or signal strength. Sensitivity and bias together provide a complete description of an observer's performance in a yes/no task.

Although signal detection theory is an indispensable tool for characterizing performance in detection tasks, it is not, at least not in its standard textbook form, sufficient to account for performance in attention paradigms. This is because signal detection theory is essentially a single-channel theory, whereas the majority of attention tasks are multichannel monitoring tasks. That is, they require the observer to monitor multiple noisy stimulus sources, or perceptual channels, for the occurrence of a signal. Moreover, manipulations of attention are often also manipulations of the observer's uncertainty about where a signal may occur. Increases in uncertainty are typically accompanied by increases in decision noise, which arise because of an increase in the number of stimulus sources the observer has to monitor. When the level of noise in each stimulus source is appreciable, increasing uncertainty will produce a decline in performance even in unlimited capacity systems.

For example, suppose an experimenter chooses to investigate the effects of attention in a yes/no task by comparing performance in a focused attention condition, in which observers are required to monitor a single display location, to performance in a divided attention condition, in which they are required to monitor several locations simultaneously. If each location is noisy—in the sense that the perceptual experience it produces is confusable with a signal—then each has some probability of triggering a false alarm (i.e., of a noise or target-absent stimulus being misidentified as a signal). As the number of noise sources increases, so too does the probability of a false alarm.

Consequently, any aggregate measure of detection performance will decrease with a change from a focused to a divided attention set. This is despite the fact that the quality of the stimulus information available at each display location does not change as a function of attentional set. Such a change would be the hallmark of a capacity-limited system and is typically what the researcher in this situation really wishes to infer. The situation is exactly analogous to the problem of multiple comparisons in statistical inference. As the number of simultaneous comparisons carried out on a set of data increases, the probability of committing at least one Type I error increases. This is despite the fact that quality of the information on which each comparison is based does not change as a function of the number of comparisons performed.

The preceding discussion implies that when one is dealing with noisy stimuli—as is the case when detecting near-threshold stimuli—capacity limitations can only be inferred once the effects of decision noise and of changes in decision noise across conditions have first been characterized. That is, capacity limitations can only be inferred from a decrease in performance with load that is greater than is predictable from an increase in decision noise alone. It is the difficulty of answering this question in a decisive way that has made the problem of arriving at a consensus about the preattentive status of detection so difficult.

The effects of uncertainty on decision making were understood and discussed by early signal detection theorists like Tanner (1961). Later authors considered ways of extending the detection theory model from single-channel to multiple-channel settings as a way to model divided attention performance (Gilliom & Sorkin, 1974; Sorkin & Pohlmann, 1973; Sorkin, Pohlmann, & Woods, 1976; Swets, 1984). Ashby and Townsend's (1986) general recognition theory extended signal detection theory in another direction to the problem of identifying multiattribute stimuli. Because a display with multiple stimuli can always be viewed as a single multiattribute stimulus, general recognition theory provides a rich source of insights for attention researchers.

However, the theorist who most succinctly laid out what was required to identify capacity limitations in perceptual identification tasks with near-threshold stimuli was Marilyn Shaw (1980, 1982, 1984; Shaw, Mulligan, & Stone, 1983). Her work provides a clear statement of the idea that, in order to infer capacity limitations, we need to demonstrate a performance decrement with load that exceeds that predictable on the basis of noise alone.

To do so, it is necessary to characterize the amount of noise that each stimulus location contributes to the perceptual decision and also how the information from each noisy location is combined to make a decision. Shaw (1980, 1982, 1983; Shaw et al., 1983) investigated a number of models for how information might be combined from multiple locations in tasks of this kind. A similar analysis was provided subsequently by Graham, Kramer, and Yager (1987). Based on an analysis of the maximum performance decrement predictable from decision noise alone, Shaw (1984) concluded that letter identification is a capacity-limited process, whereas detection of luminance increments is not.

If Shaw was the person who most clearly articulated what is needed to infer capacity limitations in perceptual identification tasks, the researcher who has most systematically demonstrated the power of Shaw's approach has been John Palmer. In a series of articles beginning in the early 1990s, Palmer and colleagues showed that a variety of visual search findings that had previously been attributed to capacity limitations could be explained by variations in noise alone.

This was the case for simple perceptual tasks like contrast-increment detection (Palmer, 1995) and line-length discrimination (Palmer et al., 1993) and for more complex judgments, in which targets were defined by conjunctions of pairs or triples of features (Eckstein, Thomas, Palmer, & Shimozaki, 2000). The latter result is particularly striking because identification of conjunction targets is viewed in Treisman's feature integration theory as the prototype of a capacity-limited task. In the wake of Eckstein and colleagues' analysis, one might be left wondering whether any phenomena are left for capacity limitations to explain! It is to the subtleties of this question that we now turn.

Visual Search for a Contrast-Modulated Target Among Distractors

Figure 9.1 shows results from an unpublished experiment from my laboratory that was similar to the experiments of Palmer and colleagues. The distractor stimuli consisted of a variable number of 15% contrast, illuminated disks, or "pedestals," presented at random locations against a uniform field. The contrast of the pedestals was chosen to make them clearly distinguishable from the background. The signal stimulus was a Gabor patch (a Gaussian vignetted sinusoidal grating) that was added to one of the pedestals. The observer's task was to decide whether a signal was present in the display and to make a yes/no detection response. The display was flashed for 50 ms and then extinguished, and the peak contrast of the Gabor patches was chosen to ensure a significant number of errors in all conditions. Peak contrast was between 5.0 and 6.5% for individual observers. The independent variable was the display size (1, 2, 4, or 8 items).

Like all of the experiments I present in this chapter, the experiment was run using a psychophysical small N design in which data were collected from a large number of sessions from a small number of observers. The data in Figure 9.1 are averaged over three observers. The small N approach allows each observer to be treated as an independent replication of the experiment, permitting data to be analyzed on an observer-by-observer basis. Advocates of such designs (like me) favor them because they allow one to evaluate the degree to which an experimental

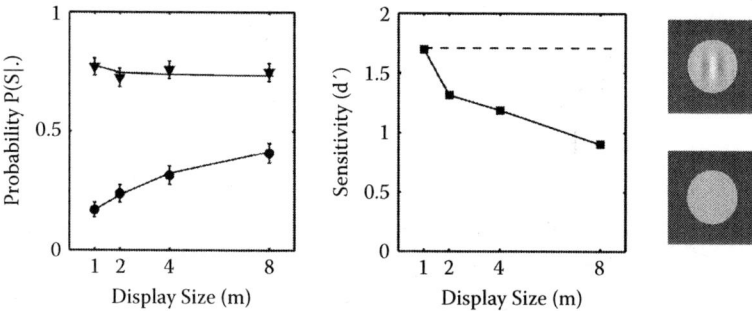

Figure 9.1 Visual search task. Observers detected low-contrast Gabor patch stimuli in displays of one, two, four, or eight distractors. The distractors were 15% contrast, circular luminance pedestals presented on a uniform background. The panel on the left shows hit rates, $P(S|s)$ (triangles), and false alarm rates, $P(S|n)$ (circles). The continuous curves are the fitted values for the independent detectors model and the error bars are pooled estimates of the binomial standard errors. The panel on the right (squares and continuous curve) shows d' calculated from the empirical hit and false alarm rates. The dashed line is the value of d, the mean of the distribution of sensory effect for signal stimuli, estimated from the fit of the independent detectors model. For the model fit shown on the left, d was the same for all display sizes. The inset on the far right shows examples of the stimuli: (top to bottom) luminance pedestal plus Gabor patch, and pedestal alone.

phenomenon is exhibited consistently across individuals. Although all of the experiments described here were originally analyzed in this way, to keep the presentation compact we consider averaged data only. The individual differences were sufficiently small in the experiments discussed here that little information will be lost by considering only averaged data.

The data in Figure 9.1 are shown in two forms: the raw conditional probabilities of hits and false alarms, $P(S|s)$ and $P(S|n)$, and the d' measure of sensitivity, calculated using the standard textbook formula (Macmillan & Creelman, 1991, p. 9):

$$d' = z(S|s) - z(S|n),$$

where $z(S|s)$ and $z(S|n)$ are the standard normal deviates (z-scores) for hits and false alarms, respectively. (We follow the convention of using lowercase s and n to denote signal and noise stimuli and uppercase letters to denote responses to those stimuli.) Figure 9.1 shows that hit rates decline slightly as display size, m, increases and that false alarm rates rise appreciably. The net result is a systematic decrease in d' with an increase in the number of distractors in the display.

How should this decrease in sensitivity be interpreted? The textbook interpretation of d' is that it is a measure of the distance between the means of the noise and the signal distributions, expressed in noise standard deviation units. It thus reflects the perceptual similarity, or confusability, of noise and signal stimuli. One might therefore be tempted to interpret a reduction in d' with increased load as evidence of some kind of capacity limitation. As capacity is distributed across more items, the mean of the signal distribution decreases and becomes more similar to the mean of the noise distribution, making noise and signal more confusable.

Conversely, as attention is focused and capacity is concentrated on fewer items, the mean of the signal distribution progressively increases, making signals increasingly more discriminable from noise. This hypothetical sharpening of discriminability with focused attention has been termed *signal enhancement* or *stimulus enhancement* in the attention literature (Dosher & Lu, 2000; Shiu & Pashler, 1994). Signal enhancement can be viewed theoretically as a local increase in the quality of stimulus information—or, more abstractly, in signal-to-noise ratio—at particular regions in the display as a function of the attentional resources allocated there.

The problem with applying this interpretation to tasks like the one in Figure 9.1 is that the decision task cannot be represented in terms of a single noise and a single signal distribution. Rather, each stimulus in the display must be viewed as contributing an additional source of noise to the observer's decision. The problem of distinguishing between noise and signal trials in this task is thus one of distinguishing between m noise sources on noise-alone trials and $m - 1$ noise sources plus one signal on signal trials.

Although we can calculate d' in a purely formal way for such experiments, as we have done here, the resulting statistic tells us nothing about how the information in multiple noisy stimuli is aggregated to make a decision. It also does not tell us anything whatever about the purely *local* perceptual similarity between noise and signal stimuli—that is, about whether focused attention leads to signal enhancement. It is wholly uninformative about this latter question because, in varying m, we have varied the total number of noise sources in the display. Without knowing anything about how these noise sources affect decision making, we cannot draw any inferences about the effects of load on the signal-to-noise ratio at individual display locations.

To go further, we need to model performance on the task. The purpose of a model is to allow us to distinguish the effects of load or capacity on the local signal-to-noise ratio (i.e., signal enhancement) from its effects on the total amount of noise in the display. Although we are seeking in this chapter to keep the technical apparatus to a minimum, we need to introduce some notation in order to fix ideas. We represent the perceptual information available at a particular display location j as a *random variable*, $X_j, j = 1 \ldots m$. A random variable is a quantity that possesses a mean and variance, but whose precise value is unknown and that may, in the context of a detection task, vary from trial to trial and possibly even from moment to moment. The random variable X_j may be thought of as representing values on a dimension of *signal strength:* Low values are evidence for noise; high values are evidence for signal. The subscript j is simply an index variable to allow us to keep track of which of the m locations we mean.

More generally, we assume that each of our random variables has a probability distribution. In the classical signal detection model, these distributions are assumed to be normal or Gaussian. We denote the probability density of X_j by $\phi(x)$ and its cumulative distribution function by $\Phi(x)$. That is, $\phi(x)$ denotes the height of the normal curve at the point x and $\Phi(x)$ denotes the area under the curve to the left of the point x.

Some readers may be a little disconcerted by the change from upper- to lowercase in these expressions. Uppercase letters are used to denote the *names* of random variables and lowercase letters are used to denote their *values*. Thus, an expression like $P[X \leq x]$ should be read as "the probability that the random variable X takes a value less than or equal to x." We use the symbol P to denote the probability of an event; other authors use "Pr" or "Prob" to denote the same thing.

We also assume, unless otherwise stated, that we are dealing with standard normal distributions—that is, distributions of random variables that have means of zero and variances of unity. The variance of the distribution of sensory effect is a fundamental scaling parameter in signal detection theory; therefore, it is not necessary to relax the unit-variance assumption unless we wish to consider models in which the variances of the noise and signal distributions are different. The density and distribution functions of a Gaussian random variable with a mean other than zero—d for example—are $\phi(x - d)$ and $\Phi(x - d)$, respectively.

Because the predictions of signal detection models depend only on the difference between the means of noise and signal distributions rather than on their absolute values, we shall, as is common practice, assume that noise distributions have means of zero and signal distributions have means of d. The value of d may, of course, vary as a function of load or attentional set. Increases in d with reductions in load or with focused attention are evidence of signal enhancement—that is, of capacity limitations.

Figure 9.1 shows the fit of a very simple signal detection model to the hits and false alarm rates from our visual search task. The model I have fitted is what Shaw (1980) called an *independent detectors* model and Smith (1998) called a *separable decisions* model, the latter terminology being derived from Ashby and Townsend's (1986) general recognition theory. A model in their theory possesses the property of *decisional separability* if decisions about one attribute of a stimulus are unaffected by its values on other attributes. In this chapter, we will revert to Shaw's terminology because most readers will probably find it more intuitive. The performance of the independent detectors model is summarized by the following decision rule:

$$P(S) = P[\text{any } X_j \geq c_j].$$

In words, this equation states that the probability that the observer responds "signal," denoted $P(S)$, is equal to the probability that any of the m strength variables exceeds its associated criterion, denoted c_j. That is, the observer responds "noise" only if *all* of the strength variables are less than their criteria; otherwise, the observer responds "signal."

The use of a subscript in the notation for the criterion c_j allows for the possibility that observers may use different criteria at each location in the display. In the context of a visual search task, such generality may seem unnecessary and artificial. Later, however, when we discuss spatial cuing tasks, we will need to allow for this possibility because it is entirely plausible that observers may adopt different criteria at cued and uncued locations. Indeed, a number of research-ers (Pashler, 1998; Sperling & Dosher, 1986) have attempted to explain some attentional phenomena using the hypothesis that people use different amounts of evidence in making decisions about attended and unattended stimuli. A hypothesis more germane to the visual search task is that people may use dif-ferent criteria for displays of different sizes. We will allow for this possibility in our subsequent analysis but do not represent it explicitly in the notation to avoid overburdening it.

In dealing with models like the independent detectors model, it is slightly more convenient to write equations for the probability of a noise response $P(N)$. Of course, $P(S) = 1 - P(N)$, so we can go backward and forward readily between the two. A key assumption of the independent detectors model—the one from which it gets its name—is that the random variables $X_j, j = 1...m$ are mutually independent. That is, the sensory effect produced by a stimulus at one location in the display is independent of that produced by stimuli elsewhere. Making use of the property that the probabilities of mutually independent events multiply, we can write an expression for $P(N)$ under the assumption that the random variables are normally distributed. When all stimuli are noise stimuli (i.e., all of the random variables have means of zero),

$$P(N) = \prod_{j=1}^{m} \Phi(c_j),$$

When a signal (mean d) is present at location i,

$$P(N) = \prod_{j=1, j \neq i}^{m} \Phi(c_j) \Phi(c_i - d).$$

These expressions state that the probability of a noise response is the product of the probabilities that each of the Gaussian strength variables is less than its associ-ated criterion. (For the reader unfamiliar with the notation used here, capital pi is used to denote "product" in the same way that capital sigma is used to denote "sum.") If we adopt the convention that the mean of the distribution of sensory effect, μ_j, is zero if the stimulus is a noise stimulus and d if it is a signal, we can then combine both of these equations into one, writing them as

$$P(N) = \prod_{j=1}^{m} \Phi(c_j - \mu_j),$$

I fitted the model in Figure 9.1 by minimizing the Pearson chi-square calcu-lated on the observed and predicted frequencies of a signal response. To do so, I assumed that d, the mean of the signal distribution, was the same for all display sizes, but the decision criteria could vary. The best fitting model had $\chi^2(3) = 0.49$, $p = .92$, and an estimated parameter vector $\{d, c_1, c_2, c_4, c_8\} = \{1.71, 0.96, 1.16, 1.32, 1.52\}$. (I have momentarily changed the notation here; the subscripts on the criteria denote the display size, *not* the particular display location.)

Evidently, as Figure 9.1 makes clear, this model provides a very good description of the data. We can compare this model to a saturated model, in which the mean of the signal distribution and the criterion both vary with display size. The saturated model has as many parameters as there are degrees of freedom in the data (four signal means and four criteria) and thus would describe the data perfectly. Our model does almost as well; almost no residual variance is left to explain.

What are the psychological implications of this result? It means that all of the decrement in performance with increasing display size in Figure 9.1 can be explained by (a) an increase in the total amount of noise in the display and (b) a compensatory increase in decision criteria as display sizes are increased. The latter assumption is needed to explain the fact that hit rates in Figure 9.1 decrease rather than increase with display size. It is consistent with the idea that observers try to compensate for the increase in false alarms produced by larger display sizes by being more cautious about which stimuli they label as "signal."

There is no evidence that any change in the discriminability of signal and noise at individual display locations occurs as a function of load. There is thus no requirement whatsoever to invoke the idea of capacity limitations to explain performance in this task. To emphasize this fact, I have plotted the estimated value of d as a dashed horizontal line in Figure 9.1 to allow for easy comparison with d' calculated from the overall hit and false alarm rates. This result echoes those of Palmer and of a number of subsequent researchers for tasks of this kind (see Palmer, Verghese, & Pavel, 2000, for a review). Where, then, is limited capacity needed? To understand this, we need to make a somewhat finer analysis of performance in multichannel detection tasks.

Models of Performance in Cued Yes/No Detection Tasks

In this section, the focus changes slightly—from visual search to spatial cuing tasks. Our analysis follows that of Smith (1998), but avoids some of the technicalities of Smith's presentation. We make no attempt to survey all possible models for performance in this task. In particular, we do not discuss the interesting Bayesian ideal-observer model of Shimozaki, Eckstein, and Abbey (2003) or any of the related, likelihood-based approaches (e.g., Palmer et al., 2000, appendix). Our goal here is to bring out certain subtleties associated with the assessment of capacity limitations, and we restrict our focus accordingly.

The independent detectors model described in the previous section embodies particular assumptions about how observers use the information in the display to make a decision. However, these assumptions are not the only possibilities. In fact, the model fitted to the data in Figure 9.1 is unlimited in capacity in not one but in two senses. It is unlimited capacity in the sense that the signal-to-noise ratio at each location in the display is not affected by load. Palmer

(1995) has characterized this as *unlimited-capacity perception*. However, it is also unlimited capacity at the level of the *decision*, in that it assumes people can make decisions about m simultaneous stimuli as efficiently as they can about one stimulus.

This assumption is expressed in the idea that decisions are made by comparing each stimulus in the display separately to an associated criterion and responding "signal" if the stimulation in any location exceeds its criterion. Such a decision rule implies that observers have complete access perceptually to all of the information in the display. As such, it differs markedly from theories like the classic single-channel theory of Welford (1959), which holds that people are only able to make a decision about one stimulus at a time. In single-channel theory, the (serial) capacity limits in the decision stage impose an absolute bottleneck on divided attention performance.

An alternative model of perceptual decision making, which does not require the assumption of quite so much processing at the decision stage, assumes that the stimulation from all of the locations in the display is simply added together to produce a composite decision variable. The value of this single variable is compared to a criterion to make a response. The decision rule in this *integration model* is

$$P(S) = P\left[\sum_{j=1}^{m} X_j \geq c\right].$$

Because only a single comparison is required to make the decision, the decision rule in this model is compatible with single-channel principles. An elaborated version of this model was proposed by Kinchla (1974, 1977) and Kinchla, Chen, and Evert (1995). In this *weighted integration model*, each of the strength variables is multiplied by an attention weight, w_j, before being summed. The decision rule then becomes

$$P(S) = P\left[\sum_{j=1}^{m} w_j X_j \geq c\right].$$

The attention weights allow for the idea that observers may place more weight on information from locations at which signals are more probable (cf. Shimozaki et al., 2003, for another expression of this idea). This could occur, for example, in cuing tasks with a probabilistic cue-validity manipulation. Note that, in the decision rule for this model, the criterion c has no subscript because the composite decision variable is computed across the display as a whole; therefore, it is not bound to any particular location.

Psychologically, the independent detectors model and the integration model represent opposite ends of a continuum, although both are derived from signal detection principles. The independent detectors model assumes unlimited-capacity decision making, whereas the integration model assumes limited-capacity—indeed, single-channel—decision making. Both models are compatible with either limited-capacity or unlimited-capacity perceptual mechanisms. That this is so underscores the fact that limited-capacity effects can arise at different levels within the system and can manifest themselves in different ways. Understanding the interplay between these various forms of capacity limitation is one of the major challenges for researchers in this area.

A third important model shares some of the attributes of both the independent detectors and integration models. In this *maximum output model*, preattentive mechanisms select the largest of the set of m strength variables, denoted X_i. Mathematically, $X_i = \max(X_1, \ldots, X_m)$. This variable is passed to the decision stage, where it is compared to a criterion to make a response. The decision rule for this model is

$$P(S) = P[X_i \geq c_i; X_i = \max(X_1, \ldots, X_m)].$$

The relationship between the independent detectors and maximum outputs models is shown in Figure 9.2. In the independent detectors model, the decision

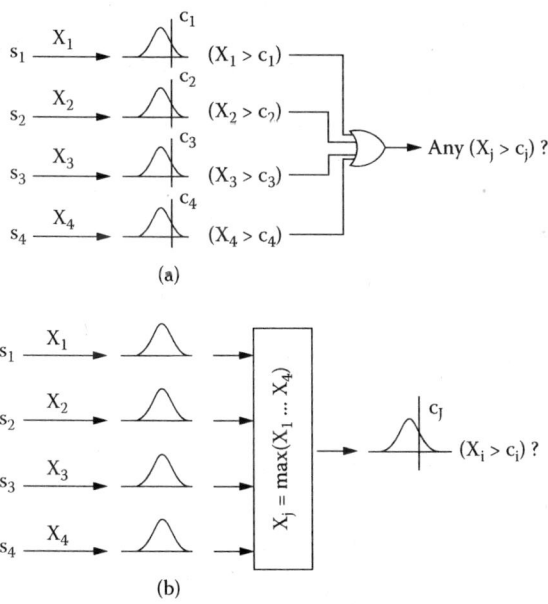

(a)

(b)

Figure 9.2   Multichannel signal detection models. (a) Independent detectors model. Each display location generates its own distribution of sensory effect. The observer compares the value of the sensory effect, X_j, at each location to its associated criterion, c_j, and responds "signal" if the sensory effect at any location exceeds its criterion. (b) Maximum outputs model. Preattentive mechanisms select the largest of the set of m strength variables, X_i. The observer responds "signal" if X_i is greater than the criterion c_i. The two models are mathematically equivalent when the criteria are equal; otherwise, they are not. The integration model is the same as the maximum outputs model, but with summation replacing the "max" operation.

requires that each of m strength variables be compared to a criterion to make a decision; in the maximum outputs model, only the largest of the strength variables is used to make a decision. The maximum outputs model is thus like the integration model in assuming a single-channel decision stage. Because the maximum outputs model embodies an additional constraint (namely, that only the largest of strength variables is used to make the decision), the expression for the probability of a noise response is a little more complex than that for its independent channels counterpart:

$$P(N) = \sum_{i=1}^{m} \int_{-\infty}^{c_i} \phi(x - \mu_i) \prod_{j=1, j \neq i}^{m} \Phi(x - \mu_j) dx.$$

To understand this equation, note that the term $\phi(x - \mu_i)$ is the probability (strictly speaking, the probability density or likelihood) that the ith strength variable takes a value of x. The product of terms of the form $\Phi(x - \mu_j)$ is the probability that all of the other strength variables take a value of less than x. The integral from $-\infty$ to c_i thus gives the probability of the joint event that X_i is the largest of the strength variables and that it is also less than its criterion. Because any of the strength variables may be the largest of the set, we need to sum over variables to get the probability that all of them are less than their criteria. The maximum outputs model has proven to be a versatile tool in the hands of Palmer and others and, in recent years, has been shown to give a good account of a wide variety of multichannel detection and perceptual identification data (Baldassi & Burr, 2004; Carrasco et al., 2000; Eckstein et al., 2000; Palmer et al., 1993).

The independent detectors and maximum outputs models make quite different assumptions about the psychological processes underlying detection and their capacity limits; however, the two models often have not been distinguished explicitly in the literature. They are frequently treated as equivalent and interchangeable (e.g., Palmer et al., 2000) because, when all of the decision criteria are equal ($c_1 = c_2 = \ldots = c_m$), the two models make identical predictions. That they do so is easy to see. When all of the criteria are the same, the probability that *any* strength variable exceeds its criterion must equal the probability that the *largest* strength variable exceeds its criterion.

The mathematical equivalence of the two models is only a little more difficult to see. When all of the criteria are equal to some common value, say c, the order of summation and integration in the preceding expression for $P(N)$ can be interchanged. The sum of terms under the integral sign may then be recognized as the derivative of the formula for $P(N)$ for the independent detectors model. By the fundamental theorem of calculus, integration of the derivative of an expression gives us the original expression. Consequently, the two formulae for $P(N)$ are equal. However, this equivalence holds only when all of the criteria are equal. Otherwise the predictions of the two models will in general be different.

To see in what ways the models differ, it is helpful to consider a specific, concrete situation. Imagine we are dealing with a spatial cuing experiment in which stimuli can appear at either of two locations, one of which is cued and the other of which is uncued. On each experimental trial, each location yields a strength variable, which we denote X_A (attended) and X_U (unattended). Let us assume that on any trial we can present a signal independently at either location. That is, we are admitting the possibility of redundant signals, one at each location. Therefore we can present any of four possible stimulus configurations on any trial: (n_A, n_U) (noise in both locations), (s_A, n_U) (signal at the attended location and noise at the unattended location), (n_A, s_U) (noise at the attended location and signal at the unattended location), or (s_A, s_U) (signals at both locations). To understand what each of the three models predicts in this situation, we consider the *decision space* for each of the models. These are shown in Figure 9.3.

The decision space is a two-dimensional coordinate space that represents the set of possible sensory effects produced by the pair of stimuli and the way in which the observer responds to them. The horizontal axis represents the sensory effect of the stimulus at the attended location, X_A, and the vertical axis represents the sensory effect of the stimulus at the unattended location, X_U. The sensory effect

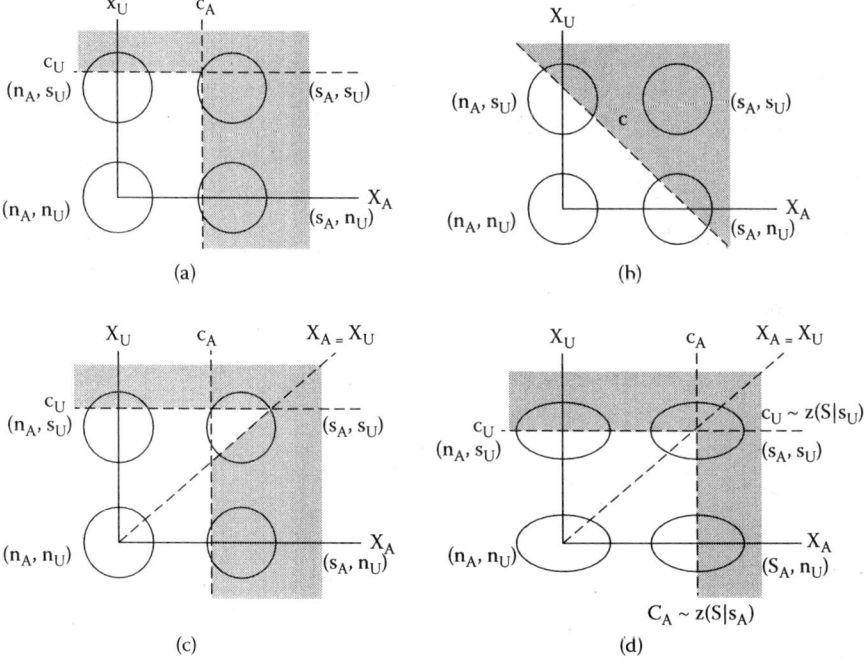

Figure 9.3 Decision spaces for multichannel signal detection models for a two-location display. (a) Independent detectors model; (b) integration model; (c) maximum outputs model; (d) maximum outputs model with equal decision criteria and unequal sensory variances at the attended and unattended locations. The observer responds "signal" if the sensory effect produced by the stimulus display falls in the shaded part of the decision space. (Redrawn after Smith, P. L., 1998, *Journal of Experimental Psychology: Human Perception and Performance*, 24, 105–133.)

produced by the stimulus display on any trial is therefore a random point in this two-dimensional space. The probability of sampling a particular point on any trial will depend on which of the four stimulus configurations is presented.

In general, the sensory effect produced by an attended and unattended stimulus pair is described mathematically by a bivariate normal distribution. Each of the four possible stimulus configurations is characterized by a different bivariate distribution. The circles in Figure 9.3 are contours of equal likelihood (i.e., probability density) for these distributions. The centroids (i.e., the bivariate means) of the four distributions are $(0, 0)$, $(d_A, 0)$, $(0, d_U)$, and (d_A, d_U), respectively. The way in which we depict the geometry of the space expresses a number of substantive hypotheses about the way in which stimuli are encoded perceptually. The relationship $d_A \geq d_U$ implies limited-capacity perception (i.e., signal enhancement), whereas $d_A = d_U$ implies the absence of any capacity limitations in perception.

The fact that the contours of equal likelihood are shown as circular reflects the assumption that the sensory effects at attended and unattended locations are uncorrelated (i.e., independent) and their variances are equal. Unequal variances and uncorrelated sensory effects result in elliptical contours of equal likelihood with the major axes aligned parallel with one of the coordinate axes. Correlated sensory effects also lead to elliptical contours in which the orientations of the major axes depend on the correlation and on the ratio of the standard deviations of the perceptual effects. Moreover, neither the size nor the shape of the contours need be the same for different stimuli. The contours would change in size, for example, if mean sensory intensity and variance were correlated. Much of the literature on yes/no detection suggests that this is indeed the case (Green & Swets, 1966).

These are some of the possible generalizations of the basic models shown in Figure 9.3. Such generalizations form the substance of Ashby and Townsend's (1986) general recognition theory and have been studied systematically by them and their colleagues (e.g., Kadlec & Townsend, 1992; Thomas, 1999). The major obstacle standing in the way of exploiting the additional generality of such models is in ensuring that they are identifiable statistically. To do so, one must ensure a sufficient number of constraints in the data to allow all of the parameters in the model to be estimated uniquely. This is an important and nontrivial matter, but one that is outside the scope of this chapter.

The contours of equal likelihood describe the distributions of sensory effect produced by the stimuli; the placement of decision boundaries in the space specifies how an observer responds to the stimuli. For each of the models in Figure 9.3, the detection region—that is, the set of points in the space that leads to a "signal" response—are shaded. For the independent detectors model (Figure 9.3a), the detection region is the set $\{X_A \geq c_A\} \cup \{X_U \geq c_U\}$. The observer responds "signal" if the sensory effect at the attended location or the sensory effect at the unattended location (or both) exceeds its associated criterion. The decision criteria, c_A and c_U, are drawn parallel to the coordinate axes, expressing the property of decisional separability (Ashby & Townsend, 1986). A model has this property if the decision about the stimulus at one location does not depend on the sensory effect produced by the stimulus at the other location.

For the integration model (Figure 9.3b), the decision space is different. This model assumes that the observer responds to a "signal" if $X_A + X_U \geq c$—that is, if the sum of the sensory effects at attended and unattended locations exceeds a criterion. Equivalently, a detection response occurs if $X_U \geq c - X_A$. The decision bound, which separates detection and nondetection regions, is therefore a straight line with a slope of -1 and a y-axis intercept of c. In Kinchla's more general weighted-integration formulation, the decision bound has a slope of w_A/w_U and an intercept of c/w_U, where w_A and w_U are the weights assigned to attended and unattended locations, respectively. Comparison of the decision spaces for the independent detectors and integration models shows that they are sufficiently different that one might expect to be able to distinguish them with the right kind of experiment.

The decision space for the maximum outputs model (Figure 9.3c) is the most interesting of the three. In this model, the observer responds "signal" only if the larger of the two strength variables exceeds its criterion. The detection region is thus the set $[\{X_A \geq X_U\} \cap \{X_A \geq c_A\}] \cup [\{X_A < X_U\} \cap \{X_U \geq c_U\}]$. This region is a little harder to visualize. To do so, note first that the diagonal line $X_A = X_U$ partitions the space into two regions. Everything to the right and below this line (including the line itself) is part of the set $\{X_A \geq X_U\}$; everything to the left and above the line is part of the set $\{X_A < X_U\}$.

These two regions correspond to the two possible outcomes on any trial: Either the maximum sensory effect is at the attended location or it is at the unattended location. (Because the strength variables are continuously distributed, the probability that they are exactly equal is zero; therefore, we can assign this event arbitrarily to one or other region without affecting any of the predictions.) For an observer to respond "signal," the sensory effect must be in the set $\{X_A \geq X_U\}$ and greater than the criterion c_A or in the set $\{X_A < X_U\}$ and greater than the criterion c_U. The union of these two regions gives the shaded region in Figure 9.3(c).

When $c_A = c_U$, the criteria intersect on the line $X_A = X_U$ and the decision spaces for the maximum outputs and independent detectors models are identical. This is the geometric counterpart of the result we showed mathematically earlier in this section. When $c_A \neq c_U$, the criteria do not intersect on the $X_A = X_U$ line and the decision spaces for the two models are no longer the same. If $c_A < c_U$—that is, if the observer adopts a less stringent criterion at the attended location—the decision space excludes the wedge-shaped region shown in Figure 9.3(c). In this region, the maximum sensory effect is at the unattended location and, although it is greater than the attended criterion, c_A, it is not greater than the unattended criterion, c_U, so no detection response is made.

What are the psychological implications of all this? As Figure 9.3(c) shows, the maximum outputs model predicts reduced *redundancy benefits* on two-signal trials. That is, the predicted increase in detection probability when a pair of signals is presented is not as great as that predicted by the independent detectors model. This is clear from Figure 9.3(c), in which a significant proportion of the two-signal distribution falls in the unshaded wedge and thus results in a noise response. However, this occurs only when decision criteria are unequal. We can therefore expect to have a chance of distinguishing between these models only in circumstances in which observers set different criteria at attended and unattended locations.

I evaluated the performance of the models in Figure 9.3 on a signal detection task similar one to the one we have discussed here (Smith, 1998, Experiment 2). Observers detected Gabor-patch stimuli presented at either cued or uncued locations in a Posner spatial cuing paradigm. To ensure sufficiently high error rates, stimuli were flashed for 60 ms and then followed by high-contrast, checkerboard pattern masks. To ensure that the parameters of the models were uniquely estimable, I used a more complex design than the one we have been discussing. Instead of using a design with just two stimulus locations, the design randomly intermixed trials with two stimulus locations (one cued and one uncued) and three stimulus locations (one cued and two uncued). All of the possible stimulus locations (i.e., two or three) on each trial were masked.

Although the parameters of the models could be shown to be uniquely estimable from the experimental design, I found it was difficult to distinguish statistically between models in which local sensitivity differed for attended and unattended locations (i.e., d_A and d_U) and models in which only the decision criteria varied (i.e., c_A and c_U). This was because the structure of the models is such that the effects of changes in criteria and changes in local sensitivity are highly correlated. However, I argued that the most consistent and parsimonious description of the data was provided by a model in which d_A, the mean of the attended distribution of sensory effect, was roughly twice d_U, the mean of the unattended distribution. Unlike the visual search task described previously, this is consistent with signal enhancement or, equivalently, with limited-capacity perception. Just why these tasks should have yielded different results is the subject of the second part of this chapter.

I also found that independent detectors and maximum output models performed systematically better than the integration model for the majority of observers. This result replicates an earlier finding of Shaw (1982); she found that the independent detector model provided the best account of the data for most of her observers and that the integration model was better for a minority of them. More interestingly, I also found that the independent detectors model performed better than the maximum outputs model for most of the observers in this sample. This means that the majority of observers did not show reduced redundancy benefits on two-signal or three-signal trials, which is the hallmark of this model. We might therefore be tempted to conclude that these results show that no capacity limitations exist at the decision stage. Observers apparently have complete access to all of the perceptual information in the display when making their decisions—at least in displays that contain no more than three stimuli, like the one used in my study.

Unfortunately, however, there is a catch. As we saw, our ability to distinguish statistically between independent detectors and maximum outputs models relies on the existence of differences in the decision criteria at attended and unattended locations. Only under these circumstances do the models make different predictions. The parameter estimates that I reported showed that estimates of c_A were systematically smaller than the estimates of c_U (Smith, 1998). This would seem to imply that the conditions needed to test between the two models were in fact present in the experiment. However, the catch is this: Estimates of decision criteria in the models are scaled in sensory standard deviation units, just as in the textbook signal-detection model. Consequently, when the models are fitted to data, differences in standard deviation at attended and unattended locations will appear as differences in decision criteria.

The situation is illustrated in Figure 9.3(d). In the model shown, σ, the standard deviation of the distribution of sensory effect, is greater for attended than unattended stimuli. The contours of equal likelihood are therefore elliptical rather than circular. The decision criteria at attended and unattended locations are equal ($c_A = c_U$), so there is no excluded wedge-shaped region in the decision space. The predictions for the independent channels and maximum outputs models are therefore indistinguishable. However, when we fit the model to data, we estimate decision criteria in z-score units: $c_A = z(S|n_A)$ and $c_U = z(S|n_U)$. If $\sigma_A > \sigma_U$, we will estimate $z(S|n_A) < z(S|n_U)$, even though the criteria are physically equal. As a result, a maximum outputs model with equal decision criteria and unequal sensory variances will look like an independent detectors model with unequal decision criteria and equal variances.

This is a rather unsatisfactory state of affairs. The reader should be convinced, I hope, that the independent detectors and maximum outputs models are quite different models psychologically, which make fundamentally different assumptions about capacity limitations at the decision stage. Nevertheless, we have just seen that what seemed our only avenue for testing between them experimentally has been closed by parameter nonidentifiability issues.

Of course, we might attempt to retrieve the situation by arguing that the assumption ($\sigma_A > \sigma_U$) used to make the maximum outputs model look like an independent detectors model is a somewhat artificial one. Why should sensory variance be greater for attended stimuli? In fact, however, my preferred model for my data (Smith, 1998) made just this assumption. In this model, the distributions of sensory effect in the model are Poisson, rather than Gaussian.

To account for the cuing effect, the model assumes that the Poisson intensities—effectively, the densities of neural spikes indicating the presence of a signal—are modulated by attention. A basic property of the Poisson distribution is that its variance equals its mean; both are equal to the Poisson intensity parameter, λ. If the Poisson intensity is higher for attended stimuli (i.e., if $\lambda_A > \lambda_U$), the model predicts signal enhancement: Signal-to-noise ratios will be higher at attended than at unattended locations. Sensory variance will also be higher at attended than at unattended locations because of the Poisson nature of the stimulus distribution. A maximum outputs Poisson model with equal decision criteria will thus look like an independent detectors model with unequal criteria. This is what my data showed.

We thus seem to have reached an impasse in which models with fundamentally different processing architectures appear to predict identical performance. However, there is a way out of this impasse, if we consider a different kind of experimental task.

The Poststimulus Probe Task

The visual search and spatial cuing tasks described in the last section are both "pure" detection tasks in the sense that they require only that observers detect the presence of signals somewhere in the display. They do not require that observers be able to localize the signals or, indeed, to report anything about them other than their presence. If, however, we assume that observers can localize the signals they detect, we can make headway on the apparently intractable problem described in the previous section.

Most researchers would probably regard this assumption as reasonable, except possibly for stimuli in crowded displays. It is consistent, for example, with the widely accepted principle of *labeled detectors* (Graham, 1989), which holds that visual analyzers code the attributes of the stimuli that activate them. This implies that an analyzer responding to a stimulus in a particular region of visual space will, by virtue of being active, signal the location of the stimulus that activated it. Such an idea is supported empirically. Johnston and Pashler (1990), for example, reported evidence of "close binding" of identity and location in visual recognition; subsequently, Cameron et al. (2002) reported high correlations between detection and localization accuracy in a signal detection task. We thus do not sacrifice too much of the purity of our definition if we assume that detection and localization are linked.

Let us agree that this assumption is reasonable. Then, instead of asking whether a signal is somewhere in the display, we can ask observers to indicate whether a signal is present at a specific location, which we designate randomly on each trial. This approach is strongly reminiscent of Sperling's (1960) partial report method, which he used to great effect to elucidate iconic memory. The attentional analogue of partial report is the poststimulus probe task, which was first used by Downing (1988). In this task, stimuli to be detected are presented in a spatial cuing paradigm like the one described in the previous section. Immediately after stimulus offset, a single display location is probed, by means of a visual marker stimulus instructing the observer to report the contents of that location.

The poststimulus probe thus reduces the decision task from a global task, in which all locations in the display are relevant to the observer's decision, to a local task, in which only the probed location is relevant. It thereby changes the signal detection problem from a multichannel problem to a single-channel problem, to which the familiar textbook signal-detection model can be applied. All a researcher need do is calculate sensitivity for attended and unattended stimuli, d'_A and d'_U, using the contents of probed locations to estimate hit and false alarm rates. The task therefore gives us a direct way to test for local variations in detection sensitivity as a function of cue condition. Of course, we are presupposing that decisions about the contents of probed locations are unaffected by noise from unprobed locations, and this entails the binding of identity and location information. If we grant this assumption, however, the method radically simplifies the problem of testing for sensitivity variations in cued detection tasks.

Since its introduction, the poststimulus probe method has been used in a number of studies to investigate whether detection sensitivity is increased locally by spatial cues (Downing, 1988; Hawkins et al, 1990; Luck et al., 1994; Müller & Humphreys, 1991; Smith, 1998, Experiment 1). All of these studies yielded reliable evidence of increased sensitivity at cued locations. Because the method uses only the contents of the probed location to compute sensitivity, it is not susceptible to the estimation problems that beset attempts to assess sensitivity variations indirectly by estimating the parameters of a multichannel signal detection model, as discussed in the last section. However, this is not all that the method can give us.

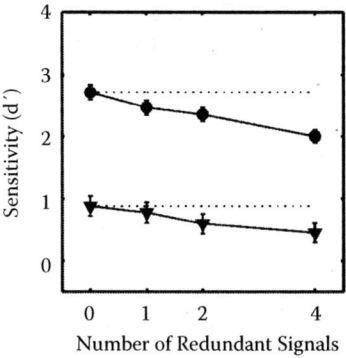

Figure 9.4 Poststimulus probe task. Observers detected low-contrast Gabor patch stimuli in eight-item displays. The distractors were 15% contrast, circular luminance pedestals. The observers' task was to detect the stimulus at a single location that was probed 500 ms after stimulus offset. The circles are d' values when the cued location is probed; the triangles are d' values when a miscued location is probed. The independent variable was the number of redundant signals in the display (0, 1, 2, or 4). The horizontal dotted lines are included for reference purposes only.

Figure 9.4 shows d' values from an unpublished experiment from my laboratory. The experiment was a cued visual search task in which observers reported the contents of a location that was probed 500 ms after stimulus offset. Each trial presented a total of eight 15% contrast pedestals to which a variable number of Gabor patch signals were added. Half of the trials were noise trials, on which a blank pedestal was presented at the probed location; half were signal trials, on which a Gabor patch was presented at the probed location. Stimuli were flashed for 50 ms and then masked with high-contrast, checkerboard masks. On each trial, 150 ms before stimulus onset, a cue was flashed at one of the stimulus locations. The cued location was probed on 75% of the trials; on the other 25%, one of the other seven locations was probed. In addition, the experiment manipulated *signal redundancy*. On noise and signal trials, 0, 1, 2, or 4 Gabor patches were presented in a randomly chosen subset of the unprobed locations. The purpose of this manipulation was to investigate the effects of signals at locations other than the one relevant to the observer's decision.

The striking result from this experiment, as Figure 9.4 shows, is that there were both cuing effects and *redundancy costs*. Sensitivity was uniformly higher at the cued location than at other locations in the display. In addition, as the number of signals presented at unprobed locations increased, sensitivity at the probed location decreased. The decrease in sensitivity with redundant signals was of similar magnitude for cued and uncued stimuli. This is not a new result. I reported a limited form of it in a task with a single redundant signal (Smith, 1998, Experiment 1), and Müller and Humphreys (1991) reported a more extensive form of it in a task in which redundancy was manipulated systematically.

Redundancy costs are not predicted by any of the multichannel signal detection models discussed in the previous section. Rather, all of those models predict redundancy gains—that is, increased detection sensitivity with increases in the number of signals in the display. This is not a reflection of a shortcoming on the part of the models but rather is simply a reflection of the changed nature of the decision task. Whereas multichannel models seek to characterize performance when observers are asked to report signals anywhere in the display, the poststimulus probe task asks them to report only the contents of a designated location.

Nevertheless, the results in Figure 9.4 are important in our attempt to distinguish between models. What they show is that an observer's ability to report the contents of the probed location is impaired by the presence of signals elsewhere in the display. Moreover, the magnitude of the impairment is increased as the number of distractor signals increases. This finding is completely at odds with the independent detectors model, which assumes that people can make decisions about m stimulus locations as efficiently as they can about one. If that were true, the identity of the stimuli at distractor locations should have no effect on the accuracy of the report at the probed location. This is intuitively obvious and follows formally from the decisional separability of the model.

However, this is not what Figure 9.4 shows; instead, the data show a significant interaction between the identity of the distractors and performance at the probed location. This is an encouraging result. We were left in the preceding section with the impression that it may not be possible to distinguish between independent detectors and maximum outputs models experimentally. However, the redundancy costs in Figure 9.4 are not consistent with an unlimited-capacity decision stage like the one in the independent detectors model. Should this then lead us to accept the maximum outputs model by default? Before we do so, we should consider what this model predicts in the poststimulus probe task.

As noted previously, the independent detectors and maximum outputs models lie at opposite ends of a continuum. The independent detectors model assumes that observers have complete access to all of the perceptual information in the display. The maximum outputs model assumes that they have access only to the largest of a set of m strength variables. This model assumes that preattentive processes do all the work, filtering out all but the most "signal-like" of the stimuli. The observer thus has access—or, strictly speaking, only need have access—to a very limited amount of the information in the display.

What are the implications of this for the poststimulus probe task? Andrew Cox investigated this question in an unpublished project carried out in my laboratory. Cox investigated the simplest form of the maximum outputs model for the poststimulus probe task. A literal interpretation of the maximum outputs decision rule states that if the largest of the strength variables occurs at the probed location, the observer compares the value of this variable to a criterion to make a decision. If, however, the largest strength variable originates elsewhere, the observer has no direct access to the contents of the probed location because it is not the source of maximum stimulation. She is therefore forced to guess and responds "signal" with some probability—for example, g. The predicted probability of a signal response is

$$P(S) = \int_{c_i}^{\infty} \phi(x-\mu_i) \prod_{j=1, j\neq i}^{m} \Phi(x-\mu_j)dx + g \sum_{j=1, j\neq i}^{m} \int_{-\infty}^{\infty} \phi(x-\mu_j) \prod_{k=1, k\neq j}^{m} \Phi(x-\mu_k)dx.$$

This equation assumes that location i is the probed location. It states that probability of a signal response is the sum of two terms. The first is the probability that the maximum is at the probed location and that it exceeds its associated criterion, c_i. The second is the probability that the maximum is at one of the other m locations and the observer guesses the presence of a signal.

Cox investigated whether this model could account for the individual-observer data from our probe task and found that it failed badly. The reason for its failure was not that it was unable to predict redundancy costs, but rather that the magnitude of the costs it predicted far exceeded those present in the data. Indeed, the reason for the failure is easy to understand. As we add signals at unprobed locations, the probability that the perceptual maximum will occur at the probed location rapidly diminishes. Consequently, the observer will be forced to guess on an increasingly large proportion of trials. This is not what the data in Figure 9.4 show. Although they show redundancy costs, the costs are much more modest than those predicted by the literal interpretation of the maximum outputs model. We are thus forced to reject the idea that observers have access *only* to the largest source of stimulation in the display.

Viewed in a larger perspective, the failure of the strict maximum outputs model should not be surprising. In its assumption that observers guess about stimuli that do not exceed a threshold or selection criterion, it resembles a *high-threshold model* (Blackwell, 1963). Such models have been discredited repeatedly; their most cogent recent critic was Palmer (e.g., Palmer et al., 2000). Among the various failures of high-threshold models, one of the most revealing is in their predictions for second-judgment tasks (Green & Swets, 1966, p. 109).

In a second-judgment task, observers are asked to perform an m-alternative forced-choice task (e.g., with $m = 4$), in which they are required to identify which of m locations or observation intervals contained a signal. On trials on which they make errors, they are asked to make a second judgment. The accuracy of second judgments is significantly above chance (one out of three in a four-alternative task), which is inconsistent with the idea that people have access only to information about the largest or the most "target-like" stimulus in the display. Like Cox's model fits, above-chance second-judgment performance implies access to a richer representation of the information in the display than a simple maximum model presumes.

Interim Summary

The failure of both the independent detectors model and the strict maximum outputs model to account for the data from the poststimulus probe task is illuminating. It shows that the two extremes of the theoretical continuum—that people have complete access to all of the information in the display and that they have access only to the single most signal-like stimulus—are false. Rather, it suggests that people have access to something less than all of the information in the display but something more than one item. I argue that what is limiting performance in this situation is the capacity of visual short-term memory (VSTM).

The proposal that VSTM limits performance in perceptual identification tasks is, of course, not novel. The role played by short-term memory factors in such tasks has been recognized since the classic iconic memory experiments of Sperling (1960). The idea that a posticonic, precategorical form of VSTM exists is likewise well established (Phillips, 1974). By "posticonic" and "precategorical," I mean stimuli encoded in a form that can survive visual masking but that have not yet been identified or categorized (see Coltheart, 1980, for a critical analysis and review). Subsequent researchers have continued to stress the theoretical connection between attention and VSTM in a number of settings (e.g., Bundesen, 1990; Luck et al., 1994; Reeves & Sperling, 1986). Rather, what is interesting here is the indirect way in which VSTM limits are manifested in signal detection.

Our analysis of visual search showed that it was completely transparent to VSTM capacity effects. A fit of the independent detectors model to the visual search data showed no evidence of capacity limitations of any kind. The sole source of performance limits was an increase in the amount of decision noise associated with increasing display size. Evidence for nonindependence appeared only in the poststimulus probe task, in which redundant signals led to reduced sensitivity at probed locations. The absence of VSTM limitations in visual search suggests that VSTM capacity is not a critical determinant of performance on this task. This was so even with displays that were larger than the four-item maximum typically assumed to be the capacity of VSTM (Vogel, Woodman, & Luck, 2006). This implies that the information needed to perform the task could be computed efficiently across the display as a whole without the need to encode individual items in VSTM. The maximum outputs model tells us what this information is likely to be: the maximum of the set of strength variables.

The situation is different for the poststimulus probe task. Because the maximum may not occur at the probed location, its value does not suffice to do the task. Rather, at least some item information must be encoded in VSTM. Depending on the efficiency of the VSTM selection processes, however, it might not be necessary to encode item information for every stimulus in the display. For example, suppose the observer could encode that stimuli exceeding a criterion occurred in a particular subset of locations—for example, locations 1, 3, 6, and 8 on a given trial. This would suffice to do the task without recourse to a guessing strategy. How well people actually do on the task in practice will depend on the capacity of VSTM and on the efficiency of the processes that pick out the largest members of the stimulus set and encode them in VSTM. We will return to the issue of VSTM selection processes at the end of the chapter. First, however, we need to consider the problem of perceptual capacity limitations.

CUED DETECTION AND VISUAL MASKING

The problem we set ourselves at the outset of this chapter—to characterize whether visual signal detection is a capacity-limited task—has metamorphosed into two problems along the way. The first was the problem of whether attention produces a local increase in the quality of the stimulus information at attended locations. We found that the solution to this problem was intertwined with a second problem: that of capacity limitations at the decision stage.

We saw that our apparent inability to distinguish between two quite different models of perceptual decision making—one assuming no capacity limitations at the decision stage and the other assuming a single-channel decision stage— could be distinguished using the poststimulus probe task. Performance on this task shows that the truth seems to lie somewhere between the two extremes: People seem to have access to something less than all of the information in the display but something more than a single extreme item. I argued that the most plausible interpretation of these findings is that what we see in this task are, indirectly, the capacity limits of VSTM.

At the beginning of this chapter, I remarked that a first-time reader of the detection literature is likely to be perplexed by its inconsistency and by the lack of consensus on core experimental findings. Part of this inconsistency can be attributed to the fact that the methodological problems in this area are complex and subtle ones. The pervasive problem, as we saw, was that changes in the overall amount of noise in the display could easily be mistaken for a change in signal quality.

But even after we winnow out the identifiable methodological artifacts, we are still left with one group of studies that appear to support the capacity-limited perception idea and another that do not. Indeed, the experiments that we have discussed in this chapter show evidence of this inconsistency. Whereas the visual search task showed no evidence of perceptual capacity limitations, the finding that cues increased d' in the poststimulus probe task suggests that such capacity limitations do exist.

Of course, these two tasks differed in a number of ways. One used a global decision task (report signals anywhere in the display); the other used a local decision task (report signals only at the probed location). One task used changes in load to manipulate attention; the other used spatial cues. This variety of methods is typical of the detection literature and is one of the reasons why it has been hard to discern consistent underlying patterns.

I have argued that the critical factor distinguishing between the two groups of studies was whether or not backward masks were used to limit the amount of information that could be extracted from the display (Smith, 2000). Specifically, I proposed that masks interrupt stimulus processing before it is complete and that attentional effects will be found in signal detection only when processing is interrupted in this way. I pointed out that, with a few, explicable exceptions, detection studies reporting signal enhancement or capacity-limited perception used backward masks to manipulate detectability; studies finding no effects manipulated detectability via exposure duration or contrast alone. My colleagues and I have developed this idea theoretically and empirically in a number of articles during the last few years and have shown it essentially to be correct. In the remainder of this chapter, I discuss some of our key findings on this topic and their theoretical implications.

The idea of a link between attention and visual masking has been suggested by earlier authors. Lu, Lesmes, and Dosher (2002) noted that Cheal and Lyon (1992) identified poststimulus masking as critical to obtaining attentional effects in perceptual identification tasks. Among a list of methodological requirements for obtaining cuing effects in accuracy tasks, Cheal and Lyon remarked on the need for "adequate masking of the targets to minimize further processing" (p. 245). The wording of this remark suggests that they saw the primary function of masks was to interrupt stimulus processing.

However, their discussion did not distinguish clearly between masks and other ways of limiting the information content of stimuli, and it did not distinguish between the effects of masks of different kinds. They also did not develop a theoretical rationale for why different ways of limiting the information content of stimuli might interact with attention differently. Rather, the article that most directly foreshadowed my argument (Smith, 2000) was on the role of *interruption* and *integration* masking in the *attentional blink* paradigm (Giesbrecht & Di Lollo, 1998).

The "attentional blink" is the name commonly given to a time-dependent reduction in the accuracy with which the second of two sequentially presented visual targets is identified. Methodologically, the attentional blink is a lineal descendent of the psychological refractory period paradigm (Telford, 1931)—a paradigm of historical importance because of its central role in the development of Welford's (1959) single-channel theory (mentioned earlier). Although the former is an accuracy paradigm and the latter a response time paradigm, both seek to vary the resources available to process a target stimulus by requiring processing of a preceding target.

The distinction between interruption masking and integration masking (Kahneman, 1968) is one of several distinctions made in the visual masking literature between masking mechanisms of different kinds (Breitmeyer, 1984). In interruption masking, processing of a target stimulus is terminated prematurely by a trailing mask; in integration masking, the target and mask fuse to form a perceptual composite whose signal-to-noise ratio is lower than that of the target in isolation. Unlike interruption masking, which only occurs with trailing (i.e., backward) masks, integration masking occurs with both forward and backward masks and is maximal when target and mask are simultaneous.

Giesbrecht and Di Lollo (1998) examined the effects of different kinds of mask on the magnitude of the attentional blink in a character recognition task. They showed, as had previous researchers (e.g., Seiffert & Di Lollo, 1997), that an attentional blink is obtained only when both stimuli are masked. In itself, this finding is not particularly surprising because it serves simply to emphasize the importance of limiting the information content of stimuli in accuracy tasks. However, they also showed that the occurrence of the attentional blink depends critically on the kind of mask that is used.

Specifically, they found a blink when the first target was masked by an integration mask or by an interruption mask, but only when the second target was masked with an interruption mask. This suggests that the blink depends on the conjunction of two factors. One is that the first-target identification task must be sufficiently difficult that it reduces the resources available for second-target processing to an appreciable extent. The other is that a backward mask interrupts processing of the second target before it is complete. In their identification of an interaction between attention and the interruption of stimulus processing by masks, Giesbrecht and Di Lollo's (1998) analysis foreshadows my own argument of about the same time.

Detection of Masked and Unmasked Targets

I tested the hypothesis that attention produces signal enhancement in detection tasks only with backwardly masked stimuli (Smith, 2000). (Remember that I am using the terms "signal enhancement" and "capacity-limited perception" as synonyms.) To test this hypothesis, I compared masked and unmasked stimuli in the same design using a Posner spatial cuing paradigm. Because the goal of this test was to ascertain whether cues produce a local increase in signal-to-noise ratio, a number of criteria needed to be satisfied for it to be convincing. Although the poststimulus probe method might seem the most direct way to test this hypothesis, the previous section showed that reporting the contents of a probed location is influenced by the properties of other stimuli in the display.

Many researchers would regard selection of a target stimulus from among a set of distractors as the sine qua non of attention; however, when testing for signal enhancement is conducted, target selection processes are a confounding effect that needs to be eliminated. Researchers such as Lu and Dosher (1998) characterize the process of selecting a target from a multielement array as one of *distractor exclusion.* This process is distinct, both logically and functionally, from attention-related changes in the local signal-to-noise ratio.

To eliminate the effects of distractors, I used a minimal paradigm developed by Luck et al. (1994) in which a single stimulus is presented, without distractors, at either a cued location or elsewhere in the display. Cues were presented 140 ms before the targets, which were displayed for 30, 60, or 90 ms. On unmasked trials, targets were flashed and then extinguished; on masked trials, they were followed by high-contrast, checkerboard pattern masks. For the comparison of performance with masked and unmasked stimuli to provide information about signal enhancement, it was important to ensure that other perceptual and decisional factors did not covary with mask condition. The most important factor of this kind is target localization.

When a single, low-contrast stimulus is presented at an unknown location and then followed by a single, high-contrast mask, the mask does double duty, simultaneously limiting the information that can be extracted from the display and localizing the stimulus perceptually. That is, it acts to resolve the observer's uncertainty about which parts of the display are relevant to the decision. When stimuli are not masked, uncertainty is not resolved in this way. As we showed earlier, uncertainty increases decision noise, regardless of whether distractor stimuli are present, because the uniform field on which the stimulus is presented acts as a source of noise when stimuli are near threshold. My colleagues and I have shown that the noise associated with spatial uncertainty can have a profound effect on the magnitude of the cuing effect in detection tasks (Gould, Wolfgang, & Smith, 2007). Consequently, no inferences about signal enhancement can be drawn if there are differences in uncertainty between experimental conditions.

To equate the uncertainty of masked and unmasked stimuli, I used a pedestal detection task, like the one described previously, in which Gabor patch stimuli were presented on top of suprathreshold contrast luminance pedestals. The idea behind this approach is that the pedestal localizes the stimulus perceptually, irrespective of whether the stimulus is subsequently masked. It assumes that localizing the stimuli with pedestals eliminates uncertainty differences between masked and unmasked stimuli.

The task is similar to that used in a previous study by Foley and Schwarz (1998) on contrast discrimination. Their study, which used unmasked stimuli, varied pedestal contrast from subthreshold to strongly suprathreshold and the number of distractor stimuli in the display. They found that when distractors were present, cues reduced contrast thresholds (i.e., increased sensitivity) at all levels of pedestal contrast. When no distractors were present, cues reduced thresholds only at the lowest levels of pedestal contrast, at which stimuli were not perceptually well localized. When no uncertainty and no distractors were present, the effect of cues on thresholds was minimal. Foley and Schwarz's results thus provide a vivid illustration of the need to eliminate the effects of uncertainty reduction and distractor exclusion if one wishes to infer signal enhancement.

The final factor that needed to be controlled in my study to allow a comparison across stimulus conditions was task difficulty. Any direct comparison of performance with masked and unmasked stimuli presented at a constant level of contrast would have resulted in large accuracy differences, thereby confounding task difficulty and mask condition. Although this may seem an obvious point, the alert reader of the attention literature will find examples of interesting results that are vitiated by problems of this kind (e.g., Bonnel & Hafter, 1998). To avoid such confounding, I set the contrasts for each observer in each condition individually to try to ensure that each performed the task at a constant of $d' = 1.35$. This required stimulus contrasts in the masked conditions that were around double those in the unmasked conditions.

When these various methodological requirements were met, I found that my conjecture about the effects of masking was confirmed. For all stimulus exposure durations, sensitivity to masked targets was higher at cued than at miscued locations for all observers. Sensitivity to unmasked targets did not differ for cued and miscued stimuli for any observer at any exposure duration. We refer to this interaction between cues and masks as the *mask-dependent cuing effect*. I have not reproduced those results here; rather, in Figure 9.5, I have shown the results from a later study by Smith and Wolfgang (2004) that replicated and extended my earlier findings.

In this study, we compared the effects of cues on the detection of masked and unmasked stimuli, and we also compared the effects of masks of different kinds. As in the Smith (2000) study, observers made yes/no judgments about pedestal Gabor patch stimuli. Unlike Smith (2000), we did not vary exposure duration; stimuli were flashed for 40 ms and then extinguished or followed by a high-contrast, checkerboard mask. Instead, we investigated the effects of masks of different kinds, using ferroelectric shutter glasses to control which eye saw the target and which the mask. In one experiment, we presented targets without masks of any kind. In another, we masked the targets *monoptically:* Targets and masks were presented to the same eye. In a third, we masked targets *dichoptically:* Targets were presented to one eye

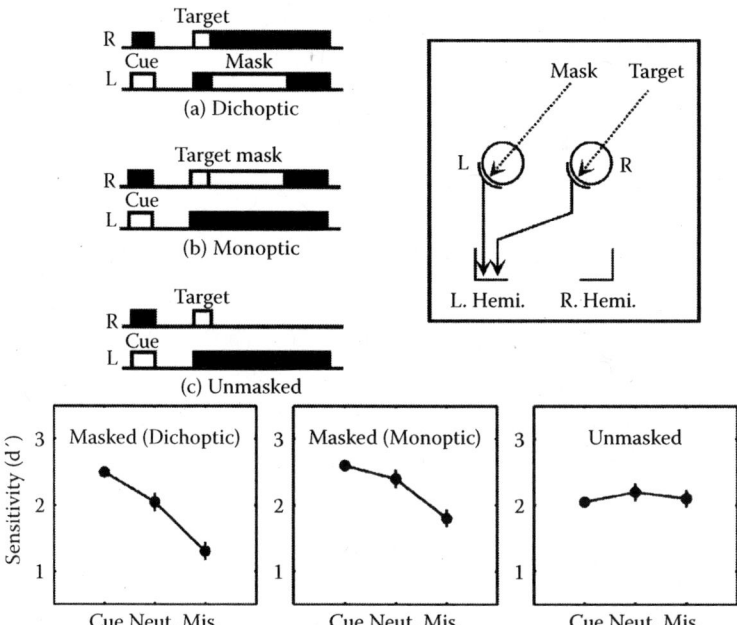

Figure 9.5 The mask-dependent cuing effect. Observers detected pedestal Gabor patches that were dichoptically masked, monoptically masked, or unmasked. Stimuli were presented at cued locations (Cue), miscued locations (Mis.), or following a neutral cue (Neut.) that provided no information about the probable location of the target. The error bars are pooled estimates of the standard error of d'. The inset at the upper left shows the sequence of events in each of the three conditions. White rectangles are stimulus events; black rectangles are periods during which the right (R) or left (L) eyes were occluded. Cues were presented only to the nontarget eye to minimize forward masking of the target by the cue. The inset at the upper right shows the afferent pathways that code stimuli under dichoptic viewing conditions. A right-visual-field target and mask are presented to the left hemiretinas of the right eye and left eye, respectively. The stimuli travel via different afferent pathways to primary visual cortex in the left hemisphere (L. Hemi.). (Data from Smith, P. L. & Wolfgang, B. J., 2004, *Journal of Experimental Psychology: Human Perception and Performance, 30,* 119–136.)

and masks to the other. Stimulus contrast was varied individually for each observer to try to maintain a constant average of $d' = 2.0$ across experiments.

Each of the panels in Figure 9.5 shows averaged results for five observers. As the figure shows, we compared performance in cued and miscued conditions to performance in a neutral condition in which the cues provided no information about the likely target location. This allowed us to assess the benefits of cuing and the costs of miscuing. We found significant cuing effects with dichoptic and monoptic masks and, as found in Smith (2000), no cuing effects with unmasked stimuli. What is particularly interesting about Smith and Wolfgang's (2004) results is that the cuing effect was preserved under dichoptic masking conditions. Indeed, it was actually slightly enhanced, as Figure 9.5 shows.

What are the theoretical implications of these findings? First, they confirm the claim that, when stimuli are equated for detectability and uncertainty reduction and distractor exclusion effects are eliminated, attention produces signal enhancement only with backwardly masked stimuli. Second, they provide insight into the anatomical locus of the interaction between attention and masks. Specifically, they suggest the interaction between attention and masks depends on the interruption of stimulus processing by the mask in visual cortex.

In an article now regarded as a theoretical and methodological landmark, Turvey (1973) used dichoptic and monoptic masks to investigate the anatomical locus of visual masking. Turvey's approach was based on the fact that when a target and a mask are presented monoptically they may interact anywhere along the visual pathway from retina to cortex. When they are presented dichoptically, they are encoded by different afferent pathways and only interact once they have reached the cortex. Any masking found with dichoptic presentation must therefore have a purely cortical locus.

Turvey used this technique to identify distinct *central* and *peripheral* components of masking, which he showed were governed by different time–energy relationships. He showed that peripheral masking occurs precortically—that is, in retina, primary afferent pathways, or lateral geniculate nucleus—by a process of target-mask integration. Central masking occurs cortically, by interruption. The magnitude of the peripheral masking effect depended on the relative energies of the target and mask; the magnitude of the central masking effect depended on the temporal relationship between the onset of the target and the onset of the mask.

More recently, Di Lollo, Enns, and Rensink (2002) have conceived of central masking as occurring by a process of *object substitution*. As in Kahneman's (1968) interruption masking or Turvey's (1973) central masking, the masking stimulus in object substitution masking is thought to displace the target stimulus perceptually before target processing is complete. Object substitution masking differs from the earlier accounts in its assumption that masking occurs via reentrant processing, mediated by feedback pathways from later to earlier stages of visual processing. However, its predicted effects on stimulus processing are very similar to those described in the earlier accounts.

To avoid involving myself in a debate about the physiological substrate of masking, in this chapter I use the term "interruption" masking in a generic way to refer to any masking mechanism in which one stimulus perceptually replaces another before processing of the first stimulus is complete. My generic usage subsumes the masking mechanisms just mentioned, as well as Francis's elegant idea of *efficient masking* (2000). This latter account models masking using differential equations similar to those governing the thermodynamics of cooling liquids.

The finding that the mask-dependent cuing effect is not merely preserved with dichoptic presentation but also slightly enhanced (Smith & Wolfgang, 2004) strongly suggests the involvement of an interruption-masking mechanism of some kind, as Giesbrecht and Di Lollo's (1998) attentional blink results implied. Turvey's analysis suggests that the central interruption component of masking will be maximized by dichoptic presentation because it prevents any form of target-mask integration prior to cortex. In his words: "In dichoptic presentation, central devices receive 'clean' stimuli, that is, inputs that are free of the possible confounding effects of the between-stimulus interference introduced when both stimuli have come to the central device via a common peripheral route" (1973, p. 14). The idea that the central, interruption component of masking is maximized by dichoptic presentation and our finding of large dichoptic cuing effects together suggest that the mask-dependent cuing effect reflects an interaction between attention and a cortical interruption masking mechanism of some kind.

My colleagues and I have reported the mask-dependent cuing effect in several studies using both central and peripheral cues as well as different kinds of decision tasks. These included a yes/no task (Smith, 2000; Smith & Wolfgang, 2004), a rating scale task (Smith, Wolfgang, & Sinclair, 2004), and an orthogonal discrimination task (Smith, Ratcliff, & Wolfgang, 2004; Smith & Wolfgang, 2007). In the latter, rather than making a "present/absent" response, observers are presented with a vertically or a horizontally oriented Gabor patch in a two-alternative, forced-choice (2AFC) paradigm and are required to identify its orientation.

The effects of attention on performance in this task were first investigated by Lee et al. (1997) and, subsequently, by Carrasco et al. (2000). Lee et al. manipulated attention via a concurrent task load and Carrasco et al. used spatial cues. Both of these sets of authors treated performance on easy discrimination tasks as, in some sense, equivalent to or interchangeable with performance on yes/no tasks—or, in our words, as a "proxy for detection."

This equivalence is justified by the findings of Thomas and Gille (1979). They showed that contrast thresholds for yes/no detection and orthogonal discrimination are the same: If an observer can detect the stimulus, she can also discriminate its orientation. This is consistent with the principle of labeled detectors, mentioned earlier, which holds that activity in a visual mechanism carries information about the visual attributes (location, orientation, spatial frequency, contrast polarity, etc.) of the stimulus that produced it. Equal detection and discrimination thresholds are predicted when the members of a stimulus pair are sufficiently different that they cease to be perceptually confusable.

In an orientation discrimination task, this will occur when the stimuli fall outside the orientation bandwidth of cortical simple cells that code the orientation of the other member of the pair. Performance will then be limited by the absolute level of contrast of the stimuli and not by their perceptual similarity. This motivates our expanded definition of detection foreshadowed earlier: Detection tasks are contrast limited; discrimination tasks are similarity limited.

The use of the orthogonal discrimination task as a proxy for detection has a number of clear advantages. One is that response bias effects are smaller and less systematic in 2AFC than in yes/no tasks. The other is that performance in 2AFC tasks can usually be modeled successfully using an equal-variance signal detection model, whereas yes/no tasks typically require an unequal variance model. Both of these features simplify the task of obtaining reliable estimates of sensitivity and of comparing sensitivity across cuing conditions. We have found exactly the same pattern of masking-dependent cuing using orthogonal discrimination as we found using yes/no and rating scale tasks, thus supporting the idea of their functional equivalence (Smith, Ratcliff, & Wolfgang, 2004; Smith & Wolfgang, 2007).

Interruption Masking and External Noise Exclusion

In the preceding section, I argued that the mask-dependent cuing effect arises because attention interacts with an interruption-masking mechanism in visual cortex. In the following section, I will outline a theory of how this interaction takes place. Before I do so, however, I should mention that other researchers have a view of the link between attention and visual masking different from the one I am proposing here.

In a series of recent articles, Lu and Dosher and colleagues have investigated the effects of attention in early vision using an elaborated signal detection model they call a perceptual template model (Dosher & Lu, 2000; Lu & Dosher, 1998). Lu and Dosher's innovation has been their use of the method of equivalent noise to investigate attentional phenomena. The method of equivalent noise originated in engineering as a way of assessing the level of internal noise in electronic devices, such as amplifiers. It subsequently came into vision research by way of auditory psychophysics as the result of the work of Pelli (1981).

The idea behind the method of equivalent noise is that one can determine the level of internal noise in a device by putting *external* noise into it as input. If adding noise into the device leads to no measurable increase in noise in its output, it can be inferred that, at the level used, the external noise is dominated by the internal noise. Systematically increasing the external noise allows one to find the point at which its effects first appear in the output. At this point, the internal noise and external noise are said to be equivalent. Dosher and Lu (2000) have used this method to characterize the attentional mechanisms operating in simple perceptual tasks. Their technique for doing this has been to manipulate attention with spatial cues while different levels of noise are added to the stimulus display.

One of their most robust findings is that cuing effects are small or absent in noiseless displays, but large when high levels of external noise are present in the display. They argue that this reflects the action of an attention-dependent *external noise exclusion* mechanism. This mechanism allows the observer to filter out noise at the target location and obtain a sharper perceptual representation of the signal, resulting in higher sensitivity (lower contrast thresholds) at attended locations. Because this mechanism only operates in high external noise displays, it is only under these circumstances that the associated cuing effects are found. Dosher and Lu (2000) have also identified another mechanism of *stimulus enhancement* that operates in low-noise displays. In comparison with external noise exclusion, the effects of this mechanism are smaller in magnitude and are found with peripheral but not central cues.

Lu and Dosher's (1998) identification of an external noise exclusion mechanism begs an obvious question: Is our mask-dependent cuing effect merely a manifestation of their external noise exclusion mechanism? To the extent that the mask can be viewed as a source of external noise in the display, this identification is plausible, as Lu et al. (2002) have argued. To test this, Wolfgang and I carried out a study in which we compared the effect of a simultaneous mask to that of a backward mask that trailed the target by 60–90 ms (Smith & Wolfgang, 2007). Our simultaneous mask was constructed, like the noise masks of Lu and Dosher, by presenting target and mask in alternating frames on a video display. We carried out a total of five experiments in which we used both noise and pattern masks (random pixels vs. checkerboards) and investigated a number of different aspects of stimulus and mask timing.

Our rationale for this study was that, if an external noise exclusion mechanism was responsible for the cuing effect, then its effects should be largest when the noise and target are in closest proximity—that is, when they are presented simultaneously. As target and mask are separated temporally, the cuing effect should decrease. To express the prediction more conservatively, the magnitude of the cuing effect should not increase with increasing temporal separation between target and mask. This is, of course, the opposite of what is predicted by an interruption masking account. This account predicts no cuing effects when targets and masks are simultaneous because no interruption masking takes place under these conditions. Rather, it predicts large cuing effects under the conditions at which interruption masking is maximal, when masks trail the targets after a critical delay, usually around 80–100 ms.

Figure 9.6 summarizes the results from one of our experiments. As in the studies of Smith (2000) and Smith and Wolfgang (2004), we used Luck's minimal paradigm, in which only a single, masked stimulus was presented, without distractors, at either a cued or a miscued location. Also, following Smith, Ratcliff, and Wolfgang (2004), we used the orthogonal discrimination task described previously.

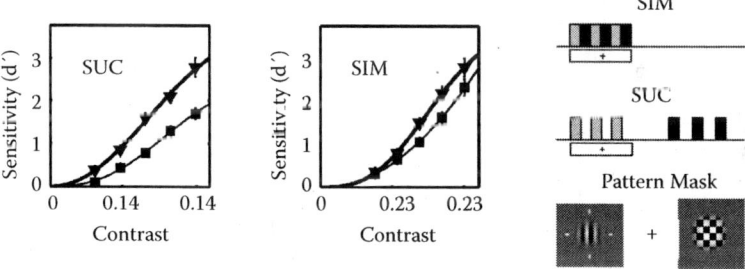

Figure 9.6   Mask-dependent cuing effect for backward, or successive (SUC), masks and simultaneous masks (SIM). Heavy lines and triangles are d' for cued stimuli; light lines and squares are d' for miscued stimuli. The symbols are the empirical data; the continuous curves are fitted Weibull functions. The error bars are pooled estimates of the standard error of d'. The inset on the right side of the figure shows the stimuli and the event sequences on SIM and SUC trials. On SIM trials, the stimulus (gray rectangles) and checkerboard mask (black rectangles) were presented in alternating 10-ms frames and integrated perceptually into a single, compound stimulus. On SUC trials, the stimulus and mask were again presented in alternating frames, but at a stimulus onset asynchrony of 90 ms. The Gabor patch was surrounded by a suprathreshold-contrast fiducial cross to ensure no differences in the time at which the target was localized perceptually on SIM and SUC trials. The fiducial cross was presented for 60 ms at the same time as the first stimulus frame. The temporal relationship of the target, mask, and fiducial cross is shown by the white rectangle labeled "+" in the inset. (Data from Smith, P. L. & Wolfgang, B. J., 2007, Experiment 4, *Perception & Psychophysics, 69*, 1093–1104.)

In our study, rather than attempting to put observers at a constant level of sensitivity, we swept out entire psychometric functions for contrast (cf. Gould et al., 2007; Smith, Ratcliff, & Wolfgang, 2004; Smith, Wolfgang, & Sinclair, 2004). Although this latter procedure requires more experimental trials, it has several advantages. One is that it avoids the difficulty of equating performance in two different stimulus conditions exactly. Another is that it avoids the complaint that in equating for difficulty, one necessarily confounds contrast. Finally, it allows one to investigate attentional effects at all levels of performance simultaneously, rather than just at an arbitrarily chosen reference level.

I have reproduced the data from only one of our five experiments here because the pattern of results in all of them was identical, irrespective of the form of the mask and of the other factors we manipulated. In each case, the largest cuing effects were obtained with a backward mask, rather than with a simultaneous mask. However, in every experiment, some observers showed smaller, but significant, cuing effects with simultaneous masks. Both of these findings are revealing. The fact that the largest cuing effect was obtained with a trailing mask is not consistent with an external noise exclusion mechanism. As we argued, this mechanism predicts the largest effect when target and mask are simultaneous—not when they are temporally separated. Rather, the large cuing effect with trailing masks is the hallmark of an interruption masking mechanism.

On the other hand, our finding of a cuing effect (albeit a weak one) with simultaneous masks cannot be attributed to interruption masking. This finding may be contrasted with those from experiments we have carried out with unmasked stimuli using the same minimal paradigm. In none of these experiments have we found a cuing effect for any observer, except under conditions in which stimuli were not well localized perceptually (Gould et al., 2007).

It therefore seems likely that what Wolfgang and I found in the simultaneous masking conditions of our experiments is evidence for Dosher and Lu's (2000) external noise exclusion mechanism. The fact that they have found large and systematic cuing effects with external noise in the display and we have found only weak and inconsistent effects probably reflects differences in the decision tasks and the kinds of stimulus displays that were used. Whereas we used a detection task (or a detection proxy), they have used more difficult discrimination tasks. Typically, they have also used displays containing distractor stimuli. As we saw previously, displays with distractors place additional demands on target selection processes and may produce larger cuing effects.

In summary, we now have good evidence that spatial cues produce signal enhancement effects in detection tasks only when stimuli are masked. The effects are large with backward masks; they are smaller and less systematic with simultaneous masks. We have seen that signal enhancement effects can only be identified unambiguously by using perceptually well-localized stimuli in displays that contain no distractors. When stimuli are not localized, either by pedestals or by other means, cuing effects can also be found with unmasked stimuli (Cameron et al., 2002; Carrasco et al., 2000), but they are abolished by the addition of markers to the display to localize the stimuli (Gould et al., 2007). Cuing effects can also be found with unmasked stimuli when distractors are in the display, as we discussed in relation to Foley and Schwarz's (1998) study. However, the cuing effects found under these circumstances are attributable to processes of target selection or distractor exclusion, rather than signal enhancement.

A THEORY OF THE MASK-DEPENDENT CUING EFFECT

During the last few years, my colleagues and I have developed a theory of attention in early visual processing that takes the mask-dependent cuing effect as its starting point. The goal of the theory is not simply to model the effect per se. Rather, it is based on our belief that the effect tells us something important about how stimuli are processed perceptually and how stimulus processing is affected by attention. We believe that an adequate account of the effects of attention in early vision requires a theory that links visual encoding, masking, VSTM, attention, and perceptual decision making within an integrated dynamic framework.

Space limits and the tutorial nature of this chapter preclude more than a cursory description of this theory, which is presented in more detail elsewhere (Smith & Ratcliff, 2009). Here I will simply try to convey how the mask-dependent cuing effect arises as a consequence of some simple and natural assumptions about how stimuli are coded in VSTM. Figure 9.7(a) shows the main elements of the current version of the theory in schematic form.

The theory assumes that decisions are made by a sequential-sampling mechanism that accumulates successive samples of noisy stimulus information to a response criterion (Smith, Ratcliff, & Wolfgang, 2004; Smith & Wolfgang, 2004). Sequential-sampling models are more complex than the simple random variable models of signal detection theory; however, they have the decisive advantage over signal detection models in that they can predict both response time (RT) and accuracy and the relationship between them. Indeed, the best sequential-sampling models not only predict the relationship between mean RT and the probability of making a correct response, but also predict the shapes of the RT distributions for both correct responses and errors (Ratcliff & Smith, 2004).

One of the theoretical puzzles in the detection literature is that the effects of attention on RT and on accuracy are different. Whereas attention has frequently been shown to have no effect on accuracy, an effect on RT is found routinely. The standard finding ("the Posner effect") is that attention shortens detection RT (Posner, Snyder, & Davidson, 1980). One of the fundamental issues that theorists in this area have had to grapple with was to explain why this dissociation should occur (e.g., Pashler, 1998; Sperling & Dosher, 1986). Our primary motivation for assuming a sequential-sampling decision mechanism was to explain the complex pattern of accuracy and RT data that we have found in attentional cuing tasks (Smith, Ratcliff, & Wolfgang, 2004).

In our theory, the rate at which evidence accumulates in the decision mechanism depends on the quality of the representation of the stimulus in VSTM. The quality of the VSTM representation depends, in turn, on the output of the early visual filters that encode the stimulus, interacting with any masking stimulus present and also on spatial attention. To predict the mask-dependent cuing effect, we make two assumptions.

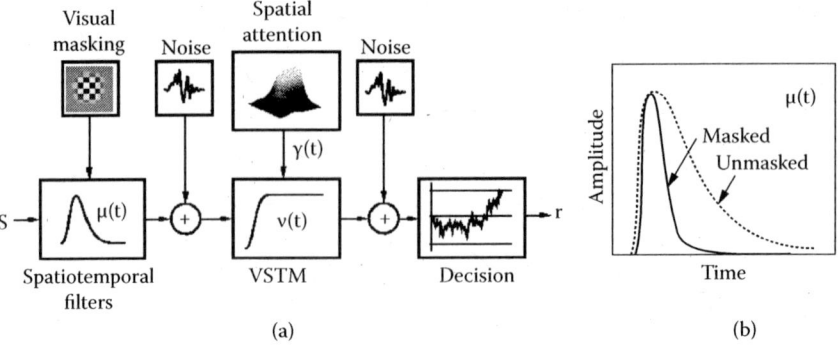

(a)   (b)

Figure 9.7 A theory of the mask-dependent cuing effect. (a) Processing stages. Stimuli are encoded by spatial-frequency and orientation-tuned filters. The filters convert a brief, rectangular pulse stimulus (s) into a smooth, time-varying encoding function, $\mu(t)$. Transient perceptual events are encoded in a durable form in visual short-term memory (VSTM) under the control of spatial attention. The VSTM trace, $v(t)$, grows to an asymptote that depends on the attention gain, $\gamma(t)$, and the contrast and duration of the stimulus. The VSTM trace is subject to moment-by-moment perturbation by noise. Successive samples of the noisy VSTM trace are accumulated over time to a criterion to make a decision (r). A second, early source of noise, analogous to the noise in signal detection theory, describes trial-to-trial variation in the efficiency of perceptual encoding. (b) Encoding functions, $\mu(t)$, for masked and unmasked stimuli. When stimuli are unmasked, they are encoded and then decay relatively slowly. When they are masked, they are encoded and then rapidly suppressed by the mask.

The first assumption is that attention affects the *rate* at which the VSTM trace is formed. When stimuli are attended, the trace is formed rapidly; when they are unattended, the trace is formed slowly. Providing that stimulus remains present long enough for the trace formation process to run to completion, the final (i.e., asymptotic) trace strength for attended and unattended stimuli will be the same. That is, attention affects only the rate of VSTM trace formation and not its final strength or quality. This is shown in Figure 9.8(a), which depicts the growth of the VSTM trace, $v(t)$, as a function of time. The VSTM trace grows rapidly for attended stimuli and slowly for unattended stimuli, but the asymptote of the two curves is the same. Carrasco and McElree (2001) provided evidence for the assumption that attention affects the rate at which stimulus information is extracted from the display.

The second assumption is one that I have already discussed: Backward masks limit the time for which stimulus information is available to later processing stages. In Coltheart's (1980) terms, masks limit the *informational persistence* of stimuli. Specifically, we assume that when stimuli are unmasked, they are encoded perceptually in a transient form that is subject to relatively slow decay. Under typical experimental conditions, the decay may be of the order of several hundred milliseconds. When stimuli are backwardly masked, however, they are encoded and then rapidly suppressed by the mask, limiting the time for which the information is available to later stages. The time course of the encoded perceptual representation, denoted $\mu(t)$, is shown for masked and unmasked stimuli in Figure 9.7(b).

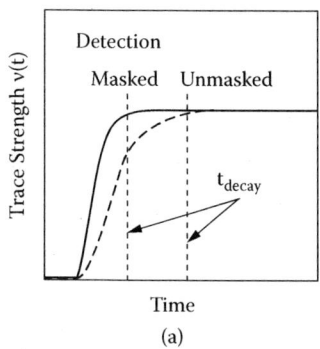 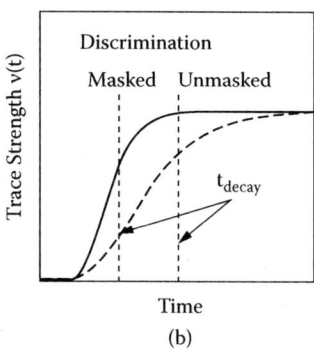

(a)   (b)

Figure 9.8   Schematic representation of the mask-dependent cuing effect in detection and the cue × mask × task interaction. When stimulus duration is long, the VSTM trace, $v(t)$, grows to an asymptote that is equal to the perceptually encoded contrast of the stimulus. The trace grows rapidly for stimuli at attended locations (solid lines) and slowly for stimuli at unattended locations (dotted lines), but both grow to the same asymptote. The asymptotic value of the VSTM trace determines the accuracy of the final response. When stimulus duration is short, the asymptotic trace strength will not be attained. With briefly presented stimuli, the final value of the VSTM trace will depend on the point t_{decay}, at which the stimulus has decayed so far that it can support no further growth of VSTM. In detection tasks, when stimuli are unmasked, t_{decay} falls on the shoulder of $v(t)$, so no cuing effect is found. When stimuli are masked, t_{decay} falls on the rising part of $v(t)$, and a cuing effect is found. The panel on the right shows the growth of the VSTM trace under the assumption that the rate at which stimulus information becomes available perceptually is slower for discrimination tasks than for detection tasks. This leads to a dilation of $v(t)$ on the time axis, which shifts the t_{decay} point for unmasked stimuli off the shoulder of the curve and onto its rising portion. This results in a cuing effect for both masked and unmasked stimuli. (Redrawn after Smith, P. L., Wolfgang, B. J., & Sinclair, A., 2004, *Perception and Psychophysics, 66*, 1056–1075.)

Because of the brief persistence of masked stimuli, when stimuli are masked, the VSTM trace formation process is prevented from running to completion. Consequently, the trace does not reach the same asymptote that it would have reached if the stimulus had not been masked. Under these circumstances, attended stimuli have an advantage because they produce a higher rate of VSTM growth. Because of this, more of the VSTM trace will have formed before the mask suppresses the stimulus. The result is that, when stimuli are masked, the final trace strength will be greater for attended than for unattended stimuli.

The theory thus predicts an interaction between attention and visual masking. When stimuli are unmasked, asymptotic trace strength will be the same for attended and unattended stimuli; when they are masked, asymptotic trace strength will be greater for attended than for unattended stimuli. The asymptotic trace strength determines the signal-to-noise ratio of the stimulus representation and, consequently, the accuracy of the final decision. The mask-dependent cuing effect thus emerges as a natural consequence of the differential persistence of masked and unmasked stimuli interacting with the differential rate of information gain for attended and unattended stimuli.

The theory also predicts the dissociation in the effects of attention on RT and accuracy. One of the determinants of RT is the time taken to form the VSTM trace. The VSTM trace grows more slowly for attended than for unattended stimuli, regardless of whether the stimuli are masked. Consequently, the theory predicts an unconditional RT advantage for attended stimuli: RT will be shorter for attended than for unattended stimuli, irrespective of whether or not they are masked. We have found this dissociation experimentally in an orthogonal discrimination task in which we measured both RT and accuracy for masked and unmasked stimuli (Smith, Ratcliff, & Wolfgang, 2004) and have replicated it in a number of unpublished studies subsequently.

Predictions for Discrimination and for Detection of Signals in Noise

Originally, I proposed that attention and stimulus persistence interact perceptually to explain the mask-dependent cuing effect in detection. Subsequently, it became apparent that the same idea could explain a number of other attentional phenomena as well. Specifically, it can explain why a mask-dependent cuing effect is found in detection, but an unconditional cuing effect—that is, one not dependent on backward masking—is found in some discrimination and recognition tasks. It can also explain why cuing effects may increase when external noise is added to the display.

To understand how it can predict these findings, we need to realize that the absence of a cuing effect in accuracy for unmasked stimuli (shown in Figure 9.8a) will not or need not occur under all conditions. Rather, it depends on the relative rates of VSTM trace formation and of stimulus decay. If stimulus decay is slow relative to the rate of VSTM trace formation, little or no cuing effect will be found because the trace will have reached its asymptotic value before the stimulus decays. If decay is fast, a cuing effect will be present because the stimulus will have decayed before the VSTM trace reaches its asymptote.

In pictorial terms, imagine a point on the time axis (denoted t_{decay} in Figure 9.8) at which the stimulus has decayed to a point where it no longer produces an increase in VSTM strength. (The idea that such a unique point exists is an oversimplification of our theory, which assumes that stimulus information decays progressively over time, but it is a useful way to gain insight into its dynamics.) Whether or not a cuing effect will be found will depend on whether the point t_{decay} falls on the rising or the asymptotic part of the $v(t)$ curve. If it falls on the asymptotic part of the curve, where the VSTM trace is essentially complete, no cuing effect will be found. If it falls on the rising part of the curve, where the VSTM trace is still growing, a cuing effect will be found. The effect of backward masking in our theory is simply to shift the point t_{decay} from the asymptote to the rising part of the curve.

This analysis implies that anything that slows the process of VSTM trace formation will increase the magnitude of the cuing effect. Imagine, for example, that the effect of some particular experimental manipulation is to slow the rate of VSTM growth by a constant multiple for both attended and unattended stimuli. Slowing the rate of growth will extend the trace formation process in time, which will appear graphically as a constant dilation of the $v(t)$ curve on the t-axis. The effect of the dilation will be to shift the t_{decay} point off the shoulder of the curve and onto its rising portion, as shown in Figure 9.8(b).

In this region, the $v(t)$ curves for attended and unattended stimuli have not yet converged. Consequently, if trace formation were terminated at this point, trace strength would be greater for attended than for unattended stimuli and a cuing effect would be found. This cuing effect is not a consequence of backward masking, but rather of the slow growth of the VSTM trace relative to the perceptual decay of the stimulus. In other words, the effect is not due to a change in the absolute value of t_{decay}, but rather of a change in its position relative to the asymptote of the $v(t)$ curve.

If we assume that the process of VSTM trace formation is slower for more difficult perceptual tasks—that is, for discrimination and recognition, as compared to detection—it follows that larger cuing effects will be found for more difficult tasks. A natural prediction of our theory is thus that there will be a three-way cue × mask × task interaction: Cues will increase accuracy only for backwardly masked stimuli in detection, but will produce an unconditional effect in discrimination or recognition.

Is the assumption of slower VSTM trace formation for difficult perceptual tasks a reasonable one? Recognition tasks and difficult discriminations often rely on information carried in the fine spatial structure or high spatial frequencies of the visual image, and such information becomes available comparatively slowly (Watt, 1987). One of the manifestations of this is a progressive lengthening of RT with increases in stimulus spatial frequency (Lupp, Hauske, & Wolf, 1976). The usual interpretation of such findings is that the channels that code the fine structure of an image respond more slowly than do those that code its coarse structure or low spatial frequencies. These findings are consistent with our assumption that VSTM trace formation is slower for difficult tasks because the perceptual information on which it is based is encoded relatively slowly.

As discussed in more detail later, the rate of VSTM growth in our theory depends on the function $\mu(t)$ in Figure 9.7(b), which describes the time course of perceptual encoding. A reduction in the rate at which stimulus information is available perceptually will reduce the rate at which the VSTM trace forms. This reduction is represented mathematically by a dilation in the time scale of the encoding function $\mu(t)$ and it leads, in turn, to a dilation of the $v(t)$ curve on the t-axis. As we saw previously, for a fixed rate of stimulus decay, the effect of such a dilation will be to move t_{decay} off the shoulder of the $v(t)$ curve and onto its rising portion. In this region, cuing effects are found.

In an analogous way, if we assume that the effect of adding noise to the stimulus display is to slow the rate of VSTM formation, our theory predicts larger cuing effects for stimuli embedded in a background of external noise. Such a reduction might plausibly come about due to competitive interactions between visual analyzers that code different spatial frequencies and orientations in the visual array. Increasing noise in analyzers that code frequencies and orientations other than those of the target may reduce the gain—that is, the rate of information extraction—in the analyzer that codes the target stimulus. A reduction in gain caused by noise is broadly consistent with noise-based gain control mechanisms like the one proposed by Rudd (1996).

In summary, our theory not only provides a natural account of why the mask-dependent cuing effect is found in detection, but also provides an account of why detection may differ from more complex discrimination and recognition tasks. In addition, it can also explain why cuing effects are increased when stimuli are embedded in noise. In either instance, the additional assumptions needed to explain these phenomena are simple and plausible ones.

Shunting Equations and Visual Short-Term Memory

In the previous section, I argued that an adequate theory of the mask-dependent cuing effect requires a theory that links visual encoding, masking, attention, VSTM, and decision making in an integrated dynamic framework. The process of VSTM trace formation is critical in this sequence of operations because it is the place where attention and visual processing interact. We model the process of VSTM formation mathematically using a particular kind of differential equation called a *shunting equation*. The distinguishing feature of such equations is that the function that drives the equation, the so-called "forcing function," enters into the equation multiplicatively rather than additively, as is the case in the usual linear system model. This gives these equations particularly desirable characteristics when short-term memory processes are modeled (described next).

The most comprehensive analysis of shunting equations has been carried out by Stephen Grossberg and his colleagues (see, for example, Grossberg, 1988, for an overview), but such equations have been proposed by a number of authors in a variety of settings. The Hodgkin–Huxley membrane equations of neurophysiology are of the shunting type (Tuckwell, 1988). These equations describe the electrochemical dynamics of neural conduction. As Grossberg has noted, the existence of shunting dynamics at the lowest level of the nervous system underscores the inherent plausibility of such equations as models of biological computation.

Sperling and Sondhi (1968) first used shunting equations in a psychophysical model of flicker perception. However, the application that is closest in spirit to our own is that of Loftus and co-workers (Busey & Loftus, 1994). Like us, they use a shunting equation to model the growth of the VSTM trace over time. However, their model is a *functional* model in which a shunting equation is used to model the growth of the proportion of correct responses over time.

Our model is a *process* model in which a shunting equation is used to model the signal-to-noise properties of the VSTM trace. The strength of this trace determines the rate at which information about the stimulus accumulates in a sequential sampling decision model. The advantage of the process model approach over the functional approach is that the former provides a computational model of both accuracy and RT, whereas the latter provides an account of accuracy only.

One can write a shunting equation to model the growth of VSTM in a number of different ways. The precise form of the equation will depend on the properties of the stimuli and on a number of ancillary assumptions about the underlying psychological processes. Here we consider the case of a sinusoidal grating patch stimulus like those used in the experiments discussed previously. The maximum luminance of such a stimulus is denoted by L_2 and its minimum luminance by L_1. To obtain the right kinds of dynamics for our VSTM model, we assume that the VSTM trace is the product of an opponent-process coding scheme in which it receives inputs from both perceptual ON channels and OFF channels. ON channels code positive contrast excursions above the background luminance; OFF channels code negative excursions below the background.

Good evidence indicates that stimulus information in the visual system is coded in this way (Fiorentini, Baumgartner, Magnussen, Schiller, & Thomas, 1990), so our assumption is plausible physiologically. We assume that the time course of perceptual information in both the ON and the OFF channels is described by a function, $\mu(t)$, depicted in Figure 9.7(b). The output of the ON channel is $L_2 \mu(t)$ and the output of the OFF channel is $L_1 \mu(t)$. The precise form of the function $\mu(t)$ will depend on the sensory response characteristics of the perceptual analyzer that codes the stimulus, the stimulus duration, and whether or not the stimulus is masked (see Smith & Wolfgang, 2004, for details).

We assume that growth of the VSTM trace, $v(t)$, is described by a shunting differential equation of the form

$$\frac{dv}{dt} = \gamma \left\{ L_2 \mu(t)[1 - v(t)] - L_1 \mu(t)[1 + v(t)] \right\}.$$

This equation has several noteworthy features. As I remarked previously, the distinguishing feature of shunting equations is that the forcing function, $\mu(t)$, which provides the input to the system, enters into the equation multiplicatively rather than additively. Consequently, when $\mu(t) = 0$—that is, when the stimulus is removed—the derivative dv/dt will also be zero and the VSTM trace will stop changing. Shunting equations thus provide a natural way of modeling the way in which a durable short-term memory trace can be computed from a transient stimulus input. (In fact, in a complete model, we would also wish to represent the way in which the VSTM trace decays over time. But because we assume that the decay occurs on a time scale that is comparatively long relative to the time course of perceptual decisions, little is lost if the decay term is omitted from the model.)

Also, assuming an initial condition of $v(0) = 0$, the VSTM trace in the preceding equation remains bounded on the range {–1, +1}, regardless of the strength of the input. Shunting equations thus provide an elegant way of solving what Grossberg has called the "noise versus saturation" dilemma. In effect, they automatically retune their sensitivity in response to changes in the dynamic range of the stimulus.

The constant γ in the preceding equation is an attention weight that determines the rate at which VSTM trace is formed. We assume that the attention weight has one value, say γ_A, if the stimulus is at an attended location and another value, γ_U, if it is at an attended location, with $\gamma_A > \gamma_U$. This relationship embodies, in an explicit way, our assumption that attention affects the rate of VSTM trace formation. Using standard techniques for solving first-order, linear differential equations (e.g., Boyce & Di Prima, 1977, pp. 11–17), it is straightforward to show that the solution of the previous equation is

$$v(t) = \left(\frac{L_2 - L_1}{L_2 + L_1} \right) \left\{ 1 - \exp\left[-\gamma(L_2 + L_1) \int_0^t \mu(s)ds \right] \right\}$$

What does this equation tell us? First, it states that, asymptotically, the VSTM trace will be equal to $(L_2 - L_1)/(L_2 + L_1)$—the Michelson contrast of the stimulus. That is, the strength of the VSTM trace encodes the contrast of the stimulus. I do not mean to imply by this statement that contrast transduction in the visual system is linear; we know the contrast response of the primate visual system is a saturating, nonlinear function of contrast (Kaplan, Lee, & Shapley, 1990). Rather, we assume that the VSTM process sits "downstream" from any perceptual nonlinearities in the processing sequence and that the effect of such nonlinearities will be embodied in the numerical values of the constants L_2 and L_1. A more accurate characterization would therefore be to say that the VSTM trace veridically represents the contrast of the stimulus as it is encoded by early nonlinear perceptual mechanisms.

Second, the equation tells us that the rate of growth is proportional to the product of the attention weight and the mean (nonlinearly transduced) luminance of the stimulus. The approach to asymptote is controlled by the area under the sensory response function $\mu(t)$. The asymptotic value of $(L_2 - L_1)/(L_2 + L_1)$ will only be attained if the area under $\mu(t)$ is sufficient to allow the VSTM formation process to run to completion. If the area is reduced, as occurs with backward masking, the process will terminate prematurely and the theoretical asymptote will not be attained.

It can be shown that with appropriate assumptions about the sensory response function and the attention gain constants, γ_A and γ_U, the model in Figure 9.7(a) predicts the mask-dependent cuing effect in detection accuracy. When combined with a sequential sampling decision mechanism, such as the diffusion process model of Ratcliff (1978), it can predict the RT, accuracy, and RT distribution data from simple detection tasks. We assume, as discussed earlier, that task difficulty (detection vs. discrimination) and the effects of added noise can both be represented by a reduction in the rate at which stimulus information is available perceptually. We model this reduction by a change in the rate properties of the function $\mu(t)$. For a fixed exposure duration, a reduction in the encoding rate leads to a reduction in the area under the $\mu(t)$ curve. Under these circumstances, the theory can predict cuing effects with unmasked stimuli as well as with masked stimuli.

Coding and Capacity Limits in Visual Short-Term Memory

To date, the theory outlined in the previous section has been applied quantitatively only to data from Luck's minimal paradigm, in which a single stimulus is presented at either a cued or an uncued location in an otherwise empty display. However, we saw previously that the nature of the attentional effects found in cuing paradigms changes markedly if distractors are in the display (e.g., Foley & Schwarz, 1998). One of the effects of distractors appears to be to create competition among stimuli for entry to VSTM. When only a single stimulus is presented, as is the case with Luck's minimal paradigm, no competition of this kind will occur. A currently open question is therefore how to extend the theory of the previous section to account for performance on tasks of this kind. I argue that shunting equations provide the right kind of theoretical and mathematical framework for extending the theory in this way.

We saw in the analysis of the visual search task that the human observer appears to function as a maximum outputs detector. Performance in such tasks is well described by a model that assumes that observers make a signal response if the largest of a set of strength variables exceeds a criterion. Although the maximum outputs model is similar to an independent detectors model and, indeed, in many situations is formally indistinguishable from it, we saw that an independent detectors model is incompatible with the finding of redundancy costs in the post-stimulus probe task. We therefore rejected the independent detectors model in favor of the maximum outputs model.

However, we also saw that a strict, or literal, version of the maximum outputs model could not be true. This model assumed that the *only* information to which observers have access is the largest of the set of strength variables. Such a model predicts redundancy costs in the poststimulus probe task that are much larger than those actually found. We were therefore forced to reject the idea that observers only had access to information about the most target-like stimulus in the display.

Together, these findings impose important constraints on any plausible theory of VSTM. The fact that performance in many simple tasks is well described by a maximum outputs model suggests that entry into VSTM is not random, as assumed by "box-and-slots" models, but rather depends on the goodness of match between a stimulus and some specified attribute of the target. The stimuli that most possess the defining attributes of the target will have priority of entry to VSTM. Increasing the number of target-like stimuli in the display will increase the competition for VSTM and produce a performance decrement. Competition of this kind appears to underlie the redundancy costs found in the poststimulus probe task. These kinds of dynamics are precisely the ones exhibited by competitively interacting systems of shunting equations.

Grossberg and colleagues have carried out a detailed analysis of systems of coupled shunting equations (see Grossberg, 1988, for an overview). Grossberg has investigated systems of equations similar to the one described in the last section, in which competitive interactions take place between equations that code the properties of different stimuli or different stimulus attributes. He has also investigated the effects of augmenting the equations with nonlinear, self-exciting feedback connections. He has shown that the particular form taken by these nonlinear feedback signals is critical in determining the kind of information that is stored in memory.

If the feedback signals are positively accelerating (e.g., quadratic), the system of equations exhibits "winner-takes-all" dynamics. The activity associated with the strongest stimulus is coded in memory and the activity associated with all weaker stimuli is suppressed. Winner-take-all dynamics are, of course, the neural network counterpart of maximum output signal detection models. In either instance, the information available to serve as the basis for a decision is the value of the largest, or most target-like, of the set of stimulus values.

Grossberg has further shown that if the nonlinear feedback signal is sigmoidal in form (i.e., positively then negatively accelerating), it endows the system with a so-called *quenching threshold*. Stimulus values above the quenching threshold are amplified and stored in memory; stimulus values below the quenching threshold are suppressed. This endows the system with a form of limited capacity property in which a subset of the largest stimulus values is stored in memory and the remainder is suppressed. These kinds of dynamics seem to capture many of the features we saw in our analysis of the visual search and poststimulus probe tasks. The fact that they do so makes us believe that the shunting equation formalism is the right one for modeling the dynamics of VSTM selection in tasks with multielement displays.

CONCLUSION

In this chapter I have provided an introduction to some of the theoretical and experimental issues involved in trying to understand if, or how and when, visual signal detection is affected by attention. I argued at the beginning of the chapter that detection is important theoretically because of the historical idea that it is, in some sense or another, a preattentive task, which neither benefits from nor requires attention. The implication of this idea is that detection differs fundamentally in its attentional demands from other visual tasks. The research described in this chapter grew out of the attempt to ascertain whether this was actually so.

Part of my aim in writing has been to try to give some idea of the subtle theoretical and methodological problems that arise in the study of attention and visual signal detection. I hope the reader will come away with some appreciation of why this apparently simple and straightforward question should have proved so difficult to resolve. More importantly, however, I hope the reader will leave with a sense that the study of attentional effects in detection has implications that are much wider than an understanding of detection per se. Indeed, I believe that the analysis of detection and its interaction with other kinds of perceptual process, such as visual masking, has the potential to illuminate the dynamic properties of spatial attention in a rich and detailed way.

REFERENCES

Ashby, F. G., & Townsend, J. T. (1986). Varieties of perceptual independence. *Psychological Review, 93,* 154–179.

Baldassi, S., & Burr, D. C. (2004). "Pop-out" of targets modulated in luminance or color: The effects of intrinsic and extrinsic uncertainty. *Vision Research, 44,* 1227–1233.

Bashinski, H. S., & Bacharach, V. R. (1980). Enhancements of perceptual sensitivity as the result of selectively attending to spatial locations. *Perception & Psychophysics, 28,* 241–248.

Blackwell, H. R. (1963). Neural theories of simple visual discriminations. *Journal of the Optical Society of America, 53,* 129–160.

Bonnel, A.-M., & Hafter, E. R. (1998). Divided attention between simultaneous auditory and visual signals. *Perception & Psychophysics, 60,* 179–190.

Boyce, W. E., & Di Prima, R. C. (1977). *Elementary differential equations and boundary value problems* (3rd ed.). New York: John Wiley & Sons.

Brawn, P. M., & Snowden, R. J. (2000). Attention to overlapping objects: Detection and discrimination of luminance changes. *Journal of Experimental Psychology: Human Perception and Performance, 26,* 342–358.

Breitmeyer, B. G. (1984). *Visual masking: An integrative approach.* Oxford, England: Clarendon Press.

Broadbent, D. E. (1958). *Perception and communication.* Elmsford, NY: Pergamon Press.

Bundesen, C. (1990). A theory of visual attention. *Psychological Review, 97,* 523–547.

Busey, T. A., & Loftus, G. R. (1994). Sensory and cognitive components of visual information acquisition. *Psychological Review, 101,* 446–469.

Cameron, E. L., Tai, J. C., & Carrasco, M. (2002). Covert attention affects the psychometric function of contrast sensitivity. *Vision Research, 42,* 949–967.

Carrasco, M., & McElree, B. (2001). Covert attention speeds the accrual of visual information. *Proceedings of the National Academy of Science, 98,* 5363–5367.

Carrasco, M., Penpeci-Talgar, C., & Eckstein, M. (2000). Spatial covert attention increases contrast sensitivity across the CSF: Support for signal enhancement. *Vision Research, 40,* 1203–1215.

Cheal, M., & Lyon, D. R. (1992). Benefits from attention depend on the target type in location-precued discrimination. *Acta Psychologica, 81,* 243–267.

Cherry, E. C. (1953). Some experiments on the recognition of speech, with one and two ears. *Journal of the Acoustical Society of America, 25,* 975–979.

Cherry, E. C., & Taylor, W. K. (1954). Some further experiments on the recognition of speech with one and two ears. *Journal of the Acoustical Society of America, 26,* 554–559.

Coltheart, M. (1980). Iconic memory and visible persistence. *Perception & Psychophysics, 27,* 183–228.

Davis, E. T., Kramer, P., & Graham, N. (1983). Uncertainty about spatial frequency, spatial position, or contrast of visual patterns. *Perception & Psychophysics, 33,* 20–28.

Di Lollo, V., Enns, J. T., & Rensink, R. A. (2002). Competition for consciousness among visual events: The psychophysics of reentrant visual processes. *Journal of Experimental Psychology: General, 129,* 481–507.

Dosher, B. A., & Lu, Z.-L. (2000). Mechanisms of perceptual attention in precuing of location. *Vision Research, 40,* 1269–1292.

Downing, C. J. (1988). Expectancy and visual-spatial attention: Effects on perceptual quality. *Journal of Experimental Psychology: Human Perception and Performance, 14,* 188–202.

Eckstein, M. P., Thomas, J. P., Palmer, J., & Shimozaki, S., (2000). A signal detection model predicts the effects of set size on visual search accuracy for feature, conjunction, triple conjunction, and disjunction displays. *Perception & Psychophysics, 62,* 425–451.

Egeth, H. (1977). Attention and preattention. In G. H. Bower (Ed.), *The psychology of learning and motivation, 11* (pp. 277–320). New York: Academic Press.

Fiorentini, A., Baumgartner, G., Magnussen, S., Schiller, P., & Thomas, J. P. (1990). The perception of brightness and darkness: Relations to neuronal receptive fields. In L. Spillman & J. S. Werner (Eds.), *Visual perception: The neurophysiological foundations* (pp. 129–161). San Diego, CA: Academic Press.

Foley, J. M., & Schwarz, W. (1998). Spatial attention: Effect of position uncertainty and number of distractor patterns on the threshold-versus-contrast function for contrast discrimination. *Journal of the Optical Society of America, A, 15,* 1036–1047.

Francis, G. (2000). Quantitative theories of metacontrast masking. *Psychological Review, 107,* 768–785.

Giesbrecht, B., & Di Lollo, V. (1998). Beyond the attentional blink: Visual masking by object substitution. *Journal of Experimental Psychology: Human Perception and Performance, 24,* 1454–1466.

Gilliom, J. D., & Sorkin, R. D. (1974). Sequential vs. simultaneous two-channel signal detection: More evidence for a high-level interruption theory. *Journal of the Acoustical Society of America, 56*, 157–164.

Gould, I. C., Wolfgang, B. J., & Smith, P. L. (2007). Spatial uncertainty explains exogenous and endogenous attentional cuing effects in visual signal detection. *Journal of Vision, 7, 13*(4) 1–17.

Graham, N., Kramer, P., & Haber, N. (1985). Attending to the spatial frequency and spatial position of near-threshold visual patterns. In M. I. Posner & O. S. M. Marin (Eds.), *Attention and performance XI* (pp. 269–284). Hillsdale, NJ: Lawrence Erlbaum Associates.

Graham, N. V. S. (1989). *Visual pattern analyzers.* New York: John Wiley & Sons.

Graham, N. V. S., Kramer, P., Yager, D. (1987). Signal detection methods for multidimensional stimuli: Probability distributions and combination rules. *Journal of Mathematical Psychology, 31, 366–409.*

Green, D. M., & Swets, J. A. (1966). *Signal detection theory and psychophysics.* New York: John Wiley & Sons.

Grossberg, S. (1988). Nonlinear neural networks: Principles, mechanisms, and architectures. *Neural Networks, 1*, 17–61.

Hawkins, H. L., Hillyard, S. A., Luck, S. J., Mouloua, M., Downing, C. J., & Woodward, D. P. (1990). Visual attention modulates signal detectability. *Journal of Experimental Psychology: Human Perception and Performance, 16*, 802–811.

Johnston, J. C., & Pashler, H. E. (1990). Close binding of identity and location in visual feature perception. *Journal of Experimental Psychology: Human Perception and Performance, 16*, 843–856.

Kadlec, H. C., & Townsend, J. T. (1992). Implications of marginal and conditional detection parameters for separabilities and independence of perceptual dimensions. *Journal of Mathematical Psychology, 36*, 325–374.

Kahneman, D. (1968). Methods, findings, and theory in studies of visual masking. *Psychological Bulletin, 70*, 404–425.

Kaplan, E., Lee, B. B., & Shapley, R. M. (1990). New views of primate retinal function. In N. N. Obsborne & G. J. Chader (Eds.), *Progress in retinal research* (Vol. 9, pp. 273–333). Oxford, England: Pergamon Press.

Kawahara, J., Di Lollo, V., & Enns, J. T. (2001). Attentional requirements in visual detection and identification: Evidence from the attentional blink. *Journal of Experimental Psychology: Human Perception and Performance, 27*, 969–984.

Kinchla, R. A. (1974). Detecting target elements in multielement visual arrays: A confusability model. *Perception & Psychophysics, 25*, 149–158.

Kinchla, R. A. (1977). The role of structural redundancy in the perception of visual targets. *Perception & Psychophysics, 22*, 19–30.

Kinchla, R. A., Chen, Z., & Evert, D. (1995). Precue effects in visual search: Data or resource limited? *Perception & Psychophysics, 57*, 441–450.

Lee, D. K., Koch, C., & Braun, J. (1997). Spatial vision thresholds in the near absence of attention. *Vision Research, 37*, 2409–2418.

Lu, Z.-L., & Dosher, B. A. (1998). External noise distinguishes attention mechanisms. *Vision Research, 38*, 1183–1198.

Lu, Z.-L., Lesmes, L. A., & Dosher, B. A. (2002). Spatial attention excludes noise at the target location. *Journal of Vision, 2*, 312–323.

Luck, S. J., Hillyard, S. A., Mouloua, M., Woldorff, M. G., Clark, V. P., & Hawkins, H. L. (1994). Effects of spatial cuing on luminance detectability: Psychophysical and electrophysical evidence. *Journal of Experimental Psychology: Human Perception and Performance, 20*, 887–904.

Lupp, U., Hauske, G., & Wolf, W. (1976). Perceptual latencies to sinusoidal gratings. *Vision Research, 16*, 969–972.

Macmillan, N.A., & Creelman, C.D. (1991). *Detection theory: A user's guide.* Cambridge, England: Cambridge University Press.

Müller, H. J., & Findlay, J. M. (1987). Sensitivity and criterion effects in the spatial cuing of visual attention. *Perception & Psychophysics, 42,* 383–399.

Müller, H. J., & Humphreys, G. W., (1991). Luminance-increment detection: Capacity limited or not? *Journal of Experimental Psychology: Human Perception and Performance, 17,* 107–124.

Neisser, U. (1967). *Cognitive psychology.* New York: Appleton–Century–Crofts.

Palmer, J. (1994). Set-size effects in visual search: The effect of attention is independent of the stimulus for simple tasks. *Vision Research, 34,* 1703–1721.

Palmer, J. (1995). Attention in visual search: Distinguishing four causes of a set-size effect. *Psychological Science, 4,* 118–123.

Palmer, J., Ames, C. T., & Lindsey, D. T. (1993). Measuring the effect of attention on simple visual search. *Journal of Experimental Psychology: Human Perception and Performance, 19,* 108–130.

Palmer, J., Verghese, P., & Pavel, M. (2000). The psychophysics of visual search. *Vision Research, 40,* 1227–1268.

Pashler, H. E. (1998). *The psychology of attention.* Cambridge; MA: MIT Press.

Pelli, D. G. (1981). *Effects of visual noise.* PhD dissertation, University of Cambridge, Cambridge, England.

Phillips, W. A. (1974). On the distinction between sensory storage and short-term visual memory. *Perception & Psychophysics, 16,* 283–290.

Posner, M. I. (1980). Orienting of attention. *Quarterly Journal of Experimental Psychology, 32,* 3–25.

Posner, M. I., Snyder, C. R. R., & Davidson, B. J. (1980). Attention and the detection of signals. *Journal of Experimental Psychology: General, 109,* 160–174.

Ratcliff, R. (1978). A theory of memory retrieval. *Psychological Review, 85,* 59–108.

Ratcliff, R., & Smith, P. L. (2004). A comparison of sequential sampling models for two-choice reaction time. *Psychological Review, 111,* 333–367.

Reeves, A., & Sperling, G. (1986). Attention gating in short-term visual memory. *Psychological Review, 93,* 180–206.

Rudd, M. E. (1996). A neural timing model of visual threshold. *Journal of Mathematical Psychology, 40,* 1–29.

Seiffert, A. E., & Di Lollo, V. (1997). Low-level masking in the attentional blink. *Journal of Experimental Psychology: Human Perception and Performance, 23,* 1061–1073.

Shaw, M. L. (1980). Identifying attentional and decision-making components in information processing. In R. S. Nickerson (Ed), *Attention and performance VIII.* (pp. 277–296) Hillsdale, NJ: Lawrence Erlbaum Associates.

Shaw. M. L. (1982). Attending to multiple sources of information: I. The integration of information in decision making. *Cognitive Psychology, 14,* 353–409.

Shaw, M. L. (1984). Division of attention among spatial locations: A fundamental difference between detection of letters and the detection of luminance increments. In H. Bouma & D. G. Bouwhuis (Eds.), *Attention and performance, X* (pp. 109–121) Hillsdale, NJ: Lawrence Erlbaum Associates.

Shaw, M. L., Mulligan, R., & Stone, L. (1983). A test between two-state and continuous-state attention models. *Perception & Psychophysics, 33,* 338–354.

Shimozaki, S. S., Eckstein, M. P., & Abbey, C. K. (2003). Comparison of two weighted integration models for the cueing task: Linear and likelihood. *Journal of Vision, 3,* 209–229.

Shiu, L.-P. & Pashler, H. (1994). Negligible effect of spatial precuing in identification of single digits. *Journal of Experimental Psychology: Human Perception and Performance, 20,* 1037-1054.

Smith, P. L. (1998). Attention and luminance detection: A quantitative analysis. *Journal of Experimental Psychology: Human Perception and Performance, 24,* 105–133.

Smith, P. L. (2000). Attention and luminance detection: Effects of cues, masks, and pedestals. *Journal of Experimental Psychology: Human Perception and Performance, 26,* 1401–1420.

Smith, P. L., & Ratcliff, R. (2009). An integrated theory of attention and decision making in visual signal detection. *Psychological Review, 116,* 283–317.

Smith, P. L., Ratcliff, R., & Wolfgang, B. J. (2004). Attention orienting and the time course of perceptual decisions: Response time distributions with masked and unmasked displays. *Vision Research, 44,* 1297–1320.

Smith, P. L., & Wolfgang, B. J. (2004). The attentional dynamics of masked detection. *Journal of Experimental Psychology: Human Perception and Performance, 30,* 119–136.

Smith, P. L., & Wolfgang, B. J., (2007). Attentional mechanisms in visual signal detection: The effects of simultaneous and delayed noise and pattern masks. *Perception & Psychophysics, 69,* 1093–1104.

Smith, P. L., Wolfgang, B. J., & Sinclair, A. (2004). Mask-dependent attentional cuing effects in visual signal detection: The psychometric function for contrast. *Perception and Psychophysics, 66,* 1056–1075.

Sorkin, R. D., & Pohlmann, L. D. (1973). Some models of observer behavior in two-channel auditory signal detection. *Perception & Psychophysics, 14,* 101–109.

Sorkin, R. D., Pohlmann, L. D., & Woods, D. D. (1976). Decision interactions between auditory channels. *Perception & Psychophysics, 19,* 290–295.

Sperling, G. (1960). The information available in brief visual presentations. *Psychological Monographs, 74,* 1–29.

Sperling, G., & Dosher, B. A. (1986). Strategy and optimization in human information processing. In K. R. Boff, L. Kaufman, & J. P. Thomas (Eds.), *Handbook of perception and performance* (Vol. 1, pp. 1–85). New York: John Wiley & Sons.

Sperling, G., & Sondhi, M. M. (1968). Model for visual luminance discrimination and flicker detection. *Journal of the Optical Society of America, 58,* 1133–1145.

Swets, J. A. (1984). Mathematical models of attention. In R. Parasuraman & D. R. Davies (Eds.), *Varieties of attention* (pp. 183–242). New York: Academic Press.

Tanner, W. P. (1961). Physiological implications of psychophysical data. *Annals of the New York Academy of Sciences, 89,* 752–765.

Telford, C. W. (1931). The refractory phase of voluntary and associative responses. *Journal of Experimental Psychology, 14,* 1–36.

Thomas, J. P., & Gille, J. (1979). Bandwidths of orientation channels in human vision. *Journal of the Optical Society of America, 69,* 652–660.

Thomas, R. D. (1999). Assessing sensitivity in a multidimensional space: Some problems and a definition of a general *d'. Psychonomic Bulletin & Review, 6,* 224–238.

Thurstone, L. L. (1927). A law of comparative judgment. *Psychological Review, 34,* 273–286.

Treisman, A. M., Cavanagh, P., Fischer, B., Ramachandran, V. S., von der Heydt, R. (1990). Form perception and attention: Striate cortex and beyond. In L. Spillman & J. S. Werner (Eds.), *Visual perception: The neurophysiological foundations* (pp. 273–316). San Diego, CA: Academic Press.

Treisman, A. M., & Gelade, G. (1980). A feature integration theory of attention. *Cognitive Psychology, 12,* 97–136.

Tuckwell, H. C. (1988). *Introduction to theoretical neurobiology, I: Linear cable theory and dendritic structure.* Cambridge, England: Cambridge University Press.

Turvey, M. T. (1973). On peripheral and central processes in vision: Inferences from an information-processing analysis of masking with patterned stimuli. *Psychological Review, 80,* 1–52.

Vogel, E. K., Woodman, G. F., & Luck, S. J. (2006). The time course of consolidation in visual working memory. *Journal of Experimental Psychology: Human Perception and Performance, 32,* 1436–1451.

Watt, R. (1987). Scanning from course to fine spatial scales in the human visual system after the onset of a stimulus. *Journal of the Optical Society of America A, 4,* 2006–2021.

Webster, M. A., & DeValois, R. L. (1985). Relationship between spatial-frequency and orientation tuning of striate cortex cells. *Journal of the Optical Society of America, A, 2,* 1124–1132.

Welford, A. T. (1959). Evidence of a single-channel decision mechanism limiting performance in a serial reaction time task. *Quarterly Journal of Experimental Psychology, 11,* 193–210.

10

Face and Object Recognition
How Do They Differ?

ELINOR MCKONE

INTRODUCTION

This chapter reviews an extensive set of findings arguing that visual recognition of faces and objects differs critically in style of computational processing. It provides a tutorial-style review of what face-recognition researchers mean by "holistic/configural" processing and describes the multiple paradigms showing that holistic/configural processing is limited to the structural form of upright faces. It then brings together several streams of literature to present a theoretical case that holistic/configural processing and part-based processing differ in patterns of sensitivity to prior experience.

Findings show holistic/configural processing is not learnable for objects, even with expertise; is insensitive to amount of experience with different viewpoints of faces; and (contrary to early ideas) does not require many years of exposure to develop in childhood. Holistic/configural processing is sensitive to experience only in that, for *faces as an entire class*, it has a critical period in infancy and that, for particular *subtypes* (e.g., races) of upright faces, it can weaken or strengthen throughout life. In contrast, part-based processing, as occurs for both faces and objects, is strongly sensitive to experience. It improves rapidly, even with experimental practice, and has no critical period in infancy for exposure to particular structural forms.

RATIONALE

My research interests lie primarily in face recognition, particularly the perceptual processes involved in face identification. In attempting to understand these processes, a fundamental question is: Are faces different from objects? The answer to this question is crucial. Without it, we do not know, for example, whether computational and neural models of face recognition must be general enough to perform recognition of all other objects also or can be limited to the (presumably easier) task of coding the structural form of faces alone. As another example, we do not know whether we should be looking for different evolutionary mechanisms to drive the visual processes of face and object recognition—perhaps deriving from their different levels of social importance or their different roles in social communication. Should we instead be searching for a common evolutionary mechanism that might drive recognition of complex visual stimuli in general?

This chapter presents a strong thesis in answer to this question. I argue that visual recognition of faces and objects differs in at least two ways: (a) the style of computational processing used to identify them, and (b) the patterns of sensitivity of that style of processing to prior experience. Specifically, I argue that *holistic/configural* processing occurs for faces but not objects, and that this "special" style of processing is insensitive to many types of adult experience (e.g., practice with objects or with unusual views of faces), although experience is required during a critical period in infancy. In contrast, part-based processing is the means for identifying objects, and this is highly sensitive to experience and can be easily learned for new classes of object even as an adult.

Note that these differences are located at the stage of "high-level perception" or "visual recognition" (occurring in inferior and lateral regions of the temporal lobe) and should not be taken to imply a claim that face and object processing will be different in all possible ways. Many other stages of the processing stream will occur in common for both stimulus types, such as early visual processing, post-recognition cognitive decision mechanisms, possible involvement of working memory in the task, and so on. It is also very likely that face and object systems share some operational principles in common; for example, all visual recognition systems show frequency effects in which reaction times are faster and functional magnetic resonance imaging (fMRI) BOLD response is lower to high-familiarity as compared to low-familiarity items.

This chapter also has several other aims. I present a somewhat tutorial-style review of the paradigms dissociating faces from objects that is designed to be useful to researchers new to the field of behavioral studies of holistic/configural processing. For readers expert in this area, certain material in the review section—particularly a discussion of the dissociation between coding of spacing and local feature information—also leads to a more detailed theoretical discussion of the nature of holistic/configural processing for faces than is possible in the standard empirical research article. This includes a critique of the different terminologies that face-recognition researchers have used (e.g., holistic vs. configural), an evaluation of Maurer, Le Grand, and Mondloch's (2002) proposal that there are subcomponents to configural processing, and an explanation of my rather different theoretical position.

Finally, I discuss the possible *origins* of special processing for faces. I expand on theoretical ideas we presented in McKone, Kanwisher, and Duchaine (2007). I consider the ability of an *experience-expectant innate template* theory and an *infant experience plus other factor* theory to explain not only the holistic/configural processing findings, but also other key observations about face recognition such as the heritability of developmental prosopagnosia. Readers should note this chapter was finalized in August, 2007, and that only research available up until that date is reviewed.

A DIFFERENT COMPUTATIONAL STYLE FOR RECOGNIZING FACES AND OBJECTS: HOLISTIC AND PART-BASED PROCESSING

In the context of the face-recognition literature, holistic/configural processing is thought to involve especially strong integration of information across the whole face region (excluding hair), which occurs at a perceptual level for stimuli that require individuation based on second-order deviations from a shared first-order configuration. First-order structure is defined as standard parts—eyes, nose, etc.—in the standard configuration of eyes above nose above mouth. By "second-order information" I mean individual exemplar deviations from this structure—for example, in exact distances between features or in exact feature shape. In the extreme view (e.g., Tanaka & Farah, 1993), holistic/configural processing comprises no decomposition into smaller parts at all, although another common idea is that it is based on some type of particularly strong reintegration following initial part decomposition.

Holistic/configural processing is usually contrasted with part-based, local, componential, or featural analysis, where parts of an object (or a face) are treated relatively independently. Empirical evidence indicates that inverted faces, scrambled faces, and objects are processed in a part-based fashion, while only upright faces are processed holistically/configurally. Evidence also indicates that upright faces receive both configural processing *and* part-based processing, rather than *only* configural processing. Thus, on many behavioral tasks, performance with upright faces will be based on a combination of the two processing types.

I now review results from relevant empirical paradigms. Except where otherwise mentioned, all results to be described come from studies using realistic face stimuli (usually grayscale photographs). Another important fact to note is that all the results to be described come from "ordinary" people—that is, typical people who are very good at recognizing individual faces but have no special expertise with the other object class or classes included in the experiment. In the literature, such people are known as object *novices*. They may have general familiarity with the object class, in its canonical orientation, but that is all. For example, most of us are familiar with upright dogs but are poor at telling apart individual dogs of the same breed. A later section deals with the topic of object experts.

Classic Holistic/Configural Paradigms

Several standard findings have been associated with holistic/configural processing. The first is the *disproportionate inversion effect* (Yin, 1969). In both recognition memory and perception (simultaneous or sequential matching tasks), all objects with a canonical upright show an inversion effect: Accuracy is higher and reaction time faster when the stimulus presentations are all upright than when they are all inverted (upside-down). However, the inversion effect for most objects is small, typically ranging from 0 to 8% in any one recognition memory experiment for dogs, cars, clothing, and so on. In contrast, the inversion effect for faces is very large, typically around 20–25% in a recognition memory experiment. This result was first reported by Yin (1969) and has subsequently been confirmed by many other studies (e.g., see first two data columns of Table 10.1; also see de Gelder, Bachoud-Levi, & Degos, 1998; Reed, Stone, Bozova, & Tanaka, 2003; Scapinello & Yarmey, 1970).

Yin's (1969) original interpretation of his results was that extracting the correct relationships between the face parts was particularly important to face recognition and that extracting this information from inverted faces was difficult. Note, however, that the disproportionate inversion effect itself provided no direct evidence for holistic/configural processing; logically, it could also have been that the style of processing for faces and objects was the same (e.g., part based in both cases) and it was merely that inversion effects on this common style were largest for faces. Similar arguments were made by Valentine (1988, 1991). Today, the disproportionate inversion effect is referred to as "indirect" evidence for holistic processing for upright faces (e.g., Michel, Rossion, Han, Chung, & Caldara, 2006). Maurer et al. (2002) explicitly noted that the mere presence of an inversion effect is not diagnostic of holistic/configural processing.

Three paradigms were subsequently designed that assess processing style more directly. These all confirm differences between upright faces and inverted faces, and between faces and objects. In Tanaka and Farah's (1993) *part–whole paradigm*, after learning whole faces ("This is Jim."), subjects are given a 2AFC recognition memory test (see Figure 10.1). In the part-alone condition, the subject sees, for example, Jim's nose and a distractor person's nose and is asked to choose Jim's nose. In the part-in-whole condition, exactly the same parts are presented, but now both are shown in the context of Jim's face (e.g., Jim's nose in Jim's face vs. Bill's nose in Jim's face). The task is either "Which is Jim?" (Tanaka & Farah, 1993) or "Which is Jim's nose?" (Tanaka & Sengco, 1997).

Results from multiple studies show that, despite the fact that the physical difference between the pairs is exactly the same in both conditions, identification is substantially better in the part-in-whole condition than in the part-alone condition (see Table 10.2; also see Pellicano & Rhodes, 2003; Tanaka, Kay, Grinnell, Stansfield, & Szechter, 1998). This corresponds to the illusion, visible in Figure 10.1, that changing one feature of the face alters the appearance of the rest of the face.

Importantly, the part–whole effect disappears for inverted faces; that is, the part-in-whole condition has no advantage over the part-alone condition (Table 10.2; Pellicano & Rhodes, 2003). Readers can appreciate this for themselves by turning Figure 10.1 upside down to see the corresponding lack of illusion. The part–whole effect has also been tested for objects, using both the Tanaka and Farah (1993) procedure and a very similar earlier procedure (*complete probe advantage;* Davidoff & Donnelly, 1990). For line drawings of houses, which one might argue are particularly easily separable into parts, there is no part–whole effect (Tanaka & Farah, 1993). For other types of objects, the part–whole effect is greater than zero, but much smaller than for faces (see Table 10.2; also see Donnelly & Davidoff,

TABLE 10.1   Inversion Decrement (Upright–Inverted) for Faces and Objects

	Task	Faces	Objects (novices)	Objects (experts)	Sig. of Expertise Increase
Dogs (Diamond & Carey, 1986, Experiment 3)	Long-term memory	20%*	5%ns	22%*	°
Dogs (Robbins & McKone, 2007, Experiment 1)	Long-term memory	23%*	3%ns	7%ns	ns
Handwriting (Bruyer & Crispeels, 1992)	Long-term memory	20%*	5%ns	9%*	ns
Dogs (Robbins & McKone, 2007, Experiment 3)	Sequential matching	11%*	1%ns	2%ns	ns
Greebles (Rossion et al., 2002)	Sequential matching	75 ms⁻	25 ms⁻	46 ms⁻	°
Cars (Gauthier et al., 2000)	Sequential matching	–	$d' = 57$*	$d' - .84$*	–
Birds (Gauthier et al., 2000)	Sequential matching	–	$d' = .05$ns	$d' = .30$ns	–
Cars (Xu et al., 2005)	Sequential matching	–	8%⁻	8%⁻	ns
		–	$d' - 0.44$⁻	$d' = 0.87$⁻	°
Fingerprints (Busey & Vanderkolk, 2005)	Face/print classification	16%*	6%ns	8%ns	ns

Notes: Because there are too many studies testing faces versus objects in novices to list all of them, only studies that also tested experts on the objects are shown; all such studies are included. Studies reported various measures, including percent correct (%), d', and reaction time (milliseconds). For novices and experts, the significance or otherwise of each inversion effect is indicated; a separate column indicates whether the increase in the size of the inversion effect from novices to experts was significant. Results are also provided for faces. Greebles are an artificial object class. Means for Busey & Vanderkolk (2005) provided by Thomas Busey (pers comm, July 21, 2006); percent correct means for Xu et al. (2005) provided by Yaoda Xu (pers comm, August 25, 2004). Adapted and expanded from Robbins R., & McKone, E., 2007, *Cognition, 103,* 34–79.

° $p < .05$.
ns $p > .05$.
⁻ Not tested or not reported.

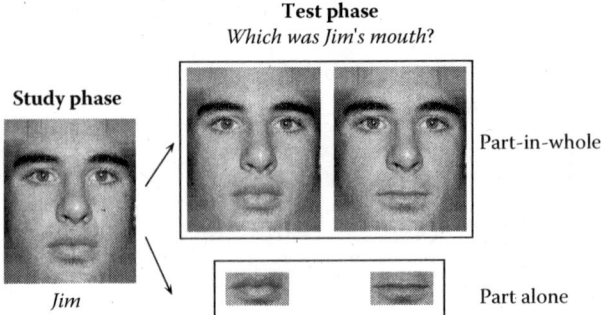

Figure 10.1 The part–whole procedure of Tanaka & Farah (1993, *Quarterly Journal of Experimental Psychology A, 46*, 225–245) and the corresponding perceptual illusion. When the face is upright, changing one feature of the face gives the illusion of changes to nonaltered regions: Replacing Jim's original mouth with one that has narrower lips increases the lip–nose distance and produces an impression of a shorter nose and more squished-up eye–nose region. The illusion disappears if the page is rotated to see the stimuli inverted.

1999). These results are consistent with the idea that what makes upright faces special is holistic/configural processing.

A number of criticisms of the part–whole method have claimed that it taps something other than perceptual holistic integration. Gauthier and Tarr (2002) suggested that, because it occurs for objects, it merely assesses an advantage of context that is generic to all stimuli. I agree that there may be some generic context component to the part–whole advantage, presumably reflecting the same sort of process that also occurs in the classic word superiority effect (Reicher, 1969; Wheeler, 1970). However, this cannot be all that there is because it fails to explain why the effect is so much larger for faces than for other objects.

Another idea is that the effect reflects merely the well established phenomenon of transfer-appropriate processing (TAP; or encoding specificity) in long-term memory; that is, memory retrieval is better in the whole condition at test because this matches the conditions at encoding, which also showed a whole face. Leder and Carbon (2005) found that the usual whole-over-part advantage was reversed when the study phase involved learning parts rather than whole faces. Again, however, this merely indicates that the part–whole effect—in the long-term memory version of the paradigm at least—does contain some component due to TAP. It does not explain why the effect is so much larger for faces than for other objects: The study–test match in the whole condition is the same for all stimulus classes.

The next paradigm is a variant on the part–whole effect, which has gone under various names but which I refer to here as the *part in spacing altered whole* effect. This was introduced by Tanaka and Sengco (1997). For faces, memory for a face feature (Jim's nose) is worse in the context of a spacing-altered version of the original face (Jim's nose in Jim's face with the eyes shifted further apart) than in the unaltered version (Jim's nose in Jim's face). This result is important in that it demonstrates that the usual part–whole advantage for faces does not come merely from the presence of extra context provided by having more features in a part-in-whole

TABLE 10.2   Results of Previous Studies, Using the Tanaka & Farah
(1993) Part–Whole Paradigm, Showing Size of the Whole–Part
Difference, Averaged Over All Parts Tested

	Faces	Inverted Faces	Objects (novices)	Objects (experts)	Sig. of Expertise Increase
Houses (Tanaka & Sengco, 1997)	11%*	–1%ns	–2%ns	–	–
Houses (Tanaka & Sengco, 1997)	15%*	0%ns	1%ns	–	–
Chairs (Davidoff & Donnelly, 1990)	11%*	–	4%ns	–	–
No objects (Pellicano, Rhodes, & Peters, 2006)	13%*	–2%ns	–	–	–
Dog faces (Tanaka et al., 1996)	20%*	–	2%ns	8%ns	ns
Cars (Tanaka et al., 1996)	18%*	–	8%⁻	6%⁻	Reverse
Biological cells (Tanaka et al., 1996)	26%*	–	16%*	10%*	Reverse
Greebles (Gauthier & Tarr, 1997)	–	–	5%ns	11%*	ns
Greebles (Gauthier et al., 1998)	–	–	7%⁻	0%⁻	Reverse
Greebles (Gauthier & Tarr, 2002)	–	–	$d' = 0.75^-$	$d' = 0.68^-$	Reverse

Notes: All stimuli were upright unless otherwise stated. All studies including objects of expertise are
included, as are sample extras that tested objects only in novices. Adapted and expanded from
Robbins R., & McKone, E., 2007, *Cognition, 103,* 34–79. Data from Tanaka et al. (1996) are as
cited in Tanaka, J. W., & Gauthier, I., 1997, in R. L. Goldstone, D. L. Medin, & P. G. Schyns (Eds.),
Mechanisms of perceptual learning (Vol. 36, pp. 83–125). San Diego, CA: Academic Press.
* $p < .05$.
ns $p > .05$.
⁻ Not tested or not reported.
Reverse = Trend in opposite-to-predicted direction for expertise effect.

TABLE 10.3   Results of Previous Studies, Using Tanaka & Sengco's 1997 Paradigm, Showing *Part-in-Whole* Minus *Part-in-Spacing-Altered-Whole*, Averaged Over All Parts Tested

	Faces	Objects (novices)	Objects (experts)	Sig. of expertise increase
Houses (Tanaka & Sengco, 1997)	7%[°]	0%[ns]	–	–
Greebles (Gauthier & Tarr, 1997)	–	–4%[ns]	0%[ns]	ns
Greebles (Gauthier et al, 1998)	–	1%[ns]	0%[ns]	Reverse
Greebles (Gauthier & Tarr, 2002)	–	$d' = 0.69^-$	$d' = 0.64^-$	Reverse

Notes: All stimuli were upright unless otherwise stated. All studies that tested objects of expertise are included, as is the original study that tested objects only in novices.

[°] $p < .05$.

[ns] $p > .05$.

[-] Not tested or not reported.

Reverse = Trend in opposite-to-predicted direction for expertise effect.

condition than in the part-alone condition. Instead, it depends on reinstating the specific arrangement of studied features. Empirical findings indicate that the advantage of whole over configurally transformed whole is strong for upright faces and absent for inverted faces (Pellicano, Rhodes, & Peters, 2006; Tanaka & Sengco, 1997); for objects it is either absent (Gauthier, Williams, Tarr, & Tanaka, 1998; Tanaka & Sengco, 1997) or weak (Gauthier & Tarr, 1997, 2002; see Table 10.3).

The next task is the *composite paradigm* of Young, Hellawell, and Hay (1987), illustrated in Figure 10.2. In the famous-face version, composites are formed of the top half of one individual and the bottom half of a different individual, and the task is to name one half (e.g., the top half). The halves are presented aligned or unaligned. In the former case, an illusion of a new person is created. Correspondingly, it is substantially harder (i.e., slower and/or less accurate) to name the target half in the aligned version than in the unaligned version.

However, as usual, this effect occurs only for upright faces rather than for inverted faces (Young et al., 1987). The same result is found in versions of the paradigm using initially unfamiliar faces that subjects are trained to name (Carey & Diamond, 1994; McKone, 2008; Robbins & McKone, 2003) and for completely novel faces in sequential or simultaneous same–different matching (de Heering, Houthuys, & Rossion, 2007; Le Grand, Mondloch, Maurer, & Brent, 2004; Michel, Rossion, et al., 2006; Robbins & McKone, 2007).

In the last few years, the composite paradigm has become increasingly popular as a good method to measure holistic processing. Logically, it has an advantage over the part–whole paradigm in that the same amount of information is present

Figure 10.2   The composite procedure of Young et al. (1987, *Perception, 16*, 747–759) using famous faces and the corresponding perceptual illusion. When the face is upright, aligning the two halves leads to a percept of a new individual and to corresponding difficulty (increased reaction time and/or decreased accuracy) in naming a target half; in contrast, the identity of each half is easy to see in the unaligned version. When the stimuli are inverted, the illusion disappears. For answers, see the "Acknowledgments" section.

on the screen in the two conditions compared (aligned and unaligned). Also, the presence of a competing response suggested by the nontarget half (e.g., the name if the face is familiar or the different-identity status if it is novel) is the same in both conditions.

Empirically, the composite effect does not reflect merely a general failure to tune out the nontarget half of the face: If this were the case, attentional competition from a (closer) aligned half would be stronger than from a (further away) unaligned half and thus the effect should be obtained for inverted faces, which it is not. Finally, the composite effect appears to show the clearest dissociation between faces and objects. The inversion and part–whole paradigms both produce a partial dissociation in which the target effect is much larger for faces than objects but is still present at some level for objects. The composite effect, however, appears to be genuinely absent for objects in novices (see Table 10.4), suggesting that it provides a purer measure of holistic/configural processing than other paradigms.

The Special Case of Spacing-Versus-Feature Changes

Another very standard approach to investigating configural/holistic processing, usually used for faces rather than objects, has been to make alterations to the face either in the distances between facial features (e.g., moving the eyes further apart) or in the appearance of individual features (e.g., changing the eyebrows). It has been common to associate sensitivity to spacing changes with configural/holistic processing and sensitivity to feature changes with part-based processing (e.g., Maurer et al., 2002). However, I think the situation is more complex than this.

The evidence for the standard idea comes from many studies that have found dissociations in the effect of inversion. Inversion influences perception of spacing or relational changes particularly strongly. This was originally discovered in

TABLE 10.4   Results of the Young & Colleagues' 1987 Composite Paradigm, Showing the Aligned–Unaligned (for Reaction Times) or Unaligned–Aligned (for Accuracy) Difference

	Task	Faces	Inverted faces	Objects (novices)	Objects (experts)	Sig. of expertise increase
No objects (Young et al., 1987)	Speeded naming	212 ms[a]	9 ms[ns]	–	–	–
No objects (Robbins & McKone, 2003)	Naming twins	8.8%*	–1.2%[ns]	–	–	–
Greebles, same-family halves (Gauthier et al., 1998)	Speeded naming	–	–	–	115 ms[ns] 0%	–
Greebles, different-family halves (Gauthier et al., 1998)	Speeded naming	–	–	–	–37 ms[Reverse] –3%[Reverse]	–
Greebles, same-family halves (Gauthier & Tarr, 2002)	Speeded naming	–	–	–42 ms[-]	12 ms[-]	–[a]
Dogs (Robbins & McKone, 2007)	Sequential matching	6.1%*	–3.5%[ns]	–0.8%[ns] 0.8%[ns b]	0.7%[ns]	ns Reverse

Notes: In both the aligned–unaligned and unaligned–aligned cases, a positive number corresponds to the direction for a positive composite effect (i.e., aligned should be the more difficult condition). All stimuli were upright unless otherwise stated. All studies including objects-of-expertise are included, as are some sample studies that reported data for inverted faces. Adapted and expanded from Robbins R., & McKone, E., 2007, *Cognition, 103*, 34–79.

* $p < .05$.
[ns] $p > .05$.
- Not tested or not reported.
Reverse = Trend in opposite-to-predicted direction for expertise effect.
[a] Across five sessions (we show only: session 1 = novices; session 5 = experts), there was a close-to-significant interaction between session and aligned versus unaligned. However, this did not reflect an increase with expertise: The composite effect started close to zero, strangely became more negative in sessions 2–4, and then returned to close to zero. The 12-ms composite effect in experts was in the context of 35-ms scanning electron microscopes for the aligned and unaligned conditions. Also note that Gauthier et al. (1998, *Vision Research, 38*, 2416) mention two additional earlier failed attempts to find a composite effect using the greeble experts from Gauthier & Tarr (1997, *Vision Research, 37*, 1673–1682).
[b] Results for two independent groups of subjects.

the famous Margaret Thatcher illusion (Thompson, 1980), in which flipping the eyes and mouth of a smiling face makes the face appear grotesque when the head is upright, but not when it is inverted. Rhodes, Brake, and Atkinson (1993; also see Bartlett & Searcy, 1993) demonstrated that, in faces made bizarre by spacing changes (e.g., moving the mouth down), inverting the face markedly reduced the perception of bizarreness. Inversion had only a weak effect, however, on perception of faces made bizarre by local feature changes (e.g., blackening the teeth).

Leder and Bruce (1998; also see Gilchrist & McKone, 2003) made less severe changes that merely made faces look more or less distinctive. Spacing changes that increased perceived distinctiveness and improved recognition memory for upright faces had weak or no effects for inverted faces, but featural changes had equally strong effects in both orientations. Using sequential same–different tasks, simple detection of spacing changes has also been found to be more severely affected by inversion than detection of featural changes (Freire, Lee, & Symons, 2000; Le Grand, Mondloch, Maurer, & Brent, 2001; Mondloch, Dobson, Parsons, & Maurer, 2004; Mondloch, Le Grand, & Maurer, 2002).

How true is the claim that feature changes show only small inversion effects? Reisenhuber, Jarudi, Gilad, and Sinha (2004) reported that inversion effects on detecting feature changes were larger when feature and spacing changes were intermixed than when they were blocked; more generally, they argued that findings of no inversion effects for featural changes were due to subjects adopting unusual strategies in blocked procedures. The latter claim, however, ignored the fact that Leder and Bruce (1998) and Gilchrist and McKone (2003) both found no inversion effect on feature change tasks using mixed presentation.

In another critique, Yovel and Kanwisher (2004) noted that Le Grand et al. (2001) and Mondloch et al. (2002, 2004) had all used the same stimulus set and that, unfortunately, this set was flawed in that the featural changes were easier to perceive upright than the spacing changes were. When Yovel and Kanwisher matched the two types for detectability in the upright orientation, the effects of inversion were equally severe for each. A criticism of the Yovel and Kanwisher (2004) procedure is that, in order to match quite large feature changes, the spacing-changed faces became quite distinctive in appearance (bordering on becoming abnormal), while the feature-changed faces were more typical.

Valentine (1991) has previously shown that distinctiveness can influence the size of inversion effects. In addition, of the previous studies, not all had feature changes that were perceptually larger than the spacing changes. Gilchrist and McKone (2003) had the reverse pattern for upright faces and yet still found that inversion influenced perception of spacing changes but not of featural changes.

Although I am not convinced by the particular explanations offered in Reisenhuber et al. (2004) or Yovel and Kanwisher (2004), the importance of their results cannot be ignored. Both studies show that large inversion effects for feature changes can occur. The same finding has also been reported by Rhodes, Hayward, and Winkler (2006); McKone and Boyer (2006); Leder and Carbon (2006); and Yovel and Duchaine (2006). This substantially undermines the supposed dissociation between spacing and features.

Taking recent findings into account, the standard description of the data needs to be changed, as follows:

Perception of *spacing* changes is always strongly influenced by inversion.

The effect of inversion on *feature* changes is much more variable: some studies find no inversion effect, some find a moderate inversion effect, and at least two find an inversion effect as big as that for spacing changes.

How can the apparently conflicting results be understood? Recent evidence suggests that results for the feature-altered faces depend on the types of feature changes. Some changes are purely "local," such as altering eye color, blackening teeth, or adding a long, thick hair to an eyebrow. Others alter the form or structure of surrounding regions of the face; for example, if a large eye is replaced with a smaller eye, then even if the new eye remains centered in the same position as the old eye, the distance from the inside edge of the eye to the bridge of the nose changes, as does the apparent shape of the eye socket.

Two studies demonstrate that shape-altering changes produce larger inversion effects than purely local changes. Yovel and Duchaine (2006) found that feature changes produced large inversion effects when the changes were in shape only (not color) and small inversion effects when changes were in shape plus color. Leder and Carbon (2006) reported larger inversion effects for feature shape replacements (eyes, nose, or mouth) than for color-only changes (with spacing changes producing a larger effect).

Overall, I agree with the standard idea that sensitivity to detailed spacing information forms a key aspect of configural processing. However, I do not agree with the idea implicit in much of the literature that *only* spacing information is part of configural/holistic processing and that any type of feature change is processed in a part-based fashion. This idea is apparent in a tendency to equate second-order information only with distances between the major features (e.g., nose–mouth distance), as if features can be treated as shapeless blobs.

Other Paradigms Consistent With Configural Processing for Upright Faces Only

The paradigms reviewed so far are widely considered the "core" paradigms. They have been used in multiple studies originating from many independent labs and are widely cited. However, many other tasks have also produced evidence consistent with the idea that configural processing occurs only for upright faces. In some cases, these tasks have also been used to test objects; in other cases, the comparison stimuli have been only inverted faces (or similar—for example, single isolated face features).

In the most abstract approach, Loftus, Oberg, and Dillon (2004) used dimensional theory and state-trace plots to investigate the disproportionate inversion effect for faces as compared to houses and cityscapes. Results showed that when proportion-correct memory for famous faces was plotted against proportion-correct memory for houses as a function of stimulus duration at study, upright and inverted data points fell on different functions. Loftus et al. demonstrated that the data were neatly described by a model in which the three independent variables (stimulus class, orientation, and stimulus duration) affected performance via their effects on two internal variables—presumably corresponding to the processing modes of holistic/configural and featural processing.

Using a *flanker variant of the part–whole paradigm*, Palermo and Rhodes (2002) found that a secondary task of matching upright flanker faces removed the part–whole effect for central upright faces. However, matching inverted flankers did not remove the part–whole effect for central upright faces. This argues that upright faces compete with other upright faces for holistic/configural resources, but that inverted faces do not; they are processed by other, presumably part-based resources.

McKone and Peh (2006) used a *memory conjunction procedure*. Test faces were old (unaltered study faces), new (completely unstudied faces), or a new conjunction of old parts. Conjunctions contained the eyes and eyebrows of one studied face combined with the nose and mouth of a different studied face. In a long-term memory test, subjects were required to say whether they had seen the face before. For both upright and inverted faces, the percentage of "old" responses to conjunctions was higher than the false alarm rate for new faces, indicating some memory of isolated face parts (also consistent with above-chance memory for single face parts in Tanaka & Farah, 1993).

Configural processing was then indicated by comparing truly old faces with conjunction faces. For upright, the percentage of "old" responses was much higher for old than for conjunction stimuli; for inverted, the two did not differ. Thus, subjects remembered which parts had been paired together for upright faces— consistent with holistic processing—but did not for inverted faces—consistent with part-based processing.

Cohen and Cashon (2001) used a related procedure in infants. Infants habituated to two female faces, then saw one of the original faces, a new face, or a conjunction formed from the internal features of one original (eyes, nose, and mouth) with the outer regions (hair, cheeks, and chin) of the other. Infants treated the conjunction face as new when the faces were upright (dishabituation to a new relationship between old parts) but as old when they were inverted (no dishabituation; i.e., the new relationship between parts was ignored).

In other approaches to demonstrating *interaction between parts*, Sergent (1984) showed subjects six line-drawn face stimuli varying on three dimensions (external contour shape, eyes/eyebrows shape, and nose–mouth spacing) of two values each. Regression analyses predicting errors and reaction times on a simultaneous matching task showed that the manipulated features contributed interactively when the faces were upright, but only independently when the faces were inverted. In Sergent's second experiment, a multidimensional scaling analysis of dissimilarity judgments between pairs of the upright faces revealed similar findings.

Yovel, Paller, and Levy (2005) tested subjects on various combinations of left or right hemifaces. The test stimulus on each trial comprised a choice of six faces, all bilaterally symmetric (i.e., the same individual on both halves). The briefly presented and masked study stimulus was a whole face showing the same individual in both halves, a whole face showing different individuals in the two halves, a stimulus showing the left hemiface only (the right face region was blanked out), or a stimulus showing the right hemiface only. If each half of a face was processed independently, accuracy for complete faces should equal the union of the observed accuracy for left and right hemifaces. For upright faces, accuracy exceeded this independence prediction for same-half whole faces (facilitation) and fell below it for different-half whole faces (interference), indicating strong interactive processing. For inverted faces, the interference effect was absent and the facilitation effect was much reduced.

Two papers have taken the approach of disrupting local information to varying degrees and showing that this disrupts identification less for upright whole faces than for other stimuli; such results argue that holistic/configural processing for faces is truly more than the sum of the parts. McKone, Martini, and Nakayama (2001) examined *categorical perception in noise*. After subjects learned two end point faces, they found categorical perception across the identity boundary in a series of intermediate morphs (better discrimination of morph pairs crossing the category boundary than of equidistant pairs drawn from the same side of the category boundary). Heavy noise was then added to the stimuli, with the idea that this would damage the reliability of information from any given local region of the face (e.g., the information extracted from the corner of the left eye might be quite different from one trial to the next). With the noise, categorical perception remained strong for upright intact faces, but was absent for inverted faces and for a single isolated feature (the nose alone).

Using similar logic, McKone (2004) introduced a *peripheral inversion task*. With increasing eccentricity, information from independent consideration of parts should degrade more rapidly than information from holistic/configural processing. For whole faces, as distance from fixation was increased, identification accuracy declined more rapidly for inverted faces (parts only) than for upright faces (holistic plus parts; McKone, 2004; McKone, Brewer, MacPherson, Rhodes, & Hayward, 2007). In contrast, for a single isolated face part (the nose; McKone, 2004) and for objects (dachshund dogs; McKone, Brewer, et al., 2007), upright and inverted performance declined at the same rate, consistent with both upright and inverted versions of the stimulus being processed only as parts.

One way of looking at the results of the categorical perception in noise and peripheral identification techniques is that, as perceptual processing is put under stress (e.g., requiring very fine discriminations, adding noise, etc.), configural processing survives more stress than part-based processing. This suggests that configural processing is more sensitive in some way; that is, it can operate on the basis of less reliable information, or less information, available from the stimulus.

In a direct demonstration of this, Martini, McKone, and Nakayama (2006) reported a saliency bias toward upright in overlaid faces. An upright version of a face was superimposed on an inverted version of the same face, and subjects adjusted the relative contrasts of the two faces until both appeared equally salient. The resulting physical stimulus contained much lower contrast in the upright face than in the inverted face. The saliency bias toward upright was found only for intact whole faces (even when lit from below); scrambled faces produced no saliency bias.

The Strength of the Evidence

To my mind, the evidence from the multiple paradigms presented previously is overwhelming: Upright faces are processed in a manner that inverted faces and nonface objects are not. The holistic/configural effects occur on directly perceptual tasks—as in, for example, the composite effect, the saliency bias, and categorical perception in noise; they also occur in tasks containing a memory component (e.g., part–whole effect). The effects occur for familiar faces (e.g., in the composite effect for famous individuals); they also occur for unfamiliar faces, as in the composite effect for novel faces, the saliency bias, and the disproportionate inversion effect on memory. The differences between upright and inverted faces occur despite the fact that these stimuli are matched in all low-level aspects, such as spatial frequency components, presence of boundaries, brightness, and so on.

When faces and objects were compared, all studies cited used identical tasks for the two stimulus classes. With the exception of Busey and Vanderkolk (2005), all required within-class discrimination (specifically, individual exemplar level discrimination). The different effects for faces and objects cannot be attributed to symmetry differences. Front views of faces are symmetric while the other object stimuli tested so far have not been, but holistic/configural effects also occur for asymmetric views of faces, such as the profile (McKone, 2008).

Also, the different effects for faces and objects cannot be attributed to baseline differences. Even though it is common for upright performance for faces to be better than upright performance for objects, many studies allow direct comparison of the size of effects (inversion, composite, etc.) because faces and objects were matched in the inverted orientation (e.g., Robbins & McKone, 2007, Experiment 1). Also, overall levels of performance seem not to matter as long as ceiling or floor effects are avoided (e.g., identification of upright objects can be easier than or equal to identifying upright faces and yet faces still show larger inversion effects; Robbins, 2005; Robbins & McKone, 2007, Experiment 3; Yin, 1969, Experiment 3).

Cases Where Faces Were Not Processed Configurally

Evidence such as that reviewed before has led to a general consensus by face-recognition researchers that faces are processed holistically/configurally, although a number of cases in the literature have not supported this conclusion. However, in the cases that I am aware of, there is almost always a simple explanation of the failure to find holistic/configural processing. Most commonly, the stimuli were of quite artificial appearance, rather than real faces. These include unnatural schematic drawings (Hannigan & Reinitz, 2000; see discussion in McKone & Peh, 2006; also see Martelli, Majaj, & Pelli, 2005; Schwarzer, 2002) and early Identikit faces (Bradshaw & Wallace, 1971). It is perhaps not surprising that artificial "faces" are processed like objects rather than like faces.

Another problem arises when attention-attracting hairstyles are used. These can provide cues to memory that outweigh the real face information (e.g., see Duchaine & Weidenfeld, 2003). I suspect this was a factor in the Loftus et al. (2004) finding, from state-trace plots, that only a single internal variable was required to describe inversion effects for faces versus houses when the faces were computer-generated rather than natural images. Given that the faces appeared somewhat unnatural in feature shape and placement and also had quite unusual hair, this single internal variable was presumably reflecting a reliance purely on part-based processing.

Occasionally, claims have been made that apparent holistic/configural processing can be attributed to decision-level effects. Wenger and Ingvalson (2002) used an unusual variant of the part-whole paradigm and showed that, in a task where subjects were required to respond "same" or "different" to two features of the face successively, apparently interactive processing between the features could be partially attributed to the response made to one feature biasing the response made to the other feature. For example, if subjects said "same" to one feature, they were likely to say "same" to the other. This seems unsurprising, but provides no evidence that holistic/configural effects in general can be attributed to decision-level effects rather than perceptual processing.

Gauthier and Bukach (2007) attempted to attribute the aligned–unaligned composite difference to a decision bias toward responding "same" in the aligned condition. However, McKone and Robbins (2007) pointed out that there is no reason why any response bias should differ between aligned and unaligned conditions when these are randomly intermixed (as in most experiments), and that the composite effect occurs not only in same–different tasks but also in naming tasks, where the issue of response bias does not arise. Finally, proponents of the decision-level idea have never put forward an explanation of how decision biases would produce differences between faces and objects in tasks with equivalent decision requirements for both stimulus types.

Consistent Evidence From Neuroimaging and Neuropsychology

The focus of the present chapter is on differences in style of computational processing, as revealed in behavioral studies. It is worthwhile briefly noting, however, that faces and objects are also processed differently at the neural level and that links have been demonstrated between these neural differences and holistic/configural processing. (For more extensive reviews, see Kanwisher & Yovel, 2006, for neuroimaging and Duchaine, Yovel, Butterworth, & Nakayama, 2006, for prosopagnosia.)

The evidence of face-specific cortical processing comes from three sources. First, in neuropsychological cases (both acquired and developmental), there is a double dissociation between prosopagnosia and object agnosia. Prosopagnosics exist who have extremely poor recognition of faces in combination with perfectly normal within-class discrimination of objects (e.g., Duchaine, Dingle, Butterworth, & Nakayama, 2004; McNeil & Warrington, 1993; Sergent & Signoret, 1992). A few cases have also been reported of the reverse pattern (e.g., Assal, Favre, & Anderes, 1984). Most famous is CK, who was severely object agnosic but could recognize faces at normal or above-normal levels, even in very difficult formats (e.g., Mooney faces, overlaid cartoons of multiple individuals; Moscovitch, Winocur, & Behrmann, 1997).

Second, neuroimaging studies using fMRI have revealed a face selective area known as the fusiform face area (FFA; Kanwisher, McDermott, & Chun, 1997) in the fusiform gyrus that responds two to three times more strongly to within-class discrimination of faces than to within-class discrimination of other objects (e.g., flowers, hands, birds, cars; Grill-Spector, Knouf, & Kanwisher, 2004; Kanwisher et al., 1997). In contrast, other areas of extrastriate cortex respond more strongly to objects than to faces (e.g., Lateral Occipital Complex; see Op de Beeck, Baker, DiCarlo, & Kanwisher, 2006).[1]

The final source of evidence comes from monkey single-cell recording studies. It has been known for a long time that monkey inferotemporal cortex contains face-selective cells (e.g., Perrett et al., 1985). Recently, Tsao, Freiwald, Totell, and Livingstone (2006) found a dense cluster of such cells. Starting from fMRI scans and using the same faces-versus-object localizer that is usually used on humans, they located a face-selective region labeled the "middle face patch." Recording from more than 100 single cells in this patch, they found 97% of visually responsive neurons were strongly face selective in comparison to a wide range of objects, including bodies and hands.

Returning to configural processing, some evidence links the human face-specific cortical areas to the core behavioral effects. In neuroimaging studies, fMR-adaptation procedures have shown that the FFA demonstrates an inversion effect on discrimination of individual faces: The BOLD reduction from repeating a face is strong for upright faces but weak or absent for inverted faces (Mazard, Schiltz, & Rossion, 2006; Yovel & Kanwisher, 2005).

More directly, Schiltz and Rossion (2006) implemented a version of the composite effect, again using fMR-adaptation to examine BOLD response in the FFA. Subjects made judgments to top halves of faces and were instructed to ignore the bottom halves; the bottom halves were either all the same (in some blocks) or all different (in others). Across each block, activation in the different-bottom condition decreased less than in the same-bottom condition, thus arguing that the FFA was integrating the top and bottom halves into new wholes. The effect occurred only when the faces were upright rather than when they were inverted; this argues that it did not merely reflect a general inability to restrict attention to the top half.

Neuropsychological evidence is also consistent with the idea that face-specific processing areas perform holistic processing. Prosopagnosics usually show weak or no inversion effects for faces (Duchaine & Nakayama, 2006), consistent with their (poor) recognition being driven by part-based processing, even for upright faces. Some even show a reversed inversion effect (Farah, Wilson, Drain, & Tanaka, 1995), suggesting that a malfunctioning holistic system can grab upright faces and suppress the part-based processing that would otherwise occur in this orientation. In further support, the opposite case of the antiprosopagnosic CK shows much larger inversion effects than controls (Moscovitch & Moscovitch, 2000).

THEORETICAL IDEAS ABOUT HOLISTIC/ CONFIGURAL AND PART-BASED PROCESSING

The empirical evidence shows that faces are recognized through computational procedures different from those used for objects. It is also clear that the theoretical difference must have something to do with local components being processed relatively independently of each other in inverted faces and objects, but being processed in a strongly dependent way in upright faces. What can we say beyond this, however? Can we be more exact about what holistic/configural processing is (and is not)?

Until fairly recently, I have been of the opinion that, really, we had little idea how to conceptualize holistic/configural processing. I have thus tended to stick to an operational definition, focusing closely on the results in the core paradigms. With the array of evidence now available, however, I think the concept of configural face processing can be fleshed out at least somewhat.

Does Holistic/Configural Processing Have Subcomponents?

A first question is whether subcomponents of configural/holistic processing exist. Maurer et al. (2002) proposed that they do. They used "configural" as an overarching term and proposed that this consisted of three subcomponents. They associated each subcomponent with particular core tasks.

The first proposed subcomponent was *sensitivity to first-order relations* (i.e., two eyes above a nose above a mouth). This was proposed to be tapped by *face detection* tasks (i.e., tasks that merely require determining a face is present, rather than identifying it). I agree with Maurer et al. (2002) that there is good evidence that detection can occur independently of identification. Prosopagnosics usually report that they can tell that a face is present and they can see the individual parts, but they just cannot make the face hang together as a person. Also, MEG and reaction time studies in normals indicate that face detection occurs earlier than face identification (Grill-Spector & Kanwisher, 2005; Liu, Harris, & Kanwisher, 2002), as might be expected.

However, some evidence (Liu et al., 2002) indicates that this detection ability relies on independent face parts (i.e., even in scrambled order) rather than relying on having a normal face configuration. This raises the possibility that, rather than coming from the holistic/configural processing stream, face detection could reflect the output of part-based analysis. Further, even if it is the case that face detection can proceed on the basis of first-order configuration, this is not logically sufficient to conclude that face identification does not also refer to first-order structure.

As evidence that it did not, Maurer et al. (2002) argued that the FFA performed face detection (e.g., activity is stronger when the background encourages perception of the stimulus as a face rather than as a vase; Hasson, Hendler, Bashat, & Malach, 2001), but did not perform face identification (no sensitivity to repetition) and was only weakly or not at all sensitive to inversion. The problem with this argument is that subsequent evidence has disproved both of the latter claims. Using the newer technique of fMR adaptation, several studies have shown that the FFA codes individual identity and that it shows strong inversion effects on identification (e.g., Mazard et al., 2006; Yovel & Kanwisher, 2005).

Maurer and colleagues' (2002) second and third proposed components were *holistic processing*—defined as gluing the features together into a gestalt—and sensitivity to *second-order relations*. Tasks proposed to tap holistic processing were the part–whole effect and the composite effect. Tasks proposed to tap second-order relations were those testing sensitivity to spacing between features (but not local feature shape). As evidence of separability, two factors were proposed to dissociate holistic processing and second-order relations.

The first claimed dissociation was in patterns of childhood development, with holistic processing proposed to be quantitatively mature early (by 6 years of age) and sensitivity to second-order relations proposed to mature much later (10+ years). I am not convinced by either half of this claim. Regarding holistic processing, Maurer et al. (2002) noted two studies that reported part–whole and composite effects no smaller in young children (6 years) than in adults (Carey & Diamond, 1994; Tanaka et al., 1998); a similar result has more recently been found in 4-year-olds (de Heering et al., 2007).

However, none of these studies matched baseline performance across age groups, leading to logical problems in making quantitative comparisons across ages. Indeed, two of these tests (Carey & Diamond, 1994; de Heering et al., 2007) produced the counterintuitive result of *larger* composite effects in 4-, 5-, and 6-year-olds than in adults. This is probably attributable simply to performance in the adult groups approaching a ceiling, but it highlights the point that, in the absence of matched baselines, it is not really possible to know whether children show effects of the same size as those of adults.

Regarding second-order relations, Maurer et al. (2002) noted two studies suggesting that sensitivity to spacing changes was very poor in young children and reached adult levels several years later than sensitivity to local feature changes (Freire & Lee, 2001; Mondloch et al., 2002). This result was also replicated in a later study (Mondloch et al., 2004). However, all these studies used stimuli that failed to match the perceptibility of the spacing and feature changes. Adults found the feature task easier than the spacing task. Thus, the results could simply indicate that development in a harder task lags behind development in an easier task.

Other results indicate no spacing-specific delay. McKone and Boyer (2006) matched spacing and featural changes for effects on perception in adults and then found that even 4-year-olds were as sensitive to spacing as to featural changes. Although they failed to match spacing and feature changes, Gilchrist and McKone (2003) instead matched baseline performance in the unaltered condition across age groups (by using a memory task with smaller learning set sizes for the younger children). Under these circumstances, 6- and 7-year-olds showed as strong a sensitivity to spacing changes as did adults.

The other claimed dissociation between holistic processing and second-order relations was based on the effects of using photographic negatives (contrast reversal). The proposal was that negation affects sensitivity to spacing changes but does not affect holistic integration. Kemp, McManus, and Piggott (1990) found that detection of spacing changes was substantially poorer in negative contrast faces than in positive contrast faces. The other half of the dissociation, regarding holistic processing, was based on Hole, George, and Dunsmore's (1999) finding that a version of the composite effect was as strong for reversed contrast grayscale faces as for normal-contrast faces.

Unfortunately, however, Hole et al. (1999) did not test the usual full composite design—namely, aligned and unaligned versions for upright and inverted faces. Instead, they tested only aligned composites and relied on the difference between upright and inverted conditions being in the opposite direction to usual (i.e., inverted was better than upright) to argue that holistic interference must have occurred for upright faces. To understand why this procedure is a problem in a contrast reversal study, consider that, in fact, the total inversion effect on naming the target half has two components: the (reverse direction) inversion effect arising from holistic interference slowing reaction times for upright but not inverted faces (i.e., the true composite effect, component A) and the (normal direction) inversion effect arising from part-based processing of the individual target half (component B).

For illustration, consider a case where the total inversion effect was −40 ms (i.e., reaction times were 40 ms slower for upright than inverted faces). Presume that, for normal-contrast faces, this is made up of a −100-ms inversion effect on holistic interference and a +60-ms inversion effect on part-based processing (i.e., A = −100 ms, B = +60 ms, total = −40 ms). In interpreting their finding of equal total inversion effects for normal-contrast and contrast-reversed faces as evidence of equal holistic processing, Hole et al. (1999) implicitly assumed that contrast reversal had no influence on inversion effects on *either* holistic interference *or* part-based processing.

There is no guarantee, however, that this is the case. A −40-ms total effect could be made up, for example, of a −70-ms inversion effect on holistic interference and a +30-ms inversion effect on part-based processing (i.e., A = −70 ms, B = +30 ms, total = −40 ms). If this pattern occurred for contrast-reversed faces, then the total inversion effect measure could fail to reveal the presence of weaker holistic processing for contrast-reversed faces than for normal-contrast faces.

Overall, I see no convincing evidence of dissociations between holistic and second-order relational tasks. There are also other good reasons to prefer the more parsimonious idea that first-order structure, second-order relations, and holistic gluing are all aspects of a single form of representation. Maurer and colleagues' proposed subcomponents (2002) associate rather than dissociate in two key ways. Large inversion effects are present on the tasks associated with all three (for holistic and second-order relational tasks, see earlier section; for face detection, think of the difficulty of seeing a Mooney face upside down).

Also, an apparent critical period in infancy applies to both the second-order relational and holistic subcomponents. Le Grand et al. (2001) tested people born with congenital cataracts that allowed no form vision until removal at 2–6 months of age. At 9–21 years of age, these patients had very poor sensitivity to spacing changes (which arose specifically with early visual deprivation to the right hemisphere; Le Grand, Mondloch, Maurer, & Brent, 2003) and a lack of composite effect (Le Grand et al., 2004).

There are also more theoretical reasons to prefer a single form of representation. The problem with associating certain subcomponents with certain experimental tasks is that, when new tasks come along, it can be difficult to slot them into the existing scheme. For example, where does the McKone et al. (2001) categorical perception in noise results fit? Maurer et al. (2002) described these results under the heading of sensitivity to second-order relations, saying that the lack of categorical perception with isolated features or inverted faces arose "presumably because second-order relational information was not available" (p. 257).

But why should the effects be attributed to this component? Showing a face inverted or the nose alone also destroys the first-order arrangement of the face and/or the potential for holistic integration. Why not assign the effect to one of these components? Similarly, to which subcomponent would the saliency bias effect (Martini et al., 2006) be attributed? Also, which subcomponent is responsible for the part-in-spacing-altered-whole effect (Tanaka & Sengco, 1997)? In this case, the manipulation is one of spacing, which would suggest second-order relations, but the method is a variant of the part–whole paradigm, which would suggest the holistic component. Overall, my point here is that the rationale for the association of particular tasks with proposed subcomponents in Maurer and colleagues' theory (2002) is not sufficiently spelled out to make it a useful theory in light of more recent evidence.

A Very Different Theory: Configural/Holistic Processing Is Not Based on Decomposition Into Eyes, Nose, and Mouth

Although it is possible to imagine many different alternative positions to that of Maurer et al. (2002), one alternative worth noting is the theory of Tanaka and Farah (1993). Maurer and colleagues' idea of a special spacing subcomponent to configural processing that is different from sensitivity to other sorts of deviations from the average template (e.g., in individual feature shape) seems implicitly based on the idea that decomposition into named-level parts provides a direct input into the formation of a configural representation.

In contrast, Tanaka and Farah (1993) suggested that the whole-face processing for (upright) faces did not decompose faces into such parts at all. In their terminology, this was *holistic processing* (with no subcomponents). Although I find their original evidence for this idea—which was merely the observation of a part–whole effect—unconvincing, more recent evidence is quite strongly suggestive of it.

This relevant evidence is that configural/holistic processing for faces can operate in the complete absence of part-based processing. Importantly, this is not to say that faces *cannot* be decomposed into parts; clearly, they can (e.g., we can describe the color of someone's eyes or the shape of his or her nose). Instead, the idea is that two independent processing routes exist that can contribute to performance on face-recognition tasks and that these branch off directly from some quite early stage of visual processing (Figure 10.3; Moscovitch et al., 1997; also see McKone, 2004; McKone, Martini, & Nakayama, 2003).

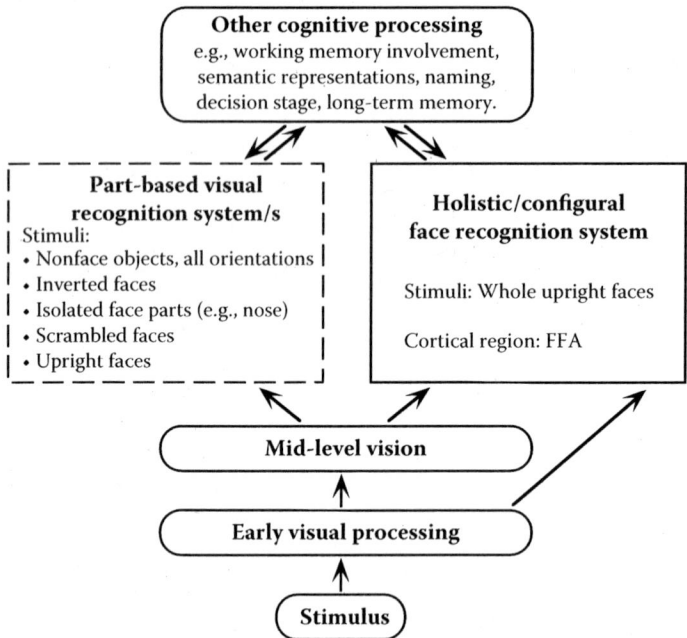

Figure 10.3   A possible neural/functional architecture in which holistic/configural processing is not derived from part-based processing as a preliminary step. This would explain
the ability of holistic/configural processing to operate in the absence of part-based processing for faces.

One route is responsible for forming a configural/holistic representation of the
whole face. The other, presumably open to nonface objects as well, is responsible
for part decomposition. Note that, in this theory, there is no arrow from the part-
based box to the configural/holistic box; that is, configural/holistic processing does
not derive from part-based processing.

The evidence that configural processing can operate without part-based processing is as follows. Patient CK, who had prosopagnosia without object agnosia, was good at recognizing faces only when they were intact whole faces in the
upright orientation. As soon as the normal configuration was disrupted, by inverting or exploding the face or by showing isolated face parts, CK's performance was
extremely poor—many standard deviations below that of controls (Moscovitch et
al., 1997). Thus, excellent recognition of whole faces occurred at the same time as
extremely poor part-based processing.

Similar results have been demonstrated in subjects without brain injury.
McKone et al. (2001) found categorical perception phenomenon in noise for upright
whole faces, despite its complete absence for the nose, which was the most discriminating feature between the particular faces tested, as well as its complete absence
for inverted faces. McKone (2004) also reported that a particular high-contrast
"Mooney face" (Mooney, 1957; Figure 10.4) was, for most people, perceivable as
a face *only* in the upright orientation. Approximately 80% of people (a number

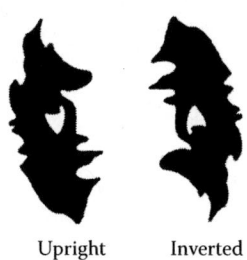

Upright   Inverted

Figure 10.4 A Mooney face (Mooney, 1957, *Canadian Journal of Psychology, 11,* 219–226) that is particularly difficult to see. Approximately 80% of people can see it upright, but not inverted—no matter how often the stimulus is viewed. The face is a young, attractive Caucasian woman lit from top-right. Rotation in the image plane causes the face percept to drop out somewhere around 90° for most people (range = 45–135° across individuals). (After McKone, E., 2004, *Journal of Experimental Psychology: Learning, Memory and Cognition, 30,* 181–197.)

based on formal data in McKone, 2004, and on hands-up tests during conference presentations) can see this particular face when it is upright but do not see it at all when the stimulus is inverted. For these people, the regions of the stimulus that form the face features are only perceived as face components when the whole face is perceived: that is, the parts do not exist without the whole.

Results from a study on learning to differentiate between identical twins (Robbins & McKone, 2003) are also consistent with holistic/configural processing operating without part-based processing. For subjects who saw a set of twins inverted, the only local feature that was sufficient for learning the twins was a minor difference in combing of the eyebrows. All subjects who successfully identified the twins reported using this strategy, and the subjects who did not report this strategy failed to identify the twins. Of subjects shown upright stimuli, however, no person reported noticing the eyebrow difference, yet all learned well and also showed an aligned–unaligned composite effect for the twins. Thus, good identification and holistic processing were possible in the apparent absence of awareness of even the most useful single local cue that could assist identification.

The Current McKone View of Configural/ Holistic and Part-Based Processing

Based on the evidence available at the time of writing, my view of the nature of configural/holistic processing is along the following lines. I think it references a detailed coding of face structure. This includes first-order information about basic face structure *and* second-order information about distances between regions of the face, *and* second-order information about exact feature shape, *and* exact face shape aspects that are less easily labeled as features (e.g., structure of cheekbones, depth of eye sockets, and angle of forehead in a profile view). Also, it intrinsically glues all these together—perhaps because they were never separated in the first place.

I also find that a useful analogy is one suggested to me by Paolo Martini and Ken Nakayama, in terms of the size of receptive fields: Although part-based processing can be thought of as applying "lots of little receptive fields" to a face or object and then summing the results, configural/holistic processing can be thought of as "one big receptive field" applied to the entire face region. (The reason for the quotation marks here is that the term "receptive field" normally refers to a region on the retina, while face and object recognition are largely size- and position invariant and the relevant cortical areas are nonretinotopic.)

Finally, an important aspect of configural/holistic processing is that it is more sensitive than part-based processing in that it can operate on the basis of less information in the stimulus. Theoretically, this might be a result of having a larger receptive field. Functionally, it may serve to enhance the perceptual salience of faces and to attract attention to them in cluttered visual settings.

It is also worthwhile to make a quick comment on what I think configural/holistic processing is *not*. Occasionally, one runs across the idea that the term "configural" implies that the representation contains only low spatial frequency information (noting that spatial frequency for faces usually refers to cycles per face width, rather than absolute spatial frequency). I see no evidence for this. All the evidence suggests that configural/holistic processing is the factor driving humans' remarkably good discrimination of so many different individual faces.

Sergent (1984) showed that low spatial frequency information, taken alone, is suitable for certain limited types of face discrimination (e.g., men from women, fat faces from thin faces), but is not sufficient for distinguishing between individuals of very similar general appearance. Indeed, in discriminating identical twins—the ultimately demanding face recognition task—it would surely be of value to consider information at all spatial scales. More directly, Goffaux and Rossion (2006) reported significant part–whole and composite effects for faces filtered to contain only high spatial frequency components, although the effects were larger for medium spatial frequency images and larger again for low spatial frequency images. Overall, low spatial frequency information may drive holistic/configural processing most strongly, although high spatial frequency detail is represented as well (also see McKone et al., 2001, p. 595).

What about part-based processing? Traditionally, face-recognition researchers have tended to focus on configural/holistic processing because it is special to faces, and they have tended to say little about what they understand part-based processing (for faces or objects) to mean. I continue that tradition here. I have little expert knowledge about the processes of object recognition, beyond knowing that the empirical literature shows differences between faces and objects. By the term "part-based processing," I merely mean some form of image decomposition after which the resulting components are treated in a relatively independent manner.

I take no particular position on whether this part decomposition is into abstract three-dimensional view-invariant components such as "geons" (Biederman, 1987) or whether it involves decomposition into much smaller image sections, as in the chorus of fragments theory (Edelman & Intrator, 2000), and so on. I also have no particular position on how context effects arise for objects (e.g., object superiority effects) or how global/local effects arise (e.g., Navon figures), beyond suggesting that these must have some explanation other than the type of perceptual integration that has been shown to occur for faces.

A Quick Comment on Terminology

In the present chapter, I have used "configural/holistic" to refer to the style of processing special to (upright whole) faces. In previous research articles, I have deliberately alternated "configural" and "holistic" across successive papers because I have seen no reason to discriminate between them in meaning. Other face-recognition researchers have used terminology differently. The Maurer et al. (2002) usage was discussed earlier: "configural" as an overarching term with "holistic" and "second-order relational" as subcomponents. Other authors use "configural" quite differently from Maurer and colleagues' use; it is quite common to see configural information closely equated with the empirical manipulation of changing spacing between features (Peterson & Rhodes, 2003; Yovel & Kanwisher, 2004). In Tanaka and Farah (1993), "holistic" was used as the general term, with no division into subcomponents. Some authors use "configurational"—again, as a general overarching term (Hole, 1994).

What are the advantages and disadvantages of the different terms? Unfortunately, all terms are far from perfect. "Holistic" captures the idea of strong perceptual integration but fails to acknowledge that orientation matters. "Configural" can be more useful in getting across the idea that orientation is important because configuration, in the sense of the arrangement of parts, is different in upright and inverted orientations. On the downside, configuration is sometimes taken by researchers to mean distances between "feature blobs," or low spatial frequency components, losing the relevance of much of the information in the face.

Of course, both terms are problematic in that they are also widely used outside the face perception literature, with different meanings (e.g., "holistic" for any processing of global structure that occurs in context and gestalt effects, "configural" to describe any sensitivity to even first-order arrangements of parts, and "holistic" for attentional field dependence). In the absence of any better terminology, I will stick with "holistic/configural" for the rest of this chapter.

FACES, OBJECTS, AND THE EXPERTISE HYPOTHESIS

In the previous sections, I described the evidence that, normally, faces are special in comparison to objects in that only faces receive holistic processing. In general, this claim is uncontroversial. (When it has been questioned, authors have appeared unaware of the key findings that were reviewed in the previous section.) Far more controversial, however, has been the question of whether faces are always special—suggesting that it is their structural form that is essential for holistic processing—or whether objects might also be processed holistically under one specific circumstance, such as in the case where a person has become an expert with a certain type of object class (e.g., a dog-show judge or a car expert). People who are expert in within-class discrimination of objects are rare, but the case is still theoretically important in that if such people show holistic processing for their objects of expertise, then this would demonstrate that holistic processing is potentially applicable to a wide range of structural forms.

Although the expertise hypothesis makes testable predictions about objects of expertise, it is fundamentally a theory about the origin of special processing for faces. The theory was first put forward by Diamond and Carey (1986; also see Carey's developmental work, e.g., Carey, 1992), who proposed that the reason why upright faces are processed holistically is that, by the time a person is an adult, he or she has had many years of experience in individuating upright faces and has become functionally expert at doing so. In contrast, inverted faces are not processed holistically because these stimuli are much rarer; adults have had little experience with them and remain functionally poor at telling them apart. Similarly, the reason for the lack of holistic processing for nonface objects (in both upright and inverted orientations) is a lack of expertise in individual level discrimination (e.g., telling Labrador 1 apart from Labrador 2).

This lack of experience arises not because appropriate visual input is not available (we may see many upright Labradors in our lifetime) but rather because there is little motivation or functional need for individuation. For faces, individuation is critical to appropriate social behavior. In most everyday cases of object recognition, however, it is sufficient to discriminate at the between-class level. We need to discriminate trees from tables but, unless we are foresters, most of us do not need to tell one tree from another.

Of course, even for ordinary people, in some cases it is important to recognize one or two individuals of an object class, such as *my* dog or *my* toothbrush. However, recognition remains poor for exemplars of the object class beyond the one or two highly familiar ones, and even the familiar items are often recognized largely by some obvious single feature (e.g., family members buy toothbrushes in different colors) or from the context (e.g., the dog in your backyard is probably your dog).

Predictions of the Expertise Hypothesis

The expertise hypothesis has been used to draw a number of predictions. The most straightforward is that objects of expertise should be processed like faces, in that both should receive holistic processing in their familiar upright orientation.

The second involves the development of holistic processing for upright faces in children. If, as Carey has suggested (e.g., 1992), face expertise takes many years of experience to achieve, then holistic processing for upright faces and corresponding differences between upright and inverted faces might emerge quite late in development. In terms of the amount of experience required to develop expertise, studies of other types of expertise (e.g., in chess or music) have indicated that 10 years or so of intensive practice is required (e.g., Gobet & Simon, 1998).

Probably partly for this reason, early developmental studies focused on the idea that there might be an "encoding switch" from part-based processing for faces to holistic processing for faces at around 10 years of age (Carey, Diamond, & Woods, 1980). In fact, the expertise hypothesis per se makes no specific prediction about the age at which holistic processing should emerge. It merely predicts that this should not occur until the child has become a "face expert"; for all we know, this could occur at 15 years, or 3 years, or as an infant.

It does, however, at least place a strong limit on the amount of experience that should be required to produce holistic processing for objects in objects-of-expertise studies. Specifically, the amount of experience required to produce holistic processing for objects should be the same as the amount of experience required to produce it for faces. The expertise hypothesis proposes only that practice is the causal mechanism. It includes no proposal that the effects of practice would depend on stage of development.

Diamond & Carey (1986, pp. 116–117) argued that a certain amount of experience with dogs, gained largely as an adult, corresponded to a similar amount of experience obtained with faces, beginning as an infant, in its ability to produce holistic processing. The same assumption that developmental stage is not critical is made by multiple subsequent tests of the expertise hypothesis (e.g., Busey & Vanderkolk, 2005; Gauthier & Tarr, 1997; Xu, Liu, & Kanwisher, 2005) in which subjects gained expertise largely or entirely as an adult. Thus, the expertise hypothesis predicts that if, say, children showed configural processing at 6 years of age, then 6 years' experience should be sufficient for holistic processing to emerge with dogs (possibly adjusted somewhat for the fact that even dog freaks probably see fewer dogs than faces).

A third prediction of the expertise hypothesis again derives from the proposed explanation of inversion effects for faces. According to the expertise hypothesis, it is the greater experience with upright faces that leads to holistic processing for upright (common format) but not inverted (rare format) faces. This then predicts that other methods of varying the natural frequency of different face formats should also affect holistic processing. One such method is rotating a face in depth; front-on views are far more common than profile views. Thus, the expertise hypothesis predicts that holistic processing should be weaker for profiles than for front views.

The first two of these predictions have been the focus of substantial empirical investigation. In contrast, the third prediction has only recently been addressed. In the remainder of this section, I concentrate on evaluating predictions one and two; prediction three is left until a later section.

Initial Evidence for the Expertise Hypothesis

The expertise hypothesis has long held sway in the literature and, indeed, had reached the status of being the zeitgeist in 2007. This is partly because it offers a coherent theoretical proposal about why faces might be special, but it is also because initial evidence appeared to provide compelling support for it. In fact, as we will see in the next section, all of this early evidence has since been refuted, but these early studies are described because they still have a powerful influence in the field. Even today it is not uncommon to see authors citing the initial papers without the corrections provided by subsequent literature.

One component of the early evidence came from studies of children's face recognition. Carey et al. (1980) reported that children's memory for faces was not affected by upright versus inverted orientation at 6 years of age. However, an inversion effect emerged at 10 years, so they therefore argued that holistic processing for upright faces emerged somewhere between these two ages.

The other component comes from Diamond and Carey's (1986) classic study of dog experts. This study tested the expertise hypothesis prediction that inversion effects on memory for dogs in dog experts should be larger than for dogs in novices and, indeed, might be similar to the size of the inversion effect for faces. One experiment showed some suggestion of this pattern, but the expertise × inversion interaction was not significant. In the follow-up experiment that became famous, mean expertise was increased to 31 years, and the breeds of the dog stimuli were carefully matched to the breeds of expertise of the show judges (this had not been done in the first experiment). A striking expertise effect was then apparent. Dog novices showed, as usual, a small inversion effect for dogs. Dog experts showed a very large inversion effect that was as large as that obtained for faces.[2]

Subsequent Falsification of the Expertise Hypothesis

Regarding the early results in children's development of face processing, there were clear problems with the initial studies. Carey and colleagues' (1980) inversion effect study suffered from floor effects in the 6-year-old group, leaving little room for inverted to be poorer than upright. Subsequent studies without floor effects have reported inversion effects in 6-year-olds (e.g., Carey, 1981), 4- and 5-year-olds (e.g., Pellicano et al., 2006), and 3-year-olds (Sangrigoli & de Schonen, 2004). In the one study that equated baseline across age groups (Carey, 1981), the size of the inversion effect was the same in young children as in adults. Using looking time and habituation paradigms, inversion effects have also been found in infants (e.g., Bhatt, Bertin, Hayden, & Reed, 2005; Cohen & Cashon, 2001).

More direct means of testing holistic processing have confirmed the implication from the inversion findings that holistic/configural processing is present in young children. The part–whole effect has been obtained in 6-year-olds (Tanaka et al., 1998) and 4- and 5-year-olds (Pellicano & Rhodes, 2003). The part-in-spacing-altered-whole effect has been obtained in 4- and 5-year-olds (Pellicano et al., 2006). The composite effect has been obtained in 6-year-olds (Carey & Diamond, 1994) and 4- and 5-year-olds (de Heering et al., 2007); in both cases, the effect was numerically larger than in adults. Sensitivity to exact distances between face parts has been obtained in 6-year-olds (Gilchrist & McKone, 2003; Mondloch et al., 2002) and 4-year-olds (McKone & Boyer, 2006). In infants, Cohen and Cashon (2001) found that a new face composed of old parts was treated as new rather than old.

In summary, data from children clearly indicate that holistic processing is present and, indeed, strong by 4 years at the latest. No data are available on children from the 1- to 3-year age range, but there is certainly some suggestion that holistic processing is present even in infancy.

Turning to objects of expertise, studies subsequent to Diamond and Carey's (1986) original dog expert studies have almost universally failed to find evidence suggesting holistic processing in experts. Regarding the basic inversion effect, no study has replicated Diamond and Carey's finding of face-sized inversion effects for objects of expertise. All relevant studies of which I am aware (as of August, 2007) are reviewed in Table 10.1. As can be seen, the general finding is better described as somewhere between no increase and a small increase in inversion effects with expertise. Importantly, this includes even in our own study that directly replicated Diamond and Carey's original design, employing dog experts looking at side-on photographs of their breed of expertise.

A likely explanation of Diamond and Carey's (1986) original result (see Robbins & McKone, 2007) is that dog experts (American Kennel Club judges) were preexperimentally familiar with the particular dogs used as stimuli (taken from AKC training manuals), along with their names. This would provide an artificial boost to memory in the upright orientation because this is the orientation in which the experts would previously have seen the stimulus dogs (e.g., in training manuals) and because having access to a name to remember as well as a picture is known to improve memory (e.g., Paivio, 1986).

It is also crucial here to reiterate the logic of the interpretation of inversion effects. Even if inversion effects do become slightly stronger with expertise, nothing in this finding per se requires that the increase must have come about because experts are learning to use configural/holistic processing in the upright orientation (cf. Valentine, 1991). An increase could arise from experts learning better part-based processing in the upright (most experienced) orientation, as is suggested by Robbins and McKone's (2007) finding of excellent transfer of expertise to contrast-negative dogs. The fact that larger inversion effects were caused by holistic/configural processing for upright faces does not mean that increased inversion effects for objects must also be holistic in origin.

The results of the more direct tests of configural/holistic processing are thus critical. Results from all relevant studies were shown in Tables 10.2, 10.3, and 10.4. The findings are clear-cut. The part–whole effect does not increase with expertise. The part-in-spacing-altered-whole effect does not increase with expertise. The composite effect does not increase with expertise; indeed, Robbins and McKone (2007) found no composite effect at all for dog experts looking at their breed of expertise, despite these experts having very high levels of expertise (a mean of 23 years' experience and the ability to match dogs as accurately as faces). Thus, improvements in performance with expertise and the small increase in inversion effects apparent in some studies must be coming from part-based processing, rather than holistic/configural processing.

Only two results in the literature might appear to challenge this conclusion (Busey & Vanderkolk, 2005; Gauthier, Curran, Curby, & Collins, 2003). In both cases, strong effects of expertise have been found on measures that the authors claimed tap holistic processing. Both used nonstandard tasks. Robbins and McKone (2007, Section 5.3) argued in detail that one of these (Gauthier et al.) definitely does not measure integration of parts into a whole at a perceptual level; instead, it measures merely the inability to ignore competing response cues from notionally irrelevant information (as in the Stroop effect). They also argued that there were reasons to doubt the validity of the other. (Busey and Vanderkolk rely on a model with questionable assumptions that has never been tested on faces.)

Finally, it is worth commenting on levels of expertise. In the face of null findings on the core paradigms, a common reply from proponents of the expertise hypothesis is that, of course, one would not expect the effects to be as big in experts as they are for faces because the level of expertise for objects remains lower than it is for faces. This is where the developmental face data come into play. The early emergence of holistic face processing disposes of the idea that perhaps experts might show face-like processing if only they were "more" expert. If babies and 4-year-old children show clear and statistically significant holistic effects for faces—despite the well known difficulties of testing in this age range (e.g., it is very easy to get no effect because the child did not understand the task), then surely the 10+ years of expertise used in many object expertise studies should also be sufficient for significant effects to show up in the much more reliable case of testing adults.

Relevant Data From Neuroimaging and Neuropsychology

Results relevant to neural substrates also support the idea that face-like processing does not emerge for objects of expertise (for review, see McKone, Kanwisher, & Duchaine, 2007). Findings from neuropsychology are the most dramatic. In cases of brain injury, the expertise hypothesis predicts that ability to recognize objects of expertise should always track ability to recognize faces (e.g., if one is damaged, both should be damaged). In contrast, the idea that faces, as a structural form, are recognized via face-specific cortical areas predicts that objects of expertise should track other objects and dissociate from faces.

Evidence clearly favors face specificity. No cases have been reported in the literature following the expertise hypothesis prediction, but a double dissociation between faces and objects of expertise has been reported. Some patients cannot recognize faces, but retain or gain expertise in individuation of objects; most famously, the farmer, WJ, could recognize his sheep, but not his family (McNeil & Warrington, 1993; also see Duchaine et al., 2004; Sergent & Signoret, 1992). Others show the converse pattern of normal face recognition with impaired recognition of former objects of expertise (e.g., Assal et al., 1984; Moscovitch et al., 1997).

In neuroimaging, seven studies have tested the expertise hypothesis prediction that a BOLD response in the FFA should increase for objects of expertise compared to the same objects in novices. Three reported no change at all in FFA response (Grill-Spector et al., 2004; Op de Beeck et al., 2006; Yue, Tjan, & Biederman, 2006), two reported very small and nonsignificant trends toward an expertise-related increase (Moore, Cohen, & Ranganath, 2006; Rhodes, Byatt, Michie, & Puce, 2004), and two reported significant increases to a level that did not approach the level for faces (Gauthier, Skudlarski, Gore, & Anderson, 2000; Xu et al., 2005). Of the five studies that also examined response in other areas of extrastriate cortex, all five reported larger expertise-related increases outside the FFA than within it (Gauthier et al., 2000; Moore et al., 2006; Op de Beeck et al., 2006; Rhodes et al., 2004; Yue et al., 2006).

Taken together, these results provide no evidence for the special relationship between expertise and the FFA that was predicted by the expertise hypothesis.

One alternative proposal (McKone, Kanwisher, & Duchaine, 2007; Xu, 2005) is that expertise effects arise primarily in the same cortical regions responsible for recognizing the objects in novices and that the small and inconsistent effects in the FFA simply reflect general attention-related increases in blood flow arising from experts being more interested in their objects of expertise than novices. Some effects could also arise from inclusion of nontarget neural material ("partial voluming"); fMRI voxels are quite large and cubic in shape, and their edges are very unlikely to correspond to the boundaries of cortical regions.

VIEWPOINT, RECENT EXPOSURE HISTORY, AND FACES VERSUS OBJECTS

The results reviewed in the previous section indicate that holistic processing is not learned with experience for objects. In contrast, improvements in object recognition with expertise appear to have their origin in improved part-based processing. This suggests a dissociation between holistic/configural and part-based processing in terms of their patterns of sensitivity to prior experience. Other ways of testing the effects of prior experience are discussed in this section. These again show face–object dissociations.

First, consider holistic/configural processing for faces. With rotation from upright to inverted in the image plane, holistic/configural processing falls off in a bell-shaped manner and is absent in the range from approximately 135° of rotation to 180° (Martini et al., 2006; McKone, 2004; McKone et al., 2001). This result could potentially be explained based on differential experience with different rotations, but two findings argue against this interpretation. Experimental practice with inverted faces does not induce any holistic/configural processing; this includes hundreds of trials of practice (McKone, 2004), thousands of trials (Robbins & McKone, 2003) and tens of thousands of trials (McKone et al., 2001). More anecdotally, I have been looking at the Mooney face in Figure 10.4 for five years and have never seen the face inverted.

The other finding is that rotation in depth (front through profile, all faces upright) has no effect on configural processing. Despite the fact that people have substantially more experience with front and three-quarter views than with profiles, McKone (2008) found that the composite effect was equally strong in all views. (Note that this also refutes the third prediction of the expertise hypothesis.)

Now consider object recognition and part-based processing in general. For objects, naming latencies increase linearly with rotation away from the canonical view in the image plane and in depth (e.g., Jolicœur, 1985; Palmer, Rosch, & Chase, 1981). These rotation effects disappear rapidly with practice (e.g., Jolicœur, 1985; Tarr, 1995), usually within 3–30 trials per stimulus. Figure 10.5 illustrates an example where the misorientation curve became flat in less than 20 exposures to each of 54 common objects (McKone & Grenfell, 1999).

People can also learn entirely new object classes easily, even when first exposed to these as adults (for readers 30+ years in age, think of mobile phones; for readers 40+, think of computer mice). Results show that part-based processing for objects

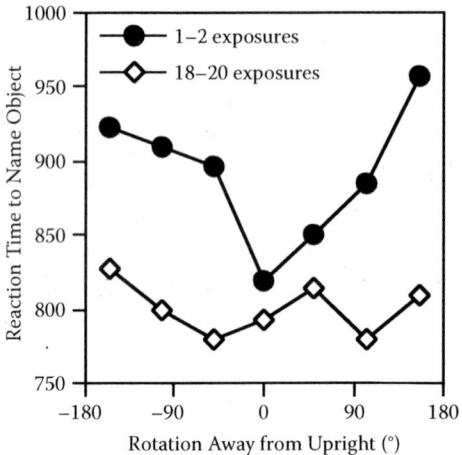

Figure 10.5   In contrast to the findings that holistic/configural processing for inverted faces shows no learning, even with thousands of trials of practice, "upright-like" processing for objects (presumably part-based) is learned very rapidly for inverted and other misoriented objects: Rotation effects disappear in less than 20 exposures to each of 54 common objects. (Results are from McKone, E. & Grenfell, T., 1999, *Perception and Psychophysics, 61,* 1590–1603.)

is strongly sensitive to experience, including very recent exposure history. The same is true of part-based processing for faces. Despite the lack of view frequency effects on holistic/configural processing, McKone (2008) found an effect of view frequency on part-based processing, as evidenced by a profile decrement that was as strong for disrupted-configuration faces (unaligned, inverted) as for intact-configuration faces (upright, aligned).

Taken together, these results argue that part-based processing for objects (and faces) is strongly sensitive to experience, including recent experience obtained as an adult, and improves easily with practice. Holistic/configural processing for faces, in contrast, seems unaffected by experience: It is always good for upright faces, regardless of depth rotated view, and always poor for inverted faces, regardless of amount of practice.

DOES EXPERIENCE *EVER* MATTER FOR HOLISTIC/ CONFIGURAL PROCESSING FOR FACES?

In contrast to the general lack of experience effects referred to previously, in two specific circumstances, holistic/configural processing is sensitive to experience. I have already noted the existence of a critical period in infancy: Cataract patients who are not exposed to faces for the first 2–6 months of life never show a composite effect (Le Grand et al., 2004). Thus, experience with faces in infancy seems to be essential to developing holistic/configural processing.

The second circumstance involves other-race effects. Holistic/configural processing is one factor involved in the poor discrimination of other-race relative to own-race individuals. Both the composite effect and part–whole effects are weaker for other-race faces than for same-race faces (Michel, Caldara, & Rossion, 2006; Michel, Rossion, et al., 2006; Tanaka, Kiefer, & Bukach, 2004). This suggests that holistic/configural processing is affected by experience with particular face subtypes. Further, normal levels of holistic processing can be induced for trained other-race individuals after only 1 hour of practice (McKone, Brewer, et al., 2007).

In summary, it seems that for faces *as an entire class*, experience matters to holistic/configural processing only in that there is a critical period for the activation of holistic processing in early infancy. For specific *subtypes* of faces (own race vs. other race), it may be that holistic processing can be switched on through experience or off through lack of it, and that this can occur quite rapidly, even for an adult. Crucially, however, this latter flexibility applies only if the face is upright.

WHAT IS THE ORIGIN OF SPECIAL PROCESSING FOR FACES?

This chapter has reviewed an extensive set of findings arguing that faces and objects differ critically in style of processing and in patterns of sensitivity of that style to prior experience. The key results can be summarized as follows. Holistic/configural processing is limited to the structural form of upright faces (in any depth viewpoint), cannot be learned for objects, and is insensitive to amount of experience with different views/rotations of faces. It is sensitive to experience only in that exposure to faces in infancy is required to activate it and that it can weaken or strengthen for particular subtypes (e.g., races) of faces. In contrast, part-based processing, as occurs for both faces and objects, is strikingly sensitive to experience. It improves rapidly with experimental practice to the point where misorientation effects can quickly disappear. It also has no critical period in infancy for exposure to particular structural forms.

What is the origin of these differences? As McKone, Kanwisher, and Duchaine (2007) have noted, it is clear that generic expertise is not the origin. Instead, they noted that this leaves researchers with two types of theories about the limitation of holistic/configural processing to the structural form of faces. These differ in whether they include an innate representation of face structure.

Perhaps the most obvious hypothesis is of an *experience-expectant innate template*. This theory proposes that a representation of face structure has developed via evolutionary processes, reflecting the extreme social importance of faces; at the same time, the visual system has maintained an independent and more flexible generic system suitable for recognizing any type of object. Within such a theory, the following components would be necessary to explain the face-recognition data I have reviewed:

- The innate "template" would code at least the basic structure of a face. The form of any such representation is not understood, but it could possibly take the form of eye blobs above nose blob above mouth blob, as in the Morton and Johnson (1991) CONSPEC theory (also see de Haan, Humphreys, & Johnson, 2002).

- The template must provide the developmental impetus not only for good face recognition (as Morton & Johnson, 1991, suggested), but also for the emergence of holistic processing and the grouping of face-selective neurons seen as the FFA in adults; how it would do so remains unknown.
- The activation of the template must rely on appropriate input during a critical period in early infancy, without which it would no longer function.
- Following a normal infancy, the coding of face structure must remain general enough to allow holistic processing to be applied to initially non-experienced subtypes of faces following practice, but it must be permanently tuned to the upright orientation of faces.
- To explain the lack of depth viewpoint effects, the template must be three-dimensional in structure or there must be multiple innate templates, each describing different views.

The experience-expectant innate template theory can explain all the results I have reviewed here, plus all other results of which I am aware. It can explain the existence of developmental prosopagnosia (e.g., Duchaine et al., 2006) and the fact that, anecdotally at least, this appears to be strongly heritable. It can explain the fact that all typically developing humans choose to individuate conspecifics (members of their own species) based on the face, rather than on some other body part. Despite extensive opportunity to develop expertise with, say, hands, adults fail to do so and remain poor at identifying these stimuli compared to faces.

It can also explain a finding that 6-month-old infants can discriminate individual monkey faces, although 9-month-olds and adults have lost this ability (Pascalis, de Haan, & Nelson, 2002). This finding is similar to the perceptual narrowing with lack of experience that occurs during infancy for phonemes of nonexperienced languages, which is usually taken as evidence for an experience-expectant innate coding of all possible phonemes.

An alternative idea is an *infant experience plus other factor* theory. In many ways, this appears to be a viable possibility. It can explain the core finding—that holistic/configural processing is limited to faces in adults—by proposing that any innate special visual ability is for the style of processing rather than the particular structural form and that this becomes tuned to faces due entirely to biased exposure to faces in early infancy, which arises from some factor other than an innate face template. That is, upright faces are the only homogeneous stimuli for which individual-level discrimination is practiced during the critical period for holistic/configural processing in infancy.

Importantly, the theory is not merely another version of the expertise hypothesis. The mechanisms supporting face expertise in the infant brain would necessarily be different from those supporting general object expertise in the adult brain. Without this assumption, it should be possible to learn holistic/configural processing for objects as an adult, but it is not. It is also important to note that this type of theory does not rule out all innate contributions, but merely innate contributions based on a visual representation of face structure. Innate contributions based on, for example, other visual preferences or auditory abilities would be possible.

In terms of explaining other relevant findings, the performance of the theory of infant experience plus other factor is rather mixed. It provides a good explanation of the choice of the face for conspecific individuation: This would arise because infants experience more faces than any other stimuli. It also provides a potential explanation of the heritability of developmental prosopagnosia: This could arise if something is genetically wrong with the "other factor," rather than with a face template; however, note that this requires specifying a reasonable other factor, which is not an easy task (see following comments).

A possible difficulty for the theory, however, is the lack of viewpoint frequency effects on holistic/configural processing and the different tuning patterns for rotations in the image plane versus in depth. The theory can explain the fact that holistic/configural processing occurs for upright but not inverted faces because inverted faces are presumably rare in infancy; however, it would then need to develop some principled explanation of why profile faces, which presumably are also rare in infancy, show configural processing as strong as that for the common front-view face.

Even more importantly, for this theory to be viable, it would be necessary to be able to identify a workable "other factor." McKone, Kanwisher, and Duchaine (2007) considered four possibilities. Three of them have clear difficulties.

Simion, Valenza, Cassia, Turati, and Umilta (2002) have suggested that infants' preference for face stimuli is based on a preference for stimuli with more elements in the upper half of the visual field. Although such a preference was certainly demonstrated with their experimental stimuli, in which the faces were cut off below the hairline, this cannot explain face specificity in real life because real heads do not have more elements in the upper half (eyes, nose, ears, and mouth are all at the midpoint or in the lower half).

Another likely sounding possibility is that face specificity could arise through attraction to faces based on infants' prenatal familiarity with their mother's voice. Again, however, the fact that such familiarity is known to exist (Kisilevsky et al., 2003; Sai, 2005) is not sufficient. Any theory based on auditory processing makes the prediction that people born deaf would be prosopagnosic, but this is not the case. The same problematic prediction arises from an explanation (Sinha, Balas, & Ostrovsky, 2007) based on an idea of infant preference for moving stimuli that produce synchronous sound (Sai, 2005).

The best "other factor" proposal of which I am aware is that face specificity could arise from faces being placed close enough to infants to be in focus more often than other stimuli (Kanwisher, pers. comm.). In a recent "baby cam" study that recorded the newborn visual world via a camera attached to the baby's head, Sinha et al. (2007) reported that faces were by far the most common stimuli presented close enough to the baby to be visible, given newborns' inability to perceive high spatial frequencies. The faces-in-focus idea leads to a potentially viable mechanism of inheritance of developmental prosopagnosia (or at least one not refuted by current knowledge): namely, unusually poor or unusually good visual acuity in infancy (or, more facetiously, being born to parents with arms of unusual length). The only evidence possibly against it is the lack of view frequency effects.

Overall, I currently lean toward the experience-expectant-innate-template theory. However, claims of innateness are always difficult to back up in that they require ruling out all alternative experience-only explanations. It remains logically possible that an alternative factor explains all the relevant data.

CONCLUSION

Although the question of the developmental origin of holistic/configural processing remains unresolved, the material reviewed in this chapter has provided a clear answer to the question of whether face processing is different from object processing: Yes, it is. This implies that computational and neural models of face recognition can be restricted to the problem of coding the structural form of faces. It also suggests that a valuable focus of future research would be whether, or how, visual representation of face structure is related evolutionarily to other functions associated more directly with the social importance of faces, including processing of eye gaze direction, facial expression, and face reading in speech and communication.

ACKNOWLEDGMENTS

Preparation of this chapter was supported by Australian Research Council DP0450636. Stefan Horarik assisted with final preparation of the manuscript. Material in the "What Could Explain All These Findings?" and "Consistent Evidence From Neuroimaging and Neuropsychology" sections is based strongly on joint discussions with Nancy Kanwisher and Brad Duchaine and is an expansion of material included in McKone, Kanwisher, and Duchaine (2007). The literature review on objects of expertise in the "Faces, Objects, and the Expertise Hypothesis" section is based strongly on discussions with Rachel Robbins and is an expansion of material previously published in Robbins and McKone (2007). I thank Galit Yovel for comments on a draft. Answers to Figure 10.2: top half is George W. Bush and bottom half is Tony Blair.

NOTES

1. Using higher resolution fMRI, Grill-Spector, Sayres, and Ress (2006) claimed the FFA was not uniformly face selective, reporting that it contained many finer scale voxels that were highly selective for non-face objects, such as sculptures. However, Baker, Hutchinson, and Kanwisher (2007) showed this was due to a mistake in the Grill-Spector et al. statistical analysis: Applying the same analysis to noise-only voxels from outside the brain also apparently revealed highly category-selective voxels.

2. Many people reading Diamond and Carey's paper are confused by the fact that the dog experts did not show better performance with upright dogs than did the novices, but instead showed worse performance inverted. The lack of upright advantage does not mean the experts were not experts: It is presumably attributable to the effect of age differences between the groups on memory. Experts' mean age was 64 years, while novices were young college students. Memory declines across this age range.

REFERENCES

Assal, G., Favre, C., & Anderes, J. P. (1984). Nonrecognition of familiar animals by a farmer: Zooagnosia or prosopagnosia for animals. *Revue Neurologique, 140*, 580–584.

Baker, C., Hutchinson, T., & Kanwisher, N. (2007). Does the fusiform face area contain highly selective subregions for nonfaces? *Nature Neuroscience, 10*, 3–4.

Bartlett, J. C., & Searcy, J. (1993). Inversion and configuration of faces. *Cognitive Psychology, 25*, 281–316.

Bhatt, R. S., Bertin, E., Hayden, A., & Reed, A. (2005). Face processing in infancy: Developmental changes in the use of different kinds of relational information. *Child Development, 76*, 169–181.

Biederman, I. (1987). Recognition-by-components: A theory of human image understanding. *Psychological Review, 94*, 115–147.

Bradshaw, J. L., & Wallace, G. (1971). Models for the processing and identification of faces. *Perception and Psychophysics, 9*, 443–448.

Bruyer, R., & Crispeels, G. (1992). Expertise in person recognition. *Bulletin of the Psychonomic Society, 30*, 501–504.

Busey, T. A., & Vanderkolk, J. R. (2005). Behavioral and electrophysiological evidence for configural processing in fingerprint experts. *Vision Research, 45*, 431–448.

Carey, S. (1981). The development of face perception. In G. M. Davies, H. Ellis, & J. Shepherd (Eds.), *Perceiving and remembering faces* (pp. 9–38). London: Academic Press.

Carey, S. (1992). Becoming a face expert. *Philosophical Transcripts of the Royal Society of London: B, 335*(1273), 95–102; discussion 102–103.

Carey, S., & Diamond, R. (1994). Are faces perceived as configurations more by adults than by children? *Visual Cognition, 1*, 253–274.

Carey, S., Diamond, R., & Woods, B. (1980). Development of face recognition: A maturational component? *Developmental Psychology, 16*, 257–269.

Cohen, L. B., & Cashon, C. H. (2001). Do 7-month-old infants process independent features or facial configurations? *Infant & Child Development, 10*, 83–92.

Davidoff, J., & Donnelly, N. (1990). Object superiority: A comparison of complete and part probes. *Acta Psychologica, 73*, 225–243.

de Gelder, B., Bachoud-Levi, A., & Degos, J. (1998). Inversion superiority in visual agnosia may be common to a variety of orientation polarized objects besides faces. *Vision Research, 38*, 2855–2861.

de Haan, M., Humphreys, K., & Johnson, M. H. (2002). Developing a brain specialized for face perception: A converging methods approach. *Developmental Psychobiology, 40*, 200–212.

de Heering, A., Houthuys, S., & Rossion, B. (2007). Holistic face processing is mature at 4 years of age: Evidence from the composite face effect. *Journal of Experimental Child Psychology, 96*, 57–70.

Diamond, R., & Carey, S. (1986). Why faces are and are not special: An effect of expertise. *Journal of Experimental Psychology: General, 115,* 107–117.

Donnelly, N., & Davidoff, J. (1999). The mental representations of faces and houses: Issues concerning parts and wholes. *Visual Cognition, 6,* 319–343.

Duchaine, B. C., Dingle, K., Butterworth, E., & Nakayama, K. (2004). Normal greeble learning in a severe case of developmental prosopagnosia. *Neuron, 43,* 469–473.

Duchaine, B. C., & Nakayama, K. (2006). The Cambridge face memory test: Results for neurologically intact individuals and an investigation of its validity using inverted face stimuli and prosopagnosic participants. *Neuropsychologia, 44,* 576–585.

Duchaine, B. C., & Weidenfeld, A. (2003). An evaluation of two commonly used tests of unfamiliar face recognition. *Neuropsychologia, 41,* 713–720.

Duchaine, B. C., Yovel, G., Butterworth, E. J., & Nakayama, K. (2006). Prosopagnosia as an impairment to face-specific mechanisms: Elimination of the alternative hypotheses in a developmental case. *Cognitive Neuropsychology, 23,* 714–747.

Edelman, S., & Intrator, N. (2000). (Coarse coding of shape fragments) + (retinotopy) ≈ representation of structure. *Spatial Vision, 13,* 255–264.

Farah, M. J., Wilson, K. D., Drain, M., & Tanaka, J. R. (1995). The inverted face inversion effect in prosopagnosia: Evidence for mandatory, face-specific perceptual mechanisms. *Vision Research, 35,* 2089–2093.

Freire, A., & Lee, K. (2001). Face recognition in 4- to 7-year-olds: Processing of configural, featural, and paraphernalia information. *Journal of Experimental Child Psychology, 80,* 347–371.

Freire, A., Lee, K., & Symons, L. A. (2000). The face-inversion effect as a deficit in encoding configural information: Direct evidence. *Perception, 29,* 159–170.

Gauthier, I., & Bukach, C. (2007). Should we reject the expertise hypothesis? *Cognition, 103,* 322–330.

Gauthier, I., Curran, T., Curby, K. M., & Collins, D. (2003). Perceptual interference supports a nonmodular account of face processing. *Nature Neuroscience, 6,* 428–432.

Gauthier, I., Skudlarski, P., Gore, J. C., & Anderson, A. W. (2000). Expertise for cars and birds recruits brain areas involved in face recognition. *Nature Neuroscience, 3,* 191–197.

Gauthier, I., & Tarr, M. J. (1997). Becoming a "greeble" expert: Exploring mechanisms for face recognition. *Vision Research, 37,* 1673–1682.

Gauthier, I., & Tarr, M. J. (2002). Unraveling mechanisms for expert object recognition: Bridging brain activity and behavior. *Journal of Experimental Psychology: Human Perception & Performance, 28,* 431–446.

Gauthier, I., Williams, P., Tarr, M. J., & Tanaka, J. (1998). Training "greeble" experts: A framework for studying expert object recognition processes. *Vision Research, 38,* 2401–2428.

Gilchrist, A., & McKone, E. (2003). Early maturity of face processing in children: Local and relational distinctiveness effects in 7-year-olds. *Visual Cognition, 10,* 769–793.

Gobet, F., & Simon, H. A. (1998). Expert chess memory: Revisiting the chunking hypothesis. *Memory, 6,* 225–255.

Goffaux, V., & Rossion, B. (2006). Faces are "spatial"—Holistic face perception is supported by low spatial frequencies. *Journal of Experimental Psychology: Human Perception & Performance, 32,* 1023–1039.

Grill-Spector, K., & Kanwisher, N. (2005). Visual recognition: As soon as you know it is there, you know what it is. *Psychological Science, 16,* 152–160.

Grill-Spector, K., Knouf, N., & Kanwisher, N. (2004). The fusiform face area subserves face perception, not generic within-category identification. *Nature Neuroscience, 7,* 555–562.

Grill-Spector, K., Sayres, R., & Ress, D. (2006). High-resolution imaging reveals highly selective nonface clusters in the fusiform face area. *Nature Neuroscience, 9,* 1177–1185.

Hannigan, S. L., & Reinitz, M. T. (2000). Influences of temporal factors on memory conjunction errors. *Applied Cognitive Psychology, 14,* 309–321.

Hasson, U., Hendler, T., Bashat, D. B., & Malach, R. (2001). Vase or face? A neural correlate of shape selective grouping processes in the human brain. *Journal of Cognitive Neuroscience, 13,* 744–753.

Hole, G. J. (1994). Configurational factors in the perception of unfamiliar faces. *Perception, 23,* 65–74.

Hole, G. J., George, P. A., & Dunsmore, V. (1999). Evidence for holistic processing of faces viewed and photographic negatives. *Perception, 28,* 341–359.

Jolicœur, P. (1985). The time to name disorientated natural objects. *Memory and Cognition, 13,* 289–303.

Kanwisher, N., McDermott, J., & Chun, M. M. (1997). The fusiform face area: A module in human extrastriate cortex specialized for face perception. *Journal of Neuroscience, 17,* 4302–4311.

Kanwisher, N., & Yovel, G. (2006). The fusiform face area: A cortical region specialized for the perception of faces. *Philosophical Transactions of the Royal Society of London B, 361,* 2109–2128.

Kemp, R., McManus, C., & Pigott, T. (1990). Sensitivity to the displacement of facial features in negative and inverted images. *Perception, 19,* 531–543.

Kisilevsky, B. S., Hains, S. M. J., Lee, K., Xie, X., Huang, H., Ye, H. H., Zhang, K., & Wang, Z. (2003). Effects of experience on fetal voice recognition. *Psychological Science, 14,* 220–224.

Leder, H., & Bruce, V. (1998). Local and relational aspects of face distinctiveness. *Quarterly Journal of Experimental Psychology, 51A,* 449–473.

Leder, H., & Carbon, C.-C. (2005). When context hinders! Learn–test compatibility in face recognition. *Quarterly Journal of Experimental Psychology, 58A,* 235–250.

Leder, H., & Carbon, C.-C. (2006). Face-specific configural processing of relational information. *British Journal of Psychology, 97,* 19–29.

Le Grand, R., Mondloch, C. J., Maurer, D., & Brent, H. P. (2001). Early visual experience and face processing. *Nature, 410,* 890.

Le Grand, R., Mondloch, C. J., Maurer, D., & Brent, H. P. (2003). Expert face processing requires visual input to the right hemisphere during infancy. *Nature Neuroscience, 6,* 1108–1112.

Le Grand, R., Mondloch, C. J., Maurer, D., & Brent, H. P. (2004). Impairment in holistic face processing following early visual deprivation. *Psychological Science, 15,* 762–768.

Liu, J., Harris, A., & Kanwisher, N. (2002). Stages of processing in face perception: An MEG study. *Nature Neuroscience, 5,* 910–916.

Loftus, G. R., Oberg, M. A., & Dillon, A. M. (2004). Linear theory, dimensional theory, and the face-inversion effect. *Psychological Review, 111,* 835–863.

Martelli, M., Majaj, N. J., & Pelli, D. G. (2005). Are faces processed like words? A diagnostic test for recognition by parts. *Journal of Vision, 5,* 58–70.

Martini, P., McKone, E., & Nakayama, K. (2006). Orientation tuning of human face processing estimated by contrast matching in transparency displays. *Vision Research, 46,* 2102–2109.

Maurer, D., Le Grand, R., & Mondloch, C. J. (2002). The many faces of configural processing. *Trends in Cognitive Sciences, 6,* 255–260.

Mazard, A., Schiltz, C., & Rossion, B. (2006). Recovery from adaptation to facial identity is larger for upright than inverted faces in the human occipitotemporal cortex. *Neuropsychologia, 44,* 912–922.

McKone, E. (2004). Isolating the special component of face recognition: Peripheral identification and a Mooney face. *Journal of Experimental Psychology: Learning, Memory and Cognition, 30,* 181–197.

McKone. E. (2008). Configural processing and face viewpoint. *Journal of Experimental Psychology: Human Perception and Performance, 34,* 310–327.

McKone, E., & Boyer, B. (2006). Four-year olds are sensitive to featural and second-order relational changes in face distinctiveness. *Journal of Experimental Child Psychology, 94,* 134–162.

McKone, E., Brewer, J. L., MacPherson, S., Rhodes, G., & Hayward, W. G. (2007). Familiar other-race faces show normal holistic processing and are robust to perceptual stress. *Perception, 36,* 224–248.

McKone, E., & Grenfell, T. (1999). Object invariance in naming rotated objects: Individual differences and repetition priming. *Perception and Psychophysics, 61,* 1590–1603.

McKone, E., Kanwisher, N., & Duchaine, B. C. (2007). Can generic expertise explain special processing for faces? *Trends in Cognitive Sciences, 11,* 8–15.

McKone, E., Martini, P., and Nakayama, K. (2001). Categorical perception of face identity in noise isolates configural processing. *Journal of Experimental Psychology: Human Perception and Performance, 27,* 573–599.

McKone, E., Martini, P., & Nakayama, K. (2003). Isolating holistic processing in faces (and perhaps objects). In M. A. Peterson & G. Rhodes (Eds.), *Perception of faces, objects, and scenes.* Oxford, England: Oxford University Press.

McKone, E., & Peh, Y. X. (2006). Memory conjunction errors for realistic faces are consistent with configural processing, *Psychonomic Bulletin & Review, 13,* 106–111.

McKone, E., & Robbins, R. (2007). The evidence rejects the expertise hypothesis: Reply to Gauthier & Bukach. *Cognition, 103,* 331–336.

McNeil, J. E., & Warrington, E. K. (1993). Prosopagnosia: A face-specific disorder. *Quarterly Journal of Experimental Psychology A, 46,* 1–10.

Michel, C., Caldara, R., & Rossion, B. (2006). Same-race faces are perceived more holistically than other-race faces. *Visual Cognition, 14,* 55–73.

Michel, C., Rossion, B., Han, J., Chung, C-S., & Caldara, R. (2006). Holistic processing is finely tuned for faces of one's own race. *Psychological Science, 17,* 608–615.

Mondloch, C. J., Dobson, K. S., Parsons, J., & Maurer, D. (2004). Why 8-year-olds cannot tell the difference between Steve Martin and Paul Newman: Factors contributing to the slow development of sensitivity to the spacing of facial features. *Journal of Experimental Child Psychology, 89,* 159–181.

Mondloch, C. J., Le Grand, R., & Maurer, D. (2002). Configural face processing develops more slowly than featural face processing. *Perception, 31,* 553–566.

Mooney, C. M. (1957). Age in the development of closure ability in children. *Canadian Journal of Psychology, 11,* 219–226.

Moore, C. D., Cohen, M. X., & Ranganath, C. (2006). Neural mechanisms of expert skills in visual working memory. *Journal of Neuroscience, 26,* 11187–11196.

Morton, J., & Johnson, M. H. (1991). CONSPEC and CONLEARN: A two-process theory of infant face recognition. *Psychological Review, 98,* 164–181.

Moscovitch, M., & Moscovitch, D. A. (2000). Super face-inversion effects for isolated internal or external features, and for fractured faces. *Cognitive Neuropsychology, 17,* 201–219.

Moscovitch, M., Winocur, G., & Behrmann, M. (1997). What is special about face recognition? Nineteen experiments on a person with visual object agnosia and dyslexia but normal face recognition. *Journal of Cognitive Neuroscience, 9,* 555–604.

Op de Beeck, H., Baker, C., DiCarlo, J., & Kanwisher, N. (2006). Discrimination training alters object representations in human extrastriate cortex. *Journal of Neuroscience, 26,* 13025–13036.

Paivio, A. (1986). *Mental representation: A dual coding approach.* Oxford, England: Oxford University Press.

Palermo, R., & Rhodes, G. (2002). The influence of divided attention on holistic face perception. *Cognition, 82,* 225–257.

Palmer, S., Rosch, E., & Chase, P. (1981). Canonical perspective and the perception of objects. In J. Long and A. D. Baddeley (Eds.), *Attention and performance IX.* Hillsdale, NJ: Lawrence Erlbaum Associates.

Pascalis, O., de Haan, M., & Nelson, C. A. (2002). Is face processing species specific during the first year of life? *Science, 296,* 1321–1323.

Pellicano, E., & Rhodes, G. (2003). Holistic processing of faces in preschool children and adults. *Psychological Science, 14,* 618–622.

Pellicano, E., Rhodes, G., & Peters, M. (2006). Are preschoolers sensitive to configural information in faces? *Developmental Science, 9,* 270–277.

Perrett, D. I., Smith, P. A. J., Potter, D. D., Mistlin, A. J., Head, A. S., Milner, A. D., et al. (1985). Visual cells in the temporal cortex sensitive to face view and gaze directions. *Proceedings of the Royal Society of London, B: Biological Sciences, 223,* 293–317.

Peterson, M. A., & Rhodes, G. (2003). Introduction: Analytic and holistic processing—The view through different lenses. In M. A. Peterson & G. Rhodes (Eds.), *Perception of faces, objects, and scenes: Analytic and holistic processes.* New York: Oxford University Press.

Reed, C., Stone, V. E., Bozova, S., & Tanaka, J. W. (2003). The body-inversion effect. *Psychological Science, 14*(4), 302–308.

Reicher, G. M. (1969). Perceptual recognition as a function of meaningfulness of stimulus material. *Journal of Experimental Psychology, 81,* 275–280.

Reisenhuber, M., Jarudi, I., Gilad, S., & Sinha, P. (2004). Face processing in humans is compatible with a simple shape-based model of vision. *Proceedings of the Royal Society of London, B (Suppl.), 271,* S488–S450.

Rhodes, G., Brake, S., & Atkinson, A. P. (1993). What's lost in inverted faces? *Cognition, 47,* 25–57.

Rhodes, G., Byatt, G., Michie, P. T., & Puce, A. (2004). Is the fusiform face area specialized for faces, individuation, or expert individuation? *Journal of Cognitive Neuroscience, 16,* 189–203.

Rhodes, G., Hayward, W. G., & Winkler, C. (2006). Expert face coding: Configural and component coding of own-race and other-race faces. *Psychonomic Bulletin & Review, 13,* 499–505.

Robbins, R. (2005). *Face and object processing: What changes with experience?* Unpublished PhD thesis, Australian National University.

Robbins, R., & McKone, E. (2003). Can holistic processing be learned for inverted faces? *Cognition, 88,* 79–107.

Robbins R., & McKone, E. (2007). No face-like processing for objects-of-expertise in three behavioral tasks. *Cognition, 103,* 34–79.

Rossion, B., Gauthier, I., Goffaux, V., Tarr, M. J., & Crommelinck, M. (2002). Expertise training with novel objects leads to left-lateralized face-like electrophysiological responses. *Psychological Science, 13,* 250–257.

Sai, F. Z. (2005). The role of the mother's voice in developing mother's face preference: Evidence for intermodal perception at birth. *Infant and Child Development, 14,* 29–50.

Sangrigoli, S., & de Schonen, S. (2004). Effect of visual experience on face processing: A developmental study of inversion and non-native effects. *Developmental Science, 7,* 74–87.

Scapinello, K. F., & Yarmey, A. D. (1970). The role of familiarity and orientation in immediate and delayed recognition of pictorial stimuli. *Psychonomic Science, 21,* 329–331.

Schiltz, C., & Rossion, B. (2006). Faces are represented holistically in the human occipito-temporal cortex. *Neuroimage, 32,* 1385–1394.

Schwarzer, G. (2002). Processing of facial and nonfacial stimuli in 2- to 5-year-old children. *Infant and Child Development, 11,* 253–269.

Sergent, J. (1984). An investigation into component and configural processes underlying face perception. *British Journal of Psychology, 75,* 221–242.

Sergent, J., & Signoret, J. L. (1992). Varieties of functional deficits in prosopagnosia. *Cerebral Cortex, 2,* 375–388.

Simion, F., Valenza, E., Cassia, V. M., Turati, C., & Umilta, C. (2002). Newborns' preference for up–down asymmetrical configurations. *Developmental Science, 5,* 427–434.

Sinha, P., Balas, B., & Ostrovsky, Y. (2007). *Discovering faces in infancy.* Paper presented at Vision Sciences Society, May 11–16, Florida.

Tanaka, J. W., & Farah, M. J. (1993). Parts and wholes in face recognition. *Quarterly Journal of Experimental Psychology A, 46,* 225–245.

Tanaka, J. W., & Gauthier, I. (1997). Expertise in object and face recognition. In R. L. Goldstone, D. L. Medin, & P. G. Schyns (Eds.), *Mechanisms of perceptual learning* (Vol. 36, pp. 83–125). San Diego, CA: Academic Press.

Tanaka, J. W., Giles, M., Szechter, L., Lantz, J. A., Stone, A., Franks, L., et al. (1996). Measuring parts and wholes recognition of cell, car, and dog experts: A test of the expertise hypothesis. Unpublished manuscript, Oberlin College, Oberlin, OH.

Tanaka, J. W., Kay, J. B., Grinnell, E., Stansfield, B., & Szechter, L. (1998). Face recognition in young children: When the whole is greater than the sum of its parts. *Visual Cognition, 5*(4), 479–496.

Tanaka, J. W., Kiefer, M., & Bukach, C. M. (2004). A holistic account of the own-race effect in face recognition: Evidence from a cross-cultural study. *Cognition, 93,* B1–B9.

Tanaka, J. W., & Sengco. J. A. (1997). Features and their configuration in face recognition. *Memory and Cognition, 25,* 583–592.

Tarr, M. J. (1995). Rotating objects to recognize them: A case study on the role of viewpoint dependency in the recognition of three-dimensional objects. *Psychonomic Bulletin & Review, 2,* 55–82.

Thompson, P. (1980). Margaret Thatcher: A new illusion. *Perception, 9,* 483–484.

Tsao, D. Y., Freiwald, W. A., Totell, R. B. H., & Livingstone, M. S. (2006). A cortical region consisting entirely of face-selective cells. *Science, 311,* 670–674.

Valentine, T. (1988). Upside-down faces: A review of the effect of inversion upon face recognition. *British Journal of Psychology, 79,* 471–491.

Valentine, T. (1991). A unified account of the effects of distinctiveness, inversion and race in face recognition. *Quarterly Journal of Experimental Psychology A, 43,* 161–204.

Wenger, M. J., & Ingvalson, E. M. (2002). A decisional component of holistic encoding. *Journal of Experimental Psychology. Learning, Memory and Cognition, 28,* 872–892.

Wheeler, D. D. (1970). Processes in word recognition. *Cognitive Psychology, 1,* 59–85.

Xu, Y. (2005). Revisiting the role of the fusiform face area in visual expertise. *Cerebral Cortex, 15,* 1234–1242.

Xu, Y. D., Liu, J., & Kanwisher, N. (2005). The M170 is selective for faces, not for expertise. *Neuropsychologia, 43,* 588–597.

Yin, R. K. (1969). Looking at upside-down faces. *Journal of Experimental Psychology, 81,* 141–145.

Young, A. W., Hellawell, D., & Hay, D. C. (1987). Configurational information in face perception. *Perception, 16,* 747–759.

Yovel, G., & Duchaine, B. (2006). Specialized face perception mechanisms extract both part and spacing information: Evidence from developmental prosopagnosia. *Journal of Cognitive Neuroscience, 18,* 580–593.

Yovel, G., & Kanwisher, N. (2004). Face perception; domain specific, not process specific. *Neuron, 44,* 889–898.

Yovel, G., & Kanwisher, N. (2005). The neural basis of the behavioral face-inversion effect. *Current Biology, 15,* 2256–2262.

Yovel, G., Paller, K. A., & Levy, J. (2005). *Visual Cognition, 12,* 337–352.

Yue, X., Tjan, B. S., & Biederman, I. (2006). What makes faces special? *Vision Research, 46,* 3802–3811.

11

Is Face Processing Automatic?

ROMINA PALERMO and GILLIAN RHODES

Normal people not only recognize faces. We seem to have an almost inde-
cent eagerness to see faces, whether they are really there or not. We see faces
in damp patches on the ceiling, in the contours of a hillside, in clouds or in
Martian rocks.

Richard Dawkins (1999, p. 266)

INTRODUCTION

*F*aces give us clues to the identity, race, sex, attractiveness, mood, and intentions of others and are therefore probably the most biologically and socially
significant visual stimuli in our human environment. It is no real surprise
then that so many of us are fascinated with faces, seeing them in clouds and on
Mars! The significance of faces in our daily lives has led researchers to argue that
faces are likely to be processed "automatically" (Öhman, 2002; Öhman & Mineka,
2001). Automatic processes have four main characteristics:

- They happen very quickly (e.g., Batty & Taylor, 2003; Öhman, 1997),
  although exactly how fast they need to be to be classified as automatic is
  far from clear (see Compton, 2003, for further discussion).
- An automatic process should happen, at least in part, unconsciously (e.g.,
  Bargh, 1997; Öhman, 2002; Robinson, 1998).
- Automatic processing is mandatory or obligatory (e.g., Wojciulik,
  Kanwisher, & Driver, 1998). Face processing that is equivalent under all
  conditions would provide evidence for mandatory processing in the strict
  sense. However, a process that always reliably occurs to some extent, even
  if it is "turned down," may still be considered mandatory.
- Processing that is capacity free, requiring minimal attentional resources
  (e.g., Schneider & Chein, 2003; Vuilleumier, Armony, Driver, & Dolan,

2001) is considered automatic. If performing another task concurrently does not alter performance on a face-processing task, then that aspect of face processing would be considered capacity free. The nature of the dual task is important, however, because a competing task involving faces may be detrimental to performance, whereas a task involving a different stimulus type may not.

In this chapter, we evaluate whether some aspects of faces are processed automatically. That is, do they happen very quickly, at least in part unconsciously, and are they mandatory and/or capacity free? We will examine these characteristics for three types of facial judgments: detection, identification, and the perception of expression. Figure 11.1 displays some of the brain regions involved in these tasks.

Processing the invariant aspects of a face for detection, categorization, and identification involves the inferior occipital gyri and areas of the lateral fusiform gyrus (which includes the fusiform face area [FFA]; Kanwisher, McDermott, &

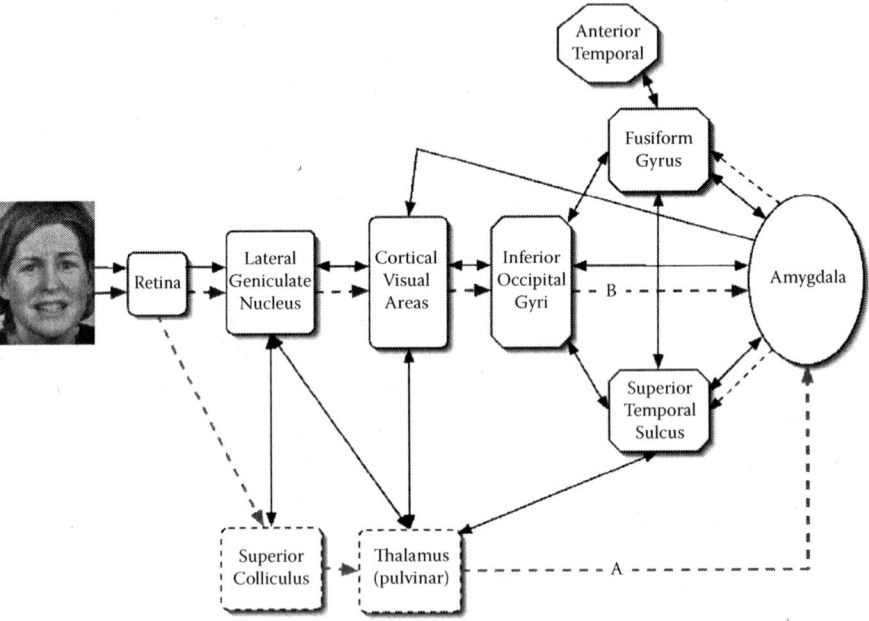

Figure 11.1   Face perception systems. The three rectangles with beveled edges indicate the core system for face perception (Haxby, J. V. et al., 2000, *Trends in Cognitive Sciences, 4*, 223–233). Solid lines indicate cortical pathways. The dashed lines labelled A represent the retino-colliculo-thalamo subcortical route for rapid and/or coarse emotional expression processing; the dashed lines labelled B represent the two-stage hypothesis (Vuilleumier, 2005a). This model is highly simplified and excludes many neural areas and connections. In addition, processing is not strictly hierarchical (i.e., from left to right) but rather involves multiple feedback connections (Bullier, J., 2001, *Brain Research Reviews, 36*, 96–107). (The face displayed is from the database collected by Gur, R. C. et al., 2002, *Journal of Neuroscience Methods, 115*, 137–143.)

Chun, 1997); more anterior temporal lobe regions are involved in the recollection of biographical information (Haxby, Hoffman, & Gobbini, 2000, 2002). A complex network of neural structures, including the superior temporal sulcus (STS), amygdala,[1] and orbitofrontal cortex, is involved in perceiving and recognizing emotion from facial expressions. Information conveyed by cortical geniculostriate pathways in occipital and temporal neocortex is needed to conduct the detailed perceptual analyses necessary to make fine discriminations between facial expressions (Adolphs, 2002a, 2002b; Haxby et al., 2000; Figure 11.1, solid lines).

Automatic processing seems most likely for facial expressions displaying threat or danger that, if rapidly detected, may confer a crucial survival advantage (e.g., Öhman, 2002; Vuilleumier, 2002). As such, a "dual-route" fear or threat detection system has been proposed; the system consists of a parallel *subcortical* route to the amygdala, via the superior colliculus and pulvinar thalamus (Figure 11.1, dashed lines labelled A), and provides a rapid but coarse analysis, perhaps based on salient individual features (de Gelder, Vroomen, Pourtois, & Weiskrantz, 1999; Hannula, Simons, & Cohen, 2005; LeDoux, 1996, 1998; Liddell et al., 2005; Morris, Öhman, & Dolan, 1999; Öhman, 2002).

Alternatively, rather than two pathways, Vuilleumier (2005a) suggested a two-stage process in which coarse information would reach the amygdala quickly via magnocellular visual pathways before more detailed parvocellular encoding and reentrant feedback (Figure 11.1, dashed lines labelled B).

DOES FACE PROCESSING HAPPEN VERY QUICKLY?

One way to judge the speed of face processing is to examine whether faces are processed more quickly than other types of stimuli. Electrophysiological studies measuring event-related potentials (ERPs) from the scalp (Bentin, Allison, Puce, Perez, & McCarthy, 1996; Jeffreys, 1989) and via intracranial electrodes in patients awaiting surgery (Allison et al., 1994) have suggested that responses to faces can be differentiated from those of other visual stimuli. In this section, we examine how quickly faces are detected and identified and compare this to the speed with which other stimuli are processed. We also examine how quickly facial expressions are registered and identified and evaluate the evidence for ultrafast and fear-specific processing by the amygdala.

Detecting Faces

Detecting a facial configuration is fast and efficient. For instance, thresholds to detect the presence of a stimulus are lower when the features compose an upright rather than an inverted or a scrambled face (Purcell & Stewart, 1988), and ERPs from frontal regions differentiate between normal and jumbled faces from 135 ms (Yamamoto & Kashikura, 1999). Moreover, single-unit recordings from primate cortex (Oram & Perrett, 1992; Sugase, Yamane, Ueno, & Kawano, 1999) and magnetoencephalography (MEG) recordings from humans (J. Liu, Harris, & Kanwisher, 2002) indicate that stimuli can be categorized as "faces" in extrastriate areas as early as 100 ms after stimulus presentation.

Event-related potential results suggest that naturalistic faces are categorized around 100 ms—much earlier than the 200 ms required to categorize objects and words (Pegna, Khateb, Michel, & Landis, 2004). Furthermore, when stimuli are embedded in natural scenes, faces (or, more precisely, humans) are detected 10 ms earlier than animals (Rousselet, Macé, & Fabre-Thorpe, 2003).

Recognizing Individuals

Extracting the finer grained information needed to identify a specific individual appears to require an additional 50–70 ms (Tsao, Freiwald, Tootell, & Livingstone, 2006). J. Liu et al. (2002) found that occipitotemporal face-selective MEG responses 170 ms after stimulus onset (known as the *M170*) were correlated with successful face categorization and face recognition (as measured with a matching task). However, those 100 ms after stimulus (labeled the *M100*) were only correlated with accurate face categorization.

Scalp ERPs over occipitotemporal sites that are maximally responsive to faces begin at around 130 ms and peak at around 170 ms (labeled as an *N170* or *N1*) and have generally been associated with face detection and structural encoding (Bentin & Deouell, 2000; Eimer, 2000b). However, recent evidence suggests that discriminating between individual faces may also be possible within this time window (Heisz, Watter, & Shedden, 2006; Jacques & Rossion, 2006a). An N170 is also seen for nonface objects and words, although often with reduced amplitude and increased latency (Bentin & Carmel, 2002; Itier & Taylor, 2004; however, see Rossion, Curran, & Gauthier, 2002).

Registering and Discriminating Emotion

Psychophysical studies measuring ERPs from the scalp of healthy participants demonstrate that emotional information from faces is rapidly registered and discriminated, from as early as 80 ms after stimulus onset (see Table 11.1 for a summary of early responses to emotional faces). Responses over occipital regions differentiate liked from disliked faces starting from 80 ms (Pizzagalli, Regard, & Lehmann, 1999) and fearful from happy faces from 90 ms (Pourtois, Grandjean, Sander, & Vuilleumier, 2004).

Frontal regions discriminate fearful from neutral faces beginning at 100 ms (Eimer & Holmes, 2002; Holmes, Vuilleumier, & Eimer, 2003), and temporal areas are involved in processing emotional information from faces from 130 ms (Batty & Taylor, 2003). Event-related potentials over temporal and frontal regions may sometimes be larger for fearful than for other basic expressions, although their response latencies are no earlier (Batty & Taylor; Eimer, Holmes, & McGlone, 2003).

Proposals suggesting that information about threat is rapidly conveyed to the amygdala via a subcortical route (Figure 11.1, dashed lines labelled A) or an initial feed-forward sweep (Figure 11.1, dashed lines lalbelled B; e.g., LeDoux, 1996; Morris, de Gelder, Weiskrantz, & Dolan, 2001; Vuilleumier, 2005a) lead to two testable predictions. First, we might expect that emotional information would activate the amygdala prior to other regions. Second, we might also expect that fearful

TABLE 11.1   Summary of Earliest Responses Found to Emotional Faces in Occipital, Temporal, and Frontal Regions, the Amygdala, and Insula

Study	Measure	Task	Key Comparison	Latency (ms)
Occipital				
Luo et al. (2007)	MEG	Judge sex of angry, fearful, and neutral faces	Onset of event-related synchrony in gamma band to fearful faces	40–50
			Onset of event-related synchrony in gamma band to angry faces	20–30
			Onset of event-related synchrony in gamma band to neutral faces	30–40
Pizzagalli et al. (1999)	Scalp ERP	Passive viewing of brief, lateralized faces	Liked versus disliked faces	80
Eger, Jednyak, Iwaki, & Skrandies (2003)	Scalp ERP	Dichoptic presentation of emotional, neutral, and scrambled schematic faces; asked to judge which stimulus appeared more "face-like"	Negative versus positive and neutral faces	80
Pourtois et al. (2004)	Scalp ERP	Judge the orientation of a bar that followed a pair of faces (one neutral, one emotional) presented in upper visual field	Fearful versus happy expressions	90
Halgren et al. (2000)	MEG	Detect repetitions of foveally presented stimuli	Happy versus sad expressions	110
Krolak-Salmon, Fischer, Vighetto, & Mauguiére (2001)	Scalp ERP	Judge sex of faces or count surprised faces (attend expression)	Neutral versus emotional (fear, happiness, disgust, surprise) when attend expression	250
Temporal				
Liu et al. (1999)	MEG	Identify emotional expression (angry, disgusted, fearful, happy, sad, surprised)	Significant change in activation to disgusted, happy, sad and surprised faces; fear delayed	130
Batty & Taylor (2003)	Scalp ERP	Detect objects among faces displaying emotional (angry, disgusted, fearful, happy, sad, surprised) or neutral expressions	Positive expressions (happy and surprise), followed by negative expressions (fear, disgust, and sadness); amplitude enhanced for fear	140

TABLE 11.1 Summary of Earliest Responses Found to Emotional Faces in Occipital, Temporal, and Frontal Regions, the Amygdala, and Insula (Continued)

Study	Measure	Task	Key Comparison	Latency (ms)
Streit et al. (1999)	MEG	Identify emotional expression (angry, disgusted, fearful, happy, sad, surprised) and categorize objects and faces	Face recognition versus emotion recognition	160
Pizzagalli et al. (2002)	Scalp ERP	Passive viewing of foveally presented faces	Enhanced amplitudes liked versus disliked faces	160
Sugase et al. (1999)	Single-unit recording from macaque	Fixation to colored dots before and after the faces	Fine-grained, subordinate information that could discriminate expressions	165
Esslen, Pascual-Marqui, Hell, Kochi, & Lehmann (2004)	Scalp ERP	Generate the emotion presented in facial expressions	Neutral versus fear	256
	Scalp ERP	Gender discrimination of emotional (fearful and happy) and neutral faces	Emotional faces elicited a larger negative peak	270
Amygdala				
Luo et al. (2007)	MEG	Judge sex of angry, fearful, and neutral faces	Onset of event-related synchrony in gamma band to fearful faces	20–30
			Onset of event-related synchrony in gamma band to angry faces	150–160
Streit et al. (2003)	MEG	Identify emotional expression (angry, disgusted, fearful, happy, sad, surprised) and categorize objects and faces	Stronger activity for emotional versus neutral or blurred faces	100
Liu et al. (1999)	MEG	Identify emotional expression (angry, disgusted, fearful, happy, sad, surprised)	Significant change in activation to:	
			• Happy expressions	110
			• Fearful expressions	150
Halgren et al. (1994)	ERP from depth electrodes	Viewing of unfamiliar faces	Faces versus words	130

TABLE 11.1   Summary of Earliest Responses Found to Emotional Faces in Occipital, Temporal, and Frontal Regions, the Amygdala, and Insula (Continued)

Study	Measure	Task	Key Comparison	Latency (ms)
Krolak-Salmon et al. (2004)	ERP from depth electrodes	Judge sex of faces or count surprised faces (attend expression)	Fear versus others (neutral, happy, disgusted) when attend expression	200
Streit et al. (1999)	MEG	Identify emotional expression (angry, disgusted, fearful, happy, sad, surprised) and categorize objects and faces	Face recognition versus emotion recognition	220
Frontal				
Streit et al. (2003)	MEG	Identify emotional expression (angry, disgusted, fearful, happy, sad, surprised) and categorize objects and faces	Stronger activity for emotional versus neutral or blurred faces	100
Holmes et al. (2003)	Scalp ERP	Attend (match identity) or ignore pairs of faces	Enhanced positivity for attended fearful versus neutral faces	100
Eimer & Holmes (2002)	Scalp ERP	Detect repetitions of foveally presented faces and houses	Enhanced positivity for fearful versus neutral faces	120
Kawasaki et al. (2001)	ERP from depth electrodes	Passive viewing of emotional faces and scenes	Changes to neuron firing rate greater in response to fearful versus happy facial expressions	120
Esslen et al. (2004)	Scalp ERP	Generate the emotion presented in facial expressions	Neutral versus happy, sad, and disgust	138
			Neutral versus fear	256
			Neutral versus angry	349
Eimer et al. (2003)	Scalp ERP	Attend (determine whether pairs of faces were emotional) or ignore pairs of faces	Enhanced positivity for all attended emotional faces (angry, disgusted, fearful, happy, sad, surprised) versus attended neutral faces	160
Streit, Wölwer, Brinkmeyer, Ihl, & Gaebel (2000)	Scalp ERP	Identify emotional expression (angry, disgusted, fearful, happy, sad, surprised) and categorize objects and faces	Face recognition versus emotion recognition	180

TABLE 11.1   Summary of Earliest Responses Found to Emotional Faces in Occipital, Temporal, and Frontal Regions, the Amygdala, and Insula (Continued)

Study	Measure	Task	Key Comparison	Latency (ms)
Insula				
Krolak-Salmon et al. (2003)	ERP from depth electrodes	Judge sex of faces or count surprised faces (attend expression)	Disgust versus others (neutral, happy, fearful) when attend expression	300

faces (which warn of an environmental threat to be avoided) and perhaps angry faces (which signify impending aggression) would be registered earlier than other facial expressions.

Despite excellent temporal resolution, scalp ERPs may not effectively measure amygdala responses due to the electrically closed structure of the neurons and the amygdala's deep position (Eimer & Holmes, 2007); thus, they are not ideally suited to test these predictions. Magnetoencephalography has superior source modeling. Most MEG studies have provided little support for the prediction of ultrarapid and fear-specific amygdala responses (see Table 11.1).

The amygdala responds more to emotional than to neutral faces from approximately 100 ms (Streit et al., 2003) and may differentiate between expressions from 110 ms (L. Liu, Ioannides, & Streit, 1999). However, other areas respond to emotional information from faces at similar latencies, such as responses over occipital regions differentiating happy from sad faces from 110 ms (Halgren, Raij, Marinkovic, Jousmaeki, & Hari, 2000). Moreover, responses to other expressions, such as happiness, appear to have earlier latencies than those to fear in both temporal regions and the amygdala (L. Liu et al., 1999).

One recent MEG study does provide support for the preferential and rapid processing of fear by the amygdala (Luo, Holroyd, Jones, Hendler, & Blair, 2007). This study is distinguished from the previous MEG studies in two ways. First, it was designed to examine both of these predictions specifically; second, it measured neuronal oscillations that occurred in the gamma band of frequencies between 30 and 50 Hz. Gamma band synchronization in response to fearful faces was found in the hypothalamus/thalamus at 10–20 ms, the amygdala at 20–30 ms, and the visual cortex at 40–50 ms. This is consistent with an ultrafast retinal–collicular–pulvinar route to the amygdala (Figure 11.1, dashed lines labelled A). Moreover, this was specific to fearful faces; responses to angry faces in the amygdala occurred much later.

Event-related potentials can also be measured by implanting electrodes intracranially into patients awaiting surgery for drug-resistant epilepsy. Intracranial ERPs have the advantage of both precise localization and millisecond timing. The limitation of this technique is that it cannot be conducted with healthy participants and it is possible that processing is delayed in medicated patient populations (Krolak-Salmon, Hénaff, Vighetto, Bertrand, & Mauguiére, 2004).

Kawasaki et al. (2001) measured ERP responses to facial expressions from electrodes implanted in frontal regions and found that fearful faces could be discriminated from happy faces from 120 ms. Krolak-Salmon and colleagues (2003, 2004) measured from electrodes located in the amygdala and insula. When participants attended to facial expression, responses to fear in the amygdala (~200 ms poststimulus onset) occurred earlier than those to disgust in the insula (~300 ms poststimulus onset), suggesting rapid, preferential processing of fear by the amygdala. However, Krolak-Salmon et al. (2004; see Cowey, 2004, for similar arguments based on single-unit recordings) argue that we cannot be sure that the amygdala response to fear is mediated purely by an ultrafast retinal–collicular–pulvinar route to the amygdala because cortical responses can occur within 40–80 ms and could provide some input.

Summary

Faces are detected and categorized more quickly than many other stimuli. Detection and crude affective categorization can occur rapidly—from 100 ms poststimulus onset; fine-grained cortical representations necessary to recognize, identify, and discriminate between basic emotional expressions are computed within an additional 70 ms. In sum, the evidence for rapid face processing is good. Current MEG and intracranial ERP studies provide mixed support for ultrafast, preferential processing of fear by the amygdala that is mediated by purely subcortical pathways. Advances in MEG methodology and further intracranial ERP studies will help to clarify the functional role of the subcortical pathway and early feed-forward processing in response to facial expressions of emotion in humans.

ARE FACES REGISTERED, AT LEAST IN PART, UNCONSCIOUSLY?

Not all visual processing by the human brain reaches conscious awareness (Rees, Kreiman, & Koch, 2002), and such processing can be thought of as "automatic" (Bargh, 1997; Öhman, 2002; Robinson, 1998). Here, we consider whether the identity and affect displayed by faces are registered even when people are unaware of this information. Conscious awareness is disrupted by some neuropsychological disorders of vision and can be simulated in healthy people by presenting stimuli very briefly with backward masking.

Can Faces Be Identified Without Conscious Awareness?

People with acquired prosopagnosia, who cannot consciously recognize previously familiar faces, sometimes show nonconscious or covert "recognition." Some show higher levels of autonomic arousal (as measured with skin conductance responses [SCRs]) to familiar rather than to unfamiliar faces (e.g., Bauer, 1984; Tranel &

Damasio, 1985). Some have access to semantic information associated with identity; they learn the names and occupations of faces better when they are paired correctly rather than incorrectly (e.g., de Haan, Young, & Newcombe, 1987). Similar nonconscious processing of facial identity may also occur in healthy participants (Stone & Valentine, 2003, 2004; Stone, Valentine, & Davies, 2001).

Are Facial Expressions Registered Without Conscious Awareness?

Covert or nonconscious recognition of facial expression in healthy people is often examined by presenting expressive faces very briefly with backward masking. Affective priming studies typically present a brief face prime (~15 ms), followed by a neutral stimulus to be evaluated. The expression depicted by the prime influences judgments of the neutral stimuli; for instance, meaningless symbols are rated as more appealing when they follow briefly presented happy, rather than angry, faces (Murphy & Zajonc, 1993; Rotteveel, de Groot, Geutskens, & Phaf, 2001; Wong & Root, 2003). Although participants appeared to be unaware of the prime expressions (Wong & Root), it is possible that the face primes were incompletely masked because they were masked by symbols rather than by more effective masks composed of a facial configuration (see Loffler, Gordon, Wilkinson, Goren, & Wilson, 2005, for a comparison of mask types).

Physiological and imaging studies typically present a brief prime face, often for around 30 ms, followed by a neutral masking face that is presented for a longer time. The studies that we review next generally find that participants were *subjectively* unaware of the face primes (i.e., they report no knowledge of the facial expressions), although *objective* awareness of the face primes (e.g., by using a forced-choice identification task) was often not assessed (see Pessoa, Japee, & Ungerleider, 2005, for more discussion).

Facial electromyography (EMG) studies reveal that people's facial muscles mimic brief (30 ms) masked facial expressions, with unseen happy faces resulting in smiles via the action of the zygomatic major muscle and unseen angry faces resulting in frowns via corrugator supercilli (Dimberg, Thunberg, & Elmehed, 2000). Fear-conditioning studies also demonstrate autonomic responses to angry faces presented below the threshold for conscious awareness. Angry faces previously associated with an electric shock evoke heightened SCRs, even when they are presented for 30 ms, backward masked, and not consciously perceived (Esteves, Dimberg, & Öhman, 1994).

Moreover, associations can be formed between aversive events and angry faces that are not consciously recognized (Öhman, Esteves, & Soares, 1995). Interestingly, masked angry (but not happy) faces evoke conditioned autonomic responses, perhaps because threatening faces have an evolutionary bias to be associated with aversive outcomes (Mineka & Öhman, 2002).

Neuroimaging studies often show that the amygdala is activated by fearful and fear-conditioned angry faces that are outside awareness (for review, see Zald, 2003). Although participants could not consciously report the expressions presented by very brief (~30 ms), backward-masked faces, functional imaging has revealed that amygdala activation was greater to fearful than happy unseen faces

(Whalen et al., 1998) and that (right) amygdala activation was enhanced for angry faces that were previously associated with an aversive sound in a fear-conditioning paradigm (Morris, Öhman, & Dolan, 1998; Morris et al., 1999).

Similar results have been found with binocular rivalry tasks, where the image presented to one eye is perceived while the image presented to the other eye is suppressed (Blake & Logothetis, 2002). For instance, fearful faces activated the amygdala to the same extent, regardless of whether they were perceived or suppressed (Williams, Morris, McGlone, Abbott, & Mattingley, 2004), and suppressed fearful faces activated the (left) amygdala more than suppressed chairs (Pasley, Mayes, & Schultz, 2004). Finally, a recent study suggests that briefly (17 ms) presented and masked eye whites from fearful faces also activate the amygdala to a greater extent than do the eye whites from happy faces (Whalen et al., 2004).

However, two recent studies found enhanced amygdala activation for fearful faces only when participants were aware of them. Phillips and colleagues (2004) found that amygdala activation present when fearful faces were shown for 170 ms was eliminated when the faces were presented for 30 ms and then backward masked. Pessoa, Japee, Sturman, and Ungerleider (2006) asked participants to report whether or not a fearful face was present on each trial and used signal detection analyses to measure objectively whether each participant was able to detect brief backward-masked fearful faces reliably.

They observed increased amygdala (and fusiform gyrus) activation for fearful relative to neutral faces when the faces were shown for 67 ms and reliably detected by participants—but not when the faces were shown for 33 ms and not detected by participants. Moreover, a small group of participants that were able to detect fear from 33 ms backward-masked faces did show differential activation, suggesting that amygdala activation may be associated with awareness (also see Suslow et al., 2006).

Investigating patients who are "unaware" of visual stimuli has also provided an insight into the unconscious processing of fearful faces. Patients with right parietal damage suffering visual neglect and extinction fail to perceive or respond to a stimulus in the contralesional (left) visual field when a competing stimulus is present in the ipsilesional field. Despite no awareness of extinguished faces, unseen fearful faces activate the amygdala just as much as those that are consciously perceived (Vuilleumier et al., 2002).

Striate cortex damage prevented patient GY from becoming aware of faces presented in his "blind" visual field. Nonetheless, when forced, he was able to choose the expression displayed by the face at above-chance levels; this is known as "affective blindsight" (de Gelder et al., 1999). The amygdala, superior colliculus, and pulvinar were activated when fearful and fear-conditioned faces were presented in GY's "blind" visual field (Morris et al., 2001), suggesting that his ability to discriminate between expressions in the absence of awareness may be mediated by a subcortical colliculo–pulvinar route to the amygdala (Figure 11.1, dashed lines labelled A) (Morris et al., 2001). Alternatively, cortical pathways to the amygdala that bypass V1 could be involved (for discussion on anatomical connections, see Pessoa, 2005; Pessoa et al., 2006; Vuilleumier, 2005a; Williams et al., 2004).

Unseen fearful and fear-conditioned angry faces do not seem to be the only facial expressions that activate the amygdala. Williams et al. (2004) found that suppressed happy faces activated the amygdala to a greater extent than suppressed neutral faces. They suggested that facial expressions that are not consciously perceived are processed primarily, and perhaps exclusively, by subcortical pathways that are able to distinguish emotional from unemotional faces but unable to discriminate between affective categories without cortical input.

However, other evidence suggests that some discrimination may be possible. A patient with total bilateral cortical blindness, who would be unable to use information in his intact visual field to help determine what was presented in the blind field, can distinguish between unseen emotional expressions at above-chance levels when given two categories from which to choose (i.e., angry vs. happy; sad vs. happy; fearful vs. happy) (Pegna, Khateb, Lazeyras, & Seghier, 2004). These expressions may be discriminated by comparing the degree of emotional arousal for each face based on amygdala activation (Killgore & Yurgelun-Todd, 2004).

Structures other than the amygdala could also be involved in the nonconscious discrimination of expression. Functional imaging studies in healthy people have revealed anterior cingulate gyrus activation in response to masked happy and sad facial expressions (Killgore & Yurgelun-Todd, 2004) and sublenticular substantia inominata activation in response to masked happy and fearful facial expressions (Whalen et al., 1998). Fearful facial expressions that were extinguished by neglect patients activated the orbitofrontal cortex (Vuilleumier et al., 2002). The role played by these areas in processing expressions that people do not consciously recognize is currently unclear.

Summary

Both healthy people and prosopagnosic patients appear to be able to encode some information about facial identity without conscious awareness. Note that this does not necessarily mean that the faces were processed without attention, because attention was directed to the location of the stimulus and, generally, no competing task used attentional resources (Pessoa & Ungerleider, 2003). Converging behavioral, physiological, neuroimaging, and neuropsychological evidence also shows that facial expressions of which people are subjectively unaware are registered, often by the amygdala.

It is less clear whether faces of which people are objectively unaware activate the amygdala; fearful eye whites presented alone seem to activate it (Whalen et al., 2004), whereas fearful faces (which, paradoxically, contain fearful eye whites) appear not to (Pessoa et al., 2006). One issue that may need to be examined in future work is that of individual differences in emotion processing (Hamann & Canli, 2004). Sensitivity to brief face presentations seems to vary across expression type (Maxwell & Davidson, 2004) and between individuals (Pessoa, Japee, et al., 2005) and could be related to anxiety levels (Etkin et al., 2004).

IS FACE PROCESSING MANDATORY?

Another characteristic of automatic processes is that they are mandatory, in that processing is unavoidable and occurs regardless of one's intentions (e.g., Wojciulik et al., 1998). Behavioral methods to test for mandatory processing include priming tasks with unfamiliar faces and face-name interference tasks with familiar faces, where participants read the names of famous people while trying to ignore photos of famous people. Functional imaging studies have compared responses to attended faces to those for unattended faces. A lack of mandatory processing is implied by a complete absence of responses to unattended faces.

In contrast, some type of response to unattended faces is indicative of mandatory processing. If responses are equivalent for attended and unattended faces, this would suggest *complete* mandatory processing, whereas attenuated responses to unattended faces would suggest *partial* mandatory processing. Electrophysiological methods have been used to assess whether processing is mandatory at various stages. For example, early processing may be mandatory, but later stages may not be.

Can You Ignore That Face?

Detecting a face may be mandatory. Participants are slower to detect the curvature of a single line when it appears in a face configuration of three curved arcs than in a meaningless configuration, indicating that facial configurations cannot be ignored even when it would be advantageous to do so (Suzuki & Cavanagh, 1995). Participants required to judge the length of lines shown at the center of the screen often noticed unexpected smiling schematic faces presented in the periphery but did not notice many other types of stimuli, including sad and neutral schematic faces (Mack & Rock, 1998).

Patients with visual neglect and extinction extinguish contralesionally presented schematic faces less often than scrambled faces and other shapes (Vuilleumier, 2000). Happy, fearful, and angry faces are also extinguished less often than faces with neutral expressions (Fox, 2002; Vuilleumier & Schwartz, 2001). Thus, processing of faces, especially expressive ones, seems to be mandatory.

Some information about the identity of ignored unfamiliar faces also seems to be processed. Khurana, Smith, and Baker (2000) presented arrays of five faces and asked participants to match the identity of two target faces and ignore the other distractor faces. Matching of the target faces was slowed when the target faces were distractors on the preceding trial (known as "negative priming"), suggesting that the unfamiliar distractor faces were represented and then inhibited. Face-name interference tasks also indicate that the identity of ignored familiar famous faces is processed: People were slower to categorize the occupation of a famous name (e.g., Mick Jagger) when it was presented with a to-be-ignored face from an incongruent occupation (e.g., Margaret Thatcher) than from a congruent one (e.g., Paul McCartney) (Young, Ellis, Flude, McWeeny, & Hay, 1986).

Load theories of selective attention propose that distractors should be processed when just one relevant stimulus is present so that spare capacity can "spill over" to irrelevant items (i.e., low attentional load), rather than when many relevant stimuli are present and exhaust all available capacity (i.e., high attentional load) (Lavie, 1995, 2000). Mandatory semantic processing of faces seems more resistant to manipulations of attentional load than does the processing of other objects, with face-name interference sustained under conditions of high attentional load that eliminated object-name interference (Lavie, Ro, & Russell, 2003).

Although mandatory processing may occur for "ignored" faces, functional magnetic resonance imaging (fMRI) evidence suggests that it may be partial rather than complete. Face-selective responses in the fusiform gyrus are larger for attended than for unattended faces (Furey et al., 2006; McCarthy, 2000; O'Craven, Downing, & Kanwisher, 1999; Wojciulik et al., 1998). Electrophysiological evidence also shows that there is at least a partial response to unattended faces; some studies show that the early components of face processing (i.e., the N170/M170) are enhanced for attended faces relative to unattended faces (Downing, Liu, & Kanwisher, 2001; Eimer, 2000a; Holmes et al., 2003; Jacques & Rossion, 2007).

Other studies have observed equivalent responses for attended and unattended faces, suggesting that the early stages of face processing are completely mandatory (Carmel & Bentin, 2002; Cauquil, Edmonds, & Taylor, 2000; Furey et al., 2006). Furey et al. presented overlapping semitransparent houses and faces and manipulated whether attention was directed toward the face or the house. They found that face-selective responses in the fusiform, inferior occipital, and superior temporal sulcal cortex were modulated by attention when measured with fMRI; however, attention had no effect on the M170 (although later face-selective MEG responses were modulated by attention). Furey and colleagues suggest that the M170 reflects a feed-forward, completely mandatory stage of face processing, whereas the slower fMRI signals are influenced by feedback and are thus able to be modulated.

Can You Ignore That Emotion?

Some evidence suggests that emotion processing by the amygdala, especially in regard to fearful or threatening stimuli, may be completely mandatory and not reduced in the absence of attention. In one study, participants matched the identity of a pair of peripheral faces (i.e., attend faces) or houses (i.e., ignore faces) (Vuilleumier et al., 2001). Responses in the amygdala to fearful faces were not significantly reduced when the faces were unattended, suggesting that fear responses mediated by the amygdala may be obligatory and not dependent upon focused attention. Equivalent amygdala responses to unattended and attended fearful faces presented at the fovea have also been reported (Anderson, Christoff, Panitz, De Rosa, & Gabrieli, 2003).

However, Pessoa, McKenna, Gutierrez, and Ungerleider (2002) argued that matching houses was not sufficiently attentionally demanding and may have allowed attentional resources to "spill over" and process the facial expressions (per attentional load theory; Lavie, 1995). They presented expressive faces at the fovea in conjunction with a more demanding secondary task (i.e., judging the orientation of two similarly oriented lines in the periphery) and found that brain regions, including the amygdala, that responded differentially to emotional faces did so *only* when participants were attending to the facial stimuli. The conclusion was that facial expression coding is not mandatory and requires some degree of attention.

Similar conclusions were recently reached by Mitchell and colleagues (2007), who found enhanced activity for fearful compared to neutral faces when participants judged the sex of the face (low load), but not when participants judged the number of syllables contained in a semitransparent overlapping word (high load). It is possible that amygdala activation is present under high-load conditions but less than that able to be detected by fMRI threshold techniques (Taylor & Fragopanagos, 2005), perhaps because it is too rapid (Mitchell et al.).

Williams, McGlone, Abbott, and Mattingley (2005) also used a more attentionally demanding competing task than that used by Vuilleumier and colleagues (2001). Participants were shown pairs of peripheral semitransparent face–house composites and asked to match either the faces (attend face) or the houses (attend houses). In vivid contrast to Pessoa et al. (2002), they found that amygdala activation was enhanced for unattended as compared to attended fearful faces.

Unfortunately, ERP evidence has not helped to clarify the picture. Vuilleumier et al. (2001) demonstrated equivalent amygdala responses to unattended and attended fearful faces with fMRI. However, an ERP experiment using a similar paradigm found that an enhanced positivity for fearful compared to neutral faces beginning about 160 ms after stimulus onset was absent for unattended fearful faces (Holmes et al., 2003).

Similarly, matching the length of two foveally presented lines eliminated differential responding to pairs of fearful and neutral peripheral faces (Eimer et al., 2003). As discussed in the preceding "Does Face Processing Happen Very Quickly?" section, because scalp ERPs may not record important amygdala activation, this is not strong evidence for an elimination of amygdala processing in the absence of attention. Instead, the diminished ERP responses for unattended faces may reflect the reduction in cortical processing measured by fMRI when faces are not attended (e.g., Anderson et al., 2003; Vuilleumier et al., 2001).

One explanation for the different patterns of fMRI results may be an interaction between attentional load and location of the faces. Peripherally presented ignored faces may activate the amygdala under both low (Vuilleumier et al., 2001) and high (Williams, McGlone, et al., 2005) attentional load manipulations, whereas a centrally presented face may only lead to strong amygdala responses under low-load (Anderson et al., 2003) but not high-load (Pessoa et al., 2002) conditions. Indeed, Pessoa, Padmala, and Morland's (2005) study with centrally presented faces demonstrated greater (right) amygdala activation to fearful than neutral faces under low attentional load but not in medium- or high-load conditions.

Enhanced processing of peripherally presented affective stimuli would be consistent with the proposal that one role of the amygdala is to direct attention to important items that are not the current focus of attention. There are more projections from the periphery to the superior colliculus (Berson & Stein, 1995). Moreover, recent evidence that the amygdala preferentially responds to low rather than high spatial frequency information (Vuilleumier, Armony, Driver, & Dolan, 2003) suggests that the amygdala may be especially sensitive to peripheral faces.

Studies varying both load and location of the faces are needed to test the interaction hypothesis outlined previously.

Another (not mutually exclusive) possibility is that amygdala responses to unattended threatening stimuli may interact with an individual's level of anxiety. Bishop, Duncan, and Lawrence (2004) used the paradigm devised by Vuilleumier and colleagues (2001) and found equivalent amygdala activation to both attended and ignored fearful faces when participants were highly anxious. In contrast, amygdala activation to fearful faces was enhanced for attended compared to ignored fearful faces when participants reported low levels of anxiety.

Similarly, participants with high "harm avoidance"—a personality measure linked to trait anxiety—showed greater (left) amygdala activation to irrelevant emotional distractors when searching for a target item in a rapid stream of pictures than those with low harm avoidance (Most, Chun, Johnson, & Kiehl, 2006). Studying how individual differences in anxiety interact with attentional load and exert an impact on amygdala activation will be an interesting area for future research.

Summary

Behavioral evidence that ignored familiar and unfamiliar faces are processed to some level indicates some mandatory processing of facial identity. Furthermore, although neural responses in face-selective cortex are reduced for ignored faces compared with attended faces, they are certainly not eliminated when measured with fMRI. Some evidence indicates that early neural responses may be equivalent when measured with MEG. Neuroimaging studies examining the mandatory processing of emotional expression have included manipulations of attentional load and also have examined individual differences in anxiety.

We expect that analysis of these variables will eventually lead to a fuller understanding of the nature of mandatory expression processing. At present, we can conclude that amygdala activation to fearful facial expressions appears completely mandatory under low attentional load conditions, but perhaps not under high attentional load conditions. An intriguing possibility is that amygdala activation to fearful facial expressions is completely mandatory for highly anxious individuals but not for those with lower levels of anxiety.

IS FACE PROCESSING CAPACITY FREE?

Another characteristic of automatic processing is that it demands relatively few attentional resources, so it should experience little disruption from competing stimuli or tasks that use these resources (e.g., Schneider & Chein, 2003):

> If face-identification performance requires little or no attentional resources, performance in the dual-task condition should suffer minimally compared to single-task performance. On the other hand, if the peripheral task requires attention, performance should be severely impaired in the dual-task condition (Braun & Julesz, 1998; Braun & Sagi, 1990; Sperling & Melchner, 1978). (Reddy, Reddy, & Koch, 2006, p. 2340)

Theoretically, the processing of faces may be mandatory without being capacity free and vice versa. In practice, however, dual-task paradigms have been used to assess both the mandatory nature and the capacity demands of face coding. The relationship exists because mandatory processing is often assumed if information about identity or expression is encoded from faces while participants are completing another attentionally demanding task.

We begin by reviewing evidence from visual search tasks, where participants actively search for a target among a number of distractors. As originally conceived, search times that did not vary with the number of distractors (commonly termed "pop-out") indicated rapid, parallel, and perhaps capacity-free processing (e.g., Treisman & Gelade, 1980). We also consider whether attentional resources are necessary to encode the configural or holistic representations by which face recognition generally proceeds. Finally, we summarize the results of dual-task experiments with expressive faces.

Searching for Faces

Simple schematic neutral or unexpressive faces do not pop out of crowded displays composed of scrambled or inverted faces (Brown, Huey, & Findlay, 1997; Kuehn & Jolicœur, 1994; Nothdurft, 1993), suggesting that face detection is neither parallel nor capacity free. Early visual studies using simplistic expressive faces reported pop-out for angry faces (Hansen & Hansen, 1988), but this has been attributed to low-level confounds rather than to valence (Purcell, Stewart, & Skov, 1996).

Hershler and Hochstein (2005) argue that faces will only pop out of backgrounds composed of nonface objects. They recently demonstrated that realistic face photographs pop out when presented among a mixture of nonface objects (e.g., cars, animals, and fruit). Because some of the distractors share low-level features with faces, Hershler and Hochstein (2005, 2006) conclude that face pop-out relies on a high-level mechanism.

Further experiments have shown that whole faces, internal face parts (i.e., eyes, nose, and mouth and cheeks), external face parts (i.e., hairline and ears), and inverted faces pop out, whereas scrambled face targets and animal faces do not (Hershler & Hochstein, 2006; VanRullen, 2006). Hershler and Hochstein (2005; 2006) take these results to mean that face search relies on a type of holistic perceptual configuration. However, VanRullen argues that face pop-out under these conditions mostly relies on low-level factors. In addition, VanRullen suggests that the Fourier amplitude spectrum may differentiate between faces and other objects and is a low-level feature.

It is now considered more appropriate to conceive of search tasks as measuring processing efficiency and/or attentional biases, with shallower slopes indicating more efficient processing of that stimulus type (e.g., see Huang & Pashler, 2005; Luck & Vecera, 2002; Wolfe, 1998). Reliable search asymmetries are found in tasks using expressive schematic faces with no low-level confounds; search for angry faces among neutral or happy faces is quicker than the reverse (Eastwood, Smilek, & Merikle, 2001; Fox et al., 2000; Öhman, Lundqvist, & Esteves, 2001). Studies using schematic stimuli suggest that angry faces may attract attention because of salient features, particularly the eyebrows (Lundqvist, Esteves, & Öhman, 1999), but that the presence of a correctly oriented facial configuration may also be essential (Eastwood et al., 2001; Fox et al., 2000; Tipples, Atkinson, & Young, 2002).

Similar search asymmetries (i.e., search for angry faces among happy faces is more efficient than the reverse) are found in studies with photographic-quality faces. Some studies suggest that this advantage may be primarily driven by the mouth region (Horstmann & Bauland, 2006), and others suggest that the eye region may be sufficient (Fox & Damjanovic, 2006). Angry faces might be detected more efficiently than faces displaying positive emotions because the rapid detection of threatening stimuli has potential adaptive value (Fox et al., 2000; LeDoux, 1996; Öhman, 1993).

Interestingly, although both angry and fearful faces signify threat, their ability to attract attention in visual search tasks using photographic-quality stimuli may vary. Specifically, when targets were embedded among large numbers of neutral-face photos, search for an angry- but not fearful-face photo was more efficient than search for a happy-face photo (Williams, Moss, Bradshaw, & Mattingley, 2005).

VanRullen, Reddy, and Koch (2004) have recently suggested that the "type" of attention measured by visual search tasks may be different from that measured by other paradigms. They point out that some targets that trigger pop-out cannot be discriminated in dual-task situations, whereas others can be discriminated in dual-task situations but do not pop out. For instance, although faces do not pop out, determining the sex and even the identity of a face is only modestly impaired by performing a concurrent letter discrimination task (Reddy et al., 2006; Reddy, Wilken, & Koch, 2004). If dual tasks are measuring independent attentional resources to those measured by visual search paradigms, then the types of conditions under which face detection occurs will determine whether attentional resources are required.

Put simply, different attentional manipulations from different paradigms are likely to result in very different effects. A greater understanding of the nature of attentional resources and the conditions under which they operate is needed before we can clarify what is needed to detect faces.

Attentional Resources to Code Identity

Recognizing facial identity appears to rely more upon the encoding of configural or holistic information than on representations of individual facial features (see Maurer, Le Grand, & Mondloch, 2002, for a review). Some evidence suggests that holistic face representations are coded with little or no attention (Boutet, Gentes-Hawn, & Chaudhuri, 2002).

Boutet and colleagues (2002) measured holistic coding of identity with a variant of the "composite effect" (Young, Hellawell, & Hay, 1987). They showed participants a series of face composites that were either "aligned" (when the top and bottom halves of two different faces are joined into a new face composite, which makes recognition of the top half more difficult) or "misaligned" (when the top and bottom halves are slightly offset, which facilitates recognition of the top half). Before seeing the face composites, participants viewed a series of overlapping semitransparent house and face images and traced the outline of the face (attend face) or the house (ignore face). Subsequent recognition was better for misaligned than aligned faces, regardless of whether the faces were previously attended or ignored, thus suggesting that facial identity is coded with little or no attention.

In contrast, other studies suggest that attention is needed to form holistic face representations of identity. Palermo and Rhodes (2002) measured holistic coding with the part–whole task. Participants are shown a face and then asked to recognize the previously seen facial parts (i.e., eyes, nose, and mouth) in a forced-choice recognition test containing two "isolated parts" (e.g., nose 1 vs. nose 2) or two "whole faces" that are identical except for the feature in question (e.g., nose 1 vs. nose 2) (Tanaka, Kay, Grinnell, Stansfield, & Szechter, 1998). For upright faces (but not those initially shown scrambled or inverted), recognition of the face parts is superior when the parts are shown in a "whole face" context rather than as "isolated parts." This suggests that upright faces are represented more holistically than other types of stimuli (Tanaka & Farah, 1993).

Palermo and Rhodes (2002) presented a central target face and two peripheral flanker faces for a brief time and then tested part–whole recognition of the target face (either the parts in a whole face or the parts in isolation). Participants who ignored the flanker faces demonstrated holistic coding (i.e., performance was better in the whole face than the isolated part condition). Participants who were required to match the identity of the peripheral flanker faces were unable to code the target face holistically, suggesting that the encoding of facial identity is attentionally demanding (see Reinitz, Morrissey, & Demb, 1994, for similar conclusions).

In a subsequent experiment, Palermo and Rhodes (2002) found that matching a pair of peripheral *upright* faces eliminated holistic coding of the target faces; however, holistic coding of the target faces was not disrupted when participants were required to match *inverted* flanker faces. Inverted faces are not coded holistically (see reviews by Farah, 2000; Maurer et al., 2002), leading Palermo and Rhodes to suggest that holistic face processing may have its own dedicated attentional or processing resources (see Young, de Haan, Newcombe, & Hay, 1990, for earlier suggestions that there may be face-specific attentional resources).

Similar conclusions were drawn by Jenkins, Lavie, and Driver (2003) after they found that face-name interference is reduced by an additional upright face but not by inverted faces or objects. These face-specific holistic resources may be quite limited, with only one face able to be coded holistically in a brief time (Bindemann, Burton, & Jenkins, 2008; also see Boutet & Chaudhuri, 2001).

Psychophysiological studies also suggest that simultaneously presented faces compete for neural representation. The N170 response to a peripheral face is reduced when participants are fixating a central face rather than a nonface object (Jacques & Rossion, 2004) and also to a centrally presented face when a task-irrelevant face is in the periphery (Jacques & Rossion, 2006b). Importantly, this sensory visual competition appears to be distinct from effects of spatial attention; attention effects begin at around 80 ms and competition at around 130 ms, even though they may act on similar populations of neurons in the occipitotemporal cortex.

The previous studies suggest capacity limits for faces presented simultaneously. Other studies have examined temporal interference by presenting stimuli sequentially in rapid succession. When two targets are presented in close temporal proximity, the second target may be missed, presumably because of a temporal attentional bottleneck; this is known as an attentional blink (AB)[2] (Raymond, Shapiro, & Arnell, 1992).

Awh et al. (2004) found that discriminating between digits impaired the subsequent discrimination of letters but not faces; they suggested that this asymmetry may be because both letters and digits are processed in a featural manner, whereas faces rely upon a separate configural/holistic processing channel. In contrast, Jackson and Raymond (2006) found that a featural discrimination task impaired the subsequent detection of an unfamiliar face and argued against the existence of a separate configural/holistic channel for faces.

Further complicating the issue of whether attentional resources are needed to encode facial identity is the possibility that very familiar or famous faces may not need attention, whereas unfamiliar faces might. Jackson and Raymond (2006) found an AB for unfamiliar faces but not for very familiar faces. Similarly, changes between two successive faces were easier to detect when one was famous (Buttle & Raymond, 2003). Observers are also much quicker to detect their own faces than those of unfamiliar people, even when these initially unfamiliar faces were presented hundreds of times; this suggests that the detection of very highly familiar faces can require fewer attentional resources than that of less familiar faces (Tong & Nakayama, 1999).

Reddy et al. (2006) asked participants to identify a peripheral face, sometimes while performing an attentionally demanding task at fixation. They found that performance under dual-task conditions was only modestly impaired, suggesting identification may be possible with reduced spatial attention. In contrast to the proposal that familiarity may interact with attention, they found little difference in performance whether the face was that of a celebrity or of a relatively unfamiliar person.

Attentional Resources to Code Expression

As discussed in the "Can You Ignore That Emotion?" section, Pessoa et al. (2002) found that responses in all brain regions responsive to expression, including the amygdala and FFA, were eliminated when the faces were not attended. They argued that facial expression coding is neither mandatory nor capacity free. In contrast, the majority of dual-task studies diverting attention away from fearful faces have found that responses in the FFA are reduced but not eliminated and, moreover, that amygdala activation is maintained, suggesting that amygdala coding is both mandatory and resource independent (Anderson et al., 2003; Vuilleumier et al., 2001; Williams, McGlone, et al., 2005).

It is also possible that emotionally arousing information reduces, rather than eliminates, the need for attention (see Anderson, 2005). In a study using words rather than faces, Anderson and Phelps (2001) found that healthy people, but not those with left or bilateral amygdala lesions, were more likely to report the second target in an AB task when the word was aversive rather than neutral. This suggests that a critical function of the amygdala may be to enhance the initial perceptual encoding of emotionally significant stimuli, "making them less dependent on attentional resources to reach awareness" (p. 308).

At least in situations of low load, the amygdala appears to respond fully to fearful facial expressions, even when attention is diverted elsewhere. However, responses by the amygdala in the absence of attention may have reduced specificity. That is, the amygdala preferentially responds to fearful expressions with attention; however, under conditions of reduced attention, it may respond to any potentially threatening expression. For example, unattended disgusted faces also activate the amygdala, suggesting that coarse subcortical input is not sufficient to discriminate between fear and disgust without attentionally demanding cortical processing (Anderson et al., 2003).

In contrast, amygdala responses to unattended happy faces are reduced compared to when they are attended (Williams, McGlone, et al., 2005). This suggests that coarse subcortical input can discriminate between threatening (fearful) and nonthreatening (happy) expressions, but not between different types of potential threat (disgust and fear).

Attention may be necessary to examine the facial features that distinguish between various negative expressions (such as the mouth for disgust and the eyes for fear), and the amygdala may be involved in directing attention to these salient facial features. Eye movement studies indicate that both primates and humans fixate upon the facial features, especially the eyes and mouth, of emotional faces (see Green & Phillips, 2004, for a review).

In contrast, patient SM has early, bilateral amygdala damage and impaired recognition of fearful expressions and appears to abnormally scan faces for emotion, with particularly conspicuous absence of attention to the eyes and perhaps also the mouth (Adolphs et al., 2005). Although she did not spontaneously explore the eye region, SM was able to look at the eyes when directed to do so. Looking at the eyes enhanced her ability to recognize fear, suggesting that her deficit might not have been in recognizing fearful expressions per se, but rather in attending to facial features that aid recognition of fear.

The results of this case study are intriguing, but they cannot explain how SM was able to recognize other facial expressions (e.g., anger) in situations in which it would seem that analysis of the eyes is important (see Vuilleumier, 2005b, for further discussion). Whereas some patients with bilateral or unilateral amygdala damage are only impaired at recognizing facial expressions of fear (Adolphs, Tranel, & Damasio, 2001; Adolphs, Tranel, Damasio, & Damasio, 1995), others also have deficits recognizing other negative facial expressions, such as disgust and sadness (Adolphs et al., 1999; Anderson, Spencer, Fulbright, & Phelps, 2000). It would be instructive to examine whether eye movement patterns in patients with amygdala lesions vary depending on which expressions can and cannot be reliably recognized.

Summary

Most evidence suggests that faces presented among stimuli matched on low-level features do not pop out, suggesting that attentional resources are needed to detect a facial configuration. The encoding of facial identity appears to require attentional resources, although, as discussed, one caveat may be that highly familiar faces require fewer attentional resources than unfamiliar faces. Faces also seem to compete for neural representation, suggesting limits to the number of faces that can be simultaneously encoded. Current evidence is consistent with the view that registration of fear by the amygdala requires minimal attentional resources, whereas more attentional resources are needed to discriminate between emotional expressions of potential threat (e.g., fear vs. disgust).

CONCLUSIONS AND FUTURE DIRECTIONS

Detecting a facial configuration is rapid and perhaps faster than detecting other stimuli. Detecting a facial configuration may also be obligatory. However, visual search studies suggest that faces are not detected in the complete absence of attentional resources.

Identifying an individual is rapid. Some aspects of facial identity are encoded without conscious awareness, without intention, and even without focused attention. However, at least for unfamiliar faces, focused attention appears to be necessary for complete activation of the FFA and to encode the configural or holistic representations generally used to recognize individuals. There may also be face-specific resources, limiting the number of faces that can be simultaneously encoded and enabling faces to be ignored only when other faces are processed.

Basic facial expressions such as fear and happiness appear to be categorized and identified rapidly (e.g., Batty & Taylor, 2003; see Table 11.1). Physiological evidence from facial EMG and fear-conditioning paradigms, behavioral evidence from affective priming studies, and neuropsychological evidence from patients with blindsight suggest that, at the very least, people are able to distinguish between positive and negative facial expressions of which they are subjectively unaware. Much of the research included in the review suggests that fearful faces are rapidly, preferentially, nonconsciously, and mandatorily registered by the amygdala, with little or no reliance upon attentional resources.

However, some evidence suggests that this may not be the case, at least not for some individuals (e.g., those that have low levels of anxiety) and for some tasks (e.g., when a competing task has a high attentional load or when conscious awareness is measured objectively). Information from faces that are not consciously perceived or attended may be conveyed via subcortical pathways to the amygdala. This information may only be sufficient to discriminate emotional faces from unemotional faces (Williams et al., 2004) or more arousing facial expressions from less arousing facial expressions (Killgore & Yurgelun-Todd, 2004), with attention needed for more precise (Anderson et al., 2003) and perhaps conscious (Pessoa, 2005) discrimination.

This chapter has focused on evaluating whether face processing is automatic. A separate question is whether faces, as significant stimuli, have a preferential bias to engage mechanisms of selective attention. For instance, some evidence indicates that faces may "capture" attention (Theeuwes & Van der Stigchel, 2006), which would suggest that visual attention would be preferentially directed toward faces rather than other stimuli. Also, some evidence suggests that faces may also "retain" attention (Bindemann, Burton, Hooge, Jenkins, & de Haan, 2005). Top-down factors affecting the allocation of selective attention to emotionally salient stimuli are likely to involve frontoparietal attention networks (for reviews see Compton, 2003; Palermo & Rhodes, 2007; Vuilleumier, 2005a).

It is not controversial to decompose "face processing" into various components, such as detection, categorization, and identification; indeed, these types of information are extracted from faces by different, but interacting, brain areas as a function of time. Similarly, we also need to delineate the various components of "automaticity" and evaluate each one separately with regard to each component of face processing. Alas, this means that there is no single "yes-or-no" answer to the question we posed at the outset: "Is face processing automatic?"

ACKNOWLEDGMENTS

We are grateful to Andy Calder and Max Coltheart for very helpful suggestions on earlier drafts of this chapter. The chapter was based in part on Palermo and Rhodes (2007). http://dx.doi.org/10.1016/j.neuropsychologia (accessed 4/25/2006).

NOTES

1. Technically, this structure is known as the "amygdaloid complex" because it is composed of a number of nuclei that are organized into a number of divisions that appear to have different functions and connections (see Davis & Whalen, 2001; Holland & Gallagher, 2004). There are two amygdalae—one in each hemisphere. Both appear to be involved in processing facial expressions; differences between the two are not clearly understood at this stage (see Adolphs, 2002b; Zald, 2003, for reviews on laterality). For brevity, we will use the term "amygdala."
2. Attentional blink tasks may not be measuring relatively early perceptual processes but rather later, postperceptual stages of processing or consolidation into working memory (see Marois & Ivanoff, 2005).

REFERENCES

Adolphs, R. (2002a). Neural systems for recognizing emotion. *Current Opinion in Neurobiology, 12,* 169–177.

Adolphs, R. (2002b). Recognizing emotion from facial expressions: Psychological and neurological mechanisms. *Behavioral and Cognitive Neuroscience Reviews, 1*(1), 21–62.

Adolphs, R., Gosselin, F., Buchanan, T. W., Tranel, D., Schyns, P. G., & Damasio, A. (2005). A mechanism for impaired fear recognition after amygdala damage. *Nature, 433,* 68–72.

Adolphs, R., Tranel, D., & Damasio, H. (2001). Emotion recognition from faces and prosody following temporal lobectomy. *Neuropsychology, 15*(3), 396–404.

Adolphs, R., Tranel, D., Damasio, H., & Damasio, A. R. (1995). Fear and the human amygdala. *Journal of Neuroscience, 15,* 5879–5892.

Adolphs, R., Tranel, D., Hamann, S., Young, A. W., Calder, A. J., Anderson, A., et al. (1999). Recognition of facial emotion in nine subjects with bilateral amygdala damage. *Neuropsychologia, 37,* 1111–1117.

Allison, T., Ginter, H., McCarthy, G., Nobre, A. C., Puce, A., Luby, M., et al. (1994). Face recognition in human extrastriate cortex. *Journal of Neurophysiology, 71*(2), 821–825.

Anderson, A. K. (2005). Affective influences on the attentional dynamics supporting awareness. *Journal of Experimental Psychology: General, 134*(2), 258–281.

Anderson, A. K., Christoff, K., Panitz, D., De Rosa, E., & Gabrieli, J. D. E. (2003). Neural correlates of the automatic processing of threat facial signals. *Journal of Neuroscience, 23*(13), 5627–5633.

Anderson, A. K., & Phelps, E. A. (2001). Lesions of the human amygdala impair enhanced perception of emotionally salient events. *Nature, 411,* 305–309.

Anderson, A. K., Spencer, D. D., Fulbright, R. K., & Phelps, E. A. (2000). Contribution of the anteromedial temporal lobes to the evaluation of facial emotion. *Neuropsychology, 14*(4), 526–536.

Awh, E., Serences, J., Laurey, P., Dhaliwal, H., van der Jagt, T., & Dassonville, P. (2004). Evidence against a central bottleneck during the attentional blink: Multiple channels for configural and featural processing. *Cognitive Psychology, 48*(1), 95–126.

Bargh, J. A. (1997). The automaticity of everyday life. In R. S. Wyer (Ed.), *Advances in social cognition: Vol. 10. The automaticity of everyday life* (pp. 1–61). Mahwah, NJ: Lawrence Erlbaum Associates.

Batty, M., & Taylor, M. J. (2003). Early processing of the six basic facial emotional expressions. *Cognitive Brain Research, 17*(3), 613–620.

Bauer, R. (1984). Automatic recognition of names and faces: A neuropsychological application of the guilty knowledge test. *Neuropsychologia, 22,* 457–469.

Bentin, S., Allison, T., Puce, A., Perez, E., & McCarthy, G. (1996). Electrophysiological studies of face perception in humans. *Journal of Cognitive Neuroscience, 8,* 551–565.

Bentin, S., & Carmel, D. (2002). Accounts for the N170 face-effect: A reply to Rossion, Curran, & Gauthier. *Cognition, 85,* 197–202.

Bentin, S., & Deouell, L. Y. (2000). Structural encoding and identification in face processing: ERP evidence for separate mechanisms. *Cognitive Neuropsychology, 17,* 35–54.

Berson, D. M., & Stein, J. J. (1995). Retinotopic organization of the superior colliculus in relation to the retinal distribution of afferent ganglion cells. *Visual Neuroscience, 12*(4), 671–686.

Bindemann, M., Burton, A. M., Hooge, I. T. C., Jenkins, R., & de Haan, E. H. F. (2005). Faces retain attention. *Psychonomic Bulletin & Review, 12*(6), 1048–1053.

Bindemann, M., Burton, A. M., & Jenkins, R. (2008). Capacity limits for face processing. *Cognition, 107,* 718–728.

Bishop, S. J., Duncan, J., & Lawrence, A. D. (2004). State anxiety modulation of the amygdala response to unattended threat-related stimuli. *Journal of Neuroscience, 24*(46), 10364–10368.

Blake, R., & Logothetis, N. K. (2002). Visual competition. *Nature Reviews Neuroscience, 3*(1), 13–23.

Boutet, I., & Chaudhuri, A. (2001). Multistability of overlapped face stimuli is dependent upon orientation. *Perception, 30,* 743–753.

Boutet, I., Gentes-Hawn, A., & Chaudhuri, A. (2002). The influence of attention on holistic face encoding. *Cognition, 84,* 321–341.

Braun, J., & Julesz, B. (1998). Withdrawing attention at little or no cost: Detection and discrimination tasks. *Perception & Psychophysics, 60*(1), 1–23.

Braun, J., & Sagi, D. (1990). Vision outside the focus of attention. *Perception & Psychophysics, 48*(1), 45–58.

Brown, V., Huey, D., & Findlay, J. M. (1997). Face detection in peripheral vision: Do faces pop out? *Perception, 26,* 1555–1570.

Bullier, J. (2001). Integrated model of visual processing. *Brain Research Reviews, 36,* 96–107.

Buttle, H., & Raymond, J. E. (2003). High familiarity enhances visual change detection for face stimuli. *Perception & Psychophysics, 65*(8), 1296–1306.

Carmel, D., & Bentin, S. (2002). Domain specificity versus expertise: Factors influencing distinct processing of faces. *Cognition, 83*, 1–29.

Cauquil, A. S., Edmonds, G. E., & Taylor, M. J. (2000). Is the face-sensitive N170 the only ERP not affected by selective attention? *NeuroReport, 11*, 2167–2171.

Compton, R. (2003). The interface between emotion and attention: A review of evidence from psychology and neuroscience. *Behavioral and Cognitive Neuroscience Reviews, 2*(2), 115–129.

Cowey, A. (2004). The 30th Sir Fredrick Bartlett lecture: Fact, artifact, and myth about blindsight. *Quarterly Journal of Experimental Psychology, 57A*(4), 577–609.

Davis, M., & Whalen, P. (2001). The amygdala: Vigilance and emotion. *Molecular Psychiatry, 6*, 13–34.

Dawkins, R. (1999). *Unweaving the rainbow: Science, delusion and the appetite for wonder.* London: Penguin.

de Gelder, B., Vroomen, J., Pourtois, G., & Weiskrantz, L. (1999). Nonconscious recognition of affect in the absence of striate cortex. *NeuroReport, 10*, 3759–3763.

de Haan, E. H. F., Young, A. W., & Newcombe, F. (1987). Face recognition without awareness. *Cognitive Neuropsychology, 4*, 385–415.

Dimberg, U., Thunberg, M., & Elmehed, K. (2000). Unconscious facial reactions to emotional facial expressions. *Psychological Science, 11*(1), 86–89.

Downing, P., Liu, J., & Kanwisher, N. (2001). Testing cognitive models of visual attention with fMRI and MEG. *Neuropsychologia, 39*(12), 1329–1342.

Eastwood, J. D., Smilek, D., & Merikle, P. M. (2001). Differential attentional guidance by unattended faces expressing positive and negative emotion. *Perception & Psychophysics, 63*, 1004–1013.

Eger, E., Jednyak, A., Iwaki, T., & Skrandies, W. (2003). Rapid extraction of emotional expression: Evidence from evoked potential fields during brief presentation of face stimuli. *Neuropsychologia, 41*, 808–817.

Eimer, M. (2000a). Attentional modulations of event-related brain potentials sensitive to faces. *Cognitive Neuropsychology, 17*, 103–116.

Eimer, M. (2000b). The face-specific N170 component reflects late stages in the structural encoding of faces. *NeuroReport, 11*, 2319–2324.

Eimer, M., & Holmes, A. (2002). An ERP study on the time course of emotional face processing. *NeuroReport, 13*, 427–431.

Eimer, M., & Holmes, A. (2007). Event-related brain potential correlates of emotional face processing. *Neuropsychologia, 45*, 15–31.

Eimer, M., Holmes, A., & McGlone, F. P. (2003). The role of spatial attention in the processing of facial expression: An ERP study of rapid brain responses to six basic emotions. *Cognitive, Affective & Behavioral Neuroscience, 3*(2), 97–110.

Esslen, M., Pascual-Marqui, R. D., Hell, D., Kochi, D., & Lehmann, D. (2004). Brain areas and the time course of emotional processing. *NeuroImage, 21*(4), 1189–1203.

Esteves, F., Dimberg, U., & Öhman, A. (1994). Automatically elicited fear: Conditioned skin conductance responses to masked facial expressions. *Cognition and Emotion, 8*, 393–413.

Etkin, A., Klemenhagen, K. C., Dudman, J. T., Rogan, M. T., Hen, R., Kandel, E. R., et al. (2004). Individual differences in trait anxiety predict the response of the basolateral amygdala to unconsciously processed fearful faces. *Neuron, 44*, 1043–1055.

Farah, M. J. (2000). *The cognitive neuroscience of vision.* Boston: Blackwell Publishers.

Fox, E. (2002). Processing emotional facial expressions: The role of anxiety and awareness. *Cognitive, Affective & Behavioral Neuroscience, 2*(1), 52–63.

Fox, E., & Damjanovic, L. (2006). The eyes are sufficient to produce a threat superiority effect. *Emotion, 6*, 534–539.

Fox, E., Lester, V., Russo, R., Bowles, R. J., Pichler, A., & Dutton, K. (2000). Facial expressions of emotion: Are angry faces detected more efficiently? *Cognition and Emotion, 14*, 61–92.

Furey, M. L., Tanskanen, T., Beauchamp, M. S., Avikainen, S., Uuteal, K., Hari, R., et al. (2006). Dissociation of face-selective cortical responses by attention. *Proceedings of the National Academy of Sciences USA, 103*(4), 1065–1070.

Green, M. J., & Phillips, M. L. (2004). Social threat perception and the evolution of paranoia. *Neuroscience and Biobehavioral Reviews, 28*, 333–342.

Gur, R. C., Sara, R., Hagendoorn, M., Marom, O., Hughett, P., Macy, L., et al. (2002). A method for obtaining three-dimensional facial expressions and its standardization for use in neurocognitive studies. *Journal of Neuroscience Methods, 115*, 137–143.

Halgren, E., Baudena, P., Heit, G., Clarke, J. M., & Marinkovic, K. (1994). Spatiotemporal stages in face and word processing. 1. Depth-recorded potentials in the human occipital, temporal and parietal lobes. *Journal of Physiology, 88*, 1–50.

Halgren, E., Raij, T., Marinkovic, K., Jousmaeki, V., & Hari, R. (2000). Cognitive response profile of the human fusiform face area as determined by MEG. *Cerebral Cortex, 10*(1), 69–81.

Hamann, S., & Canli, T. (2004). Individual differences in emotion processing. *Current Opinion in Neurobiology, 14*, 233–238.

Hannula, D. E., Simons, D. J., & Cohen, N. J. (2005). Imaging implicit perception: Promise and pitfalls. *Nature Reviews Neuroscience, 6*, 247–255.

Hansen, C. H., & Hansen, R. D. (1988). Finding the face in the crowd: An anger superiority effect. *Journal of Personality and Social Psychology, 54*, 917–924.

Haxby, J. V., Hoffman, E. A., & Gobbini, M. I. (2000). The distributed human neural system for face perception. *Trends in Cognitive Sciences, 4*, 223–233.

Haxby, J. V., Hoffman, E. A., & Gobbini, M. I. (2002). Human neural systems for face recognition and social communication. *Biological Psychiatry, 51*, 59–67.

Heisz, J. J., Watter, S., & Shedden, J. M. (2006). Automatic face identity encoding at the N170. *Vision Research, 46*(28), 4604–4614.

Hershler, O., & Hochstein, S. (2005). At first sight: A high-level pop out effect for faces. *Vision Research, 45*, 1707–1724.

Hershler, O., & Hochstein, S. (2006). With a careful look: Still no low-level confound to face pop-out. *Vision Research, 46*(18), 3028–3035.

Holland, P. C., & Gallagher, M. (2004). Amygdala-frontal interactions and reward expectancy. *Current Opinion in Neurobiology, 14*, 148–155.

Holmes, A., Vuilleumier, P., & Eimer, M. (2003). The processing of emotional facial expression is gated by spatial attention: Evidence from event-related brain potentials. *Cognitive Brain Research, 16*, 174–184.

Horstmann, G., & Bauland, A. (2006). Search asymmetries with real faces: Testing the anger-superiority effect. *Emotion, 6*(2), 193–207.

Huang, L., & Pashler, H. (2005). Attention capacity and task difficulty in visual search. *Cognition, 94*, B101–B111.

Itier, R. J., & Taylor, M. J. (2004). N170 or N1? Spatiotemporal differences between object and face processing using ERPs. *Cerebral Cortex, 14*(2), 132–142.

Jackson, M. C., & Raymond, J. E. (2006). The role of attention and familiarity in face identification. *Perception & Psychophysics, 68*(4), 543–557.

Jacques, C., & Rossion, B. (2004). Concurrent processing reveals competition between visual representations of faces. *NeuroReport, 15*, 2417–2421.

Jacques, C., & Rossion, B. (2006a). The speed of individual face categorization. *Psychological Science, 17*(6), 485–491.

Jacques, C., & Rossion, B. (2006b). The time course of visual competition to the presentation of centrally fixated faces. *Journal of Vision, 6*, 154–162.

Jacques, C., & Rossion, B. (2007). Electrophysiological evidence for temporal dissociation between spatial attention and sensory competition during human face processing. *Cerebral Cortex, 17*(5), 1055–1065.

Jeffreys, D. A. (1989). A face-responsive potential recorded from the human scalp. *Experimental Brain Research, 78*(1), 193–202.

Jenkins, R., Lavie, N., & Driver, J. (2003). Ignoring famous faces: Category-specific dilution of distractor interference. *Perception & Psychophysics, 65*(2), 298–309.

Kanwisher, N., McDermott, J., & Chun, M. M. (1997). The fusiform face area: A module in human extrastriate cortex specialized for face perception. *Journal of Neuroscience, 17*, 4302–4311.

Kawasaki, H., Adolphs, R., Kaufman, O., Damasio, H., Damasio, A. R., Granner, M., et al. (2001). Single-neuron responses to emotional visual stimuli recorded in human ventral prefrontal cortex. *Nature Neuroscience, 4*(1), 15–16.

Khurana, B., Smith, W. C., & Baker, M. T. (2000). Not to be and then to be: Visual representation of ignored unfamiliar faces. *Journal of Experimental Psychology: Human Perception and Performance, 26*, 246–263.

Killgore, W. D. S., & Yurgelun-Todd, D. A. (2004). Activation of the amygdala and anterior cingulate during nonconscious processing of sad versus happy faces. *NeuroImage, 21*(4), 1215–1223.

Krolak-Salmon, P., Fischer, H., Vighetto, A., & Mauguiére, F. (2001). Processing of facial emotional expression: Spatiotemporal data as assessed by scalp event-related potentials. *European Journal of Neuroscience, 13*, 987–994.

Krolak-Salmon, P., Hénaff, M.-A., Isnard, J., Tallon-Baudry, C., Guénot, M., Vighetto, A., et al. (2003). An attention modulated response to disgust in human ventral anterior insula. *Annals of Neurology, 53*, 446–453.

Krolak-Salmon, P., Hénaff, M.-A., Vighetto, A., Bertrand, O., & Mauguiére, F. (2004). Early amygdala reaction to fear spreading in occipital, temporal, and frontal cortex: A depth electrode ERP study in humans. *Neuron, 42*, 665–676.

Kuehn, S. M., & Jolicœur, P. (1994). Impact of quality of the image, orientation, and similarity of the stimuli on visual search for faces. *Perception, 23*, 95–122.

Lavie, N. (1995). Perceptual load as a necessary condition for selective attention. *Journal of Experimental Psychology: Human Perception & Performance, 21*, 451–468.

Lavie, N. (2000). Selective attention and cognitive control: Dissociating attentional functions through different types of load. In S. Monsell & J. Driver (Eds.), *Control and cognitive processes: Attention and performance XVIII* (pp. 175–194). Cambridge, MA: MIT Press.

Lavie, N., Ro, T., & Russell, C. (2003). The role of perceptual load in processing distractor faces. *Psychological Science, 14*(5), 510–515.

LeDoux, J. E. (1996). *The emotional brain: The mysterious underpinnings of emotional life.* New York: Simon and Schuster.

LeDoux, J. E. (1998). Fear and the brain: Where have we been, and where are we going? *Biological Psychiatry, 44*, 1229–1238.

Liddell, B. J., Brown, K. J., Hemp, A. H., Barton, M. J., Das, P., Peduto, A., et al. (2005). A direct brainstem-amygdala-cortical "alarm" system for subliminal signals of fear. *NeuroImage, 24*, 235–243.

Liu, J., Harris, A., & Kanwisher, N. (2002). Stages of processing in face perception: An MEG study. *Nature Neuroscience, 5*(9), 910–916.

Liu, L., Ioannides, A. A., & Streit, M. (1999). Single trial analysis of neurophysiological correlates of the recognition of complex objects and facial expressions of emotion. *Brain Topography, 11*, 291–303.

Loffler, G., Gordon, G. E., Wilkinson, F., Goren, D., & Wilson, H. R. (2005). Configural masking of faces: Evidence for high-level interactions in face perception. *Vision Research, 45*(17), 2287–2297.

Luck, S. J., & Vecera, S. P. (2002). Attention. In H. Pashler & S. Yantis (Eds.), *Steven's handbook of experimental psychology, Vol. 1, Sensation and perception* (3rd ed., pp. 235–286). New York: John Wiley & Sons.

Lundqvist, D., Esteves, F., & Öhman, A. (1999). The face of wrath: Critical features for conveying facial threat. *Cognition and Emotion, 13,* 691–711.

Luo, Q., Holroyd, T., Jones, M., Hendler, T., & Blair, J. (2007). Neural dynamics for facial threat processing as revealed by gamma band synchronization using MEG. *NeuroImage, 34,* 839–847.

Mack, A., & Rock, I. (1998). *Inattentional blindness.* Cambridge, MA: MIT Press.

Marois, R., & Ivanoff, J. (2005). Capacity limits of information processing in the brain. *Trends in Cognitive Sciences, 9*(6), 296–305.

Maurer, D., Le Grand, R., & Mondloch, C. J. (2002). The many faces of configural processing. *Trends in Cognitive Sciences, 6,* 255–260.

Maxwell, J. S., & Davidson, R. J. (2004). Unequally masked: Indexing differences in the perceptual salience of "unseen" facial expressions. *Cognition and Emotion, 18*(8), 1009–1026.

McCarthy, G. (2000). Physiological studies of face processing in humans. In M. S. Gazzaniga (Ed.), *The new cognitive neurosciences.* Cambridge, MA: Bradford Books/MIT Press.

Mineka, S., & Öhman, A. (2002). Phobias and preparedness: The selective, automatic, and encapsulated nature of fear. *Biological Psychiatry, 52*(19), 927–937.

Mitchell, D. G. V., Nakic, M., Fridberg, D., Kamel, N., Pine, D. S., & Blair, R. J. R. (2007). The impact of processing load on emotion. *NeuroImage, 34,* 1299–1309.

Morris, J. S., de Gelder, B., Weiskrantz, L., & Dolan, R. J. (2001). Differential extrageniculostriate and amygdala responses to presentation of emotional faces in a cortically blind field. *Brain, 124,* 1241–1252.

Morris, J. S., Öhman, A., & Dolan, R. J. (1998). Conscious and unconscious emotional learning in the human amygdala. *Nature, 393,* 467–470.

Morris, J. S., Öhman, A., & Dolan, R. J. (1999). A subcortical pathway to the right amygdala mediating "unseen" fear. *Proceedings of the National Academy of Science, 96,* 1680–1685.

Most, S. B., Chun, M. M., Johnson, M. R., & Kiehl, K. A. (2006). Attentional modulation of the amygdala varies with personality. *NeuroImage, 31,* 934–944.

Murphy, S. T., & Zajonc, R. B. (1993). Affect, cognition, and awareness: Affective priming with optimal and suboptimal stimulus exposures. *Journal of Personality & Social Psychology, 64*(5), 723–739.

Nothdurft, H. C. (1993). Faces and facial expressions do not pop out. *Perception, 22,* 1287–1298.

O'Craven, K. M., Downing, P. E., & Kanwisher, N. (1999). fMRI evidence for objects as the units of attentional selection. *Nature, 401,* 584–587.

Öhman, A. (1993). Fear and anxiety as emotional phenomenon: Clinical phenomenology, evolutionary perspectives and information processing mechanisms. In M. Lewis & J. M. Haviland (Eds.), *Handbook of emotions* (pp. 511–536). New York: Guildford Press.

Öhman, A. (1997). As fast as the blink of an eye: Evolutionary preparedness for preattentive processing of threat. In P. J. Lang, R. F. Simons, & M. T. Balaban (Eds.), *Attention and orienting: Sensory and motivational processes* (pp. 165–184). Mahwah, NJ: Lawrence Erlbaum Associates.

Öhman, A. (2002). Automaticity and the amygdala: Nonconscious responses to emotional faces. *Current Directions in Psychological Science, 11,* 62–66.

Öhman, A., Esteves, F., & Soares, J. F. (1995). Preparedness and preattentive associative learning: Electrodermal conditioning to masked stimuli. *Journal of Psychophysiology, 9*(2), 99–108.

Öhman, A., Lundqvist, D., & Esteves, F. (2001). The face in the crowd revisited: A threat advantage with schematic stimuli. *Journal of Personality & Social Psychology, 80*, 381–396.

Öhman, A., & Mineka, S. (2001). Fears, phobias, and preparedness: Toward an evolved module of fear and fear learning. *Psychological Review, 108*(3), 483–522.

Oram, M. W., & Perrett, D. I. (1992). Time course of neural responses discriminating different views of the face and head. *Journal of Neurophysiology, 68*, 70–84.

Palermo, R., & Rhodes, G. (2002). The influence of divided attention on holistic face perception. *Cognition, 82*(3), 225–257.

Palermo, R., & Rhodes, G. (2007). Are you always on my mind? A review of how face perception and attention interact. *Neuropsychologia, 45*, 75–92.

Pasley, B. N., Mayes, L. C., & Schultz, R. T. (2004). Subcortical discrimination of unperceived objects during binocular rivalry. *Neuron, 42*, 163–172

Pegna, A. J., Khateb, A., Lazeyras, F., & Seghier, M. L. (2004). Discriminating emotional faces without primary visual cortices involves the right amygdala. *Nature Neuroscience, 8*, 24–25.

Pegna, A. J., Khateb, A., Michel, C. M., & Landis, T. (2004). Visual recognition of faces, objects, and words using degraded stimuli: Where and when it occurs. *Human Brain Mapping, 22*, 300–311.

Pessoa, L. (2005). To what extent are emotional visual stimuli processed without attention and awareness? *Current Opinion in Neurobiology, 15*, 1–9.

Pessoa, L., Japee, S., Sturman, D., & Ungerleider, L. G. (2006). Target visibility and visual awareness modulate amygdala responses to fearful faces. *Cerebral Cortex, 16*, 366–375.

Pessoa, L., Japee, S., & Ungerleider, L. G. (2005). Visual awareness and the detection of fearful faces. *Emotion, 5*, 243–247.

Pessoa, L., McKenna, M., Gutierrez, E., & Ungerleider, L. G. (2002). Neural processing of facial expressions requires attention. *Proceedings of the National Academy of Sciences, 99*, 11458–11463.

Pessoa, L., Padmala, S., & Morland, T. (2005). Fate of unattended fearful faces in the amygdala is determined by both attentional resources and cognitive modulation. *NeuroImage, 15*, 249–255.

Pessoa, L., & Ungerleider, L. G. (2003). Neuroimaging studies of attention and the processing of emotion-laden stimuli. *Progress in Brain Research, 144*, 171–182.

Phillips, M. L., Williams, L. M., Heining, M., Herba, C. M., Russell, T., Andrew, C., et al. (2004). Differential neural responses to overt and covert presentations of facial expressions of fear and disgust. *NeuroImage, 21*, 1484–1496.

Pizzagalli, D. A., Lehmann, D., Hendrick, A. M., Regard, M., Pascual-Marqui, R. D., & Davidson, R. J. (2002). Affective judgments of faces modulate early activity (~160 ms) within the fusiform gyri. *NeuroImage, 16*, 663–677.

Pizzagalli, D. A., Regard, M., & Lehmann, D. (1999). Rapid emotional face processing in the human right and left brain hemispheres: An ERP study. *NeuroReport, 10*, 2691–2698.

Pourtois, G., Grandjean, D., Sander, D., & Vuilleumier, P. (2004). Electrophysiological correlates of rapid spatial orienting towards fearful faces. *Cerebral Cortex, 14*(6), 619–633.

Purcell, D. G., & Stewart, A. L. (1988). The face-detection effect: Configuration enhances detection. *Perception & Psychophysics, 43*, 355–366.

Purcell, D. G., Stewart, A. L., & Skov, R. B. (1996). It takes a confounded face to pop out of a crowd. *Perception, 25*, 1091–1108.

Raymond, J. E., Shapiro, K. L., & Arnell, K. M. (1992). Temporary suppression of visual processing in an RSVP task: An attentional blink? *Journal of Experimental Psychology: Human Perception and Performance, 18*, 849–860.

Reddy, L., Reddy, L., & Koch, C. (2006). Face identification in the near-absence of focal attention. *Vision Research, 46,* 2336–2343.

Reddy, L., Wilken, P., & Koch, C. (2004). Face-gender discrimination is possible in the near-absence of attention. *Journal of Vision, 4,* 106–117.

Rees, G., Kreiman, G., & Koch, C. (2002). Neural correlates of consciousness in humans. *Nature Reviews Neuroscience, 3,* 261–270.

Reinitz, M. T., Morrissey, J., & Demb, J. (1994). Role of attention in face encoding. *Journal of Experimental Psychology: Learning Memory & Cognition, 20,* 161–168.

Robinson, M. D. (1998). Running from William James' bear: A review of preattentive mechanisms and their contributions to emotional experience. *Cognition and Emotion, 12*(5), 667–696.

Rossion, B., Curran, T., & Gauthier, I. (2002). A defense of the subordinate level-expertise account for the N170 component. *Cognition, 85*(2), 189–196.

Rotteveel, M., de Groot, P., Geutskens, A., & Phaf, R. H. (2001). Stronger suboptimal than optimal affective priming? *Emotion, 1*(4), 348–364.

Rousselet, G. A., Macé, M. J.-M., & Fabre-Thorpe, M. (2003). Is it an animal? Is it a human face? Fast processing in upright and inverted natural scenes. *Journal of Vision, 3,* 440–455.

Schneider, W., & Chein, J. M. (2003). Controlled and automatic processing: Behavior, theory, and biological mechanisms. *Cognitive Science, 27,* 525–559.

Sperling, G., & Melchner, M. J. (1978). The attention operating characteristic: Examples from visual search. *Science, 202,* 315–318.

Stone, A., & Valentine, T. (2003). Viewpoint: Perspectives on prosopagnosia and models of face recognition. *Cortex, 39,* 31–40.

Stone, A., & Valentine, T. (2004). Better the devil you know? Nonconscious processing of identity and affect of famous faces. *Psychonomic Bulletin & Review, 11*(3), 469–474.

Stone, A., Valentine, T., & Davies, R. (2001). Face recognition and emotional valence: Processing without awareness by neurologically intact participants does not simulate covert recognition in prosopagnosia. *Cognitive, Affective & Behavioral Neuroscience, 1,* 183–191.

Streit, M., Dammers, J., Simsek-Kraues, S., Brinkmeyer, J., Wölwer, W., & Ioannides, A. (2003). Time course of regional brain activations during facial emotion recognition in humans. *Neuroscience Letters, 342*(1–2), 101–104.

Streit, M., Ioannides, A., Liu, L., Wölwer, W., Dammers, J., Gross, J., et al. (1999). Neurophysiological correlates of the recognition of facial expressions of emotion as revealed by magnetoencephalography. *Cognitive Brain Research, 7,* 481–491.

Streit, M., Wölwer, W., Brinkmeyer, J., Ihl, J., & Gaebel, W. (2000). Electrophysiological correlates of emotional and structural face processing in humans. *Neuroscience Letters, 278,* 13–16.

Sugase, Y., Yamane, S., Ueno, S., & Kawano, K. (1999). Global and fine information coded by single neurons in the temporal visual cortex. *Nature, 400,* 869–872.

Suslow, T., Ohrmann, P., Bauer, J., Rauch, A. V., Schwindt, W., Arolt, V., et al. (2006). Amygdala activation during masked presentation of emotional faces predicts conscious detection of threat-related faces. *Brain and Cognition, 61,* 243–248.

Suzuki, S., & Cavanagh, P. (1995). Facial organization blocks access to low-level features: An object inferiority effect. *Journal of Experimental Psychology: Human Perception and Performance, 21,* 901–913.

Tanaka, J. W., & Farah, M. J. (1993). Parts and wholes in face recognition. *Quarterly Journal of Experimental Psychology, 46A,* 225–245.

Tanaka, J. W., Kay, J. B., Grinnell, E., Stansfield, B., & Szechter, L. (1998). Face recognition in young children: When the whole is greater than the sum of its parts. *Visual Cognition, 5,* 479–496.

Taylor, J. G., & Fragopanagos, N. F. (2005). The interaction of attention and emotion. *Neural Networks, 18,* 353–369.

Theeuwes, J., & Van der Stigchel, S. (2006). Faces capture attention: Evidence from inhibition of return. *Visual Cognition, 13*(6), 657–665.

Tipples, J., Atkinson, A. P., & Young, A. W. (2002). The eyebrow frown: A salient social signal. *Emotion, 2*(3), 288–296.

Tong, F., & Nakayama, K. (1999). Robust representations for faces: Evidence from visual search. *Journal of Experimental Psychology: Human Perception and Performance, 25,* 1–20.

Tranel, D., & Damasio, A. R. (1985). Knowledge without awareness: An autonomic index of facial recognition by prosopagnosics. *Science, 228,* 1453–1454.

Treisman, A., & Gelade, G. (1980). A feature-integration theory of attention. *Cognitive Psychology, 12,* 97–136.

Tsao, D. Y., Freiwald, W. A., Tootell, R. B. H., & Livingstone, M. S. (2006). A cortical region consisting entirely of face-selective cells. *Science, 311,* 670–674.

VanRullen, R. (2006). On second glance: Still no high-level pop-out effect for faces. *Vision Research, 46*(18), 3017–3027.

VanRullen, R., Reddy, L., & Koch, C. (2004). Visual search and dual tasks reveal two distinct attentional resources. *Journal of Cognitive Neuroscience, 16,* 4–14.

Vuilleumier, P. (2000). Faces call for attention: Evidence from patients with visual extinction. *Neuropsychologia, 38,* 693–700.

Vuilleumier, P. (2002). Facial expression and selective attention. *Current Opinion in Psychiatry, 15,* 291–300.

Vuilleumier, P. (2005a). How brains beware: Neural mechanisms of emotional attention. *Trends in Cognitive Sciences, 9*(12), 585–594.

Vuilleumier, P. (2005b). Staring fear in the face. *Nature, 433,* 22–23.

Vuilleumier, P., Armony, J. L., Clarke, K., Husain, M., Driver, J., & Dolan, R. J. (2002). Neural responses to emotional faces with and without awareness: Event-related fMRI in a parietal patient with visual extinction and spatial neglect. *Neuropsychologia, 40,* 2156–2166.

Vuilleumier, P., Armony, J. L., Driver, J., & Dolan, R. J. (2001). Effects of attention and emotion on face processing in the human brain: An event-related fMRI study. *Neuron, 30,* 829–841.

Vuilleumier, P., Armony, J. L., Driver, J., & Dolan, R. J. (2003). Distinct spatial frequency sensitivities for processing faces and emotional expressions. *Nature Neuroscience, 6*(6), 624–631.

Vuilleumier, P., & Schwartz, S. (2001). Emotional facial expressions capture attention. *Neurology, 56*(2), 153–158.

Whalen, P. J., Kagan, J., Cook, R. G., Davis, C., Kim, H., Polis, S., et al. (2004). Human amygdala responsivity to masked fearful eye whites. *Science, 306,* 2061.

Whalen, P. J., Rauch, S. L., Etcoff, N. L., McInerney, S. C., Lee, M. B., & Jenike, M. A. (1998). Masked presentations of emotional facial expressions modulates amygdala activity without explicit knowledge. *Journal of Neuroscience, 18,* 411–418.

Williams, M. A., McGlone, F., Abbott, D. F., & Mattingley, J. B. (2005). Differential amygdala responses to happy and fearful facial expressions depend on selective attention. *NeuroImage, 24*(2), 417–425.

Williams, M. A., Morris, A. P., McGlone, F., Abbott, D. F., & Mattingley, J. B. (2004). Amygdala responses to fearful and happy facial expressions under conditions of binocular suppression. *Journal of Neuroscience, 24*(12), 2898–2904.

Williams, M. A., Moss, S. A., Bradshaw, J. L., & Mattingley, J. B. (2005). Look at me, I'm smiling: Visual search for threatening and nonthreatening facial expressions. *Visual Cognition, 12*(1), 29–50.

Wojciulik, E., Kanwisher, N., & Driver, J. (1998). Covert visual attention modulates face-specific activity in the human fusiform gyrus: fMRI study. *Journal of Neurophysiology, 79,* 1574–1578.

Wolfe, J. M. (1998). What can 1 million trials tell us about visual search? *Psychological Science, 9,* 33–39.

Wong, P. S., & Root, J. C. (2003). Dynamic variations in affective priming. *Consciousness and Cognition, 12,* 147–168.

Yamamoto, S., & Kashikura, K. (1999). Speed of face recognition in humans: An event-related potentials study. *NeuroReport, 10*(17), 3531–3534.

Young, A. W., de Haan, E. H. F., Newcombe, F., & Hay, D. C. (1990). Facial neglect. *Neuropsychologia, 28,* 391–415.

Young, A. W., Ellis, A. W., Flude, B. M., McWeeny, K. H., & Hay, D. C. (1986). Face-name interference. *Journal of Experimental Psychology: Human Perception and Performance, 12,* 466–475.

Young, A. W., Hellawell, D., & Hay, D. C. (1987). Configural information in face perception. *Perception, 16,* 747–759.

Zald, D. H. (2003). The human amygdala and the emotional evaluation of sensory stimuli. *Brain Research Review, 41,* 88–123.

12

Visuospatial Representation of Number Magnitude

CARLO UMILTÀ, KONSTANTINOS PRIFTIS, and MARCO ZORZI

NUMBERS AND SPACE

According to an influential model proposed by Dehaene (i.e., the triple code model; e.g., Dehaene, 1992), numbers are mentally represented in three ways. One is the visual-Arabic code, in which numbers are represented as strings of visual forms (e.g., <21452>). In the verbal code, numbers are represented as sequences of number-words syntactically organized (e.g., <two-thousand four-hundred and fifty-two>). In addition to the visual-Arabic code and the verbal code, Dehaene's model postulates the existence of an analogical code, based on which numbers are represented as local activations (points or regions) along a continuous, analogue *mental number line* (MNL; e.g., Dehaene, 2003; also see Gallistel & Gelman, 1992, 2000, for a different view of the MNL).

In people who read from left to right, the MNL is spatially oriented from left to right, with small-magnitude numbers represented on the left-hand side of the line and numbers of larger magnitude represented on the right-hand side. Of these three codes, the spatial one would be at the core of number meaning. That is, the semantic value of a number, its magnitude, would be conveyed by its position on the MNL.

The intuition that numerical magnitude is spatially organized so as to give rise to a kind of MNL dates back to Galton's (1880) research on mental imagery. From this work it emerged that the image of a horizontal left-to-right oriented line was the more frequently reported metaphor, even though participants less frequently reported other metaphors. Galton's findings were later confirmed by Seron, Pesenti, Noel, Deloche, and Corpet (1992). Meanwhile, the notion of a spatially organized representation of numerical magnitude had already been renewed by Restle (1970) on the basis of two phenomena, known as *distance effect* and *size effect* (Moyer & Landauer, 1967).

As with many other stimulus dimensions, it is easier and quicker to select the larger of two numbers when they are numerically dissimilar than when they are similar (the distance effect). Moreover, for a given distance, pairs of small numbers are compared faster than pairs of larger numbers (the size effect). For example, based on the distance effect, <8> and <3> are compared faster than <8> and <6>. Based on the size effect, <18> and <13> are compared faster than <28> and <23>.

The distance effect is a robust phenomenon that also occurs with multiple-digit numbers. Importantly, it is widely held to be a consistent index of semantic processing of numbers. That is, the distance effect would be evidence that number magnitudes are encoded as points (or regions) on a continuous, analogue MNL. The time to decide which is the larger of two numbers would be a function of the distance between them on the MNL. The farther apart two numbers are, the easier it is to compare them.

The origin of the size effect is more controversial. In one proposal, the MNL is held to be compressive, so larger numbers are closer together on the line than smaller numbers. Accordingly, the subjective difference between two numbers depends on their positions on the line; that is, the subjective difference between N and $N + 1$ is smaller as N increases (Dehaene, 1992; Dehaene, Dupoux, & Mehler, 1990). A different view of the MNL is that of Gallistel and Gelman (1992, 2000). In particular, they propose that the mapping is linear, rather than compressive, but the variability of the mapping increases as a function of number magnitude (scalar variability), thus causing the size effect.

There is general agreement that the SNARC (spatial number associations of response codes) effect provides the clearest and most convincing evidence of a strict link between the domain of numerical magnitude and the domain of space (e.g., Dehaene, Bossini, & Giraux, 1993; also see Mapelli, Rusconi, & Umiltà, 2003; Gevers, Caessens, & Fias, 2005, for a discussion of the relations between two effects, the SNARC effect and the Simon effect, which both depend on spatial representations). Even though the SNARC effect was first obtained in a numerical comparison task with two-digit Arabic numbers (Dehaene et al., 1990), it is typically investigated with a parity (odd/even) judgment task.

When performing parity judgments, participants respond faster with the effector that operates on the left side of space to relatively small numbers and with the effector that operates on the right side of space to relatively large numbers. In other words, even if number magnitude is task irrelevant, an interaction is obtained between side of the response and magnitude of the number. The explanation of the SNARC effect is based on the notion of an analogue, left-to-right oriented MNL with relatively small numbers on the left and relatively large numbers on the right. The SNARC effect would arise because of a spatial correspondence or lack of correspondence (i.e., corresponding and noncorresponding trials) between position of the number on the MNL and position of the response.

In addition to showing the SNARC effect when number magnitude was not task relevant and thus suggesting that the spatial representation of a number is automatically activated, Dehaene et al. (1993) clarified several characteristics of the phenomenon. It was found that the association of a given number with the left or right side of space depended on the numerical interval employed in the experiment. For example, the numbers <4> and <5> were responded to faster with the right effector when the numerical interval was [0-5], whereas they were responded to faster with the left effector when the numerical interval was [4-9].

The SNARC effect was present in left-handed participants and, in right-handed participants, when responses were executed with arms crossed, thus showing that it does not depend on hand preference or on hemispheric specialization. In contrast, it was affected by direction of reading and writing; it was reversed in people who read and write from the right to the left side, suggesting that the orientation of the MNL might depend on the way in which attention is preferentially oriented in space.

The notion of a spatial representation of numbers is widely accepted and well supported by empirical evidence. However, the properties of that spatial representation may not be invariant. For example, Bachtold, Baumuller, and Brugger (1998) found a regular SNARC effect when they asked participants to imagine numbers as arranged on a ruler. In contrast, they found a reverse SNARC effect by asking participants to imagine numbers as arranged on a clock face. If participants were required to decide whether a centrally presented number signaled a time earlier or later than 6 o'clock on a clock face, responses to small numbers were faster with the right hand, whereas responses to larger numbers were faster with the left hand. It appears that, even though numbers are always represented spatially, the properties of the spatial representation vary as a function of the instructions concerning what should be imagined. On a ruler, small numbers are on the left and larger numbers are on the right, whereas reverse spatial relations hold on a clock face.

ATTENTIONAL AND PERCEPTUAL EFFECTS OF NUMBERS

The automatic spatial coding of numbers (suggested by the presence of a SNARC effect in a parity judgment task), along with the influence of direction of reading and writing habits, has raised the issue of the relations between number magnitude and spatial attention. Fischer, Castel, Dodd, and Pratt (2003) have shown that mere perception of a number causes a shift in covert attention to the left or right side of visual space, depending on number magnitude. Participants were required to detect as fast as possible a peripheral target that was preceded by presentation of an irrelevant digit at fixation. Results indicated that left targets were detected faster when preceded by small digits (<1> or <2>), whereas detection of right targets was faster when they were preceded by larger digits (<8> or <9>). Galfano, Rusconi, and Umiltà (2006; also see Ristic, Wright, & Kingstone, 2006) confirmed the effect of number magnitude on spatial attention, even though their results were in contrast with the notion that orienting caused by number magnitude is automatic in nature.

In a study by Casarotti, Michielin, Zorzi, and Umiltà (2007), the relations between numbers and spatial attention were examined using temporal order judgments (TOJs). That is, in their study, a TOJ paradigm indexed allocation of attention. Results confirmed that, as a consequence of numerical processing, spatial attention shifted automatically to the left or right side of space. That in turn affected the speed with which sensory information was transmitted in the visual system. Given equal onset time, left-side stimuli were perceived to occur before right-side stimuli when a small number was presented at fixation, whereas right-side stimuli were perceived to occur before left-side stimuli when a larger number was presented. Importantly, Casarotti et al. found that the influence of numbers on attention orienting was specific to quantity processing and did not manifest itself in the case of non-numerical ordered sequences (i.e., letters of the alphabet).

The SNARC effect clearly depends on associations between spatial representations of responses and spatial (i.e., semantic) representations of numbers. Interestingly, evidence also suggests an effect of associations between spatial perceptual representations and spatial representations of numbers (i.e., spatial–numerical associations between perception and semantics, the so-called SNAPS effect) that occurs before response selection (Fischer, Castel, Dodd, & Pratt, 2003; Caessens, Hommel, Reynvoet, & van der Goten, 2004; Galfano et al., 2006; Ristic et al., 2006). In addition, neuropsychological findings on neglect patients, as discussed later, suggest that the MNL is isomorphic with perceptual space.

In discussing the speed of coding spatial position and number magnitude, Stoianov, Kramer, Umiltà, and Zorzi (2008) noted that the spatial coding of visual stimuli is fast and automatic (Lu & Proctor, 1995; Zorzi & Umiltà, 1995), whereas the processing of numbers is relatively slow because it comprises not only perceptual (digit recognition) but also semantic (activation of the MNL) components. Thus, they hypothesized that, in order to manifest itself, the SNAPS effect requires the concurrent activation of space and number representations, and they performed a number comparison and a parity judgment experiment to test this conjecture.

In their study, a spatial prime either preceded (forward priming) or followed (backward priming) a numerical target. Responses were verbal and nonspatial and thus precluded a response-based SNARC effect. The representations of perceptual and numerical space were likely to be concurrently activated during backward priming but not during forward priming. Accordingly, Stoianov et al. (2008) found that backward priming did lead and forward priming did not lead to a SNAPS effect.

BISECTING THE MENTAL NUMBER LINE

Zorzi, Priftis, and Umiltà (2002) investigated the issue of the spatial nature of the MNL from a different perspective: by exploring the way in which numbers are represented in patients with left (hemi) spatial neglect. Patients with left neglect, following a right parietal lesion, fail to report, orient to, or verbally describe stimuli in the contralesional left (hemi) space (for reviews, see Halligan, Fink, Marshall, & Vallar, 2003; Heilman, Watson, & Valenstein, 1979). For instance, when they have to mark the midpoint of a linear segment positioned in front of them, they systematically displace the midpoint to a subjective midpoint located on the right of the true midpoint, as if they had ignored the leftmost part of the segment.

As reported by Halligan and Marshall (1988; also see Marshall & Halligan, 1989), the rightward displacement is directly proportional to the length of the segment: The longer the segment is, the greater is the rightward displacement. However, for very short segments, a paradoxical phenomenon consisting of a leftward displacement of the midpoint (i.e., the so-called crossover effect) is observed. It is worth noting in passing that performance of normal participants in bisecting linear segments is characterized by a slight leftward error, a phenomenon known as pseudoneglect (e.g., Jewell & McCourt, 2000).

Similar effects of left neglect on line bisection were reported in studies that required the bisection of imagined linear segments (Bisiach, Rusconi, Peretti, & Vallar, 1994; Chokron, Bernard, & Michel, 1997). This is in accord with the well-known fact that neglect not only is confined to stimuli that are actually present in the environment, but also extends to images that are actively produced by the observer (e.g., Bisiach & Luzzatti, 1978).

Zorzi et al. (2002) reasoned that, if the MNL is more than a mere metaphorical concept and rather refers to a representation that is truly spatial in nature, neglect patients would show the same form of distortion in bisecting a numerical interval as they show in the line bisection task. In their study, participants were presented with two numbers (e.g., <3> and <9>), which defined the to-be-bisected numerical interval. The task consisted of telling the number that occupied the middle position in the given interval aloud (e.g., <6>). Neglect patients systematically misplaced the midpoint of the numerical interval (e.g., responding that <5> is halfway between <2> and <6>) and their mistakes closely resembled the typical pattern found in bisection of true visual lines, including the modulating effect of line length and the crossover effect with very short numerical intervals.

It is important to emphasize that neglect patients tested in the Zorzi et al. (2002) study had intact numerical and arithmetical skills. This is consistent with the observation that number processing deficits (i.e., acalculia) typically originate from lesions of the inferior parietal region of the language-dominant hemisphere (for a review, see Dehaene, Piazza, Pinel, & Cohen, 2003).

This new form of representational neglect was considered to be evidence that the MNL is more than a metaphor and that its spatial nature renders it functionally isomorphic to visual lines. Moreover, the demonstration of left–right orientation was indeed stronger and more direct than that provided by the psychophysical data from the SNARC task. Interestingly, Doricchi, Guariglia, Gasparini, and Tomaiuolo (2005) found that performance in visual line bisection could dissociate from performance in number interval bisection.

In a different context, the results of Zorzi et al. (2002) were confirmed in a study by Rossetti and colleagues (2004), where the disrupted performance of neglect patients in mental number interval bisection was ameliorated by a short adaptation to rightward deviating prisms. Further confirmatory evidence of the spatial nature of a number interval comes from the observation that neglect patients have difficulties in the processing of numbers that occupy the leftmost positions in a number interval. When required to perform a numerical comparison task, these patients took longer to respond to numbers that were located to the left of a variable reference point (Vuilleumier, Ortigue, & Brugger, 2004).

NUMBERS AND OTHER ORDERED SEQUENCES

In their seminal study, Dehaene et al. (1993) also explored whether the SNARC effect was associated with activation of elements in any ordered sequence rather than being confined to the activation of numerical magnitude only. The absence of a SNARC effect in tasks that required classification of letters of the alphabet, but were structurally similar to the parity judgment task, led Dehaene et al. to hypothesize that spatial associations are specific to the number domain. Thus, numbers seem to possess a special status because the SNARC effect occurs only with them and because their spatial nature affects human performance even in non-numerical tasks, like the orienting of attention.

However, a study by Gevers, Reynvoet and Fias (2003; also see Gevers, Reynvoet, & Fias, 2004) suggests that the spatial layout characterizing the MNL is not unique to numbers, but rather is shared by other types of ordered sequences. Gevers et al. (2003) investigated the mental representation of three non-numerical ordinal sequences, letters of the alphabet, months of the year, and days of the week. They demonstrated an association between ordinal position and spatial response preference (i.e., a SNARC-like effect), even when ordinal information was irrelevant to the task.

In Gevers and colleagues' (2003) study, the SNARC effect with letters was strong and reliable in the order-relevant task ("Does [a given letter] come before or after letter O?"), but it was significantly weaker in the order-irrelevant task (vowel–consonant classification). In contrast, a strong SNARC effect with numbers is typically found in order-irrelevant tasks (parity judgment). Moreover, Casarotti et al. (2007) have observed attentional effects (processing facilitation in one side of space depending on number magnitude) produced by number cues but not by letter cues. Therefore, the putative equivalence between numerical and non-numerical sequences is far from being firmly established.

Zorzi, Priftis, Meneghello, Marenzi, and Umiltà (2006) tried to clarify this issue by investigating the spatial representation of numerical and non-numerical sequences in neglect patients, using the same methods employed in the Zorzi et al. (2002) study. Patients completed several tasks, which included the bisection of visual lines and the bisection of number intervals, letter intervals, and month intervals. These tasks were intended to establish whether neglect affects the representation of non-numerical sequences in the same way in which it affects number representations.

The error pattern in the number bisection task showed the modulating influence of interval length and mirrored that of visual line bisection, confirming once more the left-to-right spatial orientation of the MNL (see Zorzi et al., 2002). In contrast, the bisection of non-numerical intervals was not affected by neglect. Therefore, results confirm that, as had been suggested by Dehaene et al. (1993), the existence of a strong spatial connotation constitutes a specific property of number representations rather than a general characteristic of all ordered sequences.

In contrast, the hypothesis that non-numerical sequences are spatially coded in the same way that numbers are (Gevers et al., 2003) was not supported. Neglect strongly affected the mental bisection of number intervals in the same patients whose pattern of performance with non-numerical sequences was indistinguishable from that of healthy controls. At the very least, this suggests that non-numerical sequences are only weakly associated with spatial features. These associations might be activated to a greater extent only under particular circumstances, such as in the case of judging the ordinal relation with respect to a reference point.

TWO WAYS OF ACCESSING THE MENTAL NUMBER LINE

The distinction between implicit, unconscious knowledge (assessed by direct tasks) and explicit, conscious knowledge (assessed by indirect tasks) of stimuli presented in the half of space affected by neglect is one of the most intriguing phenomena in the literature concerning neglect (for a review, see Berti, 2002). Left-neglect patients demonstrate spared unconscious (implicit) processing of information that is ignored at the conscious (explicit) level (e.g., Berti & Rizzolatti, 1992; Làdavas, Palladini, & Cubelli, 1993; Làdavas, Umiltà, & Mapelli, 1997; Marshall & Halligan, 1988).

Bisecting number intervals can be considered to be a direct task that requires voluntary access of the spatial frame of the MNL, presumably through the orientation of spatial attention. This is confirmed by the fact that neglect patients reported performing the task by forming a left-to-right-oriented visuospatial representation of the numbers comprising the interval and by subsequently attempting to locate the midpoint. The task, however, does not allow one to establish whether neglect disrupts the MNL or, rather, produces a bias in accessing and exploring an intact MNL.

In the typical SNARC task, instead, number magnitude is task-irrelevant because participants respond to the parity of centrally presented Arabic numerals. However, the very presence of the SNARC effect demonstrates that the MNL is activated indirectly and automatically. The SNARC task is an indirect task that indirectly taps into the MNL. Therefore, the number interval bisection task and the SNARC task tap, directly and indirectly, respectively, into the same number representation (i.e., a spatially organized MNL). This notion is shared by most, if not all, researchers of numerical cognition (for reviews, see Fias & Fischer, 2005; Hubbard, Piazza, Pinel, & Dehaene, 2005).

If the dissociation between explicit and implicit processing holds in the case of the representational space of the MNL, left neglect should affect number interval bisection task (i.e., the task that requires direct activation of the MNL), but not the SNARC task (i.e., the task that does not require direct activation of the MNL). A dissociation between the bisection task and the SNARC task would therefore allow one to discriminate between a deficit in accessing an intact MNL or a deficit affecting the MNL.

Priftis, Zorzi, Meneghello, Marenzi, and Umiltà (2006) compared the effects of left neglect in a number interval bisection task and in a modified version of the SNARC task. The use of a modified version of the SNARC task was rendered necessary because the left arm of neglect patients often cannot move. Therefore, participants in the study performed the SNARC task with two fingers of their intact right hand. The basic idea is that number interval bisection requires direct access and exploration of the MNL, whereas in the SNARC task, accessing the MNL is not an explicit task demand and responses do not require any explicit manipulation of number magnitude. Of course, the fact that the MNL is accessed in performing the SNARC task is attested by the SNARC effect itself.

Performance of left-neglect patients in the Priftis et al. (2006) study was impaired only in number interval bisection (direct task); it was intact in the SNARC task (indirect task). It might be argued that the dissociation reflects the activation of different numerical representations in the two tasks, rather than the dissociation between implicit and explicit processing of the MNL. However, as noted before, the consensus view in the numerical cognition literature is that the number bisection task and the SNARC task tap into the same number representation (i.e., a spatially organized MNL; Fias & Fischer, 2005; Hubbard et al., 2005). Thus, the results of Priftis et al. support the notion that neglect produces a deficit in directly accessing an intact MNL, rather than a distortion in the representation of the MNL.

NUMBER AND SPACE: UNDERLYING NEURAL MECHANISMS

No repetitive transcranial magnetic stimulation (rTMS) or neuroimaging studies have specifically investigated the neural basis of the SNARC effect. However, Göbel, Walsh, and Rushworth (2001; also see Göbel, Rushworth, & Walsh, 2001) applied focal rTMS to the angular gyrus and the supramarginal gyrus bilaterally while participants performed a number comparison task. Repetitive transcranial magnetic stimulation disrupted performance in number comparison when delivered over the angular gyri (posterior part of the posterior parietal lobe [PPL]) but not when delivered over the supramarginal gyri (anterior part of PPL). The authors suggested that the left and the right angular gyri are crucial for the use of a language-independent spatial representation of numbers (i.e., the MNL).

Because the SNARC effect is thought to depend on the MNL, it would appear that the angular gyrus should play a role in the MNL, too. In effect, the functional magnetic resonance imaging (fMRI) stimulation study of O. Simon, Mangin, Cohen, Le Bihan, and Dehaene (2002) showed significant foci of activations in the bilateral supramarginal gyrus/anterior intraparietal sulcus (IPS) and in the left angular gyrus during a simple subtraction task in which Arabic digits from <2> to <9> were to be subtracted from <11> or <15>. Note that simple subtraction tasks are also thought to elicit the MNL. It is therefore possible that both the bilateral angular gyrus/posterior IPS (i.e., posterior PPL) and the bilateral supramarginal gyrus/anterior IPS (i.e., anterior PPL) play a role in the SNARC effect.

Using rTMS, Rusconi, Turatto, and Umiltà (2007) investigated the involvement of PPL circuits in producing the Simon effect and the SNARC effect. The Simon effect (e.g., J. Simon, 1969; Umiltà & Nicoletti, 1985) is indexed by the fact that left-side stimuli are responded to faster with left-side than with right-side key-presses, and right-side stimuli are responded to faster with right-side than with left-side key-presses. As usual in SNARC tasks, participants were required to perform parity judgments on numbers ranging from <1> to <9> (without <5>) by pressing a left or a right response key. Number stimuli appeared to the left or the right of fixation (as in Mapelli et al., 2003, rather than at fixation, as in Dehaene et al., 1993, and in regular SNARC tasks). The relevant feature—that is, parity—determined the side of the correct response.

As in regular Simon tasks, therefore, the stimulus spatial position was irrelevant to the task. This way, Simon and SNARC effects were independently investigated in the same task (see Mapelli et al., 2003). Four stimulation sites were individuated on participants' scalps: left anterior PPL, right anterior PPL, left posterior PPL, and right posterior PPL. Results suggested a causal role of the anterior PPL of both hemispheres in the Simon effect and of the posterior PPL of both hemispheres in the Simon effect and the SNARC effect. This finding shows that even though visuospatial attention is involved in the Simon and the SNARC effects, the former is attributable to a manual response priming and the latter to oculomotor programming after numerical magnitude has been processed.

Overall, several attempts made to localize the neural substrates of magnitude representation point to the key role of the bilateral parietal areas that are also involved in processing of spatial dimensions. The overlap at the neuroanatomical level is consistent with the functional interaction between numerical and spatial domains, with the mental number line representation as the main theoretical construct (Dehaene, 2003).

CONCLUSION

The evidence provided so far is strongly in favor of an analogue representation of numbers, which is known as the mental number line. Its existence and characteristics were inferred by finding that the time to compare two numbers in terms of magnitude decreases as a function of the numerical distance between the two numbers and increases as a function of the size of the numbers; that small digits prime left-side responses, whereas large digits prime right-side responses in a parity judgment task; and that small and large digits prime detection of left- and right-side targets, respectively. Importantly, these effects seem to be confined to numbers and do not extend to items of every ordered sequence.

The convergence of the studies of Göbel, Walsh, & Rushworth (2001) and Rusconi et al. (2007) reinforces the claims for automatic access to visuospatial number representations, also considering that some behavioral evidence indicates that common processes are recruited during tasks addressing number magnitude directly (magnitude comparisons) as they are during indirect tasks (parity judgment and even phoneme monitoring; see Fias, Brysbaert, Geypens, & d'Ydewalle, 1996). Further converging evidence comes from neuropsychology. A defective representation of the numerical continuum has been reported by Martory and colleagues (2003), who described a patient with Gerstmann's syndrome following a focal left subangular lesion. The authors ascribed the patient's deficits to a general disorder in the manipulation of mental images of spatially related objects.

The available evidence is thus consistent with the claims of Dehaene et al. (2003), according to whom a crucial locus of the SNARC effect resides in the bilateral posterior PPL, where the visuospatial attention system would be recruited during the processing of number magnitude. Also, as Nieder and Miller (2004) note, the site where the largest population of numerosity-selective neurons can be found in posterior parietal cortex is the fundus of the intraparietal sulcus.

REFERENCES

Bachtold, D., Baumuller, M., & Brugger, P. (1998). Stimulus–response compatibility in representational space. *Neuropsychologia, 36,* 731–735.

Berti, A. (2002). Unconscious processing in neglect. In H. O. Karnath, A. D. Milner, & G. Vallar (Eds.), *The cognitive and neural bases of spatial neglect* (pp. 313–326). Oxford, England: Oxford University Press.

Berti, A., & Rizzolatti, G. (1992). Visual processing without awareness: Evidence from unilateral neglect. *Journal of Cognitive Neuroscience, 4,* 345–351.

Bisiach, E., & Luzzatti, C. (1978). Unilateral neglect of representational space. *Cortex, 14,* 129–133.

Bisiach, E., Rusconi, M. L., Peretti, V. A., & Vallar, G. (1994). Challenging current accounts of unilateral neglect. *Neuropsychologia, 11,* 1431–1434.

Caessens, B., Hommel, B., Reynvoet, B., & van der Goten, K. (2004). Backward-compatibility effects with irrelevant stimulus–response overlap: The case of the SNARC effect. *Journal of General Psychology, 13,* 411–425.

Casarotti, M., Michielin, M., Zorzi, M., & Umiltà, C. (2007). Temporal order judgment reveals how number magnitude affects visuospatial attention. *Cognition, 102,* 101–117.

Chokron, S., Bernard, J. M., & Michel, I. (1997). Length representation in normal and neglect subjects with opposite reading habits studied through a line extension task. *Cortex, 35,* 47–64.

Dehaene, S. (1992). Varieties of numerical abilities. *Cognition, 44,* 1–42.

Dehaene, S. (2003). The neural basis of the Webner–Fechner law: A logarithmic mental number line. *Trends in Cognitive Sciences, 7,* 145–147.

Dehaene, S., Bossini, S., & Giraux, P. (1993).The mental representation of parity and number magnitude. *Journal of Experimental Psychology: General, 122,* 371–396.

Dehaene, S., Dupoux, E., & Mehler, J. (1990). Is numerical comparison digital? Analogical and symbolic effects in two-digit number comparison. *Journal of Experimental Psychology: Human Perception and Performance, 16,* 626–641.

Dehaene, S., Piazza, M., Pinel, P., & Cohen, L. (2003).Three parietal circuits for number processing. *Cognitive Neuropsychology, 20,* 487–506.

Doricchi, F., Guariglia, P., Gasparini, M., & Tomaiuolo, F. (2005). Dissociation between physical and mental number line bisection in right hemisphere brain damage. *Nature Neuroscience, 8,* 1663–1665.

Fias, W., Brysbaert, M., Geypens, F., & d'Ydewalle, G. (1996). The importance of magnitude information in numerical processing: Evidence from the SNARC effect. *Mathematical Cognition, 2,* 95–110.

Fias, W., & Fischer, M. H. (2005). Spatial representation of number. In J. I. D. Campbell (Ed.), *Handbook of mathematical cognition* (pp. 43–54). London: Psychology Press.

Fischer, M. H., Castel, A. D., Dodd, M. D., & Pratt, J. (2003). Perceiving numbers causes spatial shifts of attention. *Nature Neuroscience, 6,* 555–556.

Galfano, G., Rusconi, E., & Umilta, C. (2006). Number magnitude orients attention, but not against one's will. *Psychonomic Bulletin and Review, 13,* 869–874.

Gallistel, C. R., & Gelman, R. (1992). Preverbal and verbal counting and computation. *Cognition, 1–2,* 43–74.

Gallistel, C. R., & Gelman, R. (2000). Nonverbal numerical cognition: From reals to integers. *Trends in Cognitive Sciences, 4,* 59–65.

Galton, F. (1880). Visualized numerals. *Nature, 21,* 352–256.

Gevers, W., Caessens, B., & Fias, W. (2005). Towards a common processing architecture underlying Simon and SNARC effects. *European Journal of Cognitive Psychology, 17,* 659–673.

Gevers, W., Reynvoet, B., & Fias, W. (2003). The mental representation of ordinal sequences is spatially organized. *Cognition, 87,* B87–B95.

Gevers, W., Reynvoet, B., & Fias, W. (2004). The mental representation of ordinal sequences is spatially organized: Evidence from days of the week. *Cortex, 40,* 171–172.

Göbel, S., Rushworth, M., & Walsh, V. (2001). rTMS disrupts the representation of small numbers in supramarginal gyrus. *Neuroimage, 13,* 929–926.

Göbel, S., Walsh, V., & Rushworth, M. (2001). The mental number line and the human angular gyrus. *Neuroimage, 14,* 1278–1289

Halligan, P. W., Fink, G. R., Marshall, J. C., & Vallar, G. (2003). Spatial cognition: Evidence from visual neglect. *Trends in Cognitive Sciences, 3,* 125–133.

Halligan, P. W., & Marshall, J. C. (1988). How long is a piece of string? A study of line bisection in a case of visual neglect. *Cortex, 24,* 321–328.

Heilman, K. M., Watson, R. T., & Valenstein, E. (1979). Neglect and related disorders. In K. M. Heilman & E. Valenstein (Eds.), *Clinical neuropsychology* (pp. 268–307). New York: Oxford University Press

Hubbard, E. M., Piazza, M., Pinel, P., & Dehaene, S. (2005). Interactions between number and space in parietal cortex. *Nature Reviews Neuroscience, 6,* 435–448.

Jewell, G., & McCourt, M. E. (2000). Pseudoneglect: A review and meta-analysis of performance factors in line bisection tasks. *Neuropsychologia, 38,* 93–110.

Làdavas, E., Paladini, R., & Cubelli, R. (1993). Implicit associative priming in a patient with left visual neglect. *Neuropsychologia, 12,* 1307–1320.

Làdavas, E., Umiltà, C., & Mapelli, D. (1997). Lexical and semantic processing in the absence of word reading: Evidence from neglect dyslexia. *Neuropsychologia, 35,* 1075–1085.

Lu, C. H., & Proctor, R. W. (1995). The influence of irrelevant location information on performance—A review of the Simon and spatial Stroop effects. *Psychonomic Bulletin & Review, 2,* 174–207.

Mapelli, D., Rusconi, E., & Umiltà, C. (2003). The SNARC effect: An instance of the Simon effect? *Cognition, 88,* B1–B10.

Marshall, J. C., & Halligan, P. W. (1988). Blindsight and insight in visuospatial neglect. *Nature, 336,* 766–767.

Marshall, J., & Halligan, P. (1989). When right goes left: An investigation of line bisection in a case of visual neglect. *Cortex, 25,* 503–515.

Martory, M. D., Mayer, E., Pegna, A. J., Annoni, J. M., Landis, T., & Khateb, A. (2003). Pure global acalculia following a left subangular lesion. *Neurocase, 9,* 319–328.

Moyer, R. S., & Landauer, T. K. (1967). The time required for judgments of numerical inequality. *Nature, 215,* 1519–1520.

Nieder, A., & Miller, E. K. (2004). A parieto-frontal network for visual numerical information in monkey. *Proceedings of the National Academy of Science, 101,* 7457–7462.

Priftis, K., Zorzi, M., Meneghello, F., Marenzi, R., & Umiltà, C. (2006). Explicit versus implicit processing of representational space in neglect: Dissociations in accessing the mental number line. *Journal of Cognitive Neuroscience, 18,* 680–688.

Restle, F. (1970). Speed of adding and comparing numbers. *Journal of Experimental Psychology, 83,* 274–278.

Ristic, J., Wright, A., & Kingstone, A. (2006). The number line effect reflects top-down control. *Psychonomic Bulletin & Review, 113,* 862–868.

Rossetti, Y., Jacquin-Courtois, S., Rode, G., Ota, H., Michel, C., & Boisson, D. (2004). Does action make the link between number and space representation? *Psychological Science, 15*, 426–430.

Rusconi, E., Turatto, M., & Umiltà, C. (2007). Two orienting mechanisms in the posterior parietal lobule: An rTMS study of the Simon and SNARC effects. *Cognitive Neuropsychology, 24*, 373–392.

Seron, X., Pesenti, M., Noel, M. P., Deloche, G., & Corpet, J. A. (1992). Images of numbers, or when 98 is upper left and 6 sky blue. *Cognition, 44*, 159–196.

Simon, J. R. (1969). Reaction toward the source of stimulation. *Journal of Experimental Psychology, 81*, 174–176.

Simon, O., Mangin, J-F., Cohen, L., Le Bihan, D., & Dehaene, S. (2002) Topographical layout of hand, eye, calculation, and language-related areas in the human parietal lobe. *Neuron, 33*, 475–487.

Stoianov, I., Kramer, P., Umiltà, C., & Zorzi, M. (2008). Visuospatial priming of the mental number line. *Cognition, 106*, 770–779.

Umiltà, C., & Nicoletti, R. (1985). Attention and coding effects in S-R compatibility due to irrelevant spatial cues. In M. I. Posner & O. S. M. Marin (Eds.), *Attention and performance XI* (pp. 457–471). Hillsdale, NJ: Lawrence Erlbaum Associates.

Vuilleumier, P., Ortigue, S., & Brugger, P. (2004). The number space and neglect. *Cortex, 40*, 399–410.

Zorzi, M., Priftis, K., Meneghello, F., Marenzi, R., & Umiltà, C. (2006). The spatial representation of numerical and non-numerical sequences: Evidence from neglect. *Neuropsychologia, 44*, 1061–1067.

Zorzi, M., Priftis, K., & Umiltà, C. (2002). Neglect disrupts the mental number line. *Nature, 417*, 138–139.

Zorzi, M., & Umiltà, C. (1995). A computational model of the Simon effect. *Psychological Research, 58*, 193–205.

13

Visual Memories

MAX COLTHEART and VERONIKA COLTHEART

FIVE VISUAL MEMORIES

*T*hree ways in which a visual stimulus lives on in its observer after its physical offset were distinguished by Coltheart (1980):

- The neurons of low-level vision excited by any stimulus continue to fire after the stimulus has gone. This may be called *neural persistence,* and it is studied by single-cell recording and other electrophysiological measurement techniques.
- A stimulus continues to be visible to the observer for some time after its physical offset. This may be called *visible persistence,* and a variety of methods are available for studying it: Coltheart (1980, pp. 188–205) lists seven of these and reviews results obtained with each. Visible persistence is, of course, visible; it is also short-lived. Its lifetime, as measured from stimulus offset, is inversely related to stimulus duration and stimulus energy.
- Information contained in a stimulus (such as the identity of letters when the stimulus is an array of letters) can still be processed for some time after stimulus offset This may be called *informational persistence,* and it is studied by the partial-report technique first used extensively by Sperling (1960). Informational persistence is not visible; like visible persistence, it is short-lived and of high capacity, but unlike visible persistence, its duration is unaffected by stimulus duration or stimulus energy.

How does the familiar term "iconic memory," introduced by Neisser (1967), fit in here? Uneasily. The reason is that for the first decade or so after the introduction of this term, it was used to refer to both visible and informational persistence (e.g., by Haber & Standing, 1970; Neisser, 1967; Sakitt & Appelman, 1978; Turvey, 1978).

Even 40 years later, one still comes across conflations of these two different components of cognition under the term *iconic memory* (e.g., see Koch 2004, p. 201).

These *are* different components of cognition (as shown, for example, by the fact that they are affected in different ways by stimulus duration and affected in different ways by stimulus energy, as well as by other evidence provided by Loftus & Irwin, 1998). To call them both by the same name invites confusion, so we have not used the term "iconic memory" in this chapter.

Where does the term "visual short-term memory" (VSTM) fit in here? In that VSTM holds information from the stimulus for some time after stimulus offset, it is like informational persistence; however, unlike informational persistence, its capacity is low (four or five items), it is not subject to visual masking, and it is not strictly retinotopic. Irwin (1992) provides evidence indicating that VSTM is distinct from both visible and informational persistence. Thus, this is a fourth way in which a visual stimulus can live on in the observer after its physical offset. The most common technique for studying VSTM is to present a brief visual display and then, after an interstimulus interval (ISI) long enough for visible persistence of this first display to have terminated, to present a second display (Jolicœur et al., Chaapter 7; Phillips, 1974). The subject's task is to make a judgment as to whether the contents of the two visual displays were the same or different.

Finally, a fifth item must be added to this inventory of visual memories: visual imagery. A study by Brockmole, Wang, and Irwin (2002) is especially enlightening with respect to how visual imagery is related to other items in this inventory. They used a version of the temporal integration task developed by Di Lollo (1980). Subjects saw a 4 × 4 grid. As the first display, several of the cells of this grid were filled simultaneously for 33 ms. Then the grid went blank for a variable ISI. Then, as the second display, all of the previously filled cells remained blank, and all except one of the previously unfilled cells were filled for 33 ms.

The subject's task was to identify the one cell that had been unfilled in both displays. This task is relatively easy at short ISIs because the visible persistence of the first display can be integrated with the percept of the second display, making the single unfilled cell clearly visible. As ISI increases, the difficulty of this task increases: In the Brockmole study, accuracy declined from 79% at ISI = 0 to 21% at ISI = 100 ms, an effect reported in many studies using this temporal integration technique.

It is typical in such studies to use only short ISIs. But in the Brockmole study, ISI ranged from 0 up to 5000 ms. Performance was at its worst at ISI = 100 ms (21%), but then slowly rose as ISI was increased further, plateauing at about 68% with ISI = 1300 ms and remaining at that level as ISI was increased further to 5000 ms. Brockmole and colleagues explained these results by proposing that subjects were engaged in a slow and effortful process of generating visual images. Specifically, on each trial, they built a visual image of the first display, a process that took 1300 ms to complete fully. This allowed them to perform the task by integrating a visual image of the first display with a percept of the second.

Such visual imagery represents a fifth way in which a visual stimulus can live on in the observer after its physical offset. Visual imagery is to be distinguished from VSTM by its much larger capacity (which Brockmole and colleagues estimated to be about 10 items in their experiments) as well as its very slow generation time.

INFORMATIONAL PERSISTENCE, DURABLE STORAGE, AND THE BINDING PROBLEM

In experiments reported by Sperling (1960), subjects were presented with an array of letters (say, three rows of four letters) for a brief duration (15–50 ms). At some ISI after array offset, a high, medium, or low tone requesting report of just the top, middle, or bottom row of letters, respectively, was presented. With a zero ISI, subjects averaged just over 3 letters correct out of 4—implying that at least 9 of the 12 letters from the display were still available in some form of memory after the display had been terminated. However, if subjects were asked to report as many items from the display as they could, they averaged only 4.5 letters, rather than 9.

This difference between the number of letters reported present in memory immediately after display offset when report of all was required (full report) and the number of letters estimated via the partial-report technique is the *partial-report superiority*. Partial-report superiority can be observed when physical properties of the display items other than their locations are the basis of the cueing (e.g., when letters are in different colors and letters of only one of these colors are to be reported, the cue indicating which color). As the ISI between display offset and partial-report-cue onset increases, the size of the partial report superiority decreases; at sufficiently long ISIs (say, 250 ms, depending on display conditions), the partial report superiority is zero.

In this experimental paradigm, something is persisting after display offset (namely, information from the display) and something is decaying after display offset (because partial-report performance declines with cue delay). The most natural way of thinking about this is to suppose that the display generates a visible mental snapshot that exists after display offset but fades away (loses contrast) over time. This way of thinking is encouraged by the identification of informational persistence with visible persistence. But because the evidence rules out such an identification, this way of thinking cannot be right.

This view can be shown to be incorrect in a second way. If the fading-snapshot view were correct, the reason that errors arise in the partial-report task would be that letters had faded too much to be identifiable; thus, the primary form of error would be an omission. But this is not the case. In partial-report experiments, the primary form of error (Dick, 1969; Irwin & Thomas, Chapter 6; Irwin & Yeomans, 1986; Townsend, 1973) is a position error: The reported letter was in the display, but it was in some row other than the cued row. When such errors occur, the letter is still identifiable, but only some physical property of the letter (the location it had occupied in the display, for example, or the color in which it had been presented) is unavailable, rather than the letter's identity.

Such considerations led Coltheart (1980, p. 222) to propose that "the identity of an item is stored rapidly and in a stable form early in the lifetime of a display, while physical attributes of the item are registered with more difficulty and in an unstable decaying form." The idea here is that all the letters in a 3×4 array are identified rapidly (i.e., their stored representations are activated) and without any bottleneck affecting this lexical activation process. The same would be true for nonlinguistic stimuli that also have permanent mental representations, such as familiar shapes. But activations of such representations do not represent the physical properties of the stimuli, only their identities. An A is an A whether it is red or green and whether it is in the top, middle, or bottom row of a display.

This presents a problem if the task is to select for report just those activated letters that possess a certain physical property. "The theoretical problem here is how episodic and semantic memory can be coordinated" (Coltheart, 1980, p. 223). This problem, which came to be called the binding problem, was reviewed by Di Lollo (this volume); in fact, Di Lollo lists seven different binding problems in his chapter. Assuming that letters can be thought of as objects, the particular binding problem being discussed here is the one Di Lollo refers to as *property binding* or *feature binding*: assigning the correct features to objects.

A vague solution to this problem was sketched by Coltheart (1980) based on a concept he referred to as *lexical stabilization*. First, he had to suppose that although activation of lexical entries (e.g., for letters) is rapid and free of bottleneck, these activations must decay over time; if they did not, full report would not be limited to just four or five letters from 3 × 4 displays. Then he proposed that the association of physical information (location, color, etc.) with lexical entries is also rapid and bottleneck free, but this information also decays rapidly unless subject to lexical stabilization.

A lexical entry and its associated physical information will become relatively durable if the process of lexical stabilization is applied to them. It was hypothesized that the lexical stabilization process was serial or at least parallel with limited capacity; in this case, only a subset of the items from a 3 × 4 display could benefit from it before decay. In order to explain why the majority of errors in partial report tasks are position errors (where identity information is still available but physical information is not), it also had to be hypothesized that decay of the physical information is faster than decay of activated lexical entries. Stabilized entries live long enough to be transferred to a form of storage—called "durable storage" by Coltheart (1972) and Gegenfurtner and Sperling (1993)—from which they can be reported at the subject's leisure because this form of storage is not subject to decay or masking.

Irwin and Thomas (this volume) also offer this kind of account and even some evidence in its favor. Their studies of blinking and thinking (Thomas & Irwin, 2006) led them to conclude that "blinking disrupts the maintenance of stimulus information in iconic memory (which has a very short duration) but not in short-term memory (which has a longer duration)." In particular, they pointed out that when subjects were instructed to blink in response to the letter array in a Sperling-style partial-report experiment, the resulting impairment of partial-report performance seen at a brief cue delay (50 ms), but not at longer cue delays (150 or 750 ms), took the form of an increase in position errors. Blinking did not increase the rate of misidentification (intrusion) errors. "In other words," they said, "blinking disrupts the binding between letter identity and letter position information in iconic memory."

Why does blinking have this effect? When people blink, their eyes move downward. When people make saccadic eye movements, their attention moves to the position to which the eye will be moving even before the beginning of the saccade.

Irwin and Thomas proposed that this will also be true in the case of blinking (i.e., programming a blink deflects visual attention downward even before the blink is initiated), and they provide evidence supporting this idea. This means that if subjects blink in response to the letter array in a partial-report experiment, their attention will be deflected downward.

This attention is required for binding physical information to letter identity information; correct partial-report performance requires such binding. There is a strong prediction here: Blinking should disrupt partial-report performance only for the middle and upper rows. Reanalysis of the data of Thomas and Irwin (2006) showed that this was indeed so (see Irwin & Thomas, Chapter 6, Figure 6.4).

Thus, we can now tell the following story about partial-report experiments. All of the letters in the display activate their stored representations, rapidly and in parallel without any bottleneck. If the task is full report, as many of these letters as possible have to be transferred to durable storage because the lexical activations decay quickly relative to the slow time course of serial verbal report; here, there *is* a bottleneck: "The observer does not usually begin his report until several seconds after his visual store of letters is depleted" (Sperling, 1963). All 12 items in a 3 × 4 display activate their lexical entries, but only about 4 or 5 of these items will be reported in the full-report condition. Why? It could be because the transfer to durable storage is serial and relatively slow. It could be due to a capacity limitation of durable storage: perhaps this store can hold only four or five items.

Could what is being called "durable storage" here be identical to what is called, in other chapters in this volume, visual short-term memory? That would be a convenient unification because evidence from a variety of sources suggests that VSTM has a limited capacity of four or five items, too. We return to this point later when we discuss VSTM.

What does this story have to say about partial report from brief visual displays? The idea is that binding of the physical properties of a stimulus to its activated lexical entry (the process referred to by Coltheart [1980] as "lexical stabilization") requires visual attention. A high-capacity, fast-decaying, postdisplay representation of the display—"informational persistence"—contains the required physical information. Attention must be allocated to an item in this representation if its physical properties are to be bound to its activated lexical entry. The postcue directs attention to particular items in this representation on the basis of some physical property of these items (such as their position or their color). This means that only some of the activated lexical entries (the cued ones) will have physical information bound to them. These entries will preferentially be transferred to durable storage, from which they will be reported.

The effect of cue delay occurs because informational persistence decays rapidly; the later the cue, the more likely it is that an item, even though its lexical entry is fully activated, will no longer have any representation of its physical properties in informational persistence. In this circumstance, no physical information can be bound to the activated lexical entry. The subject will know that this item had been presented, but not where or in what color. In the experiments of Thomas and Irwin (2006), the reason that blinking did not affect performance at the two longer cue delays was that the effect of blinking is to impede the cue-controlled selective attention to informational persistence, and there is no longer any informational persistence to be attended to by the time these later cues arrive.

This general account is an attractive one, but it has a general problem, which was pointed out by Coltheart (1983): The account applies only to the situation where the stimuli in iconic memory are items that have stored permanent representations (e.g., letters, digits, words, or familiar shapes) to which physical information (such as location or color) can be bound. What about stimuli that have no such permanently stored representations? Will they show the typical iconic memory effects in partial-report experiments?

According to the accounts offered by Coltheart (1980) and Irwin and Thomas (Chapter 6), they will not because the binding of physical information to permanently stored identities cannot occur if there are no permanently stored identities. The problem noted by Coltheart (1983) is that typical iconic memory effects can, in fact, be obtained with stimuli that do not have permanently stored identities.

This was shown in two studies in which the partial-report cue was direction of movement. In the study by Demkiw and Michaels (1976), subjects saw a brief display of eight dots, each moving linearly in a particular direction. After display offset, an arrow cue pointed to the location of one of the dots, and the subject's task was to indicate which direction the dot that had been in that position had been moving. Performance in this partial-report task was much better than full-report (report the direction of all eight dots) performance and declined as a function of cue delay.

In the study by Treisman, Russell, and Green (1975), subjects saw a brief display of six dots, each dot traversing a circular path, clockwise or counterclockwise, at a rate that produced apparent movement. An auditory postcue specified the particular dot about which the subject was to report direction of movement. Once again, performance in this partial-report task was much better than in the full-report task (report the direction of all six dots), and declined as a function of cue delay.

The moving stimuli in these experiments do not have permanently stored identities. Therefore, it is not possible to offer an account of why partial-report superiority is found here and why it declines with cue delay in terms of difficulties in binding episodic perceptual information to permanently stored stimulus identities—an account of the kind offered by Coltheart (1980) and Irwin and Thomas (Chapter 6). Hence, Coltheart (1983) offered a different account, one based on the concept of object files as developed by Kahneman and Treisman (1984), who said:

> We think of the perceptual system as opening an object file when an object or event is first sensed. The initial entry and the identifying label for the file simply state the location and time. As information about the features of the object is received, it is entered in appropriate slots in the file. Color, size, shape, brightness and direction of movement are specified early, but can be updated if and when they change. At some stage, the object may be identified by matching it to specifications in long-term perceptual memory. This allows retrieval and storage in the file of a name or category and of previously learned facts relating to the object, and may also guide the accumulation of further sensory information. (p. 54)

Thus, in a typical iconic-memory experiment with, say, three rows of four letters, 12 object files will rapidly be established, one for each letter. Each file will contain information about a letter's identity plus information about the physical properties of the letter as it appeared in the display, such as its color and its location. It is to this set of files that the partial-report cue is to be applied. The subject's task is to select only those files that match the cue and to transfer information about each of these files (e.g., the name of the object, if it has one, or a description of its direction of rotation in the case of the movement experiments) to durable storage. There, the information about the object is no longer subject to decay or masking and thus can be reported at leisure. There is no bottleneck in constructing the object files; these are set up rapidly and in parallel. The bottleneck comes later.

After display offset, the object files constructed from the display start to decay. If the partial-report cue is presented very soon after display offset, it can access all or almost all of the appropriate object files before they decay. Thus, information about all or almost all of them can be transferred to durable storage for subsequent report (a slow and serial transfer process in which only one object file is processed at a time). Hence, with short cue delays, partial-report performance approximates 100%.

As cue delay increases, the likelihood that a cued file will have decayed before the transfer process can be instigated will increase; hence, partial-report performance will decline with cue delay. If the task is full report, all 12 items from the display will need to be transferred to durable storage, but this cannot happen because (1) durable storage is of limited capacity (four or five items), and (2) by the time the transfer process has handled four or five object files, the remainder have decayed. Therefore, full-report performance for 12-item displays is capped at around 35% here, and hence there will be a partial-report superiority.

What is the role of visual attention here? It has already been argued (and will be argued further later) that visual attention is not needed for items to be "identified" in the sense that their stored representations are activated. But it might be that checking each object file to determine whether it contains the cued property requires visual attention to be directed to that file (which would mean that every object file constructed from the display would need to be attended to).

On the other hand, it might be that, after an object file has been selected as matching the cue (a selection process not requiring visual attention), visual attention needs to be directed only to each selected file—perhaps because such attention is needed for accomplishing the transfer process. The latter possibility seems more compatible with the blink results reported by Irwin and Thomas (Chapter 6)—given their proposal that programming a blink directs visual attention to the low row of the display and that this harms report of the middle or upper row if either of those happens to be the one cued. This is because their proposal suggests that the kind of visual attention being considered here is slow and limited in capacity.

TWO KINDS OF BLINKS

As discussed previously, Irwin and Thomas (Chapter 6) provide evidence that an oculomotor blink temporarily impairs a subject's ability to deploy visuospatial attention (at least to some parts of the display). In Chapter 7 in this volume, Jolicœur and colleagues make a related proposal about the *attentional* blink (AB) in the section heading, "Spatial Attention Freezes During the Attentional Blink."

The AB experiments of Jolicœur and colleagues (Chapter 7) occurred as follows. Subjects saw a stream of white letters, centrally and briefly presented at a rapid rate. Embedded in this stream were two targets, T1 and T2, both of which were digits. T1 was a central white digit; subjects in one condition were required to report it and in another to ignore it. The frame containing T2 displayed two digits, one to the left of center and one to the right. One digit was green and the other was red. Half the subjects had to report the green digit from the T2 frame and ignore the red digit; the other half had to do the opposite. This variation on the format of T2 in the typical AB paradigm was devised to permit electrophysiological experimentation using the event-related potential (ERP) component N2pc. This is a lateralized brain response whose occurrence is taken as an indication that visuospatial attention is being directed at the visual hemifield contralateral to the hemisphere showing the N2pc response.

An AB effect is to be expected here and was observed: When the lag between T1 and T2 was short (one intervening item), T2 report was worse than when this lag was long (seven intervening items). Jolicœur and colleagues (Chapter 7) had been assuming that the AB arose at some relatively late stage of visual processing, such as consolidation in short-term memory. Because lateralized selective spatial attention as indexed by the N2pc is an early stage in visual processing, they were surprised to find that there was no N2pc at the short lag (i.e., that the AB abolished the N2pc).

That this abolition of the N2pc was due to the AB was shown by the fact that, when subjects did not have to process T1 and only had to select the item from the appropriately colored T2 frame and report it, the N2pc was observed as a response to the T2 frame, even at the short lag. The absence of the N2pc at this short lag indicates that the AB is interfering with the deployment of visual attention—just as a real blink did in the partial-report experiments of Irwin and Thomas described earlier.

A very similar version of the AB paradigm was used by Williams, Visser, Cunnington, and Mattingley (2008). In particular, the T2 target was presented in the periphery in both the Jolicœur et al. (Chapter 7) and Williams et al. studies. In the latter study, the T2 frame had four items presented equidistantly from the fixation point; three of these items were plus ("+") signs and one was an X. The T2 task was to report the location of the X. Performance on the T2 task was worse when one item intervened between T1 and T2 than when seven items did (i.e., there was an AB) and was better when no item intervened between T1 and T2 than when one item did (i.e., there was Lag 1 sparing).

These behavioral data were exactly paralleled by fMRI (functional magnetic resonance imaging) data. Neural activity in the four regions of primary visual cortex corresponding to the locations of the four stimuli in the T2 frames was measured. It was found that this activity was smaller with one intervening item than with none or seven intervening items. Thus, when the AB was maximal behaviorally, suppression by T1 of the early visual processing of T2 was also maximal.

Evidence suggested that this suppression was not confined to the location of the T2 target, but rather was also present elsewhere in the visual field (i.e., at the locations of the three T2 distractors).

These results were interpreted within the notion of reentrant visual pathways discussed by Di Lollo (Chapter 2): "On this account, the AB arises because T1 processing prevents the iterative feedback process required for T2 identification from being completed before masking of T2 by the item presented immediately after it" (Williams et al., 2008, p. 9893). This differs from the account offered by Jolicœur and colleagues (Chapter 7), who suggested that the AB impaired the ability to direct visual spatial attention. Both accounts, though, seem to rest on the idea that items subject to the AB and, more generally, items to which visual attention has not been directed will not be identified; however, this idea does not seem tenable.

SEMANTIC ACCESS, ATTENTION, AND THE ATTENTIONAL BLINK

In an experiment reported by Allport (1977), subjects viewed a centrally fixated word for 20 ms that was followed by a pattern mask. Their task was to report this word, which they were able to do on about half the trials. This target word was accompanied by an irrelevant distractor word presented 1° above fixation, also for 20 ms, and also backward masked. Questioned after the experiment, all subjects denied ever seeing a second word or letter string on any trial. Despite this, and despite the fact that attention was not directed to the location of the distractor, that it was brief and masked, and that subjects did not have to perform any task with it, the meaning of the distractor word was accessed. This was indicated by the fact that accuracy of report of the target word was higher when distractor word and target word were related in meaning than when they were not.

The view that printed words do not require attention or task relevance for their meanings to be accessed is supported by a variety of other experiments. For example, Besner and Stolz (1999) showed that color-naming of a color patch presented at fixation is affected by the meaning of an irrelevant word presented away from fixation. Dell'Acqua, Pesciarelli, Jolicœur, Eimer, and Peresotti (2007) showed that lexical decision to a word presented to the tone side of fixation is affected by the meaning of an irrelevant word presented to the other side of fixation.

Thus, semantic access occurs for printed words when there are no spatial attention, task relevance, or awareness for these words. If such access can occur under such deeply unfavorable conditions, what of words suffering from the AB? Here, too, we find that there is semantic access despite the unfavorable condition that the word cannot be reported because of the AB. This has been shown in a variety of ways.

It is been known for many years that the N400 ERP component is of higher amplitude for a word that semantically mismatches previous words than when no such semantic mismatch is present. This result shows that the word generating the N400 must have accessed its meaning. Luck, Vogel, and Shapiro (1996) reported that N400 is just as large for a word that is unreportable because it was subject to the AB as it is for a word unaffected by the AB. This implies that attentional blinking, though it prevents report of a word, does not prevent that word from being "identified" in the sense of activating its stored semantic representation.

The same conclusion follows from the work of Shapiro, Driver, Ward, and Sorenson (1997), who used an AB paradigm with three targets rather than two. Report of the third target word, T3, was facilitated by its having a semantic relationship with the second target word, T2, even on those trials where T2 was not reported because of an attentional blink. Maki, Frigen, and Paulson (1997) found that the report of T2 in the AB paradigm was better when an irrelevant distractor between T1 and T2 was semantically related to T2 than when all distractors were semantically unrelated to the targets. This indicated that, in the AB paradigm, even distractors at least sometimes activate their semantic representations.

A similar conclusion is reached from another experiment reported by Maki et al. (1997) in which the subject was asked to ignore T1 and only report T2. Report of T2 was better when it was semantically related to the to-be-ignored T1 than when it was not. This indicated, again, that a word irrelevant to the task and that the subject is instructed to ignore at least sometimes still activates its semantics.

A comment regarding N400 is needed here. The work reviewed in this section implies not only that reportability and awareness are unnecessary for semantic access, but also that such access occurs for words on which the subject does not have to perform any task and that are presented away from the focus of attention. From this, it follows that, if the N400 is generated by semantic access, it should still occur, even when the target word is presented away from the focus of attention and the subject does not have to perform any task on it.

However, this is not so. It predicts that N400 will be smaller for a repeated word or a word that is semantically related to a prior word, even when the words are presented away from the focus of attention and the subject does not have to perform any task on it. McCarthy and Nobre (1993) presented simultaneous streams of words to either side of the fixation point. Subjects had to fixate this point while performing a task on the words in one visual hemifield and ignoring the words in the other. The attended words generated an N400 to unexpectedness; the unattended words did not.

There are two interpretations of N400: It indexes semantic access or it indexes postaccess checking. The N400 does not occur under conditions where semantic access does occur (i.e., presentation of words on which no task need be performed that are in an unattended location). Therefore, this result is inconsistent with the view that N400 indexes the semantic access process itself and instead favors the view that it indexes retrospective semantic valuation.

To take this line requires the assumption that the performance of this evaluation requires spatial attention and task relevance. Of course, the occurrence of N400 under conditions where reportability and awareness are prevented (i.e., in the AB situation) is still evidence that semantic access occurs in the absence of reportability and awareness because the execution of retrospective evaluation requires that the semantic representation of the unreportable word be available to the evaluation process.

In sum, then, words still activate their semantic representations, even when they are presented peripherally and attention is not directed to them, and they still activate their semantics even when they have been rendered unreportable by being attentionally blinked. Thus, even if the AB in the experiment by Jolicœur and colleagues (Chapter 7) described earlier prevented deployment of attention to the location of the T2 target, it would not have prevented that target from activating its permanently stored representation. One might therefore wonder what the function of this attentional redeployment is. If a shift of attention is not required for stimulus identification, why do subjects do it?

In the experiment by Williams and colleagues (2008) described earlier, the reduction in neural activity of primary visual cortex associated with the AB would not have prevented blinked items from activating their permanently stored representations because this still occurs even for blinked items. One might therefore wonder what the functional consequences of this reduced cortical activity are.

THE N2PC, FMRI, AND SEMANTIC ACCESS

In an experiment reported by Dell'Acqua et al. (2007), subjects saw a red string of letters to one side of the fixation point and a green string of letters to the other side. This display was brief (85 ms) and the two strings were forward and backward masked. The task was to make an unspeeded lexical decision to the string that was in the target color (red for half the subjects and green for the other half) and to ignore the other string. The target string was a word on 50% of trials and a nonword on the remainder; the nontarget string was always a word.

When both strings were words, they were semantically related on 50% of occasions and unrelated on 50% of occasions. Lexical decisions were more accurate when the nontarget string was semantically related to the target string than in the unrelated condition; they were more accurate when the target string was in the right visual field than when it was in the left. Once again, we find evidence that unattended words (the nontarget strings) access their semantic representations.

But this experiment has an additional important twist: N2pc responses timelocked to the onset of the letter strings were measured. A common interpretation of the N2pc is that it indexes lateralized visual–spatial attention, so one would expect an N2pc to the target strings in this experiment, which indeed was observed. But, interestingly, the amplitude of this N2pc was smaller when the two words were related than when they were not. This indicates, as did the behavioral data, that the nontarget word, despite its color indicating that it was irrelevant to the task, penetrated the processing stream up to and including the stage of access to meaning.

This relatedness effect was significant for electrode site P7 (which is over the left hemisphere) but not for the corresponding site over the right hemisphere (P8). The N2pc is considered to arise in extrastriate visual cortex, and semantic analysis occurs at later stages in the processing stream (left inferotemporal cortex). Thus, these results imply that the results of such semantic analysis may be fed back from left inferotemporal cortex via reentrant pathways to posterior visual areas while the processing required for performance of the lexical decision task is still ongoing.

Given this, suppose that in an AB paradigm, T2 is not presented at fixation, but rather is lateralized, with an irrelevant stimulus in the other visual field; a color cue is used to indicate which of the two items is to be reported. This is what Jolicœur and colleagues (Chapter 7) did, and we know from their work that an AB occurs here despite the lateralized presentation. We also know that the item that is unreportable because of AB will nevertheless still access its semantic representation.

Therefore, we would not be surprised to find that report of T2 would be better (the AB would be smaller) if, in the Jolicœur paradigm, the irrelevant stimulus accompanying T2 were semantically related to T2 (though as far as we know, this exact experiment has not been done). Even if the distractor for T2 is unrelated to T2, what would we predict about the effect of AB on N2pc? If the N2pc indexes a switching of spatial attention, there is no reason to expect it to be reduced or eliminated by the AB. However, Jolicœur and colleagues (Chapter 7) found that it was.

Thus, the AB eliminates the N2pc, and it also greatly reduces the neural response to T2 in primary visual cortex. The story to tell here is very obvious: For T2 to be identified in these experiments, spatial attention needs first to be directed to it (as indexed by the N2pc), and neural processing of T2 in primary visual cortex needs to be sufficiently strong. Obvious though it is, this story is not correct because (a) various results we have described previously show that stimuli do not need to have visual attention directed to them to be identified, and (b) stimuli are identified even when they have been made unreportable by AB. This implies that in the short-lag condition of the experiment by Williams and colleagues (2008), T2 was still identified even when the primary visual cortex response to it was very weak (i.e., in the Lag 1 condition).

We may then ask: Why is an N2pc present at long lags in the Jolicœur et al. experiment (Chapter 7) if identification of peripheral targets does not require a shift of visual attention? What is the role of the switching of attention to the T2 location in the Jolicœur paradigm if it is not to permit stimulus identification? The same question can be asked with reference to the partial-report paradigm: What is the role of the switching of attention to the cued items in this paradigm if it is not to permit stimulus identification?

When we discussed this point in relation to the work of Irwin and Thomas (Chapter 6), we suggested that visual attention is needed in the partial-report paradigm for the transfer of cued items to durable storage. A similar suggestion can be made in relation to the AB paradigm in the context of a two-stage attentional gating account of the AB (Chun & Potter, 1995; Shapiro & Raymond, 1994).

According to this account, two stages of processing are needed in the AB paradigm:

- Stage 1 is the identification of an item as a target item. This involves, in our terms, activation of the permanently stored representations of the items because, in many AB paradigms, that is the information needed to decide whether an item is a target or not (e.g., when the targets are digits and the distractors are letters).

- Stage 2 is the stage to which items that are to be reported must be transferred; this is durable storage, in our terms.

The transfer from Stage 1 to Stage 2 is accomplished by applying an attentional mechanism to the target in Stage 1. If T2 arrives while this attentional mechanism is busy with T1, T2 will be represented at Stage 1 but will not be transferred to Stage 2 and will not be reportable. This is the AB.

Given this account of the AB, suppose now that, as in the experiment of Jolicœur and colleagues (Chapter 7), T1 and T2 are presented in different spatial locations. Switching attention to the spatial location of T2 is not needed so that T2 can be identified (i.e., not for Stage 1 processing); that will happen even if visual spatial attention is not directed at the location of T1. Instead, attention needs to be switched to T2 to allow transfer of T2 from Stage 1 to Stage 2 (i.e., to durable storage), and that switch is what N2pc is indexing.

This is consistent with the work Visser, Zuvic, Bischof, and Di Lollo (1999), who, like Jolicœur and colleagues (Chapter 7), presented T1 and T2 at different locations (in some conditions), though their situation was simpler because their T2s were not accompanied by distractors. They were particularly interested in Lag 1 sparing: When there are no distractors between T1 and T2, the AB is smaller or absent. The two-stage theory explains this by proposing that the attentional gate opened by T1 has not yet been closed when an immediate T2 occurs, so T2 can enjoy the benefits of this attention (i.e., be transferred to durable storage).

Given this, one can ask the following question: Is the attentional gate tied to spatial location? If it is and if T2 is in a spatial location different from that of T1, then one will not see lag 1 sparing with T1 and T2 in different locations; this is what Visser et al. (1999) reported. This is consistent with the idea that, here, a switch of attention is needed to open a gate for a new location; this spatial switch will be indexed by an N2pc. The switch can only occur if the gate opened by T1 has closed; if it is still open, no switch will take place—hence, no N2pc. This is why the AB prevents the N2pc.

A POSSIBLE ELECTROPHYSIOLOGICAL SIGNATURE OF VSTM

In the experiments reported by Jolicœur and colleagues in Chapter 7 and discussed earlier in this chapter, a second lateralized posterior negativity, occurring considerably later than the N2pc, was noticed. It was given the name SPCN (sustained posterior contralateral negativity), and it was proposed that this ERP component is the same as the contralateral negativity observed by Vogel and Machizawa (2004) in their experiments on VSTM.

In the latter experiments, subjects saw a 100-ms memory array containing a number of colored squares and then, after a 900-ms blank retention interval, a test array of colored squares. The task was to decide whether the two arrays were the same. There were always squares in both visual hemifields, but only one hemifield was relevant to the task on any trial; the relevant hemifield was precued by an arrow preceding the memory array.

A contralateral negativity was present during the retention interval, beginning 100 ms after the offset of the memory display. The amplitude of this negativity increased with the number of colored squares in the display, up to a maximum of four items. Performance on this task is accurate up to four item displays. The authors concluded, and Jolicœur and colleagues (Chapter 7) agree, that the SPCN indexes the currently active representations held in VSTM and that VSTM has a capacity of about four items.

Given this, it is significant that no SPCN was present on the short-lag trials of the AB experiment. The interpretation of this is that nothing got into VSTM on the trials because, for the target digit to be transferred to VSTM, attention must be deployed to its location. The AB prevents such deployment (even though, as we have noted, it does not prevent stimuli accessing their permanently stored representations).

COULD DURABLE STORAGE BE THE SAME THING AS VSTM?

In the typical VSTM task, the code in which subjects hold the first display while waiting for the second display is unlikely to be phonological. Performance on this task is no better when the display objects vary on one dimension (e.g., are colored squares) than when they vary on three (varied shapes of varied size in varied colors) (Luck & Vogel, 1997), even though verbal descriptions of the first display would have to be three times as long in the latter case compared to the former. Performance on this task is not significantly impaired by concurrent verbal articulation (Treisman & Zhang, 2006).

In contrast, it has sometimes been proposed that the code in which items are held in durable storage is phonological (Coltheart, 1972; Sperling, 1963). Various lines of evidence offer support of this view. For example, as Sperling (1963) noted, errors in reporting items from brief visual alphanumeric displays are typically acoustic confusions such as writing "D" for "T" or "T" for "2." (Presumably, he had in mind here the full-report condition, which overloads durable storage, because in the partial-report condition, errors are typically location [position] errors rather than acoustic confusion errors.)

Thus, it does not seem viable to propose that VSTM and durable storage are the same thing (even though they have the same or very similar properties: both immune from decay and masking and both with capacities of four or five items). A unified model of visual cognition with brief visual displays will therefore have to include both of these systems and have to say something about how they are related. Relevant here is a problem pointed out by Sperling (1967). If all there were in the system that processes brief visual displays was the rapidly decaying informational persistence and the phonologically coded durable storage, one might suppose that the mechanism of transfer from the first to the second was covert naming. But covert naming is too slow for this job; informational persistence does not last long enough for three or four items to be sequentially converted to their spoken forms and stored in durable storage.

Sperling (1967, Model 3) proposed the existence of a distinct third mode of storage intervening between informational persistence and durable storage. The key properties of this third mode are that it does not decay as rapidly as informational persistence does and that the process of transferring information to it from informational persistence is fast enough that three or four items can be transferred during the lifetime of informational persistence.

As long as this intermediate mode of storage has these two key properties, it will serve its theoretical purpose. Thus, although Sperling's idea (1967) that this intermediate mode holds programs of motor instructions is possible, it is not required. Perhaps instead this intermediate store needed for theoretical reasons is VSTM? According to this idea, in partial-report experiments, the sequence of storage stages involved would be informational persistence to VSTM to durable storage.

This speculative proposal might be explored by the following experiment. If we accept that the presence of an SPCN indicates the presence of information in VSTM, then, if in partial-report experiments VSTM feeds durable storage, the electrophysiological signature of VSTM (i.e., the SPCN) should show up in partial-report experiments. This can be directly tested by measuring the SPCN when the subject is performing a traditional partial-report task, provided that a lateralization component is added to the task. This is simple to do: Subjects report a column from the display rather than a row. For example, displays could consist of four columns of four letters, two columns in each hemifield; the task is always to report just one column and the required column cued by a tone having one of four frequencies.

At short cue delays (within the lifetime of informational persistence), one should see an N2pc contralateral to the hemifield of the cued column indexing the deployment of visual attention to the cued column, followed some time later by an SPCN (which indexes the entrance of items from the cued column into VSTM). An electrophysiological signature of the high-capacity, fast-decaying informational persistence from which a subset of items is transferred into VSTM might also emerge.

At longer cue delays (longer than the lifetime of informational persistence), an N2pc might still be seen (the subject might still direct attention to the location of the cued column, even though no information is represented there). However, there should be no postcue increases in the amplitude of the SPCN because no additional items would be transferred to VSTM after cue onset.

Thus, it is conceivable that experiments of this kind could lead to an electrophysiological rapprochement between two currently disconnected fields: the study of "iconic memory" by partial-report techniques and the study of VSTM. If not, then students of visual cognition will still be confronted with the requirement of explaining how VSTM and durable storage fit into a unified model of the processing of brief visual displays.

REFERENCES

Allport, D. A. (1977). On knowing the meaning of words we are unable to report: The effects of visual masking. In S. Dornic (Ed.), *Attention and performance VI*. London: Academic Books.

Besner, D., & Stolz, J. A. (1999). Unconsciously controlled processing: The Stroop effect reconsidered. *Psychonomic Bulletin & Review, 6*, 449–445.

Brockmole, J. R., Wang, R. F., & and Irwin, D. E. (2002). Temporal integration between visual images and visual percepts. *Journal of Experimental Psychology: Human Perception and Performance, 28*, 315–334.

Chun, M. M., & Potter, M. C. (1995). A two-stage model for multiple target detection in rapid serial visual presentation. *Journal of Experimental Psychology: Human Perception and Performance, 21*, 109–127.

Coltheart, M. (1972). Visual information processing. In P. C. Dodwell (Ed.), *New horizons in psychology*. Harmondsworth: Penguin Books.

Coltheart, M. (1980). Iconic memory and visible persistence. *Perception and Psychophysics, 27*, 183–228.

Coltheart, M. (1983). Iconic memory. *Philosophical Transactions of the Royal Society of London B, 302*, 283–294.

Dell'Acqua, R., Pesciarelli, F., Jolicœur, P., Eimer, M., & and Peresotti, F. (2007). The interdependence of spatial attention and lexical access as revealed by early asymmetries in occipitoparietal ERP activity. *Psychophysiology, 44*, 436–443.

Demkiw, P., & Michaels, C. (1976). Motion information in iconic memory. *Acta Psychologica, 40*, 257–274.

Dick, A. O. (1969). Relations between the sensory register and short-term storage in tachistoscopic recognition. *Journal of Experimental Psychology, 82*, 279–284.

Di Lollo, V. (1980). Temporal integration in visual memory. *Journal of Experimental Psychology: General, 109*, 75–97.

Gegenfurtner, K. R., & Sperling, G. (1993). Information transfer in iconic memory experiments. *Journal of Experimental Psychology, 19*, 845–866.

Haber, R. N., & Standing, L. (1970). Direct estimates of the apparent duration of a flash. *Canadian Journal of Psychology, 24*, 216–229.

Irwin, D. E. (1992). Visual memory within and across fixations. In K. Rayner (Ed.), *Eye movements and visual cognition: Scene perception and reading* (pp. 146–165). New York: Springer–Verlag.

Irwin, D. E., & Yeomans, J. M. (1986). Sensory registration and informational persistence. *Journal of Experimental Psychology: Human Perception and Performance, 12*, 343–360.

Kahneman, D., & Treisman, A. M. (1984). Changing views of attention and automaticity. In R. Parasuraman, R. Davies, & J. Beatty (Eds.), *Varieties of attention* (pp. 29–61). New York: Academic Press.

Koch, C. (2004). *The quest for consciousness*. Greenwood Village, CO: Roberts & Co.

Loftus, G., & Irwin, D. (1998). On the relations among different measures of visible and informational persistence. *Cognitive Psychology, 35*, 135–199.

Luck, S. J., Vogel, E. K., & Shapiro, K. L. (1996). Word meanings are accessed but cannot be reported during the attentional blink. *Nature, 383*, 616–618.

Luck, S. J., & Vogel, E. K. (1997). The capacity of visual working memory for features and conjunctions. *Nature, 390*, 279–281.

Maki, W. S., Frigen, K., & Paulson, K. (1997). Associative priming by targets and distractors during rapid serial visual presentation: Does word meaning survive the attentional blink? *Journal of Experimental Psychology: Human Perception and Performance, 23*, 1014–1034.

McCarthy, G., & Nobre, A. C. (1993). Modulation of semantic processing by spatial selective attention. *Electroencephalography and Clinical Neurophysiology, 88,* 210–219.

Neisser, U. (1967). *Cognitive psychology.* New York: Appleton–Century–Crofts.

Phillips, W. A. (1974). On the distinction between sensory storage and short-term visual memory. *Perception & Psychophysics, 16*(2), 283–290.

Sakitt, B., & Appelman, J. B. (1978). The effects of memory load and the contrast of the rod signal on partial report superiority in a Sperling task. *Memory and Cognition, 6,* 562–567.

Shapiro, K., Driver, J., Ward, R., & Sorenson, R. E. (1997). Priming from the attentional blink: A failure to extract visual tokens but not visual types. *Psychological Science, 8,* 95–100.

Shapiro, K., & Raymond, J. E. (1994). Temporal allocation of visual attention: Inhibition or interference? In D. Dagenbach & T. H. Carr (Eds.), *Inhibitory processes in attention, memory, and language* (pp. 151–188). San Diego: Academic Press.

Sperling, G. (1960). The information available in brief visual presentations. *Psychological Monographs: General and Applied, 74*(11), 1–30.

Sperling, G. (1963). A model for visual memory tasks. *Human Factors, 5,* 19–31.

Sperling, G. (1967). Successive approximations to a model for short-term memory. *Acta Psychologica, 27,* 285–292.

Thomas, L. E., & Irwin, D. E. (2006). Voluntary eyeblinks disrupt iconic memory. *Perception and Psychophysics, 68,* 475–488.

Townsend, V. M. (1973). Loss of spatial and identity information following a tachistoscopic exposure. *Journal of Experimental Psychology, 98,* 113–118.

Treisman, A. M., Russell, R., & Green, J. (1975). Brief visual storage of shape and movement. In R. M. A. Rabbitt & S. Dornic (Eds.), *Attention and performance V.* London: Academic Press.

Treisman, A., & Zhang, W. (2006). Location and binding in visual working memory. *Memory and Cognition, 34,* 1704–1719.

Turvey, M. T. (1978). Visual processing and short-term memory. In W. K. Estes (Ed.), *Handbook of learning and cognitive processes* (Vol. 5). Hillsdale, NJ: Lawrence Erlbaum Associates.

Visser, T. A. W., Zuvic, S. M., Bischof, W. F., & Di Lollo, V. (1999). The attentional blink with targets in different spatial locations. *Psychonomic Bulletin and Review, 6,* 432–436.

Vogel, E. K., & Machizawa, M. G. (2004). Neural activity predicts individual differences in visual working memory capacity. *Nature, 428,* 748–751.

Williams, M. A., Visser, T. A. W., Cunnington, R., & Mattingley, J. B. (2008). Attenuation of neural responses in primary visual cortex during the attentional blink. *Journal of Neuroscience, 28,* 9890–9894.

Author Index

A

Abbey, C. K., 221
Abbott, D. F., 315, 316, 319
Abrams, R. A., 56
Adolphs, R., 307, 310, 325
Ahisser, M., 106
Allen, K., 47
Amari, S., 170
Ames, C. T., 213, 216, 224
Amiri, H., 47
Ansorge, U., 55, 158
Appelman, J. B., 349
Aramidah, M., 121
Ariely, D., 98
Aristotle, 36, 37
Armory, J. L., 305, 319
Armstrong, I. T., 195
Arnell, K. M., 205
Ashby, F. G., 226
Assal, G., 276, 290
Astafiev, S. V., 56
Atchley, P., 68, 69, 85, 86
Atkins, P., 198
Awh, E., 49, 132

B

Bacharach, V. R., 214
Bachoud-Levi, A., 264
Bacon, W. F., 74, 77, 81, 82, 86, 87, 96, 158
Bahrami, B., 28
Baker, M. T., 317
Baldassi, S., 224
Barlow, H. B., 36
Baron-Cohen, C., 45
Bartolomo, P., 45, 46, 62
Bashinski, H. S., 214
Bauer,. L. O., 126, 129
Baumstimler, Y., 123, 125, 126
Bavalier, D., 191, 197, 198, 200, 202
Bayard, S., 148
Beck, D. M., 55, 137
Bell, A. J., 170, 171
Belopolsky, A. V., 2, 3
Belopolsky, A.V., 86, 87
Bentin, S., 47, 58, 307, 308
Bergen, J. R., 104
Berger, A., 46, 51
Bernard, J. M., 341
Bertin, E., 281
Bertrand, O., 60
Besner, D., 357
Bhatt, R. S., 281

Biederman, I., 284, 290
Bischof, W. F., 30, 156, 361
Bisiach, E., 341
Blackwell, H. R., 233
Blumenfield, L., 47
Bobholz, J. A., 56
Bodanski, L., 47
Bodis-Wollner, I., 132
Boisson, D., 341
Bonnel, A.-M., 213, 214, 238
Bornhofen, C., 201, 206
Bossini, S., 338, 342
Bour, L. J., 121
Boyce, W. E., 251
Boyer, B., 271, 279
Bradshaw, J. L., 275
Braun, J., 213, 214, 241
Brawn, P. M., 213, 214
Breitmeyer, B. G., 31
Briand, K. A., 50, 51, 52
Brindley, G. S., 16
Brisson, B., 4, 147, 163, 164, 165, 166, 167
Bristow, D., 132, 137
Broadbent, D. E., 69, 70, 95, 98
Brockmole, J. R., 130
Brown, K. J., 307
Bruce, V., 44, 45
Brundesen, C., 11
Bryshaert, M., 345
Bucher, S. F., 132
Buller, J., 13, 18
Bullier, J., 24, 29
Buonocore, M. H., 62
Burger, R., 158
Burkell, J., 78
Burnham, B. R., 67, 69
Burr, D., 224
Busey, T. A., 265, 289
Butcher, S. J., 69
Buxton, R., 132

C

Caessens, B., 342
Caffera, P. A. S., 56
Cameron, E. L., 214
Campara, D., 26
Caramazza, A., 192, 196
Carey, S., 268, 279, 281, 286, 288
Carlson, L. A., 130
Carpenter, G., 18
Carrasco, M., 48, 49, 69, 214, 224, 241, 244, 246
Cashon, C. H., 273, 288
Cassarotti, M., 339

Castel, A. D., 339
Cave, K. R., 74, 85, 86, 93
Cheal, M., 236
Chen, C. Y. D., 80, 81
Chen, J. M., 305, 320
Chen, Z., 222
Cherry, E. C., 211
Choi, J., 53
Chokron, S., 341
Chong, S. C., 98
Chun, M. M., 4, 32, 94, 147, 156, 193, 201, 306, 320
Cichocki, A., 170
Clark. V. P., 214, 237
Cohen, L., 32, 345
Cohen, L. B., 273, 288
Cohen, Y., 80, 81
Cohen, Y. A., 21, 22, 45, 46
Colby, C. L., 62, 132
Collewijn, H., 121, 134
Coltheart, M., 35, 130, 167, 195, 198, 205
Coltheart, Max, 7
Coltheart, V., 191, 194, 201, 202, 203, 205, 206, 209
Coltheart, Veronika, 4, 7
Colzato, L. S., 35
Cook, R. G., 315
Corbetta, M., 56, 67, 69, 132
Coren, S., 148
Corpet, J. A., 337
Cowan, N., 98, 110, 144
Crebolder, J. M., 156, 157
Creelman, C. D., 212, 217
Crick, Francis, 9
Crowder, R. G., 194
Cubelli, R., 343
Cummington, R., 356
Curtis, B., 198

D

d'Ydewalle, G., 345
Damasio, A. R., 310
Damasio, H., 310, 314, 325
Dammers, J., 310, 311
Davidoff, J., 264
Davidson, B. J., 44, 245
Davidson, R. J., 309
Davis, C., 202, 203, 315
Davis, E. T., 213
Davis, G., 45
de Fockert, J. W., 147
de Gelder, B., 264, 308, 315
de Haan, M., 294
De Weerd, P., 28
Decaix, C., 45, 46, 62
Deco, G., 93
Degos, J., 264

DeGutis, J., 44
Dehaene, S., 32, 337, 338, 342, 343, 344, 345
Dell'Acqua, R., 4, 152, 153, 154, 155, 163, 357, 359
Deloche, G., 337
Deroost, N., 51, 52
Desimone, R., 20, 28, 68, 69
Deubel, H., 67
Deutsch, D., 70, 98
Deutsch, J. A., 70, 98
DeValois, R. L., 213
Di Lollo, V., 1, 2, 3, 18, 22, 23, 24, 26, 30, 31, 32, 34, 96, 106, 156, 158, 193, 212, 236, 240, 350, 352, 357, 361
Di Prima, B. C., 251
Diamond, R., 268, 279, 281, 286, 287, 288, 289
Dick, B., 48
Dilem, L., 50, 51, 61
DiMase, J. S., 104, 105
Dixon, P., 30
Dodd, M. D., 339
Dolan, R. J., 305, 307, 308, 315, 319
Domich, L., 13
Donk, M., 68, 69
Donnelly, N., 264–265
Dorflinger, J. M., 56
Dosher, B., 44
Dosher, B. A., 214, 218, 242
Dosher, B. A.236
Downing, C. J., 214, 230
Downing, P. E., 196, 318
Driver, J., 45, 55, 203, 305, 319, 323, 358
Dubarry, Anne-Sophie, 4
Duchaine, B. C., 271, 272, 275, 276, 277, 294
Duddy, M., 45
Dufour, A., 48
Duncan, J., 30, 68, 82, 148
Dux, P. E., 191, 194, 201

E

Eckstein, M., 214, 241, 244
Eckstein, M. P., 216, 221, 224
Edelman, G. M., 18
Edwards, T., 47
Eger, E., 309
Egeth, H. E., 69, 71, 72, 74, 77, 81, 82, 86, 87, 95, 96, 152, 158, 159, 212
Eggermont, J. J., 20
Eimer, M., 147
Elbert, T., 58
Ellis, A. W., 317
Elmer, M., 147, 148
Enns, J. T., 3, 18, 24, 30, 31, 32, 34, 96, 104, 106, 148, 212
Esterman, M., 44, 47, 58
Esteves. F., 314, 321
Etcoff, N. L., 315

Evert, D., 222

F

Fable, M., 94
Fadiga, L., 38
Fagot, C., 194, 195, 201
Farah, M. J., 277, 323
Favre, C., 276, 290
Felleman, D. J., 12
Fias, W., 342, 343, 344, 345
Findlay, J. M., 213
Fink, G. R., 340
Fischer, M. H., 339, 343, 344
Flude, B., 317
Fogassi, L., 38
Foley, J. M., 213, 245, 252
Folk, C. L., 55, 69, 74, 77, 78, 80, 81, 84, 85,
        152, 158, 159
Ford, M. A., 80
Forster, K. I., 202, 203
Frank, L., 132
Friesen, C. K., 45
Frisby, J., 11
Frith, C. D , 55, 132, 137, 147

G

Galfano, G., 339
Gallese, V., 38
Gallistel, C. R., 337
Galton, F., 6, 337
Garbart, H., 95
Garrett, R., 48
Gauthier, I., 268, 270, 271, 276, 289
Gazzaniga, M. S., 43
Gelade, G., 69, 70, 308, 321
Gelman, R., 337
Gerstein, G. L., 13, 24, 25
Gevers, W., 342
Geypens, F., 345
Ghorashi, S. M. S., 23, 158
Gibson, J. J., 16
Giesbrecht, B., 236, 240
Gillion, J. D., 215
Girard, P., 24, 29
Giraux, P., 338, 342
Girelli, M., 80
Gitelman, D. R., 56
Gobel, S., 344
Godijn, R., 67, 69, 80, 81
Goldberg, M., 132
Goldstein, R., 126, 129
Goodale, M. A., 98
Goren, D., 314
Gosselin, F., 325
Gosselin, N., 148
Gould, I. C., 237, 244

Grafton, S. T., 62
Graham, N., 213
Graham, N. V. S., 213, 216
Granner, M., 310
Green, D. M., 212, 214, 226, 233
Green, J., 354
Grice, G. R., 52
Grimault, Stephan, 4
Grossberg, S., 18, 93
Grova, Christopher, 4
Gruber, T., 58
Gurnsey, R., 104
Gutierrez, P., 50, 51, 61

H

Hafterm E. R., 213, 214, 238
Hahn, S., 71
Haller, M., 198
Halligan, P. W., 340, 341
Hamker, F., 93, 95, 96
Hammad, S., 22
Handy, T. C., 48
Harris, A., 307, 310
Harris, C. L., 198, 202
Harris, C. S , 16
Harth, E., 18
Hasson, U., 278
Hawkins, H., 45, 214, 230
Hawkins, H. L., 214, 237
Hawkins, J., 13, 14, 18, 20, 21, 36, 37, 38
Haxby, J. V., 55
Hay, D. C., 317
Hayden, A., 281
Haynes, J.-D., 132, 137
Hazeltine, E., 44, 62
Hebb, D. O., 14, 17
Held, R., 98
Heller, D., 95
Henaff, M.-A., 312, 313
Hendler, T., 309, 310, 312
Henik, A., 46, 51
Henry, G. H.
Henson, R. N. A., 195
Herd, S., 93
Heslenfield, D. J., 56
Heumann, M., 55, 158
HGordon, G. E., 314
Hickey, C., 80
Hillstrom, A. P., 96, 101
Hillyard, S., 45, 145, 147, 148, 168, 214, 230
Hillyard, S. A., 214
Hochstein, S., 96, 106
Hodsoll, J. P., 104
Hoffman, J. E., 95
Hogben, J. H., 26
Hogmen, H., 31
Hole, G. J., 280

Holroyd, T., 309, 310, 312
Holtzman, P. S., 45, 46
Hommel, B., 35
Hong, S.-K., 94
Hopfinger, J. B., 62
Horowitz, T. S., 3, 94, 104
Hubbard, E. M., 343, 344
Hubel, D. H., 11
Hubner, R., 93
Humphreys, G., 30
Humphreys, G. W., 82, 214, 230, 231
Humphreys, K., 294
Hupe, J. M., 24, 29
Hyle, M., 69

I

Ioannides, A. A., 309, 310, 312
Irwin, D. E., 71, 130, 353, 355
Irwin, David, 3
Ishai, A., 55
Isuard, J., 312, 313
Itti, L., 69, 74, 77, 95
Ivry, R. B., 43, 62

J

Jacquin-Courtois, S., 341
Jahnke, J. C., 194
James, A. C., 24, 29
Jang, Y., 32
Jaspar, H. H., 147
Jeffreys, D. A., 307
Jeffries, L. N., 22
Jenike, M. A., 315
Jenkins, R., 323
Jiang, J., 147
Johnson, M. H., 294
Johnson, M. R., 320
Johnston, J. C., 69, 74, 77, 81, 84, 85, 158, 191, 230
Johnston, J. C.l, 50, 55
Jolicoeur, P., 4, 145, 146, 147, 148, 149, 150, 151, 152, 153, 154, 155, 156, 157, 163, 164, 165, 166, 167, 168, 169, 205
Jones, H. E., 13, 24, 25
Jones, M., 309, 310, 312
Jonides, J., 45, 75, 76, 77, 86, 87, 132
Joseph, J. S., 74
Julesz, B., 74, 95, 104
Juola, J., 45, 46

K

Kadlee, H. C., 226
Kagan, J., 315
Kahneman, D., 78, 194, 236
Kamel, N., 319

Kanwahara, J., 74, 212
Kanwisher, N., 188, 194, 196, 197, 198, 199, 202, 203, 204, 206, 271, 277, 279, 285, 305, 306, 318
Kanwisher, N. G., 7, 55
Kaplan, E., 252
Kashikura, K., 307
Kastner, S., 28
Kaufman, O., 310
Kawahara, J., 23
Kawahara, J.-I., 106
Kawasaki, H., 310
Kay, J. B., 323
Keil, A., 58
Khateb, A., 307, 316
Khoe, W., 81
Khurana, B., 317
Kidd, P., 45
Kiehl, K. A., 320
Killgore, W. D. S., 316
Kim, H., 315
Kim, M. S., 74, 85, 86, 158
Kim, Y. H., 56
Kincade, J. M., 56, 132
Kinchla, R. A., 93
Kingstone, A., 45, 48, 81
Klaver, P., 165, 168
Klein, R. M., 48, 50, 51, 81
Koch, C., 69, 74, 77, 95, 213, 214, 241, 313, 320, 321
Konorski, J., 16
Koshino, H., 45, 46
Kramer, A. F., 68, 69, 71, 74, 85, 86, 87
Kramer, P., 213, 216, 340
Kristjansson, A., 96
Krolak-Salmon, P., 309, 311, 312, 313
Krummenacher, J., 69, 95
Kumada, T., 74

L

LaBar, K. S., 56
Ladavas, E., 343
Lambert, A., 45
Lamme, V. A. F., 24, 26, 27, 28, 106
Lamy, D., 96, 101
Landan, A., 44
Landau, A. N., 47, 58
Landau, Ayelet, 2
Landauer, T. K., 338
Landis, T., 316
Langdon, R., 195, 198
Langton, S. R. H., 44, 45
Lany, D., 74
Lassonde, M., 148
Lavie, N., 28, 55, 137, 147, 318, 323
Le Bihan, D., 32
Le Gros Clark, W., 10

Le, D., 49
Leber, A., 74
Leber, A. B., 82
LeBlanc, Emilie, 4
LeDoux, J. E., 307, 308
Lee, B. B., 26, 252
Lee, C., 69
Lee, D. K., 213, 214, 241
Lee, M. B., 315
Lehmann, D., 309
Leonhardt, J., 49
Lesmes, L. A., 236
Levy, J., 273
Li, Z., 69, 70
Liddell, B. J., 307
Lina, Jean-Marc, 4
Lindsey, D. T., 213, 216, 224
Lindsey, P. H., 11
Ling, S., 48, 49, 69
Liu, J., 307, 310
Liu, L., 310
Lleras, A., 32
Loffler, G., 314
Loftus, G. R., 52
Lomber, S. G., 24, 29
Long, V., 49
Love, T., 132
Lu, Z. L., 44, 214, 218, 236, 242
Luce, R. D., 61
Luck, S., 45, 110, 145, 147, 148, 168, 214, 230,
        357, 362
Luck, S. J., 48, 80, 144, 145, 146, 147, 148, 167,
        214
Luo, C. R., 192, 196
Luo, Q., 309, 310, 312
Lupianez, J., 67, 69, 82
Luzzatti, C., 341
Lyon, D. R., 236

M

Machado, L., 203
Machizawa, M. G., 165, 361
Mack, A., 98
Mackeben, M., 51
Macmillan, N. A., 212, 217
Makeig, S., 58, 170, 171
Maljkovic, V., 101
Malpeli, J. G., 13
Mangin, J-F., 32
Mangun, G. R., 43, 48, 62
Mapelli, D., 343, 345
Marenzi, R., 342, 343, 344
Marois, Rene, 4
Marr, D., 11
Marshall, J. C., 340, 341
Martin, A., 55
Martini, P., 284

Marzi, C. A., 26
Masson, M. E. J., 195
Mattingly, J. B., 315, 316, 356
Maurer, D., 321
Maxwell, W., 45
Mayer, A. R., 56
McAuliffe, J., 81
McAvoy, M. P., 132
McCann, R. S., 50
McCarthy, G., 318
McClelland, J. L., 17, 52
McCool, C., 47, 48, 55, 61, 62
McCourt, M E., 13
McCulloch, W. S., 10
McDermott, J., 306
McDermott, M. T., 80
McDonald, J. J., 80
McElree, B., 224, 246
McGlone, F., 315, 316, 319
McIlwaine, J. D., 156, 157
McInerney, S. C., 315
McKay, D. G., 198, 200
McKone, E., 5, 268, 271, 274, 275, 276, 279,
        281, 282, 283, 286, 291, 292, 293,
        296
McWeeny, K H., 317
Meneghello, F., 342, 343, 344
Mesulam, M.-M., 56
Mewhort, D. J. K., 195
Michel, C., 316, 341
Michel, I., 341
Michielin, M., 339
Michold, Kristin, O., 3
Mignard, M., 41
Miller, E. K., 345
Miller, M. D., 198, 200
Mineka, S., 305, 314
Mitchell, D. G. V., 319
Mondy, S., 201, 205, 206
Moore, C. M., 32
Moran, J., 20
Morris, A. L., 198, 202
Morris, A. P., 315
Morris, J. S., 308, 315
Most, S. B., 320
Motter, B. C., 28
Mouloua, M., 45, 214, 230, 237
Mounts, J. R. W., 74
Moyer, R. S., 338
Muller, H. J., 69, 95, 213, 214, 230, 231
Muller, M. M., 58
Mulligan, R., 215
Mumford, D., 17, 20
Murphy, S. T., 314

N

Naccache, L., 32

Nakayama, K., 51, 95
Neill, W. T., 192, 196
Neisser, U., 69, 70, 95, 212, 249, 349
Nieder, A., 345
Nobre, A. C., 56
Noe, A, 98
Noel, M. P., 337
Norman, A. D., 11
Notebaert, W., 50, 51
Nothdurft, H. C., 74
Nwachuku, I., 47

O

O'Craven, K. M., 318
O'Reilly, R., 93
Oakson, G., 13
Oh, S. H., 48, 49
Ohman, A., 305, 307, 314, 321
Olivia, A., 98
Ollinger, J. M., 132
Ongerbower de Visser, B., 121
Optician, L. M., 74
Oram, M. W., 307
Ota, H., 341

P

Paladini, R., 343
Palermo, R., 6, 273, 323
Paller, K. A., 273
Palmer, Evan M., 3
Palmer, J., 213, 216, 221, 224, 233
Pandya, A. S., 18
Park, J., 189
Park, S., 47, 48, 55, 61, 62
Parrish, T. B., 56
Parrot, J., 123, 125, 126
Pascual-Leone, A., 13
Pashler, H., 48, 93, 98, 161, 218, 230
Pashler, H. E., 245
Pavel, M., 221, 233
Payne, B. R., 24, 29
Peelen, M. V., 56
Pegna, B. N., 307, 316
Pelli, D. G., 242
Penfield, W. G., 16
Penpeci-Talgar, C., 214, 241, 244
Peressotti, F., 147
Perot, P., 16
Perrett, D. I., 307
Perry, C., 195, 198
Pesciarelli, F., 147
Pesenti, M., 337
Pessoa, L., 316, 318, 319
Phillips, W. A., 350
Piazza, M., 343, 344, 345
Pine, D. S., 319

Pinel, P., 343, 344, 345
Pinsk, M. A., 28
Pitts, W., 10
Pizzagalli, D. A., 309
Poline, J-B., 32
Polis, S., 315
Posner, M. I., 12, 21, 22, 27, 44, 45, 46, 51, 67,
    80, 81, 245
Potter, M. C., 18, 156, 187, 191, 197, 198, 199,
    200, 202
Prasada, S., 197, 198
Pratt, J., 81, 339
Presti, D. E., 51
Priftis, K., 6, 341, 342, 343, 344
Prime, D., 4
Prinzmetal, W., 2, 3, 36, 44, 46, 47, 48, 49, 50,
    51, 53, 54, 55, 58, 61, 62
Psotka, J., 36
Purcell, D. G., 307

R

Rafal, R., 46, 51
Rafal, R. D., 45, 46
Raffone, A., 35
Raichle, M. E., 12
Rao, S. M., 56
Rastle, K., 195
Ratcliff, R., 97
Rauch, S. L., 315
Rauschenberger, R., 43, 67, 69, 80, 82
Raymond, D. E., 352, 360
Raymond, J. E., 352, 360
Read, S., 48, 49, 69
Reciher, G. M., 16
Reddy, L., 320, 321
Reed, A., 281
Rees, G., 28, 55, 132, 137, 147
Regard, M., 309
Reichardt, W., 24
Reicher, G. M., 266
Reimann, B., 69
Remington, R. W., 50, 55, 69, 74, 77, 78, 80, 81,
    84, 85, 158, 159
Rensink, R. A., 3, 18, 24, 30, 31, 32, 34
Restle, F., 337
Reynolds, J. H., 69
Rhodes, G., 6, 271, 307, 323
Ricciardelli, P., 45
Richard, C. M., 45
Riggs, L. A., 122, 123, 134
Ristic, J., 45
Rizzolatti, G., 38
Robbins, R., 267, 268, 270, 275, 283, 289, 296
Robert, M., 148
Robertson, L., 44, 47, 58
Robitaille, N., 4, 147, 152, 153, 154, 155, 156,
    157, 166, 167, 168, 169, 170

Rode, G., 341
Roelfsema, P. R., 24, 26, 27
Rosen, A. C., 56
Rossetti, Y., 341
Rousselet, G. A., 308
Rudd, M. E., 249
Rummelhart, D. E., 17
Rusconi, E., 338, 344, 345
Rushton, D. N., 16
Rushworth, M., 344
Russell, R., 354
Ruz, M., 67, 69, 82

S

Sagi, D., 74
Sakitt, B., 349
Sanders, A. F., 93
Scarborough, D. L., 187
Scarborough, H. S., 187
Schiller, P. H., 24, 26
Schmidt, H., 51
Schneider, W., 23, 103, 305, 320
Schneider, W. X., 67
Schouten, J. L., 55
Schwarz, W., 213, 245, 252
Seelos, K. C., 132
Segui, J., 197, 198
Seidenberg, M., 56
Seiffert, A. E., 193, 236
Seiroff, E., 45, 46, 62
Sekuler, A., 81
Selfridge, O., 11
Sengco, J. A., 264, 266, 268
Serences, J. T., 68, 73
Sereno, A. B., 45, 46
Seron, X., 337
Sessa, P., 4, 152, 153, 154, 155
Shapiro, K. L., 145, 146, 352, 358, 360
Shapley, Rm. M., 252
Shaw, M. L., 53, 215, 216, 219
Shiffrin, R. M., 23, 103
Shimizu, N., 47
Shimozaki, S., 216, 224
Shimozaki, S. S., 221
Shipp, S., 12
Shiu, L., 48
Shiu, L.-P., 218
Shulman, G. L., 56, 67, 69, 132
Sieroff, E., 45, 62
Silverman, G. H., 95
Skinner, J. E., 13
Smilek, D., 23
Smith, E., 132
Smith, P. L., 52, 237, 244
Smith, Philip, 5
Smith, W. C., 317
Snowden, R. J., 213, 214

Snyder, A. Z., 56
Snyder, C. R. R., 44, 245
Soares, J. F., 314
Soetens, E., 50, 51
Sorenson, R. E., 358
Sorkin, R. D., 215
Spalek, Thomas, 36
Spekreijse, H., 26, 28
Spelak, T. M., 22, 23
Spence, C., 48
Sperling, G., 351, 362, 363
Sporns, O., 18
Stanley, C. M., 56
Steinman, R. M., 121, 134
Stephenson, L., 201, 206
Steriade, M., 13
Stern, J. A., 126, 129
Stillito, A. M., 13, 24, 25, 26
Stoiamov, I., 340
Stone, A., 205
Stone, L., 215
Streit, M., 307, 309, 310, 311, 312
Strock, B. D., 126
Suave, Kevin, 4
Sugase, Y., 307, 310
Suzuki, S., 317
Swets, J. A., 212, 214, 226, 233
Sylvester, R., 132, 137

T

Tai, J. C., 214
Tallon-Baudry, C., 60, 175
Tanaka, J. W., 264, 266, 268, 323
Tansy, A. P., 56
Tassinari, G., 26
Taylor, N., 54
Taylor, W. K., 211
Theeuwes, J., 56, 67, 68, 69, 71, 72, 73, 77, 78,
        80, 81, 82, 85, 86, 87, 158, 188
Theeuwes, Jan, 2
Thomas, J. P., 216, 224
Thomas, L. E., 130, 131, 132, 133, 134, 353, 355
Thomas, Laura, 3
Thomas, S. J., 48
Thorpe, S., 97, 98
Tipples, J., 45
Tjan, B. S., 290
Todd, S., 74
Tononi, G., 18
Toshima, T., 74
Townsend, J. T., 226
Townsend, V. M., 354
Tranel, D., 314, 325
Treisman, A., 34, 51, 69, 70, 78, 98, 133, 194,
        212, 308, 321, 362
Treisman, A. M., 354
Treue, S., 69, 70

Triesman, A. M., 95, 104, 114, 354, 362
Turatto, M., 344
Turvey, M. T., 349

U

Uchikawa, K., 130
Ullman, S., 74
Umilta, C., 6, 339, 340, 341, 342, 343, 344, 345
Ungerleider, L. G., 28, 55, 316, 318, 319
Unnikrishnan, K. P., 18
Usher, M., 52

V

Valentine, T., 205
Vallar, G., 340
Van der Burg, E., 68, 69
Van der Steen, J., 121, 134
Van Essen, D. C., 12
Van Wert, Michael J., 3
Van Zoest, W., 68, 69
Vanderfolk, J. R., 265, 289
VanRullen, R., 98, 321
Verghese, P., 221, 233
Verstynen, T., 44
Vickers, D., 52
Vidyasgar, T. R., 18
Virzi, R. A., 95
Visser, T. A., 106, 158
Visser, T. A. W., 156, 356, 361
Vogel, E. K., 144, 145, 146, 165, 167, 357, 361, 362
Volkmann, F. C., 123, 127, 130
von der Malsburg, C., 12, 34
Vuilleummier, P., 305, 315, 319

W

Wallace, G., 275
Walrath, L. C., 126
Walsh, V., 13, 344
Wang, V., 46
Ward, L. M., 148
Ward, R., 358
Warner, C. B., 45, 46
Watt, R. J., 44, 45
Webster, M. A., 213
Weiskrantz, L., 308, 315
Weisstein, N., 16
Welford, A. T., 222

West, D. C., 13, 24, 25
Whalen, P. J., 315
Whittlesea, B. W. A., 195
Wiesel, T. N., 11
Wilkonson, F., 314
Williams, M. A., 315, 316, 319, 356
Wilson, A., 47
Wilson, H. R., 314
Wojciulik, E., 55, 199, 204, 206, 305
Woldorff, M. G., 214, 237
Wolfe, J. M., 3, 69, 70, 93, 94, 95, 96, 98, 99, 100, 104, 105, 110
Wolfe, Jeremy, 3
Wolfgang, B. J., 237, 244
Woodley, S. J., 56
Woodman, G. F., 144, 147, 148, 167
Woodward, D. P., 214, 230
Wright, R. D., 22, 45
Wulwer, W., 311
Wundt, W., 2, 43, 62

Y

Yager, D., 213, 216
Yamamoto, S., 307
Yantis, S., 68, 69, 71, 72, 73, 75, 76, 77, 82, 86, 87, 96
Yin, C., 199, 204, 206
Yin, R. K., 263, 264, 275
Yingling, C. D., 13
Young, A. W., 317
Yovel, G., 271, 272, 273, 277, 279, 285
Yue, X., 290
Yurgelum-Tood, D. A., 316

Z

Zajone, R. B., 314
Zald, D. H., 314
Zeki, S., 12
Zeki, S. M., 148
Zenger, B., 94
Zhang, W., 362
Zhaoping, L., 95
Ziegler, J., 195, 198
Zipser, K., 24, 26, 28
Zorzi, M., 6, 339, 340, 341, 342, 343, 344
Zuber, B. L., 127
Zuvic, S. M., 106, 158, 361
Zvinyatskovsky, A., 50, 51, 61
Zwaan, L., 86, 87

Subject Index

A

Adaptive-resonance theory, 18
ALOPEX organization algorithm, 18
Artificial intelligence, neural networks of, 38
Attention
  central load, 147–148, 149
  effect of, on stimulus qualia, 47
  information selection, 67
  selective, 317–318
  visual. *See* Visual spatial attention
  visual selection, relationship between. *See*
    Visual selection
  window of, 86–87
Attentional eye blinks
  attention freezes, 152–155, 356
  attentional blink paradigm, 145, 356
  dual-task effect, 155
  electrophysiology results, 145, 146–147, 148–
    149, 154–155, 356–357, 359–360,
    361–362
  attentional blink paradigm, 150–152
  impaired deployment of spatial attention,
    156–157, 162–163
  processing load, 149, 360, 361
  psychological refractory period, 164
  repetition blindness, relationship between,
    193–194
  semantic access, relationship between,
    357–359
  spatial capture, 150–152
  visuspatial attention, relationship between,
    147–148, 149
Autoassociative memories
  action sequences, 21–22
  description, 14
  hierarchical organization, 15–16
  inhibition hypothesis, 22
  object identification, 18, 20
  observer expectations, role of, 22–23
  perceptual hypothesis, 18, 20, 35–36
  reentrant processing models, relationship
    between, 17
  routine tasks, role in, 23
  storage, 21

B

Back propogation, in artificial intelligence's
    neural networks, 38
Brain, human
  attentional resources, 211
  cortex to LGN, 114

cortical processing of faces. *See* Face
    perception and recognition
face recognition areas. *See* Face perception
    and recognition
facial expression, responses to, 324–325
fear, processing of, 312, 314–316
feed-forward models. *See* Feed-forward
    models
historical overview of theories on
    functioning, 10–11
information exchange between regions, 13
reentrant processing models. *See* Reentrant
    processing models
visual perception pathways, 9–10

C

Cell assembly, 14–15
Contextualiztion, 196
Contingent capture paradigm, 157, 158–159,
    161–162
Crick, Francis, 9

D

Distractors, visual
  Gabor patch experiments, 216–217
  Gaussian strength variables to calculate
    response, 220
  Pearson chi-squares, to calculate response,
    220–221
  visual search, impact on, 216–218
Dog expert studies, 288–289

E

Emotions, discrimination of, 308, 312–313
  facial recognition in, 308, 312–313, 318–321
Experience-expectant innate template theory,
    262
Expertise hypothesis
  falsification of, 288–289
  levels of expertise, 290
  neurophysiological data, 290–291
  predictions based on, 286–287
Eye blinks
  attention, allocation of, 135, 136
  attentional. *See* Attentional eye blinks
  cognitive processes, suppression of, 130–132
  concentration, relationship to, 3, 123–124,
    125, 129
  emotion, relationship between, 124
  endogenous, 121
  frequency, 122

iconic memory, relationship between, 130,
132, 134, 352–353, 355
inhibition of, 125–126
latency, 126
oculomotor, 355–356
overview, 121
performance, relationship between, 136–137
physical characteristics of, 122
processing demands, relationship between,
127–128
reasons for blinking, 121
reflexive, 121, 122
saccades, relationship between, 128–129,
130, 133–134, 352–353
selectivity, relationship between, 133
spatial capture, 150–152
spatial freezes, 152–155
thinking, relationship to, 129, 137
visual interruption, 122, 123–124, 124–125
voluntary, 121, 122, 124–125

F

Face perception and recognition
abstract paradigms, 272–273
artificial, 275
attention-attracting hairstyles, 276
automatic nature of, 305–306, 317
brain areas responsible for, 306–307
capacity issues, 320–321
categorization, 308, 313
children, in, 5–6, 287–288
complete probe advantage, 264
composite paradigm, 268–269
cortical processing, 276–277
decomposition of facial parts, 281, 282–283
detection of, 307, 308, 327
disproportionate inversion effect, 263–264,
266
dog expert studies, 288–289
emotions, discrimination of, 308, 312–313,
318–321
encoding of information, 322–324
experience-expectant innate template
theory. See Experience-expectant
innate template theory
expertise hypothesis. See Expertise
hypothesis
exposure history, 291–292
facial parts, 278–279, 281, 282–283
holistic process, 279–280, 281, 282,
285–286, 292–293
holistic/configural terminology, 285
infant experience, 262–263, 294, 295–296
inversion effect, 287
Mooney face, 282–283
object recognition, versus, 261–262, 269
origins of processing, 293–296

other-race effects, 292–293
overview, 261
part-based processing, 284–285
part-in-spacing altered whole effect, 266,
268
part-whole paradigm, 264, 266
part-whole paradigm, flanker variation, 273
parts, interaction between, 273–274
peripheral inversion task, performance on,
274–275
reaction time and accuracy, 47–48
repetition blindness, 205–206, 206. See also
Repetition blindness
search functions, 321–322
second-order relations, 279–280, 281, 283,
284–285
selective attention theories, 317–318
spacing-versus-features changes, 269, 271,
272
speed of processing, 313
subjective versus objective awareness,
314–316
systems for, 306
upright faces, 275, 282–283, 286–287
Fear, processing of, 312, 314–316. See also
Emotions, discrimination of
Feature integration theory (FIT), 95
Feed-forward models
binding problem, 11–12
brain mechanisms, 1–2
feature binding, 35
historical overview of theories, 10–11
inhibitory contour interactions, 32
Mumford model, 17
neuroanatomical and neurophysiological
counterevidence, 12–13
parsimony in, 26
reentrant feedback mechanisms, 114
visual perception sequence, 9
Filter theory, 211

G

Gabor patch, 216–217
Guided Search 4.0
activation map, 95, 97
architecture of, 95, 98, 104, 109–110
asynchronous diffusion, 97, 98
attention, focus of, 97–98
bottom-up selection, 95–96
conjunction search, 107, 108, 109
development, 93
error data, 93
guidance as filter, 101, 102–104
guiding representation, 105–106
object recognition, 97–98
overview, 93–94
pathways, 98–99

preattentive stage, 104–105
processing rate, 108
reaction time, 93, 98, 99, 100–101, 106, 108, 111
replication, 109–111
standard visual search, *versus,* 106
stimulus onset asynchrony, 102–104, 111
surface type, impact of, 111–114

I

Iconic memories, 130, 349–350, 355
Inhibition of return, 21–22
Involuntary spatial attention
fMRI imaging of, 56–57
span of, 56–57
Involuntary visual spatial attention
accumulator model theory, 52–53, 54–55, 61
behavior paradigms, 43–44
cortical response, 46–47
reaction time experiments, 45
serial search model theory, 52–53, 54–55, 61
temporal properties, 46

M

Memories
eye blinks, relationship between. *See* Eye blinks
iconic, duration of, 130, 340–350, 355
visual short-term. *See* Visual short-term memory
Memories, autoassociative. *See* Autoassociative memories
Mirror neurons, 38
Mooney face, 282–283

N

Number magnitude, visuospatial representation of
analogue representation of, 345
covert analogue code, 6
mental number line, 340, 341, 343–344
neural mechanisms of recognition, 344–345
overview, 337–339
SNARC effect, 338–339, 342, 344–345
spatial attention, 339–340
spatial coding, 339, 342–343

O

Object recognition
artificial faces, processed like, 275
exposure history, 291–292
face perception and recognition, *versus,* 261–262

spacing changes, 269, 271, 272
Object substitution masking, 30–34

P

Prosopagnosia, 277, 313–314

R

Random variables, impact on visual search, 218–220
Rapid serial visual presentation (RSVP)
dual target letter search, 201
face recognition, 205–206
object drawings, 204
overview, 187
processing deficits, 193
repetition blindness. *See* Repetition blindness
repetition deficits, 195
sequence speed, 206
simultaneous arrays, relationship between, 192
Reaction time
accuracy, relationship between, 47–50
Guided Search. *See* Guided Search 4.0
involuntary attention, relationship between, 45
irrelevant singletons, impact of, 78, 80
perceptual difficulty, impact of, 50–52
SOA, relationship between, 163, 164
spacial cueing paradigm, 48–49
visual selection, 84–86
Reentrant processing models
autoassociative memories, relationship between, 17
cortical connectivity, role of, 13
expectations, role of, 24–26
feature binding, 34–36
functional connectivity, establishment, 14–15
functional multiplexing, 26–28
invariant representations, 36–37
iterative, 38
neuronal function, 26–28
object substitution masking, 30–34
preattentive hypothesis, 30
primary visual cortex, role of, 25–26
proof of, 16–17
signaling, reentrant, 28
top-down influences, 17
visual stimuli, improvement of noisy/poor, 29–30
Repetition blindness, 4–5
attentional blinks, relationship between, 193–194
color stimuli, with, 203–204
construction-attribution account, 195–196

contextualization, relationship between,
196–197
critical item report, 188–189
critical items, joint report of, 189
faces, 205–206
forced-choice speeded detection, 191
forced-choice unspeeded detection, 191
index (RBI), 189–190
lexical units underlying, 197–198
memory load, relationship between, 190
memory retrieval limits, 194–195
modified token individuation theory,
196–197
morphological units underlying, 197
nonwords with lexical phonology, in,
200–201
nonwords with unfamiliar phonology, in, 200
nonwords, repetition advantages with, 201,
202–203
novel object stimuli, with, 205
object stimuli, with, 204
online detection accuracy and response
time, 191
orthographically similar word pairs, 198–199
overview, 187
phonological units underlying, 199, 204
pseudohomophone pairs, 200–201
recall levels, low, 201
reported items, with, 201
reporting the repeated item, 188
semantic unit word pairs, 199, 204
sequence recall, 188
simultaneous spatial arrays, 192–193
spatial distributed sequences, 191, 192
subspan list report, 190
token individuation account, 194
visual similarity effects, 204

S

Selective attention, 317–318
Shunting equations, 250–252
Stimulus onset asynchrony (SOA), 2
Guided Search, in. *See* Guided Search 4.0
masking, 31–32
repetition blindness studies, 192–193
response time, relationship between, 163,
164
visual selection, role in, 85–86
voluntary attention, as criterion for, 45–46

V

Visual cortex
firing rate of cells, 144–145
iconic memory, location of, 132, 137
invariant representations, processing of,
36–37

motion sensors contained in, 25
V1, 132, 137
Visual masking, 234–235
attention, relationship between, 236, 241
backward masks, 235
cueing effects, 240, 244
cueing effects, mask-dependent, 245–248
dichoptically masked targets, 238–239,
240–241
discrimination, 241
efficiency, 240
informational persistence of stimuli, 246,
247
integration masking, 236–237
interruption masking, 236–237, 242–245
masked *versus* unmasked targets, 237–241
monoptically masked targets, 238–239, 240
noise detection, 248–250
noise exclusion, external, 242–245
object substitution, 240
Visual perceptions
brain pathways, 9–10
feedback mechanisms, 1
processing sequence, 9
visual information, 2
Visual search, 3
Visual selection
attentional window, 86–87
bottom-up selection, 78, 80, 81, 95
contingent capture paradigm, 74–75
feature search, 81–84
feature singleton, 71, 74
initial selection, 70–71
interference, 82–83
irrelevant singleton paradigm, 72–74, 85
neurophysiology of, 68
overview, 67–68
processing stages, 69–70
reaction time, 84–86
search performance, 83–84
search task experiments, 75–77
singleton detection, 77–78, 82–83
singleton search, 77–78
SOA condition, role of, 85–86
top-down selection, 77–78, 81–82, 84,
85–86
Visual short-term memory
attentional blink, impairment due to, 155,
156–157
bilateral posterior distribution, 176–177
capacity limits, 234, 235, 252–254
coding limits, 252–254
dual-task paradigms, 165–167, 178
durable storage, comparison to, 362–363
magnetoencephalography data, 167–170,
171, 173, 175–176
masked and unmasked stimuli, 247
neural activity, 171

processing rate, 144
retrieval limitations, 194–195
shunting equations, 250–252
source localization, 174–178
stimulus representation, 245
stimulus selection, 252–253
storage capacity, 143, 144, 351–352
sustained posterior contralateral negativity,
    165–167, 180–181
trace formation, 246
transfer of data, 166–167
visual imagery, *versus,* 350
Visual signal detection
capacity limitations, 213, 215, 216
debate, contemporary, 212
decision space, 225–226, 227
detection, defining, 212–213
discrimination, 214
distractors, role of. *See* Distractors, visual
independent detectors model, 221–222, 223,
    224, 228–229, 233
labeled detectors, 230
masking. *See* Visual masking
maximum outputs model, 232, 233
multichannel signal detection, 223–224
poststimulus probe task, 229–233
random variables, relationship between,
    218–220
redundancy benefits, 227
redundancy costs, 231–232
sensory effect, distribution of, 226, 229
single-channel theory, 214
spatial cues experiment, 224–225
stimulus noise, role of, 214–215
unlimited-capacity perception, 222
weak, 5
weighted integration model, 222–223

Visual spatial attention, 2
attentional blink, relationship between, 144,
    149, 179
contingent capture paradigm, 157, 158–159,
    161–162, 179–180
cortical responses, modulation of, 143–144
distractors, 152, 158–159
electroencephalography results, 58, 60–61
electrophysiology results, 147, 148–149,
    154–155, 159, 161–162
failure to deploy, 146–147
filter theory. *See* Filter theory
filters, 150–151
fMRI imaging, results of, 55–57
involuntary. *See* Involuntary spatial attention
masking, relationship between. *See* Visual
    masking
nonpredictive cues, 45
overview, 211–212
predictive cues, 45
psychological refractory period, during,
    162–163
reaction time. *See* Reaction time
selection mechanisms, 144
sensory responses, 148
spatial cueing paradigm, 44–45
visual short-term, relationship to, 4
voluntary. *See* Voluntary spatial attention
Voluntary spatial attention
behavioral paradigms, 43–44
cortical response, 46–47
fMRI imaging of, 56–57
reaction time experiments, 45
span of, 56–57
spatial cueing paradigm, 44–45
stimulus onset asynchrony, relationship
    between, 45–46